Harold Macmillan, the grandson of Daniel Macmillan, the publisher, was born in 1894 and educated at Eton and Balliol College, Oxford. On the outbreak of the First World War, Macmillan left university and joined the Grenadier Guards. He served on the Western Front where he was wounded three times. After the Armistice, Macmillan joined the family publishing company, but in the 1924 General Election he became the Conservative MP for Stockton-on-Tees. He served in Churchill's wartime cabinet and though defeated in the 1945 General Election, returned to the House of Commons later that year in a by-election at Bromley. When Anthony Eden resigned in 1957, Macmillan became prime minister, serving until October 1963, when ill-health forced him to resign from office.

After his retirement, Macmillan wrote *Winds of Change* (1966), *The Blast of War* (1967), *Tides of Fortune* (1969), *Riding the Storm* (1971) and *At the End of the Day* (1972). Granted the title Earl of Stockton, Harold Macmillan died in 1986.

Peter Catterall lectures in History and Public Policy at Queen Mary, University of London. As well as editing the journal *Contemporary British History*, he has written extensively on twentieth-century Britain.

Also edited by Peter Catterall

The Macmillan Diaries Volume I: The Cabinet Years

THE

MACMILLAN DIARIES

VOLUME II

Prime Minister and After, 1957–1966

Edited and with an introduction by
PETER CATTERALL

PAN BOOKS

First published 2011 by Macmillan

First published in paperback 2012 by Pan Books
an imprint of Pan Macmillan, a division of Macmillan Publishers Limited
Pan Macmillan, 20 New Wharf Road, London N1 9RR
Basingstoke and Oxford
Associated companies throughout the world
www.panmacmillan.com

ISBN 978-0-330-43309-9

1 3 5 7 9 8 6 4 2

A CIP catalogue record for this book is available from
the British Library.

Typeset by SetSystems Ltd, Saffron Walden, Essex
Printed and bound by CPI Group (UK) Ltd, Croydon, CR0 4YY

Visit www.panmacmillan.com to read more about all our books
and to buy them. You will also find features, author interviews
and news of any author events, and you can sign up for e-newsletters
so that you're always first to hear about our new releases.

To the memory of

JOHN RAMSDEN (1947–2009)

a wise mentor who helped to inspire a whole generation of

British political historians

Contents

1964

1965

1966

List of Illustrations

Section One

1. Macmillan at work in his study.
2. On the steps of No. 10.
3. Royal Navy divers in Suez.
4. Recording a party political broadcast.
5. Lewis L. Strauss and Sir Edwin Plowden.
6. Launching the Bow Group's magazine.
7. 'Relax, bud, it's one of ours.' Cartoon by Giles.
8. 'Another little local difficulty.' Cartoon by Vicky.
9. British paratroopers bound for Jordan.
10. Col Qasim.
11. With Konstantinis Karamanlis.
12. General Lauris Norstad.
13. Fatin Zorlu and Evangelos Averoff.
14. Archbishop Makarios III.
15. With Kruschev.
16. With Rab Butler.
17. Derick Heathcoat-Amory.
18. The Shah of Iran and Queen Elizabeth II.

Section Two

19. The Hola Camp atrocity. Cartoon by Vicky.
20. The Common Market. Cartoon by David Low.
21. With Kwame Nkrumah.
22. Hugh Gaitskell, Barbara Castle and Aneurin Bevan.
23. A public address during the general election campaign.
24. Entering Conservative Central Office to applause.
25. Greeting the crowds at Maseru, Basutoland.
26. With President Eisenhower.
27. With his son Maurice.

Acknowledgements

All photos courtesy of Hulton Getty with the exception of the following:

Michael Cummings/Express Group/Cartoon Archive: 33, 49
Giles/Express Group/Cartoon Archive: 7
John Jensen 1963/Cartoon Archive: 45
David Low/Associated Newspapers Ltd/Cartoon Archive: 20
Magnum: 1
Mirrorpix: 8
William Papas/Guardian News & Media Ltd 1962/Cartoon Archive: 43
Press Association: 18, 47
Topfoto: 2
Vicky/Evening Standard/Cartoon Archive: 19

List of Abbreviations

a/c	account
ADC	aide de camp
AFHQ	Allied Forces Headquarters
AG	Attorney General
AP	Associated Press
ASLEF	Amalgamated Society of Locomotive Engineers and Firemen
BAC	British Aircraft Corporation
BBC	British Broadcasting Corporation
BG	Birch Grove (Macmillan's Sussex home)
BMA	British Medical Association
BMC	British Motor Corporation
Bn	Battalion
BOAC	British Overseas Airways Corporation
BofE	Bank of England
BofT	Board of Trade
BTC	British Transport Commission
C	Head of MI6
CAF	Central African Federation
CAS	Chief of Air Staff
CDS	Chief of Defence Staff
CDU	Christlich-Demokratische Union (Christian Democratic Union, West Germany)
CENTO	Central Treaty Organisation
CGT	Capital Gains Tax
CH	Companion of Honour
CIA	Central Intelligence Agency (USA)
CIGS	Chief of the Imperial General Staff
CND	Campaign for Nuclear Disarmament
CO	Colonial Office
CofE	Church of England
CRO	Commonwealth Relations Office
CofS	Chief of Staff
CS	Colonial Secretary

D	Dorothy Macmillan
DDEL	Dwight D. Eisenhower Library (Abilene, Kansas)
DDR	Deutsche Demokratische Republik (East Germany)
DT	*Daily Telegraph*
DV	*Deo volente* (God willing)
DWM	Department of Western Manuscripts, Bodleian Library, Oxford
EDC	European Defence Community
EEC	European Economic Community
EFTA	European Free Trade Association
EOKA	Ethniki Organosis Kyprion Agoniston (National Organisation of Cypriot Fighters)
EST	Economic Secretary to the Treasury
FBI	Federal Bureau of Investigation (USA)
FDR	Franklin Delano Roosevelt (US President 1933–45)
FLN	Front de Libération Nationale (Algerian National Liberation Front)
FM	Field Marshal
FO	Foreign Office
FS	Foreign Secretary
FST	Financial Secretary to the Treasury
FTA	Free Trade Area
G&E	E. Bruce Geelhoed and Anthony O. Edmonds (eds), *The Macmillan–Eisenhower Correspondence 1957–1969* (Basingstoke: Palgrave, 2005)
GATT	General Agreement on Tariffs and Trade
GB	Great Britain
GH	Government House
GMT	Greenwich Mean Time
H-Bomb	hydrogen bomb
HK	Hong Kong
HM	Harold Macmillan
HMG	Her Majesty's Government
HMM	Harold Macmillan *Memoirs* 6v (London: Macmillan, 1966–73)
HO	Home Office
HofC	House of Commons
HofL	House of Lords
HP	hire purchase
HQ	Headquarters

ICBM	Inter-Continental Ballistic Missile
ICI	Imperial Chemical Industries
ICS	Indian Civil Service
IMF	International Monetary Fund
IR	Inland Revenue
IRA	Irish Republican Army
IRBM	Intermediate Range Ballistic Missile
ITV	Independent Television
JFKL	John Fitzgerald Kennedy Library (Boston, Massachusetts)
K	Nikita Khrushchev
KADU	Kenya African Democratic Union
KANU	Kenya African National Union
Kings X	Kings Cross (London railway station)
LC	Lord Chancellor
LCC	London County Council
LCJ	Lord Chief Justice
LofC	Line of Communication
LTE	London Transport Executive
MA	Master of Arts
MATS	Military Air Transport Service (USA)
MBE	Member of the Most Excellent Order of the British Empire
M&Co	Macmillan and Company
MCC	Marylebone Cricket Club
ME	Middle East
MFH	Master of Foxhounds
MG	*Manchester Guardian*
MI5	Military Intelligence 5 (British counter-intelligence and counter-espionage)
MI6	Military Intelligence 6 (the Secret Intelligence Service)
MLF	Multilateral [nuclear] Force
MP	Member of Parliament
MRBM	Medium Range Ballistic Missile
MRP	Mouvement Républicain Populaire (French Christian Democrat party)
NATO	North Atlantic Treaty Organisation
NATSOPA	National Society of Operative Printers and Assistants
NCO	Non-Commissioned Officer
NEDC	National Economic Development Council
NHS	National Health Service
NUR	National Union of Railwaymen

NY	New York
NZ	New Zealand
OAS	Organisation de l'Armée Secrète (settler terrorist organisation in French Algeria)
OECD	Organisation for Economic Co-operation and Development
OEEC	Organisation for European Economic Co-Operation
OM	Order of Merit
OUP	Oxford University Press
PM	Prime Minister
PMG	Postmaster-General
POW	Prisoner of War
PPS	Parliamentary Private Secretary
PQ	Parliamentary question
PRC	People's Republic of China
PRO	Press Relations Officer
PS	Private Secretary
RA	Royal Academician
Rab	R. A. Butler
R&D	Research and Development
RAF	Royal Air Force
RC	Roman Catholic
RCAF	Royal Canadian Air Force
RMS	Royal Mail Ship
RPM	Resale Price Maintenance
SA	South Africa
SAC	Supreme Allied Commander
SACEUR	Supreme Allied Commander, Europe
SAM	Surface to Air Missile
SAS	Special Air Service
SCUA	Suez Canal Users Association
SEATO	South East Asia Treaty Organisation
SHAPE	Supreme Headquarters Allied Powers Europe
SL	Selwyn Lloyd
SofS	Secretary of State
T&GWU	Transport and General Workers Union
TNA	The National Archives (London)
TU	Trade Union
TUC	Trades Union Congress
TV	television
UAR	United Arab Republic

UDC	Urban District Council
UK	United Kingdom
UNO	United Nations Organisation
USA	United States of America
USAF	United States Air Force
USSR	Union of Soviet Socialist Republics
WD	Harold Macmillan, *War Diaries: The Mediterranean 1943–1945* (London: Macmillan, 1984)
WEU	Western European Union
WO	War Office
WSC	Winston Spencer Churchill

Introduction

Harold Macmillan was exactly a month short of his 63rd birthday when appointed Prime Minister on 10 January 1957. At the time, in the aftermath of Suez, he feared his administration might only last six weeks, rather than more than six years, which perhaps explains the delay until he resumed his diaries. It was not until 3 February, in an entry published in the previous volume, that he again took up his pen to review the formation of his government.

This was the culmination of an unusually long apprenticeship. Invalided out of the Army after service on the Western Front in 1915–16, his first public appointment was as ADC to his future father-in-law, the 9th Duke of Devonshire, when Governor-General of Canada in 1919–20. Three years later Devonshire, as Colonial Secretary, was to promulgate the doctrine of the primacy of native interests in colonial affairs. This was an early introduction to the problems of managing conflicts between settlers and natives that, in Kenya and particularly in Central Africa, were to bedevil Macmillan's premiership.

The future Prime Minister was first elected to Parliament in the 1924 general election. The new Conservative MP for Stockton was rapidly to display a primary interest in economics when confronted by the conflicts between capital and labour and the economic travails of the aftermath of the Great War. This interest was partly stimulated by his family's publishing connections with John Maynard Keynes. He shared Keynes's view that the return to the Gold Standard in 1925 could not restore financial equilibrium in response to the economic nationalism unleashed after 1918.[1] Instead of such deflationary measures, Macmillan sought ways to stimulate the economy. Interestingly, the scheme he hit upon, de-rating of industry, would see him introduce two concepts which were to remain facets of his political life. De-rating he characterised as part of a 'Grand Policy' (later he was regularly to draft documents entitled 'The Grand Design'), a series of inter-related measures to tackle unemployment and

---

1. *HMM* I, pp. 110–16, 133, 204, 360; Alastair Horne, *Macmillan 1894–1956* (London: Macmillan, 1986), p. 63.

promote industrial modernisation, re-organisation and harmony.[2] As such it would also help to further his other characteristic concept of 'interdependence', in this case 'of all classes and interests'[3] in the face of the rising socialism of the Labour party.

Although he was able successfully to promote these views to the then Chancellor of the Exchequer, Winston Churchill, he was seen as both somewhat unorthodox and self-promoting by fellow Tory backbenchers. Given his tendency to publish articles critical of the lack of clear economic direction from the party's leadership it is unsurprising that he did not commend himself to them for promotion either.[4] And then he was out of Parliament in the swing to Labour of 1929. When re-elected for Stockton in 1931 Macmillan was one of the massed ranks of supporters of the National Government landslide. He further diminished his limited prospects of advancement by continuing dissent, firstly over economic policy then, as the 1930s wore on, over foreign policy. Whilst loyal to his party and trying, through his various proposals, to forge a Conservatism able to address the economic problems of the inter-war years,[5] his open admiration for the former Liberal leader David Lloyd George can also have done little to endear him to the party leaders. After all, in some ways the only thing that united those who led the National Government coalition of 1931–40 was their dislike for the dynamic architect of the earlier coalition of 1916–22. In contrast, it was that dynamism that attracted Macmillan, who was not only prepared to flirt with Lloyd George's various cross-party schemes for a political comeback, but even resigned the party whip following the Welsh maestro's denunciation of the government's handling of the Abyssinian crisis in 1936.[6]

Macmillan thus contributed to his own lack of political progress. His open opposition to the policy of appeasement of Germany by 1936 cemented this. It did, however, also re-connect him to Churchill. And the subsequent failure of appeasement meant, as Macmillan later reminded Churchill, that both men owed much to the belligerence of the German dictator: 'He made you Prime Minister and me an Under-Secretary. No

---

2. Cited in Martin Gilbert, *Winston Churchill: Vol V, 1922–1939* (London: Heinemann, 1976), pp. 320–21.

3. Ibid, p. 254.

4. Ibid, p. 296; *HMM* I, pp. 249–50.

5. See Gilbert, pp. 261–2, 320–21; *HMM* I, pp. 250, 367f.

6. *HMM* I, pp. 315–16, 377, 456–59; Harold Macmillan, *The Past Masters: Politics and Politicians 1906–1939* (London: Macmillan, 1975), chap. 2.

power on earth, except Hitler, could have done either.'[7] On the formation of Churchill's wartime coalition in 1940 Macmillan finally entered junior office at the Ministry of Supply. He was not necessarily optimistic of further advancement. His fellow North-East Conservative new boy of 1924, Cuthbert Headlam, noted of one dinner with Macmillan:

> He is very much the Minister nowadays, but says that he has arrived too late to rise very high. I can see no reason (except his own personality) for his not getting on – even to the top of the tree – but he is his own worst enemy: he is too self-centred, too obviously cleverer than the rest of us. He never will let the other man have his say and he invariably knows better than the other man.[8]

These defects had retarded Macmillan's career. However, they were held in check now that he was part of a team striving for a cause – victory – to which he could commit himself wholeheartedly.

War then threw up further opportunities. At the end of 1942 he was given Cabinet rank as Minister Resident in North-West Africa and sent to Algiers with the tricky task of preparing for the invasion of Italy and managing relations with the Americans and French. Here Macmillan got to know two figures who were later to feature prominently when he was Prime Minister, the American commander of allied forces in that field General Eisenhower, and the prickly leader of the Free French, General de Gaulle. By the end of the war his office had expanded to cover wide responsibilities in the Mediterranean theatre. Then, with the withdrawal of Labour and the Liberals from the coalition in May 1945, Macmillan at last entered the Cabinet proper as Secretary of State for Air.

Churchill's caretaker government lasted the two months until the ballots for the 1945 election could be collected from across the country and the far-flung armed forces. When counted, Macmillan, in common with many of his colleagues, was out in the Labour landslide.

---

7. *HMM*, p. 10.
8. Stuart Ball (ed.), *Parliament and Politics in the Age of Churchill and Attlee: The Headlam Diaries 1935–1951* (London: Cambridge University Press, 1999), p. 209 (24 June 1940). See also D. R.Thorpe, *Eden: The Life and Times of Anthony Eden First Earl of Avon, 1897–1977* (London: Chatto & Windus, 2003), p. 456. Headlam was Conservative MP for Barnard Castle 1924–29, 1931–35 and for Newcastle upon Tyne North 1940–51.

However, wartime experience had moved him at last into the front ranks of the Conservative party and he was able to return to Parliament almost immediately in a by-election for the safe suburban seat of Bromley and take his place on the Tory front benches. For the first time his economic strictures were directed against a majority Labour government, rather than the leaders of his own party. The wit and superciliousness now flung at the Attlee government finally were to endear him to his fellow Tories in the changed circumstances of the post-war world.[9]

Internationally, with the Soviet Union now occupying Eastern Europe – including a substantial chunk of defeated Germany – and maintaining an enormous preponderance of military might, there was the rise of the Cold War. Macmillan has often been seen, not least because of his American mother, as fully sharing Churchill's enthusiasm for an American alliance, particularly in face of the Soviet threat that was then apparent. However, part of his criticism of what he saw as Labour's weakness in foreign policy was of their craven attitude towards the Americans.[10] To some extent this related to their failure, as he saw it, to maintain the wartime atomic alliance, unilaterally abrogated by the Americans in 1946. Restoring this relationship was one of the early successes of his Premiership. Doing so was important in order to have as much leverage as possible in Washington: otherwise, as he pointed out in 1959, Britain 'could not count on American support in all circumstances and would be less able to stand up to Soviet threats against the United Kingdom or British interests overseas'.[11]

Britain's diminished international status accordingly did not mean giving up the search for freedom of manoeuvre. Macmillan was thus less Atlanticist than he has often been portrayed, and indeed than many of his post-war contemporaries both in Britain and Europe.[12]

9. Horne, p. 302.

10. See, for instance, Peter Catterall (ed.), *The Macmillan Diaries: The Cabinet Years 1950–1957* (London: Macmillan, 2003), p. 34 (6 December 1950).

11. The National Archives, London [henceforward TNA], CAB 134/1929: Macmillan speaking at a 'Study of Future Policy' meeting, 7 June 1959.

12. Peter Catterall, 'Macmillan and Europe, 1950–56: The Cold War, the American Context and the British Approach to European Integration', *Cercles*, 5 (2002), p. 107; Peter Catterall, 'Identity and Integration: Macmillan, "Britishness" and the turn towards Europe', in Gilbert Millat (ed.) *Angleterre*

For instance, the most orthodoxly Conservative economic policy he espoused in the inter-war years was Protectionism. For Macmillan, however, the end was trade bargaining with other countries,[13] rather than the economic nationalism which, to his irritation, seemed to continue to drive American Protectionism during his Premiership.[14] 'Instead of trying to persuade the USA to adopt Free Trade' he therefore felt that Britain should be cultivating its Commonwealth and European connections.[15] Such a unit would be an equal and counter-weight of the United States, and able to close the dollar gap that had bedevilled European economies since the end of the war.[16]

Macmillan's concept of foreign policy was thus always intimately bound to international economic policy. As he was to tell President Eisenhower early in his Premiership:

> Clearly the most favourable economic climate for us to meet the communist threat is that of a steadily expanding level of world trade, in which the underdeveloped countries would feel that the future would hold increasing opportunity for them.[17]

This broad strategic context informed his approach to the rapidity of decolonisation after 1957.[18] It also informed his approach to European integration.

His preference was for a wide concept of Europe. Indeed, in 1948 he was involved in the establishment of the Central and East European Group of the Council of Europe to keep channels open to those

    ou Albion, entre fascination et répulsion (Lille: Université Lille 3 – Charles de Gaulle, 2006), pp. 167–69.

13. *HMM* I, p. 146.

14. See below p. 166 (23 October 1958).

15. Catterall, *The Macmillan Diaries 1950–1957*, p. 235 (28 May 1953).

16. Harold Macmillan, *Ruin or Recovery?*, a speech to the Empire Industries Association and British Empire League, 29 September 1949, pp. 5–7.

17. E. Bruce Geelhoed and Anthony O. Edmonds (eds), *The Macmillan–Eisenhower Correspondence, 1957–1969* (Basingstoke: Palgrave, 2005) [henceforward G&E], p. 149 (1 June 1958).

18. Tony Hopkins, 'Macmillan's Audit of Empire, 1957', in Peter Clarke and Clive Trebilcock (eds), *Understanding Decline: Perceptions and Realities of British Economic Performance* (Cambridge: Cambridge University Press, 1997), pp. 234–60; Ronald Hyam, 'Winds of Change: the Empire and Commonwealth', in Wolfram Kaiser and Gillian Staerck (eds), *British Foreign Policy, 1955–64: Contracting Options* (Basingstoke: Macmillan, 2000), p. 195.

countries now behind the Iron Curtain.[19] Macmillan understood the
French anxiety to tie in West Germany to some much tighter structure, but feared that it (a) was a distraction from the real issue of
defence against the Russians and (b) would in fact lead to the German
domination of Western Europe that the French were trying to avoid.[20]
Hence his abortive concern to widen the Little Europe being forged
by the Six Powers that signed the 1957 Treaty of Rome through
linking them into a broader Free Trade Area agreement. This nevertheless foundered, not least on American resistance, as George Ball
later put it, to 'any increase in the number of nations that have
preferential access to the Common Market as against American
producers'.[21]

By then, in any case, the international scene was shifting. The
Commonwealth preferential trade agreement reached in Ottawa in
1932 was in decline. This undermined part of the context for Macmillan's enthusiasm for an Empire/Europe bloc in the late 1940s and early
1950s,[22] even if he was still clearly unwilling to contemplate the
economic jettisoning of the Commonwealth sought by the French.[23]
The agreement reached in 1955 on West German re-armament within
the safe confines of NATO and its European arm, Western European
Union, meanwhile allayed French anxieties and made possible their
pursuit of a rather different model of European integration. Though
this pushed Macmillan eventually to respond by initiating negotiations
on the possibility of British entry in 1961, he still clearly hankered
after 'a broader European unity'.[24]

British relations with West Germany were also altered by the
advent of nuclear weapons. For Macmillan these had the paradoxical
effect of making war less likely, because of the enormous conse-

19. Catterall, 'Identity and Integration', pp. 170–71.
20. Catterall, 'Macmillan and Europe', pp. 96–97.
21. John F. Kennedy Library, Boston, MA [henceforward JFKL], NSF 175: Ball to
    Kennedy, 25 April 1962.
22. Catterall, 'Identity and Integration', p. 172.
23. Peter Catterall, 'Roles and Relationships: Dean Acheson, "British Decline" and
    Post-War Anglo-American Relations', in Antoine Capet and Aïssatou Sy-
    Wonyu (eds), *The Special Relationship* (Rouen: Université de Rouen, 2003),
    p. 122, n. 50.
24. JFKL, NSF 174A: 'Background and objectives of visit' [Macmillan to
    Washington], 21 March 1961.

quences.[25] They also rendered redundant the large armies West German Chancellor Adenauer still felt necessary for the defence of his country against the Soviet armour massed in Eastern Europe and surrounding the divided city of Berlin. Instead, Macmillan sought to reduce both the tensions and costs resulting from maintaining numerous conventional forces in Central Europe by shifting towards a strategy based upon nuclear defence, whilst trying to allay fear of nuclear warfare. His Moscow trip in early 1959 was thus for him a sensible way of trying to kill several birds with one stone: by reducing nuclear tensions in Europe which – as the 1955 Strath Report pointed out – could result in the obliteration of Britain; by responding to the Soviet initiatives over the previous year on nuclear test moratoria which had spoken to concerns in the West, reflected not least in the founding of CND in 1958; and thereby also reducing the costs of stationing troops in Germany which were a constant drain on the exchanges. His efforts to do so were, however, partly for reasons of West German domestic politics, not to endear him to Adenauer; a situation that de Gaulle, following his return to power in France in 1958, was to exploit ruthlessly.[26]

If the post-war world in which Macmillan came to political prominence was very different, so too was the domestic political scene. Always in favour of rationalisation of industry, he found it difficult to criticise Labour's nationalisations. His inter-war enthusiasm for planning, however, had been about direction in order to help capitalism work more effectively, not as an end in itself. The excesses of Labour bureaucracy were lambasted in a Conservative policy document in 1951 partly authored by Macmillan: 'Where Socialists propose to freeze, to control, to tax, and to mutilate, Conservatives propose to create wealth and to expand and liberate the efforts of the community.' This excessive direction was depicted as leading to a misallocation of resources, not least in Labour's new National Health Service.

---

25. Catterall, *The Macmillan Diaries 1950–1957*, pp. 454, 459 (21 and 25 July 1955).

26. Sabine Lee, *An Uneasy Partnership: British–German Relations between 1955 and 1961* (Bochum: Universitätsverlag Dr. N. Brockmeyer, 1996), pp. 72f; Peter Catterall, 'The singularity of Suez in postwar Anglo-French relations 1945–63: Une Entente mal entendue', in Antoine Capet (ed.) *Britain, France and the Entente Cordiale since 1904* (Basingstoke: Palgrave, 2006), pp. 135–38.

Meanwhile Labour, having boasted it would build 400,000 houses a year to make up for the stock lost in the war, had in fact managed little more than half that figure.[27]

Macmillan, however, despite an interest in housing going back to the inter-war years, little imagined that it was he who would be called upon to remedy this deficiency when the Conservatives under Churchill narrowly won the 1951 general election. He had hoped to become Minister of Defence, though when he later held this portfolio in 1954–55 he was to discover that this was essentially an exercise in responsibility without power, which continued to lie with the service departments over which he was nominally in charge. Creating a better-co-ordinated Ministry of Defence, in two bouts of reform at the start and end of his Premiership, was to be one of Macmillan's lasting legacies.

Macmillan initially regarded his new job in 1951 as something of a poisoned chalice. In practice, however, Churchill supported Macmillan in all his battles for resources with Chancellor of the Exchequer Rab Butler. And in delivering the key election pledge of building 300,000 houses per year by 1953 Macmillan cemented his place in the hearts of the party faithful. As Churchill later reminded Macmillan, 'You were disappointed at the time; but it made you P.M.'[28]

When Churchill was eventually prevailed upon to retire from the Premiership in April 1955 he was replaced by Anthony Eden, who was in turn replaced at the Foreign Office by Macmillan. Macmillan was now at last in an office he had long coveted. His tenure, however, was short. The relationship with his predecessor was not always easy and in December 1955 Eden moved a reluctant Macmillan to replace Butler at the Treasury.

The end of Butler's Chancellorship had been fraught, not least in light of Labour's success in depicting his emergency Budget of October 1955 as a desperate redress for the pre-election giveaways of his previous effort in April. Macmillan thus inherited a fiscally constrained position. He was very aware of the need for savings 'to make foreigners feel we are in earnest' in the run-up to his 1956 Budget.[29] Whether, later in the year in his bellicose response to the Egyptian nationalisa-

---

27. *Britain Strong and Free: A Statement of Conservative and Unionist Policy* (London: Conservative and Unionist Central Office, 1951), pp. 14, 26, 29–30.

28. See below p. 598 (25 September 1963).

29. Catterall, *The Macmillan Diaries 1950–1957*, p. 548 (8 April 1956).

tion of the Suez Canal, he bore in mind sufficiently the sensibilities of these foreign sterling-holders – and especially the Americans – has long been a matter of historiographical controversy. What is not in doubt is that it was selling in New York, American blocking of British drawing rights at the IMF, and suggestions of oil sanctions that led to Macmillan counselling a ceasefire on 6 November. His subsequent robust defence of the action against the Egyptians, not least to backbench Tories in the 1922 Committee, nevertheless helped to secure him the succession to the Premiership when Eden resigned in ill health early the following year.

Resolving the fallout from Suez – from arranging compensation for the Egyptian nationalisation of British property to the proxy war which broke out against Nasser-backed nationalists in South Arabia during his final year in office – was to cast a long shadow over the Macmillan government. This was not Macmillan's only challenging inheritance on becoming Prime Minister. An armed struggle with nationalists in Cyprus, ongoing since 1955, was only to be resolved in 1960. Sterling remained weak. Full employment, which had become seen as a *sine qua non* of government policy since 1945, rendered the economy prone to inflation and balance-of-payments crises. Industries such as cotton and shipbuilding were in long-term decline, producing in turn regional patterns of unemployment.

Other challenges were yet to emerge, such as the gradual break-up of the Central African Federation, or the series of scandals culminating in the Profumo affair, that would dog his last years in office. Fairly regularly, as a weekend exercise of review, Macmillan would summarise these problems and reflect on how to tackle them in the diary which he kept up throughout his Premiership. By organising these diaries into years, and listing at the head of each annual section the principal themes running through each year, I have tried to provide a ready guide to the matters which seemed to Macmillan to either become or remain pressing during the relevant twelve months.

Macmillan had first kept a diary long before. His many letters to his mother during the First World War effectively form a war diary of his military service. His *War Diaries*, published in 1984, covering his period as Minister Resident in Algiers, Greece and Italy 1943–45, similarly began as letters to his wife, Dorothy. They, however, soon graduated into a regular journal. He began keeping a diary again in August 1950. Over the next six years he filled 22 black-bound foolscap notebooks. A 23rd, covering the final stages of the Suez Crisis, appears to have been destroyed.[30] The diary only picks up again with an entry on 3 February 1957, in what Macmillan treated as a new series of diaries. This entry, in which he reviewed events since his accession to the Premiership, appears as the closing item in the first volume of these diaries, published in 2003.

Over the next ten years he was to write just under 510,000 words, entered in the same foolscap notebooks. There are 23 of these for the period of his Premiership, crammed with a forward-leaning, large, somewhat linear script. Having been wounded in the right hand at the Battle of Loos in 1915, even Macmillan as he later reviewed his diaries when preparing his memoirs would find some words challenging to decipher. He would write on the right-hand page and then, often, start again at the front on the left-hand page before moving on to the next notebook. During the period of his Premiership each volume contains some two-to-three months of diaries. A further three notebooks carry on the diaries down to May 1966. In these Macmillan, despite standing down from Parliament at the 1964 general election, continued to comment on the course of British politics. Although he eventually found the House of Lords the perfect place for an old gentleman – 'you're never more than 40 yards from a bar or a loo'[31] – he did not, however, resume his parliamentary career until accepting a hereditary peerage as Earl of Stockton in 1984, just two years before his death. Instead, he returned as Chairman to the family publishing firm and set about its modernisation following the long and quixotic reign of his elder brother Daniel.[32] These final years of the diary record abroad the company's expansion in newly independent Africa, and at home the impact on business of the tax policies of the first Wilson government. Then, suddenly, they stop. Macmillan never seems to have explained why he resumed a regular diary in 1950, though even before he became Prime Minister there are all too obvious hints that he was aware they provided a mine of material for his subsequent memoirs. Nor does he give an explanation for their cessation. Dorothy's fatal heart attack, the day after the final entry, nevertheless surely provides it. Despite the hurt his wife's long affair from 1929 with his fellow Tory MP Bob Boothby clearly caused him (see the rare, oblique reference to this in

---

30. Ibid, p. 607, n. 68.
31. Private information.
32. See Alan Maclean, *No, I tell a lie, it was the Tuesday* . . . (London: Kyle Cathie, 1997), chap. 10.

the entry for 21 April 1961), there seems little doubt of the strength of his emotional tie to her. With her death he does not seem to have had the heart to continue the diary.

Nor, perhaps, did he feel so much the need. This is not to imply that the diaries necessarily served as a sanctuary to which Macmillan retreated. The idea of a tension between Macmillan's inner and outer life to which too many of Macmillan's biographers have been drawn[33] – perhaps seduced by his own tendency to use the image of the swordsman or the gownsman – cannot be used to explain the keeping of so activity-focused a diary, however literary its form. The passages of introspection are short and pithy, prompted either by his health or by something he was reading. Indeed, if it is apt to speak of Macmillan's inner life, then it was primarily expressed in his voluminous reading. Although they had a wireless at Birch Grove, Britain's first television Prime Minister only had a set in the servants' hall. Instead, even during his Premiership he could manage to read over 100 books a year, getting through seven on his 'Winds of Change' tour of Africa in 1960, one of which was a novel set in Nkrumah's Ghana. He may have occasionally read as soothing relief, sometimes after enumerating in his diaries the problems currently faced by his government. This does not mean that his reading, any more than the writing of his diaries, represented an escape by Macmillan to any specific inner life.[34]

Both his reading and his diaries make clear his distaste, at the opposite extreme, for empty, swordsman-like heroics. Macmillan might have been gifted the mock-heroic persona of 'Supermac' by the left-wing cartoonist Vicky,[35] with malicious intent that went awry. Not that he harboured any illusions that he was actually playing that role. He was far from being the showman sometimes depicted, simply distracting the British from their long-term decline. His 'never had it so good' speech in 1957, for instance, was a warning of the threat posed to the prosperity of the whole community by self-indulgent

---

33. See in particular Anthony Sampson, *Macmillan: A Study in Ambiguity* (London: Allen Lane, 1967), p. 260; Richard Davenport-Hines, *The Macmillans* (London: Mandarin, 1993), pp. 161, 273; Charles Williams, *Harold Macmillan* (London: Weidenfeld & Nicolson, 2009).

34. Peter Catterall, 'The Prime Minister and his Trollope: Reading Harold Macmillan's Reading', *Cercles*, Occasional Paper 1 (2004).

35. *Evening Standard*, 6 November 1958. 'Vicky' was the pseudonym of Victor Weisz (1913–66).

strikes and resulting wage-push inflation, however much it may have
been deliberately misinterpreted as a mere exhortation to conspicuous
consumption by his political opponents after their 1959 election defeat.
Instead of grand gestures he went for grand inter-connected designs. In
his 'Grand Design' paper of December 1960, for example, written
partly in face of the impending imposition of the Hallstein tariffs by
the six countries of the recently formed European Economic Community, the initiation of European negotiations was simply part of an
overarching scheme for liberalising international trade and aid: this
was designed to tackle the stop-go cycle bedevilling the UK economy;
consolidate resistance to communism both in the West and the former
colonies; and thereby help to reduce the military costs of the Cold
War. When in his famous diary entry of 28 January 1963 he later
reflected, in that hyperbolic vein to which the diaries are occasionally
prone, that 'All our policies at home and abroad are in ruins',
Macmillan was, of course, referring to the totality of these goals rather
than, as too many commentators have assumed, just the impending
end of the European entry negotiations the following day. These
negotiations were more of a contingent policy device for achieving
wider policy ends. And by that stage, anticipating a breakdown in the
talks, he had already begun preparing some kind of alternative. The
grandiose title of his October 1962 'Modernisation of Britain'[36] Cabinet memorandum should not distract too readily from the fact that
Macmillan was defaulting to expansionism of the domestic economy
and the incomes policy elaborated earlier in the year.[37]

This resort to domestic expansionism was because his preferred
alternative of global liberalisation and trade expansion was being
closed off. Having sought Commonwealth/European alternatives to
relying internationally on America, ironically, Macmillan found that
he made most progress with the latter. Again ironically, this was
particularly true in his relations not with the Administration of his old
wartime buddy Eisenhower, but under his youthful successor Kennedy.
That Macmillan's penchant for personal diplomacy worked on an
Irish-American President but not on his West German or French
counterparts reflects not that Kennedy was necessarily more susceptible

---

36. TNA, CAB 129/111, C(62) 201.
37. See Department of Western Manuscripts, Bodleian Library, Oxford
    [henceforward DWM], MS Macmillan, dep. c. 356: 'Notes for remarks to
    Cabinet', 28 May 1962.

to the blandishments of the older man, but that he shared Macmillan's global framework, whilst the visions of the even older de Gaulle and Adenauer were for their own good reasons fixed more upon Europe. The launching of the Kennedy Round and the shared pursuit of the Test Ban Treaty thus reflected a coincidence of interests never quite achieved with the more sceptical Eisenhower Administration.

Macmillan's global vision was summed up in the word 'interdependence'. This has often been taken erroneously to refer almost exclusively to Anglo-American relations. Macmillan certainly used it in that context in October 1957,[38] when the American furore over the Soviet launch of the *Sputnik* satellite provided the opportunity to persuade the Eisenhower Administration to 'pool all our resources to fight them – financial, military, technical, propaganda?', paving the way for the restoration of nuclear information sharing.[39] However, its wider import became clear when, at an Anglo-American meeting on 23 October 1957, he talked of unity among 50–60 allies, though with Britain and America acting as 'an inner core working in unison gradually extending by example and influence their own harmony and confidence to all the free world'.[40] The pursuit of interdependence, by giving poorer countries access to world markets and raising their productivity, would also benefit the richer, both in terms of trade and security, not least by reducing the attraction of communism to those sections of the globe then heading to independence. This had a domestic analogue: it is no coincidence that he used this vision of global interdependence as a means of introducing to an initially sceptical Birmingham audience the related merits of trying to help economic expansion in the depressed areas of the country on 9 January 1963.[41]

Nor is it coincidence that he ended the famous diary passage of 28 January 1963 with the words 'We have lost everything, except our courage and determination'. All too easy to see as a rhetorical grasping at straws, it expresses a deeper truth about Macmillan's view both of personality and history: that above all he valued character, not least

---

38. Catterall, 'Identity and Integration', p. 174.
39. See below p. 64 (9 October 1957).
40. Dwight D. Eisenhower Library, Abilene, KS, Whitman File, International Series [henceforward DDEL], Box 23: memorandum of conversation, 23 October 1957, 'Closer US–UK relations and Free World Cooperation'.
41. *Birmingham Post and Gazette*, 11 January 1963.

those characters who struggled to overcome circumstances.[42] Character
and the resilience Macmillan tried to show in repeatedly finding new
ways to pursue his 'Grand Design' were central to his thought. His
reading preferences indicate that he developed this penchant for
'unflappability' long before Hailsham claims to have coined the phrase
in 1958.[43] In contrast, Butler's apparent deficiencies of character were
key reasons why Macmillan felt he should not become Prime Minister.
The fact that Butler failed to seize his opportunities during the crucial
days of October 1963 simply reinforced this fact for Macmillan.[44] As
Churchill himself had observed when advising the Queen to send for
Macmillan rather than Butler in 1957, 'Harold is more decisive.'.[45]

Character was not gender-specific. One of the historical characters
Macmillan most admired was Elizabeth I. Amongst his contemporaries
Lady Diana Cooper clearly continued to exercise a fascination,[46] whilst
space has made it impossible to reflect fully in this edition his close, if
sometimes a little exasperated, friendship with the twice-widowed Ava
Waverley. He may not have thought much of the capabilities of most
female Tory MPs,[47] but his one reference to Margaret Thatcher makes
clear that he recognised her qualities. Nevertheless, for Macmillan,
character clearly included manliness. This is a term he seems to see
particularly exemplified by the Cabinet solidarity over the 1958 Jordan
or 1959 Nyasaland crises. Another comment on 5 September 1963
associates it with vision and moral strength. Interestingly, after Denzil
Freeth's arrest Macmillan observed, 'There is nothing unmanly about
being drunk, and very good precedents among my great predecessors'.[48] Macmillan's sympathies with Freeth were no doubt
informed by his awareness of the battles his own son Maurice fought
with alcoholism. What was unmanly was not being drunk but being
out of control, either through drink or other failings. This perhaps
explains Macmillan's bafflement when it became apparent that too

---

42. Catterall, 'The Prime Minister and his Trollope', pp. 8, 13 f.
43. Lord Hailsham, *A Sparrow's Flight* (London: Collins, 1990), p. 317.
44. See below p. 612 (19 and 20 October 1963). See also Catterall, *The Macmillan Diaries: 1950–1957*, p. 314 (6 June 1954).
45. John Colville, *The Churchillians* (London: Weidenfeld & Nicolson, 1981), p. 188.
46. Maclean, pp. 167–68.
47. See below p. 257 (30 October 1959).
48. See below p. 466 (25 April 1962).

many of the Cabinet were being neither solidaristic nor sexually continent during the Profumo scandal.

Manliness, then, was about self-control. Macmillan, unlike Alan-brooke,[49] did not keep a diary just to let off steam. There is certainly nothing in it about Dorothy and Boothby, though there are other, sometimes intemperate, personal judgements. There are also exasperated passages in the diaries, as when the European Free Trade Area negotiations failed in 1958, but these match the mood he then expressed in government memoranda as well.[50] Indeed, the diaries can help to contextualise these displays of emotion. They also show how calculating these could be, at least on some occasions. When, for instance, on 5 December 1962 Dean Acheson claimed that 'Great Britain has lost an empire and has not yet found a role',[51] Macmillan's diary entry helps to amplify his comment that this presented 'One of those rare opportunities . . . . which can be seized with great <u>internal</u> political advantage. It might be a turning point in our fortunes, which are low at the moment.'[52] It also served to provide an external political advantage by putting the Americans on the back foot in the upcoming Nassau negotiations, from which Macmillan returned triumphant with their agreement to supply Polaris missiles.[53]

It is important to remember that this occasional need to dissemble is a necessary part of the weaponry of any successful politician. It is a tactic, pursued once the course has been decided. Macmillan, however clear he might have been about long-term goals, was nevertheless not always as good as he pretended at deciding on the course. This is apparent in his vacillations over Suez in 1956. And on occasion he toyed with the idea of floating and devaluing the currency as a way out of the economic constraints presented by the post-war Bretton Woods system of fixed exchange rates, a drastic measure to contemplate at the time as a unilateral act – not least because of its implications for Commonwealth members of the Sterling Area with currencies

---

49. See Alex Danchev and Daniel Todman (eds), *War Diaries 1939–1945: Field Marshal Lord Alanbrooke* (London: Phoenix, 2002).

50. See, for example, James Ellison, *Threatening Europe: Britain and the Creation of the European Community 1955–58* (Basingstoke: Palgrave, 2000), pp. 191, 207.

51. See Catterall, 'Roles and Relationships', p. 115.

52. TNA, PREM 11/4057: Macmillan to Bligh and de Zulueta, 7 December 1962.

53. Catterall, 'Roles and Relationships', pp. 115–17.

tied to the value of the pound – but one which would certainly have made the domestic expansionism of the early 1960s easier to pursue.[54]

Vacillation is equally apparent as he agonised over whether and when to relinquish office in 1963. It is in the scope that they offered privately and in real time for thinking through these dilemmas that the diaries appear to have served Macmillan's purpose. Dorothy's sudden death, when he had just finished a volume, may have seemed like the prostate problem which struck him with equal suddenness just when he had made up his mind to continue in the Premiership: an act of God that not only brought his marriage but the continuing need for the discipline of the diaries to an end.

There are occasional glimpses that Macmillan saw this as a (sometimes trying) discipline. In the entry for 12 March 1958 he complains, 'The trouble is that I get tired always [having] to "do" the diary every night. (Actually I am writing this on Saturday 15th)'. It was a discipline he did not always keep up. The diaries for the period of his Premiership do not have suspicious gaps like the one covering collusion and denouement at Suez in 1956. Nevertheless, there were clearly a number of occasions when he simply failed to enter it up, sometimes for a few weeks. One such was when he went to Moscow. Instead, there was a flurry of letters to Eisenhower. He did, however, review the trip in his diary on his return to London. When he went to Africa in 1960, in contrast, he noted:

Although I have not been able to keep up the diary since Jan 5 till Feb 7, there are (a) the programmes of each country .... (b) the Salisbury and Cape Town speeches (c) there will be (as on the last tour) a printed record, compiled by Norman Brook. A copy of this should be available for my records.[55]

Accordingly, he felt no need to review the tour in his diary on this occasion.

Nevertheless, such gaps are rare. Occasional slips in dating suggest that he was writing up an entry later. And there is certainly a tendency for weekend entries to be longer and more reflective. This is particularly true after wide-ranging visits from figures like Kennedy or de Gaulle. However, generally Macmillan seems to have been able to keep up his

54. See below p. 57 (4 September 1957); Lewis Baston, *Reggie: The Life of Reginald Maudling* (Stroud: Alan Sutton, 2004), pp. 195–96.

55. DWM: 'Harold Macmillan Diary', 13 February 1960.

almost daily discipline. This gives an immediacy lacking in, for instance, the diaries of contemporary figures like Richard Crossman or Kenneth Younger, written up at weekends or even weeks later.[56] On the other hand, unlike Younger's considered efforts, Macmillan often does not seem even to have bothered to check the previous entry before writing the next one. The result is a fair amount of repetition, not to mention inconsistency of spelling. Nor is that the only inaccuracy. Figures drift: at one point in late 1962 the cut in the purchase tax on cars is 33.3% rather than the 25% eventually effected. It is not always easy to tell whether such shifts reflect ongoing policy discussions or simple misremembering. And issues come and go, reflecting the priorities on Macmillan's desk on a particular date. The stories thus taken up are, however, sometimes left unresolved, as his attention has to move on to some other matter.

A particular example is the crisis in Laos. Suddenly brought up the agenda by the Americans in late 1960, Macmillan can only observe, 'They back a certain Phoumi – we, I don't quite know why, prefer Phouma.'[57] No one should expect prime ministerial omniscience on a hitherto obscure crisis not his own that abruptly climbs the agenda at the moment of a change of administration in Washington. Laos troubles the prime minister, and thus the diary, for a while, before fading back into obscurity.

This illustrates one of the problems of assessing how and why a diarist constructs their account. It is easy to assume that topics intrude because they are important either because they bulk large in the diarist's working life, or because they are, like reading or shooting for Macmillan, key interests. But Macmillan does not always record events or issues which seem on the face of it, not least from the amount of attention they receive in Cabinet or in his own papers, to be important stories. Importance, clearly, is not the same as interest. Things that interest Macmillan, or strike a chord with him, will get recorded. For instance, notwithstanding his apparent blind spot about the merits of the Euston Arch, he obviously cared about architecture. Matters such as the 1962 Cuban missile crisis can fill pages. In contrast, the Robbins Report into higher education receives one perfunctory mention from the then Chancellor of Oxford University. Concorde goes unrecorded until the Labour government in 1964 thought about cancelling it. The

---

56. See 'Editing Political Diaries', *Contemporary Record*, 7/1 (1993), pp. 104, 127.

57. See below p. 341 (8 December 1960).

Plowden Report into the control of public expenditure in 1961 and the founding of the National Economic Development Council the following year – both matters in which Macmillan might be expected to take a great interest – are not even obliquely referred to. Nor is the audit of empire Macmillan commissioned in 1957.[58]

The same goes for the people in Macmillan's life. An encounter with an old wartime colleague is sometimes recounted with more interest than a conversation with a Cabinet minister. This perhaps reflects a generation gap which became more marked after the Cabinet reconstruction of 1962 brought in a number of younger men. Thereafter there is little indication that Macmillan mixed socially with his senior colleagues, except Home, in the way he had with Kilmuir or Salisbury.

When he does record encounters or correspondence the entry may not appear on the relevant date. Thus a speech by the Prime Minister of the Central Africa Federation, Sir Roy Welensky, to the Conservative backbench Commonwealth Affairs Committee on 16 March 1961 went unmentioned in the diary until eight days later. The diary often records what Macmillan was thinking about that day as much as what actually happened. This is particularly the case when, as in this particular entry, he was reviewing developments over the past few weeks. As a result, the dates mentioned in the diary at times are only an approximate guide to when events actually occurred, or even to when Macmillan became aware of them.

Macmillan's source for events such as Welensky's speech was his PPS, Samuel Knox-Cunningham. There is a fat file of Knox-Cunningham's reports on backbench committee meetings in Macmillan's papers at the Bodleian Library, Oxford.[59] The above is, however, one of the rare occasions when Macmillan directly refers to such intelligence, because it mattered. Otherwise, it seems, Knox-Cunningham's reports formed part of the furniture of Macmillan's world, unremarkable because they were always there.[60] Concorde and Plowden were presumably unremarkable for similar reasons: Macmillan knew what he thought of them, did not feel a need to record every twist and turn and, in the

---

58. This is probably because it was set up on 28 January 1957, before Macmillan re-started his diary: see TNA, PREM 11/2617.
59. DWM, MS Macmillan dep. c. 354.
60. Jad Adams makes a similar point to explain significant silences regarding daily episodes in Tony Benn's diaries in 'Editing Political Diaries', p. 117.

and, in the case of the former, was happy to leave his son-in-law Julian Amery to get on with it.

In editing his diaries for publication I have tried to interfere as little as possible with Macmillan's text. His tendency to contract words like 'which' or 'Parliament' has largely been left untouched, as has the sometimes irregular punctuation. Misspellings of proper names have generally been corrected or standardised (he transliterated the name of the Iraqi dictator Qasim in three different ways!).

Names pose other problems as well. These diaries throng with them. Historical and literary allusions abound. Not only are there so many names, but large numbers have subsequently changed. Countries, cities and even institutions have all been re-labelled since 1966. Even during the period covered by the diaries some figures regularly changed their names through ennoblement or, following the 1963 Peerage Act, renunciation. This vast supporting cast of sometimes ghostly characters need their roles clarified and contextualised in one way or another. I have taken the line that historic or literary figures whose provenance is not clear from the text are best explained by a footnote, whilst potted biographies of contemporary figures of significance are provided at the end of this volume in a set of Biographical Notes, along with a further appendix detailing the personnel of Macmillan's successive Cabinets. Recurring items, events or places are explained by footnote, usually at their first appearance. So are important contextual matters, such as the political complexion in this period of the national press.

I have also sought to contextualise the diaries by providing some cross-referencing with the accounts of other actors. This approach seemed particularly appropriate for some of the more controversial moments covered. For instance, I have drawn extensively upon the memoirs and biographies of others involved when footnoting the events culminating in Macmillan's resignation in October 1963.

Omissions have, of course, had to occur to reduce the original text to less than half its length. It has been possible to achieve some of that by cutting out repetitions. To a much greater extent than in the first volume, however, it has also been necessary to omit Macmillan's reading, social activities and family life. It was also tempting to leave out now familiar material first reproduced in Macmillan's memoirs. Some certainly proved expendable. It became clear, however, that many of these passages had only been partially reproduced, without ellipses, in the memoirs. This is true, for instance, of the sections on the 'Night of the Long Knives' – Macmillan's famous Cabinet reshuffle in 1962. Sometimes these unacknowledged omissions reflect personal sensitivities still current at the time the memoirs appeared. With the passage of time it should now be possible to reproduce the expurgations.

Where I have omitted material I have indicated the fact with ellipses. In general I have tried to select discrete passages or paragraphs, whilst also necessarily flagging the omission of superfluous diversions or repetitions. Occasionally, to obviate the need for a footnote, an explanatory date or name has also been inserted into the text within square brackets.

Editing a diary is a very distinctive way of getting to know your subject. Instead of making sense of who they were, it involves the somewhat different process of making sense of and explaining as concisely as possible what they wrote. It has throughout been a challenging but intellectually very rewarding task. No doubt I have occasionally fallen into error. Nevertheless, I hope that, on the whole, Harold Macmillan would consider that I have proved a worthy amanuensis.

PETER CATTERALL
May 2010

1957

Surviving the Suez crisis – rapprochement with the Americans – Treaty of Rome, the establishment of the EEC and the British Free Trade Area alternative – Makarios' release from the Seychelles and the continuing Cyprus crisis – Bank Rate 'leak' – the Rent Act – Sputnik and the renewing of nuclear secrets sharing with the Americans

8 February[1]

.... Civil Estimates are up by £280m. Service estimates etc are still £155m. We have got the Cabinet to agree about £15m cuts in Civil Estimates and a new 'Health Stamp' to bring in (say) £34m and give back some of the insurance character to the Health scheme. We hope to get £50m out of the Germans. We shall cut our men in Germany – Army 80,000 to 50,000 – aircraft 420 to 220 front line. We hope for £50–£100m of economies as well. All this has meant intense work .... However, ministers are working well and I am admirably served in the Private Office. One of the more agreeable aspects of my new job is the weekly audience. This is usually on Tuesday evenings. The Queen is not only very charming, but incredibly well informed. Less agreeable, are visits and letters from the Archbishop of Canterbury [Fisher]. I try to talk to him about religion. But he seems to be quite uninterested and reverts all the time to politics. After a long negotiation, my meeting with the President [Eisenhower] has now been arranged. I was very unwilling to go to Washington.[2] The Americans, with great generosity and good feeling, suggested Bermuda. Of course, this (being British soil) makes all the difference to us. But I was afraid that the French wd be hurt; or, worse still, want to make it a Tripartite meeting. However, they too have behaved very well, and agreed to go on their own to Washington. We have now settled in No 10.[3] It is very comfortable. I have a good room as a study, next to Dorothy's 'boudoir'. (She has arranged a working sitting room upstairs) The house is rather large, but has great character and charm. It is very 'liveable'. René Massigli came to luncheon yesterday – in very good form .... René thinks that Mollet will last quite a bit – but we must hurry with our plans for European unity ....

---

1. The only previous entry for 1957, detailing Macmillan's rise to the Premiership, appears in volume 1.
2. This would have made him appear a supplicant after the breakdown of Anglo-American (and Franco-American) relations over Suez.
3. 10 Downing Street, the Prime Minister's official London residence.

One of the remarkable things about the recent crisis has been how we have somehow adjusted ourselves to the new conditions . . . . In spite of the oil cuts, industry is going on pretty well. Yesterday, because of market conditions and considerable funding by the Bank – £200m in the last few weeks – we knocked ½% off the Bank Rate. The House of Commons is very quiet – almost tame. Our only anxiety is a by-election in N Lewisham, where we shall (on form) lose the seat.[4] However, our people are working very hard.

9 February (Saturday)
. . . . In thinking over our immediate problems, they seem to be

  a) <u>UN and Israel</u>. As long as Israel refuses to leave Gaza etc U.N. will declare her in default and may try sanctions.[5] UK opinion will <u>not</u> stand for this. But if we stand out, Arab opinion is still more inflamed agst us. The Americans are behaving very weakly over this, with legalism and pedantry.
  b) <u>Syria and Egypt</u> have an excuse, owing to a). Syria will not allow the Mediterranean pipe-line to be mended and Egypt may close the canal.
  c) <u>Nasser and the canal</u>. He may refuse passage to British and French ships.
  d) <u>Canal dues</u>. Nasser will claim full dues. If we refuse, we don't get our oil.[6] If we accept, we lose face terribly. (We might even lose our majority in the House) Here again Dulles uses fine words but does nothing . . . .

If we can get over these immediate troubles, we might manage fairly well. The Budget will not be easy. When the Civil Estimates come out,

---

4. Labour took the seat on a small swing, with an Empire Loyalist intervention. This was the Conservatives' first by-election loss since they gained a majority of 60 in the 1955 General Election.
5. Having occupied the Egyptian territory of the Sinai during the 1956 Suez War, Israel had then withdrawn from all except the Gaza Strip and the Sharm el-Sheikh Heights on the Tiran Straits. Whilst they were reluctant to withdraw from Gaza, the starting point for years of *fedayeen* raids into Israel, or from the Heights, to protect their shipping, Syria and Egypt insisted that neither oil pipelines nor the Suez Canal would re-open until they did so. This finally occurred on 7 March 1957.
6. Britain was largely dependent on Middle Eastern oil, most of which was carried through the Suez Canal.

people will have a shock. The Farm Price Review is due – and of course, the farmers will do their Oliver Twist act as usual[7] . . . .

11 February
Cabinet at 10.30. . . . Israel problem was discussed and Cabinet approved the line wh F.S. and I had worked out. . . . This is a) we cannot vote for sanctions agst Israel b) in order to put ourselves as right as possible with Arab world, we shall try to get a 'moderate' motion sponsored by (say) Canada, which wd call for a fair settlement . . . .

13 February
I have contracted a slight chill, so I stayed in bed till it was time to go to the HofC (3.30) for the defence debate. The news from America is better. The State Dept are at last frightened by what they have done. They are trying to settle Israel's demands, and may end up in 'guaranteeing' her free passage of the Aqaba straits and the Canal![8] Yesterday, they were threatening 'sanctions'. The Americans have also suggested quite a sensible plan for payment of Canal dues. Whether Nasser will agree, I don't know. I shd say not – unless the Americans pay some blackmail. However, all this is encouraging.

14 February
Churchill to luncheon (alone) It seemed strange for me to be entertaining him at No 10. He has aged, but is still very well informed and misses little that goes on . . . .

The North Lewisham figures were announced at 12 midnight. We lost by 1100 votes. The third candidate (Empire Loyalist) took 1500 votes – no doubt largely, if not entirely, Conservative votes. So really we have done rather better than we expected. Nevertheless, there is an obvious swing away from us – 5% or so – which must be corrected if we are to win the next election.

15 February
A long Cabinet in the morning. I did not find my colleagues too depressed about the by-election. Anyway, we took or confirmed some

---

7. That is, to ask, like the eponymous character in Charles Dickens's *Oliver Twist*, for more.
8. The Americans in the end offered Israel guarantees, but these proved ineffective.

pretty 'tough' decisions – all of which are right and essential, but will (I suppose) be 'unpopular'. We decided to go ahead with the Rents Bill, with some modification to Clause 9, to retain the principle of decontrol but smooth out the transition a little.[9] This had already been proposed by the Minister. We confirmed our decision to raise another 10d on the Insurance stamp, and thus get some £34m a year towards the ever-growing cost of the Health scheme. We decided to offer, and if necessary, impose a firm financial settlement on the farmers . . . .

16 February
It has turned very cold – a good deal of snow last night. Shepilov (Soviet For Secy) has been dismissed and Gromyko has taken his place. As usual, there is much speculation as to the significance of this; as usual, no one really knows. We came last night (for the first time) to Chequers.[10] D and I; Carol and Mark (Faber), Catherine and Julian Amery,[11] with Louise. The children enjoyed it very much. L[ouise] is about 5 and Mark is 6. Neither of them had been in so large a house and they were very pleased at the adventure of going all over it. [Oliver] Cromwell's letters; the T.V.; and the telephone exchange were the chief points of interest. I left at 10.15 for London airport, to 'see the Queen off' to her state visit to Portugal. I took Mark with me. We have here the advantage of secretaries, typists etc – so it is easier to get work done all the time than at B.G.[12]

17 February (Sunday)
. . . . The Sunday press is fairly sensible – except the *Express* which demands an immediate General Election and has a bitter personal

---

9. When Housing Minister in the early 1950s Macmillan had favoured decontrol of rents to help finance repairs and encourage a more efficient private-rented sector. Although concerned about the political risks of concomitant rent rises, the government decided to introduce a Rent Bill in October 1956. All-party concern at resulting hardship, especially at the top end of the market, however, induced the Cabinet at this meeting to extend the period during which there could be no change in rents from six to fifteen months and to make premiums on decontrolled properties illegal for three years.

10. The Prime Minister's country residence, in Buckinghamshire.

11. Carol, who married Julian Faber, and Catherine, who married Julian Amery, were Macmillan's daughters.

12. Birch Grove, Macmillan's country house in Sussex.

attack on me.[13] I'm afraid this is the beginning of what will be a sustained campaign. It's all the result of the European Free Trade policy, for which Lord Beaverbrook has a fanatical hatred . . . .

18 February
. . . . The Israeli refusal to withdraw from Gaza or the Gulf of Aqaba is creating a fresh crisis in U.N. . . . . [W]ill Egypt react by stopping General Wheeler from finishing the work of clearing the canal?[14] From our point of view, the situation is very bad, for until Israel's terms of withdrawal are agreed with U.N., there seems little hope of the Canal being re-opened or the Syrian pipe-line restored. This again means a heavy financial loss for Iraq, which we shall have to support ourselves in some way, in order to keep Nuri [al-Said] Pasha in power.

I had Iain Macleod (Minister of Labour) to dinner alone. He is very able and full of ideas. I am very anxious to get legislation in the autumn to deal with Pensions on a wide basis. The Socialist scheme, which will soon be coming out, will be unsound but attractive[15] . . . .

---

13. Macmillan refers to a broad range of contemporary newspapers, both national and regional, in these diaries. It might be helpful to give some indication of their general political affiliations. The Beaverbrook press – the *Daily Express*, *Sunday Express* and London *Evening Standard* – were Conservative but reflected the maverick, pro-imperial politics of their proprietor. Other Conservative-supporting newspapers were the *Daily Mail*, *Daily Sketch* and London *Evening News* (all Rothermere-owned), the *Daily Telegraph* and, amongst the regionals, included the *Yorkshire Post*. It might be argued with less conviction that *The Times*, owned by the Astor family until 1981, should be included in this list. The only remaining Liberal-supporting newspaper, the *News Chronicle*, merged with the *Daily Mail* in 1960. The *Daily Herald*, 49% owned by the TUC and with an official line of supporting the Labour Party, also had its difficulties. In 1961 a majority share was taken by the Mirror Group, which acquired the rest of the shares and renamed it the *Sun* in 1964. Labour's most influential supporter in Fleet Street was the *Daily Mirror*, which in this period had a circulation peaking at 5 million in 1965, over half a million more than its nearest rival, the *Daily Express*. Its Sunday version, the *Sunday Pictorial*, became the *Sunday Mirror* in 1963. The remaining most politically influential newspapers were the leftish *Manchester Guardian*, renamed the *Guardian* in 1959, the liberal-inclined Astor-owned Sunday paper, the *Observer* and the Communist Party's *Daily Worker*.
14. The British general Raymond Wheeler was in charge of the UN salvage force.
15. In May Richard Crossman's *National Superannuation: Labour's Plan for Security in Old Age* suggested a supplementary earnings-related pension on top

The 'Kashmir' problem (which is quite insoluble) is now before the Security Council and is causing us great anxiety.[16] India is, of course, supported by Russia and Indian opinion is being inflamed by Nehru against the UK. There is even a threat to leave the Commonwealth. The United Nations seems to be turning out an institution for causing the maximum of international trouble. Yesterday, UK, Greece and Turkey had a battle in New York over Cyprus. Last week, it was France and the Algerian question.[17] So it goes on.

19 February
. . . . Chancellor of the Ex[chequer] announcement after questions. The Opposition put on a great show of indignation, but I thought it rather synthetic . . . . I feel sure we were right to increase the Health contribution rather than increase the Charges or reduce the benefits . . . .

20 February
The Press is divided, more or less as one wd expect on the Government economy scheme. £57m is (after all) not a negligible sum. *Times* and *D.T.* good; *Mail* also. The *Express* (which ought to support us) is opposed. This means that all the Beaverbrook press (except, curiously enough, the *Evening Standard*) are under orders from Nassau[18] to attack all along the line . . . .

----

of the existing flat-rate scheme. Outlines of the scheme had been heavily used in Labour's successful campaign in North Lewisham.

16. Kashmir had been disputed between India and Pakistan since independence and partition in 1947. The UN calls for a plebiscite on the territory's future in the early 1950s had been reiterated in a UK-led resolution on 24 January 1957. India retaliated with moves, furiously resisted by Pakistan, formally to integrate Kashmir and issue it with a new constitution. As both sides became more bellicose another UN resolution on 15 February remitted the problem to a mission led by Gunnar Jarring, the Swedish ambassador to the UN. This achieved little, though at least for a time reversion to war between India and Pakistan was averted.

17. France had been arraigned by fifteen Afro-Asian states for 'extensive military repression' and violation of the Genocide Convention in its conflict with nationalists in Algeria. The French hotly disputed the right of the UN to interfere in what was to them part of Metropolitan France before a compromise resolution calling for a 'peaceful, democratic and just solution' was carried in the UN General Assembly on 15 February.

18. Where Beaverbrook lived most of the time, in the Bahamas.

I impressed on M. Elath (Israeli ambassador) the need for a gesture from their side. British public opinion was strongly in favour of a 'package' deal. If Israel withdrew from Gaza and the Aqaba strip, she shd have guarantees from UN on which she could rely. We were taking this line firmly in Washington.

21 February

.... We have got a Treasury-Oil Company agreement about advancing £5m this year and up to £20m next financial year to Iraq to help her Budget, which is being very much knocked about by the closing of the pipe-lines. The doctors are very upset about our appointing a Royal Commission on their claims. They threaten a strike, but I don't think anything will happen. They are really pretty well paid, with some exceptions which we can meet at once. Luncheon for Mintoff (P.M. of Malta) who is here to negotiate for 'integration'.[19] His price is very high, but I got Bevan to talk sense to him – which he did.

At question time, it became clear that feeling was running rather high, on both sides of the House, about the President's speech on the radio last night. His approach to the Israel problem seems to us all very legalistic and one-sided. Of course, we can't say what we are doing behind the scenes, so we got all the blame. Our honour and our interest are in conflict. We want the Israelis to retire as soon as possible – so that the Canal clearance can continue and pressure be turned on Nasser. We are anxious about the oil-producing countries if 'sanctions' are imposed – whichever way we vote for sanctions, for we don't think Israel has had a fair deal. Even abstention must injure us in the Arab world and might shake our position at home. So, at all costs, we must work for a settlement . . . .

23 February

.... The great 'defence' week-end began today. There arrived for luncheon at Chequers For Secy, Ld P[rivy] Seal, Ld President, Minister of Defence, Chancellor of Ex, Chief Whip [Heath], Sir Norman Brook, Sir R Powell (MofDefence) Marshal of the Royal Air Force Dickson (Chief of [Air] Staff) We began work at 3pm and went till 6. Again

---

19. There were problems over social security arrangements and the desire of the Catholic Church in Malta to retain its privileged status. In the end Mintoff in 1958 dropped the idea of integration into the UK and started to press for independence.

from 6–7.30 and from 9.30–11.30. Duncan Sandys had prepared a paper, as a basis for discussion . . . .

24 February

I went to Church at 8am. At 10.30 the 'school' started work and went on till luncheon. Alec Home (Commonwealth Secy) came for luncheon. We had a short interval for a walk and started again at 3pm and finished at 6pm. We have had a very successful conference; some definite decisions (such as cutting forces to a figure of 380,000) have been reached. Other difficult questions, like the size of our nuclear and atomic effort; the size of the bomber force etc etc have been much clarified and the ground prepared for definite conclusions . . . .

25 February

. . . . We have at present more 'balls' in the air than I can remember.

In Foreign Affairs, these are, (a) Israeli–Egypt (b) Clearance of Canal (now held up by Egypt) (c) Canal dues – short term (d) long-term Canal settlement (e) Syrian pipe-lines.

In Commonwealth, (1) Indian–Pakistan dispute over Kashmir. Indian threat to leave Commonwealth. (2) Discussions with Malta, about to founder on Mintoff's intransigeance.

In defence (1) British forces in Germany, and our desire to reduce, resisted in WEU and NATO (2) German support costs; the Germans are wriggling out of the £50m agreement wh seemed 'in the bag' a week or two ago[20] (3) Cuts in forces – and new pattern of forces.

In Home Affairs
(1) High Civil Expenditure
(2) The doctors' claim to £20m
(3) Old Age Pensions
(4) Budget prospects.

If everything went right, we should still have been [in] difficulties. But of course, hardly anything ever goes right. If the Europeans don't obstruct us too badly, I really think our new defence policy may work out pretty well. Duncan Sandys is both able and obstinate – great qualities. The Minister of Labour is good too. The ridiculous and perhaps very widespread strike, starting at Briggs, extending to Fords, and perhaps reaching eventually to half the engineering industry seems

---

20. This represented German reimbursement towards the costs of stationing British troops in West Germany as agreed in the 1954 London agreement.

to have been called off, at least temporarily, by his effort. If this proves a firm settlement, it will redound much to the credit of the Govt.

26 February

.... I gave a large dinner (32 people) for the Foreign Ministers attending the Western European Union meeting. I gather that the reception of our plan for cutting our forces was pretty chilly . . . .

27 February

According to the newspapers (I have not yet seen the telegrams) Pearson launched his plan in U.N. yesterday. The Americans are said to be concocting a plan on similar lines. There seems no talk of immediate sanctions agst Israel. But the Canal clearance is equally being held up.

However, when I got to the Cabinet room, the newspapers were proved – as usual – wrong. Pearson made his speech, but did not move his resolution. Very bad telegrams both from Washington and New York. The administration have ratted again – going right back on Dulles' statement to Caccia and the President's telegram to me. They are talking (in Washington) of the matter 'not being negotiable' and (in New York) of accepting a motion for sanctions against Israel. We had a talk (F.S.; Ld S[alisbury] and I) after the defence committee (which met at 11am) and sent off telegrams of instructions . . . . We told them to abstain on the Asian–African motion of sanctions, and vote for the Pearson resolution (if it were moved) but to try for one or two further amendments in it . . . . All this is very bad. At home, abstaining will be thought weak; but even that may put us at further risk with the oil-producing states. All this drawn-out argument prevents the Arab world from settling down, and keeps the heat off Nasser.

.... M Mintoff (P.M. of Malta) came to see me. The negotiation is still alive, but not very flourishing. He is going back to Malta to reflect. The claims wh he puts forward are very extravagant and not very encouraging for the future of the 'integration' plan . . . .

28 February

A great row is threatened about an indiscretion by David Eccles, President of the BofT, which is alleged by all the press to be a 'Budget leak'. I had a rough time after questions – Gaitskell, Bevan, Wilson – all joining in the 'Hue and Cry'. I felt sure that they were going to use this as an extra piece of pressure against a Government which is going through a bad patch. The by-elections all show a swing away from us – 4% it is now or 5%, against (I believe) 7% <u>before</u> Suez (which is interesting)[21] Eccles' slip is a very small and venial one, and I was determined to protect him by drawing all the fire on myself. This I did so successfully that we are to have a vote of censure against me on Monday for not having demanded his resignation! I think the younger members of our party (and most of the press) thought that I was too unyielding and counter-attacked too vehemently. But I felt that Bevan's pretended moderation was a trap. (His indignation when I didn't fall into it proved this) B wanted Eccles to apologise. I remembered that Dalton apologised – the first day.[22] On the second, the hunt started again and he was out . . . .

2 March
. . . . Krishna Menon came at 11.45 and stayed till 12.30 this morning – one long whine, but very clever. He puts on a wonderful act. In a curious way, he is sincere as well as false – a strange mixture. The real reason why Nehru won't give way at all about Kashmir is, according to M, that he fears that after his death India may fall apart. So he sticks rigidly to his legal rights, as successor to the British in India . . . .

3 March (Sunday)
. . . . One piece of good news – the negotiations with Germany about 'support costs' have finished successfully – at the official level. The Germans have agreed to recommend a payment of £50m for 1957–8. We have now to get agreement from W.E.U. (and NATO) to our proposed reduction to 50,000 men (from 80,000). I think this agreement means that the Germans will support us. It is the French who are going to be difficult . . . .

5 March
. . . . The Israeli Govt has decided 'as an act of faith' to withdraw their forces from the Gaza strip and from the shores of the Gulf of Aqaba.

---

21. The only recent by-elections, on 28 February, had been in Camarthen, won for Labour by Megan Lloyd George from the Liberals without Conservative intervention, and Wednesbury, where a small positive swing helped Labour to retain the seat.

22. Hugh Dalton had been forced to resign as Chancellor of the Exchequer in 1947 after he unwisely passed on budget secrets to a reporter. Eccles had made reference to a possible reduction in Entertainments Duty.

This follows a most complicated negotiation, in which it looks as if the American passion for being liked by everybody has got them into the position of being trusted by nobody . . . . It will be interesting to see whether the Israeli withdrawal will affect the Syrians and the pipelines. I shd imagine that they will think up some other excuse, for the men who are in control of Syria at the moment are just Russian stooges. (This, alas! the Americans do not yet admit) I fear that the Russian grip on the country will get too strong for any reaction to be possible, unless something is done soon . . . .

6 March

. . . . Reception at 7.30 – for the celebration of the 'independence' of Ghana (Gold Coast) At 9.15 I had to do a broadcast and TV about this.

7 March

Another long day. Cabinet 10.30–1.15 with many difficult questions, including MPs' and ministers' salaries. In view of all our troubles (including the doctors) I persuaded Cabinet to put this off till July. There was a long discussion about the agricultural price review and the usual pressure to give in to the farmers. We eventually agreed to settle at £12m (⅓ above the minimum under the long term guarantee) but not to give more on milk, eggs etc – in other words, to concentrate the subsidies (as far as possible) on those commodities which the nation needs. This at least makes sense.

. . . . At 6pm I had to go to the 1922 Ctee.[23] In spite of all the difficulties, they seemed in good heart. I warned them that the next two by-elections (polling today) wd be bad. But we must stick it out, or we shd be rattled out . . . . Warwick and Leamington result came through at 11pm. It is very bad. The Socialists[24] have gained 5000 votes and there is a new feature. It is, perhaps, to be explained by the spread of Coventry workers into this area and the loss of the great personal following which Anthony Eden had. We held the seat by 2200 (a fall of 11,000). Bristol was better; no Socialist gain of votes and the usual 5% abstention of Tories. We held the seat easily.[25]

---

23. The forum of the Conservative parliamentary party.
24. The term conventionally used by Tories to describe the Labour party at the time. This by-election followed Eden's resignation from Parliament.
25. Following Monckton's elevation to the peerage: the Tory majority was over 14,000.

8 March

. . . . Very unexpectedly, the Syrians have suggested that the pipe-lines should be mended and the oil flow. If this is really a genuine move, it is very encouraging . . . . The Americans are being very difficult about our proposed 'force reductions' in Germany and this will encourage the French to be the same. We _must_ get a settlement in the next 10 days, if we are to settle the Defence White Paper and the Budget. I pray that we shall not be forced to denounce our Treaty obligations.

9 March

Altho' the election results are discouraging, I am not dismayed. Actually, they are better than the pre-Suez one – Tonbridge.[26] Everything now depends on whether our firm policies can bear fruit in time. Whatever else we do, we must not run away from our responsibilities. The Syrian move gives me some hope that Nasser may be reasonable – or, at least, not too unreasonable. The last ships will soon be cleared from the Canal . . . .

There is grave danger of a strike in the shipyards and engineering works throughout the whole country. Iain Macleod (MofLabour) is a very sane, sensible, as well as intelligent man. But this time the masters seem determined to fight. They were incensed at getting a wage demand ten weeks after the last wage settlement. The 'moderate' leaders have so often found that their warnings proved wrong (i.e. the masters have in fact given in every time, usually under Govt pressure) that they are now disregarded. The Govt has been preaching my 'price plateau' and cannot conscientiously urge the employers to give in. So it looks like a clash and perhaps a long dispute. This may spread to the railways and end in something like a general strike. The only way out might be arbitration.

Left London airport at 9.35 and arrived Le Bourget at 11.45 (French time). . . . We had a very long; and rather unpleasant, argument about our force reductions in Europe. Altho' the French military, and even the Quai d'Orsay[27] officials were quite understanding, both

---

26. The Tonbridge by-election of 7 June 1956 had seen the Conservative majority in this rock-solid constituency slashed from 10,000 to 1,600. Curiously, Macmillan made no mention of this at the time.

27. The location of, and therefore the conventional term for the French Foreign Ministry.

Mollet and Pineau were bitterly hostile. This is chiefly due to an imminent debate in the Assembly, and Mollet's fear that he will be attacked by Mendes-France as having 'betrayed' the Paris agreement.[28]

After nearly two hours arguing, we passed from the subject without any progress having been made. I took a very tough line and made it clear to them that we would have to make these reductions. We had no alternative. The discussions on the Common Market and the European Free Trade Area were on a calmer plane. The French have got what they want, but they have put us in a great difficulty. If it had not been for the question of our forces in Europe, I would have attacked the French for the way in which they managed the last stages of the negotiations for the Common Market, esp the inclusion of the French Colonial Empire. This was got through at the last minute, and makes great difficulties for us[29] . . . .

10 March (Sunday)

. . . . Lord Ismay came to the Embassy about 12 and we had a talk a) about Cyprus, and the plan for a NATO 'mediation'[30] b) about our forces in Europe. He was, as usual, very sensible and helpful. Both these are pretty tricky subjects. But I think Ismay can, and will, help to steer the best available course . . . . We left the airport about 5pm. The usual press conference etc. I read a speech in French. At London airport, the press, BBC, TV, ITV – all the works. A mass of work on my return – all troubles! . . . .

---

28. The 1954 agreement which set up the WEU, negotiated by Pierre Mendes-France.

29. The 'Common Market' was the conventional term used to describe the EEC set up with the signing of the Treaty of Rome on 25 March 1957 by Belgium, France, West Germany, Italy, Luxembourg and the Netherlands. The difficulty with the inclusion of the French colonies was that, whilst it gave them preferential access to European markets, similar suggestions would have derailed Britain's decolonisation strategy and had been hotly rejected by newly independent Ghana. It also conflicted with Britain's desire to keep agriculture out of their attempts from 1956 to negotiate a European Free Trade Area as a way of squaring the circle between the Common Market's customs union and Britain's maintenance of preferential tariffs with the Commonwealth.

30. Ismay offered NATO mediation between the three members involved, Britain, Turkey and Greece, a task carried on by his successor as NATO Secretary-General, Paul-Henri Spaak.

11 March

. . . . I had the Board of M&Co[31] to luncheon at No 10. . . . They all seemed to enjoy it very much. D had a tea party – the 4th of her series, for Conservative MPs and wives. They seem a great success . . . .

At 5.30, I had a conference about the doctors. We decided to give 10% at once to the lower-paid hospital staffs. We shall probably give 5% rise to the rest. But we shall insist on the Royal Commission doing the permanent job – that is, to find a permanent system wh will be in substitution for the quite impossible Spens system.[32]

12 March

. . . . A very long Cabinet – Farm Price Review was the most difficult and left undecided . . . . Another Cabinet at 4.30. Farm Price Review again. There was so sharp a disagreement between the Chancellor of the Exr and the Minister of Agriculture, that we could not finish. I arranged to go on with one or two colleagues tomorrow . . . .

13 March

. . . . I am anxious about the situation wh is developing, as either Chancellor or Minister of Ag might resign – the latter the most probable. Heathcoat Amory is an awfully nice fellow – rather slow, but very sensible. I think he feels that we ought to trust him more. We could not agree and met again at 7.30 – still leaving it open. But we got a very clear picture of the alternatives. We can get an 'agreed settlement' with the former at £14m extra, with ¼d on milk, or an 'improved settlement' at £13m, with nothing on milk. Milk is really the crux. Logically, since supply is too great, it seems absurd to give even a synthetic ¼d. But the cost of production has gone up by 2½d (on one calculation) and 1d (on another) So there is some case for giving this small easement.

D and I dined with the American Minister, to meet the new

---

31. The family publishing firm.

32. The Spens Committee had established doctors' remuneration on a generous basis at the setting up of the NHS in 1948, and also offered salary increases in line with inflation. By the mid-1950s the government was increasingly concerned about the cost of this arrangement. Whilst paying the 5% mentioned here, Macmillan therefore also set up a Royal Commission under Sir Harry Pilkington, which in 1960 proposed a new salary system for the medical profession.

ambassador. I got very late and in day clothes to the dinner, which was a very agreeable one. The new ambassador is rather difficult to understand, since he tries to speak without opening his mouth (like the French ambassador) He is a great personal friend of the President's, and was with him at Algiers in some capacity. Whitney is enormously rich. His wife was married to James Roosevelt (the former President's son)

14 March

I called a Cabinet for 10am to settle the Farm Review question. I had made up my mind to go for the agreed settlement, in spite of the embarrassment about milk (wh is technically wrong) But, really, we have so much trouble coming to us that we must try to have some friends and preserve the firm agricultural base of the party, in the House and the country . . . .

Minister of Labour's industrial report was gloomy. Shipbuilding seems pretty bad; general engineering almost as hopeless; railways very bad too. Sir John Forster will only award the railwaymen 3%, which they will certainly refuse. I am working hard to get him to <u>postpone</u> his award for at least a week. This will give us some breathing space. But it's all pretty bad. Peter Thorneycroft (Chancellor) behaved very well about the Farm Price Review. I think he really felt that it was the right decision from the wider political point of view. But it helped him, as Chancellor, to have the Cabinet take the decision collectively and after 3 full discussions . . . .

15 March

A very heavy day. In the morning papers, there was an account of leaflets distributed in Cyprus by EOKA, offering to call off terrorism if the Archbishop Makarios were released. The language of these leaflets, referring to the United Nations resolution and other rather sophisticated expressions, confirms what we heard from the Turks that this development had been prepared in Athens (the leaflets are said to have been composed by M. Pallis)[33] and that the object is to avoid, at all costs, the collapse of terrorism as the result of British action.

Of course, the press here and the Archbishops and Bishops here, with their usual sentimentality, will regard this as a 'change of heart',

---

33. Alexandros Pallis was an official in the Greek Ministry of Information who had served in London earlier in the decade.

and a 'conversion to constitutional methods' and so on. What we have
to do is a) not to relax the pressure on the terrorists at the critical
moment b) not to lose Turkish support c) to satisfy home and foreign
opinion (and especially *The Times* newspaper) that we are dealing with
the new situation in an 'imaginative' way . . . .

11.15. Minister of Labour. There seems little hope that the Ship-
yard unions will accept the offer of arbitration. . . . The truth is that
we are now paying the price for the Churchill–Monckton regime –
industrial appeasement, with continual inflation.

11.30. Foreign Secretary. He had not yet taken in the Cyprus
development, and seemed rather upset about the decision to hang a
young man for having fire-arms (actually he had committed some
brutal murders, which he admitted) The curious thing is that this
hanging (which everyone here said wd be fatal and about which the
American Govt had the impudence to send a message to me) was
followed by the EOKA move. This shows that the hanging had no
effect on the EOKA decision, which is either the result of the desperate
position into which the gangs have been driven, or just a ruse to get
time to reform (this was certainly the purpose of a similar move last
August) The F.S. accepted this view. For my part, I am as anxious as
anyone to get clear of Cyprus. But I think we must try to reduce our
liabilities in an orderly way. I am not persuaded that we need more
than an airfield, either on long lease or in sovereignty (like Gibraltar)
Then the Turks and Greeks cd divide the rest of the island between
them . . . .

12.15. Colonial Secy. We had a talk about Cyprus and a possible
plan for dealing with the situation. I think that we should build on the
NATO 'conciliation'. This gives us a more respectable entry into a new
position than the EOKA pamphlets. I rang up Ld Ismay in Paris, and
arranged with him to send his letters to the UK, Greek and Turkish
representatives at NATO forthwith. Also, to eliminate from his proposal any request that it shd be confidential. He would ring back at
4.30pm today, to say what he had been able to do. So we arranged a
Colonial Policy Ctee for 4.30 . . . .

3pm. Home Secretary (Rab) and Norman Brook. . . . It looks as if
the Railway Strike will come, within a week or 10 days. The power
stations, and the docks will be out, in sympathy for the engineers.
Nationalised transport (but not private hauliers) will come out. So it
will really be the 1926 position – practically a General Strike. The
emergency organisation is working well. The regional organisation is

being re-activated, we have quite enough troops (soldiers, airmen and sailors) without bringing back any from Germany. But it will be a fierce struggle. However, there is no alternative, if the issue comes. Rab is convinced (from what he has heard in the lobbies of the House of Commons) that this is a political plot, between the Communist and extremist union leaders and the parliamentary Labour Party. Since they cannot get the Govt out by Parliamentary means, and since they have not been able to get us 'rattled' by ordinary methods or even the swing of Gallup polls and by-elections, they hope to finish us off by creating an untenable industrial situation. This seems to me a possible explanation; but I don't think it covers the whole position. I think the unions have got their own way for so long (since 1939) that they cannot imagine that there is any point at which they can meet firm resistance. At 3.30, Ministers of Labour and Transport. We discussed means by which the Railway crisis could be put off a bit. Sir John Forster's arbitration award (which will touch off the row) is not yet published. I shd like him to postpone publication as long as he can – anyway till next Friday. The difficulty is that the T.U. member of the arbitration tribunal knows that the report is really ready.

4.30–6. Colonial Policy Ctee. We worked hard at the Cyprus problem and eventually agreed a document which would a) be circulated for Monday's Cabinet b) be sent to Turkey for information. I think it is about right. We accept the NATO offer; we 'assume' that the Archbishop will now recommend the end of violence – in wh case we will welcome him from Seychelles (but not yet let him go back to Cyprus) But I feel that a) the Turks b) some of the Cabinet, will jib at this . . . .

16 March

Minister of Labour came at 10.30am. Nothing can now stop the shipbuilding strike. I discussed with him the germ of an idea which I have had. When the arbitrator's award comes out about the railways – giving 3% – it is regarded by us all as the signal for yet another row. Could we make use of it in another way? Could the shipbuilders say that a) they had already accepted arbitration b) that it was now obvious that an arbitration award wd be about 3% c) that they wd therefore give 3½% at once, if the whole thing was called off? Then engineering wd perh follow suit. If the railwaymen then struck, they wd be very unpopular. They might, in their circumstances, accept 3½% also. Macleod promised to study this and discuss with Mills.

D and I motored to Chequers, arriving for luncheon. We had
Foreign Secy, Chancellor of Ex and Mrs Thorneycroft, Sir Norman
and Lady Brook; and Freddy Bishop (my principal P.S.) I had a talk
with the Chancellor about Budget prospects (assuming the industrial
situation doesn't get too bad) For one reason or another – the 'cuts'
we have made, in civil and service estimates, as well as a more
realistic estimate of 'below the line' costs, the 'gap' will be much less
than we expected in December. So I believe that we could afford to
reduce taxation by about £100m. This might be divided as follows
(a) £25m for relief of overseas investment – for profits 'ploughed
back' (b) £25m for sur-tax payers (c) £25m for children allowances
etc (d) £25m cut in purchase tax on articles in common use. There
would be some changes in entertainments tax, but these wd be self-
balancing.

At 6.30, the whole school met! We went through the Minister of
Defence's White Paper from the point of view of a) Foreign Office b)
Treasury . . . .

17 March (Sunday)

I started work at 8.45 and dictated a new version of the White Paper.
This seemed generally approved when we met at 10.30am . . . .

We motored to London . . . . At 8pm Duncan Sandys (Minister of
Defence) came to dinner and I showed him my redraft of the White
Paper. Fortunately, he accepted this. At 10pm Macleod (Labour) and
Mills (Power) came to talk about the industrial situation. We agreed
that they shd discuss my plan for some move by the shipbuilders with
Hunter. They wd also take soundings with Braby (Engineers) to see
whether they wd contemplate any move. I am getting very worried
about the railways – and perhaps the coal-miners. This prospect is
already having a very bad effect on sterling.

18 March

. . . . Left on 2.35 for Leicester. After the usual reception, visit to
Lord Mayor etc, I went to a quite comfortable little suite at the
hotel. I telephoned to Minister of Labour (we had had a 'scrambler'
put in) There was not a very encouraging report. Both the shipbuilders and the engineering employers are unwilling to make a
move.

Meeting at Simon de Montfort Hall – absolutely packed – 3000 in
audience. It was not a ticket meeting, except for 400 Young Conser-

vatives on the platform. There was some rather tiresome heckling by 'Empire Loyalists' (imported from London) but otherwise the speech went very well[34] . . . .

. . . . At midnight I got a message from London that the WEU talks were going pretty well. Just before going to sleep (about 1.30am) the news came of a complete agreement.

The French were very difficult and unhelpful throughout. The Germans got more reasonable. I think that Adenauer is only worrying about his election.

19 March

Left Leicester at 9am. At 11.30, we had a meeting (to be kept very secret) about the industrial situation. Macleod came and with him Sir Brian Robertson ([British] Transport [Commission])[35] Mr Brady (Engineering) Mr Hunter (Shipbuilders) Sir Colin Anderson (British Employers Federation) The talk was useful, but inconclusive. Braby – who is [a] weak and rather stupid man – shewed all the rigidity of weakness and stupidity. Hunter (who is excellent) was much more helpful. Sir Colin Anderson was useful. The general agreement reached was that Sir Brian should settle the railways at any reasonable figure – say 4% – as soon as possible. He would not be regarded as having sold the pass by private industry if he did this. On the contrary, it was essential to get this out of the way as soon as possible. I tried to persuade Hunter at least to re-start negotiations with his unions while this was going on. Even if they proved abortive, it would encourage the more moderate elements in the railway unions if they felt that discussions were going on elsewhere. These discussions went on till 1pm – when the Colonial Policy ministers came – on Cyprus . . . .

Ld Salisbury (Ld President) and Alan Lennox-Boyd (Colonial Secy) took diametrically opposing views. At one time, both had offered – or

---

34. The League of Empire Loyalists was launched by the right-wing journalist A. K. Chesterton in April 1954 as a reactionary, anti-semitic organisation. Its intervention in the February 1957 North Lewisham by-election cost the Conservatives the seat. Noisy heckling of speakers was one of its key tactics, but by the end of the 1950s it was in decline. In 1967 it was one of the far right groups which merged to form the National Front.

35. Established by Labour's 1947 Transport Act nationalising inland transport, the British Transport Commission was abolished in 1962.

threatened – to resign. However, by 2.15pm we agreed on quite a good formula. In effect, Ld S gave in . . . .

20 March

We arrived at Bermuda punctually at 10am (local time) (about 2.30pm Greenwich time) We had a good, but rather tiring flight.

The Governor; the local notabilities; a naval guard of honour; a Durham Light Infantry band; and a great proportion of the inhabitants of the island were there to greet us. I said a few sentences of thanks. . . . and then we drove off to the Mid-Ocean Club – which has been taken over for both the delegations – at a vast cost to the British tax-payer! . . . .

President Eisenhower made his arrival by sea at 4pm. . . . The President seemed very well – bronzed and alert. He had rather a tiresome cough; but as I have caught a shattering cold myself, we are evenly matched in this respect.

Foster Dulles flew in from Washington about the same time. We met him at the Club. He seemed very well – and very little changed in spite of his severe illness.

President and Foster dined with us – Selwyn Lloyd and myself – at 7.30 and stayed till 10.30. In the car (some 20 minutes drive) Pres had talked very freely to me – just exactly as in the old days. There were no reproaches – on either side; but (what was more important) no note of any change in our friendship or the confidence he had in me. Indeed he seemed delighted to have somebody to talk to! In America, he is half king, half prime minister. This means that he is rather a lonely figure, with few confidants. He told me very frankly that he knew how unpopular Foster Dulles was with our people and with a lot of his people. But he must keep him. He couldn't do without him. Nor cd he find a substitute. Governor Herter (now under secretary) was a fine man, but with poor health. No one had the combination of intellectual and physical stamina that Foster had. He wd stay probably for 2 more years. Charlie Wilson (Defence) would go quite soon. George Humphrey was very anxious to be relieved, but President wd try to keep him on.

At the dinner, which was very good, the talk was rather general, with a good deal of war reminiscences etc. After dinner, we really got down to it – a broad review of the general situation in the world. Nothing very startling was said and nothing settled; but the atmosphere was very good – I thought, in view of all the circumstances surprisingly so. They did most of the talking; we were most reticent. But it is clear that we are not going to be the 'suppliants' or 'in the dock' at this conference.[36] It is rather the other way round.

21 March (Thursday)

The Conference opened at 10.30. I made an opening statement, which I had prepared pretty carefully .... I made it rather clear that the British people felt 'let down' by America. They were puzzled and sore. The President took this up rather sharply in his reply, which was very gracious and very fair. But I think we managed to take the offensive at the start ....

Telegrams keep pouring in from London – chiefly about the strikes. The Cabinet is clearly divided about the wisdom of buying off the railway strike and asked for my decision – or at least, guidance. I felt no doubt. We really cannot stand a railway strike, probably followed by a mining strike ....

22 March

The President .... came to this afternoon's meeting, but much of the morning meeting we left to the Foreign Secretaries. This is all to the good, because it allows work to proceed, with sub-ctees of officials etc, while he and I have a series of informal chats[37] ....

The Cabinet has, it seems, accepted my advice. Ld Mills; Henry Brooke; Dr Hill; and (I fear) Minister of Labour were rather unhappy about the decision but acquiesced.

23 March

.... The Americans produced a frightful 'draft' communiqué – full of the usual high-faluting verbiage about United Nations, Self-Determination and what not – with no relation whatever to what we had in fact discussed, either in private or plenary session. I persuaded the President to cut all this out – to have a short communiqué – two sentences – with a list of agreements reached and subjects discussed in an annexe. He agreed – and sent written instructions to Foster Dulles. We lunched with President. Foster Dulles didn't much like the President's decision about the communiqué; but he accepted it.

---

36. In the aftermath of the Anglo-American disagreements over Suez in 1956.
37. Agreements reached included the co-ordination of strike forces and the storage of American nuclear weapons on UK bases.

The rest of the day I sat in my room (vile weather continues) while British and American parties of officials worked on the protocol and the communiqué. The protocol is my idea. It means a signed set of agreements on a number of actual decisions. None of them are published – but they represent the solid achievements, and range from understandings of policy, to actual agreements on guided missiles. I don't think we have been able to have this procedure since the great war conferences. Thus the communiqué loses its prime importance. So often it has been the only real result of the Conference. By this method, it is just propaganda . . . .

. . . . Bob Murphy came out today and I had some private talk with him. He said 'Why, oh why didn't you get to Cairo? I was just praying that you would get there'. I think he loves the President, but finds Dulles pretty difficult. Bob said 'You think you have got him somewhere, and then he seems just to slip out at the end'.

President; Foster; For Sec; and I had dinner together. We had a long discussion on the United Nations – its use and future. I found Ike much less dogmatic about this than I expected. He has a sort of semi-religious faith – but it is not blind faith. He seemed very much oppressed by America's abandonment of the old League of Nations – a sort of sin for wh they must try to make amends.[38] Foster was more cynical. He just thought there was no way of doing without U.N. but thought that if, in future, US and UK policies were thought out beforehand and brought closely into line, we cd probably still manage the majorities there. I think the general conclusion was that we must get working together again at U.N. I said that this involved Cabot Lodge being willing to co-operate with Dixon (U.N. representative) which he doesn't do at present. Dulles (who thoroughly dislikes Lodge) approved this sentiment. President, who owes a great deal to Lodge and has given him Cabinet rank, was silent.

24 March (Sunday)

. . . . A whole sheaf of telegrams have been arriving – personal from Butler; personal from Lennox-Boyd; personal from Lord Salisbury. The first two (supported by Governor Harding) want to accept Archbp's statement as satisfactory; let him out from Seychelles; and announce changes to mitigate emergency regulations. The last strongly disap-

---

38. Despite the role of President Woodrow Wilson in initiating the League of
    Nations at the end of the First World War it was never ratified by Congress.

proves, and in fact threatens resignation. F.S. inclines to Ld S's view, but I don't think Hoyer Millar does – so long as we inform Turkey. Finally we agreed a line wh F.S. undertook to support a) say Archbp is – as usual – equivocal and logic-chopping b) say we can make no bargain with him or EOKA. The emergency regulations will be mitigated as and when Governor decides c) all the same, let him go d) Inform Turks. e) No commitment to be given in Parl about 'negotiations' with Makarios .... Meanwhile, altho' the rail – and I hope the coal – strikes are 'off', the shipbuilding and engineering are not yet settled ....

27 March

Arrived at London Airport at 3.30 and was met by Butler. After the usual press, radio, and T.V. ceremonies we drove to London .... It seems clear that Ld Salisbury is bent on resignation over the release of Makarios. But I am sure that we had better let him go now. We may never find a better opportunity and we can't keep him indefinitely in the Seychelles. The Colonial Secy <u>and</u> the Governor are very strongly in favour of this course.

Salisbury came to see me after dinner. He was very charming, but seemed determined to resign about something ....

28 March

A full morning with Cabinet. There was a long discussion about Makarios. Some ministers supported Salisbury, but the weight of opinion was in favour of the course proposed by the Colonial Secy. I had revised the statement considerably – to make it clear that there was no bargain of any kind, and that we could only reduce the severity of the emergency regulation in the light of events ....

From 4.15 to nearly 7 we had a full Cabinet on the Defence White Paper. We are in a great dilemma. If we say that we are aiming at forces of 375,000 by 1962, we shall start off a great row in NATO, and esp in Germany. We may even lose our £50m. But if we <u>don't</u> say this, our whole plan becomes ridiculous ....

31 March (Sunday)

.... The press foretells the early collapse of the Government, as the result of Ld Salisbury's resignation;[39] the Suez failure; Makarios and

---

39. Two days earlier, Makarios was released from detention in the Seychelles and went to Athens on 17 April. He was not allowed into Cyprus.

Cyprus; the strikes; and the general sense of malaise. The *Sunday Express* is particularly virulent .... For my part, I think it's much better to have lost Salisbury over Cyprus than over the Canal. The doctors (or rather the BMA)[40] have decided to boycott the Royal Commission. I think this will lose them sympathy.

In pondering over Lord Salisbury's resignation at this particular moment I came to this conclusion. All through history the Cecils, when any friend or colleague has been in real trouble, have stabbed him in the back – attributing the crime to qualms of conscience.

1 April

An enormous team of 'egg-heads' arrived at No 10 and we worked through the speech with their help.[41] The work was only finished at 1pm. I lunched alone and then rested till 2.45. I have never been so strained or nervous before a speech. According to the press, the continuance of the Govt and the unity of the Party depend entirely on my performance.

12 midnight. The debate is over. By some miracle, the speech went very well and our boys were delighted. I ended with the Tories (temporarily) united and the Socialists split in two. This was by devoting a great part of the speech to the Bomb and the Bomb testing and challenging Gaitskell to say whether he wd continue or abandon the tests if he were in my position. He faltered; wobbled; hedged – and so lost both wings of his party. So we have got over this particular fence ....

2 April

A very long Cabinet, in which the White Paper on defence was finally agreed. This has been a terrible labour. Sandys has been very patient. P.Q.s went well today. I am beginning to gain a more confident manner in dealing with them. Just before the end of questions, I heard the welcome news that the shipbuilding and engineering strikes had both been called off. This is very good. Another hurdle surmounted – and no concessions ....

---

40. The British Medical Association, effectively the doctors' professional organisation.

41. In a debate initiated by Macmillan on the Bermuda talks, in which he defended the continuance of nuclear testing.

3 April

A long Cabinet – mostly about what I call 'the water-jump' – i.e. the Suez Canal. More by good luck than by good management, we seem to have scrambled over the other hurdles. But I don't see how we can fail to take a toss at the canal hazard . . . .

4 April

. . . . Lord Salisbury's resignation has left scarcely a ripple on the surface. The Cabinet, much as they all like him personally, feel like a man who has got rid of an inflamed tooth.

Altho' the men have gone back to work pretty well, there is an ugly feeling in the industrial world. This is political, and inflamed by the Communists and Left-Wingers. In the House of Commons, Gaitskell has made a shameful surrender to the Left Wing and has now shifted his ground about the bomb tests. He demands 'postponement'. Of all proposals, this is the most idiotic . . . .

5 April

The Defence White Paper, on which we have worked so hard, has at last been published. It has had, on the whole, a very good press. Since it makes it clear that <u>all</u> our defence – and the economies in defence expenditure – are founded on nuclear warfare, it throws the Socialists into still greater confusion[42] . . . .

7 April

With Ayr to face, I could not go to Church, but dictated bits and pieces for my speech . . . . The Scottish Unionist Conference (to which I go as Leader of the Party) is at Ayr. This is close to the little town of Irvine where my grandfather went as a bookseller's apprentice at the age of 10 (in 1824) We are to stay with Hamish Maclehose, the grandson of his greatest friend[43] . . . .

8 April

. . . . Dulles and Caccia have had a long conference about the next step

---

42. Its key theme was reduction of conventional forces and costs, including the end of conscription by 1962, with instead reliance upon nuclear forces as deterrence.

43. The firm of Robert Maclehose and Co. Ltd continued to print many Macmillan books.

with Egypt. The American negotiations have <u>not</u> been successful altho'
the Egyptians have made some minor concessions. What are we to do
now? The Americans might agree to continue the negotiations. Alternatively, they (or we) cd appeal to the Security Council. There are
objections to both courses. For Secy and I thought some kind of
combination of these cd perhaps be made. USA to <u>report</u> to U.N.
Security Council; proposal to hold a conference or to continue unilateral negotiations (with representation of user countries to advise US
delegation) under cover of this, we and other countries might make 'de
facto' arrangements (with least danger of Egyptian intransigeance or
counter-claims) for opening canal and passing our ships through. Our
whole problem is how to use the Canal with the minimum of short
term loss of face. In the long term, we must hope for enough pressure
on Nasser to bring him down.

I called a Cabinet for noon and put the whole case before them (I
am very anxious to secure and engage their collective approval and
responsibility, for we are now approaching the most critical phase in
the life of the Govt. After an hour's discussion, there was a general
measure of agreement for the course wh I proposed . . . .

Lord Beaverbrook came to luncheon with me – alone. I had not
seen him for some time – over a year, I think. He looked remarkably
well – hardly aged at all. (He affects to think himself very ill) We had
a very good talk – for 1¼ hours, in a very good temper, but only really
fencing. We never got to grips on Europe . . . .

. . . . He said that Gaitskell was a great asset to me. I must be
careful to preserve him. Bevan would be far more dangerous.

Max was very scornful of Salisbury. He was not dangerous. I
said that he was a very old and dear friend (Max of course hates
him) but that I felt he had not chosen a very good ground for
resignation . . . .

9 April

Cabinet at 11. The Americans have accepted our plan for the next
steps with Egypt . . . . The Cabinet agreed that we must try to cover
our decision to use the Canal (if Nasser is willing to accept transferable
sterling) by a) appeal to Security Council b) recommendation of all
maritime nations in SCUA. Further telegrams must be drafted to
Washington . . . .

The Chancellor opened his Budget at 3.30 and spoke for 1½

[hours] or more. It was an admirable speech – well constructed and well delivered. We have kept pretty well to the plan. Apart from minor changes in Entertainment Tax (living theatre and sport freed; £6m relief to cinemas, balanced by £1m on T.V. licences) the 'give-away' is £100m, divided in to equal parts – £25m for overseas trading companies, £25m for surtax relief, £25m for Children's allowance, £25m for Purchase tax cuts. The Opposition seemed rather dazed; our chaps were very pleased.

10 April

The Budget has had a good press on the whole. Naturally, the *Daily Herald* and the *Daily Worker* attack the sur-tax concessions – 'a class Budget'. But I don't think this will cut much ice. More serious will be the campaign of the Old Age Pensioners. But we can't do anything about that until the autumn.

A series of visitors filled the morning – Haley (Editor of *The Times*) – who seemed to approve of the Govt but nevertheless lectures us daily in the best grandfatherly style. The trouble with *The Times* is that the proprietor is a nonentity and the Editor is a prig . . . .

After luncheon, Ormsby-Gore (to arrange the daily telegram to Washington about Suez); then meeting with Junior Ministers at 5pm. 6–8 I talked with a group of right-wing and rather dissident Tory MPs, gathered in Maurice [Macmillan]'s house. I think this was a useful exercise, in view of the approaching Canal crisis . . . .

11 April

. . . . P.Q.s went well today – chiefly because they didn't go at all. I had 18 to answer and didn't get through more than 3 or 4 before stumps were drawn at 3.30.

Addressed 1922 Ctee. A good reception. There is no doubt that the MPs are in good heart.

After dinner worked on the speech for Ayr, till it was time to leave for the night train.

12 April

. . . . Everything has begun to leak about the Canal, and the For Secy seemed rather concerned. Another trouble is the Japanese threat to take us to the International Court about an H-Bomb test. I agreed with the For Secy that we must immediately file at United Nations a document stating that we withdrew our adherence to the Court (We did this before, over Buraimi)[44]

The [Ayr] meeting took place at 7.30 – nearly 4000 people, in a vast cinema theatre. The speech was long – it took an hour to deliver – and I thought rather heavy. As it dealt largely with the Budget and Home Affairs, there were a lot of figures. I began with a reference to Eden (to whom I had telephoned during the day. He is in Boston, in hospital) Then I went on about my own forebears – Arran, Irvine etc. The audience was quick to take points and responsive. They gave us a good reception . . . .

15 April

Cabinet at 10am. We had a very long discussion on the Suez position. It was agreed to support the Americans in continuing their negotiation at Cairo. Mr Hare (now called Mr Tortoise), the American ambassador, is conducting this in a leisurely, but able, manner. Meanwhile, we are trying (not without success) to keep the ships of all countries out of the Canal. Of course, one of our chief anxieties is not whether we ought to send British ships through the Canal, but whether Nasser will allow us, except on absurd terms – for instance, compensation for damage at Port Said. (No one in the press or Parliament seems to realise this)

We were also given the latest account of the situation in Jordan. For the present, the little King seems to be holding his own. But these two factors (Jordan and the Canal) made the Cabinet willing to agree to go on with petrol rationing.[45] I am sure this was wise politically.

We settled the doctors' interim payment at 5% . . . .

. . . . At 3, I had a meeting with Minister of Labour and officials. I want to get ready to launch a new industrial policy. (I also want preparations against a possible railway strike next year)

---

44. In October 1955 Britain intervened militarily in support of Muscat and Abu Dhabi in a boundary dispute with the Saudis at Buraimi oasis.

45. Under Egyptian pressure Jordan had just abrogated its treaty with Britain but then, on 10 April, King Hussein dismissed the pro-Nasser government. For the rest of the month Macmillan was anxious as to whether he would survive this coup. Meanwhile, the petrol rationing imposed following Suez was relaxed but not ended until 14 May.

16 April

.... Defence debate. Duncan Sandys opened with an admirable speech, only marred by a slight mix-up about strategic and tactical nuclear weapons. Brown followed. Considering the absurd position which the Opposition have got themselves into over the Bomb, I thought he made a gallant effort. Of course, he had to go back on his robust broadcast statement. The Opposition amendment is contradictory and ridiculous, for it attempts a compromise between two diametrically opposed views.[46]

17 April

.... The defence debate was resumed .... Dick Crossman made a very able, but torturous, speech. Two years ago he was <u>for</u> the Bomb; now he is against it. The debate was wound up by John Strachey for the Opposition. If his voice were not so high and querulous, he wd be an effective speaker. He had, of course, to walk on a tight-rope – and he knew it. But I thought he did it well. I finished – with a 40 minute speech – which seemed to go pretty well ....

21 April

Easter Sunday. Church at 8am and at 11am – crowded both times. I read the lessons (Exodus 12. 1–14 and Revelation 1. 4–18) The gardens were open (for some charity of Dorothy's) from 2.30–7. As it was a lovely day and there was curiosity to see both the gardens and the house (wh was open) as well as the P.M. and his family, a great many people came. 700 cars were packed in the field opposite the house; altogether 2000–3000 people came ....

25 April

.... D and I dined with Churchill at Chartwell[47] and motored home to B.G. after dinner. He was in good form – tho' getting very deaf. Nor does he say much now; for the first time in his life he listens. All this is rather sad – for the fight has gone out of him ....

---

46. The debate was on the Sandys Defence White Paper signalling an end to National Service and an emphasis on nuclear deterrence that Labour claimed was excessive; a compromise position between those like Brown – who in his broadcast a fortnight earlier had defended British nuclear weapons – and other Labour figures moving towards a unilateralist position.

47. Churchill's country residence in Kent.

4 May

. . . . I am told that Lord Salisbury is organising a campaign against me and is in touch with Eden about it. I have written several letters to Eden and had but short acknowledgements; but I have seen letters that he has written to others[48] . . . .

5 May (Sunday)

. . . . Chancellor of Ex rang up to say that the expected talks between the representatives of the Bank of Egypt and Bank of England at Basle had not come off. They will not start till tomorrow (Monday) This is a great nuisance. It is not clear whether this is deliberate or just bad luck. First, the Governor of the Bank of Egypt (who should have gone to Basle on Friday) got influenza. Next, 3 of his colleagues were to arrive Saturday and talk on Sunday. Now they failed to turn up till Sunday evening. Meanwhile, how are we to hold back the other maritime countries? We have managed to keep them back for 2 or 3 weeks after the real breakdown of the American negotiations with Nasser. But they are getting very restless. It is impossible to foresee what line Nasser will take. But I feel sure that if he accepts transferable sterling it will only be after much haggling concerning the No 1 a/c.[49]

7 May

Left London Airport at 10.30am and flew to Wahn, the airfield for Bonn. We arrived about 12.30 and were met by Dr Adenauer and the members of his Govt . . . .

The first subject tackled – which lasted from 4 to 6.30 and a little later – was defence . . . . It was clear from the start of the talks that the Germans – esp the Chancellor – were both suspicious and ill-informed. Their military concepts were based on those of the past –

---

48. Eden and Salisbury were old and close friends who shared similar misgivings about the government's Suez policy, though he urged: 'I beg you to keep these outpourings to yourself. I just had to tell someone. I am not well enough to figure in this business at this stage . . . . Harold will no doubt be shrewd enough to know of them, from what I wrote to him' (Hatfield House, Papers of 5th Marquess: Eden to Salisbury, 12 May 1957). He had also expressed his doubts about the policy to Home and Poole, though this hardly amounts to a plot.

49. Egypt was a member of the Sterling Area and its sterling balances held in this account were frozen at the time of the Suez Crisis. Negotiations stalled but resumed in the autumn. A financial settlement between the two countries was only finally concluded in 1959.

large numbers of divisions, on both sides, armed with conventional weapons and waging a long-drawn out war. Naturally the British 'cuts' have alarmed them. They foresee a dangerous period between the British reductions and the creation of the new German army. They excuse, but cannot explain, the slowness with which the German military effort has developed. I thought it better to be absolutely frank, esp as I was told that the Chancellor is so old and powerful that no one really tells him the truth. However, I felt that the afternoon's discussion has shaken the Germans but left them rather sore. We dined with the Chancellor – white tie, decorations etc. I made a carefully prepared speech – about ¼ hour – about Europe during the last century – our failures and follies, and now our opportunities. It appears that this speech had a great effect on the Chancellor and some of his colleagues . . . .

8 May

The Bank negotiations between the Bank of England and the Bank of Egypt have gone unexpectedly well and I have authorised the initialling of the agreement. This authorises a special transferable sterling a/c to be opened – primarily for canal dues and other outgoings.[50] If the Egyptian Govt sticks to it, our great head-ache is dealt with.

The talks this morning began at 10.30 and lasted till 12.30. They were about the Russians; the future of Germany; disarmament etc. They went very well. Yesterday's dinner seems to have done a great deal to improve the atmosphere . . . .

4.30–6.30. Resumed talks. This time we discussed the European Common Market and the proposed Free Trade Area. We are very anxious about all this – but the Germans were, or professed to be, entirely on our side. They would regard the union of the 6 Messina[51] powers as a disaster if it were <u>not</u> followed by the Free Trade Area. The talks also comprised our so-called 'Grand Design' – for the simplification of the various European organs. Here the inclusion of NATO has made the Europeans rather suspicious. But the Germans agreed that all this shd be pursued, <u>after</u> the ratification of the Rome

---

50. This enabled British shipping to resume using the Suez Canal, authorisation for which was publicly announced on 13 May.

51. A reference to the negotiations in Messina, Sicily in 1955 which started the process leading to the Treaty of Rome.

treaties. It is clear that they still have grave suspicions of the French. They fear that it will be the EDC story all over again[52] . . . .

9 May
. . . . Arrived London Airport at 5.15. After usual press and radio and T.V. interviews, left for No 10.

At 6.30 we had a meeting of ministers (not a full Cabinet) The results of the SCUA meeting were reported to us, with the rather tiresome French reservation.[53] Some ministers felt very distressed by this . . . .

10 May
The Foreign Office spokesman must have done a good job, for the press does not pay much attention to the French gesture. There is a general acceptance of the fact that the SCUA resolution means that the boycott is off . . . .

11 May
Working party at Chequers. Butler, Thorneycroft, Macleod, Boyd-Carpenter (Pensions) Charles Hill, Ted Heath. Also Norman Brook, and Fraser (Treasury) and Freddy Bishop (Private Secy) They arrived for luncheon. We worked from 4–8pm and after dinner till midnight. I think we did a lot to 'clear the air'. The Labour Party Pension scheme (produced by R Crossman) comes out next Sunday. We had, by some means or other, obtained early copies . . . .

12 May (Sunday)
. . . . The most interesting talk which I had with Adenauer I forgot to record. After dinner at the British Embassy on Wednesday night the atmosphere was very relaxed and the Chancellor in a very good form – sometimes serious, sometimes gay. He told me 'I don't know how it is with you, but there are at least 4 members of my Govt who think they wd be better than I am as head of it – and 2 of them are sitting on that sofa!' We talked a great deal about Germany and the Devil. He believes in a personal devil. He said that no one who had lived through the years of Hitler cd fail to believe in the Devil. He said, 'I

---

52. The abortive scheme for a European Defence Community killed by the French in 1955.

53. The French were reluctant to lift the boycott of the Canal.

tell you, what I could not say to any German, no one realises the harm that Nazism has done to the German soul. It is by no means cured yet. We have got rich again too quickly. I don't want us to get strong again too quickly. I hate uniforms, the curse of Germany. You will see that our generals in conference are like yours, in civil clothes. I see great dangers ahead. That is why I yearn so for European unity and (in view of France's weakness) for British participation'.

A told me that when he was in prison, his cell was immediately above the Nazi torture chamber.

A told Selwyn Lloyd that Foster Dulles had told him a) that Bermuda was a failure b) that the British had no foreign policy and were finished. I am considering a) talking to the American ambassador about this or b) writing to the President. I have always rather liked and stood up for Foster Dulles. But it may be that people are right in dubbing him 'double-crosser' . . . .

13 May

I made the Suez statement after questions – in as simple and matter-of-fact terms as I could. There were many fewer questions, from either side of the House, than I expected. But there was rather a tense calm – like that just before a storm.

The Tory dissentients are beginning to organise themselves – under Lord Hinchingbrooke and Mr A Maude. The former is an eccentric Whig, the latter an able but disappointed politician, somewhat soured because he has seen others pass him in the race. (How well I remember the feeling!)

14 May

. . . . There are to be two days debate [on Suez] – a vote of censure. I have decided to open <u>and</u> wind up. Gaitskell will speak first – I shall follow . . . .

15 May

. . . . Gaitskell opened the debate. The first part of his speech was scarcely an attack at all – the second half was more effective. He had obviously been warned to avoid the hysterical mood and tone of his autumn speeches on Suez – with the result, his speech, altho' able and well argued, was rather muted in tone. When I got up it was clear that the Opposition were determined not to let me repeat my answer to Gaitskell about the H Bomb. So they kept up a sort of wave of laughter, jeers, cat-calls etc – just not enough for the Speaker to interfere, but very disconcerting. This quite spoiled the serious parts of my speech – esp the long passage on the future transit of oil – and made me rather fumble other parts. But all I could do was to go on – as manfully as I could – till I got to the end. It was not a success. However, the material was quite good for the record. The whips are doing their best, but the situation is not good. 8 Conservatives (led by Hinchingbrooke and Maude) have announced their intention both to abstain in the division and to refuse the whip. It is thought that the abstentionists must total 20 and may reach 30. (The latter figure wd be serious and make it difficult for me to go on) James Stuart (who came to dinner) thinks it will be about 16 in all. No very notable speeches were made today. Maude failed – the best of the dissentient Tories was Raikes. Maude was elaborate and gave an impression of insincerity (falsely, I think) Raikes was rather noble. I started to work after the debate on tomorrow's wind up. Much will depend on this.

16 May
The press is not bad on the matter and substance of the debate. My speech is called 'below recent form' by the *Manchester Guardian*, which criticises also certain phrases as banal. The *Express* is violent, and in spite of Lord Beaverbrook's dislike of Lord Salisbury has started to laud Lord S to the skies. 'The Suez Betrayal' is Max's line. 'Eden was deserted by his colleagues' (which in view of Jamaica is strange!)[54] *Times* was correct and quite fair. *Daily Telegraph* did its best. The Chief Whip this morning thought [a revolt] would not reach 20, altho' the French Govt 'fight to the finish' attitude has made some impression.

. . . . The H Bomb was successfully exploded yesterday.[55] (I got the news last night) This has filled the papers today, to the great detriment of the Crossman pensions scheme, and the advantage of the Suez situation! I had a private notice question from Gaitskell over the Bomb; but he did not press it very hard. Younger began for the Opposition, with an able, bitter speech. The Foreign Secretary fol-

---

54. His fragile health undermined by the Suez Crisis, Eden had flown to Jamaica to recuperate from 23 November to 14 December 1956. The debate was effectively a no-confidence motion.

55. This was the first successful British test, though the first megaton test was not until November and thermonuclear devices did not enter service until 1961.

lowed. He did very well and got a good sympathetic reception from most of our people. The press, the Socialists, and the dissidents are making a dead set at him and trying to force me to ask for his resignation (He has offered this to me, but I have of course refused it) Selwyn Lloyd has some very great qualities (incidentally, he is tremendously efficient and quick) But naturally this persistent attack on him (coupled with his private troubles – his wife has abandoned him shamefully and gone off to live with some other man) has rather shaken him . . . .

17 May

Well, it's over. A good majority – 49 – with only 6 more abstentions over the original 8 – making 14 in all.[56] This is a great triumph for Ted Heath and his team of whips. Bevan, whose speech was to have been absolutely devastating, failed completely. He spoke for 45 minutes – was rather dull and made a great error in resting too much of his case on the Bulganin letters to Eden. (Even the Socialists, after Hungary, don't much like Bulganin's Pecksniffian lectures)[57] It was rather like my speech yesterday, tho' (I think) worse. He had 2 good jokes, and that was all. I rose at 9.30 – with enough material to last 20 minutes only! (It was vital to go on till 10, because of the whipping) However, some interruptions, partly by Bevan and partly by Dick Stokes got me through. The speech was as great a success as yesterday's was a failure. After the division was taken and the figures announced, the whole Tory Party stood up and cheered me. At the Speaker's chair, I turned and bowed. It was an extraordinary and spontaneous act of loyalty, which touched me very much.

How odd the English are! They rather like a gallant failure. Suez

---

56. The original eight, who actually resigned the Party whip, formed the core of the 'Suez Group' and were Lord Hinchingbrooke, Lawrence Turner, Sir Victor Raikes, Angus Maude, John Biggs-Davison, Paul Williams, Anthony Fell and Patrick Maitland. Some 30 Conservative MPs had previously signed the Early Day Motion criticising the government's policy towards Egypt.

57. Bulganin's note theatening force in response to Suez was delivered to Eden on 5 November 1956. At the same time Suez provided opportunity for the Soviets to reverse their decision to pull out of Hungary and instead crush the multi-party regime recently established there, an operation which started on the day before Bulganin's note. This hypocrisy was certainly worthy of Mr Pecksniff, a character in Charles Dickens's *Martin Chuzzlewit*.

has become a sort of Mons retreat.[58] Anyway, we're through this particular trouble – at least for the moment. But it's very exhausting!

It is amusing to read the accounts in the different newspapers of last night's debate. With perhaps the exception of *The Times* and the *D.T.*, every writer has to suit the bias of the editor or proprietor. You wd hardly believe that they were describing the same events . . . .

19 May (Sunday)

There was an amusing telegram from Gladwyn Jebb about the French political crises describing a talk with M. Pineau, the Minister for Foreign Affairs. 'He did not seem at all confident of the Government's prospects and seemed to think that the chances were about 50–50. If they did fall, he said sardonically "The best system for France might be to have no government at all, but only a well-organised Opposition which wd command the unswerving allegiance of all parties" ' . . . .

21 May

Lord Salisbury is said to be meditating a fierce attack on the 'Suez surrender'. Considering that he was party to all the decisions and the strongest supporter of 'evacuation' in the whole Cabinet,[59] this is not without its comic side (to those who know) I hear that he is in touch with Eden, and will try to get him to support a movement against the new Govt (no doubt with the help of the 8 in the House and others who might join) I don't feel that S will succeed. He knows (or shd know) that he is just whistling to keep his courage up.

I had a meeting with Lord Chancellor, Home Secy and others about the Cairo trials. If these men are condemned to death, it will have a very bad effect here, unless the sentences are at once commuted. I don't believe Nasser will really allow a death sentence to be carried out. This is not the practice of civilised countries (except in times of war) We agreed to ask Mrs Pandit to bring the matter to Nehru's attention informally, in the hope that he might intervene[60] . . . .

---

58. A fighting British retreat in August 1914 which, in delaying the German onslaught at the start of the First World War, became a tactical and moral victory.

59. Salisbury in fact argued for indefinite deferment of the operation.

60. On 10 May four Britons (and four others *in absentia*), a Yugoslav and 11 Egyptians were put on trial in Cairo charged with spying for Britain. Three of

24 May

. . . . The For Secy came in at 3.30 and I got Chancellor of Ex; Ld Home and one or two others to agree our final instructions to our representatives at Paris on the China trade question.[61] The Americans are being very stiff and bringing tremendous pressure on the Europeans. But I feel that we must be quite firm on this. Harold Caccia doesn't believe it will lead to any grave or lasting breach – partly because opinion in the Democratic Party is moving towards a more realistic view of what the administration calls 'Red China'; partly because of the absurdity of a boycott to which Sweden and Switzerland do not adhere . . . .

31 May (Friday)

This has been a very heavy week, with Cabinet or ministerial meetings all the time. We have had good <u>defence</u> meetings (altho' very long and tiring) and have made progress with what I have called 'Round Two'. 'Round One' was to fix the total of manpower. Now we have to fix the equipment and dispositions – how many bombers, fighters etc, and estimate the cost. This is an immense task. But we made some progress. Finally, we must come to Round Three (the first steps in which I hope to take next week) That will be to consider how we could integrate and reorganise the administrative functions in the 3 Services (4, if you add Ministry of Supply) with a quite new set-up under the Ministry of Defence.

We have had Malta – where Mintoff is behaving very badly, in spite of all our generosity, and where he is trying to mobilise the Opposition against us. (I saw a deputation led by Griffiths. Crossman was on it and rather offensive)[62] Then we have had long meetings on

---

the Britons were a month later sentenced to five or ten years in gaol, while the rest were acquitted.

61. Whilst the US had a total embargo on trade with China, Britain supported the general line in Western Europe of uniting the lists of goods embargoed against sale to Russia and China, instead of continuing to discriminate against the latter. Opposing this, Eisenhower in a 24 May letter warned that this could prove 'a terrific psychological blunder . . . . and possibly even lose all the areas of the Southeast that have strong Chinese minorities' (see G&E, p. 56). It was not until 14 August 1958 that Britain and most other NATO countries greatly relaxed trade restrictions to both the Soviet bloc and China. The Americans only relaxed restrictions to the Soviets.

62. Labour enthusiastically supported the Malta integration plans.

Cyprus. The Archbishop (Makarios) has written and published an impudent, but quite clever, letter to me. A good deal of time had to be spent on the reply. We also are getting on a little with our plans for some solution. Perhaps partition will be the only way out . . . .

. . . . Read [Sir Walter Scott's] *Rob Roy* in evening, before starting off for the train to Newcastle. I have spent most of the day (with the help of George Christ)[63] in writing a speech for tomorrow, at Stockton[64] . . . .

1 June

. . . . It was strange to drive down the old High St, now so modern and smart and prosperous, then so drab (but more beautiful) The old cobbles are gone; old Georgian houses have had their fronts 'Woolworthised' – still, it's a fine street. We drove through Thornaby (now no longer part of the constituency) to the race-course.

There was a crowd of about 3000. They listened patiently to the speech; took the jokes and sarcasms very quickly; and applauded satisfactorily at the end.

But after the votes of thanks – which were very well done by Jack Simon (Middlesborough MP) and Longbottom (candidate for Stockton) the warmth of feeling began to display itself. D spotted old Mrs Keith (one of our best canvassers, now aged 95) and went straight up to her – at the back of the stand. Great enthusiasm. We all embraced each other. We spent half an hour or more talking to the people, signing autographs etc . . . . We dined with the Dugdales and drove back to Stockton to catch the night train . . . .

2 June

. . . . Mr Stassen (US representative at the disarmament sub-ctee) has filed an extraordinary set of proposals,[65] without telling us or the

---

63. George Christ usually provided first drafts for Macmillan's setpiece speeches.

64. Macmillan had been Conservative MP for Stockton in 1924–29 and 1931–45.

65. The UN Disarmament Commission had been set up in January 1952. In response to a Russian offer Stassen proposed the negotiation of a test suspension of 12 months, linked to a cut-off in the production of fissile material. Macmillan complained to Eisenhower on 3 June that 'if the Russians react favourably to any proposals invoking an early cut off date for the production of fissile material for military purposes, the effect upon the British weapons programme and our capacity to defend ourselves will be most serious' (G&E, p. 60).

French – or, it seems, the State Dept. Nor has he given copies to anyone except the Russians! Is this America's reply to our becoming a nuclear power – to sell us down the river <u>before</u> we have a stockpile sufficient for our needs? . . . .

3 June

. . . . M. Jules Moch (French representative at disarmament conference) came to see me later in the afternoon. It seems that Stassen returned from America without instructions. He kept hesitating and delaying. Some instructions must, therefore have come for him before he saw the Russians. Stassen told Moch (whether truthfully or not) that he had never intended to give any paper or memoranda to the Russians. He had meant to read over his ideas, which were informal and did <u>not</u> bind the American Govt. But after he had been through the memoranda orally with the Russian delegates, he was asked for copy in writing – and weakly gave it. I think this is rather thin. The memorandum (of wh we have obtained a copy – first through the French and subsequently from Stassen) is about 30 pages of closely type-written material, and cast in official language, suitable to the Heads of a Treaty. The proposals are drafted as <u>formal</u> proposals, altho' there is one reference in the contrary sense. The French are very angry about all this . . . . Of course, the real trouble is that the disarmament subctee is not really the place for serious negotiations – if that is what we are considering. The great powers must first get together and then negotiate as a unit with the Soviets.

5 June

After a meeting of defence ministers at 10.15, D and I left for Epsom at noon. We lunched in the Jockey Club stand and walked about and watched the racing till 4.30. Knowing nothing of racing, I was able to enjoy (as I did) seeing a lot of old friends. I had a <u>very</u> good reception from the crowd . . . .

Foster Dulles rang up, to apologise. Stassen had no authority! They are trying to get the document back! (This seems rather naive) . . . .

11 June

. . . . Oliver Poole came to luncheon today and we discussed all the difficulties of the Party. He offered to resign his position as Chairman at any time. But I told him to carry on – at least for the present. He is very clever and very fair and frank – and I like him. Our talk did us both good and we understand each other well. His difficulty is one which any other Chairman wd have, esp one not in the Cabinet – that is, having to follow Lord Woolton, the best publicist and salesman in the country . . . .

12 June

Motored early to London. F.M. Ld Montgomery came at 10.30. He had little to say, except about his 4 day visit to President Eisenhower – partly at the White House – partly at the Gettysburg farm. He rests (in bed) for one hour in the morning and one hour before dinner. He sees practically nobody – no ambassador etc. Milton Eisenhower (his brother) comes every morning at 9am. Al Gruenther, every evening. These two are the powerful '*eminences grises*',[66] Gruenther having taken the place of Bedell-Smith. Foster [Dulles] comes occasionally; Humphrey also (till his resignation) Sherman Adams 'runs' the Cabinet business (so far as there is any coherent Cabinet system) Hagerty (an important figure) runs the press and publicity. There is growing criticism of this strange system; but Ike's power has by no means yet waned. Everyone watches Nixon and keeps in with him, for fear Ike shd die. (The whole scene, (as described by Monty) is more like the days of the Roman Empire than a modern democratic state) According to Monty, the President wd still like to deal with UK on special terms – a partnership basis. But this view is by no means universal.

Ronnie Knox came this morning from Oxford, where he delivered his Romanes lecture . . . . Poor Ronnie is dying and he knows it and bears it with great fortitude . . . . After the operation which he had some time ago the cancer has come again – in the liver, where it must be fatal, in a few months or perhaps weeks. The only comfort is that no friend I have is better prepared for the journey.

13 June

I took Ronnie to Paddington Station and left him in the hands of a friend, to travel back to Wells. I fear we shall not meet again. He was calm, but I'm afraid when I had left him I cd not hold back my tears . . . .

---

66. Grey eminences – powers behind the throne. Milton Eisenhower was President of Johns Hopkins University 1956–67, and Gruenther was – like Bedell-Smith – a retired general.

15 June

. . . . The weather is glorious – almost tropical, except for a NE wind or breeze. I'm afraid it's a 'drying' wind, and there is already something of a drought. The pheasants are now dying, for want of insect life.

Colonial Secretary came at 10.15 and I shewed him a telegram which I had sent (rather hesitatingly) to the Governor of Cyprus about the recent trials of terrorists. F[ield].M[arshal]. Harding is rather 'touchy' about the prerogative. So we always have the dilemma – either a perhaps ill-judged hanging, or the Governor's resignation! . . . .

Attended the unveiling (in Dorset Square) of a plaque to commemorate the Free French HQ. It was terribly hot, and I nearly fainted. The Queen Mother (nearly twenty minutes late, as usual!) did it beautifully . . . . As I fully expected, the Russians have made full use of Stassen's rather naive diplomacy. They now propose suspension of all nuclear tests, and agree to a plan for policing this suspension. They say nothing about production of fissile material or of weapons. This puts the Americans, who have always insisted on linking tests and production, in a hole . . . .

16 June

We did not go to Church. Worked all the morning on papers, and dictating. Miss Barker took the place of another girl yesterday. She is a very good and quick short-hand writer and also manages the little office here very efficiently . . . .

18 June

I went to see Anthony Eden, arriving about 1pm. I lunched with him (alone) in the cottage[67] and left about 3.45. I was surprised to find him as well as he seemed to be in body and as relaxed in mind. He had put on a stone since he had left the hospital, and although rather thin, he seemed pretty well covered again. But he told me that he was incapable of any effort. He did nothing and could do nothing without the return of fever. He will stay at the cottage (which, in fine weather at any rate, is really charming) until October, when there will be an x-ray examination. If, as he hopes, this shows the condition of the duct to be sound, he will begin to do more. He doesn't need (financially) to go on Boards (of Banking or Insurance) which is good. It would not be very dignified

---

67. At Broadchalke, Wiltshire.

for a former Prime Minister (altho' I shall certainly go back to M&Co. But a family business is different)

He might take on Red Cross or Shakespeare Theatre or National Gallery or something of the kind. He might write – if so, it will not be about Suez only, but about the whole story of the struggle against dictators, from 1930 onwards. The three great decisions of his life were 1) His resignation from Chamberlain's Govt in 1938 2) His decision to send the army to the relief of Greece in 1940 3) Suez. About the last, he talked calmly and moderately. Ld Beaverbrook had been to see him, trying to persuade him that he had been abandoned by his colleagues! (After the Jamaica incident, this is a difficult proposition to maintain) But he (Eden) was only anxious that I shd (once immediate problems were resolved) put the whole issue in its proper perspective before the electorate. It was significant how the Socialists kept off Suez. This meant that we shd not be afraid to talk about it. Eden has great political flair, and this may well be good advice. I have been too occupied up to now in conducting a retreat (like Sir John Moore etc)[68] to be able to write about it . . . .

Harold Stassen and Selwyn Lloyd to dinner. We had a long talk about disarmament. I took a very tough line with Stassen and I think he was a bit shaken. Anyway, he has agreed to alter the text of his reply to the Russians, in order to make it less difficult for us. The tests and the 'cut-off' (of material) are the fatal things for us if they come too soon.

21 June

. . . . Sir E Plowden to see me, about the US submarine *Nautilus*. We don't want this visit. The Americans, untruthfully say (for commercial purposes) that our Calder Hall reactors are not safe. The Admiralty replies by inviting (without a word to me) the US atomic submarine to Plymouth!

D and I went to Lords (Walter Monckton is [MCC] President this year) for test match – England v West Indies. A good afternoon's cricket . . . .

24 June

. . . . Dr Nkrumah, P.M. of Ghana, came at 11am. He was in a very

---

68. The commander of the British forces in Spain, killed during the successful retreat to Corunna in 1809.

merry mood and certainly has considerable charm. But there is, I wd think, a good deal of *faux bonhomme*[69] about him. Cabinet from 11.45 to 1.15 on disarmament. There was a long and rather difficult discussion. I read to my colleagues my correspondence with the President and tried to give them the whole background, as well as make clear to them the terrible dilemma in which we find ourselves, between the Scylla of Test Suspensions and the Charybdis of 'cut-off' of fissile material.[70] After much discussion, the Cabinet agreed to our proposed position, with the Americans, French and Canadians, but in the amended form which I got Stassen to agree . . . .

The Cabinet met again at 3 to 5.30 and from 6.30 to 8. There was a tremendous lot of business to get through, which had accumulated during the holidays. The difficult question of MPs' and ministers' salaries was put back on the order paper by my direction, for I felt (on reflection) that the previous decision to put up Cabinet ministers from £5000 to £6000 was wrong. With the £750 of the Parliamentary salary wh we propose to allow ministers to draw, it wd be an increase of £1750 – too much at one go! . . . .

In between the Cabinet meetings, I had calls from Mr Louw (S Africa) and the new Canadian P.M., Mr Diefenbaker. The former is not a very attractive personality. But he made himself as pleasant as he could. The latter I thought very engaging – naive, but strong – modest, but quite impressive.

25 June

Mr MacDonald (New Zealand) called at 10.30. He is representing S[idney] Holland, the P.M. I spoke to him about my desire to visit N.Z. in the New Year. He said he wd inform Mr Holland, whom he knew wd be delighted. I asked particularly that it should be kept secret, as there had been so many disappointments in the past – first Attlee, then Eden. This he promised faithfully.

After MacDonald – who is a fine, open, and typical N.Z. character – came Sir Roy Welensky. He is also a very likeable man – the best type of Trade Union leader, who has developed morally and intellectually as his responsibilities have grown. Then Mr Suhrawardy – vain,

---

69. Macmillan indicates that he considered Nkrumah a shifty customer.
70. In Greek mythology Scylla was a many-headed sea monster living in a cave adjacent to the whirlpool Charybdis. Mariners had to navigate a cautious path between the two.

clever, voluble, but courageous. He has certainly gripped a dangerous position in Pakistan, and seems determined to succeed. His hatred for Nehru and N's friends (like Krishna Menon) is extreme and he makes no effort to conceal it . . . .

P.Q.s – on the House resuming. The H-Bomb is temporarily displaced by 'Telephone Tapping'.[71] I answered a question by saying that I wd be very glad to discuss the problem with Gaitskell and Grimond. I think this has rather cut the ground from under their feet . . . .

27 June

Two meetings of the [Commonwealth] Conference. A talk with Grimond and Gaitskell. I have decided to set up a small ctee of Privy Counsellors about 'telephone tapping' . . . .

28 June

. . . . [Commonwealth Conference] Session from 10.30–1. We have now completed a 'tour d'horizon' on Russia, Europe, Middle East, SE Asia, and Far East. On the whole, the discussions have been good. It's clear to me that the Indians are not so certain of themselves as they used to be. Suez has shaken them, because they have learned that there is a point when Britain will react. Their financial position is very bad; their moral position over Kashmir is untenable. But they are still powerful and subtle. The Ceylonese (the present Govt is 'fellow-travelling') naturally side with India, in general neutralism. Everyone else is more militant and stout-hearted than before. Canada has a man, instead of a stuffed shirt.[72] Nkrumah seems, curiously, to be leaning to Pakistan rather than India. I tried to summarise the whole discussion at the end of this morning's session, and my effort seemed well received. I took rather a robust line, to stiffen our real friends, and I think did so without offending India, altho' obviously Nehru did not agree. Krishna Menon came in the afternoon – smooth and false as

---

71. The issue had blown up on 6 June with a question from Labour MP Marcus Lipton to Butler about telephone intercepts. On 28 June a committee under Sir Norman Birkett to investigate the use of prerogative powers in this area was set up, recommending in late October stricter supervision of this activity.

72. A reference to the recent surprising Conservative victory at the Canadian elections, after which Diefenbaker had replaced Louis St Laurent as Prime Minister.

ever. Then a long conference with Suhrawardy about Kashmir – not very conclusive, but not bad . . . .

29 June

Dorset [North] by-election worked out very well – we won by 3000. Of course the press will call it 'fall in Tory vote'[73] – but all the same it marks quite a change. The press is annoyed by the Committee of Privy Counsellors (wh was announced yesterday) because it has rather stopped the fun. So they are a bit sour. *The Times* has gone quite mad, and thinks that all secret service work shd stop . . . .

30 June

Church in morning. Rather unexpectedly the Begum (Suhrawardy's daughter) came with us. She said she likes all religions. Last week she went to a RC church. A terribly hot day, ending in a thunderstorm. By the evening, I was quite exhausted, having talked (or been talked at) by all the Prime Ministers both collectively and individually.

4 July

The Conference has gone on all the week, morning and evening – and, on the whole, has gone well. The discussions have been frank and candid. There has been a good deal of disagreement – but a wide measure of agreement as well. On European trade – and the proposed Free Trade Area – the PMs and ministers have been sympathetic and sensible – tho' naturally vigilant. On anything affecting alliances or arms, Nehru has been 'neutral' – but not disagreeable. Krishna Menon (his evil genius) has been odious. I think he is the nastiest man I know (tho' perhaps even he has redeeming virtues. Who knows? Anyway, Mrs Pandit doesn't think so) . . . .

5 July

The sensational changes in the Russian Govt leave us rather uncertain as to where we stand on disarmament. Our proposals have had a fairly good press, and the fact that USA, UK, France and Canada are united is good. When they were put forward by the F.S. on Monday, the Russian delegate (Zorin) was very 'cagey' – we did not know why at the time, but we assume because of the Palace revolution going on in the Kremlin. Molotov; Malenkov; Kaganovitch; and Shepilov have

---

73. It fell by 4,000 and there was a small swing to the Liberals.

been ousted. (A few years ago, they wd have been shot; but this seems
not obligatory any more) The position of Gromyko (who has always
been one of Molotov's men) is obscure. B[ulganin] and K[hrushchev]
are more firmly established than ever – with the help of the army,
under Zhukov. On the whole, it may mean a more flexible policy
towards the West. But it may be more a personal struggle for power
than a conflict of policies.

Final meeting of Commonwealth Conference at 10.30 .... The
last point was Diefenbaker's invitation to the Finance Ministers of the
Commonwealth to meet in Ottawa in September 'in order to make
arrangements for a Financial and Economic Conference of the Commonwealth'. Fortunately, I had arranged for this meeting to be in
'restricted session' – only PMs and their representatives. The Canadian
P.M., having just won a spectacular election, is still the victim of his
election oratory.[74] He is a fine man – sincere and determined; but I
fear that he has formed a picture of what can and cannot be done with
the Commonwealth today wh is rather misleading. Menzies (Australia)
reacted violently. He would have nothing to do with it. An item in the
communiqué on these lines would only raise a lot of false hopes. An
Economic Conference, if it were to be held at all, could only succeed if
great and expert preparation preceded it. If it were written up to great
importance and then failed, it would be a major disaster. (All this, of
course, is true; but poor Mr D looked first puzzled, then pained, then
indignant) MacDonald (N.Z.) followed Menzies – tho' less violently.
S Africa said the same as Australia, but more contemptuously. (The
Orientals stood aloof – Nehru amused, Suhrawardy puzzled) I let it
run a bit (for it suits us that D shd not believe everything that Lord
Beaverbrook tells him) but then I stepped in to rescue D from the
critics. After some discussion a formula was agreed to say that 'The
PM of Canada had invited the Commonwealth Finance Ministers to
have their normal meeting (after the International Bank meeting) this
year in Ottawa'. Altho' this did not, of course, give Mr D what he
really wanted, he seemed much relieved and accepted the compromise.
After it was all over he thanked me most warmly for my help. Indeed,
he said he could not have gone back to Canada without something of

---

74. During the elections Diefenbaker had attacked the Liberals over Canada's trade
    dependence upon the US and proposed the strengthening of Commonwealth
    ties.

the kind to build on. I heard later that he was to dine with Lord Beaverbrook. I hope he will not fail to tell him what happened . . . .

Nehru to luncheon. He seemed more relaxed. He likes to talk alone and he speaks more freely and less circumspectly in this way. He pressed me again to come to India after Christmas. After luncheon, we sat in the garden (a hot summer day again) and were soon joined by Suhrawardy (P.M. Pakistan) Since these two men are on the worst of terms and <u>never</u> meet – in India or in London – this was rather a risk. But the talk – wh lasted an hour – went off very well. . . . I have just a hope that they may reach some settlement about the Indus waters, and both agree to accept the International Bank's proposal.[75] If they could only get this question cleared up, it would make the approach to Kashmir much easier . . . .

7 July

. . . . 'Cyprus' conference at 4pm . . . . It really is one of the most baffling problems which I can ever remember. There are objections to almost every possible course. Altho' for the moment the terrorist movement is quiescent, Harding (the Governor) thinks that Archbp Makarios will start it up again after the next U.N. session. In any case, it will take us more troops than we can afford to hold the island through the next few years. (The Socialists will give it away anyhow, if they get in) If we give it to Greece, there will be war between Greece and Turkey. If we 'partition', it is a confession of failure – means civil war in the island, and perh war between Greece and Turkey. We really want only air-bases for ourselves, for Baghdad pact and general M.E. and Persian Gulf defence. We hammered out a new plan[76] – wh seemed quite good late at night, but will perh not look so good in the morning . . . .

11 July

A long Cabinet on Cyprus . . . . I have tried the party pretty hard over Suez. I don't now want a panic about 'Selling out in Cyprus'. Then there is 'disarmament' – where the Russians have refused our proposals, and are obviously going to concentrate on 'suspension of

---

75. This was achieved with the 1960 Indus Water Treaty.
76. This was what Macmillan called the 'Macmillan Plan', involving sovereign British bases, a tridominium of Britain, Greece and Turkey over the island and separate Greek and Turkish assemblies for communal affairs. The Baghdad Pact was a 1955 defence arrangement of Iran, Iraq, Pakistan, Turkey and Britain.

Tests' . . . . Then there is a new flutter about 'the economic situation' – a heavy fall of 'gilts'[77] and a good deal of popular alarm at the recent price increases of coal, gas, electricity, transport etc (nevertheless, I think the public are at last beginning to realise the connection between wages and prices) In addition, we have telephone-tapping, MPs' salaries, and so on, as well as compensation to British refugees from Egypt (an awkward one) For all these reasons, I am not too keen on starting a new policy on Cyprus until <u>after</u> the House has risen . . . .

15 July

. . . . The 'Rising Price' problem – otherwise inflation – continues to fill the press. Thorneycroft (Chancellor of Ex) has done his best to <u>warn</u> people. But, as I used to find, one is apt to <u>scare</u> the City and the foreign bankers without producing much effect on the T. Unions . . . .

18 July

10am. Defence Ctee. A very dangerous revolt (aided by Saudi Arabia) has broken out against the Sultan of Muscat.[78] If this spreads to the Persian Gulf, the situation may be very serious. We agreed certain plans, subject to Cabinet approval . . . .

19 July

. . . . On the whole, the House of Commons situation is <u>not</u> as good as a few weeks ago. I think this is a) reaction from Suez b) opposition to European Free Trade c) cost of living and Old Age Pensioners. The Party in the country is <u>not</u> in a good mood. But I think we shall get through to the end of the session without disaster. If we <u>can</u> do that, it's more than I thought possible 6 months ago.

26 July

Quite a lot has happened since my last entry – altho' only a week. I went to Bedford on Saturday – a large crowd in the football ground. The speech was well reported in the Sunday press, and I think helped

---

77. Government bonds issued to raise funds on the capital markets.
78. Treaty relations with the Sultan and Cold War anxieties led to British involvement in suppressing this Saudi-backed revolt under the Imam Ghalib bin Ali, though this was only successfully completed in late 1959. The Saudis had severed diplomatic relations with Britain after the Buraimi incident in 1955.

to steady things a bit.[79] The bus strike began – and now looks like ending. There has been a good deal of ugly feeling, sabotage and violence. The Covent Garden porters are on strike – but the effect seems very small.

We have had lots of Cabinet, Defence Ctee meetings, luncheons, dinners – the usual crowded end of July. The Imam's [Ghalib bin Ali] rebellion in Muscat continues. Whether we can put it down or contain it seems doubtful; we cannot operate by land (it is too hot) and we have to be careful about air attack .... Last night I wound up the debate on inflation, in a fighting speech which seemed to rally the party. There were two abstentions. Martin Lindsay (who is a worthy fool) and Lancaster (who is just an ass).[80] However, we got a majority (I don't know how) of 63. Harold Wilson was pretty good – but laid himself too open to retort. Gaitskell was poor. Thorneycroft was admirable. Old Herbert Morrison intervened with a valuable and courageous little speech. Altogether, I was relieved to get this debate over. I think we shd now be all right till November (unless there is some unexpected catastrophe) ....

29 July

Cabinet at 11.30. Pensions. A very good talk – decision postponed till Cabinet on Friday. We have to decide a) the additional sum to the Old Age Pensioner b) the additional contribution from employer and employed c) whether to prepare a 'graded' pension scheme on the top of the present one. The sums involved are enormous.

.... We had a heavy afternoon – chiefly discussions among

---

79. This speech, on 20 July, contained the celebrated, and later frequently misrepresented, remark: 'Let's be frank about it; most of our people had never had it so good.' Contrary to myth, it was largely concerned with warning not to endanger prosperity and full employment by letting inflation rip. The phrase did not originate with Macmillan. In *The Goon Show*, 'The Mystery of the Fake Neddy Seagoons', first broadcast on 29 November 1956, the character Eccles says 'This is livin' – I never had it so good,' though there is no evidence that Macmillan consciously borrowed the phrase.

80. The debate was on the government's decision to establish a Council on Prices, Productivity and Incomes. This followed the conclusions of a Court of Inquiry into the wage dispute in the engineering industry in April 1957. In calling for tougher action to curb wage-push inflation at its end, Conservative MP Martin Lindsay had intimated that another Tory MP would join him and Colonel C. G. Lancaster MP in abstaining in the division.

ministers about the next steps to be taken in the European Free Trade problem. I have persuaded my colleagues chiefly concerned (CofEx; BofT etc) that we need one man charged with the task of preparing and conducting the preliminary negotiations. They have accepted this, and so has Reggie Maudling – Paymaster General. He will do the job admirably . . . .

30 July

. . . . The [Muscat and] Oman affair goes slowly on. We spend as much time on its details as if it were a real war. But it really isn't easy. We want the Sultan to clear up the rebellion. We want him (if possible) to do so with his own troops – on the ground (His troops are quite hopeless) We want the matter brought to an end quickly. But how can a few hundred troops finish it up, when the area is large and mountainous, and the climate conditions bad? However, Burrows (Political agent) and Sinclair (Air Marshal) are both good men, and I am glad to see them sending us joint telegrams (as FM Alexander and I used to do from Greece and Italy)

31 July

I am having a lot of trouble about a Scottish row – Niall Macpherson (under secy for Scotland) is accused of 'tampering with the liberty of the press' by getting the proprietors of a small newspaper in his constituency to dismiss the editor. The proprietors (National Liberal)[81] are for Macpherson; the editor (Liberal) against. This ridiculous row has been elevated into a great scandal; P.Q.s and protests to me, from Labour and Liberal MPs. There is now a hostile motion on the paper (supported by Grimond) and I have told the Chief Whip that we must dispose of it by debate if necessary . . . .

We had a Defence Committee this afternoon from 4–7.30. There has been a lot of talk in the newspapers about Cabinet divisions on defence. Curiously enough, the Cabinet has not discussed defence for a long time. But I think all this gossip comes from the Service Depts and possibly the Chiefs of Staff. The First Sea Lord [Mountbatten] is a

---

81. The Liberal Nationals split from the Liberal party over economic policy in 1931, adopting the name National Liberal in 1948. Closely aligned with the Conservatives after 1947, several government MPs like Macpherson sat as National Liberals. The party formally assimilated with the Conservatives in 1968.

strange character and tries to combine being a professional sailor, a politician, and a royalty. The result is that nobody trusts him. I have a feeling that he is at the bottom of all this newspaper intrigue . . . .

1 August

. . . . The debate on Niall Macpherson's alleged misbehaviour came off this evening. I spoke for 20 minutes or less, and managed to squash the accusation. The Opposition (Lib and Labour) was very weak. Gaitskell behaved lamentably. He allowed the whips to be put on; but (altho' he was in his place when I sat down) he hadn't the courage to answer me. In the circumstances, he ought not to have pressed the motion. We won easily, and our boys were very pleased at a) my loyalty b) my success in the debate. All this helps, with so many divisions and disaffections in the Party on more serious affairs.

2 August

11–1.15. Defence Ctee. This was a most successful morning and we really made great progress. We have at last definitely fixed
1. Size of Bomber Force till 1962
2. Number of Megaton Bombs
3. Defence expenditure 1957–8

We have now to embark on special studies of
   a) Air defence of GB. Is it possible and with what weapons?
   b) Tactical atomic weapons for the Army. Need we make any, or can we rely on Americans
   c) Role of the Navy.

But we have agreed the principles which are to guide these studies and I have asked them to be completed by the autumn.

Cabinet at 2.30. We had a short talk about one or two points wh had come up in the last day or two, but the main talk was about Pensions. We definitely settled the additional sum to be 10/-; contribution (total) to rise to 17/6; a 'grad[uat]ed' scheme on top to be worked out. Two Bills will be required – one in November, the other in February.[82]

Everyone is so exhausted at the end of a really terrible year (July

---

82. This involved an immediate increase in pensions and a decision, after a lengthy Cabinet battle, in favour of the Treasury scheme for graduated contributions and pensions.

1956 to August 1957) that the Cabinet began to wrangle and almost
to quarrel. So I sent them away . . . .

8 August

Winston and Clemmy Churchill came to luncheon. We got the Kil-
muirs to come over, and it was a very pleasant party. W was in pretty
good form, and remarkably quick either on very old questions (where
his memory is most retentive) or on very new ones (which he has not
had time to forget) He was splendidly indignant about Ld Altrincham's
(Ned Grigg's son) foolish attack on the Queen in the *National Review*
and the T.V.[83]

9 August

. . . . The Oman operation has met with rather more and better organised resistance than seemed at one time likely. But those on the spot
seem confident. The press is terrible – it gets worse every day. There is
a kind of masochism wh has seized them, which is infuriating. Nothing
is right; everyone is wrong. I think this reflects the tremendously high
standard of comfort and well-being of the people. When things are really
difficult, even the press does not complain very much . . . .

12 August

All day at Aldermaston – the atomic weapons establishment. It is a
remarkable place – 6000 people employed – £20m a year. It's worth it
if it helps to prevent wars. Sir W Penney is a splendid character, and –
as at Harwell – I was struck by the keen and buoyant atmosphere of
the place . . . . Of course, the tragedy is that, in defence of the same
cause, the American and British effort has to be duplicated, instead of
shared.

13 August

. . . . Oman seems to be over. I am much relieved. The operation has
been brilliantly conducted, when one considers the difficulties of terrain

---

83. John Grigg, who had succeeded his father as 2nd Baron Altrincham in 1955,
    suggested that the Court was 'complacent' and 'out of touch' and too closely
    associated with the upper classes, views he reiterated in a television interview
    with Robin Day. These widely misinterpreted comments reflected Altrincham's
    strong support for a constitutional monarchy which he wished to be national,
    unifying and above class divisions.

and climate – with only 3 companies of Cameronians and very second-rate Arab troops . . . .

23 August
Personal messages from Foster Dulles in Syria. The Americans are still uncertain, but I think realise that something must be done.[84] In my reply, I suggested that Syria may be the Czechoslovakia we need to make a NATO for the Middle East. Can the Baghdad Pact be extended and remodelled . . . .

27 August
Cabinet. A very good meeting, all the better for only 8 out of 17 being present.

1) <u>European Free Trade</u> etc. Maudling gave us a picture of the position and we agreed on the best line to take about agriculture. We shall try to omit this from the Free Trade Area agreement, but propose instead a separate 'Statute'.

2) <u>Canada</u>. I pressed strongly for a bold and imaginative approach. This is very important, both politically and for economic reasons. We must not 'drag our feet'. On the contrary, we should – if anything – overbid Mr Diefenbaker.

3) <u>Syria</u>. I gave the Cabinet a broad picture of the messages wh I had received from Washington and the draft of my proposed reply. This question is going to be of tremendous importance. The Americans are taking it very seriously, and talking about the most drastic measures – Suez in reverse. If it were not serious (and really satisfactory) it wd be rather comic . . . .

I had offered the Chairmanship of the Party to Quintin Hailsham (coupled with Ld President and deputy leader of the HofLords) He professed – quite genuinely – inability to do so great a job. But he will think it over.

I dined alone at No 10. The Chancellor of the Exr came at 9.30 and left at midnight. We had a long talk about the weakness of sterling (we lost $200m this month) and the inflation. We covered the whole ground and I promised to let him have a memorandum. We <u>must</u> be bold; caution is no good. All our political future depends on whether we can combine prosperity with stability . . . .

---

84. About Soviet infiltration there. The 1948 Communist coup in Czechoslovakia had helped to prompt the founding of NATO in Europe.

29 August
Ld Hailsham has accepted, if Oliver Poole can be persuaded to stay on
and help. This is just what I want. I saw Poole later in the day, who
has generously agreed to become deputy chairman. He will do 'organisation'; Hailsham political leadership and ideas. This should make a
very good combination.

I went this morning to Westminster Cathedral – a requiem mass
for Ronnie Knox. It was a very fine ceremony. But I must say that our
Anglican Burial Service is much nobler. Father Davy preached a good
sermon – or rather address – about Ronnie. He must have realised that
there were many non-Catholics present, and dealt generously with his
Anglican life and tradition.

. . . . I went to see John Waverley, in Saint Thomas' Hospital. Poor
Ava knows now that he has a malignant cancer.[85] But he has not been
told. He looked very grey and thin; but he was in good form, talking
and arguing in the old style . . . .

3 September
I had a good talk with For Secy last night. The Oman affair drags on –
in the sense that the rebel leaders (with some of their supporters) have
fortified themselves in a mountainous position (4 or 5 thousand feet up)
The choice is a) to blockade them b) to try to 'winkle' them out. Both
courses have their objections. There is public opinion; the United
Nations; the nervous state of the Arab world; the idiotic British press;
the danger of the infection spreading; the problem of air attack . . . .

4 September
I telephoned to the For Secy last night. We decided to go ahead in
Oman – at least for a limited period. If the operations against the
remaining rebels failed, (owing to difficulty of terrain, supply etc) to
lead to early success, it would be best just to blockade them in the
mountains. The troublesome thing is that (in these days of radio
communication etc) they may be able to claim that they exist as a
'movement' or even as a separate state . . . .

Meanwhile, it is clear that the states cast by US govt for the role of
'Prince Charming' do not seem very anxious to play the part. Iraq
(without Nuri) has a weak Govt; Jordan is weak too (and the two

---

85. A Cabinet colleague during and after the war, Waverley died on 4 January
    1958.

[Hashemite] Royal families have had a tremendous quarrel) Lebanon is a frail plant. The Turks wd probably play up, but then what about Russia?

The collapse of the Franc[86] and the tremendous rise in the Mark has meant a very bad month for us on the exchanges – the worst since Suez. But the actual balance of payments position is good and so is the trade balance. So we must hold on. At the Chancellor of the Ex's request, I am circulating my memorandum on inflation etc to the Cabinet.[87] I'm afraid the pressure will grow during this month, owing to the meeting of the International Fund and Bank at Washington. If only we cd get into a position of reasonable equilibrium and fairly settled world conditions, it would be a great relief to 'free' the £ and escape from this perpetual opportunity for the speculator to profit out of our slender reserves . . . .

6 September

. . . . Cabinet met at 3pm and I explained to them the Syrian situation. The Americans are now definitely in favour of a 'retrieving' operation in Syria . . . . They want us to be committed to this decision. Naturally, a British Cabinet, while being ready to accept a 'retrieving' operation as an <u>aim</u>, wd like to know by what <u>method</u> it is to be reached. However, my colleagues were impressed by the importance of not discouraging the Americans (now they are in this mood) and I think recognised the immense stake. For unless Russian influence in M East can be stopped, Britain and Europe 'have had it' (as they say) Only the Americans can bring the power to bear a) to stop Arabs etc from falling b) to risk the consequences – i.e. Russian threats to Turkey, Iran, etc c) to stop this degenerating into global war – by the American air threat to Russia – still at its strongest moment in history (in ten years – or less – the trans-continental rocket will alter the balance) . . . .

7 September

. . . . This M.E. position weighs very heavily on me; the responsibility cannot really be shared with the Cabinet. I have to try to weigh up the pros and cons. Apart from what advice we are to give the Americans, what part do we ourselves want to play? Stand on the side lines and

---

86. Effectively devalued on 12 August.
87. This emphasised controlling the money supply rather than the eventually chosen solution of raising interest rates.

cheer? Or take a leading role? (The Americans will expect <u>moral</u> support, but do they want or shd we demand <u>active</u> participation?) . . . .

8 September (Sunday)
. . . . The Beaverbrook Press attacks the Foreign Secy (and through him, the P.M.) violently and unscrupulously. They have now sunk to the level of *Confidential* (a scandalous American paper) During the F.S.'s short holiday in Spain, he was walking down the street with a friend and his wife. The lady was in the middle. The *Express* photographer (who had followed S Lloyd to Catalonia) took a picture. The husband (on the right) was cut out. The picture (containing the lady and the F.S.) was then published in the *Express* under the caption 'F.S. on holiday. Who is the senorita?' Even Beaverbrook could stoop no lower . . . .

10 September
. . . . Nuri Pasha came to see me. He looked much better. 3 months out of office and his 'cure' in England have done him good. He was not very hopeful about the situation. But he felt that if nothing were done, the whole of the area wd gradually slide into Communism. He is going back to Iraq and will do his best . . . .

11 September
    9.45. Foreign Secy.
    10.30. Mr Geoffrey Lloyd.
    11.15. Julian Amery.
    11.30. Mr Macdonnell (Canadian minister [without portfolio])
    12 noon. Sir E Plowden.
    12.30. Mohammed Ali (ex P.M. Pakistan)
    1.15. Luncheon of Mr Casey (Australia)
    4–6. Chancellor.
    6. Sir R Powell (defence)
    8. Dine with Ld Mills.
A good day for holiday time! . . . .

15 September
I spent Sunday at B.G. (D at Islay) Ld Mills came down for the day, and we had a long talk about the plans to 'hold the inflation'. We both feel that the broad policy of a) holding Government investment to the

same money back as last year and b) the Bank's advances to the same as last year, is the right policy. This really means that the people can have present standards of living and full employment. If they insist on fresh all round wage increases, they will create unemployment, because there won't be enough money to pay. But, in addition to this endemic problem of British costs and prices, there is the epidemic attack of the £ by international bears. The losses incurred by the authorities, drawing on the gold and dollar reserves, were formidable in August and will be worse in Sept. Can we hold on? Or shd we let the £ go? In any event, it is some comfort to feel that the same cure (roughly) is right for both diseases . . . .

17 September

Cabinet at 3. A great deal of drafting and re-drafting of the statement had been going on. The Treasury wanted to relate it primarily to the attack on the £. I have resisted this stoutly – and successfully. What the British people are waiting for is the answer to the 64000 [dollar] question – how to stop rising prices and fall in value of money. They will (perhaps) accept measures to deal with these problems. But they regard an exchange crisis (which they do not understand) as some kind of a swindle organised by foreigners. Cabinet approved policy and draft. But the great question remained to be answered. The Bank want to raise Bank rates by 2% – a thing practically without precedent (5%–7%) After much argument, this was left for me and Chancellor to settle . . . .

20 September (Friday)

The 'bomb' burst yesterday. The Chancellor of the Exchequer's announcement about a) credit base and bankers' advances b) government investment was issued at 11.45am; the Bank Rate increase to 7% (from 5%) was issued to Stock Exchange at same time.

Naturally all stocks and shares fell rapidly, from the best 'blue chips' to gilt-edged. The Chancellor gave a short I.T.V. message. This morning, (so well was the secret kept) that the press seemed dazed. On the whole, the serious papers give full support. *D.T.* excellent; *Times* quite good; *Yorkshire Post*, very good. What is interesting, is that the *Daily Mirror* has no reference at all to the whole subject. The Opposition will, I think be cautious. Since they aspire to office (and no doubt feel confident about the next election) they will try to be 'statesmanlike'.

I had a meeting with the Chancellor and the Treasury this morning.

Various papers are to be prepared about possible developments and what we ought to do in certain circumstances. The Deutsch-Mark is really the key. I doubt whether we shall be able to persuade the Germans to help.[88] What pressure can we mobilise against them? . . . .

22 September (Sunday)
I did not go to Church, as I wanted to get ahead with the [Party] Conference speech.[89] There also arrived last night a most formidable document from Washington – the very secret report of the Anglo-American working party on Syria and the M. East. Foster Dulles (on whom the mantle of Anthony Eden seems to have fallen) is desperately anxious to do something. But what? This has been the task of the working party to discover. The situation is very like that over Suez. How to find an occasion or reason for intervention? Yet, if nothing is done, there may be a rapid, and perhaps fatal, deterioration in the M.E., with its ultimate loss to Russia. With the report, came a mass of telegrams from New York (where the For Secy and Dulles both are, for the U.N. assembly) and some difficult decisions. The fact is that the friendly Arab states (Iraq; Jordan; Lebanon) are weak internally and uncertain what to do. Nuri has gone to Istanbul, and will wait a call to Baghdad. But without Nuri, the present Iraq Govt is weak and timid. King Hussein (of Jordan) is anxious to start real pressure on Syria, by whose subversive and brigand forces he is all the time threatened. Even King Saud is said to be alarmed at the spread of Communism. All the same, nothing is done . . . .

24 September
Two meetings this morning – one F.O. and Treasury, on the best way to take up (if at all) Colonel Hatem's proposals for a [renewal of the financial] negotiation. I am not very anxious to get involved in talks with Col Nasser. On the other hand, the move comes from him and from the Parliamentary point of view I wd like to see progress with the compensation of our nationals by some means . . . .

26 September
A new row. It is alleged that there was a 'leak' about the intention of

88. The Bundesbank did help to stabilise sterling.
89. In this period the party leader usually only attended to address the Saturday post-Conference rally.

the Govt to raise the Bank Rate. Since I only agreed to this on Wed morning, and since the dealings on Wed evening (after the Stock Exchange had closed) were very small, I think this improbable. We have had careful enquiries made; but no trace can be found of any irregularity. Harold Wilson has written a letter to the Financial Secy, demanding an official, or rather a judicial enquiry. In the absence of the Chancellor of the Exr, Enoch Powell came to see me to discuss his reply. The Governor is quite happy; so is the Chairman of the Stock Exchange that we should refuse. I therefore authorised the F[inancial] S[ecretary] to send his reply and publish it at once (as Wilson had done) The Lobby were seen and took the decision (with background explanations) well enough. Wilson at once published a further protest and said it wd be raised when Parlt met. No doubt there will be trouble in some of the newspapers tomorrow. It is, of course, true that the Chancellor saw a few newspaper editors (*Times*, *M.G.* etc) about the general policy (investment cuts; restriction of credit base etc) But he naturally never mentioned the Bank Rate . . . .

29 September (Sunday)
. . . . The Socialists seem now to be going to promise to repeal the Rent Act. No doubt this will win some support, but if the election doesn't come soon, people will have got used to it. When I think of all the fuss about the bread subsidy, the milk subsidy, the removal of the housing subsidy and all the other grievances, one wonders how long the Rent Act will 'run' as an issue[90] . . . .

1 October
Brendan Bracken came to dinner last night.[91] He was very amusing and very encouraging. I need the latter – the *Express-Chronicle* Gallup polls show another slide away from us – 7% swing. What is

---

90. The Rent Act does not seem to have played a significant part in the 1959 General Election, but revelations during the Profumo Affair in 1963 of the extortionate activities of the recently deceased landlord, associate of Stephen Ward and lover of Mandy Rice-Davies, Perec Rachman, revived it as an issue. Rachman had replaced sitting tenants with West Indians at high rents in often subdivided properties in places like Notting Hill. It should, however, be noted that he largely moved out of private renting after 1958. Following their narrow victory in 1964 Labour were to reintroduce a measure of rent control.

91. Former Conservative MP, long-term close confidant of Churchill and chairman of the *Financial Times*.

rather discouraging is that this followed the Govt's recent decisions. Perhaps it only reflects nervousness about the 'crises'. The Labour Party conference started in Brighton yesterday. Their mood is (naturally, I suppose) one of exultation over our difficulties. All pretence of 'statesmanship' or 'defending the £' is thrown aside. They have promised 'Repeal of the Rent Act' and the purchase by municipalities of some 6 million houses. (As this will cost between £2 and £3 thousand million, it hardly seems a good anti-inflationary measure!) Harold Wilson made quite a good old-style attack on me personally – ducal grouse-moors and all that. Cousins, curiously enough, was more restrained . . . .

3 October

Lord Kemsley to luncheon – alone. His press give us consistent support and he never fails us. Apart from the *Sunday Times* – which is beating the *Observer* hollow – his provincial evening papers are important. He is not unduly depressed by the swing against us. He feels that the Socialists are producing their election programme too soon. The 'nationalisation' plans can be riddled [sic], when they are understood. The threat is now much more alarming than when it was confined to one or two industries. Now every business is under notice.

4 October

A Bevan, at the Socialist conference, has come out with a passionate defence of the H-Bomb![92] The *D.T.* has a leader headed 'Bevan into Bevin'. The Bevanites are furious; the rank and file of the constituencies voted pretty solidly against him and the platform – but the unions (in spite of Cousins, who was voted down in his executive) voted solidly for the Bomb! Of course, all this is very satisfactory from a national point of view. From a narrow political point of view, it makes them more dangerous.

Harold Wilson has come back to the charge about the alleged leak of the 7% Bank Rate. He delivered at 6pm tonight a long argumentative letter to Enoch Powell . . . . but making this time a definite statement of a leak from a 'political source'. He published the letter on the tape and wireless at 6pm. After consulting Norman Brook, Bishop,

---

92. Bevan, Labour's shadow foreign secretary, merely pointed out that unilateral disarmament by Britain would mean sending her representatives 'naked into the Conference Chamber'.

and Chief Whip, I got my reply . . . . to him, to B.B.C., and to press by 9pm. I rejected his general demand for a roving enquiry into vague rumours. I went on to say that he now made a specific allegation, for which he said he had evidence. If he wd send it to us, I wd refer it to Lord Chancellor for advice as to whether further investigation was called for . . . .

5 October

Ld Hailsham made a very fine broadcast last night. It was certainly a wise step to put him in as Chairman. What will happen during the next 2 years, no one can say – or even if we can keep the Government going for that time. At the moment, the whole thing is swinging <u>away</u> from us – but has it swung to Labour? Gaitskell is trying to attract the middle vote. But will he lose the enthusiasm of the Left. (The H-Bomb is perhaps the real test) I think he will probably succeed – but he has made a tactical mistake in trying to get his troops rallied too early. If I can keep the battle off for 2 years, it is quite likely that they will quarrel again. My problem is, of course, very similar. If we cannot bring back the traditional strength of the party to the fold – small shop-keepers, middle class etc – we have no chance. But we also need at least 3 million Trade Union votes . . . .

7 October

A long Cabinet 3–6. Maudling came for first time and handled the European Free Trade problem quite admirably. He is really a first-class brain. Before the Cabinet, Mr Harold Wilson, accompanied by Mr James Griffiths (*vice* Mr Hugh Gaitskell) called. I had the Lord Chancellor with me. They seemed rather nervous, but produced a story about a Mr X (who was under my 'patronage') and a conversation with a Mr Y (who was under my control) Mr Y had claimed that he had full knowledge of the Bank Rate decision. I assumed from this that Mr X must be a civil servant or a Bishop and Mr Y an employee of the Conservative Central Office. Mr Wilson demanded that a Judge shd make the preliminary enquiry – not the Lord Chancellor, because of the peculiar position of X and Y. It was a very full day, because in addition to the Cabinet, there was a meeting about the Egyptian financial negotiations; due to start in Rome – quite a tricky subject. However, after discussing it with Ld C[hancellor] and Norman Brook, I decided to reject Wilson's rather impudent demand and ask him to produce his evidence to the Lord Ch[ancellor] . . . .

9 October

. . . . Admiral Strauss, of the US atomic energy, came at 3 and we had a long talk. As a result I have sent messages to Foster Dulles and to the President. The first (agreed with the For Sec) is about the U.N. disarmament debate. Shall we have to make some concession to the demand for a cessation of tests? Could we impose on ourselves some voluntary limitation? The message to the President says this – in view of the extent of Russian power and technical capacity (the 'satellite' launched this week has, of course, struck public imagination)[93] couldn't we now pool all our resources to fight them – financial, military, technical, propaganda etc. This wd include getting rid of the McMahon Act. This Act was to make sure that America's secrets were not sold or betrayed to Russia. But it was relevant to the situation in 1950 [sic]. It's quite absurd now . . . . S[trauss] is really in favour of an abrogation or repeal of the McMahon Act.[94]

10 October

For Sec in the morning . . . . We are both rather in favour of offering the Governorship of Cyprus to [Sir Hugh] Foot. Harding cannot go on much longer, for health reasons. There is a lot to be said for reverting to an ordinary Colonial Governor, and Foot (now in Jamaica) seems to be the best man available . . . .

15 October

. . . . Luncheon for Mr Krishnamachari (Indian Finance Minister) We had a frank and useful talk after luncheon. He quite realises that we

---

93. The Russians launched *Sputnik*, the first artificial satellite, on 4 October, only a month after the first successful Soviet test of an ICBM. This heightened the already growing sense in the West of the Soviet technological threat. As Macmillan wrote to Eisenhower on 10 October: 'This artificial satellite has brought it home to us what formidable people they are and what a menace they present to the free world. Their resources and knowledge and their system of government will enable them to keep up the pressure for a very long time to come – perhaps two or three generations. After that we must hope that the Communistic ideology will be spent and that their people will revert gradually to ordinary human behaviour' (G&E, p. 86).

94. In 1946, in spite of various secret wartime agreements, the US Congress passed the McMahon Act, virtually prohibiting any inter-allied exchange of nuclear information.

cannot do much. But I undertook to ask both Eisenhower and Adenauer to see what they could do. A financial collapse of India wd be very serious and we must try to avert it. The trouble is that Nehru has not made things easier for the American administration to get anything through Congress in favour of India. The Germans have plenty of money, but no real experience for foreign lending or the machinery for organising it . . . .

16 October
. . . . The Russians are making more and more inflammatory speeches and statements about Syria and the M.E. . . . . Foster Dulles and the President want me to come over for a talk, if it can be arranged without attracting too much attention or causing alarm . . . .

18 October
The Lord Chancellor has delivered his report on the alleged 'Bank Rate Leak'. Although it completely exonerates all concerned and quite definitely advises me against a formal enquiry, it is not easy to decide the next step . . . .

22 October
. . . . Left London Airport at 11.30pm for Washington. As far as I can see, the press have taken my decision about 'Bank Rate Leak' pretty well.

23 October
. . . . We got to Washington at 9.15am and were met by Foster Dulles and the For Secy . . . .

Foster Dulles soon began to reveal the new ideas with wh he is struggling. He realises that America cannot stand alone, still less 'go it alone'. I responded, with quite a romantic picture of what US and UK could do together – practically the last act of *Apple Cart*.[95] But I added that our unity must be not to rule but to serve the world. Foster said this represented the President's inmost thoughts. The problem was how to do it. We continued our talk till luncheon. Harold Caccia (who is a tremendous success here) told me that

---

95. The final act of George Bernard Shaw's *The Apple Cart* (1929) posits an Anglo-American reunion.

a) the Queen's visit has made a tremendous effect here. She has buried George 3rd for good and all.[96]

b) The Russian success in launching the satellite has been something equivalent to Pearl Harbor. The American cocksureness is shaken.

c) President is under severe attack for first time.

d) Foster is under still more severe attack. His policies are said to have failed everywhere.

e) The administration realises that their attitude over the Canal issue was fatal and led necessarily to the Suez situation.

f) The atmosphere is now such that almost anything might be decided, however revolutionary . . . .

7pm. At the White House. The President; Dulles; For Sec; and I. Drinks etc, with mostly reminiscent chat till dinner. The President seemed much better than at Bermuda. He was brisk; confident; and seemed more sure of himself. He complained a good deal about 'politicians' and the attacks upon himself. (This is a new experience for him. Up to now, he has been immune)

After dinner, the real talk began. I felt that Foster was rather feeling his way. So I let him make the running. The conversation was rather scrappy, and the Pres, while agreeing to the need for full [nuclear] cooperation in principle, seemed unwilling to discuss just how it was to be done in practice. However, Foster was persistent, in his slow laborious way and at one time I thought we shd get down to real business. But we didn't . . . . The only point which seemed to get home was when I told the President that if we couldn't get all this done in the next two or three years, with all the advantage of our close friendship, it was unlikely that our successors wd be able to do the job.

When we got back to the Embassy I was tired – and a little depressed. For Secy was more hopeful.

24 October

I thought about it all during the night and came to the conclusion that it wd be best to let the hand play itself. We would ask for nothing, but see what they had for us. At 10am there was a 'plenary' meeting at the

---

96. The Queen's first state visit to the USA, only the second by a British monarch after her father's visit in 1939, was from 17–21 October to mark the 350th anniversary of the founding of Virginia.

White House – in the Cabinet Room. The Americans start early, for a meeting of the National Security Council was just ending as we arrived. The Cabinet Room is a fine and dignified room – with a good picture of George Washington.

We fielded our full team. The Americans, in addition to Pres and Dulles, had the new Secretary of Defence [Neil McElroy], the under-secretary [Christian Herter], Allen Dulles (Intelligence), Admiral Strauss (Atomic), American ambassador in London [Whitney], Dillon (State Dept) and various other 'experts'. The President opened with a little speech – perfect in form and very good in substance. He went very far – further than I dared hope last night. Then I spoke – a little 'sentimentally' – but I think they liked it none the worse. (I had prepared nothing, but trusted to the spirit moving me. I thought how pleased my mother wd have been to see me, as British PM, in the American Cabinet Room, addressing a meeting presided over by the American President.) Foster spoke next, very well. Then Selwyn Lloyd – short, clear, and effective. Then the President asked Allen Dulles to give his appreciation of Russian military strength and future potential. It appeared that we have 3–5 years of superiority. [Sir Patrick] Dean agreed – it was a 'joint appreciation'.

At this point, the President produced a directive (obviously pre-pared by Dulles and agreed at the National Security meeting) It set up two committees, one headed by Powell and Quarles – on collaboration on weapons, etc; the other headed by Plowden and Strauss, on nuclear collaboration. This was agreed; as well as a communiqué to be given to the Press announcing these two committees, which were to report tonight. I could hardly believe my ears – such rapid progress, to be publicly announced. This done and agreed, the President adjourned the meeting and we left the White House at about 11.30.

Dulles came to luncheon again at the Embassy. We had a talk afterwards, and he produced the draft of a 'declaration', to be called 'declaration of common purpose'. I glanced at it, and saw, embedded in a lot of verbiage, para 3 – the end of the McMahon Act – the great prize! . . . .

7pm. At the White House – drinks and talks before dinner. All the same party as at the plenary session. Another committee (in addition to the two technical committees) had formed itself – Norman Brook and Libby Merchant. By dinner, a redraft of the declaration was available; and later (after dinner) the reports of the two technical committees, as well as one on <u>general</u> cooperation, through working parties, over the whole field of our relations, political, economic, propaganda, foreign policy etc. This is to be very secret to avoid the jealousies of Commonwealth countries as well as all other allied countries.

There was a lot of chaff between us all about the 'declaration of interdependence' as the title. The Pres rather like the idea – but on reflection we all thought it a little too dramatic. Fortunately, both he and I had made some very similar amendments in the draft. But everything of substance remained. I heard that Admiral Strauss was getting rather alarmed about the phraseology of para 3. (McMahon) But I have high hopes that the Pres and Secretary Dulles will stand firm. Incidentally, at the plenary session this morning, the President rather shocked some of his people by referring to the McMahon Act as 'one of the most deplorable incidents in American history, of wh he personally felt ashamed' . . . .

25 October
Plenary meeting fixed for 10.30. Before this actually took place (it was a trifle delayed) we heard that the American atomic team had made an effort for a modification of para 3. But it seems that the President stood by his words.

1. The Declaration was finally approved, with two small verbal changes.
2. The agreements on a) general cooperation b) weapons c) nuclear were agreed and initialled.
3. We stated that the British Govt would not press for admission of Communist Chinese Govt to U.N. without discussion and agreement of US.
4. US agreed to regard Hong Kong as a joint defence problem and discuss ways and means with us.

(I think that 3 is a very small price to pay for all we have obtained. It is very carefully worded, not as an agreement but as a unilateral statement of HMG's policy . . . .

. . . . Dulles came to see us off at the airfield. The job is done – and I must frankly say better done than I expected . . . .

27 October
Arrived London airport at 7.30am. Press conference; T.V.; I.T.V. What a barbarous practice. Drove straight home, arriving about 9.15am . . . . They had a good shoot yesterday – 180 pheasants. I am sorry to have missed it . . . .

29 October

MPs back to work – like boys to school! I had a number of questions, wh went quite well. Also statement about Washington and the accident at Windscale. Members seemed in a relaxed mood. Gaitskell made one foolish intervention; but I squashed him.

Thorneycroft opened the debate – a good, serious speech – delivered simply and straightforwardly. Harold Wilson made a very clever speech in reply; witty, well-informed, but too long and too indecisive. He could not make up his mind whether there <u>was</u> or was <u>not</u> a financial and economic problem to be solved. I had a speech ready to deliver on 'Bank Rate Leak' – but Wilson's short reference to it was such an obvious retreat, that I decided (after discussion with Chief Whip) to leave it alone.

30 October

. . . . Edwin Plowden (Atomic Energy Authority) called – in a great state of emotion – about the report on the accident at Windscale. He wants to offer his resignation. I dissuaded him, as best I cd. But the problem remains – how are we to deal with Sir W Penney's report?[97] It has, of course, been prepared with scrupulous honesty and even ruthlessness. It is just such a report as the board of a company might expect to get. But to publish to the world (esp to the Americans) is another thing. The publication of the report, as it stands, might put in jeopardy our chance of getting Congress to agree to the President's proposal . . . .

31 October

. . . . There was a Cabinet this morning – mostly on the economic situation. It is going to be very difficult to hold the balance between firmness and truculence. A great deal depends upon the tone wh we adopt. If the T.U. leaders think that there is any chance of weakening, they will press forward. On the other hand, they will seek to make a grievance of our intransigeance . . . .

5 November

. . . . The Russians have launched another and larger 'satellite' (with a 'little dawg' in it) which has created much alarm and despondency

---

97. Windscale in Cumbria had been developed from 1946 to produce weapons-grade plutonium. An error in the cooling process resulted in a fire in Pile 1 on 10 October 1957, releasing radioactive isotopes into the atmosphere.

in US. The English people, with characteristic frivolity, are much more exercised about the 'little dawg' than about the terrifying nature of these new developments in 'rocketry'. Letters and telegrams were pouring in tonight to No 10, protesting about the cruelty to the dog.

.... I have, by tradition, to make a long speech expounding all the items in the Queen's Speech,[98] more or less seriatim. This makes a dull speech – and mine was pretty dull. But I succeeded in my two objectives

    (i) to lower the temperature of the 'class war' – that is, to set out simply and clearly our line about wage increases, arbitration etc.

    (ii) to launch the concept of 'inter-dependence'. This will annoy Ld Beaverbrook, Lord Hinchingbrooke, Sir Kenneth Pickthorn and other 'isolationists'.[99] But it is our only hope . . . .

6 November

Mr Mintoff (P.M. of Malta) at 10.30 – a low, blackmailing type, but very clever. Cabinet 11–1.15 – a great deal of difficult stuff. The Treasury and the Ministry of Defence are at daggers drawn about pay etc. There was rather a difficult situation developing between their heads (Thorneycroft and Sandys) but I think today's discussions will help to make a détente. The 'wages' problem is easing. Of course, we don't know what the unions will do. But it's clear that no one is really 'spoiling for a fight'.

D and I had a private luncheon today. Hugh Cudlipp (Ed of *Daily Mirror*) was the pivot round which the party was built. He is able, and not unreasonable – altho' naturally, like all such journalists, without any scruples about truth, morality, good feeling and the like. But he is by no means 'sold out' to the Socialists. He is critical of their faults and failures.

Dinner for Spaak – usual company of politicians, business men etc. Eric Bessborough[100] (who used to be with me in Algiers) came – also

---

98. The annual address by the Sovereign to both Houses of Parliament outlining the Government's programme for the coming year.

99. Macmillan is referring to opposition from amongst fellow Conservatives in Parliament.

100. Lord Bessborough was a Conservative peer who went on to hold junior ministerial office under Douglas-Home.

Tom Williamson (TUC) Alf Robens (Labour MP) The latter was obviously sincerely anxious to avoid an industrial row this winter . . . .

7 November

I lunched with 5000 'Directors' (the Institute of Directors) and addressed them afterwards in the Festival Hall. I spoke 'off the cuff'[101] for 10–15 minutes. I think it was just what they wanted to hear and it certainly went very well. When 5000 men who have had 30% chopped off their holdings (gilts and equities) and are paying 8% for money stand up and cheer, it's quite a sign of good feeling and understanding.

Read novel about the end of the world (thro' radiation following nuclear war) by Nevil Shute. It is called *On the Beach*. Well done, rather too long, but none the less impressive . . . .

8 November

I made a statement in the House at 11am about the Windscale accident. I have published a long White Paper (the substance of Penney's report) and this seemed to satisfy the House. At least, no one asked about publication in full. Of course, it will take a few days before public opinion is expressed . . . .

There are a number of subjects which I had to deal with this afternoon, the chief being Cyprus. We want M Spaak to try to bring Greece and Turkey together over this. He (S) has some vague ideas about 'independence' (but without external affairs or defence) We have some vague ideas about military 'enclaves' for UK; 'condominium' for the rest . . . .

9 November

. . . . 6.50 arrived at Guildhall[102]. . . . My speech was not as well received as I was. It was intended to make people think, not excite them – being variations on the theme of 'interdependence'. This has two advantages – 1) it is the great problem of the future 2) it takes the heat off the industrial war at home . . . .

10 November (Sunday)

. . . . The more I think about the 'interdependence' theme (wh is really only a variation of the Churchill speeches after the war) the more I feel

---

101. Having decided John Wyndham's speech draft would not do.
102. To address the Lord Mayor of London's Banquet.

the vital importance of the NATO meeting in December. This will set a pattern. The chief problem will be to get practical measures going. The Continentals, frightened of the nuclear, will want larger conventional forces. But these are even more expensive and they will not, in fact, produce much themselves . . . .

11 November
. . . . One of the most urgent things is to get a really good agenda for NATO. The Germans are very shy about nuclear and want conventional armies. The French seem in a rather dazed condition – until Algeria is conquered, evacuated or conciliated, they are immobilised. Spaak is working hard on the right lines. But it won't be easy to get down to brass tacks. If we could get ourselves into a better posture, there might be another meeting with the Russians. But it is too early yet. I believe I cd get the idea into the President's head that it shd happen while we are both in command.

Meanwhile, the home front continues obscure. The £ is responding to treatment, but at a very high price. The T.U.s are being fairly cautious. But the transport claims are gathering – buses, railway clerks, and the NUR etc . . . .

13 November
On reflection, I reached the view that we must now set up the Judicial Enquiry into the alleged 'Bank Rate Leak'.[103] Altho' no *prima facie* evidence has been produced to me or to the Lord Chancellor, there has now been an imputation against the honour of distinguished men. Oliver Poole has written me a letter 'demanding' an enquiry. Thorneycroft is in the same mood. We discussed all this during this morning and my conclusion was upheld by the leading colleagues whom I had in . . . .

14 November
. . . . I made my statement after questions, in spite of my cold and bad voice. It shocked Mr G[aitskell] and his men, because it was not in the

---

103. When he went to Washington the previous month Macmillan was determined to avoid this. However, comments in the Commons on 12 November by Labour MPs Harold Wilson and Sir Leslie Plummer implying that the Conservative Party deputy chairman was involved in the alleged Bank Rate leak forced his hand.

mealy-mouthed apologetic form which they were expecting, but
launched as a violent counter-attack upon Wilson and Co – all those
who had used 'privilege' as the protection for libel. Our chaps liked it
very much . . . .

15 November
. . . . My cold is gone deeply to the chest and I greatly fear pleurisy or
pneumonia. Doctor Richardson wants me to go to bed, but there are
400 Kent men and women who have bought tickets to dine and listen
to me at Maidstone tonight!

17 November (Sunday)
It is now about 6pm, and I have woken up after nearly 48 hours sleep
– under various drugs. I got through the Maidstone dinner all right –
without any notes or any ideas of what to say and with plenty of
brandy. Apparently it was a huge success. It seems also that my speech
moving for the Judicial Enquiry was regarded by the press as one of
my best. Certainly on both these occasions the cheering was tremendous. My chest is better tho' not quite right. I am weak (from the
drugs) but I feel mentally rested. I am at home – D is here, no one else.
My room at B.G. is a very lovely one, and full of memories.

18 November
Dozed most of yesterday and this morning. Left by car about 2.30 and
got to No 10 in time for a meeting of the Defence Ctee. We agreed in
principle – and indeed in practice – two important papers. The first
dealt with atomic artillery for the Army. We have decided to rely
entirely on US except for one 30 mile range rocket (Red Rose) We
agreed the shape and form of the modern fleet. (This, without the
resignation of the First Lord and Board of Admiralty was a real
triumph) . . . .

20 November
Defence Ctee in the morning – dockyards were chief subject. We also
had a restricted meeting (a few leading ministers) about . . . . 'what is
Fighter Command for?'[104] This is difficult to solve on technical grounds
and politically dynamite. A huge sum of money is spent on it, but I

---

104. It nevertheless survived until 1968.

don't believe they could protect us from Russian bombers – at least enough wd get through to destroy the island . . . .

21 November
. . . . Worked all afternoon and evening on Liverpool speech. It will be rather dull, I fear. But I have made too many speeches lately and have exhausted my material. Besides, the situation (at home, at least) is one that needs careful handling and an atmosphere of calm – if not boredom is what we need. This is not conducive to epoch-making platform speeches!

1 December (Sunday)
The last 10 days have been rather hectic – nothing but speeches, dinner[s], Cabinets, P.Q.s and all the rest – coupled with a frightful cold and a journey to Liverpool and back, as well as to Paris! Far the most important thing, really, has been the Paris meeting with M. Gaillard, the new French P.M. After much discussion here, we decided to stand in with the Americans in making a small, almost token, delivery of arms to Tunis – now an independent country. This upset the French very much[105] – but it was their own fault, for they have 'dithered' about this for weeks and even months. The fact that there was no French Govt for five weeks did not make things easier. The French press worked the thing up, and added all kinds of usual accusations about 'perfide Albion'. We and the Americans were accused of a) trying to dominate NATO b) doing the French out of the oil exploitation in Sahara c) preventing France becoming a nuclear power – etc etc. However, altho' it was rather sticky to start with, I think the Paris meeting did good. I liked the young and energetic P.M. (Gaillard) and I felt that he was a man of considerable power and character . . . .

The HofC (and the *Daily Mirror* led critics) have suddenly got excited about the H-Bomb being in the hands of American bombers based in this country. All the pro-Russians and all the pacifists and all the sentimentalists (inspired by the clever politicians) have tried to

---

105. Tunisia had gained independence from France in 1956. The Algerian nationalist FLN, however, used its territory to launch raids into Algeria, prompting French reprisals. Accordingly, early in 1957 President Bourguiba appealed for arms, and when the French refused to supply them accepted them instead from the British and Americans.

work this up into a sort of 'finger on the trigger' campaign.[106] The only thing is to remain quite calm and see it through. I had to deliver a speech in the House – about Lord Balfour,[107] moving that a statue be put up to him. It took me a long time and infinite trouble to compose this speech – but the papers scarcely reported it. What a thing is fame! Hardly anyone today has even heard of AJB! . . . .

3 December
Cabinet at 11. A long discussion about Wales. I have to decide whether or not to make a Secretary of State . . . .

5 December
. . . . P.Q.s – mostly the American bombers again. Wales to be settled – SofState or not? A great many formal and constitutional arguments are now being adduced by the Home Office (who are passionately opposed to the change) Meanwhile, the Chief Whip suggests the title 'Chancellor of the Principality of Wales' (But this would require legislation?)[108] . . . .

6 December
. . . . We had a long meeting (of For Sec; Chancellor of Exr; Lord President; and Minister of Defence) about a new series of H-Bomb tests. It is just possible that (if the McMahon Act is repealed) we shall get the knowledge we require from America. But one of the main reasons that we have made so much progress with the American administration is that we are a nuclear power on our own. I felt that to stop now wd be like giving up 'in the straight'. Ministers agreed . . . .

13 December
After a very full day at No 10, we left for Paris on the night ferry, arriving about 10am. We drove straight to the Embassy. The weather

---

106. A reference to the *Daily Mirror's* attempts to portray Churchill as a warmonger in the 1951 election.
107. A. J. Balfour was Conservative Prime Minister 1902–05.
108. The Home Secretary had been given the additional title of Minister of Welsh Affairs by Churchill in 1951. After 1957 this responsibility was given to the Minister of Housing and Local Government. Nothing came of the discussions Macmillan mentions here, and Wales had to wait until Labour came to power in 1964 for its Secretary of State.

was fine, but bitterly cold. I thought I wd try the ferry, for fear of fog. But it was not very comfortable.

14 December
.... Foster Dulles came at 11.30 and stayed to luncheon. He seemed rather vague about this NATO meeting, and to be wondering now whether we had been wise in 'writing it up' so much. He seemed to think it could be just a sort of 'jamboree'. We wd accept the American nuclear rockets, give 3 cheers for ourselves and 1 for Uncle Sam and then go home. This attitude seemed foolish to me – but Foster has no other ideas at present ....

15 December (Sunday)
The President arrived yesterday afternoon and had a great reception from the people of Paris. He stood up in the open car, waved his arms to the crowd, and generally delighted them all with his manner. Tunisian arms are forgotten – or ascribed to the wicked Dulles. Last night Gaillard (French P.M.) came to a small dinner at the Embassy. He was much relaxed since I was in Paris a few weeks ago .... The paradox of France is this. The mass of peasants and bourgeois classes have (under their beds) more gold than the gold and dollar reserves of the Bank of England and HMG. The French Govt and Bank have nothing. The French 'rich' classes have two or three times this wealth in Switzerland and are continuing to export capital. Here, it is the opposite. Such wealth as we have, the Bank and the Govt get hold of – and dissipate! Which country, France or England, is intrinsically the stronger? ....

I had a private talk with Adenauer about 'support costs' for 1958–9. I told him that we were not bluffing. We simply could not afford to spend £50m a year, in perpetuity, across the exchanges. He promised to deal with this personally – and with me. He hoped to send me some reply early in January. On the general question of NATO, the Germans were reserved. They don't want the IRBMs in Western Germany. But they don't want to have to say this openly. They would like a decision on 'military' grounds, which in fact was against W Germany as a suitable site. I said I thought that if this decision really was sound, some price should be got for it. What would the Russians pay?

The Chancellor has aged – but is still very much the master of his Govt and of Germany. I think he is very anxious about the future. He would like to see W Germany definitely bound up with the West – through NATO or other means. That is why he was so keen on EDC, the European Army, the 6 Power Common Market plan, the Free Trade Area – in a word, everything which wd range Germany in the ranks of the civilised countries. But he knows how far his people (ever since Bismarck) hanker after Eastern dreams. When he is dead, he fears that his people will fall for the bait – unified but neutral Germany. Some will accept it from genuine patriotism – to get unification. Others will see the advantages of neutralism – and hope to play off one side against the other. Others again will just be weary of all these struggles. With all this in mind, Adenauer is not saying much – esp to his colleagues . . . .

16 December

10am. I called to see the President. He was sitting in a large room, on the first floor of the American Embassy, and seemed very pleased to see me. We had nearly an hour's private talk – if a talk can be called so, when the large folding doors on the landing outside are wide open, and the police, G-men,[109] Hagerty (Press) and others are lounging about this gallery. However, the President seemed to take no notice of them – so I decided to conform to this.

He told me a good deal about his illness[110] – a subject with which he is obsessed. He was determined to come to Paris. Had the doctors forbidden him, he would have taken it very badly (everyone in the American entourage confirms this, and says he would have resigned forthwith. This explains a) Dulles having decided to let him go b) D[ulles]'s extreme anxiety about him) . . . .

The official opening of the Conference took place at 12 noon . . . . Everyone made the usual prepared speeches. On the whole, the tone was quite good, but no one seemed to have any idea how the conference was to go on. I made a speech, like a wind-up in the House, from notes wh I had made during the discussion, supplemented by some prepared passages. The effect of speaking in this way was electrifying. Everyone listened and the contrast between this method and the droning along of the prepared texts seemed to enchant them. Apparently, they never do this in their new Parliaments. I ended by saying that instead of a peroration – and, I added, I have a lovely one

---

109. Nickname for FBI agents, coined in the 1930s.
110. Eisenhower had suffered a mild stroke in November.

all ready – I will make two practical suggestions. First, let an agenda be prepared – political and military – one for Tuesday; the other for Wednesday. Let it be discussed on the morning of each day by the Ministers of Foreign Affairs and in the afternoons or evenings by the Heads of Government. Secondly, let us decide to stay till Thursday – when we can agree the communiqué. It is bound to take the whole morning. Let us announce this decision at once. These proposals were unanimously agreed . . . .

17 December
The Heads of Government did not meet till 4pm and made pretty good progress on the political and economic decisions. I supported strongly a further offer to Soviet Russia – a meeting of Foreign Secretaries to 'break the deadlock'. The Americans didn't much like this, but finally agreed. (I talked it over with Dulles behind the scenes and he behaved very reasonably. I told him that I thought this was necessary if we were to get acceptance of nuclear weapons by the NATO alliance) . . . .

18 December
The same procedure. The Foreign Secretaries and Ministers of Defence met in the morning and early afternoon. We were not summoned till 5pm. But everything went through satisfactorily. The Scandinavians behaved quite well. They accepted that the alliance shd be armed with rockets – but they don't want them in their own territories. The Germans were very non-committal . . . .

19 December
A full meeting (plenary session) at 11am. The communiqué was agreed by 1.15, when we broke up (rather like schoolboys) The British delegation has every reason to be satisfied. For, without us, the thing wd have been an absolute shambles. We have got the Americans to take a more realistic view of the psychological and political situation in Europe . . . . On the political and economic side, we are beginning to get the Europeans out of the 'Maginot Line'[111] complex and begin to look to their flanks. Suez – altho' a tactical defeat for us – is in this sense beginning to be vindicated strategically. The Americans, of course, are now completely converted – too late – and wish

---

111. The ineffective inter-war defensive system built by the French to guard against another German attack.

devoutly that they had let us go on and finish off Nasser. The French were always realistic; but now, even the more idealistic European Govts have begun to realise that the life of Europe depends on the M. East. (Far East developments, as in Indonesia)[112] have alarmed them considerably. We now, at least, have diagnosed the sickness. But, alas, we have no agreed remedy, nor is it easy to find one. However, if we can get this 'outward look' accepted and digested, it should make it easier for us to press on with our two major ends 1) acceptance of concept of 'balanced forces' in Europe 2) less demands for Europe and a more sensible approach to the NATO force plan in the spring.

All this, of course, depends on our being able to get a reasonable settlement of the 'support costs' problem with the Germans.

Altogether, the Conference has been a success. The American and French press (whom I saw yesterday) have been very generous to the British leadership. Our own press is, of course, hostile and rather silly . . . .

We left at about 6pm and after I had done a British Press Conference, as well as TV, and ITV, at the Embassy. A good flight home and at No 10 by 9pm.

20 December

. . . . Debate [about the Paris discussions] began at 11am with a speech by For Secy. He was not at the top of his form; but considering the work he has done during recent days and the short time available for preparation, it was adequate. Anyway, he made no mistakes and took a tough line about Russia. Bevan followed – with a rambling speech – some good phrases – the chief purpose of which was to make as much mischief as possible while trying to unite the essentially divided Opposition, some of whom are pro-Russia, others defeatist and others sound loyal supporters of NATO and the Bevin tradition. George Brown (who belongs to the last group) wound up as best he cd. I did not feel that his heart was in it. I ended and the division was at 5. We had a bad division (39 majority) with some sick (unpaired)[113] and some deliberate abstentions (Ld Hinchingbrooke and the rump of the Suez

---

112. A rebellion led by colonels opposed to Sukarno's regime started in late 1957 in Sumatra with covert Anglo-American backing.

113. Pairing is an arrangement whereby MPs of opposing parties agree not to vote if one or the other is absent.

group) Altogether, it was rather damping – after all our labours. We thought (in Paris) that we had done pretty well. But we had a cool reception at home! . . . .

21 December

. . . . The press and the public (or some of them) have worked themselves into an orgy of defeatism. The *Daily Express* has joined the hunt, with the *Herald* and *Chronicle*. I am said to have lost touch with public opinion in England, because I have not already set out for Moscow, to see Kruschev. All this is pure Chamberlainism[114] . . . .

22 December

. . . . I went to London after tea and had a long talk with the Chancellor of the Exchequer. He is very worried about the Civil Estimates, which shew a great rise for 1958–9 – nearly £200m above the out-turn for this year. Most of this is due to inescapable causes – the Old (being pensioned) the Young (at school) and the Agricultural Subsidies which rise automatically as world prices fall. (This is, of course, a gain to the Balance of Payments but a loss to the Exchequer) The Chancellor wants some swingeing cuts in the Welfare State expenditure – more, I fear, than is feasible politically.

23 December

. . . . 11.30–1.15. A tremendous discussion on the future of Fighter Command. The SofS Air and the CAS are in a very exciting, resigning mood. I explained to them that I had asked the Minister of Defence to prepare a paper with all the arguments <u>against</u> the usefulness of the fighter in a nuclear age. I had asked the SofS for a reply. We must now argue it out, as dispassionately as possible. We decided to adjourn till Saturday.

3–7. A long discussion, partly about civil estimates, partly about future policy for the Conservative party. Chancellor of Exr; Ld Privy Seal; Minister of Labour; Ld President – a very useful talk, which will help both the future and the immediate problems. The Chancellor is feeling in a very determined (also resigning) mood. The rest are bitterly

---

114. A reference to the flight by the then Prime Minister (1937–40), Neville Chamberlain, to treat with Hitler at Munich in 1938: this mood was stimulated by Bulganin's note of 11 December calling for an immediate ban on nuclear tests.

opposed to his main proposal, which is to abolish the children's allowance and thus save £65m (2nd child only) I summed up impartially, but laying most stress on the need to win the battle on the wages front.[115] We must not be deflected from this . . . .

---

115. Macmillan had in August urged the Cabinet to aim to follow Thorneycroft's recommendation of freezing the Civil Estimates for 1958/59 to the same level as the current year. His hint here that this might drive up inflation marked a subtle shift in his position.

1955

1958

The Thorneycroft resignations – Commonwealth tour – Defence reorganisation – railway and bus disputes – Algeria and de Gaulle's return to power in France – Revolution in Iraq and crises in Lebanon and Jordan – continuing crisis in Cyprus – race riots – failure of the Free Trade Area negotiations – Russian ultimatum on Berlin

6 January (Monday)

Since Christmas, a crisis has been developing, slowly but inexorably, in the Cabinet – as far as I can see, carefully planned by the Chancellor of the Exchequer and the Treasury ministers. As far as I can judge, the Treasury officials have had no hand in it and have disapproved of it. It came to a head this morning, when a formal letter was sent to me by the Chancellor of the Exchequer, offering his resignation. Thorneycroft's letter (which was clearly written some days ago) the date of the month was type-written – the day filled in by hand!) was accompanied by letters from Birch (Economic Secy) and Enoch Powell (F.S.T.)

Ever since Christmas (I had only Boxing Day off) there has been a tremendous pressure of work growing up .... To all this has been added more or less continuous meetings either of the whole Cabinet or of a group of ministers, trying to settle the Defence Estimates, and the Civil Estimates, for 1958–9. Thorneycroft argued strongly, throughout all the discussions, that the expenditure for this year (including supplementaries) should not be exceeded [in] 1958–9. Thus our policy would be complete and logical in its three aspects. Capital investment and Bank advances are already to be held to 1957–8 levels. Govt expenditure shd be the same. This sounds very well in principle, but has considerable difficulties in practice. The margin to be covered began at £150[m].[1] We got it down, by accepting many economies, some very awkward, to £50m odd. There we stuck. On the Friday Cabinet (which last[ed] 4 hours) Thorneycroft behaved in such a rude and *cassant*[2] way that I had difficulty in preventing some of the Cabinet bursting out in their indignation. We adjourned on Friday night (Jan 3rd) on the understanding that we would take up the work on Monday, after a small meeting of ministers on Sunday evening. On Saturday (after a day's shooting at Birch Grove) I returned to No 10

---

1. Actually £153 million.
2. Brusque.

.... Sunday 5th, I saw the Chancellor at 10.30am and made an appeal to him – on personal and public grounds – not to threaten us any more but to tell the Cabinet that he would work along with his colleagues and accept the collective view. The defence estimates could be finalised (as was necessary) at once, and further discussions about the Civil Estimates could continue for at least another 3 weeks. This work cd go on during my absence overseas and results agreed by telegram. He looked uncomfortable; said he had not finally made up his mind; but I got the impression that he had made up his mind to resign, unless he got his full demand. (It struck me that he was in an excited mood, and he had obviously been pushed on by the Treasury ministers, Birch and Enoch Powell. The first is a cynic; the second a fanatic. In light of this talk, I suggested that instead of the small meeting, the whole Cabinet had better meet on Sunday evening – so that he might 'sleep on it'. This was arranged.

.... Yesterday (Sunday) I motored to Chartwell and lunched with Winston. I told him what was going on. He was very indignant with Thorneycroft and promised his full support. He could hardly believe in a resignation. (The parallel with Ld Randolph Churchill is curious!)[3] Butler; Sandys; and Macleod came at 4.30. Home and Kilmuir at 5.30. The Chancellor is now making two demands – at least £50m, to be drawn from Defence or Civil Estimates or both. Duncan Sandys (by really remarkable efforts) has got the defence estimates below last year, and that to include £35m of extra pay, allowances etc and £20m of once for all compensation to officers etc compulsorily retired. He has now made [a] further offer of £18m. As regards civil, Chancellor has suggested either £65m (less £20m refund or redistribution to larger families) by abolishing 8/- a week family allowance or by abolishing school meals, welfare milk etc at cost or reduced prices, and also putting up Hospital charges, opthalmic charges etc and/or increased Health insurance stamp. The ministers concerned have studied these proposals – of wh they were given no notice by the Chancellor[4] – but there are almost insuperable technical difficulties about some of them (e.g. Hospital charges; school milk; opthalmic charges etc) The only

3. Seeking cuts in defence expenditure and personal advancement, Churchill's father, Lord Randolph, resigned as Chancellor of the Exchequer in 1886, never to hold office again.

4. The family allowance cut for the second child had been discussed and rejected by Cabinet in early 1957.

'clean' proposals are a) another Health Insurance 'stamp' or b) abolition or cut in 'children's allowances'. But the new stamp (fixed by
legislation in the autumn) only starts in February and to abolish the
2nd child allowance affects 3–3½ million families – amounts to a
10% wage cut in low-paid homes – and seems hardly a wise start to
the wage struggle which confronts us. (Lord Mills, Macleod and
others feel this very strongly) At the meetings of my most trusted
colleagues (before the Cabinet) there was incredulity about the resignation, altho' most agreed that Nigel Birch and especially Enoch
Powell were egging him on. We decided to see what happened at the
6.30 Cabinet, before deciding on tactics. This Cabinet – though less
painful – was no more fruitful than Friday's. Defence Minister stated
his position very clearly. He would do all he could to help farther,
but must warn us that to abandon the pay and allowances proposals
for the services wd mean the loss of any hope of all-regular forces;
the resignation of SofS War and of CIGS. The social ministers (represented in Cabinet by Macleod) gave their considered views on the
practicality (apart from the desirability) of the proposed cuts. Chancellor re-stated his position very firmly, but less offensively than at
earlier Cabinets. He left the door open, but made it clear that he
would not accept much less than the full £150m. Other ministers
spoke. Ld Home (who had not been at Friday's Cabinet, where Chancellor had behaved really disgracefully) could scarcely conceal his rage
– and contempt. Ld Chancellor made again (as on Friday) a noble
plea for unity. We adjourned at about 8.40 – I asked Cabinet to
reassemble at 10.30.

Dorothy was with me at dinner (having come up from B.G.) We
also had Butler, Macleod, and Heath (Chief Whip) We discussed the
position – still confused as the Chancellor had left the door open.
Sandys was very keen that if he went it shd be clear that he went on
'family allowances' 'welfare milk' etc. Macleod thought he was
obsessed and dominated by Powell. Butler was really shocked at the
irresponsibility by which Cabinet was asked to make great changes of
policy at a few days notice, without study or preparation. He was also
offended by Thorneycroft's rudeness and egotism. I still thought he wd
retreat, if we could get him a few more economies to save his face (I
was proved wrong) At 10.30 we reassembled and I 'summed up' for
about 40 minutes. Cabinet quietly dispersed. Most thought that my
statement (which I tried to make fair and balanced, as well as very
flattering and generous to the Chancellor) would succeed in avoiding

the crisis.[5] It was however clear to me by dinner that the greater danger was the complete disintegration of the Cabinet – Treasury Ministers; Defence Ministers; Labour and Social Ministers – all might resign (for different reasons) and there wd be no alternative to the resignation of the Govt; a Labour administration; a dissolution; an election in which the Conservative Party wd be in a hopeless and even ridiculous position, without policy or honour. This must at all costs be avoided. In the last attempt to avoid a break I saw the Governor of the Bank at 9.30 today (Monday). He was to see the Chancellor at 10. But he was not very helpful. He is nice, but stupid – anyway about politics. I suspect that he has had a hand in all this.

7 January (Tuesday)

Yesterday (Monday 6th) was an extraordinary day. At 10.30 I received (without any covering note of personal regret) a formal – and very contentious – letter of resignation from the Chancellor of the Exr, together with 2 letters from EST and FST. Thorneycroft's letter was in brutal terms, calculated, if unanswered, to do the maximum injury to sterling. It sought to give the impression that he alone in the Cabinet stood against inflation. Cabinet met at 11. I read out the letter, which was received with a good deal of indignation. We proceeded to other business – of which the new plan for Cyprus was the most important.[6] The Governor (Sir Hugh Foot) attended. I am not very hopeful about it, for I don't think either the Greeks or the Turks will play, whether locally or nationally. However, it will help us to have Sir H Foot's plan, both for opinion inside and outside UK.

After Cabinet, I offered post of Chancellor of the Exr to Heathcoat Amory – now Minister of Agriculture. He was rather hesitant, but accepted . . . . also Hare to Min of Agric (from War Office) Soames to W.O. Jack Simon to be FST – no EST, but Maudling (now Paymaster General) to help with economic work of Treasury. This has only left a few minor posts to be filled. We also had composed a reply to the letter wh Thorneycroft wrote to me . . . . as well as listening for an

---

5. £100 million of expenditure reductions had been agreed and Macmillan argued that the remaining £50 million was only 1% of government spending and therefore manageable.

6. The plan for the retention of UK sovereign military bases with a tridominium shared by Britain, Greece and Turkey over the rest of Cyprus that had developed since the previous summer.

hour (3–4) to a deputation from TUC about H-bombs. This remarkable feat was due to the way in which everybody has helped me. Butler has been excellent throughout. The Chief Whip superb. Freddy Bishop works quietly and efficiently. And Sir Norman Brook is always a tower of strength . . . .

We started off from London Airport this morning as planned. I felt sure that this was the right course to follow. Almost the whole Cabinet came to see me off. This was intended, obviously, as a mark of respect and loyalty. I said a few words to the BBC, TV etc, which I had prepared last night, about the Commonwealth trip and 'our little local difficulties'. This will annoy a lot of people, but I think it will give them a sense of proportion. I cannot believe that, if and when the truth is known, Thorneycroft will get much support . . . .

19 January

. . . . I can only record here very general impressions [of the Commonwealth tour].[7] First, of India after ten years of independence. The country is much more sure of itself. So are the Government. At the same time the whole judiciary also. The Army is British and is treasuring the old regimental traditions. The Parliamentary and 'democratic' system is ours – and so is much of the ordinary way of living. All this, now that the bitterness of the struggle is over, even Congress[8] men are beginning to remember. There is also the contrast between the way the British made the 'transfer of power' and what was done by the French and the Dutch.

The second impression is of the supremacy of Nehru (altho' this is not quite what it was) Malcolm MacDonald said that Nehru at a distance seems a very great figure; seen nearer, he begins to shrink in stature. There is something in this, for he is undoubtedly arrogant and (whatever he may have been in the past) very fixed in his ideas. His speeches (or monologues) are 5 or 6 well-tried records – the rise of Asian nationalism; the new Communism in Russia, and its renunciation of war; etc. Nevertheless, he is able, full of charm, cultivated, and ruthless – all great qualities in a leader.

The third feeling I had was the very strong position of the British –

---

7. The first, and last, grand tour of the Commonwealth undertaken by a British Prime Minister.

8. The Congress Party of India, dating from 1885, which under Nehru led India to independence in 1947, remained in power until 1977.

esp business men. They are liked and trusted. They have to compete for business, but that does them no harm. Socially, they stand higher than under the old regime, which was dominated by soldiers and civil servants.

Nehru treated me with great courtesy. We stayed at his own house – instead of staying at the President's palace, formerly Govt House. This is a very unusual compliment . . . .

We were entertained to a banquet in the President's House – with all the pictures of the Viceroys on the walls and all the pomp and circumstance unchanged. We were also the chief guests at a garden party there – also in the old style, with the old Viceroy's guard in their splendid uniform; the trumpeters; the military secretary and ADCs. We had a very interesting afternoon in some Indian villages, where thousands of people turned up, danced, sang and cheered my speech to the echo!

It is certainly true that the warmth of our reception surprised – and perhaps a little annoyed – the Congress ministers and their friends. When Kruschev and co came, there was greater applause in the drive from the airport. But it is said that platoons of soldiers were put into 'plain clothes' to lead the cheering. There was nothing of the kind for us. Each time we appeared, the welcome grew. It could not have been 'inspired'.

To go from India (especially from New Delhi) to Pakistan, is like going from Hampstead or North Oxford to the Border country or the Highlands. Iskander Mirza, the robust President of Pakistan and his wife (a Persian lady) are *grands seigneurs* – very charming hosts, not too intellectual, and good food and wine. (Nehru's food was uneatable. It was European, but like a bad boarding house)

Pakistan is poor; politically unstable; in a state of religious turmoil (the mullahs have large tho' rather uncertain power) without a 'political' class – without so large an ICS tradition as India, and practising corruption on the grand scale. (The President told me that Suhrawardy, the last Prime Minister, scooped £4 million in his short premiership. Noon, the present P.M. is said to be honest)

The one stable element in this situation is the Army – the Air Force and Navy are also reliable. East Pakistan,[9] more advanced and richer, is drifting to Communism – or may easily do so. The old Moslem League, orthodox and rigid, is supported by the mullahs, but less and

---

9. Bangladesh, since becoming independent in 1971.

less by the people. The Services – esp the Army – are excellent. I saw something of them all. The men were smart and the officers (esp in Air Force) young and intelligent.

We had a wonderful visit to the Khyber Pass (flying over [in] our Britannia aeroplane to Peshawar) Here all goes on as before – Khyber rifles; medals; regimental HQ; polo; even the Hunt. The tribesmen are all . . . . armed to the teeth. But they are quieter now and many of their sons come in to the new university at Peshawar . . . .

From Pakistan – which we were sorry to leave, for staying with the President was like being in a very comfortable country house – we went to Ceylon . . . . The Prime Minister (Mr Bandaranaike) is a sort of local Nehru – except that he has only just got into office and had nothing to do with Ceylon obtaining independence. He clearly models himself on Mr N; dresses like an Anglo-Catholic priest at the altar, stole and alb; takes an interest in world politics; is a very rich man and the son of a very rich man; is westernised (he was Secretary and Treasurer of the Oxford Union, where he was at Christ Church); makes friends with everyone, and is himself partly Conservative and partly advanced Socialist, as is his Govt. (One of his ministers is leader of the Dockers Union which has defied the Govt and brought the port to a standstill)

However, the people seem happy, and were wildly enthusiastic. We had royal progresses wherever we went. Ceylon has not yet had the energy to declare herself a Republic, so there is still a Governor General, in whose charming and antique house (Dutch by origin) we stayed in great comfort. The Europeans bow and curtsey to him – and some of the Ceylonese. He does the job well.

I had a long and quite sensible talk with the P.M. . . . . I told him that he could 'socialise' or 'nationalise' his companies; port and harbour companies and the like without much harm. But I begged him to let alone the rubber and tea estates, on the efficiency of which the whole economy of the island depends. (The deterioration and almost disintegration of the Indonesian economy now going on is a useful object lesson for Ceylon politicians) In a curious way, the political life is more like that of Whig politics in the 18th century than one would suppose. The leading figures have a 'following' (like the Bedfords or the Rockinghams) But the Govts formed comprise men of very different points of view.

Of course, the danger here (as elsewhere throughout the East) is the collapse of the agreeable, educated, Liberal, North Oxford society to whom we have transferred power, in the face of the dynamism of Communism, with all the strength of Russian imperialism behind it . . . .

A lot of work arrived from London. Thorneycroft has made a considerable impression by his 'moderate' speech to his constituents. The debate (which is due in a few days) will be rather tricky. Cabinet have not yet agreed precisely what further economies (if any) are necessary to reduce the 'gap' to £50m or less. I have had excellent telegrams from Butler, setting out the problem, and asking for guidance. This we got off before leaving Singapore. Then I must write another letter to Bulganin about 'Summit talks' and all that. I have got a perhaps crazy idea of offering to go myself to Moscow to discuss a) agenda b) procedure, with Kruschev[10] . . . .

24 January

(At Dunedin, New Zealand) My Moscow plan did not please the Cabinet. But it has persuaded them that we must, in the next reply to Bulganin, be a little more positive about the 'Summit meeting' on the basis of proper preparation. We can, I think, by this means test the Soviet sincerity. If they refuse all preliminary work, it will show that all their peace talk is really propaganda . . . .

This is a most attractive country and the people extraordinarily friendly and loyal. They are in temporary financial trouble, because during the last few years of high prices for wool and dairy products – as well as meat – they have had a terrific buying and spending spree. Now they have no sterling reserves and have been forced to make import cuts. But the prices could not last indefinitely, and even at present levels the farmers are doing very well. Wool prices seem to be recovering (except merino) and the British market still absorbs a vast export of milk products and meat.

---

10. Bulganin had written again on 8 January 1958 denouncing the West's intentions, and calling for an end to nuclear tests, the outlawing of nuclear weapons, implementation of the proposals put forward in October 1957 by Polish foreign minister Adam Rapacki for a nuclear-free zone in the two Germanies, Poland and Czechoslovakia, and a Summit. Macmillan had replied to the Rapacki Plan on 14 January, asking for Soviet co-operation in control procedures. His subsequent suggestion of a trip to Moscow for exploratory discussions met with opposition from Cabinet colleagues who felt little could come of it.

There has just been a general election. The Conservatives[11] have lost (by 2 seats) and old Nash (75; a Radical more than a Socialist) has become P.M. He is rather vain and talkative, but sound and loyal. I have found him very easy to get on with.

It may be possible to help them to some extent by our new 'anti-dumping' legislation. They do not complain so much of our British production as of the sale of foreign produce below (as they allege) cost price in the British market . . . .

The news from home is better. The 'Bank Rate' Tribunal seems to have reported in a most satisfactory way and the Opposition leaders must wish that they had not committed themselves to this mare's nest.[12] On the economic debates – following Thorneycroft's resignation – we have just heard of our excellent majority – 62. This is very good and I am awaiting with interest the full account of the discussion. Meanwhile, the Cabinet seems to have been working well and loyally on the 'estimates' problem. It has been argued that the stamp should be increased by 8d[13] – but no cuts in the welfare services . . . .

31 January

. . . . The Americans have suddenly turned very nasty about our proposed reply to Bulganin. They do not seem to understand the feeling either in our country – or perhaps in their own. They are now pressing for a very negative reply from me to B's last letter. They are almost threatening. With so much at stake (e.g. financial support; McMahon Act etc) it is difficult to know quite how to handle the situation . . . .

Although we did very well in the division last week, it is clear that Thorneycroft made a very good speech and is playing his hand very well. I am beginning to suspect – behind his rough and uncultured

---

11. The New Zealand National Party.
12. The tribunal found the allegations that the raising of the Bank Rate the previous year had been leaked to be wholly unsubstantiated and exonerated all those who had been accused.
13. This increase in national insurance contributions (conventionally known as 'the stamp' because initially stamps had been issued to record payments) had in fact been agreed by the Cabinet in Macmillan's absence on 22 January. Ironically, this had been a change the Cabinet had sought to avoid during the Thorneycroft battles, but was forced into when a further £40 million of costs were found in early January. Various forms of creative accounting were used to square the rest of the figures.

manner, rude and *cassant* to an extreme, a deep plot. He may be calculating on another 'sterling crisis' this autumn and the break up of the Govt in conditions wh wd allow him to seize the leadership of the party from me and Rab. The immediate election, of course, would be lost. But he is young, and could afford to wait for the next . . . .

I am beginning to feel the disadvantages of my absence from London, for it's very hard to keep track of all that is going on. However, from the broader point of view, this Commonwealth tour has been worth while.

3 February
After some very good days in Canberra, with really useful talks with Menzies and his ministers, we set off again and had three days in Queensland . . . .

. . . . The F.O. have proposed a new draft on 'Bulganin' wh the For Secy thinks will do. It shd meet the American anxieties without abandoning my own position (actually, now that the Americans have successfully launched their own 'sputnik' they will be in a better temper)[14] . . . . I do not suggest any particular date for the Summit meetings, but I do suggest that the 'preparatory work' (whether by Foreign Secretaries or diplomats) should start forthwith[15] . . . .

10 February
. . . . We shall lose Rochdale, I fear, by a lot. The Liberal intervention in all these by-elections is very annoying. If it is done at the General Election on a large scale our position will be hopeless.

14 February
We arrived at London airport about noon, having been away nearly 6 weeks . . . . The Rochdale by-election (on Wednesday) where our vote fell from 20000 or more to 7000 and we were behind the Liberal (who polled 17000) has been a tremendous shock.[16] I was, of course, asked a question by the BBC and ITV interviewers. I said that the govt cd

---

14. The first American satellite, *Explorer 1*, was launched on 31 January 1958.
15. This reply to Bulganin was published on 10 February.
16. The Rochdale by-election on 12 February saw Tory support fall from 51% to 20% of the poll and the party beaten into a poor third in a seat held since 1951.

continue to carry on its work and that a single incident in a campaign did not settle the issue . . . .

16 February

. . . . Hailsham has – very foolishly – made an attack on the Liberals. This has done a lot of harm to us. I am beginning to wonder whether his lack of judgement does not outweigh his brilliance.

17 February

. . . . Nuri Pasha came to see me. He is going back to Iraq today and expects to take on the Premiership again. He is full of plans – some of them rather dangerously vague – for detaching Syria from Egypt. He wants us to get the Ruler of Kuwait to join, in some form, the Iraq–Jordan union.[17] The problem we have is to head Nuri off impossible or dangerous schemes, which are bound to fail, without losing his confidence or injuring his will to resist Egypt and Russia. The Americans (according to Nuri) have given him promises of 'support' – but his story does not quite tally with what they have told us. However, we will clear this up. Meanwhile, Nasser has started to threaten the Sudan.

18 February

. . . . I had a talk with Gaitskell (Leader of the Opposition) and I hope persuaded him to take a fairly reasonable line in the debate. At this time (esp after Rochdale by-election, which has upset the exchanges, and frightened many allied countries) we do want to get as near as possible to a 'bi-partisan' foreign policy. But I'm afraid Bevan and Bevanism are still very strong in the Opposition . . . .

20 February

Today has been a terrible day. First, I had to go to a throat specialist to be x-rayed. Dr Richardson came to see me yesterday, and seemed rather alarmed at the state of my larynx and chest . . . . With so many speeches (30 formal ones, as well as 'whistle-stop' ones) my voice has been overstrained and the throat is permanently inflamed. I thought

---

17. Syria and Egypt had announced a union to be known as the United Arab Republic on 1 February 1958. In reaction on 14 February the inter-related Hashemite kings of Iraq and Jordan announced the union of their states in an Arab Federation.

perhaps it was the start of a cancer, but the throat specialist relieved my fears.

Defence Committee at 10.30 – two rather difficult problems. What are we to do in Oman. Talib (the rebellious chieftain) still holds out in the mountains. If we 'bomb' him out with aircraft (as we cd easily do) there will be a terrible row and 'world opinion' will be inflamed against us. If we leave him, he will prob[ably] start the whole thing off again after Ramadan. He has about 600 tribesmen and might get others to rally to him[18] . . . .

Foreign Affairs debate continued. Bevan was incredibly bad. He bungled his speech from the start and told so transparent a lie about his speech at Brighton[19] as to shock even his friends. The Foreign Secy followed, with – unfortunately – a speech almost as bad. It was really tragic. He had a wonderful situation and opportunity, and failed altogether. He is <u>so good</u> in the work that I really cannot think of anyone who could be more efficient. But he has – for the moment – lost his nerve in the House . . . . The Chief Whip told me that the so-called Independents (the Suez Six)[20] <u>and</u> some others, <u>and</u> the Liberals would vote against us or abstain.

. . . . At 7pm I talked over the situation with For Secy and Chief Whip, and decided to wind up the debate myself. I spoke for 20 minutes only – had a completely quiet house – and got great applause from our side. We got a good majority – 66. Poor Selwyn is very distressed, and I did my best to comfort him. He is <u>so</u> good and <u>so</u> loyal.

21 February

I had a talk early this morning with F.S. The press are loudly demanding his resignation – all except the *D. Telegraph*, which is behaving admirably and *The Times*, which is aloof and grandly ignoring everything . . . .

---

18. Talib was the brother of the rebellious Imam. In the end it took a land campaign to dislodge the rebels from the Jebel Akhdar.

19. This was a debate initiated by Bevan on delays in convening a Summit. For his Brighton speech see above p. 62.

20. Probably the hard core of the Suez rebels: the 'Bedford Group' (Lord Hinchingbrooke, Lawrence Turner, John Biggs-Davison, Paul Williams, Anthony Fell and Patrick Maitland), so called because they used to meet in the Bedford pub near Pont Street.

American Ambassador came in the morning. I shewed him a telegram which I sent yesterday to the President, urging that we should now <u>do</u> something about summit talks. The Americans do not seem to realise the anxieties of Europe . . . .

Luncheon with Michael and Pamela Berry . . . . The *D.T.* has been <u>very</u> good lately. But I am always anxious about Pam. She told me that the Thorneycrofts are very angry with her for 'deserting' them.

Alec Home (Commonwealth Secy) came after lunch, for a general talk as well as the specific question of whether the Queen shd accept an invitation to Ghana. I said I hoped she would do so, but offered to discuss it again with her. At 9.30 I 'appeared' on T.V. It was a 'questioning' by 3 journalists from *Observer*, *Economist* and *New Statesman*. I think it went off pretty well. This is an easier technique than the 'monologue' . . . .

24 February

I had <u>all</u> ministers <u>not</u> in Cabinet; all ministers of state; and all under-secretaries to a sherry party at No 10. I think these little gatherings help to keep the administration together . . . .

26 February

. . . . I have had 2 or 3 very difficult days with Selwyn Lloyd. He feels that his position has been so weakened a) by his failure in the House b) by the attacks upon him, that he is of no use to the Govt. He sent me a letter offering his resignation. I think he is very sensitive and cannot bear the charge that he is 'clinging to office'. But I really cannot have another resignation – altho' from a different cause. Selwyn is quite sincere and <u>most</u> friendly. But he is definitely shaken in nerve . . . .

27 February

The Cabinet approved our plan on support costs. Broadly it is to open a negotiation on the basis of our stating our military intentions for (say) 3 years. It will cost us a good deal in currency, but I don't really see how we can just leave NATO. The Germans may be got to offer something for this year.

. . . . There was a great 'flap' this morning over an extraordinary statement by a certain Colonel Zink – an American 'Eagle Colonel' of the Air Force – who claims to be about to take over <u>operational</u> command of the Rockets and Rocket bases in England. As this is in direct contradiction to a) the terms of the agreement,[21] published last Monday b) what we told Parlt on Monday and the debates yesterday, Colonel Zink has put his foot in it on the grand scale! (The awkward thing is that the Americans originally asked to man the missiles until our men were fully trained, but we refused – or at least 'stalled'. Zink may have heard some rumours of this.) However, I will say our Embassy did very well . . . . The American alliance is continually being put in jeopardy by the folly of American officers, in all ranks. General Norstad (SACEUR) has just made a very silly speech – or interview – about the missiles.[22] Americans will feel quite differently about all this when their own country becomes a target . . . .

The defence debate ended tonight. Shinwell made an admirable speech, attacking the pacifists etc. Strachey made a good speech at the end, attacking his own pacifists and the 'nauseating hypocrisy' of the Liberals. Christopher Soames wound up with a really first-class speech – simple, effective, well-delivered. As a first performance in a big debate it was admirable, and fully justified my choice of him as Secretary of State for War. It was also a risk for him to 'wind up', but I am very glad I decided not to speak myself. They would have said it was a 'one man govt' etc etc. Now we have found a new debater to strengthen our team.

We had a large meeting – Chancellor of Exr; Ld Privy Seal; Maudling (Paymaster) with Treasury officials, including Leslie Rowan and Prof. Hall, who are just back from Washington. It was a pretty depressing meeting, because it is clear that the Americans have no idea what to do about their own 'depression' and still less about the approaching 'world slump'. I wish I could persuade the American administration that the Free World cannot be defended by H-Bombs if it is allowed to fall into trade collapse and large-scale unemployment.[23]

I have taken on Anthony Barber as my P.P.S. *vice* Bobby Allan, who has gone to Admiralty as Parliamentary Secretary.

---

21. The 22 February agreement specified that any launch decisions regarding the Thor IRBMs being established in Britain had to be taken by the two governments jointly 'in the light of the circumstances at the time'.

22. Norstad wanted a unified command of the missiles under NATO.

23. Persistent current account imbalances (not least with Europe) and resulting central bank monetary tightening had prompted a recession in the US, but consumer expenditure held up and by the end of the year the economy had recovered.

28 February

The Opposition have demanded a 'vote of censure' on the working of the [1957] Rent Act. This, of course, is just 'politics' but it is good politics. There is a wave of hysteria about evictions in October. I still believe it will not be justified. But fear of a future event is a good method of political agitation. I fear it may lose us the Kelvingrove by-election (where K[atherine] Elliot is standing in Walter [Elliot]'s seat) I had a talk with Butler this morning about how to handle the debate etc.

Meeting of Ministers at 11.30 to discuss the state of the financial negotiations with Egypt. I feel in my bones that there will be a tremendous row about all this, whatever the result. Actually, the Egyptians are so keen to get some of their 'blocked' sterling that they are being pretty reasonable in the negotiations.

I lunched alone with Ava Waverley. I'm afraid she is in a bad way. She has suffered 6 months of knowing that John was dying of cancer. Now her eyes have gone wrong and she can scarcely see. She has no child; no relations; and, altho' she has many friends, they are largely busy people (like me) who cannot give her all the attention she needs. I am really very concerned about her.

2 March (Sunday)

Woke at 8am. Finished Harriette Wilson – a curious book.[24] I must have read it before, but I had quite forgotten it. I think the great demi-mondaine have disappeared or at least do not play so great a part today . . . . This type really depend on the institution of marriage being strict and divorce impossible or rare. Now people marry for a year or two and then pass to the next period of what is really licensed concubinage. Since the so-called 'upper classes' are as corrupt as they can be, these ladies, like Harriette Wilson, are cast out by 'real ladies' – the daughters of their friends. I think the old way was really best . . . .

4 March

I got M. Spaak to come round at 9.45 and I told him about the messages which were passing to and from Washington . . . . Actually, the situation of the different countries in NATO is strange. The French

---

24. Harriette Wilson (1786–1846) was one of the most celebrated courtesans of her era, numbering the 1st Duke of Wellington amongst her lovers. She recorded her amorous adventures in memoirs first published in 1825.

are not much alarmed about the H-Bomb. They do not think it will be used or that the Russians will dare attack so long as the Americans have their bases. The Italians <u>don't</u> want 'Summit talks' at all – for they are about to have elections, and the Christian Democrats have to take the line that Communism is an accursed thing and the Communists untouchables.[25] The Benelux countries are resigned. UK and Scandinavian countries are <u>for</u> summit talks, in the hope of some good coming out of them. American public opinion is definitely against talk. Canadians neutral.

10.15. Minister of Defence; Sir R Powell; Sir E Plowden etc. We have definitely decided on a 'test' in April – just after the recess! We shall not take a decision about the 2nd or 3rd test in this series until later.

I asked for a paper setting out what wd be our position if we agreed to a) suspension of tests b) cut off of materials, at a Summit Conference. (Of course, much depends on what the Americans wd give us if McMahon Act is amended)

11.30. A long meeting about Lancashire and cotton imports from India, Pakistan, and Hong Kong. The Colonial Secy is very intransigeant about this. If we <u>force</u> Hong Kong to conform to an agreement wh India and Pakistan seem ready to make, he will resign. If we accept his view, we shall lose a lot of Lancashire trade .... and 9–14 Lancashire seats! This dilemma was not resolved by lunch time.

I delivered an hour's speech at a London Conservative Rally in Central Hall, Westminster. A good audience and a good reception. But, in spite of their courage, they seem to feel the tide going against us. Will it gain in impetus, or turn in the next two years. It will soon be necessary to consider whether we wd do a more patriotic thing if we went to the country now – riding for a fall, but not too severe a one. I do not myself think that this is yet necessary or desirable ....

6 March

.... A ridiculous and tiresome night. The House sat late – till nearly 4am. After midnight, the first editions of the morning papers began to come in. The *Daily Herald* had a most circumstantial story – in the headlines – saying that Duncan Sandys (Minister of Defence) was to go to Moscow on my instructions to try to deal direct with Moscow, by-passing Washington and the NATO alliance, and reach a separate

---

25. This is perhaps why the Russians had suggested Italian participation.

arrangement with them. This of course was given to the *D. Herald* by the Russian Embassy and they fell for it. Unfortunately, Sandys could not be found anywhere. He had gone home after a broadcast and gone to bed and neither by telephone nor by going to the house could he or his house-keeper be raised. Finally we got the story, early on Friday morning of

7 March
Chief Whip; Sandys; Harold Evans; Hoyer Millar (F.O.) came round at 10 to discuss 'l'affaire Sandys'. It seems that, while I was on my tour, he got an invitation to Moscow – as other ministers often do. Since 'Hungary',[26] these were not accepted, until quite recently. After consultation with F.S., he 'accepted in principle' with no date fixed or likely to be. We drew up, with some difficulty, a statement to [the] Press, which I hope will 'kill' the story. But it was a bore to be deprived of sleep for practically one whole night on this account . . . .

10 March
Since the Foreign Secretary is away in Manila, I have had most of the work to supervise. Indonesia is the new worry. There is a rebellion against Sukarno started in Sumatra. Java is in Sukarno's hands and is more or less Communist. The rebels are anti-Communist. If the West supports the rebellion openly, a) it will not help the rebels, because the West means the Dutch b) it may mean Russian intervention c) it may mean splitting Indonesia into two, with Java going Communist and Russian for keeps. It is not an easy position. The Americans and ourselves are giving 'covert and disavowable' help to the rebels, for it is obviously a good thing to let them have a chance. Unfortunately the Java govt has all the aeroplanes . . . .

14 March (Friday)
We had a meeting of Chancellor of Exr, Commonwealth Secy, President of BofT, Paymaster General about Cotton. It is a <u>most</u> difficult question. But I think we have persuaded the Colonial Secy to let us have one more try at 'voluntary' limitation [of exports to Britain] by Hong Kong. If this cd be done, we have a good chance of getting the same from the Indian and Pakistani industries . . . .

---

26. The crushing of the Nagy regime in Hungary in November 1956 by the Russians.

We have lost Kelvingrove.[27] It is very sad. Mrs Elliot is 'out' by 1600 votes. It is, I suppose, largely due to the Rent Act, wh affects very much the 'better' wards . . . .

7pm. I had Chancellor of the Exr and Ld Privy Seal (Butler) to talk and supper. We argued for some hours about the state of the economy and what should now be done. The Treasury think that the 'boom' or the 'inflation' is still on. Butler and I have our doubts. We all agree about trying to win the wages battle now upon us – bus and railway. But, if and when these are over, we need an expansionist policy again. Anyway, there are the facts, wh I have checked with Compton, the statistical expert. Since my Budget speech in 1956, about 'looking up trains in last year's Bradshaw', much more is being done by sampling and 'spot checks' to get up-to-date information. Based on this, we estimate that <u>Investment</u> in the <u>Public Sector</u> will be the same in 1958–9 as in 1957–8. In the <u>Private Sector</u> it will be about the same – perhaps a little up. But (and this is very significant) its character will change, altho' remain the same in money terms. There will be a much less proportion of <u>building</u> (this was 11% down in last quarter of 1957) but a greater proportion of <u>plants and machinery</u>. This means, of course, the working out of plans made 2 or 3 years ago, with less <u>new</u> investment, which <u>starts</u> with the building. On the <u>consumption</u> side, purchasing power will be up by about £300m on a total of £13,000 million. This takes account of last year's wage increases, now working into the system, as well as allowing for a general 3½% rise in 1958–9. It takes, however, no account for more unemployment or for reduced overtime. Both these have no effect, rapid or substantial on purchasing power. The Budget surplus <u>above</u> the line will be £383m. The total <u>below</u> the line[28] (shown in the new way wh I introduced in the 1956 Budget) will be £600[m]. Problem, do you increase, or reduce taxation, or make no change? We had an argument about this all the evening. Derry Amory is [a] splendid man, in that he is both humble and firm. We all agreed that in terms of adding to purchasing power, £50m, £100m or £150m was negligible. It was a question of psychological effect. The Chancellor has a good, but humble, little package

27. Katherine Elliot failed to hold the Glasgow seat vacated by the recent death of her husband, Sir Walter Elliot. The Conservative vote fell by 14% to 41% and, although they briefly regained this constituency in 1959, this contest marked the start of the collapse of their support in the West of Scotland.

28. After adjustments to levels of public expenditure.

up to £50[m]. (£10m off Cinema Duty; £30m off Purchase Tax, and a few oddments, useful but not spectacular) I want 6d <u>off</u> the Income Tax (£100[m]) This wd give a fillip to the economy, and cheer up the Conservative Party no end.[29]

15 March (Saturday)

I stayed in London last night, and motored down to see Anthony Eden, at a house wh he has borrowed near Newbury .... He talked only about politics, and chiefly about Suez – which is, naturally, an obsession. Yet I feel sure that, however tactically wrong we were, strategically we were right. If the Americans had helped us, the history of the Middle East wd have been changed. Now, I fear, Nasser (like Mussolini) will achieve his Arab Empire and it may take war to dislodge him. Yet (in these nuclear days) limited war is difficult and dangerous ....

17 March

.... David Eccles (BofT) came to luncheon (alone) He is always fertile of ideas, but the follow through is not so good. SofS for Scotland in the afternoon. The battle of the 'strip-mill' is about to be started at Cabinet level. It just amounts to a struggle between Wales and Scotland. Unfortunately, on purely economic grounds, Wales has the advantage[30] ....

Derry Heathcoat Amory told me a wonderful story about his father and the American [1929] slump. Just before the crash, Alec Spearman – who was their broker and adviser – told them to sell everything. (They had a large holding of American shares, having sold a business they had there. It was a very big sum) Spearman came down to the West Country to see Derry and his brothers. There was no time to be lost. They went out to look for their old father, who was MFH and out hunting. When they approached him to get permission for the sale, he had a fox in a furze-brake, the hounds after him. 'American stocks' said the boys to their father. 'There he is – there he is' cried the father. 'We really must ask you about the stocks' replied the boys. 'To hell

---

29. Income tax nevertheless remained at 8/6 (42.5%) in the pound, the level since 1955, until it was reduced to 7/9 (38.75%) in 1960.

30. There was a perceived need for a fourth mill to produce strip steel in the UK. The Scottish firm Colvilles initially showed little interest, thinking local demand would be limited. Scottish politicians were, however, keen on the project, arguing that it would help promote employment and economic development.

with the stocks! There goes the fox! Tally-ho – tally-ho.' And so it
went on. The fox ran well, but hounds changed to another and
another. The boys could not get their father's attention till evening.
But, at dinner, the old Baronet was tired. The next morning, they
heard the news. The market had crashed. 'That' said Derry 'was
probably the most expensive fox in history'.

18 March
Cabinet. Colonial Secy has agreed my plan for Cotton, and Sir Frank
Lee is off to Hong Kong quite soon. If anyone can bring it off, he
will . . . .

Mr de Valera came at 5pm. It was rather a queer performance. He
is now old, and blind. The revolutionary fire has gone and he cannot
understand why we are so bored with Ireland and so glad to be rid of
her, after all these weary centuries. He kept trying to raise the question
of partition; but I wd not allow him and kept turning the subject . . . .

19 March
A meeting about the Rent Act took place before the Cabinet. I had
Brooke (Housing); Ld Chancellor; Ld P[rivy] Seal; Chief Whip; SofS
Scotland (Maclay) and Chancellor of Exr. Brooke feels that while we
can stand absolutely by the broad principle of the Act, the evictions in
October will be rather higher than will be politically 'wearable',
without some 'ambulance' treatment. This wd really mean an amending Bill, dealing with a right of appeal to the County Court in 'stay of
execution' for 6 month periods, in case of hardship. Of course, it will
be called a 'climb-down' but I am rather impressed by the view [of the]
Minister of Housing – who is both intelligent and courageous.[31]

Malta is flaring up – with their impossible P.M. – Mintoff – trying
to blackmail and bully HMG. In view of all this, the Conservative
Party is by no means so keen on 'integration' as a year ago. Gaitskell,
Griffiths, and Callaghan – what a crew! – came to my room to try to
bully me in their turn.

---

31. Rents affecting some 800,000 privately renting households had been
    decontrolled by the 1957 Rent Act. The intention had been that increased rents
    would incentivise landlords to fund repairs. There was, however, also concern
    that landlords could evict tenants with only four weeks' notice to take
    advantage of the higher rents, hence Brooke's move to provide for lengthening
    this period in new legislation.

5–6.30. Meeting on Defence Organisation. Minister of Defence; 3 Service Ministers; 4 Chiefs of Staff. I began by asking the Chiefs to state their feelings – or grievances – about the present system. This they did – not by any means all agreeing with each other as to the cause of the difficulties. After an hour or more of this, I outlined the scheme which I had worked out with Sandys and Norman Brook[32] . . . .

20 March

. . . . P.Q.s – a fairly even duel today. We had a long meeting of the 'Steering Ctee'. This is a policy ctee of the <u>Party</u> – and only deals with <u>party-political</u> questions. We have done some good work on policy questions. Our chief talk today was on how to treat the Liberals and the Liberal revival. Some say 'do a deal with them' – others 'fight to exterminate them'.

I gave a dinner to Bankers, Merchant Bankers, and Stock Exchange magnates. Afterwards, I had a fascinating talk with Robarts (National Provincial) He is a <u>strong</u> advocate of the 'floating' pound[33] . . . .

24 March

. . . . The 'rebels' are losing out in Indonesia, in spite of as much 'covert' help as we and US can give them quietly. This means, unless they can hold on and some compromise emerges, a Communist regime in Indonesia with all that this means for SE Asia[34] . . . .

27 March

Ld Beaverbrook came to see me. He stayed ¾ hour. He looks no older – and is just as irresponsible as ever . . . . B thinks the Liberal revival will not come to much.

I gave dinner at No 10 to a small party to discuss financial and economic questions. Politicians three (Heathcoat Amory; Butler; HM) Bankers three (Cobbold; Robarts; Monckton) A fascinating discussion

---

32. Essentially this clarified the functions of the Minister of Defence and created a Chief of Defence Staff.

33. Macmillan had toyed with the idea of floating sterling from the post-war system of fixed exchange rates since the currency crisis of the previous year. In the event this did not happen until the system broke up in 1972.

34. Although the rebellion dragged on for three more years the decision of the CIA in May to end support sealed its fate.

and <u>little</u> agreement. Butler and Robarts passionate for a 'free' pound; Governor Cobbold hesitating and pointing out with great clarity the dangers. I feel that we must <u>not</u> think of this until we know what is going to happen to European Free Trade.

28 March

We <u>lost</u> the Torrington by-election by 200 votes. Actually, this is 2–3000 <u>better</u> than we expected and it is certain that in the last few days our candidate has been gaining ground. But it is irritating to lose by so little and I'm afraid the triumph of the Asquiths (Violet Bonham Carter and her son)[35] will encourage the Liberals elsewhere. The Liberal campaign is quite unscrupulous – they have no policy but opportunism, exploiting every grievance and promising protection or Free Trade, or anything else according to the demands of each constituency . . . .

29 March

By train to Wakefield, arriving about 5pm. A meeting of the officers of the Mid-Yorkshire Conservative Federation at Hemsworth. This was a very pleasant little meeting of a gallant band of workers who keep the party flag flying in hopeless seats – with Socialist majorities of 10, 20, or 30,000. No Conservative minister, let alone a Prime Minister, had ever been near them. Dorothy and I had a wonderful reception and it was really rather a moving occasion . . . .

1 April

. . . . 10.30–1. Cabinet. The most important topic was the H-Bomb and the 'Summit' talks. During the week-end two dramatic events have taken place.

1) Gromyko has announced the unilateral decision of the Soviet Govt to suspend all nuclear tests. (As they have just completed a large and accelerated series this is a bit thin as propaganda for ordinary

---

35. Mark Bonham Carter, grandson of the Liberal Prime Minister (1908–16) Herbert Asquith, was the victorious Liberal. The Conservative share of the vote fell by 28% and a Tory majority of 9,312 became a Liberal one of 219. Macmillan, as he makes clear in *The Past Masters: Politics and Politicians 1906–1939* (London: Macmillan, 1975), had always been drawn to Asquith's great rival and successor as Prime Minister, David Lloyd George.

folk, but has naturally had a great effect on people like the Editor of the *Daily Mirror* and on the Radicals and Socialists generally) . . . .

2) After weeks of arguing, the U.S. Govt and now <u>all</u> the NATO Govts have approved our idea of sending a short and clear reply to Russia about the summit meeting. I actually drafted this paper myself some weeks ago . . . . At that time Dulles did not like it at all. But he changed his view – just in time, after a good deal of coaxing. (The President, judging from his messages, has been more flexible all through; but of course he generally bows to Dulles in the end)

Then we had to get NATO support. For the substance, this was easy enough – only one or two amendments being made to our text. But then came the problem, who was to deliver the note in Moscow? On this, the NATO representatives argued for several days; Italy, Turkey, Greece; Belgium – all wanted to join. For Italy, owing to a General Election, this had some importance. Finally it was agreed, after a lot of telephoning and telegraphing, that this <u>note</u> should be <u>delivered</u> by the Geneva Conference Powers – UK, France, US – but that this would be without prejudice to the question of what powers wd actually take part in a meeting of Foreign Secretaries or Heads of Governments.

Gromyko's speech was Monday afternoon. The Allied Note was given in on the same afternoon and published at 5pm. (6 o'clock news) It was 'a dam' close run thing'.[36] Actually, I think our note about the Summit almost cancelled out the propaganda effect of the Russian decision on Tests. I had, of course, to explain all this to the Cabinet, and get their general approval for the line I wd take in HofC – that is, to stand quite firm on <u>tests</u>.

The other main subject at Cabinet was the proposed statement about the Rent Act. The Cabinet approved the Minister's statement and proposed Amending Bill (giving 'evicted' tenants an appeal to the County Court) but with some hesitation and reluctance. (Altho' everyone is rather disappointed about Torrington, I think our morale is still quite good) . . . .

Questions went pretty well. Since the Labour Party are trying to cover their deep internal divisions on the whole question of defence by a compromise – 'no more tests till the Summit' they were outwardly in a strong position. However, I stoutly maintained our position and got

---

36. A misquotation of Wellington's remark after his victory at Waterloo in 1815 that 'It was a damned nice thing, the nearest run thing you ever saw in your life.'

general support from the House. All the patriotic Labourites had seen through the cynicism of the Russian propaganda line. 3 megaton tests in a week – then, no more tests.

I gave dinner for Dag Hammarskjöld – Secretary General of U.N. He was very pleasant and quite interesting, but he speaks so indistinctly as to be barely comprehensible. He had just been to Moscow. Krushchev is supreme, without challengers, and very confident of his own and Russia's strength. He will make no concessions. We must have Summit talks, but we shall achieve nothing serious, except perhaps on Tests – that is, if we are ready to stop. On most weapons and scientific developments – esp in 'space science', the Russians are ahead of the West. Thus H (incidentally confirming what our own Intelligence services tell us)[37]

2 April

. . . . John Morrison (Chairman of 1922 Ctee) is worried about Quintin (Ld Hailsham) I told him that we must wait a little to see how things develop. Ld Hailsham had had a frank talk with me and is only anxious to help in the best way possible. I would certainly not yield to clamour agst him because we had lost these by-elections. Morrison seemed satisfied, but thought that Hailsham wd not prove balanced enough in judgment to be successful as Chairman. I said we must wait and see . . . .

3 April

. . . . To all our other difficulties, the almost certainty of a Railway, Bus, Dock and general Road Transport strike is now added! The Railway tribunal will give its award a week today. Whatever it is – 3% or nothing – the unions will not accept.

After Cabinet, we had a talk with a small group of ministers. It is hard to find a way out. The Govt cannot, once again, reject the arbitration and offer more. Yet I don't think the men can accept a 'nil' award, esp if the arbitrator puts the blame not on the Transport Commission but on its Bankers, who refuse to lend any more money to finance growing deficits. The Bankers are HMG, so the strike will be against the Government . . . .

---

37. There was then a widespread, if erroneous, belief in both Washington and London, even before *Sputnik*, that the Russians possessed and were increasing a technological lead over the West.

10 April

I had to go to London this afternoon for a meeting at No 10. Sir John Forster's award is out. It recommends <u>no</u> wage increase at all to the railway workers. Unfortunately, altho' the Employer's representative on the Tribunal supports Sir J.F., the Trade Union representative has issued a minority report – this, in effect, proposes an increase to meet [the] rise in cost of living since last year (say 3%) and then to study how further increases cd be made. So, if the strike comes, it will really be on this. Sir J.F. has, however, 'passed the buck' firmly to HMG by saying a) that Railway wages are on the <u>low</u> side, compared with other nationalised and some private industries b) that since the Transport Commission is bankrupt and HMG (the bankers) have in effect refused to lend any more money, he has no alternative to a 'nil' award.

Chancellor of Exr; M of Labour; M of Power; Chancellor of Duchy; Chief Whip. We had a useful talk – chiefly about the publicity side. The important things to get over are

a) the large difference between wage rates and average earnings, e.g. Porter. Basic rate 7/7/0 – average earning 9/9/6.

b) That HMG are giving railways £50 and £60[m] to meet deficit (current) as well as £150m or more for capital.

c) That it is <u>not</u> just railway wages that are at stake. It is whether or not we have another wage spiral throughout industry.

At the same time, I am very anxious that the Govt, while firm, shd not seem to be obstinate. Above all, we must not 'challenge' the T. Unions (as people like Ld Hinchingbrooke wd like) We must appeal to the unions, and try to take ourselves some constructive initiative.

11 April

. . . . A strike, if it comes, will be terribly damaging. For, as it goes on, the present good feeling will change, and bitterness begin. The middle classes are so angry, that the spirit of Liberalism (now the same as Poujadism)[38] will encourage the class war. I am desperately anxious to

---

38. An anti-tax and xenophobic revolt of small shopkeepers and artisans led by the populist politician Pierre Poujade, which sprang to prominence briefly during the 1956 French elections. Poujadism only bore passing resemblance to thinking either in the Liberal Party or in liberal economic circles such as the recently founded Institute of Economic Affairs, though there is some evidence to suggest similar views were current amongst disgruntled middle-class voters switching to the Liberals in these years.

avoid a strike if we can find a way out wh does not mean either letting down Sir JF and his award or abandoning the fight against inflation just when it may succeed.

Meeting of some ministers at 10am. I am circulating a paper on the 'initiative' which HMG might take at the right moment. (It is really based on the idea that we might <u>accelerate</u> the capital programme, and the management and men might agree on 'economy through efficiency' – no restrictive practices; shutting up branch lines <u>and accepting</u> redundancy as inevitable etc etc) . . . .

Motored back to No 10, for Defence Ctee meeting on 1) Aden 2) Malta c) Yemen. We decide to arrest (if possible) the 3 Jifri brothers who are doing such harm in the Aden Protectorate. This may (if it comes off) prevent one of the Sultans (who is [in] the hands of these rascals) from breaking his treaty with us, and declaring that he and his country are joining the Egypt–Syria combination. (We know that this is being plotted, with Nasser's help)[39]

After this meeting (wh was a long one) we had to take some steps to reinforce the troops in Malta. Yemen is the most difficult of all. We are fired at all the time by guns from the other side of the border.[40] If we retaliate, we are accused of killing women and children.

The Defence Ctee was followed by an adjourned meeting on my proposals (proposed by Sandys and myself) for reorganising and redefining the Defence structure. Altho' the Service Ministers and the Chiefs of Staff have calmed down quite a bit since the last meeting, there was an under-current of jealousy and dislike of Sandys. (This, of

---

39. Muhammad al-Jifri founded the South Arabian League, to press for an independent Southwestern Arabia, in 1951. He was expelled from the British colony of Aden in 1956. However, he and his two brothers were subsequently to become advisers to the pro-nationalist 'Ali, Sultan of Lahj, one of the potentates in the British-governed Aden Protectorate. Convinced that the Jifris were negotiating Lahj's entry into Nasser's United Arab Republic, the British attempted unsuccessfully to seize them on 18 April 1958. They fled, but 'Ali was deposed and replaced by his more pliant brother Fadhl.

40. Imam Ahmad of Yemen, the Aden Protectorate's northern neighbour, had signed a tripartite agreement with Nasser and King Saud of Saudi Arabia in April 1956 and was now establishing a nominal attachment to the UAR. Meanwhile, a frontier conflict along the Yemeni–Protectorate border had become a low-intensity proxy war of raids and subversion between Britain and Egypt since 1955.

course, is because he has really tried to <u>be</u> a Minister of Defence and to carry out the job wh I asked him to undertake) . . . .

15 April
Cabinet at 11. The Geneva Conference on 'Territorial Sea' is giving a lot of trouble. All the Afro-Asians want an extension to 12 miles, in order to annoy the Israelis by closing the Gulf of Aqaba. The Icelanders and the Canadians (and lots of others) want to protect their fishing. The maritime powers are isolated, and in spite of much help from U.S., almost powerless[41] . . . .

Budget opened by Heathcoat Amory in a good speech, and was well received. The Socialists only voted against the proposal to equalise Profits Tax[42] . . . .

16 April
The Press is <u>very</u> good on the Budget. The reductions in Purchase Tax are popular; the general economic presentation given by the Chancellor was much praised.

I met Dr Adenauer (the German Chancellor) at Northolt at 2.15 and drove with him to London. We began our talks (at 4.15–5.30) with a review of Russian policy; Summit talks etc. He had with him von Brentano (Foreign Secy) and Dr Erhardt [sic] (Economics) The Queen gave a dinner at Windsor – to wh D and I were bidden and the Germans throughly enjoyed themselves. The old Chancellor sat between the two Queens, and flirted with both.

17 April
We met all the morning (in the old Treasury Board Room) and reached complete agreement about all the major questions. The Russians (according to the Germans) can best be tackled and shewn up by making 'controlled disarmament; conventional and unconventional' our main demand . . . .

---

41. As a traditional naval power Britain's interest was to defend the existing three-mile territorial waters limit and freedom on the high seas, not least for her fishing fleet. The Icelandic declaration of a twelve-mile limit on 1 June 1958 was to provoke the first Cod War. By 1964, however, Britain was not only forced to accept these new limits, but had also extended her own.
42. They saw the new single rate of 10% as a replacement of taxation on reserves.

18 April

. . . . Luncheon at the Mansion House, after wh we composed (in a remarkably short space of time) a very good communiqué, saying all the things we wanted said. 'Support costs' are settled, so far as the Germans are concerned. We now have to try to get NATO and WEU to agree. The chief trouble will be about our proposed reduction to 45,000 men.[43]

Sir Brian Robertson came to see me in the afternoon, and I agreed with him a statement from No 10, wh will invite the unions to see me next Tuesday. We cannot give in on the subsidy to wages. All we can offer is acceleration of the modernisation programme . . . .

19 April

. . . . Adenauer seems to be delighted with the visit and feels that it has been an immense success. It has certainly helped to counteract the poison which the French have been pouring into his ears . . . .

22 April

In response to my invitation, issued last Friday, Sir Brian Robertson accompanied by some of his principal officers, Mr Greene (NUR) Mr Hallworth (ASLEF) and Mr Webber (Railway Clerks) and their supporters came to No 10 at 3.45. The meeting lasted just over 2 hours. Sir Brian introduced the deputation shortly; then each of the 3 union secretaries spoke; then Sir Brian, in his capacity as Chairman of the Transport Commission. The unions asked for an increase of wages and argued that the arbitration tribunal would have granted this if it had not been for the financial difficulties of the Railways and the Government's refusal to lend more than the £250m for current needs. The Chairman of the Commission said that he could not pay any more wages at present, and therefore accepted the Tribunal's findings. However, he felt that if the Govt wd reconsider their attitude to the Modernisation Plan (capital required £1500m) and help in one or two other

---

43. On 10 July Macmillan wrote to Eisenhower that 'I feel that our European allies have not yet understood the advantage to them of all regular British forces . . . . This will be a very powerful force and to be compared favourably with a much larger force of non-regular troops' (G&E, p. 156). In the event, despite complaints from Norstad and a brief and unfulfilled suggestion of sending an extra 5,000 men during the 1961 Berlin crisis, British forces in West Germany were to remain at this reduced level.

ways, things wd improve. I then put forward the Govt's position (speaking generally from a brief wh had been agreed at a meeting of Ministers chiefly concerned last night) I said that what was needed was a concerted effort. The Commission shd attack the problem of making fresh economies with greater urgency, and work out detailed plans; these wd no doubt involve closing some lines and stations and other fairly dramatic measures. Manpower must be saved. The unions shd agree on accepting redundancy and in getting rid of any remaining restrictive practices etc. Provided this were done, the Govt wd (as a matter of urgency) consider any scheme for increasing the tempo of modernisation.

The unions asked a lot of questions after this, but in a very amicable and reasonable tone. A good deal of whisky was consumed.

Finally, they agreed to have a meeting with Robertson tomorrow afternoon to discuss the various statements made and esp to consider the Govt's proposal . . . .

23 April

The Press has been excellent about the Railway Crisis and has set out the Govt's position very well. I think both the Ministry of Transport and Harold Evans (my PRO) must have done a good job with the lobby journalists etc. Even the *Herald* is not too bad; the *D Mirror* is favourable. I heard in the late afternoon that the union leaders had agreed to the plan wh I put to them and at least to see how it wd work out. The test will come, of course, as to <u>when</u> a new claim or a wage increase is likely to come . . . .

29 April

. . . . The British H-Bomb Test was made successfully from Christmas Island yesterday. I expected a great row in the House – but in fact Gaitskell (when I counter-attacked quite vigorously) collapsed like a pricked balloon . . . .

1 May

9.30 Defence Committee on Cyprus. The Chiefs of Staff are against any plan whether Partition, or a modified Partition, or a 'Tridominium'. They want us to 'soldier on' and try to defeat EOKA. The Cabinet took a different view, and supported the 'Tridominium' idea. This is noble and ambitious and can only have any chance of success if we put it forward with confidence. It was agreed to set to work and try to devise a plan and a timetable . . . .

.... After dinner, a meeting of Ministers to discuss the Bus and Railway situation. Nothing can avert a Bus strike. The Railway strike is in the balance.

2 May

Another 2 hours on the siting of the new strip mill – the Cabinet is divided between Scotland and S Wales. All the economic arguments are for Newport. But the social and political arguments seem to favour Grangemouth . . . .

6 May

The Chief Whip is very anxious about the Parliamentary side of the Railway situation. The Conservatives are waiting anxiously to see what we do. Peter Thorneycroft (with Birch and Enoch Powell) are ready to pounce. On the other hand, I am more anxious about the Industrial and practical side. It is not going to be easy to keep the people fed and in good heart unless they are absolutely with us. This means that the Ry unions must have rejected an offer wh everyone wd regard as fair and reasonable. Then we have to consider sterling. A strike will put the £ down. But to 'give in' to 'an inflationary demand' wd (it is said) do more harm still in the longer run . . . .

7 May

.... 2.30. Meeting of ministers on Ry and Bus disputes. We are going on working at some plan to settle the railways consistent with our general policy. This really means – savings, economies, improvements etc – which are to produce £10 or £12m to finance an increase of pay . . . .

10 May

Macleod has called the parties together. (This is a slight farce, when one of the parties is a Nationalised Industry, of wh the Govt is both equity holder and banker) It seems that after a 6 hours debate a motion was carried 13 to 10 for an immediate strike by NUR Executive. ASLEF and the Clerks Assocn are more cautious.

The meeting has been adjourned till Tuesday – so we are safe for a few more days. The emergency organisation has been very carefully prepared – as far as is possible in 'peace' – and will (I hope) work reasonably well . . . .

11 May (Sunday)

Drove to Chequers from Kings X, arriving about 8am. I found there For Secy; Colonial Secy; Sir Hugh Foot (Governor of Cyprus). Sir N Brook; Mr Melville (Col. Office) Archie Ross (F.O.); F Bishop . . . .

Apart from one or two outstanding matters on Summit Talks, Geneva, Indonesia, Lebanon etc which took an hour or so, we spent the day (with short luncheon interval) on Cyprus.

The Governor was very helpful and I was impressed by his fervour. After several hours discussion, a new draft was prepared, wh embodied a) Governor Foot's plans for <u>internal</u> self-government b) our original plans for the <u>external</u> solution of 'Tridominium'.

I left Chequers at 6 and got to No 10 by 7.30. Meeting of Ministers about the Railway dispute. Butler; Heathcoat Amory; Ld Mills; Macleod; Watkinson; Chief Whip (Heath) We ended at 11. (Cake, soup and sandwiches were supplied and a lot of time thus saved) At first Ministers were very much against any variation of what General Robertson has offered – something in October and a 'review' in July. This certainly will not avoid a strike. Of course, some Ministers and a lot of the Party want a 'showdown'. But I don't think they realise how it may end. Even if we win (wh is doubtful) it will be at a heavy cost.

The orthodox Treasury doctrine – invented by Thorneycroft and more or less adopted by Heathcoat Amory is that no advance of wages at all is to be conceded <u>unless</u> it can be got out of economies. I accept this – but I do not personally think it can be applied absolutely literally. (The Chief Whip – loyal as he is – seems to be with the orthodox, not to say Brahminical group) At present, General Robertson's economies amount to £10m a year. But since they take some time to fructify, the view still is that they shd not be translated into any pay increase till October. So all my efforts have been concentrated on getting <u>more</u> economies. If we cd get the total to a rate of £12½m p.a., this wd justify paying out sooner. (£10m = 3% on wages) In other words, it wd be legitimate to anticipate for 3 months, if the <u>total</u> of the savings were increased by a quarter. I finally got the Ministers to accept this view (Butler supported well – also Macleod) and we must now await tomorrow's Cabinet.

12 May

. . . . 5–7. Cabinet. After much discussion, and a review of Robertson's latest economies, it was decided to authorise him to offer an increase

of 3% in July. The Chief Whip is very unhappy about this and
obviously thinks it will break the party and allow Thorneycroft to do
on me 'tit for tat' (like Palmerston on Johnny Russell)[44] Some other
Ministers (including the Chancellor of the Exr and Dr Hill) were very
reluctant to agree but did so out of loyalty to me. But I am sure I am
right. Public sympathy is (on the whole) with the Railwaymen. The
cost of living figure (owing to potatoes and tomatoes) will go up by
TWO points on May 23rd, and who knows what Ld Justice Morris
may give the Coal Miners. If we are to face a strike, which we can
only break by volunteers and full public sympathy, we must get into a
better posture . . . .

13 May
. . . . 3.45 Cabinet. We had meant to confine the discussion to the
Cyprus plan. But – as so often – other urgent matters had to be
dealt with. In the first place, a great crisis is blowing up in the
Lebanon. Nasser is organising an internal campaign there against
President Chamoun and his regime.[45] This is partly Communist and
partly Arab Nationalist. Russian arms are being introduced from
Syria and the object is to force Lebanon to join in the Egyptian–
Syrian combination. In other words, after Austria – the Sudeten
Germans. Poland (in this case Iraq) will be the next to go. Fortunately the Americans have learned a lot since Suez, and the Bermuda
and Washington visits are beginning to shew results. The Cabinet
agreed that we wd join with U.S. in saying to President Chamoun
that if he decided to ask for military help to preserve the independence of Lebanon we wd give it. Telegrams accordingly had to be
drafted and approved. Then we got back to the new Cyprus plan.
However this conversation had to be interrupted, for General Robertson rang up to say that he had offered 3% in July (or rather from
June 30th) together with the enquiry into Railway wages, but he did

---

44. After Palmerston's dismissal as foreign secretary in 1851 he had his revenge the
following year in assisting the fall of Lord John Russell's government over its
militia proposals.
45. Chamoun's support for France and Britain in 1956 had angered Nasser. A
Christian, his stance increased tensions in a religiously divided country, as did
the apparent rigging of the 1957 elections. Lebanese Muslims greeted the
foundation of the UAR with enthusiasm. In May a general strike was
proclaimed, whilst Muslims in Tripoli took up arms.

not think they would accept anything but June 1st or even earlier. They might also ask for 4%. After some discussion, we agreed to stand by our offer (or rather General R's offer) whatever the consequences . . . .

14 May

. . . . There has been a great flare up in France, still in a state of political confusion. The Generals in Algeria have set up a Committee of Public Safety. Whether it is to be followed by an attempt at a *coup d'état* in Paris is obscure. M. Pflimlin is forming a Govt. No doubt the politicians will now rally, in fear of the Army . . . .

The latest news of the Railway position is that the <u>clerks</u> and <u>ASLEF</u> have definitely accepted. <u>NUR</u> have asked to see General R[obertson] again tomorrow . . . .

15 May

. . . . The Chief Whip is nervous about the Party and the Railways. *The Times* has written a very silly leader called 'The Price'. (Printers wages were put up by 6½% a few weeks ago!) . . . .

4–5pm. Meeting of Ministers concerned (that is almost half the Cabinet) to hear from Maudling the latest state of play on European Free Trade area. The confusion in France (they have had no govt for 6 weeks or so, and now they are threatened with a *crise de régime*) makes progress very slow. We shall have to make some concessions – the question is how far we are to go . . . .

It seems that Thorneycroft made an attack at the 1922 Ctee, but did not really press it home. The Party is grumbling about the Ry settlement. But when they get to their constituencies they will find a good deal of sympathy for the Railwaymen . . . .

17 May

. . . . [T]he news of the proposed Anglo-American military help to the Lebanon has leaked in Washington! It seems that Dulles had a confidential talk with the Senate leaders. One of them must have talked and it is all in the morning's *Washington Post* . . . .

The Russians have made a tentative proposal about a scientific committee to enquire and report on the practicality of detecting nuclear tests. This is at least a small move forward, as we proposed this ourselves nearly a year ago and have repeated it since. One of the problems is that the Russians have addressed only US and seem to want to leave out UK and France. It would be very dangerous to agree to this . . . .

20 May

The House of Commons is unaccountable. We expected yesterday great trouble over both Cyprus and the Lebanon. After much discussion between Ministers, we decided that Colonial Secy shd make the statement on Cyprus . . . . The Governor had done a good deal of work with his friends in the Labour Party, and all went off quite well. As regards Lebanon, in spite of the American leak, there was no trouble. It seems to be generally known that we and the Americans have given some guarantee to President Chamoun and that troops are ready to go. But for some reason even the extreme left of the Labour Party have made no protest . . . .

21 May

Cabinet 10.30. The Icelanders look like declaring the 12 mile limit unilaterally. If they try to arrest our trawlers, we shall have to take action to protect them. This will lead to trouble with Canada (who want to do the same thing) and with U.S.A., who are afraid that Iceland (wh is very Communist-minded) will go out of NATO and the Americans may lose their base . . . .

The French situation is still obscure. The P.M. (Pflimlin) seems to be putting up quite a fight. But de Gaulle has taken up a pretty good strategic position[46] . . . .

We had a meeting of the 'Steering Ctee' of the Party in the evening . . . . There was a rather desultory discussion about the Liberals. The general view was that we shd <u>not</u> attempt to enter into any negotiation with them on a national basis – at least at present. Machiavelli said that 'princes should either be annihilated or conciliated' (or words to that effect)[47] In the long run, we must either make a union with the

---

46. The coup leaders disliked the weaknesses of the Fourth Republic and feared that it would abandon the Army's defence of *Algérie Française*. The restoration of de Gaulle to power was an obvious alternative, though the General was concerned to take care that his ascent to power was by constitutional means, not as a beneficiary of the junta in Algiers.

47. The quotation, from *The Prince*, chap. 3, is 'Men should be either treated generously or destroyed, because they take revenge for slight injuries – for heavy ones they cannot' (translated by Allen Gilbert).

Liberals or fight them *à l'outrance*.[48] Meanwhile, we shall allow – but not encourage – Conservative associations to adopt candidates against sitting Liberals.[49]

28 May

We got back to London this morning after 5 <u>very</u> pleasant days in Scotland. We played 2 rounds of golf on Monday and one yesterday. The weather was very good for 3 out of the 5 days.

The French crisis is still unresolved. The army are in virtual command of Algeria and now of Corsica. They threaten to seize different areas of France and perhaps to attack Paris by parachute troops. Pflimlin has resigned. President Coty is consulting the various party leaders. Anti-de Gaulle demonstrations are taking place in Paris . . . .

The bus strike continues. Mr Cousins has tried – and apparently failed – to get the Railwaymen in. He now threatens to withdraw 6000 men who drive the oil delivery vans, and then paralyse all road transport. He also threatens to stop the Electric Power stations. This, of course, is pure blackmail . . . .

29 May

10am. Meeting of Ministers (Chancellor of Exr; Defence; Ld Home; with Sir E Plowden etc) The purpose was to discuss the position on nuclear weapons and tests. Our last test (a few weeks ago) was successful. Nevertheless it is absolutely vital for us to complete this series in Sept. If all goes well, we shall need only 2 explosions; but if (as is very possible) we have a failure in the new and very special system wh we want to test, we shall need 2 more. We should complete everything by October 31st (at latest) and prob[ably] before. Can we hold on against a) the public and political pressure now b) the extension of this pressure wh is likely to follow [the] U.N. report on medical effects?[50] These are the questions we must face. But if we give up now, we shall <u>not</u> have a reliable weapon or one wh the

---

48. To the extreme.
49. Local arrangements in Bolton and Huddersfield nevertheless survived until 1964.
50. The last test was on 23 September. Meanwhile, the United Nations Scientific Committee on the Effects of Atomic Radiation (set up in 1955) finalised its first report on 13 June 1958.

enemy cannot neutralise. This last is really the vital point. Yet until
[the] McMahon Act is amended or a new agreement made with US)
we cannot even discuss the problem with them. However, the news
about this is good. The Amending Bill has passed the Committee stage
and there is just a chance of an agreement being concluded in time
to lie 30 days on the table <u>before</u> Congress adjourns. But it will be
a race against time. And everything depends on it! For, if we get a
really good working agreement, it is unlikely that we shall need any
more tests – except perhaps just this last series, to put us in a better
bargaining position. However, <u>with American</u> working arrangements
made, our autumn tests are not a '<u>must</u>'. Without them, these are
absolutely vital to the safety and strength of Britain and we must go
on . . . .

11am. David Eccles came. He is going to Spain for a visit and will
have to call in [on] President Franco – or rather, General Franco.[51]
David is a <u>very</u> good Minister, but he always wants to do the work of
another department. His early business connection with Spain makes
him keen to do some diplomacy.

Our trade with Spain is good but could be much increased. He is
going primarily to the Barcelona Fair. But I don't want him to discuss
Gibraltar! . . . .

12 noon. Ld Rochdale, Sir C Clegg etc about the Cotton Imports
from the Commonwealth. It looks now as if we <u>may</u> get voluntary
agreement by India and Pakistan <u>industrialists</u> to a quota to be <u>policed</u>
here by HMG. The problem remains – will Hong Kong industrialists
agree? We must do what we can. But Colonial Secy will <u>never</u> agree to
compulsion. The arguments are very balanced, but I feel we might
bring our <u>influences</u> in favour of such a voluntary limitation . . . .

2.30. Meeting of Ministers on Industrial Situation. We were told
that TUC were meeting at same time. We agreed on <u>Petrol</u> notices to
public and to garages; also plans for troops.

4pm. Defence organisation – Min of Defence; Service Ministers;
Minister of Supply; 4 Chiefs of Staff. I had circulated a revise of the
paper two days before and also done a little bit of talking to individuals. Although the atmosphere was not good, it seemed to me likely
that we shd get through without resignations. Of the Chiefs of Staff,
two – Dickson and Mountbatten – are keen supporters of the new

---

51. Spanish dictator since his victory in the 1936–39 civil war.

scheme.[52] Gerald Templer [CIGS] (who leaves anyway in a few months) and Boyle (CAS) are opposed . . . .

At about 7.30pm Macleod (Labour) and Sir W Neden came along for a talk. The Minister had received a deputation from the TUC and asked for further Govt intervention in the Bus strike, in order to prevent the danger of a spreading of the strike to other fields, either controlled by T&GW or by other unions. He said he wd reflect on his reply, and if (as he expected) it was that he cd not see any ground for a Ministry of Labour intervention he wd tell them as soon as possible. In that event, the TUC deputation wd wish to see me . . . .

30 May

10am. Chancellor of Exr; Lord Mills; and Minister of Transport. We discussed the line for me to take with TUC. 11–1. TUC deputation – 6, including the two secretaries, Vincent Tewson (nice but ineffective) and Woodcock (left-wing; intellectualist and therefore tricky, tho' agreeable) Yates – Chairman – is a good sound fellow. Willis, the printer's man, is extreme. Tom Williamson (Municipal and General Workers) charming, honest, and weak. Collison (Agric Workers) – nice fellow. The discussion was very friendly, but rather ineffective. It was clear that

a) TUC want to avoid a General Strike – or even _any_ spreading of the strike

b) that they have been and are still frightened of Cousins – partly because of his size (1¼m members) and partly because of his character.

c) they are desperately anxious that Cousins should be helped out of the position into which he has got, if HMG or Transport Bd can do so. All the same, each one of these men individually _hates_ Cousins just as much as he is frightened of Cousins.

I made it clear to them

a) that we were going to maintain essential services – petrol, light etc.

b) we did not want a showdown. We wanted a fair settlement.

---

52. In May 1957 Macmillan suggested uniting the three service ministries and the Ministry of Supply into a single defence department. Service opposition ensured that these new proposals, to revamp the Cabinet's Defence Committee and to create a Chief of the Defence Staff, were more modest in scale when implemented later in 1958.

I took them all through the Bus dispute; the industrial court agreement; the moves which Sir J Elliot had made, improving on the award in some respects. What had Cousins done to match all this?

I took them all through the way I had personally handled the Railway problem; the way the TU leaders had helped me had led to a settlement wh was generally approved by all moderate people. It ended with

(i) an agreed Press statement

(ii) an agreed statement of what they had asked and what I had replied. This would be useful to them for their afternoon meeting of the whole TUC Executive . . . .

I had to go at 5pm to have two upper teeth removed . . . . It was quite an operation (because my teeth are so strong and so firmly fixed to the bone) . . . . It took 40 minutes. Dr Richardson kindly came and took me back to No 10. I was rather shaken by it all and of course a good deal of poison is let loose – so penicillin etc is necessary. I went to bed on returning from Harley St.

The TUC had their meeting. They seem to have been pretty firm with Cousins and told him to re-open his talks with Elliot. Of course, this cannot lead to anything – since (I hope I am right) Elliot will only talk on the basis of my paper (wh I had arranged with Robertson last night) But action is delayed, and – in a way – I think this helps . . . .

31 May

. . . . De Gaulle looks like getting enough votes in the Assembly to become P.M. by <u>constitutional</u> methods.[53] This is of great importance. Everything turns on the Socialists, whom Mollet is trying to lead into acquiescence if not to active support of de Gaulle.

Read *The Political System of Napoleon 3rd* by a young man called Theodore Zeldin . . . . The book is (in the Namier tradition) very well documented and clearly founded on good research. It is well written, and (with present troubles in France) quite opportune. It is published by M&Co . . . .

4pm. Minister of Transport rang up. Cousins has asked to see Sir J. Elliot. They are meeting now. Minister said that he had heard from T.U. sources that Cousins now wanted to settle. The question is, can he? . . . .

---

53. He had been appointed Prime Minister of France on 29 May and was confirmed in office by the National Assembly on 1 June.

11pm. After a discussion lasting 3 hours or more the LTE and Cousins separated for a pause. After the interval, Sir John Elliot put forward a plan, based on Point 3 of the paper which I had given to the TUC on Friday. M of Transport, M of Labour, Sir Wilfred Neden were consulted. I tried – but failed – to get hold of the Chancellor of the Exr. But it seemed not to go beyond what the Cabinet (or rather the group of ministers concerned) would approve. So I authorised M of Transport to tell Sir J.E. that we thought his formula a good one. However, Cousins and Co did not accept it – altho' they did not reject it outright. At 10.15 or so the negotiators packed up for the night, to meet again tomorrow . . . .

2 June

. . . . The TUC asked to see me again, but I refused to see them, since Mr Cousins was due to report to his delegates and until he had done so, I could not accept the breakdown of the negotiations as final . . . .

My grand-daughter, Theresa Amery – aged about 4 – was taken to Tussaud's where she saw an effigy of me. She said, not in great concern over this supposed event but in annoyance at being kept in the dark – 'Well – I do think somebody might have told me that grandpapa was real'.

3 June

The strike continues. How far Mr Cousins will be able to spread it, is not yet clear. Meanwhile a bad position is building up in London docks – where half the men are out – unofficially – in support of the Smithfield meat porters . . . .

4 June

They telephoned . . . . the result of the TUC meeting with Cousins. He asked for a general strike! This they turned down flat. Then he asked for support in extending the strike to railways, oil, power stations etc. This they equally opposed. They then passed a resolution urging him to negotiate again on my formula. The meeting lasted 5 hours and was very stormy. This is really very good.

6 June

Meeting of Ministers at 10. There seems some more hope about the docks. Nothing on 'bus' strike. We made all the plans for troops if power stations and oil men come out, but no one expects this to happen this week-end. I do <u>not</u> want to use troops in the docks if we can manage without, for this inevitably means spreading the strike to all other ports . . . .

Politically, the 'bus' strike etc should do us no harm. But much depends on the 5 by-elections now going on. Voting is next Thursday in all. If we can hold 3 which are our seats all will be well. If not, it will be a great blow, and might force me to an earlier election than I would like.

We left London Airport at midnight, in a Britannia . . . .

7 June

We had to turn back after about 2 hours flight, owing to a faulty oil valve in one of the engines. We got back to London airport, on 3 engines. There was then some consultation – fortunately we were able to have the defect repaired . . . .

We arrived at Washington about 11.30. Foster Dulles was there to meet us, as well as Harold Caccia and his wife. Almost immediately on arrival we got down to work – there was a lot to be done to prepare an agenda etc. Sir E Plowden arrived for talks about the proposed agreement to be made in pursuance of the amended McMahon Act. There is every hope now that Congress will pass the Act by the end of July[54] . . . . Dinner with Foster Dulles – a small party; Mrs Dulles (Janet) Mr and Mrs Herter; the Caccias; the Vice President (Nixon) and his wife and ourselves. We had an excellent dinner (as regards food and drink) and I had hoped that we could have some good and useful talk afterwards. Chris Herter (under Sec of State) is a particularly interesting and thoughtful man. But both at the dinner and afterwards – when the ladies had left – the Vice President poured out a monologue which extinguished any spark of conversation from whatever quarter it might arise. This spate of banalities lasted for 3 to 4 hours. We withdrew – battered and exhausted, about midnight. Janet Dulles kept her head better than most of us. Whenever the Vice President had a pause for breath (every twenty minutes or so) she said to the company in general 'When we were in Saigon we had birds nest soup'. But even this failed to stop Nixon for more than a moment . . . .

---

54. The agreement, signed on 3 July, permitted the exchange of classified information. It was extended in July 1959 to also permit purchases and exchange of fissile and thermonuclear material.

8 June (Sunday)

. . . . Harold Caccia and I, with Bishop and Zulueta, left Washington in the Britannia about 11.30 and reached Indianapolis airport about 1pm. There we were met by various dignitaries – including the Governor and the Mayor, as well [as] by Mr Pulliam, the owner of the *Indianapolis Star* and other newspapers. All the route, about 30 to 40 miles, was lined with people, who gave me a tremendous welcome. There were banners with 'Welcome Mac' or 'Welcome Home' across the streets in the villages. It was really most touching . . . . At President Humbert's house[55] were assembled all the Faculty of the University of DePauw. Finally, about 3.45, we left in an open car for the stadium. A large crowd was gathered in the streets; and in the stadium was about 6000–7000. After the playing of the National Anthem etc, the 'Commencement Exercises' began. This meant the conferring of degrees on some 400 'graduating' young men and women and of some MAs and doctorates on a few more advanced worthies. Finally, punctually at 5.30 began a ceremony which was on a more or less nationwide TV hook-up. (It [is] said that at least 20 million people will have seen it – perhaps 40–50 million!) The Dean read the citation and Dr Humbert introduced me and conferred the degree. My speech began at 5.35 and had to end at 5.59 precisely.[56] We had taken a lot of trouble about the content – and also about the length. The speech ended at 5.59 – just in time. It was well received by the local audience. But of course, all depends on its effect upon the larger audience – the whole American people – to whom it was addressed . . . .

We drove back from Greencastle to Indianapolis, arriving at the Marriot Hotel about 7.30. Mr Pulliam gave a dinner to about 30 guests – mostly 'publishers' and editors of local and neighbouring newspapers . . . . It was a pretty good collection of those who both make and reflect Middle Western opinion. After dinner, they asked questions for nearly an hour. I am bound to say that I was amazed at the change in the 'isolationist' Middle West since the old days. Moreover, where they are changed, they will stay changed. For they are folk who are fixed in their ideas. Mr Pulliam gave me a beautifully framed

---

55. Russell Jay Humbert was president of DePauw University 1951–62.

56. Eisenhower had invited Macmillan to give the Commencement address the previous June. Apparently Macmillan's maternal grandfather had been amongst the first graduates of the DePauw medical school.

portrait of my mother (an old photograph, really) which had been
found somewhere . . . .

9 June
We flew back to Washington, arriving in time for luncheon . . . . At
3pm we were received by the President at the White House . . . .
Among other things, the President and I initialled an agreement about
the use of Bombs or War-heads under <u>joint</u> control. So far as the bases
are concerned, wh the Americans have in England, this regular agreement replaces the loose arrangement made by Attlee and confirmed by
Churchill[57] . . . .

10 June
Left White House with President Eisenhower at 10.20am. We travelled
by helicopter, arriving at Baltimore at about 10.45. There we drove in
an open car to the 'Campus' of Johns Hopkins University . . . . The
President and I were received by the President of the University, Dr
Milton Eisenhower (brother to Ike)

After the usual ceremonies, in the course of wh both Ike and I were
given Hon degrees of Doctor, speeches were made. Both the Eisenhow-
ers said very nice things about me. My speech was shorter than the
DePauw one – about 15 minutes – but on the same general theme. In
spite of the anxieties of the British Treasury, I think it's as well to go
on 'plugging' the same point. 'Economic interdependence is every bit
as necessary as military'.

. . . . At 3pm we went to the State Dept for a further spell of
discussion. This time it was interdependence in fields <u>other</u> than
military – i.e. economic and propaganda.[58] Mr Anderson (U.S. Treas-

---

57. This document extended to the air forces the 22 February joint agreement.
58. On 1 June 1958 Macmillan had written to Eisenhower arguing 'I think that
    you and Foster [Dulles] have always consistently felt that our military defences,
    however strong, against communism would never be sufficient by themselves.
    Indeed, the more the communists see that they will not get anywhere by
    military aggression, the more they will turn to other methods – diplomatic
    pressure, subversion and of course economic infiltration. We cannot altogether
    complain about the last. Indeed, it should be the field in which we would want
    to meet, and defeat, the communist challenge. Believing in the virtues of the
    democratic way of life, we ought to be able to show the rest of the world,
    including in the end the communist countries themselves, that democracy can
    give the best results' (G&E, pp. 148–9).

ury) was interesting, genial, well-briefed, but not inspiring. He succeeded George Humphrey, and has (I fear) succeeded to some of H's
rather conventional ideas. But the movement will be too much for him.
American public opinion is moving towards my conceptions. Even the
Middle West, once so anti-British and isolationist, is changing. After a
good session with Anderson and his assistants, where Doug Dillon was
very helpful, we changed to Allen Dulles and his team. I think we
made some progress here towards coordination of Anglo-American
effort in propaganda and counter-subversion.

11 June

. . . . [Foster] Dulles put forward some very far-reaching ideas about
the future, on wh we must really do some work and have another
meeting to discuss. What he wants to work towards is a unified system
of government for the Free World. Both he and the President feel that,
while this sense of unity and understanding exists between us, we
should try to create something definite to leave to our successors.

We left Washington airport at 5pm. Dulles and many others came
to see us off. 7pm. Arrived Uplands RCAF station, Ottawa . . . .

13 June

At 10am, I was received in the [Canadian] HofC, which was full.
Senators attended. The Speaker of the Senate made a short introductory speech, followed by the P.M. I spoke for 25 minutes. The speech,
which was partly in French, was very well received . . . .

14 June

Arrived London Airport at 8am London time. . . . I got the news of
the 5 by-elections. These have turned out very well indeed for us – a
great change in the last few months[59] . . . .

19 June

Gaitskell, Bevan and Griffiths came (at their request) to see the F.S.
and me about Lebanon. Bevan was more robust than the others. I
refused to give any pledge that we would not intervene in any

---

59. On 12 June there were by-elections in Argyll, Ealing South, Weston-super-
    Mare, and Labour-held St Helens and Wigan. Despite a swing away from them
    the Tories comfortably held the three seats they were defending.

circumstances. (They really accepted that such a <u>public</u> pledge would be a fatal encouragement to Nasser and his party in Lebanon) . . . .

The Bus strike is over – but I fear that Sir John Elliot (alias Blumenfeld) has almost given away the fruits of victory by a most foolish statement. I had to mobilise the Chancellor of the Exr and the Minister of Transport to bring pressure on General Robertson. The whole strike has been about the arbitration award, which was based on a <u>differential</u> rate between central and outside bus drivers. If Sir J E gives (say) up to 4/6, (against 8/6 now agreed for Central men) we can get away with it. If he gives 5/- or 6/6 or 7/6, we might as well have <u>not</u> had the strike – with its inconveniences and financial losses – and given in 6 weeks ago . . . .

23 June

Edward Beddington-Behrens gave a large luncheon at Claridges in aid of the movement for European Free Trade. Harold Drayton was in the chair,[60] and a lot of leading figures in finance and industry were present. By a curious chance, I went straight from the luncheon to a meeting of ministers to discuss what (if anything) can be done to save the European Free Trade area project, which is being strangled to death by the French. Maudling, who is going to Bonn tomorrow, was authorised to tell the Germans that we were almost at the end of our patience. But if this fails, it means (in my view) the end of much more than trade cooperation in Europe. I don't see how NATO could survive.

. . . . 7.30 dinner given by Alderman Black MP – a leading Free Churchman[61] – to which came about 30 deacons, ministers, elders etc of the Methodists, Baptists, Congregationalists, Presbyterians etc. I talked about 1) Russia and the Summit talks 2) the H Bomb and disarmament 3) U.N.O. On the whole (for I was very frank) I think the meeting did good. There was an hour or more of discussion afterwards – wh was useful . . . .

24 June

The row about defence reorganisation gets worse and worse. The

---

60. The chairman of United Newspapers, Drayton was treasurer of the UK Council of the European Movement.

61. Cyril Black, Conservative MP for Wimbledon 1950–70, was a Baptist and a leading temperance advocate.

Chiefs of Staff are divided into two groups and the Service Ministers are angry with the Minister of Defence. The real truth is that Duncan Sandys, altho' an able and efficient minister, is disagreeable and *cassant* in relations with other ministers or officials. When you get to know him well, you begin to like him. But he is obstinate and fatiguing to deal with. I think he must have German blood . . . .

26 June

Cyprus debate. This went off very well, partly due to the efforts of Sir Hugh Foot with the opposition leaders. After much dispute amongst themselves, the Socialist 'Shadow Cabinet' decided not to have a division. But when this was put to the Party this morning, there was much argument. In the end, the majority agreed not to vote.

Callaghan, who spoke after Alan Lennox-Boyd, performed his task with great skill. Bevan, who wound up before me, with such obvious dislike of being sensible and moderate that it amused everybody, including himself [sic]. Actually, the decision of the Opposition has great importance. For it must have persuaded the Greeks that, even if the Socialists win the next General Election here, they will be no nearer to *Enosis*.[62] Bevan in particular made it clear that by 'self-determination' they did not mean the imposition of majority rule on the minority . . . .

29 June (Sunday)

We left London Airport at 3.45 for Paris. The party consisted of the Foreign Secy; Sir W Hayter; Sir A Rumbold; Mr Con O'Neill; P de Zulueta; John Wyndham; Maurice Macmillan etc.

On arrival at Orly we were met by General de Gaulle. There was a guard of honour; a band; and a very large crowd. The General – whom I had not seen for many years – was all affability and charm – quite remarkable. I made a little speech in French (which seemed to please him) He was accompanied by Couve de Murville (his Foreign Minister) Joxe, and ambassador Chauvel. It was a beautiful Sunday afternoon – and a very large crowd was out the whole way from Orly to Paris. They all seemed very relaxed and in a most friendly mood. I drove with the ambassador (Jebb) and the F.S. in the next car behind. I have never seen a French crowd cheer in such a friendly way. (The last time I was in Paris we were not at all well received. It was when poor M. Gaillard was P.M. and we had supplied arms to Tunis)

---

62. Union with Greece.

At first I thought that all this was laid on by order – then that it was all for the General. The latter was partly true, except that he was not in our procession. I think really it was a sign of the popular feeling of hope. At the moment, everyone is confident that the General's policy will succeed. No one knows what it will be – all the same it commands general confidence . . . .

30 June

. . . . It was astonishing to me to see de Gaulle in his present mood. He has, of course, aged a lot. He has grown rather fat; his eyes are bad and he wears thick spectacles; he no longer smokes chains of cigarettes (indeed, he does not smoke at all) His manner is calm, affable, and rather paternal. But underneath this new exterior, I shd judge that he is just as obstinate as ever. I spoke very strongly to him about the Free Trade area, and the fatal political results wh wd follow the present French attitude. But he clearly was neither interested nor impressed . . . . His present view is that France is rich, if confidence can be restored (That also is true) His motto is '*L'intendance suit toujours*'.[63] I am very apprehensive about European Free Trade, for M. Pinay (who de Gaulle has made Minister of Finance) is a small man, with a small mind, and completely dominated by the French *patronat*.[64] As regards the new French constitution, this has been entrusted to Mollet. De Gaulle says that the plebiscite will be held on it on Sept 30 or Oct 1st. No one seems (including D.G. or M) to know what it will be – but it will no doubt try to create a greater stability for governments – perhaps by placing the power of dissolution in the hands of the P.M. and/or by giving greater power to the President. Many people think that de G will then go himself to the Elysée.[65]

De G told me that all French citizens will take part in the plebiscite – including Algerians. Then Algerian deputies will be elected – some by separate, some by common voting lists. When they have been duly elected, he will deal with them – he will offer integration, autonomy, or any other plan. He will put the burden of choice on them. If they choose integration, it will be expensive for France in the short term,

---

63. Variations on this enigmatic comment recur in de Gaulle's discourse and broadly indicate his view that material considerations are always subordinate to political ones.
64. The business community.
65. The presidential palace.

but the great potential wealth of the Sahara will make it bearable in the long run.

.... We left Orly at 5.30.

1 July

.... After P.Q.s (wh were not very difficult today) I saw Gaitskell. After all the Socialist protestations regarding 'Life Peers'[66] – they would never touch it etc etc he had produced 5 or 6 nominations! ....

4 July

.... At 5pm I had Reggie Maudling (Paymaster) who had just returned from Paris. He could make no progress at all with his European Free Trade negotiations. Pinay is hostile; Couve de Murville is waiting on de Gaulle's decision. I fear it looks as if the whole of this great effort will break down, foiled by the selfishness and insularity of the French ....

6 July

.... At 9.15[pm], meeting with SofS Colonies; Governor Luce of Aden; and various officials. Emergency action has [had] to be taken in Lahj (one of the largest of the Aden Protectorates) The young Sultan has gone over to Nasser (as we know from secret sources) and some of his people have already crossed into Yemen. He will have to be deposed.[67] The other sultans or chieftains appear to be loyal.

13 July (Sunday)

This has been a very hard week, and I got down to B.G. yesterday tired out. Apart from the usual luncheons and dinners, wh seem to crowd this part of the year .... there have been three major issues within the Cabinet. After many weeks (or months) of argument, the defence reorganisation question was brought to a head by me. I told the Service Ministers and the Staffs that I wd now write my own paper and let the Cabinet decide .... Lord Selkirk (First Lord) has been good – but he disagrees with the First Sea Lord (Mountbatten). CIGS (Gerald Templer) is charming but difficult. Christopher Soames (a very young SofS) is (like all young ministers) too anxious to defend his ministry and its powers at all costs. Geordie Ward is delightful in every

---

66. Introduced by the Life Peerages Act passed in April.
67. See footnote 39.

way, and torn between loyalty to C.A.S. and to me. There was a long and fruitless discussion on Thursday. I worked with Norman Brook on amendments to White Paper (including a preface) and these were finally agreed at a long Cabinet on Friday. Some ministers thought I could have made a statement and done without a White Paper. But I objected to this with the argument that even St Athanasius couldn't have answered supplementaries 'off the cuff' without an agreed text. Really, this argument was almost theological, when we got to the relations between the Chiefs of Staff. There was even a sort of 'filioque' clause, about the responsibilities of Service Ministers[68] . . . .

The other large question which has worried us all has been going on for months – pensions. The present Old Age Pensions scheme is approaching bankruptcy. The Socialists have put out a plan (Crossman's) – attractive but unsound. What are we to do? We have had a number of plans, but no decision. I have kept it in play because the Cabinet was deeply divided on the question of 'contracting out', to take care of existing schemes (which are said to cover some 8 million workers altogether) At last a 'compromise' scheme has been produced and everyone has agreed.[69]

The third point of controversy has been about Lancashire Cotton. The President of the Board (Eccles) and the Colonial Secy (Lennox-Boyd) have ceased to be on speaking terms – they are only on bawling terms. Indian and Pakistan Cotton industries have made a voluntary limitation agreement, subject to Hong Kong. But H-K is shy; and SofS, quite rightly, takes the line that, as trustee for colonial interests, he cannot press H.K. unduly. He cannot order. Yes, but can he suggest? On this, another metaphysical argument has been carried on with violence between the two ministers. I did not take this to Cabinet, because all of them are against the Col Secy, and he might easily resign. I cannot lose him, for he is a fine man, with noble qualities. Finally, they agreed to my settling the matter – which I did. I hope that on the

---

68. This attempt to encapsulate the doctrine of the Trinity was probably not in fact written by the fourth-century St Athanasius. The 'filioque' clause, which ostensibly lay at the root of the schism between the Eastern and Western churches in 1054, relates to whether the Holy Spirit proceeds from the Father *and* the Son (Western Church), or not.

69. The compromise simply involved the Treasury conceding that members of existing occupational pensions could contract out of its graduated scheme agreed the previous August.

basis wh I settled, Ld Rochdale and his colleagues will go to Hong Kong and get at least a temporary agreement. This cotton problem is really a terrible one. Free entry is part of the whole 'Ottawan' system.[70] If we go against it, the whole structure will collapse . . . .

14 July[71]
. . . . For[eign] Sec[retary] rang me up to say that there had been a revolutionary 'coup' in Baghdad – that the King, Crown Prince and Nuri Pasha had been murdered . . . .

A luncheon party for Prince Da[o]ud – Prime Minister of Afghanistan[72] – was not particularly well timed! However, the PM was very pleasant – talked good French and left early.

The publication of the White Paper on Defence no longer seemed to present great difficulties! So easily does a larger trouble obscure a smaller one.

I saw Gaitskell at 5.30 at HofC, and gave him what news I had about Iraq. Meanwhile, President Chamoun (Lebanon) has asked for help and addressed his request to Britain, U.S. and France. I called a full Cabinet in the late afternoon (6pm) and there was a long discussion. The general feeling was uncertainty as to what the American policy really would be. Nothing cd be more fatal than for the Americans to go to the Lebanon and rest content with that or soon retire in favour of a UN force. We had to carry, on our economy, all the evil effects that might follow – in Iraq, Syria, and the Gulf. Our sterling oil might dry up and what real guarantee had we from U.S.?[73] . . . .

I went with Alan Lennox-Boyd and Chief Whip to dine at Bucks.[74] On getting back (10.45 our time) a long conversation with President

---

70. The system of preferential tariffs between Commonwealth markets introduced at the 1932 Ottawa conference. A three-year agreement with India, Pakistan and Hong Kong was finally announced on 30 September 1959, just in time for the general election.

71. This and the following few entries were all written up on 20 July.

72. Prime Minister 1953–63 and, after overthrowing his cousin King Zahir, President from 1973 until his assassination in 1978.

73. Most oil from the Middle East, except that from Saudi Arabia, was denominated in sterling. This gave Britain financial benefits, for otherwise dollars would have to be used to buy oil.

74. Bucks was one of the three London gentlemen's clubs to which Macmillan belonged. The others were the Carlton (closely associated with the Conservative Party) and the Beefsteak.

Eisenhower . . . . It soon became clear that the Americans had taken the decision, and the fleet was approaching Beirut. I said 'You are doing a Suez on me', at wh President laughed. The conversation became almost impossible to carry on with an open line . . . .

15 July
Cabinet. I read my telegrams to President Eisenhower, and gave an account of the conversations. After much debate, there was unanimous support for giving U.S. our 'moral support'. Chancellor of Exr was, with a good deal of heart-searching, quite firm on this. He felt (as did many others) that on this the Americans are on good legal grounds, both of the U. Nations Charter and by the ordinary rules of international law . . . .

16 July
. . . . The debate was opened by Selwyn [Lloyd], in an excellent speech – short, objective and well expressed. It was very well received. Bevan followed with a weak speech. Gaitskell wound up for the Opposition, and I for the Government. There was no vote. The whole atmosphere, tho' charged, was different to Suez. Apart from it being merely a matter of moral support to an American 'intervention', the Opposition made little attempt to challenge the legality of the decision. It was a matter of its wisdom. Of course, they kept trying to extract promises that British troops would not be used. But I avoided, or evaded, this. It seems that there was a tremendous dispute in the 'Shadow Cabinet' and in the Labour Party meeting about voting. Gaitskell (who is clearly trying to 'live down' his Suez performance, seems to have carried the day against Bevan . . . . I think my 'wind-up' speech was well received in all parts of the House. I tried to argue the case very objectively and to keep the temperature as low as possible. D was in the Gallery. As I went to my room (behind the Speaker's chair) where D was to meet me, Bishop gave me a telegram from Amman – it had just arrived – it was written out in long-hand – not typed yet. It was soon followed by another. One was a message from the King, sent through our ambassador; the second, a further plea, still stronger and more poignant from almost the last survivor of the Hashemite family.

I called the Cabinet; the Service Ministers and the Chiefs of Staff. (Foreign Secy and Chief of Defence Staff had already left for Washington) All were scattered, after the debate but all were finally collected by about 11pm.

There followed a very remarkable – and perhaps historic – Cabinet meeting in my room in the House of Commons. I don't think I have ever been through anything of the kind.

The political, diplomatic, Commonwealth, United Nations, Middle East difficulties were all put over and over again by me and Ld Privy Seal. The Staffs described what could be done – and it was precious little. 2 Battalions of paratroopers to be flown in from Cyprus to Amman, to hold the airfield and give succour to the King. But militarily .... with a supply by air only if the Israelis agree to over-flying; no sea base; no real purpose or future – since we cannot attempt to invade Iraq – and even if we wanted to do so, it could not be through Amman.

I telephoned twice to Dulles during the 3 hours discussion. I made each minister express his view, without any lead from me. (I was determined not to repeat Anthony's mistake and let them say – if this venture was attempted and proved a disaster – that they had not been properly informed). As at recent Cabinets – on the Lebanon – I had the Attorney General all the time.

Dulles thought it rash but praiseworthy. He could not promise troops, but wd give moral and logistical support.

The Chancellor of the Exr was on the whole in favour of an act of 'honour', however militarily dangerous. He had no legal doubt (as at Suez) and he carried a lot of weight. The Staffs were 'for', but on political not military grounds. I kept asking them questions to test the difficulties. The Foreign Office .... seemed quite sure that the Israeli consent would be forthcoming. Sir D[erick] H[oyer] M[illar] had seen the ambassador. It would be almost a matter of force. (This proved to be a disastrous judgment) Finally, I asked for 10 minutes by myself. I went with Rab and Norman Brook into another room, and tried to make my decision. We all thought the Cabinet were determined to do this rather 'quixotic' act and that we wd not forgive ourselves if the King were murdered tomorrow, like the Royal Family of Iraq. Moreover, the Arab world (on the Gulf etc) might be more moved by our inaction than by some reaction to the loss of all our friends in Iraq.

I came back into my room – where all were assembled – I tried to sum it all up again – pro and con. Then I went round the room. All were 'for'. So I said 'So be it'. The Cabinet dispersed about 3am.

.... Norman Brook undertook to coordinate the work. In fact, he did not go to bed at all that night. I got to bed about 3.30am, having been assured that everything would be done that needed to be done.

17 July
One thing – alas – had <u>not</u> been done – or too lightly done, with too much taken for granted. This mistake – wh I am convinced would never have happened if For Secy had not been away in Washington – nearly led to a terrible disaster, wh wd (I think) have resulted in the collapse of all our policies and the fall of the Govt.

I was woken up at 8 – and told that a) we had started the flight from <u>Cyprus</u>, <u>over</u> Israel, <u>without</u> obtaining the permission of the Israeli Govt. Some machines (with about 200 men) had gone into Amman. Then the order was given to stop and other machines had to go back. At 10am Gaitskell was coming – fortunately he put this off himself till 1. We had tried telephoning (poor Norman Brook spent 3 hours trying to get through) We had tried telegrams. But nothing seemed to get through and certainly nothing came back.

Cabinet at 11. I told them only a little of the difficulties, and then left Rab to carry on the routine business . . . .

What was I to say in the House? I must announce the facts at least, at 3.30. But what were the facts? No one seemed to know. I waited throughout the morning in my study – trying to deal with other work and hide my sickening anxiety. All we knew was that the Israeli Govt was still sitting. Brook (who thought it was his fault) was almost in tears. F Bishop and the other P.S.s were very kind and sympathetic.

Gaitskell came at 1pm – alone. I was just beginning to tell him about the political situation in Amman . . . . when a small bit of paper was brought to me. 'The Israeli Govt has agreed'. Altho' I was not sure whether this meant agreed to flying in 2 battalions as a once for all action or 'agreed to their daily supply by air over Israel' (a matter to cause great trouble and anxiety later) Nevertheless here was immediate relief. I told G what we had done (trying to look as calm as possible) and asked how he would like it handled. Perhaps he and his two friends (Griffiths and Bevan) could come at 2.45 and we could agree how to handle it in Parliament. This was agreed. I said that I thought the debate cd be arranged as the Opposition preferred. Perh other business (it was a Supply day)[75] could stop at 7pm, and we could then debate these events.

No lunch – an encouraging call from Anthony Eden – composing the statement. Can we conceal or obscure the trouble with over-flying?

---

75. One of the days in the parliamentary calendar allotted to the Opposition to choose the subject for debate.

Prob[ably] in the first statement, at all events. Ted Heath (Chief Whip) very wisely suggested that we should <u>offer</u> the adjournment at 7pm. This avoids the 'motion' under the Standing Order, with all the Opposition standing up in support – a dramatic gesture wh we shd be able to avoid. When G and his friends came, I suggested this. A short statement; not too many supplementaries; a debate at 7. This was accepted. So it was my job to make a statement at 3.30, an opening speech at 7pm, and a 'wind up' at 9.45pm.

More by good luck than good management, it all turned out pretty well – from the Parliamentary angle. G was quite good, and very restrained, following me. Bevan, who had asked for 35 minutes, sat down after 20 minutes, having completely lost the House and a large part of his reputation. The Opposition, having decided <u>not</u> to vote yesterday – on the American intervention in the Lebanon – very unwisely decided to vote today. My last words at 9.58 were 'I ask myself this question. If it was not right to vote against America yesterday, why is it right to vote against Britain today'

This thrilled the House and in particular our side. It was the only 'partisan' thing I have allowed myself throughout the crisis. But it is a phrase which will stick. We got a majority of 62 in the division – Liberals <u>against</u> us; some Labour (notably G Brown) <u>abstained</u>. All the Conservatives (and some Labour) stood up in my honour as I walked out of the House – under the clock – into the members lobby. It was really a great tribute.

Back to No 10 – more telegrams, meetings and troubles. But, anyway, I feel the House of Commons is in a good mood. There is none of the rancour of Suez. I tried (and I think) succeeded in making them feel how difficult and balanced was the decision wh we had to take. In the country generally I think there will be a sense of the gravity of the situation – but I hope also a sense of unity.

18 July

<u>Defence Ctee</u> (including Service Ministers) at 11am. We have much to decide. The Gulf is very uncertain – but we have plans for Bahrein and Kuwait, in case of need. But there is the usual dilemma. Shall we go in now? If so, it is 'aggression'. Shall we wait? If so, we may be too late.

Kuwait, with its massive oil production, is the key to the economic life of Britain – and of Europe. The 'ruler' is an enigmatic figure. He is in Damascus 'on holiday'. Will he return? He has seen Nasser. Has he sold out to Nasser? No one knows. We have <u>no</u> troops at all in Kuwait. So we might lose the airfield, wh means fighting yr way in. Can we get the ruler to ask for a battalion or a ship now? All these questions are asked, but not resolved.

Sultan of Muscat called at 12.30 – for a courtesy call. We have at least concluded our agreement with him, including even the cession of Gwadar to Pakistan.[76]

Chancellor and M of Defence – talk at 4.30 on defence estimates for next year. This was useful – for we must keep on at our normal work and not allow the 'crisis' to absorb us and our energies. Meetings continued most of the evening.

Ben-Gurion and the Israeli Govt have turned difficult again. They are trying to withdraw their permission for overflying, on the plea that they did not understand it to include daily supply – 10 machines or so each day. However, I doubt if they will press it to an issue at once . . . .

20 July (Sunday)
I heard last night of Mr Krushchev's 'panic' appeal for an immediate summit meeting. This will need careful handling . . . .

21 July
The *Mirror*, *Herald*, etc have lost their heads, screaming for immediate acceptance of Mr K's threatening demand for a meeting on Tuesday! . . . .

I have told the Chiefs of Staff that we <u>must</u> open the sea route to Aqaba and an LofC from Aqaba to Amman. It is not impossible in spite of their protestations. Now that Dickson is back, we shall get something done. The Israelis are getting very troublesome. Ben-Gurion (under pressure from his [coalition] Cabinet) has written me a letter of protest. I have tried a 'soft answer'. The truth is that an extreme party in Israel think that Jordan had better 'collapse' and that they can then seize all territory up to the West Bank. Others are frightened by the Soviets, or sympathetic to them. I am trying to get logistic aid from [the] Americans – both for oil supplies for Jordan and for our own troops . . . .

22 July
Cabinet at 11. I explained to them the plan wh Dulles has suggested

---

76. Gwadar was a small Omani enclave on the coast of Baluchistan.

to For Secy. Let there be a so-called Summit meeting – but let it be held in U.N., in New York, and under Article 28 (to which, fortunately, Arthur Henderson specially drew my attention yesterday in the House) this article allows special meetings of the Security Council to be attended by Heads of Governments.

In addition, of course, there could be <u>informal</u> meetings, wh wd amount to a sort of private summit 'on the side' and without anything like the publicity. The Cabinet liked this idea very much. I therefore got hold of Gaitskell and suggested that the For Secy might open the debate, to outline our plan. This was agreed.

F.S. made another excellent speech. Bevan followed in a rambling, meditative and quite harmless speech – taken from an article in last week's *Observer*. Foreign affairs debate droned quietly on until 10. No division!

The Israelis are protesting, but not stopping our airlift. We are working hard at trying to open up a proper line of communications. Without this, Jordan will just wither away . . . .

27 July (Sunday)
. . . . All yesterday I struggled (to no avail) with the French, who have now sent a reply to Moscow on quite different lines to that which we and the Americans have sent. The French don't want the Security Council concept; don't want to go to New York; but <u>do</u> want the original Russian proposal – a meeting of the 5 Heads of Govt (India included) at Geneva. But even that they <u>don't</u> really want very much and only at leisure, after 'calm preparation'. On the other hand, US and UK (who have troops in Lebanon and Jordan) <u>don't</u> want delay but <u>do</u> want to press forward with some short-term solution to L[ebanon] and J[ordan] . . . . The great thing in our favour consists of the American army – 11000 strong – in Lebanon. We must <u>not</u> let the Americans take this body of men out of the country in response to some fake U.N. gesture . . . . Nasser cannot now be won over by kindness – or even money. But I still doubt whether he wants to be sold out – body and soul – to the Russians . . . .

Foster Dulles came at 11 . . . . Foster feels that the Soviet Govt is frightened. I said that I thought that they were frightened at the idea that we might be moving into Iraq. Now that they know that we are not going to do so, they will be reassured. So they will go back to propaganda . . . .

The Persian Prime Minister (Iqbal) called, with a Persian rug as an offering. This is most embarrassing. All I give him, it seems, is a picture of myself in a silver frame.

I went to meet him at London airport at 11pm. He arrived at 1am. So perhaps I deserved the rug . . . .

At 7.30 we had a 'working dinner' at 1 Carlton Gardens – 3/3 a side – of the Baghdad Pact powers (less, alas, Iraq!) . . . . Two things were clear 1) the Turks don't now intend to invade Iraq, altho' they think they can keep up a lot of pressure on the northern borders of Iraq shd the new Govt go wrong. 2) With considerable logic, Turkey – and Iran and Pakistan will agree – feels that if Iraq is not to be attacked, her new Govt shd be recognised.

28 July

Baghdad pact meeting all day. Since we are the 'host' government, I presided . . . .

. . . . [T]he critical decision was taken by Foster Dulles in the course of the early afternoon. After discussion by telephone with Washington and the President, he devised a formula by which (in effect) U.S.A. becomes a full member of the Pact, making separate arrangements with each of the countries. This the President can do without a Treaty (wh only the Senate can make) resting on the authority given him recently by Congressional resolution. Naturally this public declaration was the real highlight of a meeting otherwise darkened by failure and tragedy.

As regards Iraq, everyone wants to 'recognise' the new Govt. The Moslem powers will begin; we will follow. The future of the Pact – now much fortified by American adhesion – will not be pressed to a definite conclusion as regards Iraq. We shall not expel them; we shall wait for them to retire (wh they can legally do with 6 months notice) or to resign (without notice) This seems wise.

After the meeting (which ended about 5.30) Foster and I (with Selwyn and ambassador Whitney) went into a huddle in my room at Lancaster House about Kruschev's latest reply. With considerable skill (and much vituperation) K has fastened on the difference in substance between the French position on the one hand and the UK/US on the other. We agreed a line of reply. We shall stick to the meeting under the aegis of the Security Council, but with 'informal' talks as well. We wd prefer New York, but wd go to Geneva. Telephone talk with President Eisenhower confirmed this. It was a great help having the

Russian reply (wh came over the tapes as we were conferring) before Foster left to get his plane . . . .

29 July

. . . . At 3.30 the last stages of the Baghdad Pact meeting – in private session. Then the usual communiqué – wh everyone argues about and the public scarcely reads! We broke off in good heart, in spite of all the troubles and dangers.

The news from Jordan is not good. However, we seem to have less trouble with Israel since the Americans have been doing the 'overflying' with their logistical aid to us.

At 9.30pm M. Menderes (Turkish P.M.) with M. Zorlu . . . . came to No 10 on a secret visit. They came through the garden door, from wh also they left some 3 hours later. It was a curious talk. What it amounted to was this. Turkey now accepts, in full, the British plan for Cyprus. The Turkish Govt (which a few weeks ago was inciting riots against it, both in Cyprus and in Turkey) now regards it as fair, honourable, statesmanlike, well-balanced! But – and here is the point – it must be 'the plan, the whole plan, and nothing but the plan'. It is so beautifully constructed – say the Turks – that the slightest alteration or amendment will destroy its equilibrium and mar its symmetry. (The object, of course, is to make it quite certain that the Greeks – who want some important amendments – will reject the plan) If we, the British, will undertake to carry out the plan without amendment, the Turks will cooperate – will call off violence – and will abandon all their other claims – partition, a military base etc.

. . . . I said that we were very gratified to feel that the Turks now thought our plan a good one. We meant to go on with it and wd rely on their help. But the question of procedure must be considered. I had told Parlt (and the world) that I wd go to Athens and Ankara to try to get our plan accepted. While I understood that the Turkish acceptance was conditional on the plan remaining substantially unchanged, I must retain the right to discuss and perh[aps] accept Greek amendments. I wd then put them to the Turks . . . .

30 July

. . . . I forgot to record the sequel to last night's Turkish party . . . . The Turks, who had intended to leave at 2.30pm, stayed on and asked to see me again. To this I agreed, and they came at 9.30. But this time I made them come through the front door. As they didn't want to be known to be doing more than say 'goodbye' this ensured a reasonably short meeting. Having thought over how to treat them, it seemed the best thing was to express amazement – and some resentment – at their behaviour .... I made it clear that I should not hold them to their acceptance of the British plan _if_ (as was indeed probable) I had to ask them to consider amendments later (to meet the Greeks) They wd be absolutely and honourably free to accept or reject them. Finally, I said I thought all their attempts to put into a sort of legal form what we had agreed as gentlemen, had better be torn up – which they were. The Turks had really no alternative to accept this – wh they did as gracefully as possible ....

31 July
10.30 to 1. Cabinet. A lot of work, but very successfully completed. Final agreement on pensions, subject to some details. Agreement on the immediate injection of £30–£50 millions of Govt expenditure on Housing, Hospitals, Roads etc – with special regard to the areas where some unemployment is developing. (Nothing will be said about this – for it will be thought too little by some, too much by others. No doubt, later on, supplementary estimates will be required. At the same time, there will be certain relaxations as to the amount of deposit on Hire Purchase transactions. These will be announced in a few weeks. (In addition, the Chancellor of the Exr has told me that he hopes to be in a position to recommend ½% _off_ Bank Rate quite soon)

The Chancellor of Exr is really handling the economy with great skill. Cautious where necessary, but not afraid of bolder action. He is worth 20 Thorneycrofts!

1 August
.... At 11.15 I saw the Colonial Secy, partly to tell him about Wednesday night's Turkish comedy and partly to discuss another row wh has developed between him and the President of the Board of Trade about Hong Kong textiles. They cannot agree about the instructions to the Governor and as to how far he can be told to advise the Hong Kong manufacturers to accept the voluntary agreement. I had tried my hand at a draft myself and asked him to take it away and let me know if he agreed it. (This, an hour or two later, he did) ....

10.30pm. For Secy, M of Defence, Chief of Defence Staff, and Sir [Fre]D[erick] Hoyer Millar on Jordan. It is clear that we need another battalion – partly to strengthen our position in Amman, and partly to secure the new LofC from Aqaba. I agreed to this – rather reluctantly, for I hate committing our troops in penny packets all over the place. But there was a long argument – not resolved till midnight – as to the means of transport – by air, or by sea? We finally agreed to ask Ben-Gurion for permission to 'overfly', giving as a reason for despatching this battalion the opening of the new LofC (wh he will like) The position in Jordan is precarious and may blow up at any moment. God grant that we can avoid a disaster. But, of course, our force is too small for any real conflict – if, for instance, the Jordanian army deserts the King. Its only use is to strengthen the hand of his Govt and provide an element of stability. The danger is that it might be overwhelmed. I do not think a mob cd do this. But if the Jordanian armoured division went over to Nasser, we shd have difficulty in extricating our troops. So it is – and will be – a continual worry, until we can get a U.N. force in their place.

2 August

. . . . The Russians have sent a note to the Israelis protesting against Anglo-American violation of their air-space (They have sent a similar protest to Italy) The Israelis, partly out of fear of the Russians, but more (I think) to try to force a 'guarantee' of some kind out of UK and US govts, have ordered us to cease the air-lift at once. The Israeli Cabinet meets this morning to consider its reply to the Soviet note. Much telephoning and telegraphing to Washington and Tel Aviv went [on] during the night. We must have two objects a) to continue the air lift if at all possible b) not to let the Soviet Govt get the immense propaganda victory involved . . . .

3 August

. . . . The results are bad 1) the Israelis have insisted on the air-lift stopping tonight.[77] The Americans have agreed – so we have had to agree 2) the Americans are not anxious for us to send a cruiser from Cyprus with the troops to Aqaba, since this means going thro' Canal. They asked us to send [a] merchant ship . . . . After our final talk we decided to send the extra battalion from Aden, thus avoiding the risk of trouble in the Canal.

. . . . The news from Cyprus, in the war of terrorism, is depressing. 2 more British soldiers have been murdered . . . .

---

77. Limited overflying was in the end allowed to continue until 10 August.

4 August

.... After dinner, I got the news of EOKA's decision to declare a
truce, till August 10th. Then – if <u>provoked</u>, terrorism wd be resumed.
It seems difficult to interpret this . . . .

5 August

.... Sir Hugh Foot has made two recommendations following the new
developments in Cyprus – one wise, the other foolish. A very large
operation is going on – 2000 or more troops emplaced – following on
the arrests made some days ago. It is hoped that a number of the worst
terrorists are in the circle. No doubt Grivas and the inner circle will
contrive to escape – as they have before. But if to continue this
operation constitutes 'provocation' we must take this risk. To stop it
wd be to abdicate all authority. The Governor, and all his advisers,
take this view . . . .

The Governor's bad idea was to go at once to Athens, to see
Makarios. This wd be foolish, and we have stopped him doing so. The
reason for Grivas' [ceasefire] gesture (wh was obviously planned with
Archbp Makarios, since the Archbp made a statement 2 hours later) is
thought to be either that the trap is really closing on them, or (more
likely) that Makarios feels that the latest outrages have really begun to
alienate world opinion – esp after appeals by the 3 Prime Ministers.
We agreed (in a joint telephone conference) that . . . . I shd now offer
to go to Athens and Ankara. We are asking the views of our ambassadors in these two places and also of Sir Hugh Foot. If I were able to
make this journey, I should take the Governor with me . . . .

6 August

.... 4.30. Governor of Bank. He still wants to bring the two rates
together – perhaps this autumn, thus concentrating the whole sterling
market in London, instead of letting the transferable market be more
or less permanently transferred to Amsterdam. Of course, this is really
'convertibility' with all that is implied.[78]

---

78. Convertibility, which had proved so controversial at the start of Churchill's
    1951–55 government, had effectively been achieved by its close, though the
    process was not completed until the 27 December 1958 ratification of the
    European Monetary Agreement and the consolidation of the transferable and
    resident rates for sterling. Thereafter sterling had to trade within a single,
    narrowly defined margin (+/– 0.75%) with the dollar.

5–6.15. Israeli ambassador. Elath is a clever man, but very voluble. Of course, the Israelis want to squeeze us in view of our troubles in Jordan. They ask for a) a new guarantee b) a huge list of arms c) a sort of partnership agreement. I think we can do something, but not all that they want . . . .

I heard later that both the Greek and Turkish Prime Ministers accepted. So I shall leave tomorrow.

7 August

. . . . We took off at 2pm in an RAF Transport Command Comet, and got to Athens about 6pm, where we were met by Mr Karamanlis, (Greek Prime Minister) Sir R[oger] Allen (British ambassador) etc. We drove to the British Embassy. It has been repainted and the marks of the bullet holes – which were many – removed. Otherwise, it had not changed much since the days of the siege in 1944–5. How well I remember those extraordinary scenes! The evacuation of the front rooms; the sniper shots if one ventured into the garden; the midnight communion on Christmas Eve, 1944; the telegram (given to us immediately after the service) announcing the arrival of Churchill and Eden on Christmas Day; the abortive conference in candle-light with the Communists; the Field Marshal's serenity (Ld Alexander) the ambassador's scholarly charm (Sir Rex Leeper) and all the tragi-comedies of those months.[79] Our reception by the Greeks was cool, but correct. In spite of Cyprus (which has been worked up into a mountain) the old Anglo-Greek friendship has deep roots. Dinner at Embassy – British only. The ambassador was very pessimistic.

8 August

First meeting at 10.30 . . . . I began with a big appeal for Peace and the Seven Year period. I claimed that this was all the more necessary because of [the] state of world politics, esp in Middle East. Partnership was a fine ideal, and a noble one. Greek Prime Minister replied at considerable length, with a frank objection to partnership with Turks, who were essentially barbarians (he did not actually say this but implied it) I suggested 'cooperation', pending partnership. This discussion (which with translations was rather slow) continued till 1pm. At the end, I had got them to agree to two principles as desirable 1) end

---

79. See Harold Macmillan, *War Diaries: The Mediterranean 1943–1945* [henceforward *WD*] (London: Macmillan, 1984), pp. 601f.

of violence 2) 7 year period, with provisional solutions but without prejudice to final solution. We agreed to meet at 6pm to start on detailed discussion of [the] British plan. This seemed to me some advance. For if one wholly rejects a plan, it does not seem logical to examine the different points . . . .

At 6pm the talks were resumed . . . . It seemed that the Greeks – apart from their dislike of partnership as a principle, since this was equivalent to admitting *de jure* a Turkish 'presence' in the island, had four points. 1) 4 to 2 on the [Governor's] Council was unfair. Population wd entitle them to 4 to 1. 2) There was no joint assembly. 3) They disliked the proposals for dual nationality. 4) They hated the two governmental representatives on the Council.[80] It was not clear whether it was their presence on the Council or their presence on the island in any capacity to which they object. We did not press for clarification.

Altho' the Greeks affected to attach equal weight to these four objections, it soon became apparent that they really feel far more keenly about the Governmental representatives than about the other points. Of course, for the same reason, the Turks regard this – I am sure – as vital. It is for this that they are abandoning the [demands for a] base and territorial partition . . . .

9 August

Woke early – a hot night and a hot day coming. Wrote up diary, and thought about how to handle the last meeting, which began at 10.30. I started off with an expression of 'disappointment' that the P.M. and his colleagues had not accepted the British plan, or at least acquiesced in it. They had rejected [the] Radcliffe plan two years ago;[81] now they wished devoutly that they had not done so. For the Turks had accepted Ld R's constitution, wh cd by now have been in force – with a single

---

80. The new British proposals, developed since June, envisaged self-government with four Greek Cypriot and two Turkish Cypriot ministers, as well as representatives of the Greek and Turkish governments, on a Governor's Council drawn from separate Greek and Turkish Houses of Representatives. Cypriots would be able to have dual Greek, Turkish or British nationality. To try to neutralise the continuing Greek demand for *enosis* and the Turkish for partition, it was an interim proposal, initially for seven years.

81. Published on 19 December 1956, Lord Radcliffe's Plan envisaged internal autonomy in Cyprus with a legislative assembly composed of Greeks and Turks.

legislative assembly. If they rejected this new plan, or made it unwork-
able by violence and terrorism, the end wd certainly be partition in its
worst form – territorial partition, with Turkish bases etc. I felt that the
Greek Govt were not rising to the level of world events, as well as
acting contrary to their real interests. I could not understand this,
which was unworthy of them. Nor did I feel that an intransigent
attitude wd gain them world sympathy. All this was very sad for me.
As a minister in Churchill's Govt I had seen something of Greek
heroism in war, and helped them to the best of my ability in their
struggles against Communism, wh (without our aid) wd have overwhelmed them in 1944–5. The affection of the British people for the
Greek people was as strong as ever. But we had made great sacrifices
since the war. We had seen the old Empire fade away into a new
concept. Independence was over; interdependence must take its place.
Modern Greece shd set an example and not lag behind. In reply, as I
hoped and expected, Mr K[aramanlis] became quite emotional. They
hated the Turks; they had fought them for 500 years; they wd fight
them for Greek liberty whenever and wherever they could. They cd
not be humiliated by the Turks. A Turkish veto on Greek aspirations
was humiliating. Having got all this off his chest, he felt better and we
discussed very calmly the four points until lunch time. It became clear
that it was only really the point about Governmental Representatives
wh distressed them beyond bearing. Anything that might be done
about a) dual nationality – to postpone it b) unitary assembly – to
have it as an aim, wd be all to the good. The meeting closed about
1.15pm and we all went off to luncheon (Greeks included) at the
British Embassy, where the atmosphere was very friendly . . . . We left
Athens at 4.30, with usual farewells etc. The crowd was not hostile,
but not particularly friendly. Karamanlis and Averoff were personally
very charming.

   It is difficult to form a very precise impression, exc[ept] that the
Government is frightened of Makarios, frightened of Parliament, and
frightened of the rise in the Communist vote at the last (May) elections
– this partly due to Russian propaganda about 'British imperialism in
Cyprus'. So the Govt clearly cannot 'accept' the plan. But I have not
come to sign a treaty or even an agreement. Can the Greek Govt
'acquiesce' in the plan and cooperate at least to the extent that is
inherent in the plan itself. Makarios will probably persist in violent
opposition to the plan – unless, perhaps, he is attracted by the prospect
of returning to the island. The big stumbling-block is, of course, the

Governmental Representatives. But the Turks cannot abandon this, wh
is of cardinal importance for them.

We arrived at Ankara about 6.30. Here we were met by M.
Menderes (P.M.) and M. Zorlu (For Secy) The Turks had obviously
decided to make my welcome a marked contrast to that in Athens. A
band; a guard of honour; a large and applauding crowd. After the
usual ceremonies (including radio etc) I drove with P.M. the twenty
miles to the capital from the airport. In Ankara, the population was
all in the street, and applauding – occasionally by subdued cheers,
more often by clapping. Clearly, the order had gone out to give me
this friendly reception. Our ambassador, Jim Bowker, thought that
there was a mixture. The Govt's wishes for a friendly reception had
obviously gone out. A hostile demonstration could, however, be got
up more easily. He thought that in this large turn-out – wh included
middle class shopkeepers and traders – there was perh[aps] an element
of genuine friendliness.

The British Embassy here is very well situated – on the hill above
the city, about 3000 feet (the city is some 2300–2500 ft) above sea
level. It is a fine building. Unfortunately, poor Jim Bowker had shut
the Embassy, since he gives up this post (after 4 years tenure) in a few
weeks. So I stayed at the Governmental guest house (comfortable, but
rather Russian – that is showy bathrooms, but taps that don't work
etc etc) However, since there was no security in this building, I spent
most of my free time in the Embassy, wh was only a few hundred
yards away .... After dinner, wh was quite good and not too
elaborate, the first talk began. I explained to P.M. what had happened
in Athens. The Greek Government clearly accepted the two main
principles – no more terrorism and a seven year provisional settlement.
This was satisfactory. But they had raised points upon certain aspects
of the plan, wh I explained. The Turks took a very rigid position and
affected to be surprised, after our secret talks in London, that we shd
even discuss any amendments. As they had told us in London the plan
was well-conceived, well-designed, with a perfect balance and equilibrium. Not a word cd be altered without disaster. This moved me to
enquire why in that case the Turkish Govt had stimulated spontaneous
riots against it of hundreds of thousands of people throughout the
length and breadth of Turkey. The Turks, who have no shame, were
not at all put out by this retort .... [and] (through Zorlu, who is one
of the stupidest – except for a low cunning – rudest, and most *cassant*
men I have ever met) still maintained their admiration of the perfect

harmony of our plan. In a word, they wanted 'the Bill, the whole Bill, and nothing but the Bill'[82] . . . .

10 August (Sunday)

Meeting at 10.30. The Turks were very rude, and accused us of bad faith. I was rude back, and they withdrew, rather sullenly, but replied by saying that they wd not even consider any amendments emanating from the Greeks or calculated to help them. They cd not tolerate a Greek veto! I kept appealing for at least some discussion of these points – but they refused. On the contrary, while the Turks wd accept the plan as it stood, any amendments wd lead them to propose amendments of their own. On this, the meeting ended – at my suggestion – at about noon . . . .

Meeting at 4.30. After discussion with all my own advisers, I told the Turks that we intended to implement our policy, and we hoped that it would be in a form with which – as each stage developed – they would be able to cooperate. There was really nothing more to be said. They agreed and the meeting hardly took an hour . . . .

11 August

We left Ankara airport at 12 noon. Once more, a very friendly drive thro' the city, and a band and guard of honour on the air-field . . . . Menderes and Zorlu were at the airport to see me off. Everything was most friendly – but again I felt it all rather Russian. You do not get much sense of heart or feeling behind these smiling faces and pleasant gestures . . . . Everything is black and white – there is no such colour as grey. You are friend or enemy; if you are friend, you must want to destroy the enemies of your friend. If you don't do this, whenever you can, you are no friend.

We arrived at Nicosia airport just after 1pm and drove to Govt House. Very few people had been told – for security reasons – of my plan to come to Cyprus, altho' I had determined to do so before we left London . . . .

3pm. Took off in 2 helicopters. Foot and I in one; Freddy Bishop and Philip de Zulueta in the other. We flew over the hills which lie south of Nicosia, over Episcopi, to Akritiri . . . . I went round the great

---

82. A popular cry during the Reform Bill controversies in 1831–32, this phrase seems to have been first used in the *Spectator* on 12 March 1831 and rapidly passed into the political and cultural lexicon.

air base, and talked to a number of officers and went into various messes. We also drove (in a jeep) round the married quarters. I was quickly recognised, and everyone seemed very pleased to see me. Morale was clearly high. Off again by helicopter to a village called Lyssa, in the Limassol area. Here we landed in the square outside the church. An operation was going on. A cordon of troops (3rd Bn Grenadier Guards and a company [of] Royal Scots Fusiliers) had been put round the village some days ago and was still maintained. The population were confined to their houses, and only allowed out at stated times for stated purposes. A search of every house and of the church had revealed a lot of arms, including 20–30 bombs. One haystack (wh was a cache) for some reason blew up, much to the delight of the troops. 6 very dangerous men were arrested.

The Bn was commanded by Col Britten – son of Charles Britten who was in the 4th Bn with me at Loos (in 1915) The officers, NCOs and men were scrupulously clean, and looked in splendid shape. One company was paraded in the school-room for my benefit (they being in reserve and not actually in the cordon) and I spoke a few words to them. I found all this very moving and I almost broke down in speaking, for it all recalled so many memories . . . .

After this I saw the Mayor of Nicosia (Dervis) and the Mayor of Kyrenia (Demetriades) Mr Dervis (not an unattractive character, something between Mr [Glenvil] Hall M.P. and Mr Harold Davies M.P.)[83] talked for 40 minutes without drawing breath. He gave the history since the British occupation and made rather a good case against our chops and changes of policy. The rest was a diatribe against the Turks, the Police, and this man Foot (who was proving nothing but a fraud) Then we had the leaders of the Turkish community – Dr Kutchuk (the very opposite to Dervis – for he could scarcely speak, and then only in Turkish and in a hoarse whisper) and Mr Denktash – his deputy, a very able and voluble lawyer. They said almost all that the Greeks had said, but the other way round. The most interesting thing was that they attacked the new British plan – so clearly the word to support it has not yet come from Ankara . . . .

. . . . From 11.30pm we worked on telegrams, 1) draft British statement 2) draft telegrams to Athens 3) to Ankara. These were on the assumption that we decided to carry out the plan, with some amendments to please the Greeks and <u>one</u> to please the Turks. But this

---

83. The Labour MPs for Colne Valley and Leek.

is really the point to settle in London. Our object in working out all this tonight was to get these telegrams immediately to both Athens and Ankara, and get the ambassadors' advice. Since this took longer than we had allowed for, we put the aeroplane back ½ hour. Ultimately, we left at about 2am local time.

12 August (the glorious twelfth!)[84]

. . . . We arrived at London airport after 4½ or 5 hours flight and drove immediately to No 10. Here I found Dorothy, who had come up last night to meet me. I stayed in bed till noon, the time fixed for the first meeting. I was <u>very</u> tired, for yesterday was really a very long day.

Defence Ctee at 12. Several decisions about Jordan, Aden etc. The local command (Cyprus) want to send another battalion to Jordan but I have refused. We do not want troops to be more and more sucked into this affair. Unless some stabilisation of Jordan under U.N.O. can take place pretty quickly, we had better leave . . . . I have suggested that a few 25 pounders wd be more useful.[85]

3–6. Cabinet. About 8 members present, including Ld Chancellor, Chancellor of Exr, President of BofT, Dr Hill, Minister of Transport, Ld Home – otherwise various under-secretaries, including Ormsby-Gore (F.O.) and Ld Perth (C.O.) . . . . On the N Zealand demand either to be allowed to break or revoke the Ottawa agreement,[86] I am in daily touch with Mr Nash (New Z Prime Minister) The trouble is that they want to use 'quotas' and 'bilateral trade agreements' in the Socialist or Communist spirit. But at home public opinion will support New Zealand, however badly they behave. We are still appealing to them to wait for talks at Montreal . . . .

19 August

The *News Chronicle* published a 'Gallup Poll' which was very favourable

---

84. The start of the shooting season.

85. The following day he wrote to Sir Patrick Dean also suggesting recruiting a few Soho Greeks to interrogate Cypriot terrorists.

86. Australia had earlier finalised a downgrading of the Ottawa system in February 1957. New Zealand had been seeking similar adjustments since April 1957 and in a message on 8 August Nash had threatened to give six months' notice of termination of the Ottawa Agreement before the upcoming Commonwealth Trade and Economic Conference in Montreal. In the event the threat was withdrawn and a new trade agreement was eventually signed in August 1959.

to the Conservatives <u>and</u> to the Prime Minister. On this showing, we could win an Election now. Therefore everyone is speculating about the likelihood of an autumn election. These polls are encouraging (when they are good) and we tend to regard them as of little value (when they are bad) The truth is that the great British – and esp London and English – democracy is very fickle.

The Greek ambassador called at 11am. He was very charming and rather sad. For he clearly feels that his Govt are behaving weakly and foolishly. I went over the 4 points – the only points – wh the P.M. had made in Athens in criticism of the plan. The first . . . . was obviously unimportant. On the other three – the comprehensive popular assembly in the future; the joint nationality; and the presence of the Governmental representatives on the Governor's Council, I had met the Greek Government's wishes either in whole or in part. The ambassador brightened a little and wrote this down. But really he had little to say. He did however add that perhaps the return of Makarios to Cyprus wd be now the only way out. He said, quite frankly, that his presence in Athens made the Govt's position impossible . . . .

I was looking forward to a quiet evening, and leaving tomorrow morning for Bolton Abbey.[87] But tonight (about 10.30pm) two telegrams arrived from Selwyn wh raise the most serious questions. The Americans (led by the President, who seems determined to show his strength) want to announce abolition of nuclear tests as from Oct 1st.[88] What will be the effect a) to our programme b) on our relations with France, the Americans are too much in a hurry even to consider. I shall have to put off my journey and deal with this tomorrow. I made a first draft of a possible reply to the Americans . . . .

20 August
Sir N Brook (Cabinet Office) Sir Patrick Dean (F.O.) Sir R Powell (Ministry of Defence) and Sir E Plowden (Atomic Energy), with O'Neill (F.O.) and one or two others came at 10am. Meanwhile, another

---

87. An estate belonging to Macmillan's nephew, the 11th Duke of Devonshire, where Macmillan had regularly shot since the 1920s.

88. The Americans wanted to announce not abolition but a one-year suspension on 21 August to coincide with publication of an UN expert report on the possibilities of monitoring testing. Macmillan succeeded in getting them substantially to shift their position, including deferring the start of suspension until 31 October.

message – personal from the President – promising (if we agreed to suspension of tests on the basis of their proposed declaration) full information 'so far as law permits'. I told my advisers that I thought this message shd be answered separately and that I shd ask straight out the 64000 dollar question 'Does the law permit US to give us full information on "vulnerability" of the Bomb and on making small bombs, but with megaton power.' . . . .

21 August

. . . . The President has sent a most categorical reply, pledging himself and his Govt to give us <u>all</u> the information on nuclear weapons wh we need and declaring that the law allows him to do so . . . . The Americans have altogether changed their plan – at our suggestion – because they are not now offering to abandon tests <u>absolutely</u> but only if Russians agree to negotiate on the control system. From our point of view, I think that we can rely on the American promise, wh replaces this not altogether satisfactory 'bilateral' agreement made under the McMahon Amendment Act. This will save us both time and a great deal of money . . . .

23 August

. . . . The first of our Christmas Island tests was done today – a small kiloton 'trigger' explosion. The megaton test is timed for Sept 8th or so. The question now arises about going on with it. In principle, we can rely on the latest American understanding. In practice, it might be as well to have the knowledge wh we shall get from this test.

The Greek Govt are in great difficulties, and there are gloomy telegrams from our ambassador in Athens. The Greeks, he says, will threaten – and perhaps be compelled – to leave NATO. Or the present govt will fall and be succeeded by one of a 'neutralist' character. I rather doubt this. Meanwhile, EOKA have issued a rather strange threat – which seems to be more urging a political boycott of the British plan than a resumption of terrorism. Makarios is to go to U.N. – for the regular assembly. But I doubt if he will make much headway. The Turks have not yet replied – but I feel sure that they will ultimately accept the plan and perhaps instruct their people to play their part . . . .

25 August

. . . . A long talk with For Secy (Ld P[rivy] Seal also present) about all the problems – and they are manifold and baffling. The most important thing is to persuade the Americans to support Jordan financially (we [are] making a modest contribution) for at least a year. This is the only chance of getting our troops out and yet Jordan staying firm. If the regime were to collapse immediately after our departure it wd be a heavy blow to our prestige at home and in the M. East . . . .

28 August

. . . . Now a new trouble is developing in the Far East. The Chinese are threatening to attack the famous 'off-shore' islands about wh we used to hear so much in 1955. This puts the Americans – and to a lesser extent ourselves – in a difficult situation. If the Americans abandon the Chinese Nationalists, it will be a great blow to their prestige and may even endanger their hold on the Pescadores and on Formosa. If they help the Chinese Nationalists to repel an invasion (the islands are only a couple of miles from Amoy) they may fail, if they stick to conventional weapons. If they attack the Chinese airfields with nuclear weapons, the fat may be in the fire with a vengeance.[89] Our dilemma also is great. Our own view is that the Chinese (Communists) have an unanswerable case to the possession of these islands (we distinguish – apparently on good juridical grounds – between these and Formosa etc) Eden stated this view in 1955, and Churchill took the same line – (in private, he wrote very strongly to the President) But if we abandon the Americans – morally, I mean; they need no active support – it will be a great blow to the friendship and alliance which I have done so much to rebuild and strengthen. If we support them, the repercussions in Far East, India, and thro' the Afro-Asian group in the Middle East will be very dangerous. At home, Parliament and public opinion will be very critical of any change from our public position 3 years ago. So there we are!

29 August

. . . . On the Far East, it is said by some that Kruschev arranged all this (or agreed to it) during his recent visit to Peking. Since the Communist bloc seemed to be losing the initiative somewhat in the Middle East, the plan is to regain it in the Far East. Also, seeing that British and

---

89. After the first crisis in 1955 the Americans had fortified the islands with, amongst other armaments, howitzers capable of firing nuclear shells, hence Macmillan's anxiety about escalation after the Chinese started shelling the islands on 23 August.

1. Macmillan at work in his study at Birch Grove. US ambassador David Bruce described him thus in a despatch to Rusk of 13 December 1961: 'I am neither an intimate nor a friend of the PM. Few apparently are. His play, to use a gambling expression, is close; and his inmost thoughts are seldom open to penetration. He is a political animal, shrewd, subtle in manoeuvre, undisputed master in his Cabinet house . . . His opponents think him a cold-blooded but formidable individual. Some liken him to Disraeli, though he lacks the flamboyance . . . his clothes are sometimes compared with those of English dukes who have been accused of dressing in the cast-off garments of Irish beggars, though this does Macmillan a sartorial injustice.'

2. Macmillan on the steps of No. 10 prior to the party to mark Derick Heathcoat-Amory's retirement as Chancellor, July 1960.

3. Royal Navy divers begin the task of clearing the block ships from the Suez Canal after the 1956 Suez Crisis.

4. The new Prime Minister recording a party political broadcast in Downing Street, 17 January 1957.

5. Prelude to restoring Anglo-American nuclear cooperation: the heads of their respective countries' atomic energy commissions, Lewis L. Strauss (left) and Sir Edwin Plowden, wait to meet Macmillan at Washington airport, October 1957.

6. Macmillan launches the Bow Group's magazine, *Crossbow*, in October 1957 flanked by (left) Colin Jones, its first editor, and (right) the future Chancellor of the Exchequer (1979–83), Geoffrey Howe.

7. Carl Giles's laconic take on the transatlantic anxiety sparked by Sputnik in the *Daily Express*, 9 October 1957.

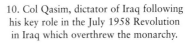

"Oh, just another little local difficulty over a mere £50 million . . ."

8. Vicky's comment on Selwyn Lloyd's efforts to get German support for the stationing costs of British troops in Germany from Ludwig Erhard in the *Daily Mirror* 14 January 1958. The caption refers to Macmillan's dismissal of Peter Thorneycroft's resignation the week before as a 'little local difficulty'.

9. British paratroopers board an aeroplane bound for Jordan during the 1958 crisis.

10. Col Qasim, dictator of Iraq following his key role in the July 1958 Revolution in Iraq which overthrew the monarchy.

11. Greek Prime Minister Konstantinos Karamanlis greets Macmillan at Athens airport in August 1958.

12. General Lauris Norstad at his desk as NATO Supreme Allied Commander Europe.

13. Turkish Foreign Minister Fatin Zorlu (left) with his Greek counterpart Evangelos Averoff in London for talks about Cyprus in February 1959.

14. Archbishop Makarios III in London for talks on the future of Cyprus in February 1959. As a result of the talks Makarios, who had been exiled by the British authorities on 9 March 1956, was allowed to make a triumphant return to the island on 1 March 1959.

15. On his trip to Moscow in February 1959 Macmillan shakes hands with Khrushchev under portraits of Marx and Lenin.

16. Macmillan outside 10 Downing Street with Rab Butler, before the Budget Cabinet on 6 April 1959.

17. The Chancellor of the Exchequer, Derick Heathcoat-Amory, holds up the despatch box as he leaves the Treasury to deliver his Budget speech, 7 April 1959.

18. The Shah of Iran, Mohammad Reza Shah Pahlavi, on his visit to London, seen here riding in state with Queen Elizabeth II on 5 May 1959.

American policy is united and firm in M. East, a wedge can be driven in over these wretched 'off-shore' islands. Another view is that the Russians do not like this at all, and are seriously alarmed of it leading to war. Nuclear war wd destroy Russia; but the Chinese are said to have reminded them blandly that it could not do much harm to China. Two or three hundred million people might be killed, but that would be tolerable and rapidly put right. Such are the divergent explanations of the experts of this new trouble wh threatens us.

31 August (Sunday)
We have had two fine days at Chequers .... Chancellor of Exr came to luncheon yesterday .... [and] said he wished to give up at the end of the Parl (whenever that might be) I said this was impossible, but he stuck to it ....

1 September
To London. Meeting of atomic experts, just returned from U.S. The talks have gone off very well. Two important facts emerged. 1) Americans are doing ten more kiloton tests before end of Oct and wd not wish us to stop before them. 2) In some respects we are as far, and even further, advanced in the act than our American friends. They thought interchange of information wd be all give. It will be a good deal of take. They are keen that we shd complete our series, esp the last megaton, the character of wh is novel and of deep interest to them. This is important, because it makes this final series complementary rather than competitive – and therefore easy to defend in Parlt ....

Cyprus. Another EOKA murder. I fear the 'truce' is ended ....

2 and 3 September
A full afternoon, followed by a dinner, and talk with Ld Mills. I think he has found an answer to the problem of the new strip-mill – S Wales or Scotland. It is worthy of Solomon. One in each country![90] ....

We discussed Middle East oil position at length. Ld M feels that we have no alternative but a rear-guard action. We shall be 'squeezed' out of the profit – the immense difference between 'access' to oil and having production, marketing etc in our own hands. If we are gradually squeezed, we cd perh[aps] stand it. If we were suddenly threatened with seizure, we shd have to fight for it ....

---

90. A costly decision, and neither Llanwern nor Ravenscraig thrived.

5 September

.... Foster Dulles has sent (at request of President and in his name, more or less) a most important message. It makes it clear that the President and the administration hope, by a tough line on Formosa and the islands, to <u>stop</u> the threatened invasion. But it may turn into a blockade, and this is the purpose of the 12 mile territorial waters claim announced today by Peking (incidentally, if this were enforced, Hong Kong also wd be untenable) If the Nationalist Chinese cannot deal with the blockade themselves, U.S. will help. This may or may not lead to direct Chinese–American attacks on each other. But the 'Red' Chinese may attack Quemoy etc by air. In this case (they have <u>not</u> so far done any air bombing – only gun-fire) the Americans can only reply by attacks on the 'Red' Chinese airfields on the mainland. To be effective, this will prob[ably] have to be with nuclear weapons, (kiloton capacity) This may lead Russia to join in. We shall thus be on the brink of world war 3. All this is very clearly set out by this message, in (for Americans) very clear, simple, and restrained language.

6 September

.... Last night there was a tropical storm all over the S of England – the most spectacular in our history, says the Press. The harvest in East Anglia and the South will now be finally ruined, I fear. What is almost worse is that the potato crop is beginning to go mouldy. We are certainly not having much luck in my period of office. When I think of all the troubles since 1956, I feel we have had almost more than our share – and now the weather.

I composed, and sent off last night without consultation with my colleagues (there were none to consult) a long reply to Foster and the President. I tried to set out, as objectively as possible, the point of view of the public in UK and in each of the Commonwealth countries. None of these will support, whole-heartedly, the U.S. position. How can we get into a) a better posture b) a posture likely to cause the Russo/Chinese to halt. a) is – on the surface – contrary to b). If the Communists really believe that America will go to war about the off-shore islands – and if they believe that U.K. and other[s] will back them up – there <u>will</u> be no war.[91] For the Russians, anyway, don't want world war 3 – not now. But if our public opinions and Parlia-

---

91. This probably explains why Chinese Premier Chou En-lai on 6 September
    offered negotiations, leading to a resolution of the crisis by early October.

ments (thank goodness, ours is <u>not</u> sitting) show hesitation or weak-ness, then Communists may feel that U.S. will not really have the nerve to 'go it alone' (I think they will be wrong) So there may well be an invasion of the islands. If U.S. goes on, there may be world war. If U.S. gives in, there will be a collapse of the anti-communist front (SEATO etc)[92] all through the Far East. This will affect M East and eventually Europe. It will be a Munich.

This is the dilemma. I put to the Americans the only idea I have. But whether it's a 'runner' I do not know. It is suggested by some words of Dulles to Lord Hood. It is this. Could we not get all the friends of U.S. to

1) Denounce any attempt to alter status quo by armed force
2) Support U.S. – and anyone else – who will take this line, pending at least action in U.N. or outside
3) Support 'demilitarisation' of islands – and perhaps a zone on mainland, for a period . . . .

Colonial Secy, Sir H Foot, John Addis (F.O.) de Zulueta (my P.S.) to dinner. We talked after dinner in the long gallery. There was general agreement on two propositions

a) We must go on with the Cyprus plan, to the best of our ability, hoping that the Cypriot Greeks will – gradually – accept the advantages of local self-govt wh the plan gives them.
b) It would – on the whole – be best to allow Makarios to return <u>after</u> Oct 1st (when Turkish representative <u>can</u> arrive and Greek could – and he would)

Whether this offer shd be made now (wh wd be best) or later, depends on the Turkish reaction . . . .

7 September (Sunday)

I went to Church with Governor Foot and read the lessons (Jeremiah xxxi and Luke vi) . . . . 6–7.30 discussion on the 'race riots' in London and the problem of West Indian immigration into U.K.[93] Sir Hugh (so lately in Jamaica) was helpful. Indians and Pakistanis have now stopped (we have 50000 inside the country) This has been quietly

---

92. A weaker analogue of NATO lacking joint command structures, the Southeast Asia Treaty Organisation was established by Dulles in 1954.

93. On 23 August there had been racial disturbances in Nottingham, and a week later fighting between white youths and West Indians broke out in Notting Hill, in West London, continuing intermittently for several weeks.

negotiated by Ld Home with the two Governments, who (for some reason) are much against their people (except students etc) coming to this country. It was decided that Home Secy, Colonial Secy, and . . . . M of Labour shd see the W Indian ministers (Manley etc) who have hurried over here . . . .

8 September

. . . . After the Cabinet had broken up, we got the early editions of the *Evening Standard*, giving a most circumstantial account of a bitter rift in the Cabinet about Makarios. This being a complete invention, and Col Secy the keenest supporter of the Governor's proposal, is really too bad. I authorised, before leaving for Chequers, a pretty full account of today's Cabinet, for 'background' use of Lobby[94] and Press.

9 September

Stayed in bed all day. I am suddenly feeling very old and tired. But I think a day's rest will do me good. I really need a complete holiday; but I see no hope of this. I may get my 12 days in Scotland, but I shall be 'in charge' – wh means anxiety over the telegrams all the time . . . .

Worked on papers. Mr K[hrushchev] has now issued a warning to the Americans – or else. I find this rather comforting. I doubt if he wd threaten war if he really meant it . . . .

11 September

. . . . I was shewn an article in the *Evening Standard* by Randolph Churchill, wh gave the appearance of an authorised interview with me, under the heading 'Mac backs Ike'. The rest of the Press have got tremendously excited, and it was necessary to issue a statement from No 10 making it clear that Randolph C had no authority to give my views on the Far Eastern problem. The trouble was that his article gave the impression that we would give military support to U.S. This is, of course, absurd. They do not want this. But they do need moral support, wh (in spite of all the complications about the islands) I intend that we should give.

---

94. The parliamentary lobby correspondents, who would be given non-attributable briefings by Macmillan's Public Relations Adviser, Harold Evans. See Harold Evans, *Downing Street Diary: The Macmillan Years 1957/63* (London: Hodder & Stoughton, 1981), pp. 47f.

12 September

The Churchill article and the statement from No 10 has made a terrible hullabaloo. It was really very tiresome of him. Actually, he came to see me on Wednesday afternoon, to get a message from me to Winston (for the golden wedding) and to shew me the wonderful 'Book of Roses' which the Churchill family (and many leading artists) are giving to Winston and Clemmie. We got chatting about Far East and Cyprus. He went off and wrote a 'feature article' – making no references to his talk with me – which would have been quite all right. Unfortunately, the Editor asked whether he had seen me. Randolph said yes – and the article appeared as an interview. The *Mirror* and the *Daily Herald* are very offensive – the rest of the Press make a lot of the story, but seemed quite 'understanding'. They all know their Randolph! However, I am <u>very</u> upset about it, for it's the first big 'gaffe' since I became P.M. and was quite unnecessary . . . .

Large luncheon party for Mr Manley (P.M. Jamaica) and other West Indian notabilities who have arrived here in connection with the so-called 'Racial Riots'. Butler and Alan [Lennox] Boyd have been dealing with them, and seem to have got on well. We can, I hope, reduce the rate of immigration <u>without</u> legislation.[95] At least, we must give this a trial . . . .

13 September

. . . . Left London Airport (in a Hermes of the Queen's Flight – lent by her kindness) at 12.45. Arrived Wick at 3.45. Dorothy met me there with her car (she has been in the North of Scotland for some days)[96] and we drove to Langwell . . . . I hope to get 10 days holiday, unless something terrible happens. We have Ann Barker and a scrambler telephone – so urgent business can be done . . . .

16 September

Gaitskell sent me a letter yesterday evening – arriving at No 10 at about 8pm – asking a lot of questions about our policy in Far East and our relations with U.S. Govt. It was a 'governessy' sort of letter, written after a meeting of the Labour 'Shadow Cabinet' . . . . The text was telephoned to me just before dinner; by 9pm I had the text of a draft reply (based on a draft wh I had prepared before leaving London)

---

95. Numbers fell in 1959 but rose again in 1960.
96. Presumably staying with Bob Boothby.

for I had been told of this meeting and the probability of the letter from G) . . . .

It was rather mean of G to <u>insist</u> on publishing his letter immediately. He actually sent it to the Press <u>before</u> it reached No 10. But we got our reply to the Press in time for all except the first editions, and this apparently made a profound impression in Fleet St. They thought it quick work to receive a letter practically at John O'Groats and get off the reply between 8 and 10 at night.

John W[yndham] insisted on sending our reply to H.G. by hand to Hampstead and kept him up pretty late. Then the Press mercilessly rang up G all the rest of the night, asking if he wd send a further reply. All this incident took place last night (interrupting dinner somewhat) . . . .

17 September

A wonderful holiday. No boxes; no letters; no papers – only a certain amount of telephoned messages and telegrams. The new Tory pamphlet *Onwards in Freedom*, wh goes with the start of the recruiting campaign, was officially launched yesterday by Butler. It seems to have had a good reception in the press . . . .

20 September

We left Tillyfourie with sorrow – after 3 lovely days. Not a drop of rain since I began my holidays – a whole week, and the rain-coat never taken out of its bag. The grouse were plentiful, very strong on the wing, and naturally a good deal poached . . . .

21 September

. . . . The Foreign Secy has had long talks with Dulles and now with the President. The Americans seem in a very reasonable mood, but do not see how to handle the next stages in the Far East. However, the supply position seems better – the islands can somehow be kept going, it appears, by use of tank-landing craft and amphibious tanks . . . . The President has told Selwyn Lloyd that he is against the use of even tactical atomic weapons in a limited operation . . . .

4 October (Saturday)

. . . . We had a long defence ctee yesterday about Muscat, where the rebels in the mountains are making a lot of trouble. All the same, I think a punitive expedition, in the present state of nervousness in the Arab world, is too risky.

Foster Dulles has made one or two statements suggesting a compromise over Matsu and Quemoy but Chiang has reacted violently. It is clear that he can blackmail the Americans pretty thoroughly . . . .

If all goes well, our troops are to start to move out of Jordan on Oct 20th. Of course, there are great risks in leaving, but perhaps greater still in staying. Cyprus goes on; this time the Turks have behaved with great moderation and good sense. Instead of sending an ambassador from outside as their representative, they have appointed the Consul General who is already in the island. This has had a good effect in NATO, and Spaak is still trying to find some compromise. However, it was quite impossible for us to have 'postponed' the operation of the plan. If we had done so, we shd have lost the Turks for good, and civil war wd have begun. Meanwhile, violence is increasing. Two women, soldiers' wives, were shot yesterday, one fatally. This will, of course, enrage the troops. Makarios has issued a declaration, wh (tho' cleverly drafted, in wh the word 'fight' might be given a metaphorical meaning) is really an open incitement to violence and murder.

The Labour Party conference has been going on all the week. They started in rather a depressed mood; but they have done well during the proceedings and definitely improved their position. Gaitskell has made 3 speeches – on Far East, on economic situation, and on the H-Bomb – all of wh seemed to me to be effective. It is clear that he has firmly established his leadership. If they win the General Election, he will be in a strong position. If they lose he will be thrown immediately to the wolves. The essential confusions and contradictions of socialism remain – but the divisions have been skilfully papered over.

Our chief danger lies in the shadow of unemployment. If this goes much above 2½% – certainly if it goes above 3% – we shall be hard put to it. I feel that the American situation may help and our exports continue to increase as the American recession ends. New Delhi may help (in World Bank conference etc) if more credit can be made available to primary producers. But it will not be easy to 're-expand' in time for next year's General Election – that is if the present deflationary tendencies continue. Yet wages go on rising – in spite of all our efforts – and we may really begin to 'price' ourselves out of foreign markets. The truth is that economics is not a science – hardly even an art. It's a gamble . . . .

D and I gave a luncheon yesterday at No 10 for Mr and Mrs Pulliam (of Indianapolis) . . . . Pulliam told me that opinion in U.S.

was a) very critical of the administration's <u>handling</u> of the Far East
b) intensely grateful to HMG for their dignity and forbearance. Had
it not been for b) there wd be a great danger of a swing back (esp in
Middle West) to isolationism . . . .

8 October

. . . . Left London Airport at 10am. For Secy, being laid up with a
chill, did not come but sent David Ormsby Gore in his place . . . .

We got to Wahn Airport at 12.30 (Bonn time: 11.30 our time)
where the Chancellor met us . . . . Dinner (for about 20) at 8pm. The
Chancellor, who is a great expert on wine, produced one bottle after
another of Rhine wine, and made me take a glass from each, explaining
at the same time the different qualities.

The most serious question raised at our talks, both before and after
dinner, was the memorandum which General de Gaulle sent privately
to President Eisenhower and myself regarding the present organisation
for the defence of the Free World. In this (which was given privately
and securely to us both a few weeks ago) the General sets out his ideas
for reform. He is rightly critical of NATO, which may well turn into a
kind of European Maginot line, regardless of its flank. But he suggested
a world organisation, under an Anglo-American-French triumvirate.
NATO wd be the European branch of this; other parts of the world
similarly. Of course, the whole purpose is to claim for France 'as a
coming nuclear power' a special position, with Britain and America.[97]

The President and I have kept his confidence scrupulously. But
with incredible folly (wh has almost stupefied the Quai d'Orsay) the
General gave a copy to Spaak – on a personal basis – and allowed the
<u>German</u> and <u>Italian</u> ambassadors in Paris to see it. Altho' none of
the other NATO governments – not even the French or Italians – have
actual copies of the memorandum, they have a pretty good idea of its
contents and are naturally enraged. Knowing that this had happened
and that I wd be put in a difficult position when I saw Adenauer, I
asked de Gaulle what I was to do. He replied that I could certainly

---

97. Congressional lack of enthusiasm for this had been fully discussed at
    Macmillan's meeting with Eisenhower on 9 June 1958. De Gaulle seems to
    have had little illusion that his tripartite proposals would work, but they gave
    him the excuse he needed gradually to disengage from the NATO command
    structure.

discuss with Adenauer his (de Gaulle's) ideas in general terms. (He seems still to be quite unaware of the effect of his action)

I found the Chancellor very concerned. In the afternoon, with the various officials present, he tried to control himself. After dinner, in a small group, he shewed his disgust and resentment. He had trusted de Gaulle. They had met for confidential talks only a few weeks ago. De Gaulle had seemed to be loyal and open.[98] Now he had struck this cruel blow at Germany and at the Chancellor's policy of Franco-German friendship etc etc. I tried to calm him as much as I could. I had a much longer experience of de Gaulle than almost anyone. He was apt to treat his friends with this curious ineptness and rudeness. It was because of his mysticism and egoism. But I felt sure that the best way to deal with this, before it went too far, and caused real trouble in NATO, was to get the General to write another memorandum, leaving out the offensive parts, wh could be circulated and discussed in NATO. The President and I wd have to consider how to deal with his request for the Anglo-American-French 'directorate', there was nothing for the French to join. Of course, US and UK had rather special relations – arising from history, language, the last war, the Churchill–Roosevelt and now the Macmillan–Eisenhower friendship. But we had never tried to 'institutionalise' this. Nor wd we do so.

One of Adenauer's staff had asked (before dinner) of Sir A Rumbold whether I wd give A a copy of the memorandum. I did not think I cd do this honourably. I cd not go beyond the letter and spirit of de Gaulle's agreement as to what I shd say to A. So I told this straight out to the Chancellor, at the beginning of the talk after dinner, and I think he understood and respected my scruples. Moreover, A might wish to write me 'private and personal' letters. He wd not do so with confidence if I had acceded to the suggestion that I shd give a copy of a similarly private memorandum from de Gaulle to another person. Of course, the great 'gaffe' wh de G committed was to give a copy to Spaak. Yet (as I told the Chancellor) this was a proof of clumsiness but also of innocence. I think it wd never enter into de G's head to doubt the general acceptance of the thesis that France is to be treated on a different level to any other power – equal certainly to UK and

---

98. Adenauer had initially been hostile to de Gaulle's return to power and it was, ironically, apparently Macmillan who urged him to meet with the new French leader. Adenauer was charmed by de Gaulle's protestations of Franco-German friendship, and was therefore deeply suspicious of his tripartite proposals.

also to US. His 'nuclear' claim is absurd. They have not any nuclear capacity and cannot have any H-bomb capacity without a diffusion plant.[99]

9 October

We met at 10am and by 11.30 had covered all the field wh we had intended. A communiqué was easily agreed. In a restricted session, Adenauer shewed me a draft letter to Spaak – very discreet, esp about me – saying that all this wd soon leak in public, and asking Spaak to discuss with de G how the position can be regularised – perhaps by circulating another, but inoffensive, memorandum as soon as possible. The Chancellor is still very hurt and angry. I do not think he will ever trust de G again.[100] From my side, my chief purpose in these talks has been to get Adenauer to help over the Free Trade Area. The Germans have up to now been very good. But with Prof Erhard away and the growing Franco-German rapprochement, German officials have been telling A that it is the British who are being obstructive. I think I can exploit his anger with the French over the de G memorandum to some account. At 11.30, I had a large press conference – press of all nations, 250 or more. There was nothing much to say, but the atmosphere was good . . . .

The rise of the unemployment figures from 1.9% to 2.2% has given the Socialists a good chance for criticism. The 'shadow' of unemployment is our real danger. Of course, even 3% (wh the figure will go to during the winter) is still within the famous Gaitskell definition of 'full employment'.[101] But it is something to be watched. I am awaiting the return of the Chancellor of the Exr and the meetings of the Cabinet next week to discuss the present state of the 'economy' and what steps to further stimulate (if any) we ought to take. We must be careful not to plunge into another inflation. But we must equally

---

99. Diffusion plants are facilities for producing weapons-grade uranium. Although France tested its first atomic bomb on 13 February 1960, it did not explode a nuclear device until 24 August 1968.

100. A completely mistaken assessment. In practice, de Gaulle's proposals drew Adenauer's attention to the different quality of the Anglo-American relationship and it was Adenauer's attitude towards Macmillan which was to cool from this point.

101. Stated by Gaitskell as Chancellor of the Exchequer in a Commons written answer on 22 March 1951.

try to stop too great a deflation. (I have had a good memorandum from Roy Harrod on all this)

We left Wahn airfield at 12.30 and got to London airport at 1.40. Drove to No 10 . . . .

We heard of the Pope's death this morning. The Chancellor was grieved, for he said he had been a life-long friend. He was much interested in the succession . . . . The Pope was a noble and saintly man. I shall always remember my talks with him in Rome during the war and his sympathy and understanding.[102]

11 October

The Blackpool Conference ended today. It has, I think, been a great success . . . . Apart from interruption by Empire Loyalists, my speech went well enough. It took us a lot of work to prepare, but it ended up a good speech. It lasted an hour . . . .

18 October

A great row has developed between Ld Hailsham and Mr Chesterton (degenerate nephew of the great GK)[103] about the Empire Loyalists at Blackpool. Litigation is threatened, tho' I doubt whether it will happen. Poor Ld H has written to *The Times*, (in answer to Mr C) and to the Press generally, at great length . . . . The truth is that the audience got rather excited, esp some loyal old ladies (who resented the interruption) and the professional stewards were rather rough, by ordinary tho' not it seems by Blackpool standards.

Cyprus is still being discussed in NATO. Spaak (who has apparently fallen for the charms of Zorlu) is being very good to us and bringing a lot of pressure on the Greeks. It looks as if a conference may now be possible. Of course, this is really a fatal blow to the Greek thesis that the Cyprus problem has nothing to do with the Turks . . . .

20 October

. . . . All Lancashire is in a ferment about the Textile Industry . . . . The 64,000 dollar question is how to get a 'voluntary' agreement with India, Pakistan and Hong Kong to limit imports into UK of grey cloth and (latterly) 'made up' goods. The feeling about this is intense. Yet

---

102. Pius XII (1939–58). For Macmillan's wartime audiences with him, see *WD*, pp. 585–7, 763.

103. In fact he was the cousin of the author G. K. Chesterton.

free entry is guaranteed by Ottawa, nearly 30 years ago, and is in the spirit of Montreal. The newly emerging countries <u>must</u> be allowed some exports of manufactured goods if they are to achieve the progress on wh their hearts are set. But the effect of this on Lancashire, with its declining <u>exports</u> of textiles, is – so they say – catastrophic. My task was to persuade them to make <u>some</u> counter-offer to the Hong Kong proposal for voluntary limitation . . . . But I do not yet know whether I have persuaded them to allow Lord Rochdale and Sir Cuthbert Clegg to continue this negotiation . . . .

22 October
I had a good talk today with the Chancellor of the Exr on the 64000 dollar question – is it a boom, is it a slump? Is it slack water? If the last, will the tide go in or out? The people have now a pathological fear even of a little unemployment. Yet 1% means <u>over</u> employment and a financial crisis. 3% means almost a political crisis. The figures in November will shew another increase – 2.8% or so.

It is a great pleasure to talk with Heathcoat Amory, after having dealt with Thorneycroft. The former is <u>very</u> intelligent, flexible, and courteous. The latter was fundamentally stupid, rigid, and *cassant*. We agreed on the things we <u>might</u> do to 'reflate' the economy a little, but we did <u>not</u> reach a final agreement about what to do . . . .

23 October
'Doug' Dillon (Banker and chief economic adviser to State Dept) called this morning. He . . . . seemed to hold out real hope of some action to increase world credit. But he admitted that it was an almost impossible task to fight against the traditional restrictionism and protectionism of his countrymen on tariffs, quotas etc.

24 October
. . . . Cabinet 10.45 to 12.45 . . . . Both Brooke (Housing) and Eccles (Trade) were excellent and imaginative. I summed up and it was left for me to make proposals as to actions to the Chan[cellor] for some 'reflationary' measures. Chan[cellor] accepted this, and it gives me just what I wanted. It is a heavy responsibility, for the whole future of the Party depends on whether a) we ought to reflate b) we <u>can</u> reflate – in time for a General Election. a) means – can we risk <u>another</u> inflation if we go too far b) means – how long does it take to stop a slump, if it takes 2 years to halt a boom? . . . .

25 October

A glorious autumn day. Bright sun, no wind. Walked in the woods morning and afternoon. Read Mont[gomer]y's memoirs. The book is badly composed, has much padding in it, but it <u>does</u> tell a story and give an impression of this strange, egotistical, brilliant, and Cromwellian figure – who is perhaps the best 'battle commander' we have ever had, Wellington included. But he was no Marlborough. To him, a British friend is a man to be patronised, a foreign ally one to be insulted.

The Greeks have refused the proposed Cyprus conference. After all these weeks, in spite of – or perhaps because – the British and Turks having agreed on every point, they have run out. It's Makarios who has bullied poor Karamanlis, Averoff and Co into this absurd position . . . .

26 October

. . . . The outlook for the European Free Trade Area seems bad. The French are determined to exclude U.K. De Gaulle is bidding high for the hegemony of Europe. If he cd get peace in Africa and hold on to the Sahara oil, he might achieve it . . . .

28 October

Opening of Parlt. For the first time the ceremony, from the Queen leaving Buckingham Palace to her return, was televised. The commentary was by [Richard] Dimbleby and very well done . . . . I am sure that the effect has been good. The whole history of Parliament is enshrined in these ceremonies. Nor can it do the people any harm to be reminded of the antiquity and continuity of the realm . . . .

I spoke in the debate – about 45 minutes. It went well and our people seemed pleased. We have a good programme, which will be lively and (in parts) popular. The only shadow remains 'unemployment' . . . . it

31 October

Morning with Mr D[iefenbaker]. His talk was interesting, but rather diffuse. His relations with U.S. are good – but he is much firmer than his predecessor, who left everything to Mike Pearson. D is essentially a romantic. I think the problem of dealing with him is the same as with the adolescent boy – how to explain to him the facts of life without shocking his idealism. (D is also a very clever and rather unscrupulous politician. But this often goes with romanticism and idealism)

In the afternoon, For Secy, Chancellor of Exr, President of BofT, and Paymaster-General about the European Free Trade negotiations. Maudling has handled the whole affair with great skill and patience. He thinks that the French must soon declare their hand. At present, they have just wasted time. But even the 5 (their partners in the Treaty of Rome 6 powers) are shocked and angry at French insincerity and trickery. We must wait till the end of November. If the French make no move, we shd break off the negotiation. We must consider what, if anything, we and the other powers (Scandinavia; Switzerland; Denmark; Austria) can or ought to do, either in the political or economic sphere . . . .

D and I went to Covent Garden for 'Boris Goodanoff [sic]' The chief singer was a Bulgar – but from the Russian point of view a renegade! So Malik (the Russian ambassador) who was in our box, left hastily before the singer cd be brought in to be introduced!

I am not a musician enough – or indeed at all – to know whether it was a good rendering. It was certainly dramatic – but it was also very long 7–11.30 . . . .

3 November

Mr Diefenbaker came at 11am, for more general talk. He is certainly a strange man. He has enthusiasm, energy, faith. But he is ill-informed and seems to be lacking in any power of precise ratiocination . . . .

The debate on the Socialist amendment [to the Queen's Speech] began today with a very amusing speech from Harold Wilson, attacking me. I was the central theme and pivot of his speech. (This is the new Socialist line. I feel it does not do me much harm) . . . .

5 November

A small ministerial meeting took up all the morning with Operation Unicorn. (This is the code name for bringing the two rates of sterling together)[104] No decision to be taken finally till the end of the month, when the French position shd be clearer . . . .

---

104. Since February 1955 the transferable rate of sterling had been at a 1% discount to the official rate, providing effective convertibility. With the strengthening of reserves full convertibility could now be pursued, co-ordinated with the French and West Germans, and was introduced across Western Europe on 29 December.

6 November

A quiet morning. Couve de Murville came in for a few minutes before luncheon. He is here for one day, to talk about European Free Trade and also about de Gaulle's ideas for NATO etc. He made it pretty clear that the French were still trying to stall and I told him so, roughly. It was a painful discussion, esp with an old friend . . . .

Mr McCone and Sir E Plowden to see me at 4pm. Mr McCone has proved a very reasonable negotiator and he has not pressed us unduly on the exchange of full atomic information on the civil side. Altho' we believe and practise full publication of scientific and technological information, we are not willing to exchange drawings of industrial designs, exc[ept] (as agreed with the President) in the military field. Actually, this is a very important matter for us, as we have a very good lead in this sphere . . . .

8 November

Our first shoot at B.G. It has been a poor season – no wild birds and tame birds have not done well . . . .

Motored to London for British Legion Festival of Remembrance at the Albert Hall. Dinner afterwards and short speech. Queen, Queen Mother, Princess Margaret etc etc. All these ceremonial duties and functions are becoming more and more oppressive to a Prime Minister and makes it necessary to work further and further into the night.

14 November

This has been a pretty busy week. A statement on Cyprus; a statement on an allegation of misuse of departmental facilities for party ends; (enquired into by Brook) another similar case (this one blown sky-high) attacking Eccles; a long Cabinet; meeting of Defence Ctee – and all the usual meetings and ministerial conferences. All the problems remain unresolved . . . . There has been a protest about some remarks of mine to the Czech ambassador made by the Czech govt to F.O. It was rather silly of me to get drawn into an argument at a party last week.[105] But altho' I hate this sort of distracting incident, one cannot avoid them now and then. I hope it will do no political harm at home . . . .

---

105. Macmillan apparently made critical remarks about Czechoslovakia and the Communist system to its ambassador Miroslav Galuska at a Swedish diplomatic party.

16 November (Sunday)

.... The For Secy wd <u>not</u> receive the protest, on the ground that it referred to a private conversation. The British press is sympathetic to me – all the same, it was a perfectly unnecessary scrape to get into and I am very angry with myself . . . .

17 November

De Gaulle has replied – obscurely and not very satisfactorily – to my letter about the Free Trade Area.[106] He suggests bilateral negotiations – a little later on (i.e. <u>after</u> the French elections) We had a meeting this morning of ministers chiefly concerned. The right tactics for the moment seem to be to hold off for a bit and let other countries bring pressure on the French. The first hurdle is Jan 1st. If the French act in a discriminatory way against us and the other 11 countries,[107] I fear this must mean the disintegration of OEEC and other European institutions. But they <u>could</u> easily avoid this in one of two ways. They could claim their escape clauses, and lower their tariffs <u>neither</u> to the 5 nor to the 11. (Similarly with quotas) Or they could extend their concessions to all Europe . . . .

18 November

.... I made the long-awaited statement on the new strip mill. As with Solomon's judgment, neither the Welsh nor the Scottish members are altogether pleased. There is to be one mill by Colville's (at Motherwell) – another at Newport. But, on the whole, the House accepted the decision as wise and the Scottish members know that, on purely economic grounds, the whole project would have gone to Wales . . . .

19 November

.... Chancellor of Exr and Butler for a talk this evening on the estimates and the Budget prospects. The position is very uncertain –

---

106. De Gaulle had never supported the FTA plan, but had delayed showing his hand in deference to the support for it of his five partners. During what turned out to be the final meeting of the Maudling Committee on 14–15 November the French made their objections brutally clear.

107. The other members of the Organisation for European Economic Co-operation, set up to administer Marshall Aid in 1948. The OEEC was indeed wound up as a result of economic divisions in Europe and replaced by the OECD in 1961.

but we <u>must</u>, by hook or crook, have an encouraging Budget. Our aim shd be a reduction of £200m in taxation . . . .

21 November

A most unfortunate new trouble. Ian Harvey (under secy, FO) and a very nice chap, was arrested on Wednesday night in St James' Park and has been charged with indecent behaviour with a young guardsman. If (as I fear) he is guilty, it means that he must resign his post in the Govt <u>and</u> his seat in Parlt.[108] I saw him this morning, and did my best to comfort him. But it [is] a terrible thing and has distressed me greatly . . . .

23 November

. . . . Bob Menzies has won his general election in Australia – wh is a very good thing. Nkrumah (P.M. of Ghana) is announcing today a declaration of intention to join with Guinea (lately French)[109] I fear that the French will suspect us of having plotted this (which is, of course, absurd) and some of the Commonwealth countries may object. But I think that there may be advantages. The Balkanisation of Africa is not good, and if some of these little countries join together on becoming independent, I see no great harm . . . .

24 November

. . . . The chief thing is to do what we can to disabuse the French of the idea that this is yet another example of '*perfide Albion*'. They are very suspicious of the £10m bribe with wh cocoa-rich Ghana is trying to buy impoverished Guinea. They believe, (wrongly, of course) that the Governor of the Bank of England can prevent an independent Commonwealth country from using its sterling balances as it wishes.

Lunch for Sir Roy Welensky (Prime Minister of the Federation) He seemed in excellent form, having won his election so easily.[110] He still

---

108. He did. Male homosexuality was not legalised until 1967.

109. France had recently offered new colonial arrangements to its African colonies. Guinea alone rejected this in a referendum. On independence on 2 October the departing French stripped it of financial support and much more, leading Nkrumah to step in with a £10m loan. The Ghana/Guinea amalgamation also announced proved abortive.

110. The Central African Federation had been created in 1953 out of the territories of Northern and Southern Rhodesia and Nyasaland (now Zambia, Zimbabwe

objects to two points in the proposed constitution for Northern Rhodesia. Over one of these – approval of candidates of tribal chiefs – I feel we shd meet his views. On the other, nomination by Governor of two African members of council, I think he is perhaps right theoretically. He says such a <u>statutory</u> provision is contrary to the whole concept of a multi-racial or partnership state. In practice, however, I think it necessary in the early stages of constitutional progress.

28 November

This has been <u>Nixon</u> week, and any work done (apart from P.Q.) has had to be either very early in the morning or very late at night. We have dinners, luncheons, speeches galore .... Dinner at No 10 (followed by evening party) went off quite well, as we had a lot of guests outside the ordinary Whitehall[111] and embassy lot – e.g. Isaiah Berlin and Jack Wheeler-Bennett. The dinner (last night) at the American Embassy, to which the Queen came, was excellently done and everyone enjoyed it very much. I had <u>some</u> serious talk with Nixon, and the For Secy more. On the whole, I thought N much improved since I saw him in Washington. His manners were better (he did not talk <u>all</u> the time) and he seemed more restrained. His views on atomic tests etc seemed to me more sensible than 'present State Dept thinking'.

.... The European trade picture is darkening. We had hoped that the suggestions of the 6 for Jan 1st would be fairly reasonable, and might even avoid <u>all</u> discrimination. But I fear this will turn out [not] to be true and the results of the French proposals (wh they have persuaded the Germans to adopt) will be very serious indeed.[112] Meanwhile Mr K[hrushchev] has hotted up the Berlin row, 'good and proper'. It is a 6 months ultimatum.[113] I was glad to see a leading

---

and Malawi). The African National Congresses of the three territories (of which only Southern Rhodesia had a substantial white settler presence) opposed the Federation and boycotted the (restricted franchise) elections.

111. Conventional term for the government Civl Service, after the London street where many of the major departments of state are situated.

112. Although the tariff changes to be introduced by the EEC on 1 January 1959 minimised discrimination against non-members, French proposals for discriminatory quotas (on, for instance, car imports) were viewed very seriously in London.

113. Having demanded the withdrawal of Allied troops from the city on 10 November, the Soviets followed this up with a note on 27 November declaring all existing arrangements for Berlin null and void, and arguing that West Berlin

article in *Financial Times* (a responsible paper) about European trade. It ended by suggesting that the people of Britain cd hardly be expected to accept economic blows <u>from</u> Europe and receive military blows in defence of Europe – Berlin, W̄EU, NATO etc . . . .

The *Daily Express* are publishing next week (in serial form) the Suez chapters of a Life of Sir Anthony Eden wh has been written by Randolph Churchill. This is said to be a vitriolic attack on Anthony Eden, as well as a most damaging (if believed) and wounding criticism of the Govt as a whole. I fear it will revive the whole controversy, wh will not do us any good . . . .

4 December

. . . . [A]t 5.30 Dr Erhard and a lot of tough Germans. He came on a hurried mission from the 6 Powers asking that <u>no</u> further meetings either of the Maudling Ctee <u>or</u> of OEEC shd be held till the end of January! The offer of the 6 was <u>not</u> a negotiation; it was a statement of what they wd do on Jan 1st. Dr E seemed rather embarrassed (as well he might be)[114] I rejected this plea altogether . . . .

7 December (Sunday)

Stayed in bed all the morning working. Talked to F.S. The U.N. vote on Cyprus was very favourable. It may be that the Greeks will now be a little more flexible. Arms for Indonesia. Sent a telegram to Menzies warning him that we must now sell them <u>some</u> arms. If not, they will look only to Communist countries.[115]

A new row over alleged atrocities by the military in Cyprus. If we yield to the demand for an independent inquiry, we shall break the spirit of the security forces. Many PQs about Suez. It really is troublesome to start up all the controversy again. However a) we must not seem unduly disturbed b) much better <u>now</u> than in a few months time. The German Chancellor (Adenauer) has suddenly invited himself to

---

should be demilitarised as a free city within six months or all Soviet powers there would be handed over to the East German authorities.

114. Erhard publicly announced his support for the FTA plan in February 1957, but shifted his position in late 1958. There was still considerable support for it in the Bundestag (the West German parliament).

115. On 27 August Macmillan had told Australian Foreign Minister R. G. Casey that Britain would not sell Indonesia arms, but on 18 October he noted to Selwyn Lloyd that now Australia's elections were out of the way they could go ahead.

London. He, of course, wants to talk about Berlin. I shall talk to him about European trade.[116]

At Geneva, it seems as if the Russians are giving some ground on H-Bomb Tests, and getting nearer to our position that cessation of Tests and International Control must go together . . . .

9 December

. . . . Sir Winston and Lady C to luncheon. He is very unhappy about the Randolph Churchill row. In the House, I had a large number of PQs and the supplementaries developed into a sort of Suez debate. I tried to throw as many red herrings as possible across the path of the hounds – including threat of an early General Election. I think at the end of a quarter of an hour, honours were even . . . .

10 December

. . . . Sir Arthur Penn came to see me about the Queen Mother's finances. I'm afraid she finds that her expenses far out-run her income. So, alas, do most of us today. It is not an easy problem. The Queen Mother says, cheerfully, that if necessary she will resign or emigrate! I hope we may be able to find some way of helping with the inevitably heavy costs of Clarence House etc[117] . . . .

12 December

Dr Richardson at 9am. He made a thorough examination and found me in good physical shape.

10am. Meeting of ministers about

a) 'Unicorn' – i.e. bunging the official and transferable sterling rates together. This involves 'convertibility' – in its modern and technical sense – that is, of sterling (other than capital transfers) held by non-residents. It was agreed to go ahead in principle, but the timing to be left with Chancellor of Exr and For Secy together while in Paris next week. We believe that the Bank of

---

116. In the event Adenauer caught a cold and cancelled the visit. His policy on Berlin was also decisively rejected on 7 December in *Land* elections there which Adenauer had tried to turn into a vote of confidence in his foreign policy.

117. Her Civil List allowance had been fixed in 1936 at £70,000 and not subsequently increased. Macmillan abortively explored ways of tackling this with Penn, her treasurer, without raising a furore in Parliament in 1959 and the allowance was not eventually raised until 1970.

France is trying to persuade the French Govt to <u>devalue</u> and to go convertible. In other words, what we proposed to do from strength, they want to do from weakness. But I suspect a French plot to put the blame on us and thus create another grievance.

b) Our tactics in OEEC and subsequently. The proposals of the 6 for January 1st are not acceptable, because (in the case of the French but not of the other five) they are discriminatory. This threatens the whole OEEC structure. We can – of course – retaliate on French lines etc. But the discussion, which lasted all the morning, confirmed my view that we hold very few economic cards . . . .

14 December (Sunday)

Drove to Chevening (with D) to luncheon with Ld Stanhope. He is now 78, with one leg cut off a year or two ago, but very merry and bright. He shewed us all round this wonderful house, full of lovely things, with a splendid library, and especial relics of Chatham and Pitt.[118] His intention (having no heirs and no relations) is to give everything – house, furniture, books, 3000 acres of land, £1m of money, to the nation. He wd like the house to be a sort of 'Chequers'.[119] It is a princely gift . . . .

Dined with Alan Lennox-Boyd, (Colonial Secy) . . . . [D]iscussed Lancashire and Hong Kong. I think I have now persuaded him that in default of a 'voluntary agreement', the Govt will have to <u>impose</u> one. I still believe, that under this sanction, we may be able to get a 'voluntary agreement'.

16 December

. . . . There was a debate on Suez (1½ hours on the adjournment) tonight. Anthony Head made a good speech. Soames (SofS War) wound up very well for us. There was a row, but no real indication of the line the <u>Front</u> Opposition bench means to take. I think they will want to see what they judge to be the national reaction. At present, the demand for an 'enquiry' – by Select Ctee or otherwise – is confined

---

118. The Earl of Chatham (William Pitt the Elder) was Prime Minister 1766–68 and his son, William Pitt the Younger, Prime Minister 1783–1801 and 1804–6.

119. Since 1980 this Kent stately home has been used as the country seat of the Foreign Secretary.

to a few Back Bench 'Left-Wingers'. However, it is perhaps significant that Bevan came in last night to support (an unusual thing for him nowadays) the old Bevanites.

17 December
. . . . The For Secy reported from Paris the extraordinary new political developments – that is, the talks between the Greek and Turkish Foreign Ministers, as well as the tripartite discussion fixed for tomorrow. We thought Foot (the Governor) ought to know of all this, in view of two executions fixed for tomorrow. This we arranged he shd have – tho' of course we shall be told that HMG is interfering with justice. However, even if still remote, it is a great prize. Peace in Cyprus would radically alter our whole military picture . . . .

21 December (Sunday)
Church in morning. Motored to London for conference with senior ministers – Butler, Selwyn Lloyd, Lennox-Boyd; Heathcoat Amory; and Duncan Sandys. (Ld P[rivy] Seal and Home Secy; For Secy; Chancellor of Exr; Colonial Secy; Minister of Defence) We began at 6pm and ended at midnight. I gave them supper. It was a useful exercise, in these hectic days, where there is so little time for real discussion and consultation. Each gave a general picture of the chief problems of his own department.

22 December
A very tiring day. Defence Committee (grand parade of them all) 10.30–1.15 . . . . [W]e have got down from £1567m (demanded by depts) to about £1520m. We should get a bit lower. But we cannot take any <u>dramatic</u> decisions this year.

23 December
. . . . Operation <u>Unicorn</u> (convertible sterling) is now to take place on Saturday. The operation will be regarded as a European one, with France, Germany etc agreeing. The Opposition here will be violently opposed – but the European aspect (that is, if the others don't 'rat' at the last moment) will make it more difficult for them . . . .

The Hong Kong–Lancashire agreement seems now assured. H-K seems to have chosen the first of the alternatives I gave them, and fortunately that most agreeable to Ld Rochdale and the Lancashire Ctee . . . .

31 December

. . . . Colonial Secy at 11am. I had prepared a directive to the
Governor, wh C.S. accepted. He is told <u>not</u> repeat <u>not</u> to relax the
pressure on EOKA and above all not to enter into any kind of
discussion or negotiation with the terrorists. Even if the present talks
really led to a 'solution' (as between Governments) it is more than
likely that EOKA wd continue – rather like the IRA in Ireland.
<u>Executions</u> are another thing. I think the Governor has done right to
commute in the cases now before him.

11.30. For Secy . . . . He left me notes or proposals on <u>all</u> the
immense range of problems, wh cover Berlin, the H-Bomb Tests,
Egypt, Libya, and all the rest. He really is an extraordinarily capable
and efficient man – as well as a wonderfully agreeable man to work
with. He feels a great sense of gratitude and loyalty to me oopersonally,
for I have really been able (by moral support, in private and in public)
to help him through a bad time. He had to go into hospital this
afternoon, for an operation to remove his tonsils. So I am to take over
the Foreign Office . . . .

1959

Berlin, East–West relations and Macmillan's trip to Russia – Cyprus agreement – Nyasaland crisis starts to undermine the Central African Federation – EFTA negotiations – Hola camp scandal in Kenya – the print strike – the start of efforts to control nuclear tests – General Election victory – preparations for a Summit

1 January

Went to Foreign Office in the morning. Then Minister of Education (to plan the Education Drive)[1] then Chief Whip (about by-elections etc) then (in afternoon) a very long meeting about U235 and other materials for the nuclear programme, military and civil. We have a chance of buying U235,[2] partly for cash and partly for plutonium (of wh we have too much and the Americans have too little) from U.S. This means another 'bilateral agreement', under the amended McMahon Act. The price of American material (because of their cheap power) is only about ⅓ or ½ of our price. Moreover, we shd have to spend £60m on a plant. After a very good discussion (Chancellor of Exr; Minister of Defence; Sir E Plowden; Sir N Brook; Sir P Dean; Sir W Penney; Sir W Strath) we authorised Strath and Penney (who are going to Washington shortly) to negotiate on these lines. What I fear is the Americans trying to get us to part with some of our 'civil' patents and secrets – wh we must resist . . . .

5 January

. . . . The Berlin 'crisis' is approaching and we have (as yet) no agreed policy with our allies. The Paris declaration only papered over the cracks.[3] Are we really prepared to face war over Berlin? If so, just in what way are we to play the hand, so as to get the Russians sure that we are serious and ready to come to a serious conference. I feel sure (altho' the Americans so far are not quite agreed) that we must not

---

1. This envisaged a five-year £300 million programme of secondary school building.
2. A fissile (and rare) uranium isotope used in nuclear weapons. Under this amendment of the 1958 Mutual Defence Agreement tritium was also obtained for warheads.
3. Before the NATO Council met, on 14 December 1958, the British, French, Americans and West Germans rejected the Russian note of 27 November 1958 about Berlin.

over play our hand. If we do, the Russians will see through and call our bluff. I doubt therefore whether we can make the question of whether Russians or East Germans approve the bills of lading or punch the railway tickets into a *casus belli*.[4] What matters is whether civil and military supplies actually reach Berlin . . . .

Cyprus is relatively calm, but there seems little news of any further Turko-Greek talks. Zorlu (Turkish For[eign] Minister) is under a good deal of pressure in Turkey. He is now accused of abandoning the sacred cause of 'partition'. In the same way, Averoff is accused of abandoning *enosis*. So – by a curious logic – both approach, necessarily, to a compromise wh is very similar to the hated 'Macmillan plan'.

We have agreed a telegram to Black (of IMF)[5] who is trying to negotiate preliminaries with Nasser and Co to a financial agreement. I do not want our men to go to Cairo unless there is a very fair chance of a settlement. In many respects I don't like them going to Cairo at all. Discussions in Rome are more dignified. But they are much more protracted, since every point has to be referred back. It looks as if the chances of agreement were about fifty-fifty . . . .

7 January
. . . . 6pm – Anthony Nutting. He talked about himself and his plans. His divorce is now probable quite soon – for desertion, wh is nowadays fairly respectable . . . . He wants to get back into Parliament. I advised him to wait till after this General Election, and then try for a by-election. This will be the best for him and his resignation over Suez will by then not be a subject of controversy[6] . . . .

12 January
. . . . [M]eeting of ministers on the Economic situation. Some progress towards 'Reflation' – but the Chancellor of the Exr (urged on by the Treasury) [was] rather stiff. He still fears another inflationary boom.

---

4. Cause of war.
5. Eugene R. Black Sr was in fact President of the World Bank 1949–63.
6. Nutting resigned as Foreign Office minister on 3 November 1956 over Suez. At the time he was certainly being hounded by the *Daily Express* over his American mistress. Dissuaded at the time by Macmillan from making a resignation statement, he later made his case in *No End of a Lesson* (London: Constable, 1967). He did not return to Parliament.

For 6 months or more I have had the opposite fear – the approaching slump. Fortunately, we have done something – by reduction of Bank rate, and by credit squeeze, abolition of Hire Purchase restrictions, and (by immense pressure from me) by injecting another £50m into the Public Investment programme. But I am still not sure that this is enough . . . .

16 January
We got back early this morning from an exhausting, but very exciting and inspiring trip. Darlington; the Hartlepools; Thornaby; Stockton; Billingham; Sunderland; Haverton Hill; Birtley and Newcastle.

It was very cold – snow everywhere – but fine. We had a most touching reception in Stockton, and everywhere the people were very friendly. It was really extraordinary. Of course, all this means very little when it comes to voting . . . .

I was, however, concerned about the future – the immediate future – of heavy industry in this area. Order books are thin; and I feel sure we must do more 'reflation' if we are to avoid a serious increase in unemployment.

This was confirmed to me by Minister of Labour after the Cabinet. The January count (taken on Monday) will shew an increase of 86000 – 2.8% in all. This will cause a great Parliamentary outcry and some real alarm. Of course, the bad weather will have had some effect – esp on building workers etc – but I don't like it. I had a talk with Chancellor of Exr, but found him unmoved.

Cabinet at 11. The chief item was to approve the Egyptian financial treaty. There will be some political troubles about this, but it is clearly right and not unfavourable to our commercial interests.

We had a talk about Pensions. It _may_ be necessary to have another increase this year. Cost of living has gone up 5% or 6% since the last rise . . . .

5.30 Kit Steel (our ambassador in Bonn) came for a talk. I did _not_ get much illumination from him, except that Chancellor Adenauer is in a bad way and ageing rapidly. The rest of them (Brentano etc) are unable or unwilling to think out anything new in these circumstances. At one moment, A is violently pro-French and pro-de Gaulle, at another highly critical. He is still, it appears, fond of me. About Berlin etc, he stands (officially) for absolute rigidity and a solid front against Soviet Russia. Behind the scenes, he wrings his hands and says that Russia and the West are like two express trains rushing to a head-on collision .... The most important thing is to decide whether we (including Adenauer) <u>really</u> want a unified Germany or not, recognising that it seems hardly possible to get any unified Germany except as neutral or neutralised ....

18 January (Sunday)
.... I have decided to send telegrams to Washington expressing my anxiety and my desire to make some progress. I wd like, above all, to go to Washington for talks with Dulles and the President. This method has worked very well during the last 2 years. But with French jealousy and German suspicion, it may be too dangerous. It seems therefore that I had better make a more complicated plan. For a long time, there has been a sort of outstanding invitation to go to Moscow. Of course, the invitation might not be renewed. But it is worth trying. In that case, I wd go to Bonn and Paris, and finally to Washington ....

19 January
.... Dined with Ld Mills and went through the economic paper. Broadly, I disagree with the official Treasury view that the danger is a boom. I think (and Ld Mills agrees) that the danger is a serious slump. My plan is
   a) To inject another £50[m] capital expenditure on public a/c into the economy at once. It can only begin to have some effect in 5 or 6 months time. This wd be <u>in addition</u> to the £50m we have already done.
   b) To bring the Budget date forward from April 7th to March 17th and so get the stimulus wh we hope the Budget will provide as soon as we can.
This will be a difficult battle – but I must make an effort to get one or other (if not <u>both</u>) of these ....

22 January
.... The Egyptian Treaty is hanging fire and may go sour altogether. We <u>cannot</u> sign (it has been initialled) without a clear understanding about having a British agent in Cairo to operate the 'desequestration' and other financial clauses affecting British citizens. Such an agent must have immunity and right of cyphered communication. The Egyptians are saying that we are demanding full diplomatic relations restored. This is not the case. We need a machinery to implement the agreement. I hope this is a genuine misunderstanding and can be

cleared up. But I fear that Nasser may have got 'cold feet' and shrink from rebuilding his bridges with UK even to get £46m [of blocked sterling balances]. He too, I have no doubt, has his 'Suez Group' . . . .

The American reply has come in the most friendly terms. They say, in effect, that they have complete confidence in me and I must do whatever I think best[7] . . . .

6.15–8.15. For Secy, Chancellor of Exr, Ld Privy Seal, Minister of Labour, Minister of Power, Chief Whip. My economic plan fully discussed, but no conclusions reached. I told them, before we began, about my Russian and American plans. They approved initiative in the foreign field; I hope they wd sympathise with my desire to show equal initiative on the Home Front. Ld P[rivy] Seal supported me fully; also Ld Mills. Chancellor of Exr reserved his decision – or his final decision, but gave an analysis wh rather depressed me. He (with Treasury) believe in the doctrine of automatic recovery. I do not . . . .

23 January

In the afternoon, I motored to see Field Marshal Ld Alexander. He is living in a rented house, near Virginia Water. In spite of his very serious illness, I found him in good spirits – as gallant and attractive as ever. He has had two serious heart attacks, from the second of which he nearly died . . . . Alex was obviously very pleased with his O.M.[8] It reminded me of the time when he learned that his appointment as Field Marshal, altho' announced before Montgomery's, was ante-dated ahead of him. He did not say anything, but I remember smiled in a rather peculiar way, showing me the telegram. It was (I think) at Caserta or perhaps in Rome – in 1944. We had a good gossip – chiefly about the war and Churchill and other familiar topics – wh old men and old comrades cannot turn over too often when they meet.

He told me something new about Monty and Alamein. Of course the battle – as battles always do – went quite differently to what had been planned. In the penultimate stages, Monty was really stuck. Practically all his forces had been engaged; he had only one substantial formation left to throw into the battle. If this failed, the whole thing

---

7. Macmillan's claims of allied support for his Moscow initiative in this entry, and the one for 5 February, are somewhat disingenuous.

8. The Order of Merit, an honorary title established in 1902, restricted to 24 members and in the sole gift of the monarch.

wd have to be called off – not a complete failure, but no victory and no 'follow-up'. There was a meeting between Alex and his Chief of Staff and Monty and his staff. Monty did not know what to do and asked for suggestions. Dick McCreery (Alex's CofS) suggested the place and character of the attack – the last throw. (I dare say it was really Alex who thought of it, but he attributed it to Dick M) Alex agreed. After some discussion, Monty accepted the plan, wh was put into effect (I think it was the Australian attack along the coast, but I cannot quite remember about this) and all went well. Some weeks afterwards, Alex heard that Monty was complaining everywhere of being 'interfered' with while fighting his battle by the Commander in Chief and his staff. Actually, said Alex, Monty on this morning was at his wits end and very grateful for help . . . .

26 January

. . . . Chancellor of Exr and I dined together and we had a good talk about a) the content b) the date of the Budget. I am sure that he will be able to give us something pretty good in content – altho' of course falling short of some absurdly optimistic forecasts. On date, it is still between March 17th and April 7. March wd be unorthodox; it might create a violent fit of 'electionitis' (and so hold up instead of stimulating business expansion) But we would save 3 vital weeks.

27 January

The trade negotiations with France drag on – as the French intend. Meanwhile, the discrimination agst U.K. and the 11 Europeans not in the Treaty of Rome has begun . . . .

After the division (Pensions Bill) we had a meeting of our (adjourned) employment committee. Nearly all ministers supported me in asking for more 'reflation'. But the Chancellor was very guarded. I think the 'Treasury' is giving him as bad advice as it has to every Chancellor in turn. Certainly the Bank of England is very timid and 'orthodox'. I have a greater belief in Roy Harrod. Meanwhile, the Treasury have got into a terrible mess over the Egyptian financial agreement. After initialling, the F.O. has discovered that there is complete confusion over the schedules as between 'sequestrated' property (to be returned) and 'Egyptianised' (to be compensated) As a result, the compensation claims may be £10–£12m higher than we expected, and the £27½m wh we are to get correspondingly inadequate. There is an explanation, of course; but a lame one.

31 January
(At Birch Grove) I got down last night in time for dinner – after a tiring week, with a mass of engagements, mostly useless! I feel rather depressed and frustrated. Abroad

1) No answer from Russians; my proposal has clearly surprised them
2) Egyptian treaty hold up – no easy way out
3) Cyprus – we have postponed publication of electoral list legislation and also of new muncipal system, in the hope of assisting the Averoff–Zorlu talks – but nothing seems to be happening
4) Germany. I saw van Scherpenburg yesterday (head of [the foreign trade division of the] German F.O.) He seemed quite negative
5) U.S.A. No 'give' at all on the electrical contracts – wh is a scandalous story. No 'give' either on the great world issues, and no ideas . . . .
6) France – no 'give' at all regarding the trade discrimination. No ideas about Europe. De Gaulle is determined to break up NATO.

At home

1) Unemployment growing. I feel in my bones that both Treasury and Ministry of Labour are wrong – unemployment will get worse, not better.
2) Public opinion is going against us. We have now dropped behind Socialists in Gallup poll.
3) Party is not too good. Sir D Robertson (Caithness) has just resigned the whip.[9]
4) Southend election – bad. We dropped enormously and Liberal did not. Another Torrington.[10]

Against all this, it is a glorious morning here, bright and sunny; I shall go for a walk in the woods and forget all these worries. Read all of an excellent novel last night and most of another (both Macmillan books) . . . .

---

9. This was over the handling of transport and agriculture issues in Scotland. Robertson sat as an Independent MP until his retirement in 1964.
10. This was the Southend West by-election of two days earlier, at which Paul Channon replaced his father, Sir Henry 'Chips' Channon as MP, though with his majority slashed from over 18,000 to 8,000 and the Liberal beating Labour into third place.

I agreed a proposal of the Governor Foot to make a statement about military operations in Cyprus. The Averoff–Zorlu talks are by way of continuing. We get a very confused picture of Greek opinion, even from secret sources . . . .

1 February (Sunday)

. . . . A lovely day – cold wind but sunny. A good deal of telephoning, chiefly with For Sec. The situation in Persia is worrying and the Shah shewing signs of weakening to Russian pressure. The Minister of Defence is seeing him today. It wd be very serious if Iran were to leave the Baghdad Pact . . . .

2 February

. . . . Lunched with James Stuart. He seemed to be ready to leave David Robertson alone in Caithness. He will prob[ably] rejoin us before the General Election. James is agst an early Budget or a summer election. His judgment is usually pretty good . . . .

I heard after luncheon that the Russian Minister had called at F.O. and given the Russian reply. All my anxieties are removed. They have accepted the date; the length of the visit; and the terms of the announcement. This will be 3.30 on Thursday. This is an immense relief, for we rather 'stuck our necks out' in making the proposal, and a rebuff (wh wd have leaked) wd have been damaging as well as embarrassing . . . .

3 February

Ld Hailsham, Ld Poole, Mr Butler, and Chancellor of Exr at 11 to discuss the attitude we are to take to the steel industry's 'Quiz' on nationalisation, wh has infuriated the Socialists. I was against a formal statement from Conservative Central Office. But Ld H will make a speech to chaff them and rub in the fear they have of their nationalisation plans being brought to public attention.

Cabinet at 11.30. I told my colleagues about Russia – all approved, and were even enthusiastic. The rest of the business was concerned with the problem of how to help the British horticultural industry – a ticklish problem, because of its European repercussions.

. . . . Meeting of Ministers (after one of D's tea parties to MPs) at 5. We definitely decided against an early Budget, but for another £30m or so of reflationary Govt expenditure on capital a/c. I am very pleased about this . . . .

Good news from Teheran. It looks as if the Shah has decided to stay loyal and turn down the Russian overtures . . . .

4 February

. . . . There is some difficulty about <u>how</u> to make the announcement about Russia. We <u>must</u> wait till tomorrow, because of informing Paris, Bonn, Commonwealth PMs, NATO etc . . . .

Our operations in Muscat seem to have been very successful. The mountain has been occupied by a small, highly trained force (Life guards etc) and there is now some chance of a temporary period of quiet there . . . .

3pm. Col and For Secretaries. Shall we let Makarios back into Cyprus? I wd rather like to do so now; but agreed to await the result of the next Turko-Greek meeting. We believe that this will be next week at Zurich, with both Foreign Ministers and Prime Ministers of the two countries. I do not anticipate that they will reach agreement. But there is some chance that they will make progress and meet again. The question, however, will soon arise as to whether and when we shd intervene – either ourselves, or with Spaak's assistance . . . .

. . . . At 5.30 I saw Haley (Editor of *Times*) to tell him about Russia. He was the same as usual – outwardly friendly and flattering. But he is not trustworthy.

Foster Dulles had 5–7 with For Sec. He is not able to dine out. He has to eat some strange foods and rest to digest them. But Janet came to a dinner at No 10 wh Dorothy gave (wives only) and FS and I had a sandwich together, awaiting his arrival at No 10 at 9pm. I had some talk <u>alone</u> with him – and then the usual conference. For the British – For Secy, Hoyer Millar; Rumbold (with Bishop to take a note) For the Americans – Foster Dulles, Libby Merchant (Under Secretary) Ambassador Whitney . . . .

At the earlier conference, (of wh I was given a record) the two Foreign Ministers had dealt with Iran, Egypt, Indonesia etc. Having got these out of the way, they had begun on Berlin. Here Foster had 'thought aloud'. The impression he gave was that he had <u>completely abandoned</u> the Pentagon plan and the idea of a large convoy of tanks, with perhaps a division or more of troops and artillery, to force and hold the road and rail approach. He put forward a much more modest and much less spectacular form of 'probe', to be followed by political pressure – in U.N. and by other means. It was (I thought) necessary that he shd restate this view to me, in the hearing of his American colleagues. For he <u>must</u> speak on the same lines in Bonn. This does <u>not</u> mean that we shd abandon our position in Berlin or desist from a 'tough' point of view. But it means that while we must present a firm and united front to the Russians, we must not deceive ourselves. Above all, we must not slip into the 1914 position – mobilisation sliding into war. I thought this exposition of the case very ably done. F.O. knows that it is the opposite of what Murphy and the Pentagon have been saying for weeks, almost accusing us of being weak and defeatist – perhaps traitors – because we did not swallow the military plan without thought. I suspect that it is the President who has over-ruled the soldiers. Indeed, when we were alone, Dulles as good as told me this.

The Berlin problem leads on to the wider question of Germany and European security. I threw out various ideas – really to try out the Americans. We might propose 'thinning out' – without national discrimination. We might even propose something much more ambitious – Russian troops to leave Poland, Hungary, and Czechoslovakia – at a price. This price might even be the neutrality of Germany.[11] To my surprise, Foster Dulles was not unduly shocked. He seemed to be ready to discuss new ideas. This may be partly the result of having lost control of Congress and therefore having to accommodate the views of the Administration and the Senate. Senator Fulbright (who is powerful) has been expressing views on these lines . . . .

5 February
. . . . I made the statement about my visit to Russia after questions.[12] It went all right. Gaitskell and his party were rather put out, I thought. They were uncertain whether to praise or damn our initiative . . . .

. . . . The French (who I thought wd be upset by the visit to Moscow) are not at all concerned. Adenauer is rather put out; but I think will be comforted by the emphasis wh I have given (and got over to the Press etc) to the idea of this journey as a 'reconnaissance' <u>not</u> a 'negotiation'.

6 February
No definite news from Egypt. But it looks as if the Egyptian Govt will

---

11. More thoroughgoing than the Soviets' 1957 Rapacki Plan, this was nevertheless almost a straight lift of Labour's 1957 'Gaitskell Plan'.

12. Macmillan had first visited Russia in an extensive tour in 1932, whilst Gaitskell was planning a visit.

not yield and will demand that the Treaty be signed as initialled. However, we have left it to Mr Black to 'play the hand' and if he makes it clear that Egypt will get nothing from the World Bank unless she is reasonable, this intransigeant position may change . . . .

The Press is good about my visit to Russia. The Left-Wing Press tries to conceal its chagrin – and does not find the exercise too easy. The Press has followed very well the lead I gave in Parliament and in the Lobby. 'A reconnaissance, not a negotiation'. This avoids the danger of rousing hope wh will afterwards be disappointed . . . .

David Eccles came after luncheon – talk about Russia and trade possibilities. He is a strange creature. He is the <u>most intelligent</u> man in the Cabinet. He has real genius. But he has two faults. He makes a bad impression on people (it is just a rather self-satisfied manner – actually he is a modest man) and he lacks 'follow up'. He doesn't <u>drive</u> through his ideas. He throws them out, for someone to pick up or not.

At 4pm Chancellor of Exr; Min of Defence and others on Raw Material for Nuclear Weapons. Now that we have the American agreement, we can make quite favourable 'purchase' and/or 'exchange' agreements with them. A useful meeting and some important decisions taken.

6pm. US ambassador (Jock Whitney) He came to deliver a very apologetic message from the President about the British tender for the Arkansas dam, wh had been set aside. President says he was not told about this till too late. In fact, it was just a political job, to help a Republican election.[13]

. . . . Read a novel *No Love for Johnnie* by a Labour MP called [Wilfred] Fienburgh – now dead – (in a motor accident) If he hadn't died, the other Labour MPs must have killed him. It proves what I have often said 'The Labour movement began as a Crusade. It has now become a racket'. This book is reasonably well written, and is a terrible picture of Labour MPs in the House, and their life and intrigues. I also read a curious (privately printed) correspondence between Ld Rosebery and Mr Labouchere. 'Labby' wanted to be ambassador in Washington. In spite of pressure (tantrums as regards Mr Gladstone) Ld R resisted and comes well out of the correspondence. Rosebery's position is pretty equivocal. 'Labby' was a thorn in the flesh of the weak Liberal govt of 1892, and the plan was to buy

---

13. Four days later Macmillan, however, wrote to Eisenhower of his relief that the Greers Ferry Dam contract had in fact gone to the British company Parsons.

him off by an Embassy. What is amusing is that Washington was regarded as obscure and unimportant.

7 February
.... We had a meeting of officials about Moscow. Apart from policy, there is a terrible lot to be settled – in the way of detail. One of the troublesome things is the espionage. Even in our own Embassy, we cannot talk or read secret documents except in one room ....

8 February (Sunday)
Another – rather heavy – box came last night. So I stayed in bed in the morning and did not go to Church. I called in to see Ava Waverley on my way home yesterday. She has to go to hospital today for a serious operation. She is so wayward and sometimes so affected, that I am not sure whether she is anxious to recover or not. She is, of course, very lonely since John's death, and has no relations. She has many friends, but no really intimate ones to rely upon – except, curiously, Dorothy and me.

Rab Butler is laid up with 'flu' and a high temperature. This [is] rather a bore, as there is a lot to be done before I go to Moscow in clearing up matters at home. There is a great row developing about 'Horticulture'. The growers want protective duties on tomatoes etc. But tomatoes are very important in the 'cost of living' index, on wh wages throughout industry depend. Can some other way be found? For ordinary agricultural products, we have 'support prices' not tariffs. This has hitherto been said to be impossible for vegetables and flowers. Is this true? For all this investigation and decision, I am depending on Rab. The political impact is quite important – in Essex, Bedfordshire, and elsewhere. However, I had a talk with Rab this morning on the telephone. He seemed better and hoped to be at work by Wednesday or Thursday ....

10 February
.... Late in the evening, For Sec rang up to say that he expected M. Zorlu (Minister of F Affairs, Turkey) and M. Averoff (ditto Greece) to propose a visit to London tomorrow (11th) This is getting very interesting. What one fears is that they may join in asking us more than we can concede. But we only need our 'Gibraltars'.[14]

---

14. The sovereign military bases eventually secured at Akrotiri and Dhekelia. A number of 'Retained Sites' were also negotiated elsewhere in Cyprus.

11 February

The bad news (60,000 extra) about unemployed has come out. All the Press take it calmly (except the *Herald* and *Mirror*) *Manchester Guardian* sensible. I am worried, because I don't know whether we have done enough reflation and when the tide will turn.

Chief Whip, Tony Barber, Harold Evans – conference on TV, and other similar problems during coming weeks. Having (by some miracle) a day with no appointments till 5pm, I stayed in bed till then. There is such a lot to <u>think</u> about and so little time for thinking . . . .

Roy Harrod came in the evening. He is still very critical (and I think rightly so) of the Treasury and the BofE. By their obsession with the problem of 'funding' they are continuing to narrow the credit base at a time when it shd be expanded. They shd be using 'open market' operations to create <u>more</u> money – by buying securities, not selling. I am trying to compose a paper on all this, and his help will be useful.

12 February

. . . . Cabinet at 11.15 and again at 5.30. We dealt with Horticulture (Tax on Cut Flowers <u>will</u> be increased) Education (50% grants for Church Schools to go to 75%) We had also (in the morning) a statement of the Cyprus situation. We authorised the F.S. to continue the talks on certain understanding 1) our 'bases' to be under British sovereignty 2) other points – e.g. Radar station – to be ours in perpetuity 3) full facilities – harbours, roads etc 4) special arrangement for Nicosia airfield. Many other questions will have to be settled – but this is a start. F.S. made a short statement <u>after</u> questions, wh was well received.

<u>All</u> the Press is good – except the Beaverbrook Press which calls it a 'sell-out' and makes a most violent series of attacks – headlines, leaders, and cartoons, against me and F.S. . . . .

14 February

. . . . I have started to read Lloyd George's *War Memoirs*.[15] The first two volumes throw an extraordinary light on the government machine of those days – no Cabinet papers, no Cabinet minutes, no Cabinet

---

15. During the First World War David Lloyd George was successively Chancellor of the Exchequer (1908–15), Minister of Munitions (1915–16) and Prime Minister (1916–22). He significantly influenced Macmillan's early career. His somewhat self-serving memoirs were published in the 1930s.

secretariat – a P.M. without much power of initiating policy, and none
of 'follow up'. Of course, this suited Asquith admirably – for he was
more a judge than a man of action.

15 February (Sunday)
.... Colonial Secy (Alan Lennox-Boyd) and Sir H Foot (Governor of
Cyprus) arrived .... The position is this – the Greeks and the Turks
have agreed the Zurich concordat. This deals with the Govt of the
Island, the various constitutional arrangements etc – including the
'built-in' Turkish veto through the mechanism of the 'Vice President'.
But it left us to make our demands. This we are now putting into
writing. The Gk and Turk ministers say that we can 'have what we
like'. The Gk says (but I do not believe him) that Archbp Makarios
has 'agreed to everything'. I feel sure that the prelate is going to make
trouble.

16 February
.... Talk with Gaitskell about Cyprus and Germany. He is not a big
man ....

17 February
.... I worked on my paper on 'Money', in wh I am trying to demolish
the Treasury and the Bank of England! Roy Harrod has sent me a
paper about 'open market operations'. Just as Montagu Norman[16]
was obsessed by the gold standard so Cobbold is obsessed by 'funding'. So he is selling securities when he ought to be buying – at least
this is what I feel (supported by Roy Harrod and others, including
Ld Monckton, Midland Bank)

Statement on Marlborough House in Commons. The Queen is
making a truly noble gift to the Commonwealth by handing over this
historic palace as a Commonwealth meeting place. I said that I felt
(when the time came for P[rince] of Wales to be married and need a
house of his own) Parliament wd not forget its obligation. Typically,
both Gaitskell and Grimond welcomed the gift, but sheered right away
from the obligation ....

5pm Defence Ctee. Arms to Iraq, were approved in principle. But

---

16. Governor of the Bank of England 1920–44. Macmillan was thus calling for an
    expansion of the money supply.

we must consult with Americans, Pakistanis, Turks, and Iranians (i.e. our partners in the Baghdad Pact).

Audience at 6.30. Just as I was leaving for the Palace, I heard the terrible news that Mr Menderes and his party had crashed in an aeroplance outside Gatwick. 10 or 12 were believed to have been killed; but the Turkish P.M. himself was said to be safe, tho' very much shaken .... Menderes was coming to the Cyprus conference, and was to have dined with me at No 10. After a great deal of discussion and consultation, it was arranged that our dinner shd be put off till 9pm and only the Greeks to come. The Turks (including Zorlu) went to the London Clinic (where Menderes was taken) and to other hospitals.

The dinner was naturally rather sombre, owing to this tragic affair. But I had very good talks with both Karamanlis (Greek P.M.) and Averoff (For Secy) Altho' they had got the Archbishop's consent to the Zurich agreement and had warned him that we shd have to retain sovereignty in our bases, the Greeks obviously feared that he wd 'rat' . . . .

18 February
There were no formal meetings of the full conference today expected, owing to Mr Menderes being in hospital and out of respect for the victims of the disaster. However, there was a meeting of the 3 Foreign Secretaries, in wh a good deal of progress was made on the assumption that agreement could be reached. At the same time, the Archbishop seemed to be quite intransigeant. At 5pm I heard that the Gk and Turkish Govts were 'fed up' and wanted to go home!

However, Selwyn Lloyd – who has managed all this with consummate skill – got a full meeting called at 7pm (but without Prime Ministers) Once more, the UK, Greek, and Turkish Govts expressed their agreement with the Cyprus plan. M. Kutchuk (Turkish Cypriots) also agreed. The Archbishop (who, so Selwyn reported, seemed nervous and not sure of himself) stated his objections, which were <u>all</u> concentrated on the <u>Zurich</u> agreement – that is, on the Greek–Turkish constitution for Cyprus etc. He made no reference to the <u>London</u> declaration – that is, the British requirements. Since the newspapers have widely reported that the Archbp objected to our retaining <u>sovereignty</u> of the Bases, and since this is vital to us both militarily and politically, I was very glad to hear that he had <u>not</u> in fact taken this line. In a struggle about this, we shd have been very hard pressed here

– by the Socialists, by the Liberals, by all the wet-fish Press (especially the Astor-owned Press) If we had stood firm on sovereignty as against leases, we wd have been accused of being the wreckers. If we had given in, we shd have had a Parliamentary crisis with the Party. Selwyn Lloyd – seeing how firm Averoff and Zorlu continued, adjourned the meeting at 9.15pm. He told the Archbishop that the Zurich-London agreements stood as a whole. What the conference – indeed what the world – would want to know was whether the Archbp – as leader of the Greek Cypriots – would say 'Yes' or 'No' – would open the road to Peace or bar it. Let him think about it – and give his answer in the morning. So this was agreed.

I went to F.S.'s flat at 10pm and heard all the story from him. Colonial Secy and Foot were there. We discussed our plans – if Archbp said no; if he said yes. If no, we wd have a full meeting of the National representatives (UK; Gk; Turkish) and deplore Archbp; reaffirm our plan and our belief it wd be acceptable when understood. (Averoff has said – if he says 'no' now, he will say 'yes' in a week) We must then set up the machinery to take the necessary steps, just as if he were to say 'yes' . . . .

19 February
An extraordinary day. Col Secy rang at 9am (followed quickly by For Secy) The answer is 'yes'. The Cyprus agreement is therefore made! . . . .

I went to Lancaster House at 3pm. Full meeting of conference had been called for 3.30. We worked out our plan – signing first. Speeches after (we must make sure that the Prelate does not raise any point or wriggle any further) . . . .

. . . . After the signing was safely over, I made a little speech, the others followed.

Then we all went into the gallery, for refreshments etc. I had quite an interesting talk with Archbp Makarios, whom I saw for the first time. He was not at all as I had pictured him. I had thought of him as a big man – like Archbishop Damaskinos.[17] Not at all; 5' 8" or so, at the most. Without the beard, not a strong face. Good hands, flexible and artistic. I would have said agreeable, subtle, intelligent, but not strong. This explains, perhaps, his hesitations.

The eating and drinking over, Mr Karamanlis and I drove together

17. Archbishop of Athens and Regent of Greece 1944–46 (see *WD*, pp. 581f).

to the London Clinic. We were taken up to the room, into which a mass of people forced themselves, including a Foreign Office messenger with a fine silver ink-pot! We all signed and after some little talk with P.M. Menderes, withdrew. Menderes seemed all right and <u>very</u> happy – as well he might be.

The Greeks are delighted – altho' they realise that they have <u>not</u> had the best of the bargain. They could have done better by accepting the Radcliffe Plan <u>or</u> the Macmillan plan. But all our friends – and they are legion – like the ambassador and others, are delighted that the long Anglo-Greek dispute is over and that our old friendship can be renewed . . . .

We drafted statement on Cyprus from 6–7 in my room. I entered the House at 7 and spoke for fifteen minutes or so. The agreement was well received. Such Conservative doubts as there may have been seemed resolved by what I said.

Gaitskell made the mistake of a sneering (instead of a generous) reply – and I <u>went for</u> him. This was very pleasant for our Party, and they cheered rapturously.

At 9pm I had to listen to a dreary 'wind-up' by P Noel-Baker (père) who is as great a bore, but not such a cad, as F Noel-Baker (fils)[18]

Having had no time to compose a speech, I wound up for some 15 minutes, saying nothing in particular, but <u>not</u> (I fear) particularly well. However, it was a very thin House.

Chancellor of the Exr came to No 10 at about 10.30pm and we had 1½ hours on Budget prospects. He has some <u>Capital</u> ideas, and the Budget shd be very exciting.

20 February

A good Press – except, of course, Ld Beaverbrook's papers. Gaitskell had a <u>very bad</u> press all round.

Stayed in bed till 11am. Rab Butler at 11.30 – plans for my absence. I also saw Dr Hill and others about propaganda concerning Cyprus. This is important. It is necessary to show a) that British interests are protected b) that it could not have been done before, and certainly not by multilateral concession to Greeks or to Greek

---

18. Philip Noel-Baker, the Labour MP for Derby South, held various Cabinet posts in the 1945–51 Attlee government and in 1959 was awarded the Nobel Peace Prize. His son, Francis, was Labour MP for Swindon.

Cypriots. Turks had to be in – or civil war certainly, Greek–Turkish war probably, would have followed . . . .

4 March

We got back yesterday, at about 6.15pm from our Russian journey. Just before leaving, I finished Lloyd George's *War Memoirs* – more interesting to me now than when I read them years ago. One of the main impressions is the bad arrangements for a PM in those days, and the lack of any properly organised relations with Foreign Office and Service Depts. The absence of anything like the Chiefs of Staff organisation is very noticeable and had very bad effects. The contrast today is very great. I am admirably served in the Private Office. The Cabinet Secretariat has become a very efficient machine. The relations with Service Depts are pretty well tied thro' M of Defence and Chiefs of Staff (tho' there is certainly a weakness still here) and with other departments, including Treasury, our organisation works pretty well. I also read a book on Peter the Great[19] . . . .

We left for Moscow on Saturday Feb 21st. The journey took about 4 hours (in a Comet) It was not, unfortunately, possible for me to take the diary – too risky, in view of the continuous and highly skilled espionage to which we were subjected.

The account of the trip has since been written up and I suppose will be circulated to the Govt and others. I can only now record some general impressions.

In the first place, the ten days of our visit were absolutely filled from morning to night. Three large dinners – at the Kremlin in Moscow; in Kiev; in Leningrad. Two large receptions – at the British Embassy in Moscow and at the Kremlin. Three Ballets – Moscow, Kiev, Leningrad – all admirable in their different ways. Hours and hours of unofficial and fairly relaxed talks with Kruschev, Mikoyan and Gromyko. Hours of 'official' conferences, with more officials present on each side. Luncheons; tourist visits to special places in the 3 cities; visit to universities, collective farms, shipyards, factories and so on.

The second impression – dominating everything else – was the strange experience of being surrounded by friends and advisers – Foreign Secy; Sir N Brook; Sir P Dean; Sir A Rumbold; Bishop; de Zulueta; Sir P Reilly (ambassador) and all this staff and yet being practically

---

19. Tsar of Russia 1682–1725.

unable to communicate with them at all, by word or writing, except in one room in the Embassy in conditions of great discomfort, inside a plastic tent with a gramophone record playing continuously. This is because you cannot speak in the residences, town or country, put at our disposal. Every room is 'wired'. You cannot speak in a car, or train, or even outside the house, if it be a small compound or garden. There is a danger of the apparatus picking up what you say. In the British Embassy, in spite of constant searches, the modern methods are so good and the modern mechanisms so unobtrusive, that (with so many foreign servants etc) there can be no security (except in the one room – as I have described) This makes everyone rather jumpy and is a very unpleasant feeling. Those who stay long here either disregard it or get very irritable and nervy. (I don't myself think that an ambassador should stay more than 2–3 years)

The third impression is more banal. The consumption of food and drink is tremendous. The food (except for caviar, smoked salmon and similar pre dinner delicacies, is not good. The drink (other than vodka – wh is very good) is bad – with the exception of some quite nice white wine from the Caucasus. Soviet brandy is just poison.

The fourth impression, was how nice and how friendly all the people are. I spoke to many – crowds in the streets, in the factories, outside the places where we dined and outside the 'residences' put at our disposal. These gatherings – wh grew in size as the visit proceeded and my speaking to them in this way got known – were uniformly good mannered and attractive.

Some of the crowds were clearly anxious about Peace and War. The propaganda was terrifying. Everyone in Russia seems genuinely persuaded that the Americans, and probably British, have decided on a surprise attack – a 'bolt from the blue'. Everyone asks anxiously whether we are going to keep the Peace. They are kept absolutely ignorant of all the provocations of Soviet policy all over the world.

The fifth – and clearest – impression of all is that Mr Kruschev is absolute ruler of Russia and completely controls the situation. The uneasy period after the death of Stalin is now over.[20] The attempt at a 'directory' has not lasted. The First Consul is in authority.

Mr K is a curious study. Impulsive; sensitive of his own dignity

---

20. The Soviet dictator died in March 1953: see vol. 1, p. 216. Macmillan here compares Khrushchev's subsequent climb to power with that of Napoléon in post-revolutionery France.

and insensitive of anyone else's feelings; quick in argument, never missing or overlooking a point; with an extraordinary memory and encyclopaedic information at his command; vulgar, and yet capable of a certain dignity when he is simple and forgets to 'show off'; ruthless, but sentimental – K is a kind of mixture between Peter the Great and Lord Beaverbrook. Anyway, he is the boss and no meeting will ever do business except a 'Summit' meeting. Neither Mikoyan (a clever Armenian, who cringes to K) nor Gromyko (For Secy) who is afraid of him, will ever do any real negotiation on any essential points . . . .

We had expected to find difficulties about telegrams from England and conducting affairs while away (as one can do in most capitals, at any rate) But we had not reckoned on the difficulties of decyphering and cyphering telegrams, or of consultation etc, owing to the tremendous espionage system.

We were very well treated – apart from this – and all the different residences and 'dachas' put at our disposal were made as comfortable as possible. Food and drink were lavish.

The visit fell into three parts or phases. The first days – Saturday night, Sunday, Monday – everything was smiles. Then, (after Tuesday – when K made a party speech wh was offensive to us, both in content and timing) I had a straight talk with him on Wednesday. He chose to take offence and say that we had 'threatened him' and 'insulted him'. At Thursday morning's conference (in the Kremlin) he was rude and provocative – talking about the Strang visit in 1939[21] and what Eden had said to him in 1956, and the result – our humiliation in Suez. I replied that I cd not accept such talk, and brought the meeting to an end. K then said that – owing to tooth-ache – he wd not be able to go to Kiev with us – a special honour wh he had announced during phase 1. I said I was sorry about the tooth-ache. No doubt I shd have the pleasure of meeting at Kiev his married daughter (who lived there, as he had told us) He said he thought it unlikely. Mr Mikoyan and Mr Gromyko wd not – unfortunately – be able to come to Leningrad with us, as had also been announced during the honeymoon period. We left the meeting. All this began to leak to the Press (or, rather, was put out by the Russians, including the ridiculously oriental story of the tooth-ache) Many ambassadors (esp U.S., French and German) were saying

---

21. The Soviets were offended in June 1939 when Chamberlain responded to their overtures for negotiation in face of the German threat by sending not a senior minister but William Strang, a Foreign Office official.

that the only reply was to ask for my Comet aeroplane and go home. Most of the English press took the same line in their cables home. The *Daily Chronicle* next day called my journey a 'monumental flop'.

I had a meeting at the Embassy (in the special cell) when we got back from the Kremlin (about 11.30am) and decided to take no notice at all of all this childishness and go on with the programme. This ended phase 2. Phase one, marriage and honeymoon. Phase two, quarrel. Phase three, reconciliation. The story of phase 3 was simple. We went off to Kiev as planned – without K, Mikoyan, Gromyko – but with ambassador Malik and one of the deputy foreign secretaries. At the dinner, K's daughter appeared – the only woman, except a woman minister. Next day, a message from Moscow – 'I would be glad to know that K's tooth was better. The dentist had used an excellent and new British drill!'

Then, when we got to Leningrad, we found both Mikoyan and Gromyko to greet us. They never left us. A luncheon was added to all the dinners, ballets etc in our honour. Mikoyan paraded everywhere with me and spoke to the crowds with me. At the Monday meeting, (a very long and important meeting) a really useful and constructive discussion. At the Kremlin party (Monday afternoon) Mr K made a helpful speech (of wh he courteously sent me the text) I was allowed to make my T.V. broadcast to the Russian people without any censorship or interference. Next day, further friendly talks; (including a talk <u>alone</u> with Mr K) no trouble about the communiqué; a ceremonial signature in the Kremlin Imperial State apartments; a drive to the airfield with Mr K, in his car; a fine band and military parade. Home Tuesday night – March 3rd – where I was met by Butler, Ld Kilmuir etc. On reading the British Press, I found that the 'monumental flop' of a few days before was being universally acclaimed as a 'triumph'. All we <u>really</u> did was to keep our heads – but that is something in this world.

It is hard to see why the Russians behaved in this way. It helped me enormously. In order to keep straight with the Western allies, I <u>had</u> – at some point – to take a '<u>tough</u>' line on Berlin and the consequences of unilateral action by the Soviet Govt. This was <u>not</u> easy to do, altho' necessary. K's public speech (esp its rather 'Limehouse' character)[22]

---

22. Lloyd George's speech in Limehouse on 30 July 1909 attacking the House of Lords for rejecting his 'People's Budget' precipitated a constitutional crisis. For a time 'limehousing' went into the language as shorthand for political vituperation.

enabled me to do this, but in reply. He took offence, or pretended to take offence, and then realised his mistake. Prob[ably] (as so often) the simplest explanation is the right one. He had this party speech fixed long ago – a sort of 'Blackpool' speech.[23] He did not realise how it would be taken as an insult to me. He tried to cover his mistake by taking offence at my protest. He saw that he had acted foolishly and impulsively and then made amends.

We have been loaded with presents. I have a gun (shot-gun) beautifully made, with gold fittings, an elk's head; a malachite box; a china figure; a box of records; caviare etc. We gave the Russians some fine presents – the chief being a wonderful Queen Anne walnut cabinet – also, some very good wedgewood china. The problem of 'financing' these outward presents and 'dealing with' the inward ones is quite difficult. In theory, we ought to 'turn over' our presents to the Treasury – to be sold at auction or in a jumble sale. But it wd seem that this strict procedure might have awkward results.

Cabinet at 11.30 – For Secy and I gave an account of what we had learned in Russia and of what we proposed to do. We are to visit Paris, Bonn, Ottawa and Washington. We want a negotiated settlement, because we do not believe that (in spite of all the brave talk) the allies will face war over not the right to supply Berlin but the insistence that USSR and not DDR police or customs officials shall issue the necessary permits. However, we (Britain) must not get in to the position we got into at Munich (1938) I will be no Mr Chamberlain. We must therefore talk ourselves quite boldly about preparations for war and see what de Gaulle and Adenauer say in response. What wd be the worst thing of all for the West wd be a humiliating climb-down after talking big . . . .

I made [a] statement in HofC on the Russia trip. All the Conservative Party rose and cheered when I came in, led by Winston Churchill!

A long talk with Heathcoat Amory about a) monetary policy b) Budget. Treasury and Bank of England are rather sticky about a) However, altho' they are not yet buying securities in the open market (as they should be doing) they have stopped selling and have lately even bought a little. On b) the prospects for a stimulating Budget are distinctly good.

---

23. A speech to the party faithful. British party conferences then frequently met in Blackpool.

5 March

A most troublesome situation is developing in N Rhodesia and Nyasaland. A sort of reign of terror has been brought about thro' the 'extremist' native leaders, supported by the Socialist Party and papers like *Manchester Guardian* and *Observer*. There is a most regrettable division of responsibility between the various Governments concerned. It looks as if the Federation plan, altho' economically correct (since Nyasaland is not 'viable') is regarded with such great suspicion by 'advanced' native opinion as to be politically unacceptable. In Kenya, a similarly dangerous position is developing.[24] I must try to get the facts and take a hand in this affair, or it may prove really difficult as well as politically damaging at home : . . .

D and I left by air for Belfast. We stayed the night with Ld and Ly Brookeborough.[25]

6 March

A terrific programme, including – (morning and afternoon) visit to a Machine Tool Factory (Hughes), Short and Harlands (aircraft) and Harland and Wolff (shipbuilding) I had the most enthusiastic reception from the workmen, such as I have never experienced in England or Scotland. Luncheon – Ulster Unionist Party and half-hour speech (wh seemed to please them) De Valera has started to let IRA criminals out of detention, so more trouble is beginning on the Border.[26] I referred to this, which has pleased Belfast, but angered Dublin . . . .

---

24. Kenneth Kaunda's recently formed Zambian African National Congress was banned by the authorities in Northern Rhodesia in March 1959. A State of Emergency was declared in Nyasaland on 3 March and Hastings Banda and other nationalist politicians arrested, with 52 Africans killed by security forces in the ensuing disorder. On the same day in Kenya prisoners held for their part in the Mau Mau uprising had been beaten by guards at the Hola detention camp, 11 of them to death.

25. Lord Brookeborough was Prime Minister of Northern Ireland 1943–63.

26. A border campaign into Northern Ireland was launched by the IRA in December 1956 and continued until February 1962. It was combated by the use of detention without trial on both sides of the border, a practice which continued after de Valera's return to power in 1957. Its use in the Irish Republic, however, was challenged using the European Convention on Human Rights by Gerard Lawless. The progress of this case and declining IRA activities led the Irish to discontinue internment in February 1959.

8 March (Sunday)

.... I am trying to get the Allies to send a really forthcoming reply
to the last Soviet note, instead of the usual quibbling answer. I am
quite convinced that we can have no effective negotiation with anyone but Kruschev. We ought therefore to propose, right away, a Summit meeting. I wd like this as early as possible, but wd accept end
of July or early August. This wd prob[ably] have the effect of getting
Mr K to take no dangerous or provocative action till then. It wd
force the Allies to concentrate their minds on the real problem – an
acceptable compromise on Germany and Berlin. It would (incidentally) give me the maximum of manoeuvre regarding our own General
Election.

9 March

Left for Paris at 9.45 .... The French really agree with us entirely
over the German problem. But they are trying to pretend that we are
weak and defeatist, and that they are for 'being tough'. The purpose
of this is to impress Chancellor Adenauer, and keep his support in
their protectionist attitude towards European economic problems. I
concentrated therefore a good deal of my talk, esp after dinner, on the
practical measures wh ought now to be taken to prepare for war –
calling up reservists, organisation of civil defence, more troops to
Germany, evacuation of children from Berlin etc. This surprised and
alarmed them very much.

10 March

To the Elysée at 11.30. I had a good talk with de Gaulle – first alone,
then with Debré, For Secy, de Murville etc.

De Gaulle rather put out of countenance his team, by admitting
right away that one cd not have a nuclear war in Europe on the
question of who signed the pass to go along the *autobahn* or the
railway to W Berlin – a USSR sergeant or a DDR sergeant. In his
view the only question which wd justify war wd be an actual physical
blockade. I asked 'did he say this to Adenauer?' He admitted that
he had not. It wd depress him. He also thought the Russians shd be
kept guessing. On the 2 Germanies, de Gaulle also said that reunion
was impossible without war, and that France and Britain cd not fight
such a war. But the 'idea' of reunification shd be kept alive in order
to give some comfort to the German people. This is 'the light at the
end of the tunnel' idea, about wh much has already been said. '*La*

chose-Allemande[27] – that must be kept alive. Meanwhile there shd be practical cooperation on economic, supply, and cultural matters between the two Germanies. What Dulles had called 'confederation' shd be pressed. Again, I asked 'Had he said this to Adenauer?' He said 'Non'. It was clear that the French (who are getting money and support from Germany on a big scale) expect Britain or America to put this forward .... Gen Norstad came to see me yesterday. He was very distressed at de Gaulle's open flouting of all his NATO obligations. The French are now withdrawing the [Mediterranean] fleet from NATO command.[28] He begged me (as did the State Dept) to take this up with de G, wh I did – without getting much satisfaction ....

We left Paris at 7pm ....

11 March
Cabinet in morning. I had left instructions for some stronger action in Nyasaland and some real effort to get public opinion on our side. Between the Commonwealth and Colonial Offices, things have rather slipped and I felt this was doing us harm. After a long discussion the following course of action was agreed and I have given Norman Brook the task of coordinating it.
1) Ld Perth to visit Nyasaland and report next week
2) Intelligence reports which led Governor to propose and Col Sec to agree to 'state of emergency', arrest of leaders etc to be published in White Paper as soon as possible, so far as this can be done without disclosing sources.
3) Send out a judge and perhaps two senior Privy Councillors to inquire into causes of disturbances and riots in Nyasaland and report ....

The wider problem – can the Federation continue in the present form? – must be studied further before the Constitutional Conference agreed for 1960 ....

The 'Nasserite' revolt in Iraq has failed. But this may mean that the present regime will go more and more Communist. We are in a bad position here – between the devil and the sea[29] ....

---

27. The German issue.
28. Followed by the Atlantic fleet in 1965.
29. This Nasser-inspired revolt in Mosul was defeated by Iraqi dictator Qasim,

12 March
Left London airport at 9.30 for Bonn (the time in Bonn is one hour later than London – so we did not arrive till about noon German time) We were met by Chancellor Adenauer, Foreign Minister Brentano and other ministers and officials . . . .

The conference began at 3.30 and lasted till 6.30 . . . . The first half of our conversation was a full account, given in detail by FS, of what happened in Russia. I then gave a sort of appreciation. We then had an account of the Chancellor's six days in Russia, a year or two ago. Also, a very long speech giving his views on Russia generally, and the future of Western Europe. This was all rather pessimistic. The Germans then launched quite an attack upon us about 'disengagement', which they seemed to think we had agreed in principle with the Russians. We argued that 'limitation and inspection in an agreed area' was the only way to avoid 'disengagement' wh we too thought very dangerous. It took an hour or more of quite heated discussion to get these suspicions out of their heads. The Chancellor was slow to understand and seemed to cherish some resentment. I was pretty sharp with him, and this had some effect. Von Brentano and his colleagues told Selwyn Lloyd afterwards that they were themselves perfectly satisfied. The Chancellor had got hold of the wrong end of the stick; but this talk would do a lot of good . . . .

13 March
10.15–12.30. Private talk with Adenauer. This was very useful altho' very diffuse. I think I got him round to my view of a Summit conference. Meanwhile, telegrams came in showing a) that the Americans are against us b) that the French have ratted – and gone back on what de Gaulle and the others had more or less agreed . . . .

We left Bonn at about 5.45 (German time) and got to London airport just after 6, (London time) . . . .

15 March
Adenauer has rather gone back (like De Gaulle) on what we thought had been arranged. But I hope we shall be able to clear it up. The Americans are yielding a little about the Summit, but are still averse to

strongly backed by the Iraqi communists. The Egyptians at the time convinced themselves that Britain had a significant hand in this defeat.

a fixed date. I have refused to move, so <u>no agreed</u> answer can be made
to the last Russian note until I have seen the President . . . .

16 March

All day's debate on the financial agreement with Egypt.[30] Chancellor
of Exr opened – with a dull but sufficient speech, explaining the
provisions. Gaitskell followed with an admirable speech, attacking the
whole Suez episode, and ending with a call for my impeachment (this
was the only mistake. It was a bit too melodramatic) It was one of the
best speeches I have heard him make. The debate then collapsed – or
rather dragged itself along in a very thin house. Then Bevan wound up
– amusing, but light. I rose at 9.23 (earlier than I had thought – but
Bevan suddenly stopped) The first 10–15 minutes were about the
agreement – wh I think I explained better than the Treasury [brief] wh
the Chancellor had read out, and gave some assurances about further
help to individuals. The rest of the speech was on the general Suez
question. It was thought to be effective and was very loudly cheered
by our side. My comparison of Bevan to 'a shorn Samson, groping
about the front Opposition bench, filled with a bevy of prim and
ageing Delilahs' (or some such phrase) brought the House down. We
got – very strangely – a majority of 70 – altho' both sides had 3 line
whips and it was a vote of censure.

17 March

. . . . In the afternoon, P.Q.s – and a series of visitors. Signor Pella
(Italian Foreign Minister) an old friend, urbane and courteous. He
wants Italy to be a member of any 'Summit' meeting. Then F.M. Ld
Montgomery – very full of the only subject in wh he takes a really
deep interest – himself . . . .

18 March

2am. Left London airport in Comet – with For Secy, Norman Brook,
Hoyer Millar, etc etc.

　　7.30am. Arrived at Ottawa (Canadian time – 12.30 London
time) . . . .

　　10–12. Talk with P.M. . . . . He and his ministers are <u>very</u> sympathetic with our point of view and agree completely with us about

---

30. The recently negotiated agreement that Egypt would pay £27.5 million
　　compensation for British properties which had been nationalised.

how to handle the Berlin and German problem. This is partly due to confidence in us (D[iefenbaker] has always been very friendly with me personally, dating from the Commonwealth Prime Ministers Conference) and perhaps even more results from their deep suspicion – amounting now to active dislike – of the Eisenhower administration. Canada feels always anxious about being absorbed by USA. The Conservative victory is partly a reflection of this sentiment . . . .

19 March
Left Ottawa airport about 10 and arrived Washington at noon . . . .

Dinner at Embassy – Vice President and Mrs Nixon; Mr and Mrs Herter; Mrs John Foster Dulles; Mr and Mrs Allen Dulles; Mr and Mrs R Murphy; Ld and Ly Cromer etc etc. I sat between Mrs Nixon and Mrs Foster Dulles. Mrs N was agreeable, even gushing – she is a pleasant enough woman, with some claim to beauty, but in the rather hard American way. Janet [Dulles] was as delightful as ever – but she looked, not unnaturally, pretty tired and worn.

The position about Foster seems to be still obscure. He has had a new and very fatiguing treatment which may or may not succeed in 'retarding' the spread of the cancer. Nobody sees him, except the President – who goes every other day. He reads papers and summaries of telegrams and rings the State Dept. He is still Secretary of State. Governor Chris Herter, Under Secy of State, acts more or less as wd a Minister of State or Under Secy in England, in the absence of his chief. This has now been the position for several weeks and is causing a good deal of confusion at such a critical moment.

Janet Dulles wants him to resign. She told me that she wanted to take him away from Washington – to the South – for a bit. She clearly feels that he cannot live very long, and wd like to make his remaining time as happy as possible. But I fear that to keep working is his idea of happiness, and that he clings to the job. The President, out of loyalty to his friend – whom he trusts and reveres – will not ask for his resignation.

20 March
F.S. and I went to White House. President met us and we motored with him to the Walter Reid Hospital. Foster Dulles was sitting up, in dressing gown, and altho' very thin and even emaciated, talked with conviction and vigour. But it was even more of a monologue than ordinarily, and his views much more inflexible than they had seemed at our last talk. It was a strange scene. The President sat on a sofa; For

Secy and I sat in low arm-chairs in the sitting room of this 'Hospital suite', furnished in a sort of Claridges style,[31] while Foster – in another chair, higher and harder, discoursed on Communism, Germany, Berlin etc. He was <u>against</u> almost everything. He was strongly against the idea of a <u>Summit</u>; he didn't much like the Foreign Ministers meeting. He thought we cd 'stick it out' in Berlin, and that the Russians wd not dare to interfere with us. There wd be no war – unless the Russians challenged it.

The President did not say anything. I said a few words (wh I afterwards regretted, because I felt I ought not to have argued at all with this dying man) Foster could <u>not</u> have been nicer or more genuinely glad to see us. He had particularly asked to see me and took my hand and held it clasped in his two hands for quite a few moments when we said goodbye. It was a splendid exhibition of courage and devotion. But I felt that his illness had made his mind more rigid and reverting to very fixed concepts . . . .

. . . . We left about 12.30 and drove to some Naval installation where the helicopters were waiting. We had about 35–40 minutes in the air and got eventually to Camp David (FDR's 'Shangri-La') about 1.30.[32] The President has to rest <u>before</u> a meal – so luncheon was not till about 2.15. The President was in capital form, very glad to escape from the White House. This is a delightful spot, 1800 feet up, surrounded by woodland, overlooking a wide valley with the mountains beyond. There is a main hut or bungalow – a large 'sun-parlour' – with also room for 10 or 12 to eat. My bedroom; the President's; Herter's; and Selwyn Lloyd's are in this main building – very simple but very comfortable. The rest of the party live in huts – some with one and some with two bedrooms – which are scattered about the camp. We have brought with us Brook, Caccia, Hoyer Millar and Bishop as <u>permanent</u> members of the Camp party. Others are flown in, as wanted, and return to Washington – by helicopter.

The talks began at about 3 and lasted – on and off – till dinner. The whole of today was taken up with the draft reply to the last Soviet note and how to phrase our references to the Foreign Ministers and the 'Summit' meeting. At times, we got quite heated – indeed I made an

---

31. An upmarket London hotel.
32. Macmillan had been invited to the Presidential country retreat in Maryland, established by Roosevelt and now renamed after Eisenhower's grandson, on his return from Moscow.

outburst just before dinner,[33] and said I would have to send a separate note, and we must 'agree to differ'. President got quite animated. Eventually, I said that each side had better produce their own drafts, going as far as they could to meet the other's point of view – then we could 'sleep on it' and reach a final conclusion the next day. This was agreed.

The fact is that the President – left to himself – is _very_ reasonable and wants to help. He especially wants to help me. (He took me out for a drive alone in his car to his Gettysburg farm in the course of the afternoon) – as a break between the discussions and was most friendly and intimate. He spoke freely about Foster – a few weeks must decide whether the disease cd be 'retarded' or not. He thought it unlikely that he cd go on.[34] But whom cd he appoint? Herter was good – but after his own and Foster's illness, was it wise to have a man who could only walk with crutches? Foster has been ringing up from the Hospital to find out what is happening and of course Murphy and Libby Merchant take the rigid State Dept view. Herter is himself much more flexible. He is also a really charming man. As he has been a long time (20 years or more) in politics, he is much more aware of public feeling than the State Dept officials. Ambassador Whitney is helpful and has quite an influence with the President.

After dinner the great problem of the draft reply was left aside. We had a film, called 'The Great Country' or some such name.[35] It was a 'Western'. It lasted three hours! It was inconceivably banal.

Our news from home seems good .... Both the Harrow and Belfast by-elections have gone well.[36] There is much talk of an early election in all the papers.

33. The American memorandum reports that 'The Prime Minister became exceedingly emotional. He said that we were dealing with a matter which in his judgment affected the whole future of mankind. He said that: "World War I – the war which nobody wanted – came because of the failure of the leaders at that time to meet at the Summit. [Sir Edward] Grey instead had gone fishing ...."' (DDEL: Whitman File, International Series, Box 24). At a meeting that evening Macmillan referred to a concern that the Soviets could deliver eight missiles against Britain, killing 20 million, hence the pressing need for a Summit.

34. Dulles resigned on 15 April and died on 24 May.

35. Presumably the Oscar-winning _The Big Country_ starring Gregory Peck, released in October 1958.

36. The day before, the Tories retained Harrow East – following Ian Harvey's resignation – and Belfast East, despite small swings to Labour.

21 March

We <u>agreed</u> a compromise on the reply to the Soviet Govt at 10 am, after only half an hour's talk between President and me . . . .

We sent off the necessary telegrams. The French and Germans – as well as NATO – must now be consulted. But I hope the reply can be got off early next week. No doubt the French (and perhaps the Germans too) will make trouble, because they always dislike an Anglo-American agreement . . . .

We then passed to our ideas as to 'limitation and inspection of forces in an agreed area'. The President (in spite of almost universal disapproval of his military advisers) rather liked the idea. He quite saw that we <u>must</u> have something constructive if we are to resist the dangerous Rapacki plan and what is called 'disengagement'.[37] The President felt that we shd work out big and imaginative proposals and not always be driven to a purely negative position. General Twining winced at this.

Then we had a long discussion on Atomic Tests and the Geneva conference. The American experts gave an interesting exposition of the latest scientific theories, all of wh are quite different from the conclusion of the scientists a year ago and on wh the Geneva conference is based. It is clear that we are in a difficult position, as the Americans are very unwilling to abandon anything <u>unless</u> the Russian side of the agreement can be effectively policed.[38] It now seems that underground tests up to quite high levels (10 and perh[aps] ultimately 50 or 100 kilotons) cd escape detection. The Geneva view was 5 kilotons only. It was decided to postpone further discussion till tomorrow. After dinner, we had another film – very bad – but we got to bed early . . . .

---

37. This 1957 proposal for nuclear disengagement in Central Europe clearly favoured the East because it would leave Soviet preponderance in conventional forces in place, whilst denying the West the ability to balance that with nuclear deployment.

38. During his visit to Moscow Macmillan had written to Eisenhower on 24 February suggesting an annual limit on inspections as a way of getting the Russians to drop their absolute veto on having any. Khrushchev had told him 'he regarded the Western purpose in asking for mobile inspection teams to investigate suspected nuclear explosions as exclusively designed to permit ground inspection throughout the Soviet Union in order to locate missile bases' (G&E, p. 217). At Camp David some discussion of limits began.

22 March

We .... had a good talk on economic questions. We deployed, with some vigour, our grievances – on tariffs, quotas, and cancelled contracts. The situation is getting worse not better. There is a threat that all 'electrical' contracts are to be forbidden.

President and Mr Herter both proclaimed their own belief in 'liberalising' trade. But they were very eloquent about their difficulties. Congress is hostile; lobbying and log-rolling is rife; the Republican Party is just as uncontrollable as the Democrats and the Democrats (for all their talk) just as Protectionist as the Republicans. It was rather a pathetic reply to our protests. For the first time in our talks, Pres was really embarrassed . . . .

I asked what wd happen if the Russians were <u>not</u> unyielding about control. Pres said that we should take the agreement – at least for 3 or 4 years – and let underground testing go hang. He knew his advisers wd be shocked, but both he and Foster thought the political gain wd outweigh any technical disadvantage. I was very glad to hear this.[39]

We left Camp David by road at 4pm. Before leaving, Pres shewed me the underground fortress wh has been built – a sort of Presidential command post in the event of atomic war. It holds 50 of President's staff in one place and 150 defence staff in another. The fortress is underneath the innocent looking huts in wh we lived, hewn out of the rock. It cost 10 million dollars!

On the drive to Washington (wh took about 1½ hours) Pres talked at large about the future of the world. He is certainly a strange mixture. With all his crudity and lack of elegance of expression, he has some very remarkable ideas. He thought that USA, UK, Canada, Australia etc should make a Federation and combine in something like the European Common Market (to start with) ending in a political merger or Federal constitution. This wd be the only way to resist Communism and to create a force strong enough to attract the neutral world. He developed this theme at some length – monetary tariff, and all other policy cd be unified and our power <u>together</u>, wd be much more – 3 or 4 times more – than our power

---

39. After further correspondence, Macmillan wrote on 8 April 1959 to Eisenhower, welcoming the fact that 'we are prepared to agree to a comprehensive ban on all nuclear tests, in spite of the risk that the Russians may in fact be able to carry out certain tests which the system could not identity as such' (G&E, p. 236).

separately – however closely we work together. For our present co-
operation depends too much on personal factors, like our own
friendship . . . .

23 March
. . . . At 6pm a party given by Vice-President Nixon at his house –
there were the leading Senators and Congress leaders, Republican and
Democrat. They gave us quite a 'gruelling' for an hour or more. This
was a most useful exercise, as these are the men who really control
Congress. We normally only see the Administration. In our country
any visitor who sees the Ministers also sees the Parliamentary leaders.
Here, where Congress and the Executive are altogether separate, we
are always apt to forget this difference.

24 March
. . . . We left Washington at 9am (Washington time) in the Comet,
arriving London airport about 9.30pm (London time) . . . .

3 April
. . . . Meeting of Ministers about European Trade. The *modus vivendi*[40] with the French (chiefly on quotas) has at last been negotiated
and is not too bad. What we have to consider is what to do next. If
we could make some agricultural concessions to Denmark, we might
be able to organise another European grouping with the Scandinavian
countries, Switzerland, and Austria. But here, the problem is our
pledges to British farmers. We can only really 'get out' of them by a
General Election and a new series of undertakings.[41] At luncheon at
No 10 were Butler, Hailsham, Poole, Macleod, Ted Heath, and Derry
Heathcoat Amory. We discussed the next General Election for 3
hours. On the present form, and after a most careful analysis of every
constituency in the light of a) the agent's report b) the Liberal intervention c) the state of the various Gallup polls, Central Office say
that a dissolution now wd give us a majority of 13 in HofC. The
questions to be answered are –

---

40. Means of living (with).
41. The government had pledged both to exclude agriculture and horticulture from
    European trade negotiations and to consult the National Farmers Union on
    negotiations.

1. What will be effect of Budget
2. Where shall we stand on June 11th (the proposed polling day)
3. Will we be any better in October . . . .

A complicated situation is arising in Central Africa. Ld Home is out there and is doing his best with Sir Roy Welensky etc. But the settlers are in a dangerous mood. If the Labour Party gets in here, I have no doubt that they will secede and either declare their independence or join S Africa . . . .

6 April

. . . . Budget Cabinet at 3. The Chancellor of the Exr gave the outline of his proposals – most of which many already knew. I and the Ld Privy Seal alone were privy to the whole scheme. Beer (2d a pint reduction) was rather a surprise. So – to some – was 9d off Income Tax. Purchase tax reductions were obviously right. The repayment of post war credits is likely to be very popular. The restoration of 'initial allowances' should help investment in the private sector[42] . . . .

9 April

Budget has been <u>very</u> well received in the country and by the Press. The only attack has been 'Why nothing for the Old Age Pensioners'. Actually, we have done this class in the community exceptionally well – as a leading article in *The Times* showed very forcibly today. But Gaitskell and co will exploit the old people quite shamelessly. The 64000 dollar [question] remains – when? I am feeling more and more <u>against</u> a 'snap' election . . . .

   Dr Adenauer has – quite unexpectedly – announced that he will stand as his party's candidate for the post of President. The present man – Heuss – is due to retire shortly . . . . Some time ago, there was an effort by the Chancellor and the CDU[43] to get Erhard to stand. He managed to resist the pressure to 'kick him upstairs' . . . . Some say that it will be not so completely 'upstairs' as some believe and as the practice of President Heuss wd suggest. There <u>are</u> residual powers in the President's hands wh Adenauer might develop. Nor is it clear

---

42. In fact it was investment allowances which were reintroduced at 20% whilst initial allowances were reduced from 30 to 10%. This offered businesses the incentive of 120% tax relief on investment in plant and machinery.

43. The ruling right-wing party of West Germany, the Christlich-Demokratische Union Deutschlands (Christian Democratic Union).

<u>when</u> the election is to be. All that <u>is</u> certain is that yet another element of doubt and uncertainty is introduced into an already complicated and obscure situation. For who will really direct German foreign policy during the next critical weeks? . . . .

20 April

Cabinet at 6pm. I stayed at home till after luncheon. Everyone (including excited Lobby correspondents) thought the Cabinet was to decide on a dissolution and the wildest rumours were current. Actually, it was the 64000 dollar question – shall we continue to supply the Iraqi army with arms or not? If we do, Nasser will get very angry and may go back on the whole financial agreement – which is anyway not being implemented very satisfactorily. If we don't, the Iraqi Govt (who are already half-Communist) will go finally into the Russian control and will get all the arms they need from Russia. A very long discussion ended in a great support of the F.O. – that it was worth trying to save Iraq . . . .

23 April

. . . . A long Cabinet – ranging from Obscene Publications Bill to Dollar Liberalisation! I refused to allow a decision on the Treasury proposals to remove more dollar restrictions. The country is in rather an anti-American mood at the moment. The President's decisions on the Electrical Contracts and the wool tariff have been bitterly resented. At the same time, the foolish talk about war with Russia which flows daily out of the Pentagon has exasperated people of all parties here. It certainly makes my task much more difficult.

. . . . The President of the BofT announced the new help for the cotton industry this afternoon. There are 3 basic principles 1) Reorganisation and where necessary destruction of obsolete and obsolescent plant. The Govt will contribute ¾ to the cost. 2) New machinery. HMG will contribute ¼. 3) Compensation agreement for redundancy to be made between employers and T Unions as a pre-condition for 1) and 2) . . . .

24 April

The Opposition have committed themselves – thro' Gaitskell and H Wilson to a bitter attack on the Cotton scheme. This is both foolish and dishonest . . . . A very long day – 9am to midnight . . . . 6 or 7 speeches – impromptu – we covered many Lancashire towns, including Oldham, Rochdale, Bury, Stockport, Manchester. D was with me. It was really a most heartening experience. With the masses of people whom we saw – they waited in large numbers in the streets – there was scarcely a 'boo'.

25 April

. . . . The more I think of the visit to Lancashire the more pleased I am.[44] Of course, I don't mean that the people who were so polite and friendly will all vote Tory. But I cannot believe that such courtesy and so little bitterness are not good signs. It is very different to the mood of 1945 or even 1950 . . . .

4 May

Mr Gaitskell, walking in the rain yesterday afternoon – a May day march to Trafalgar Square – made a vulgar and violent attack on me. He accused me of having arranged with President Eisenhower to back or condone our foreign policy in order to help the Conservatives at the next General Election. His speech has received almost universal condemnation from the Press. He is a contemptible creature – a cold-blooded, Wykehamist – intellectual and *embusqué*.[45]

Another telegram from Welensky. After a talk with Commonwealth and Colonial Secretaries, I got off a reply. The plan for a Commission to report on Central Africa is going ahead slowly.[46] But since it depends – to some extent – on the Opposition appointing their Privy Councillors, I fear they may try to wreck it by boycotting it . . . .

6 May

Several problems – of the kind that cause great trouble at elections – are looming up. First – and far the most important – can we organise another European Free Trade area out of the European countries not in the Rome community? It is obviously in our interests, industrially and commercially. But there will be the Commonwealth objections (altho' this plan cannot in any way injure Commonwealth interests) There will also be some price to be paid to Denmark – perh[aps] in

---

44. Lancashire was then seen as an important electoral barometer.
45. Someone who found a safe post in war time.
46. This was decided upon by Cabinet on 17 March 1959, to prepare the ground for a review of the Central African constitution.

bacon and/or blue cheese. But this – altho' very small – may arouse British farmers agst us . . . .

10 May (Sunday)
The Shah arrived at 11.30,[47] with his Minister of Foreign Affairs – Hekmat – and his ambassador Nakhai. The former of these is a scholar and historian, and very deaf. The latter is a poet, and very *distrait* . . . .

Talks from 11.30–1.15 and from 3.30–5.30. Anthony Eden took part in the morning and left after luncheon. In the morning, we exchanged views on the general situation – which means Russia. I thought the Shah very intelligent and very moderate. He speaks excellent English, and expresses his thoughts with distinction as well as with clarity. He very much shares our motto 'firm but flexible'. By this method, Persia has managed to survive. He agreed with our policy towards Iraq and Col Qasim.[48] He fears Nasser more.

In the afternoon, we dealt with special subjects – military and civil aid; problems of the Gulf etc. There was a good deal of pressure for more of everything. Persians are all born Oliver Twists . . . .

For Secy left today for Geneva. The Powers have already begun to squabble about the shape of the conference table. The Americans say 'square'. The Russians insist 'round'. There is a deep significance in this, because of the question of Poles or Czechs (and on our side perhaps Italians) attending. The British propose 'oval' – thus admitting only the German 'observers' (East and West) whose presence has already been agreed . . . .

14 May
. . . . Meeting of Ministers in the morning – about Railways and Coal. The position of both these nationalised industries is as bad as it could be. The truth is that we are at the beginning of the end of the coal age. Oil is cheaper and easier to handle . . . .

24 May
. . . . The For Secy got back on Friday and I had a long telephone

47. Mohammad Reza Shah Pahlavi, Shah of Iran 1941–79.
48. This included, after Qasim repudiated the 1955 defence agreement, withdrawal from British bases in Iraq by May 1959.

conversation with him. The Press all assumed that I wd cut short my holiday to see him in London. I therefore thought it better to do no such thing, and retain the reputation of being 'unflappable'. Actually, largely owing to Selwyn's initial effort, the Conference has at least got started. On my advice, he decided to 'lie back' and let the rest get into a muddle. The French and Germans (out of jealousy) are only too ready to accuse us of weakness and Chamberlainism. '*Nous sommes trahis*'[49] and all that. So the F.S. has ranged himself (without undue fervour but with complete loyalty) behind the others. When the Americans began to realise that the Conference might rapidly come to an end, and the Russians revert to the old 'ultimatum' policy, they got alarmed. The French and the Germans (who only want to <u>seem</u> strong and have no real desire for trouble) have also changed their tune . . . .

Apart from trouble in Buganda[50] and more trouble in the Kenya prison camps (wh in the absence of the Colonial Secy is referred to me) the chief interest has been David Eccles's trade negotiations in Moscow. He has run into rather difficult weather but I shd not be surprised to see the Russians give in, if we are 'firm and flexible'. The trouble is that the colleagues here (Minister of Agriculture and Chancellor of Exr) are rather suspicious of David Eccles and afraid that he may give something away in order to get his agreement. So a good deal of telegraphing has gone on; but it has ended now in a short and cryptic telegram – just arrived – to say that 'everything is agreed'. Tho' <u>what</u> is agreed is unknown. I do not worry unduly about this, for the agreement is rather a 'face-saving' affair. What matters (export credits; orders by Russians; increased purchases by U.K.) is something not covered by the formal agreement, wh is more an expression of intentions than a contract . . . .

26 May

. . . . Dulles died on Sunday, after a gallant struggle. This is sad; but he could not have survived long. With many faults, he was a great man, and a great support to the whole Free World. If he was weak and

---

49. We are betrayed (by British appeasement of the Soviets). The foreign ministers' conference was intended to prepare the way for the impending heads of government summit.

50. A kingdom within Uganda headed by Kabaka Mutesa II, whose supporters were opposing plans for an independent and unified Uganda unless it was to be headed by the kabaka.

vacillating over Suez and Nasser, he has done all he could since then to repair the damage . . . .

The fall in the unemployment figures has come out at 50,000 decrease (4000 above the estimate wh I had been given) This is good. At the same time, the cost of living has remained unchanged for a year. So we have really brought off the double.

The Chancellor of the Exr came to dinner with me alone. He seemed rather low. I believe it is partly because he lives this strange hermit life and (unless he remembers) hardly eats. Anyway, we had a good talk. He is very sensitive and very conscientious and rather a man to worry. He is now worried about having reduced the Beer Duty (£36m) and generally having had a too reflationary Budget. (All this is because sterling has not been quite so strong in recent weeks) The estimates for Govt expenditure next year are very high; the tax concessions (in a full year) must reduce the revenue – or so the experts say. But they cannot quite tell whether the expanding economy will be able to make up for this and the revenue (even at a lower rate of taxation) prove unexpectedly buoyant. Heathcoat Amory will stand at the Election – but he wants (if we get in) to give up the Treasury and either take a less exacting post or retire altogether . . . .

27 May

The Opposition are clearly going to start a new hare – all the rest, Rent Act; Cost of Living; Unemployment etc etc having failed. This will be 'Africa'. They will try to show that the Tories are being reactionary etc and to get on their side that Liberal opinion – esp among the young – which animated the Scottish Church Assembly in their discussion of the Central Africa problem. I have decided to get together an 'Africa Ctee' of Ministers. This must meet weekly and hammer away until we can get out a coherent and simple line of policy. This afternoon I had a long talk with Mr Blundell, who is the leading European in Kenyan politics and has just launched a new approach which seems on good lines . . . .

28 May

. . . . The Cabinet decided to proceed with the Bill to raise the State contribution to Church schools. We shall be attacked by the Free Churches (chiefly by the Baptists) but with the greatly increased cost of building, I think it is fair. Both the Roman Catholics and the Anglicans have agreed to the proposed 'compromise'. Our political risk is that Liberals (in despair of finding anything else) will pitch on this issue to revive their fortunes in certain parts of the country where the Free Church tradition is strong[51] . . . .

1 June

The Times has published an extraordinary article – in the centre page – stating, among other things, that I have decided to replace Selwyn Lloyd as For Secy 'shortly'. This would not matter much in the ordinary way, but it has made a tremendous row at home and overseas, because a) foreigners regard *The Times* as 'inspired' b) the Geneva conference is reaching a critical point and the article must react on Selwyn's position and reputation. All sorts of rumours are going about, including the allegation that some other minister inspired the article. We issued 'guidance – not for attribution' from No 10. But I am very worried by all this . . . .

4 June

. . . . The African problem, in all its forms, looms up more and more ominously. The Socialist Party wd of course agree to 'one man, one vote', for Kenya and Rhodesia and face the results. Even the right wing (like Mr Gaitskell) are uncertain. G has an intellectual dislike of and contempt for British settlers.

A most unfortunate incident in one of the Mau Mau camps (only the 'hard core' rebels and fanatics remain) has put us in difficulties in Parl and we have now to face a vote of censure.[52] The Scottish Church is getting worked up about Nyasaland. We shall probably get a bad report from Mr Justice Devlin and his ctee.[53] I have set up an 'African Ctee' – wh will meet every week, to try to work out a policy and give us a grip on the situation . . . .

---

51. Free Church opposition to state funding for church schools had assisted the Liberal electoral victory in 1906. The 1959 Education Act, which raised the state's contribution to the capital costs for these schools to 75%, passed relatively without incident.

52. Eleven of the remaining detainees from the Mau Mau rising in Kenya of the early 1950s died at Hola Camp on 3 March. The Kenyan colonial government initially claimed that this was a result of drinking contaminated water, though police evidence that they were killed had already been raised by Barbara Castle in the Commons on 26 March. An Opposition censure motion was debated on 16 June.

53. An inquiry set up into the March events in Nyasaland.

Gaitskell, Griffiths and Callaghan – the three musketeers, a Professor, a Professional Preacher and an Irish Corner Boy came to see us this afternoon. We have been in negotiations for a 'bipartisan approach' to African problems. This was the third meeting. As I expected, their position had hardened. Seeing nothing else to clutch at – full employment has been restored and the economy is stable – they cannot resist trying to exploit the African situation . . . .

5 June

. . . . Guy Mollet came to see me and stayed to lunch . . . . Mollet told a story wh amused me about the Russians. When he was talking to Bulganin and Kruschev, they suddenly became convulsed with laughter. They tried but cd not contain themselves. M said 'What is the joke? Can't I share it?' They shook their heads, but still shook with amusement. They just could not contain themselves. M insisted. 'Let me share the joke'. K to B 'Shall we tell him'. B 'No, no'. K 'Oh well, we might as well'. Mollet 'Well, what is it?' K 'It's just this. It's really so funny. It's – I can hardly go on, it's so funny – it's – well, its that you are sitting in Beria's chair!!' (They had shot their colleague B a few weeks before [in 1953]. As M observed, 'A somewhat grim sense of humour'.) . . . .

6 June

Old Adenauer has suddenly done a complete volte-face. Angry at not being able to get the party to take Etzel as his successor, he has suddenly decided (while Erhard is in Washington) not to stand for the Presidency after all, but to remain as Chancellor. He represents this as due to 'international dangers' and hints darkly that it is all due to British weakness towards Russia. I suppose Etzel will now be forced to become President. It is an extraordinary drama – rather reminiscent of Hitlerian days . . . .

7 June

All day conference at Chequers on 'Future British Policy'. The idea was to draw up a paper – for the use of the next Government. The first part would try to assess 'The Setting' – what is likely to happen in the world during the next 10 years. The second part wd deal with 'U.K.'s resources' – the gross national product; the calls for expenditure on Pensions, Education, Defence etc wh are more or less inescapable. The third part would be about 'The Objectives' – what Foreign,

Commonwealth and Colonial and Economic policies we ought to follow. Today's meeting was to agree the skeleton – the general outline of the work – and to cast the parts . . . .

8 June

Adenauer seems to have a bad press, all over the world. Even the French seem rather shocked. The Americans – whose darling A has always been – seem taken aback. But I have no doubt that the old man will get his way – at least for the moment. But I think he will have weakened his authority, and that even Germans will be less prone to believe all the rather malicious stories which he had been spreading about British statesmen and their policy of 'appeasement' . . . .

Africa Committee. We are in a real jam about the incident at Hola Camp in Kenya, where 11 Africans were killed and 20 or more injured in a riot. The Opposition have put down a motion demanding a 'public inquiry'. The C.R. Secy is much against this; Ld Hailsham and Minister of Labour are for it, one much more vigorously than the other. We had the afternoon on this and continued at 10.30 for another 1½ hours or more. I foresee a serious split . . . .

10 June

Cyprus Committee (with the Governor, Sir Hugh Foot) The task of putting the rather hastily arranged agreements with formal documents is quite a big one. We have a committee of all concerned in Cyprus. Archbp Makarios is being helpful . . . .

Meanwhile, the F.S. is confronted with a crisis at Geneva, and the telegrams are pouring in. I do my best to keep up – but often my replies are too late for another change in events. I feel that the excessive legalism of the West has (as I always foresaw) got us into a jam. I only hope that we shall not now lose the Summit . . . .

12 June

We dined with the Danes at their Embassy last night. Rather heavy going. Mr Hansen is a pleasant and intelligent man – called a Socialist in Denmark. He wd here be a Conservative in England. He came to No 10 at 10am today and we had a very useful hour's talk about the proposed new European grouping – the Seven.[54] I tried to persuade

---

54. Involving Austria, Britain, Denmark, Norway, Portugal, Sweden and
    Switzerland, this European Free Trade Association was intended to provide an

him a) That I regarded this as a bridge, not an act of trade war against the Rome powers b) That I did not think the 6 wd retaliate. Many of our friends in the 6 had expressed their pleasure at what was going on. c) That we must not wait and not try official negotiations with the 6 until our organisation of the 7 was formed d) That he should send his Foreign Minister as soon as possible to negotiate with us on the agricultural problem on a <u>bilateral</u> basis.

Mr Hansen was rather cautious at first. He seemed particularly anxious about possible retaliation by Germany and Italy against Denmark's agricultural exports. But he finally seemed to agree to all these propositions, and Mr Krag is to come about June 22nd. The meeting of ministers of the 7 should be towards [the] end of July, <u>after</u> meeting of Nordic Prime Ministers on July 12 . . . .

Two telegrams from Selwyn this morning. Herter went to see Gromyko and accused him of 'threats'. G denied this. The strong (and a little exaggerated) indignation of the Western powers <u>may</u> have a good effect and serve to smoke out the Bear a bit. It is rather a risk to start talking about 'ordering your aeroplane' (esp as it was found that Herter's was not in fact available) but it <u>may</u> come off . . . .

13 June

'Trooping the Colour'. This is the first year of the Saturday trooping – and a great success. The crowds were enormous, and very enthusiastic . . . . We left at 3pm for a fête at Mill Hill (2000 people – and a short speech) and at Alexandra Park (6–7000 people and a long speech) We had a mild dose of 'Empire Loyalists' at the latter, but they were very ineffective. Anyway, they got mixed up into a 'Ban the Bomb' party . . . .

The Foreign Secy (whom I had not seen for 4 weeks or more) came to dinner . . . . Unfortunately, it wd seem that little or no progress has been made with the Russians. Nobody knows what to do next. One plan (a very bad one) is to adjourn the Foreign Ministers' meeting for one, two, or three months. Nothing, to my mind, could be worse. The Soviet Govt wd preserve its monolithic front – with its controlled Press and Radio. The West wd be thrown into a Babel of confusion. Debates in our Parliament wd be unavoidable and damaging.

---

alternative for European states unwilling to countenance the customs union of the EEC. There was also a stillborn aspiration that it might provide a stepping stone to a future multilateral European organisation.

Another idea is to break off *sine die*,[55] <u>without</u> plans for a Summit. This is, to the British, utterly unacceptable.

Meanwhile, the Americans – who are being much more reasonable with Herter in charge – have drafted a new paper, with proposals wh the Russians may at least be ready to discuss. If so, enough 'progress' can perhaps be made to 'justify' (in President Eisenhower's mind) a Summit conference . . . .

Another plan (wh greatly to his credit Herter tentatively proposed to Selwyn Lloyd) is that on the breakdown of the Foreign Ministers' Conference, I (as P.M.) shd issue an invitation to Eisenhower, de Gaulle, and Kruschev to meet in London (or any other acceptable place) to 'discuss the situation'. This would be a sort of 'informal' Summit. I like this plan very much.

14 June (Sunday)

. . . . Bob Menzies came at 5pm. We were alone and had a splendid talk (including dinner) till 10pm. We covered a lot of ground. He was in great form and full of vitality. He talked very frankly about his own future (he is 64 years old) I don't think he wants to go on as PM of Australia more than another year or two. He has already done 12 years as PM. He would perh[aps] like a Life Peerage and some kind of job (or series of jobs) in the life of the Commonwealth. For instance, had he now been free, he cd have taken the chair of the proposed Commission for Central Africa. He gave an extraordinary account of Dulles' funeral (he happened to be in Washington) wh was bungled to an amazing extent. He himself sat in a motor-car, with Madame Chiang Kai-Shek for 2½ hours in a queue! He thought the President well and active. Since the death of Foster Dulles he has had to exert himself more. M thought he could really do it if he tried, but he admitted that the Pres seems puzzled and did not really do a great deal of steady work. Much of each day is spent resting . . . .

In the course of the evening I received a message from the F.O. Rumbold had sent a message to say that Herter had tried 'his' idea (that is my invitation to the other 3) on the President, but that his reaction had been negative . . . .

---

55. Indefinitely.

15 June

Motored to London, with Menzies, whom I had invited to attend our Cabinet . . . .

John Boyd-Carpenter made a statement about another £32m for the impoverished old people (by raising National Assistance) The Opposition were much taken aback. We had long conferences about the Hola debate tomorrow. Alan Lennox-Boyd was unwilling to start (after Soskice who opens for the Opposition) But I have persuaded him to do so. This leaves us more room for manoeuvre, and if necessary I shall have to wind up myself. The Attorney General has prepared a good legal speech, wh must be delivered and put on record some time during the debate. Things have not been made easier by the incredible folly of the Colonial Office in recommending an MBE (announced on Saturday) to one of the men whose conduct has been impugned.[56] C.O. is a badly run office, but there is really no excuse for this . . . .

16 June

(Midnight) The debate has gone off 'as well as could be expected', but it has been an anxious day. Soskice (ex A[ttorney] G[eneral]) opened for the Opposition with a clever and well constructed speech, based largely on the Coroner's report. He ended with a bitter, but not ineffective, personal attack on Sir Evelyn Baring and the Colonial Secy. Perhaps this was rather too highly coloured – for everyone on both sides of the House respects Lennox-Boyd and knows how much sympathy and devotion he has brought to his task. Col Secy followed. His speech was very long, but in the main succeeded in its purpose. He frankly admitted the mistakes and muddles of the Hola tragedy. But by giving the whole story of Mau Mau, and particularly by a vivid story of how the original 80000 detainees had been brought down to under 1000 by the 'rehabilitation' work, he did succeed in putting this unhappy incident in its proper perspective. Callaghan wound up for [the] Opposition, in his usual Irish corner-boy style. Attorney General had difficulty in getting his speech listened to, but it was very good.

---

56. This was John Cowan, Senior Superintendent of Prisons in Kenya. On 11 February 1959 he produced the 'Cowan Plan', purportedly to improve discipline in the detention camps. It advised that prisoners who refused 'should be manhandled to the site of work'. The beatings after such a refusal led to the massacre at Hola.

Our majority was 59 – so far as we know, no abstentions – at least on our side.

17 June
The Press is not good about Hola, but not too bad. The *Manchester Guardian* has a very bad Parliamentary account of the debate, headed 'Mr Lennox-Boyd's Failure'. But the leading article was fair and reasonable. Naturally, it seems terrible that 11 men shd die in this way, and no prosecutions or resignations.[57] The Col Secy has been well supported by the Cabinet, altho' at one time I feared a split. So he owes us something. I feel there must be a 're-shuffle' in the Kenya administration . . . .

18 June
The Western Powers have put a paper to the Russians wh marks a great advance and is far better 'presentationally' than any former statement. Gromyko was to have given his reply today. But he has not received instructions and the meeting is postponed till tomorrow. Selwyn Lloyd has done an excellent job in getting his colleagues towards this position. Nevertheless, we have a very weak position, both in argument and in fact. For, if the Russians make a treaty with East German Govt and withdraw themselves, what can we really do? None of the Western Powers (in spite of all the 'Emergency Planning') have faced realities so far. I am much torn as to what to do. De Gaulle will not play with me or anyone else. Adenauer is now half crazy . . . . Eisenhower is hesitant and unsure of himself (Either of the Roosevelts wd have been more active) We alone can take an initiative, but with Germany madly suspicious and France jealous and America uncertain, no one will follow my initiative except Kruschev! It is an infuriating situation but I feel that the public opinion of all countries (including the smaller NATO powers) is on our side . . . .

22 June
Early to London – a good talk with Selwyn [Lloyd] in the morning. After Geneva, what? . . . . K[hrushchev] can do one of two things. He can invite us to a Summit. It will be equally embarrassing to refuse or

---

57. As a result of the disciplinary inquiry the Kenya Commissioner of Prisons and the Hola Camp Commandant took early retirement. This report prompted a further Labour censure debate on 27 July.

to accept. If we refuse, then K has every moral justification for immediately making his peace treaty with the Eastern Germans and handing over all Russian obligations. Or – K can not bother to invite us to the Summit – but proceed at once to his unilateral action. S.L. sees all this. But we are at a loss as to how to make the Americans understand. Herter has been very helpful – but (altho' he is just beginning to realise how much he has been misled by State Dept and Pentagon) he has not the authority that Dulles had, either with State Dept or with the President.

A separate and more immediate problem has arisen over the weekend from the Colonial Secretary's renewed offer of his resignation over the Hola affair. I keep telling him that it wd be a fatal mistake and quite uncalled for. But (with all his extraordinary charm and real ability) he is a highly-strung, sensitive, and rather quixotic character. I tell him that to resign now over this affair would

a) be a great blow to HMG at the most critical period before the General Election, when all is going well otherwise
b) wd be a very sad end to his splendid career as Col Secy
c) wd upset the whole colonial service, whose loyalty and devotion he can command
d) would have very bad – even dangerous effects in Kenya and Africa. It might make the extreme Africans feel that they had now got the white men on the run.
e) That it would involve Sir Evelyn Baring's resignation. This wd really be a tragic end to a fine career of voluntary service in Africa.

24 June

. . . . Defence Ctee – 4–6. The most important question was that of our forces in Germany. We are bound under the W.E.U. Treaty and cannot easily escape. So far, by agreement, we have come down from 86,000 men to 55,000. We now want to get down to 45,000 (or perh[aps] 50,000) After long discussion; it was agreed that F.S. shd discuss this 'off the record' with General Norstad . . . .

25 June

Mr Gaitskell (with help of Mr Bevan and some of the T Unions) has produced a 'compromise' policy on the H Bomb. I fear it may have a rather specious success. The idea of a Nuclear Club – or rather a Club of countries who agree not to have nuclear weapons – may be attractive. I am anxious not to comment on it yet, but let the battle inside the Socialist Party develop. (Ld Hailsham – impulsive as ever – has already 'sailed in' with a speech to the Women's [Conservative] Conference wh was rather crude)[58] ....

The Printers' strike (all printing establishments except National Newspapers, Stationery Office etc) is spreading and becoming rather bitter. It may (since its leader, Willis, is a Communist) spread to London and to Government printing. The National newspapers (the Provincials are all stopped) hardly dare report it. The Labour Party in the HofC are rather ashamed of it (the unions have refused arbitration) and scarcely mention it. It is a queer (and rather ominous) situation ....

11.30. Steering Ctee. (This is a Party – not a Govt Ctee) We saw the first draft of the Election manifesto.

.... I have read this week 3 'scientific' stories by John Wyndham (not my J.W.) of a sort of Jules Verne type. They are good – well-written – and hold the attention. *Triffids* – *Kraken*, *Chrysalids*. They all arise (of course) in the period just before or just after the world has destroyed itself with H-Bombs ....

29 June

.... [S]at in the summer-house reading *The New Machiavelli* by H G Wells in the afternoon. I had not read it since 1913. It is really admirably written and rather moving. The portrait of the Sidney Webbs is excellent and must have seemed very funny at the time. The slighter sketch of Arthur Balfour is sympathetic and good. What is strange is the change in public morality and the attitude to divorce. Although the circumstances of the hero's abandonment of his wife and seduction of a young lady wd still be regarded as rather bad, and wd no doubt call a temporary halt in a political career, I don't think they would be fatal. After all, I have sat in Cabinets with Eden, Monckton, Thorneycroft who were all divorced ....

---

58. *Disarmament and Nuclear War: The Next Step*, published by Labour the previous day, proposed reductions in conventional forces and international agreement on conversion of nuclear stocks to civil use, abolition of delivery means and of weapons of mass destruction. On 25 June Macmillan wrote to Hailsham suggesting he convene an *ad hoc* Cabinet committee to study Labour's policy as it 'may command considerable support' (TNA: CAB 21/3909).

30 June
. . . . Apparently both Willis and the head of NATSOPA, Briginshaw
are Communists or Crypto-Communists. They are therefore anxious
to spread the strike as much as possible, regardless of the real industrial
issues or the effect. All the unions have steadily refused any form of
arbitration, which the Employers have repeatedly offered. Macleod
explained the situation to the Cabinet today. He proposes to invite the
ink-manufacturers, employers and union leaders to meet him to discuss
this issue. He thinks the T Union leaders will refuse. The Labour Party
are remaining quiet in the HofC. Not one question from Robens, who
generally bubbles over with excitement and self-importance at any
dispute. I suppose they feel that the Unions' case is so bad that the
public will not sympathise . . . .

2 July
Late last night we got the reply from Washington. It is really _very_
satisfactory. In effect, the President has accepted our analysis of the
situation – the strategic and tactical weakness of our Berlin position.
All the old nonsense about 'occupying the road and rail communications' or 'sending the tanks through' is (by implication at least)
abandoned. The Americans seem willing to concentrate on trying to
get an acceptable political settlement, probably of a 'provisional'
character . . . .

A long meeting of ministers about the Stockholm plan (European
Trade Area of the Seven) We are soon coming to the crucial problem
here. Can we bring off such an agreement (wh is vital for British
industry) without a violent reaction from the Agricultural interest.
Altho' the concessions we shall offer to the Danes are really very small
and will _not_ hurt the British farmer, nevertheless the farmers will raise
the old cry '_nous sommes trahis_' and it may cost us enough constituencies to lose a General Election.

3 July
Still very hot. Meeting of Ministers at 10am, on the future of the
Aircraft industry – a terrible tangle. The trouble is that these new
machines are immensely costly and it seems impossible to get enough
orders for any one type to make them pay . . . .

5 July
Another glorious day. Read Almeric Fitzroy's reminiscences. 2 vols.

He is no Greville.[59] But I found the years 1900–1914 very interesting. It describes a way of life and a civilisation as remote as that of Queen Anne . . . .

. . . . Read Sir Algernon West's diaries. Sir A.W. (after retiring from the Treasury) became a sort of Private Secy (at the age of 65) to Mr Gladstone in the last Premiership.[60] (He was a sort of Lord Cherwell in his relation to Churchill) The account of the last Government is extraordinary and certainly confirms Lord Rosebery's version of the end. But all these Liberals – Morley, Harcourt etc – hated each other bitterly. It is strangely like the Labour Party today. Perhaps this lack of loyalty and discipline is inherent in the parties of the Left.

6 July

Two hours and a half with Sir Roy Welensky. It was very hot, and we sat in the garden at No 10. Alec and Alan (Commonwealth and Colonial Secretaries) were there. We had only general talk, in which we made some progress. He is, I think, sincere and at least progressive. But he is very sensitive and liable to outbursts of angry indignation. There can be no doubt that he would not shrink from secession if he thought the Europeans ill treated from London. At the worst, he cd join the Union of S Africa.

These talks were preliminary to the two points to which I want to bring him

a) A reasonable Commission – with 5 or 6 Africans on it
b) A declaration of policy in favour of the multi-racial concept and giving Nyasaland a prospect of self-govt . . . .

7 July

Cabinet at 10am. The chief item was the Anglo-Danish agreement. This is an essential preliminary to the Stockholm conference and the organisation of the 7 – a European Free Trade group in opposition to the 6 – Stockholm v Rome. The stakes in this affair are very high – no less than the survival of the industrial life and strength of Britain. For

59. Fitzroy was Clerk to the Privy Council under Victoria and Edward VII. Charles and Henry Greville were early nineteenth-century political diarists admired by Macmillan.
60. The nineteenth-century Liberal leader, W. E. Gladstone, was Prime Minister 1868–74, 1880–85, 1886 and 1892–94.

if we cannot successfully organise the opposition group – Scandinavia; Denmark; Switzerland; Austria etc – then we shall undoubtedly be eaten up, one by one, by the 6. Already I have heard of plans for American factories – wh were to have been built in Scotland, North Ireland or an area of unemployment in England – being cancelled. These are to be built in France or Germany, where the pull of the 'Common Market' attracts them. Unfortunately, we have to pay a price – and, because it comes at this particular time, it may well cost us Conservative success in the General Election. For – altho' removing the 10% tariff on Danish <u>bacon</u>, with the same on <u>luncheon-meat</u>, amounts to nothing real – certainly no real injury to a home industry which is protected by <u>price</u> support (not by the Tariff) yet the combination of a) suspicion natural to farmers b) Sir James Turner (Ld Netherthorpe) who has turned nasty c) Ld Beaverbrook and his press may well lose us 10 to 12 precious seats in the agricultural constituencies. However, the Cabinet – with full knowledge of the risks but equal knowledge of their duty – decided to go ahead and give instructions to Maudling and Hare (our negotiators) accordingly. As for the tariff, we agreed to remove all the 10% in <u>three</u> successive bites, starting on July 1, 1960. Later in the day, I heard that the Danes (who had asked for every other kind of concession – on milk, butter, cheese etc – wh we refused) wanted a) a better formula on <u>future</u> agricultural interventions b) the Tariff to <u>go</u> in <u>one</u> swoop – July 1, 1960. I called Cabinet at 2.30 and it was agreed to <u>stick</u> to our formula on <u>future</u> interventions – there must be no equivocation or misunderstanding here of any sort, esp as regards our right to fix our <u>price</u> support for pigs as we like. But we gave our negotiators latitude to accept the abolition of the small Tariff (10%) in <u>two</u> bites instead of <u>three</u>. Later in the day I heard that the Danes (after telephoning to their Cabinet) had agreed. So, if our Parliament and the Danish Parliament acquiesces, this is settled and the first step taken to organising the Seven. Already the Germans are beginning to talk in a very different way and even the French seem alarmed. I have every hope that if the Seven can make an agreement and get it ratified by the end of the year, the Six will be ready for a reasonable negotiation between the two groups.

8 July

. . . . Foreign Affairs debate. Over 90° outside the Chamber; much cooler inside. For Secy began with a factual speech – our hopes and fears for Geneva. Bevan answered, with a very good speech – witty and well-argued, quite his old form. He only spoilt it by being too long. Gaitskell wound up with rather a 'governessy' speech. I replied, with an adequate but by no means impressive effort. So far as we were concerned, we wanted the debate to be quiet. Our opponents hardly referred to us, but concentrated on the great issue which is splitting the Socialists in two – H-Bomb disarmament or Non-Nuclear Club. (I cd not help reminding the House that the non-nuclear club means that British foreign policy must be still more dependent on America. Yet, for years, the Socialists have urged us to be more independent of America) Nevertheless, Gaitskell is showing considerable courage in handling this affair . . . .

The Printers' strike is now approaching the end of the 3rd week. Very large sums of money must have been lost, esp by the Provincial and Local newspapers, the magazines and Journals. I fear that M&Co will have a pretty heavy loss over *Nature* and *The Nursing Times* . . . .

However, the pressure to settle has <u>not</u> come from the Master Printers (who <u>are</u> involved) or from the Provincial and Local Newspapers (who <u>are</u> involved) but from the National Press. These expected to be out of the dispute. (Like the Poles, they will be attacked in a few months time when Hitler Willis has finished with the Provincial Czechs) They have been involved in an obscure dispute about ink. For the ink firms (employing NATSOPA men) are involved and also are largely owned by the National Press. So it has looked, every day, for the last fortnight as if the National Press wd stop, from shortage of ink, which has been declared black!! The Provincial Press has, of course, rather wanted for this to happen. For it wd certainly bring the strike to a close more quickly. The Opposition (in Parlt) debated this affair on Monday last – but (with the exception of a foolish speech by George Brown in the provinces) the Labour Party – with their eyes on the election – have been quiet. Moreover, the Printing Unions (who ought to be trying to extend the strike to the National Press) don't want to lose the contributions to their funds from the heavily paid (£30–£60 a week at the *Daily Telegraph*) National Press employees. There has been a great clamour from the Left that Walter Monckton shd be chosen as 'referee' or 'conciliator' . . . . This wd not (I think) be acceptable to the Master Printers (tho' it might be difficult for them to refuse) It <u>would</u> go very badly with the Party in Parl. Indeed (labouring under the false idea that HMG have put forward Monckton) our stalwarts are already very angry. It <u>might</u> upset the Party in the country and undo all the good wh the Bus Strike did us last year. For Monckton is now regarded as a weak minister, who, as the pliant tool of Churchill, avoided trouble at all costs in the years of Churchill's last Govt, and so brought about the inflation. This is not altogether fair; but there is enough truth in it to make it damaging – and dangerous at this moment. So I (with Butler) saw Monckton late tonight and he readily agreed not to let his name go forward.

Today (July 9th) has been a very heavy day. I sent for Lord Netherthorpe (Sir James Turner) head of the National Farmers Union. He tried to bully me (about the Danish treaty) and I tried to be as firm and as rude as I dared. Since he _is_ rather a bully, he seemed surprised at being challenged . . . .

A very long meeting took place of ministers concerned about Distribution of Industry. There has been a very good report by officials.[61] Now that we are back at 1.9[%] unemployment (that is, _no_ unemployment) for the country as a whole, we must try to concentrate on the weak spots – N Wales; parts of Lancashire; Scotland. But we must obviously not do this by general measures (more reflation; reduced taxes etc) For, with 1.9[%] figure for U.K., such measures would inevitably result in a renewed inflation, with all that this means to our balance of payments and to sterling. We must therefore treat the disease differently . . . .

Lunch with Butler – alone. He is in good form, full of ideas. His hope is that we shall win by 20 or so. I suppose his further hope would be for me to resign after a year or two . . . .

12 July
. . . . Ld Birkett has undertaken to act, in rather an indeterminate capacity, in the Printers' Strike. I feared, at first, that the Printing Employers had yielded on the point of 'Arbitration'. But after talking to Minister of Labour (Macleod) I learned that the Unions had in fact accepted the Master Printers' definition of the function of 'Referee' – with all its implications about 'Productivity'. This, of course, is the

---

61. A committee of officials led by the Board of Trade reported on 18 June on the working of the Distribution of Industry Acts 1948–58. It concluded that the idea of development areas should be replaced by intervention where needed, through enhanced development control, allowing capital grants for buildings and plant, and extended powers to tackle derelict sites. This became the basis of the 1960 Local Employment Act.

real point at issue. The Printing industry has always been riddled with 'restrictive practices'.

13 July

. . . . Japanese Prime Minister and his advisers. I don't think the talks amounted to very much – but Mr Kishi seemed pleased. The afternoon discussions were with the Chancellor of the Exchequer and the President of the B of Trade. But I don't think we have much to give him even here. Article XXXV of GATT is the bone of contention.[62] But we really cannot allow ourselves to be flooded with cheap Japanese goods, without any control . . . .

More discussions and development about the Nyasaland report. Rab and Chief Whip came over at 10.30pm and we discussed this and Central Africa generally till nearly 1am. We must have a debate on Federation and my talks with Welensky and the proposed Commission. We must have a debate on Devlin (but the report is not yet signed, still less printed) We must have a debate on the despatches from Col Secy to Governor of Kenya and his reply about Hola. All this to be fitted into the last few days [of the session], with all the risks of an exhausted HofC at the end of a hot summer! My chief theme throughout was that a Minister must either resign or be supported up to the hilt by his colleagues. I am hopeful that resignation (wh wd shake the Govt, since it must include Ld Perth and Julian Amery) can be avoided. For this would certainly shake the strength of the Govt and public confidence in it just before the Election. But it may be that the Report will be too critical to accept. Can it be rebutted?

Incidentally, I was away in Russia when the Devlin Commission was chosen. Why Devlin? The poor Lord Chancellor – the sweetest and most naïve of men – chose him. He was able; a Conservative; runner-up or nearly so for Lord Chief Justice. I have since discovered that he is

---

62. Concern about dumping of Japanese textiles on the British market had played a part in British reluctance to accept Japanese entry to the GATT, finally achieved in 1955. With a booming economy in the late 1950s seeking export markets, Japan pressed for a commercial treaty with Britain. The British, unwilling to open their markets to Japanese competition, however, invoked the safeguard of Art. 35, which avoided them having to apply the full liberalising of the 1947 GATT Treaty in their trade relations with Japan.

a) <u>Irish</u> – no doubt with that Fenian blood that make Irishmen anti-Govt on principle
b) A <u>lapsed</u> R.C. His brother is a Jesuit priest; his sister a nun. He married a Jewess, who was converted and has <u>remained</u> a Catholic.
c) A <u>hunchback</u>
d) Bitterly disappointed at my not having made him Lord Chief Justice.

I am not at all surprised that his report is dynamite. It may well blow this Govt out of office . . . .

16 July

One of the most ridiculous of all our 'chores' is 'seeing people off'. I left No 10 at 8am, returning at 10am – for the sole purpose of seeing Mr Kishi for a few minutes before he left London Airport . . . .

20 July

. . . . I asked the Ld P[rivy] Seal (Butler) to come at 10.30 and the Colonial Secy at 11. I talked over with the former the tactics wh I proposed to pursue in the Cabinet. This met at 11.30. Every member of the Cabinet had received the Devlin report last Sat[urday] morning. This morning (11.15–11.30) they were asked to read the <u>Governor</u> [of Nyasaland, Robert Armitage]'s reply – wh is to be published at the same time. This is a pretty good document. It has been written at Chequers in 2 days (Devlin & Co had several months) largely by Lord Chancellor, Attorney General, and Julian Amery. Before the formal meeting began (Ministers sat in the Cabinet room, reading these documents) Rab and I and Alan Lennox-Boyd sat in the garden. Alan L-B once more pressed on me his readiness to resign and thought this the best way out. Rab agreed with me that such a decision wd be a) <u>wrong</u>. Colonial administration in the dependent colonies wd break down if HMG were to betray them. b) <u>impolitic</u>. A rather difficult debate in the HofC with perhaps a few Tory abstentions is one thing; hardly a ripple over the constituencies. But the resignation of the 3 Colonial ministers – Lennox-B, Perth and Amery, together with the dismissal of the Governor, would be a major event at a most critical time. But in order to satisfy C.R. Secy, I told him that I would <u>not</u> give the Cabinet much of a lead. I wd let each express his view before I expressed mine. Then we shd know the unbiased view of each minister – not a view tinged with loyalty to me as P.M. Accordingly, I opened the discussion very briefly, setting out the case. I called on the lawyers first. The Lord Chancellor and the A.G., followed by Ld Hailsham. (I had some anxieties about Ld H, but I need not have been concerned. He was fine and noble) After these, the Cabinet in order, round the table, ending with the Ld P[rivy] Seal on my left. Every single one said, with absolute conviction, that we must stand by the Nyasaland Govt and the Colonial Secy. (I told them that the Col Secy had placed his resignation in my hands – this was part of my short preliminary remarks) This was a fine performance and most impressive. Mr Gladstone used to call his last Cabinet 'the Blubbering Cabinet'.[63] This is a 'Manly Cabinet'.

I told them, after the decision had been taken, that had it gone otherwise, I shd have not continued as P.M. But I had thought it unfair, before the decision, to offer such a temptation to such a brilliant and properly ambitious set of men as composed the Cabinet. This broke the tension – and after a short discussion on tactics, Press, debates etc, the Cabinet dispersed . . . .

21 July

. . . . I made a statement in the House announcing the Advisory Commission for Central Africa. Mr G[aitskell] was pretty sour, but foolishly asked a large number of questions and made it quite clear what he will say tomorrow in the debate. This makes preparation easier . . . .

Rested most of the morning and worked on speech for debate on Central Africa. Gaitskell opened – 1 hour – rather academic, waspish rather than rude – quite effective. I answered. 40 minutes. My speech was rather heavy and except in the last five minutes little life or colour. But I think it succeeded in the main object – to damp down the general temperature. After this, the House was almost completely empty till the wind-up. Callaghan for them – vulgar, violent and most helpful in driving back our doubters into the fold. Colonial Secy ended with the best speech I have ever heard him make and one of the best speeches I have ever heard in the House of Commons. Majority 50. Grimond and his few Liberals praised my plan and voted against us!

---

63. This was the fractious 1892–94 administration. See Macmillan's comments on West's diaries above, p. 230.

23 July

I am getting more and more worried about the foreign situation. If we are not careful, we shall drift into war. At somebody's suggestion, I took up an idea of sending some observations about Russia and Mr K[hrushchev] to Vice-President Nixon. It seems he had asked for this. I sent it <u>through</u> the President and this gave an opportunity for saying something about getting on with the plan for finishing Geneva and moving to the Summit. To my great regret, the President has replied with a very odd message – wh seems to be going back on everything that Herter promised to Selwyn . . . . He reverts to the old theme that the Summit is a sort of post-graduate course, wh the boys can only take if they first graduate with honours (at Geneva) . . . .

The Chancellor of the Exr and Paymaster-General (Maudling) have pulled off a big thing in Stockholm. It looks as if the European Trade Association (or Stockholm group) will really come into being.

 . . . . Chancellor of Exr, Minister of Defence and I had a talk about Defence estimates, wh seem to be rising steeply. We fixed a 'target' of £1610m and hope that the Minister can work down to this.

The rest of the evening was taken up with brooding and talking about the President. Shall I make a public statement, disassociating Britain from the allied position? A great responsibility. But so it is to drift along with the tide – with a half-crazy Adenauer, a cynical and remote de Gaulle, and an amiable but weak President . . . .

Read Lord Morley's *Recollections* volume 1.[64] I find these 19th century memoirs soothing. They had just as many difficulties and crises as we do. But they did not live in the terrible world produced by 2 wars, with its frightful losses and the prospect of a third. Moreover, they had solid comforts – esp servants!

24 July

The Devlin Report is published today. The so-called 'serious' Press has been excellent. *The Times* has a good news-story and a robust and sensible leading article. *D Telegraph* equally good. *Manchester Guardian* bad headlines but a <u>very</u> good and <u>very</u> fair leader. *D Mail*,

---

64. John, 1st Viscount Morley, served as Irish Secretary in Gladstone's last Cabinet (1892–94) and under Rosebery (1894–95), as India Secretary (1905–10, 1911) and as Lord President (1910–14). He was also, for many years, chief literary adviser to M&Co.

D Express, good. *D Chronicle* very hostile. *D Mirror* 'goes to town' in a big, hysterical way. The Party seem pretty steady. The *'fron-deurs'*[65] – who make the mistake of opposing on everything – are quite active – Lord Lambton (one begins to realise what poor Lord Grey suffered at the hands of his son-in-law in the Reform Cabinet)[66] Enoch Powell (who is a sort of Fakir) and one or two others. We have put a good motion on the order paper, and the thing will have to be fought out on Tuesday. I do not want to speak, if I can avoid it, because it looks weak – esp as Gaitskell is not speaking. Actually, the Party are more worried about Hola than about the Nyasaland incident . . . .

26 July (Sunday)
. . . . A serious crisis has developed in the field of Foreign Affairs. It has cause[d] me great annoyance – alarm – and even anger. It is not (as some of my colleagues seem to feel) the result of American bad faith, but rather of their stupidity, naivety, and incompetence. What has happened is this. The President (some days ago) sent a message through Koslov (who is a deputy prime minister of the USSR and was visiting Washington) inviting Kruschev to go to U.S. in September, to come to Washington for 2 days; and then, if there is a Summit at Quebec, to return to U.S. for a fortnight's trip. He also said that he (the Pres) would be glad to pay a return visit in October.

This message does several things
   a) It sabotages an immediate Summit (end of Aug or Sept 1st)
   b) It practically rules out <u>any</u> early Summit except the end of Sept. This, in turn, sabotages our General Election
   c) It means – no Summit till November or December
   d) Instead of acting – as President hoped – to make K more accommodating at Geneva, it has had the opposite effect.
Mr K – with great skill – replied that he would be delighted to visit America in September. Of course, if there was a Summit, he wd attend it. But Summit or no Summit, he accepted the invitation and

---

65. Originally used to denote those who slung stones at the windows of the supporters of royal government at the start of the French civil war of 1648–53, *frondeur* has gradually come to mean anyone opposed to those in authority.

66. Lambton's forebear, John Lambton, 1st Earl of Durham, served as Lord Chancellor in the government of his father-in-law Earl Grey in 1830–34. His talent was tempered by tactlessness and touchiness.

wd be delighted to have President in Russia later on. As for Geneva, he had never attached much importance to these negotiations.

This has put the President into a great difficulty. His invitation was (or was intended to be) linked with a Summit and he hoped to make the Russians less intransigeant at Geneva. Mr K has taken the bait, but avoided the hook.

Herter has confessed all this to Selwyn. He is himself distressed and hurt .... H has not dared tell the French or the Germans. The Russians may leak the news at any time. The President doesn't now see how he can get out of the invitation, esp as he has no written document to appeal to. So, this foolish and incredibly naïve piece of amateur diplomacy has the following results

a) He has made any further 'progress' at Geneva less likely. The Russian position will harden

b) He will have a very difficult task in explaining to the American people that there is _no_ progress at Geneva and yet he has asked K to have a jolly visit to America

c) There will be no Summit

d) The French and German governments and people will be suspicious and angry

e) My own position here will be greatly weakened. Everyone will assume that the 2 Great Powers – Russia and U.S.A. – are going to fix up a deal over our heads and behind our backs. My whole policy – pursued for many years and esp during my Premiership – of close alliance and co-operation with America will be undermined. People will ask 'Why shd U.K. try to stay in the big game? Why should she be a nuclear power? You told us that this wd give you power and authority in the world. But you and we have been made fools of. This shews that Gaitskell and Crossman and Co are right. UK had better give up the struggle and accept, as gracefully as possible, the position of a second-rate power ....

Ministers were very angry indeed when I unfolded this story to them. I purposely did not try to under-estimate the dangers or excuse the failure of my diplomacy ....

27 July
.... At least we have more latitude in fixing our election, which (with a Summit in Sept) would have been a close run thing. A still more embarrassing feature of the President's plans has now been

revealed. He proposes to go on his travels in <u>October</u>, with visits to Japan, India, Pakistan, and Russia (the return visit) If he does not come to U.K., this will be an insult to the Queen and to our whole nation which will never be forgiven. I have told F.S. so to advise Herter. After all, we put all our forces – by land, sea, and air – under his command. He has had a State visit from the Queen, and a second visit a few weeks ago. But I feel sure that, on reflection, he will see the absolute necessity for treating us properly . . . .

The 'Hola' debate began about 10pm and lasted till 3am. It was not an easy affair, because the Kenya Govt had really muddled it. But the Colonial Secy put up a good case for the action we had taken and the administrative reforms we had made. The Opposition muddled the attack – in two ways. By taking it on the Appropriation Bill there could be no vote. By taking it late at night (wh since they control the business on this day they cd have avoided) they got no press. Yet, on a vote, there might well have been quite a number of Conservatives voting agst the Govt or abstaining.

I had a meeting of the Aircraft Industry Ctee at 9.30. We made good progress and have decided to support the VC10 for the new long-distance aircraft. I think we may also be able to devise a plan, by cooperation between Vickers and de Havilland, for the Viscount replacement[67] . . . .

31 July

. . . . Prepared press release in case the visit of K[hrushchev] to U.S. is (as we expect hourly) given out officially in Washington. I have decided to welcome and acclaim this as a great and statesmanlike act! I welcome it as following the initiative wh I took myself by going to Russia earlier in the year! I feel sure this is the best line to take . . . .

It is strange to think that this Parliament is now over. Unless something dramatic happens in the foreign field to prevent it, I shall ask for dissolution at the end of Sept, with polling day Oct 8th or Oct 15th. Curious to reflect that within this short time I shall know whether I have to have another period as P.M. or leave it all – probably forever . . . .

---

67. Vickers' VC10 jet airliner, still in development as a replacement for the Viscount, had run into financial difficulties. Purchases of VC10s by nationalised airlines and the consolidation of the British aircraft industry into BAC and Hawker Siddeley in 1960 was used to address these problems.

1 August

A quiet day .... My head feels clear enough, but I have a sort of horror of people. So to stay in bed, to work or read, is a great relief. I think it's the perpetual interviews, discussions, committees of ministers, Cabinets, Parliamentary Questions, talking to MPs, luncheons, dinners – and all the rest – which got on one's nerves ....

Worked on telegrams etc (in and out to Geneva, Washington etc) most of the morning. I also got off messages to Menzies, Diefenbaker, Nehru and Walter Nash. I like to send them 'gossipy' messages now and then ....

The Printers Strike is settled at last. It has been a very extensive struggle for both sides. But I hope it means some real peace for 2 or 3 years.[68]

2 August

.... [T]he President's invitation to Kruschev is to be published tomorrow. I shall issue a statement welcoming this initiative. The President has sent me a telegram suggesting a 'Western Summit' at the end of the month. De Gaulle is likely to refuse – in wh case the President will come to London ....

5 August

.... We have had a remarkably good Press about the President's gesture. It is all attributed to my pioneering in the early months of the year. Indeed, the political climate is remarkably good ....

6 August

.... After dinner, a good talk with the Foreign Secy, who got back yesterday from Geneva. His account was modest about himself, but it is clear to me that he has established a very strong position for himself in the diplomatic world. Herter was helpful, but his health is poor and he is not a strong character. Couve de Murville is able, cynical, and moody. His staff dislike him very much and say he is impossible to work with .... Of course, he serves a master, not (as Selwyn does)

---

68. The employees had initially pushed for a 40-hour week and a 10% pay increase. After a dispute of over six weeks, involving over 100,000 workers and costing over £20 million, the former Law Lord, Lord Birkett, was able to negotiate agreement on a 4.5% increase and 42-hour week, in return for some productivity improvements.

a colleague. De G[aulle] receives him in audience about once a week. At Cabinet, each Minister (Finance, For Affairs, Interior, Education, etc) says his piece, for the information of the others, and then leaves. M Debré the P.M., is 'plus royaliste que le Roi'[69] and is therefore a trouble to de G. For instance, de G wd like to pursue, and has initiated, a liberal policy in Algeria. Debré's main preoccupation is to hamper and emasculate it in every way he can . . . .

The Conference at Geneva <u>ought</u> to have succeeded and <u>would</u> (For Secy and I both feel) have succeeded except for the President's 'gaffe'. From the moment Mr K[hrushchev] had secured <u>both</u> the invitation and the promise of the return visit, Gromyko made no step forward and several steps back . . . . Selwyn feels a great sense of frustration and is very fatigued. 9 weeks or so in that daily round of talk, argument, lunching, dining – without any chance for relaxation – with people who aren't even your friends! . . . .

No one here has suggested that the Eisenhower–Kruschev visits are 'negotiate with Russia behind our backs' or a 'sinister deal between the 2 great powers, at the expense of smaller powers'. On the contrary, in U.K., as indeed throughout the whole world, this is said to be the result of the Macmillan initiative earlier this year. The British broke the ice. In some countries, this is welcomed; in others, deplored. But I am relieved that this is the interpretation of history wh is universally accepted. It was the danger of the other interpretation wh so alarmed and angered the Cabinet . . . .

22 August

. . . . There has been another 'Gallup Poll' wh reports increased support for the Conservative Party and for my Premiership. When these polls are adverse, we criticise their accuracy and minimise their importance. When they are going our way, we must not over-rate their meaning or effect. However, I don't think things can get any better and may get worse. So I have written to the Queen, warning her that I may shortly be asking for a dissolution . . . .

24 August

I drove from B.G. to Chequers last night. Worked all the morning on speeches, T.V. broadcast, and other details for the President's visit. The T.V. broadcast will be important. The Socialists are very angry

---

69. More royalist than the king.

and will of course try to denigrate it. Moreover, it will be very difficult to avoid it being rather banal. If it comes off, and I can say some things of real importance (without offence) it should have a good effect for the General Election. For the real issue must be whether they want a Conservative or a Socialist P.M. to conduct the diplomatic negotiations at a Summit . . . .

26 August
. . . . Dined in London with Cecil Harmsworth King (*Daily Mirror*) A party of 'industrialists'. Both Cecil King and Hugh Cudlipp seem to think we shall win the General Election . . . .

27 August
. . . . Left for London Airport at 5.30pm. President Eisenhower arrived punctually at 6.45. After speeches etc, we drove in an open car together to the American Embassy. The distance is 17 miles. It took us nearly 2 hours. There was a wonderful turn-out all along the route, and great enthusiasm . . . .

29 August
I have definitely decided the date for the Poll – October 8th. This means prorogation and dissolution on Thursday and Friday 18th and 19th. I am not quite sure on what date to make the announcement or whether to go to Balmoral.[70] I rather want to keep the Queen's prerogative in its integrity, and for this an audience is better than a written submission. But of course the Press will draw its conclusions . . . .

Talks began at 3 and lasted till 5pm. We covered all the European ground, including Berlin, Summit etc. My real purpose is not to make any new agreement with President in all this, but to try to keep the position quiet and fluid during the next few weeks . . . .

President got pretty restless after these 2 hours. These talks with 8 or 10 advisers on either side are rather unreal and do not suit him or me. But Herter and Selwyn Lloyd had made good progress on a lot of topics yesterday and will do more work together here, reporting their results to President and me. This is really what Eisenhower likes . . . .

---

70. The Queen's Scottish residence.

30 August (Sunday)
An hour's talk – 9.30 to 10.30am on the problem of the Geneva 'Tests' Conference. The only people present were President; Herter; Selwyn Lloyd and myself. In spite of the restricted meeting, Pres seemed rather ill at ease. I knew this to be the result of the division – some deep cleavage – of view between the Pentagon and the State Dept. The Pentagon want to go on with tests, in order to make the refinements which their experts hope for – this partly for the small 'tactical' weapon, to be used at 1000 yards range; partly for the 'anti-missile' missile – which seems anyway almost a fantasy. (Our own Defence experts really agree with the Pentagon, but in our system they do not have the kind of independent life and authority wh the military chiefs have in U.S.) The State Dept sympathises with the British view (P.M. and For Secy) wh wants a 'comprehensive agreement', bringing all nuclear tests by USA, USSR and GB to an end. The laymen (British and American) are not impressed by the argument about 'underground' tests and esp the theory of the 'large hole'. These methods wd be tremendously expensive, and in the end wd probably not escape detection, by one means or another. In the circumstances, I confined myself to expressing my own views very strongly. I told Pres that we ought to take risks for so great a prize . . . .

31 August
President and I motored to St Paul's from Chequers. The crowds were so great that we changed into an open car. The East End of St Paul's and the American chapel are now really magnificent and an immense improvement over the old reredos. Bishop Wand [of London] and the notorious Canon Collins (fellow-traveller etc) took charge of us. Canon Collins afterwards gave a ridiculous and offensive interview to the press.

I spent most of the afternoon pondering over the TV discussion with the President, wh was due for 7.20pm to 7.40pm, in the pillared room at No 10. The whole house has been filled with technicians and workmen of all kinds. After the television, I have a dinner party of some 40. The guests are invited for 7.15, and there are T.V. sets in the various rooms for the viewers . . . .

1 September
Altho' the Press normally dislikes (and naturally) the Television and the Radio, our talk has had a tremendous Press, on the whole favour-

able. The *M[anchester] Guardian* thought I wrote my own 'commercials' – meaning that I said some things in praise of Britain wh might be thought things in favour of the Conservative Party! But it is clear that there was an immense viewing audience and that it was well received. Apart from the actual performance 7.20–7.40, extracts were shewn at 9 and the whole thing was done again at 10.30. Sound Radio also carried it. Dorothy was in the West Highlands, but she listened to the radio. My colleagues (there was a Cabinet at 10.30) were very enthusiastic.

Worked all day on the General Election programme. There is a tremendous lot to arrange – Prorogation Councils, Dissolution, Announcement, visit to Balmoral and a mass of other details . . . .

4 September

I have managed to persuade Lord Monckton to take the Chairmanship of the Central African Commission. This is a very great triumph and will make people regard the Commission as something serious. As soon as we get formal agreement from Welensky, Whitehead and the local governors, we will announce it. It will (among other things) help us here in the General Election . . . .

5 September

. . . . The Laos trouble is blowing up and we had a lot of telephoning. The President and I had a talk. I think we must go to U.N. in the first instance. The trouble is that it's an impossible country – at least, that part in wh the Communists are penetrating – a sort of Malayan jungle[71] . . . .

7 September

Left Benson airfield (RAF) by a Heron of the Queen's Flight about 1pm. Reached Dyce airport (near Aberdeen) about 3.15. Sir Michael Adeane met me and we motored to Aboyne, where James Stuart was waiting at The Huntley Arms. Sir M Adeane went on in the car to Balmoral. I stayed and had an hour or so with James. He is all for the early election, on wh I have decided. As regards Scotland, he does

---

71. The civil war against the Communist insurgents of the Pathet Lao had recommenced in July. The British had recently been successful in the similar jungle war against Communist guerrillas during the Malayan Emergency (1948–60).

not foresee much change. He puts possible losses at 5, possible gains
at 3 . . . .

11 September
I think Mr Gaitskell has made a very good start – rather too good, I
fear. He redeemed a terrible T.V. [party political broadcast] of smear
and calumny by some sensible words at the end. He also spoke pretty
well at the T.U.C. conference. Our manifesto – wh is sound and
sensible, but naturally not dramatic – was 'launched' at a Press Conference today. I took the chair and introduced it. The questions from
the journalists were good. Butler and Hailsham were with me. I then
did 4 minutes about the manifesto on the T.V. news . . . .

12 September
. . . . Mr Thomson, the purchaser of the Kemsley empire,[72] came to
see me yesterday. He is a Canadian 'card'. He is trying to buy more
newspapers in England. He seems to have a lot already, both in
Canada and UK. He made it clear that he did not intend to take any
political position. His instructions to his editors and managers are
only to make as much money as possible. He wants (he says) his <u>news</u>
to be objective (no slant) but his editorials must say what 'the community' will like. This is really the point of view of Lord Astor to
The Times, but more crudely expressed. I rather liked Mr Thomson.
He said, in addition, that he believed in the Rotary motto – Service
not Self: Honesty is the Best Policy etc. I should judge that he wants
a Peerage and will hope to get [one] from me or Gaitskell . . . .

13 September
Sunday Press reasonable. Even the *Observer* is not too bad. Mas-
singham, their political correspondent, is hedging. Malcolm Mugger-
idge in the *Pictorial* is very violent (all the *D Mirror* group are being
very offensive – smear and personalities and no argument. This is <u>not</u>
what I expected, when I saw Harmsworth King and Cudlipp. But it
may be preparatory to a change of tone at the end) M M calls me a
'Turf Court Bummaree' – I wonder what he means.
    . . . . We did a lot of good work yesterday. Since G[eorge] Christ
and I began we have done

---

72. Lord Kemsley sold his press empire, of which the flagship was the *Sunday
    Times*, to Roy Thomson in 1959.

Gramophone Record
Election Address
Introduction to Press Conference
Message to Party Workers
Message to Candidates.
In addition, we have finished full scale (45 minute) speeches for
Bromley (adoption meeting)
Manchester
Birmingham
Swansea.
This covers speeches for the first week's tour, except the ¼ hr
or 10 minute 'whistle stop' speeches. George is working on a form
for these. We have also to do some newspaper articles. In addition,
we have done the draft of the <u>sound</u> broadcast, wh comes at the
end of the first week. So we are fairly well on. Of course, we must
allow for last minute changes, or taking out one section and introducing another, according to the way the Election seems to be
turning. We have also to do a speech on agriculture etc for Tewkes-
bury . . . .

16 September
. . . . After luncheon, I saw three Ministers. First, the Chancellor
of the Exr – in good form and hopeful about the Election. But he
is weary and talks of giving up his office, altho' (if we win) he wd
like to serve in a less arduous post. I told him that we cannot jug
the hare till we have caught it, and that he must not think of a
change anyway. Then Alec Home (Commonwealth) with only departmental points. Then Duncan Sandys (Defence) He would like to be
Foreign Secy. Failing that, he wd prefer to remain at Defence – but
he wants a <u>complete</u> reorganisation, and centralisation of the Higher
Ministerial control and commands – an old scheme, but full of difficulties. Duncan is ambitious, but loyal and thoroughly ready to
serve as I may decide. (All this talk seems to me to be taking victory for granted and I don't like it. We must concentrate on the
Election) . . . .

17 September
. . . . The House met at 11am. A favourable speech by Mr Speaker;
followed by short valedictory speeches from me and Gaitskell and

Wade (for the Liberals) All over by 11.30 when Black Rod appeared.[73] One Labour member (Rankin) cheated and began an oration about unemployment and poverty in his constituency in Scotland. This was received in silence – none more indignant than the Opposition. After the ceremony in the Lords, we returned to the Commons. I walked there and back with Mr Gaitskell – leading the procession behind Mr Speaker. G seemed rather grumpy – but I expect I struck him in the same way. When it came to the procession of MPs to say goodbye to Mr Speaker and shake his hand, I made Winston go first. This was liked by the House and the spectators.

I had all ministers (not in Cabinet) and ministers of state, under secretaries, parly secretaries, and whips in both Houses to a sherry party in No 10. They seemed to enjoy it. Ld Selkirk made a nice little speech, to wh I replied. The *News Chronicle* Gallup Poll, published yesterday, shows no change in the position . . . .

19 September
. . . . Mr K[hrushchev] has made a speech about disarmament in the U.N. 'Scrap the lot' is his policy. The passages about 'control' are vague. But as a 'propaganda' effort it seems pretty good. We must, however, follow it up (on the lines of the For Secy on Thursday at U.N.) and <u>not</u> seem to oppose K but rather pin him down to concrete plans.

The Labour Party manifesto is published in full. It is full of promises and seems attractive to those who ask nothing more. But it is quite unrealistic. The bitterness of the attack on me and the For Secy – on the City and the rich executive class – on all the 'Establishment' is pretty strong throughout. But there is nothing unexpected . . . .

22 September
All our people were depressed yesterday by the *Daily Mail* 'Gallup Poll' wh shewed our lead had reduced from 7% to 3½%. But today the rival *Daily Express* poll shows our 7% lead maintained. So there is a tremendous battle among the experts. Ld Poole, who came yesterday afternoon, was calm – but thought we shd have to stiffen up the attack pretty soon. I thought I could use the whistle-stop speeches

---

73. Black Rod, a senior official of the House of Lords, was bringing the royal command to prorogue Parliament. The retiring Speaker, W. S. Morrison, had been in post since 1951.

for this. The Socialists had a very successful TV last night – much better than ours. Gaitskell is becoming very expert. All their campaign so far is concentrated on dirt (against Tories and businessmen) with bribes to the Old. They are trying to make it a Pension Election. While we must defend this flank, we must not let ourselves be diverted from the main theme – Peace and Prosperity.

27 September (Sunday)

. . . . The Labour Party have – so far as policy goes – one immense bribe – 10/- at once for the Old Age Pensioners. Considering their numbers, this is a dangerous 'pressure group'. If they win, it will be on this bribe and nothing else.

I have taken the only possible line and declared that I will not enter into a public auction. All the same, this is our weak point.

The fact that their T.V. performances are better than ours and that they are stirring up a lot of mud over some shady City Jews who have done a disreputable 'property' deal, does not matter so much. The latter may even recoil – for these particular rich Jews are all the particular friends and supporters of Labour – Howard Samuel, [Victor] Mishcon (LCC), [L. C.] Cohen (Eastbourne) etc.[74] But the Press has up to now been leaning to them, chiefly because they are getting livelier news from Transport House[75] than from our Central Office. We are trying to put this right.

---

74. A scandal broke on 16 September after the collapse of shares in companies controlled by shady property dealer Harry Jasper. Jasper, born a Berlin Jew, circumvented the credit shortage by buying companies, selling their assets and then leasing them back, prompting Harold Wilson to attack the 'casino mentality of the City of London', whilst Gaitskell had on 26 September used the scandal as a means to attack the 1957 Rent Act. Samuel was a property developer with a minority stake in the Labour-supporting *New Statesman*; Mishcon a City lawyer, LCC councillor and Labour candidate for Gravesend; and Cohen the managing director of the Alliance Building Society who was in fact standing for Labour in the election for Brighton Kemptown (not Eastbourne). Although the *Daily Express*, in particular, played up alleged links between Labour and the management at Jasper, these three do not seem to have been directly involved in the management of the company. At the start of October the government set up an inquiry which led to new controls to prevent another Jasper in the 1960 Building Societies Act.

75. The headquarters of the T&GWU in Smith Square in Westminster, which had been shared with the TUC and the Labour Party since 1928.

My impression is, up to now, that we have lost ground in the first 10 days. How much, we cannot tell. The Gallup and allied polls will certainly reflect this during the coming week. If everyone keeps calm, it will be all right. If our people begin to panic, the result might be serious.

It is rather a strange feeling to lie in bed in this room at No 10 (wh I have occupied for nearly 3 years) and wonder whether I shall be here in 10 days time . . . .

28 September
Daily Mail poll bad – down to 2% lead. But I still feel confident. A very good afternoon tour. ¼ hour speeches at Acton; Uxbridge; Ealing; and Chiswick – with shorter calls at 3 or 4 other constituencies. Excellent reception.

President E[isenhower] and Mr K[hrushchev] have parted without quarrelling! Indeed, the communiqué, about no force but only negotiation, is excellent and should help me.

I answered Mr Gaitskell's absurd idea about getting all this money out of 'business expansion'. If so, why didn't he do this in 1951, instead of putting nearly £400m more in taxation[76] . . . .

9 October
The General Election is over. We have got a majority of 100 over all parties, having gained some 29 seats and lost 3 or 4.[77] We lost Devon [North] to the Liberals, but to my great joy we got back Torrington from them (Lady Violet Bonham Carter has been routed)

The Election campaign was so exhausting during the last 10 days that I could not keep the diary going. I made major speeches in Glasgow; Bradford; Halifax and Nottingham – and some 10 to 11 speeches every day as well – of 15 minutes each. The weather was fine the whole time and the crowds in each place ranged from 3000 to 6000. It was an extraordinary experience.

In the last few days, I felt we were doing better. My last broadcast, which was largely due to the good advice I got from Mr Norman Collins, was a real success. I did it alone – without interviewers or

---

76. In a speech in Newcastle that day Gaitskell claimed that all his election promises, including the pension increases, could be funded out of economic growth without requiring increases in income tax. Macmillan's subsequent rubbishing of this claim proved a turning point in the election.

77. The Conservatives won 365 seats, Labour 258 and the Liberals 6.

gadgets – and standing up. The *Observer*; *Mirror*; and *Spectator* were virulent in opposition. *The Times* came down on our side at the end; so did the *Mail* and the *Express*. The various polls became somewhat ridiculous, because the number of 'don't knows' kept growing. We did <u>very</u> well in the South and the Midlands; not so well in Lancashire. In Scotland there was a slight swing against us. Altogether, the result is remarkable. I don't think any Party has won three times running, increasing its majority each time.

Dorothy and I spent Thursday–Friday night (8th–9th) at No 10, watching the T.V. At first, it was rather anxious, esp when the two Salfords swung against us. David and Sylvia Kilmuir came in about midnight. By 1am it was clear that we would win and Gaitskell (interviewed by T.V.) 'conceded' the Election. (a curious modern Americanism) We went to bed at 4am, happy but exhausted.

To Bromley at noon – for our own count. My majority was up by 2000.[78]

I went to Central Office at 2am this morning and had a fine ovation. D went with me. Tonight, I went again for Press Conference, and T.V. I tried to keep a humble note, stressing the need for national unity . . . .

11 October
. . . . It is hard, without some thought and study, to analyse the Election result. The Liberal vote (with twice the number of candidates) nearly doubled. Much is made of this in the Press and it is perhaps exaggerated. What I think happened is that the Liberals (for the first time) took more from the Socialists, in many places, than from us. This may prove important. The great thing is to keep the Tory Party on <u>modern</u> and <u>progressive</u> lines.

18 October (Sunday)
After much effort, I got the Cabinet settled and published by Thursday. Alan Lennox-Boyd leaves us, much to my regret. He has been an outstanding Colonial Secretary, for 5 years of growth and development in all the Overseas Territories. If he has had bad luck over Kenya (the Hola Camp) and Nyasaland, these are very small affairs in comparison to the wonderful work which he has done. Iain Macleod is to succeed him. Fortunately, that was his ambition. Geoffrey Lloyd leaves also

---

78. Macmillan won 27,055 votes, to Labour's 11,603.

. . . . He has been an adequate, and in some ways resourceful, Minister of Education. But he hates office routine and seemed quite glad to be relieved of it. I have put Eccles back there. He doesn't like giving up the BofTrade and being apparently 'demoted'. But he will soon inflate himself again (he is naturally a buoyant character) and will do a good job. My chief problem has been about the Chairmanship of the Party. Ld Hailsham, with Ld Poole gone, (he has had to go back to business) is really not safe. After much effort and quite a lot of emotional scenes,[79] we have at last got everything arranged. Butler is to be Chairman of the Party and Hailsham is to be Ld Privy Seal and Minister for Science. H is in a very over-excited condition and keeps giving ridiculous 'Press Conferences' – but no doubt he will quieten down soon. The appointment of Butler as Chairman is very good symbolically. It shews the world that, after our great victory, we intend to remain progressive and not slide back into reaction.

Defence I have given to Watkinson and Transport to Marples. These are both 'self-made' men . . . . and will both do well. I have, with some difficulty, persuaded Duncan Sandys to take over the Ministry of Supply – break it up – and form a new Ministry of Aviation.[80] The present position of the aircraft industry is very bad. Aubrey Jones failed to grasp the nettle. If anyone can tackle the job, Duncan Sandys is the man. (I offered Ministry of Works to Aubrey Jones, but he declined)

The service ministers have presented no problem. I have made no change except to substitute Lord Carrington for Lord Selkirk as First Lord. (Lord S is, very patriotically, going to Singapore as High Commissioner)

There is a great problem – not yet resolved – about the Speakership. A strong 'moderate' opinion has appeared, in the Party and in the Press, that we ought to have a 'Labour' Speaker.[81] But if this means

---

79. Hailsham later alleged that Macmillan mistakenly thought him involved in a divorce case at the time and that he was being moved for personal reasons. Macmillan's views on divorce were no doubt flavoured by the advice he received in 1931 that divorcing Dorothy because of her affair with Boothby would ruin his own political career.

80. Military supply and aircraft production had been combined in the Ministry of Supply in 1946. The former function was now returned to the War Office, whilst the latter, and responsibility for nuclear weapons, went to the new ministry.

81. At this point something which had not happened before.

1959

253

Mitchison (who is 'gaga') or Jones [?] (who is a fellow traveller)[82] or [W. R.] Williams (who is a buffoon) it is not a reasonable idea. If, however, Sir Frank Soskice (ex Solicitor General) a man of parts, intelligence, and integrity will stand, I think we should try to get our Party to accept him. Rab has seen Gaitskell on my behalf and told him just this. G was ungracious and called it 'blackmail'. He thinks he shd have the Speakership as a Labour 'perquisite' and nominate whom he likes. This is a quite intolerable position. I think it will work out that Soskice will not be allowed to accept – so it will end in our nominee, the present Solicitor-General, Hylton-Foster. The chief trouble to me is that I am now absolutely stuck and cannot complete the administration. For if Hylton-Foster does become Speaker, all sorts of consequential changes follow. So I must 'wait and see'.

I was sorry about Aubrey Jones – a nice, sincere, and shy creature. But he is not really fitted for the rough and tumble of politics and industry. He is the son of a coal-miner. But he looks like, and is like, a rather overbred and slightly effete younger son of a duke.

I still have to face Lord John Hope, who (like all his family) regards himself as a man of great political importance and of considerable political quality. The trouble is that he is useless in the House. (He is good on the platform) Hopes have always run a strong mutual admiration society among themselves. His father (the late Lord Linlithgow)[83] was conceited and second rate. But he is an agreeable fellow, and I cannot bear having to wound his feelings. He is under-secy at Scottish Office (wh he has done well enough) but wants to be Minister of State, Foreign Office – which is quite out of the question. Could he be Minister of Works?

I also have to get a Minister of Power, in place of Ld Mills (who stays in the Cabinet, without portfolio, as Paymaster-General) But nothing can be done till the Speakership is settled . . . .

The Labour Party, as we would expect, are engaged in a tremendous postmortem about the General Election. The Right wants to drop Socialism and Nationalisation. The Left wants more Socialism and more Nationalisation. I think Gaitskell will ride the storm without too much difficulty, for there is really no one else. Part of the pressures

---

82. Someone seen as a Communist sympathiser. It is unclear to whom Macmillan is referring.
83. Viceroy of India 1936–43.

building up against him result from dislike of his 'intellectual' friends
and his aloofness from the rank and file . . . .

22 October

Rather a hectic 3 days. We have got over the Speakership problem,
with the unanimous election of Hylton-Foster, the Solicitor General.
We offered the Opposition, if they would allow Sir Frank Soskice to
stand, to get our people to support him. But Mr G wd not part with
him, and then tried to turn this act of generosity into a grievance . . . .
The Press gave it no support; and Hylton-Foster's speech of acceptance
was so good that everyone realised that he was far the best choice.

De Gaulle has refused the President's suggestion for a Western
Summit in October and a full Summit in December. Not content with
doing this by private messages to Eisenhower and to me, he has
published a long and argumentative communiqué. He accept[s] a
Summit in the 'spring' (I suppose after his bomb has been exploded)
but he rejects the idea of a rather tentative meeting, to be followed by
others. He wants it to be comprehensive and 'decisive' – a sort of
Congress of Vienna. He has invited Kruschev to Paris (I suppose in
order to be on a level with the British and Americans – 'keeping up
with the Joneses') All this has infuriated the President and is very
embarrassing to me – esp in view of what I said during the Election.
However, I dare say it will get sorted out somehow.

I have – with great difficult – completed the Administration. It is
terribly painful getting rid of colleagues, and very hard to choose the
right ones for their first job.

I have [been] making some experiments – Richard Wood (39) to
be Minister of Power. My excellent PPS, Tony Barber, to be Economic
Secy at Treasury. We have got 8 new boys – which isn't bad . . . .

. . . . Poor Adenauer, who usually 'sucks up' to de Gaulle, accepted
the American invitation to the Western Summit in October, before he
heard that de G was going to refuse! . . . .

23 October

. . . . After luncheon, Governor of Cyprus – who was fairly cheerful.
Then For Secy – chiefly on appointments, within and without the
Office, during next 3 and 4 years. I want Hoyer Millar to stay – he is
so solid and reliable. Even when he is away shooting (as he usually is)
he gives a sense of confidence. He shd be kept on another 2 years or
so (if he agrees) and be succeeded by Harold Caccia. Gladwyn Jebb

shd become a Life Peer (and help the Govt in various ways) and Bob
Dixon go to Paris . . . .

27 October

HofCommons at 11. Black Rod summoned us to the HofLords. The
opening of Parlt was by commission, in view of the Queen's pregnancy.
It was a dull affair – without any of the uniforms and great pageantry
that we have when the Queen opens Parl in person.

The House met again at 2.30. The mover (Tiley of Bradford) made
a good speech – very Yorkshire.[84] The seconder (Gardner – Billericay)
made a more polished effort. Both good. Gaitskell poor – he seemed
to have nothing left in him. I am told that Transport House promised
him a majority of 25 right up to the last moment. So he must have had
rather a shock on Election night. I spoke for 35 minutes. It was pretty
successful, altho' I was anxious about 'Summitry'. However, the whole
House (including most of the more serious Labour members) were
sympathetic. They all knew that de Gaulle was just 'showing off' in
order to annoy the President and me.

Party for new members and their wives at No 10 (we have 75 new
members altogether) D ran this admirably, as usual. Her sisters,
daughters, daughter-in-law and friends rallied round . . . .

Dined at The Club[85] . . . . Derry Heathcoat Amory (a new member)
was there and in good form. The Governor [of the Bank of England]
was (as we all are) astonished at the weakness of the Radcliffe
Report.[86] The only advantage is that it unanimously whitewashes the
'establishment'.

29 October

. . . . A long, but useful Cabinet. We discussed the Betting and Gaming
Bill. I was struck by the extraordinary ignorance of some of us (like

---

84. The debate was on the Queen's Speech setting out the legislative programme of
the government. The motion was moved by two backbench Conservative MPs,
Arthur Tiley and Edward Gardner.

85. An exclusive political dining club founded by Sir Joshua Reynolds in 1764.

86. Set up in May 1957 in the face of anxieties about rising inflation, the
committee into the working of the monetary system under Lord Radcliffe
sacrificed clarity for unanimity, whilst broadly rejecting concentration on
interest rates or the money supply rather than control of total demand as the
means of tackling inflation.

Henry Brooke) and the uncanny knowledge of others (like Iain Mac-leod)[87] .... The Bill will be controversial; there will be trouble with the Churches Anti Gambling Society [sic];[88] and so on. But a) it's the first year of the Parlt b) it really <u>must</u> be done if the whole Police force is not to be corrupted c) it will amuse Parlt and let the private members have a chance . . . .

A long and very good discussion on the Stockholm negotiation . . . . The Norwegians are being very truculent over fish. We decided to give them a concession on canned or frozen fish. Whether they will be satisfied or not, we cannot tell. But we might try to work out a compromise through the Swedes. Of course, the home fishing industry will be indignant – but the stakes are <u>very</u> high. For if Stockholm fails, I feel very unhappy about the future of British exports to Europe.[89]

De Gaulle has proposed a 'Western Summit' (with Adenauer 'to come along later') on Dec 19th. President Eisenhower is disgusted at the delay, but not disposed to argue any more. So then I have agreed. But we have <u>refused</u> his proposed date – April – for the real summit. What Mr K[hrushchev] will now do is obscure. He may well turn nasty and start sending ultimatums again about Berlin. Then – through the folly, first of the Americans and then of the French, we shall have lost all the ground wh I gained by the Moscow visit . . . .

30 October

. . . . A great flurry – For Office, Commonwealth Relations Office, Colonial Office. A grave dilemma is presented to us. The Moroccans have put down a resolution in United Nations Assembly calling on the French to abandon the Bomb Test (atomic, we think) wh they have planned to set off in the Sahara. The Nigerians, Ghana, and other Africans are terribly upset. It is an emotional reaction, for it is very unlikely that the Test will do any harm – certainly no more in Africa than elsewhere. They even talk about 'leaving the Commonwealth' if we do not vote for the resolution.

On the other hand, if we do, the French (who always supported us

---

87. Macleod had been a professional bridge player in the 1930s. The most significant aspect of the legislation was the legalisation of betting shops.

88. The Churches' Committee on Gambling.

89. This stumbling block in the EFTA negotiations was resolved by Britain removing tariffs and raising the quota for imports of fish from the Scandinavian countries, enabling the agreement to be signed in Stockholm in November.

and USA on similar resolutions in the past) will be deeply offended. I had talks with the 3 Secretaries of State singly and jointly and we have agreed on a telegram to Washington and New York. We must try to get some kind of resolution wh the French might accept (or, at least, understand <u>our</u> voting for) which will pacify the Africans.

The whole thing is all the more tiresome – and ridiculous – because everyone knows that the test will in fact take place, resolution or no resolution. But just as we have a) trouble with Nigeria and Ghana and b) are desperately trying to 'mend our fences' with France, it is most vexing to have this problem . . . .

On the whole, the new Administration has been well received. Miss Irene Ward ([Conservative MP for]Tynemouth) who is mad, has written a foolish letter to the *D.T.* But she carries no real weight. The trouble is that none of the women MPs have a real brain. I can think of none (at present) who could be a Minister . . . .

I still feel very tired – mentally – and without any real desire to work on problems. I seem to have neither resilience nor initiative. But perh[aps] today and tomorrow and half Sunday in bed or resting will put me right . . . .

10 November

. . . . Dinner for the Guinea President – full rig, wh they like. Reception afterwards. It is strange to hear these gentlemen pouring out bitter criticisms of France in faultless and idiomatic French – the only language they have, except a large number of barbaric dialects. I spoke in French, in proposing the health of the President – wh seemed to go down pretty well.

Read Hugh Dalton's memoirs – quite interesting. The intrigues and hatreds among the Socialists of the 20th century remind me of the same thing among the Liberals in the 19th – esp. the second half. No doubt parties of the Left are more prone to quarrel than those of the right. They attract cantankerous types . . . .

16 November

. . . . A tiresome and inconclusive interview with Gaitskell, who was accompanied by Bevan and Callaghan. (Home and Macleod with me) They are torn between joining and refusing to join the Central African Commission. They will make a decision on firmly political grounds – at least Gaitskell will. Bevan is clearly more favourable than G. This delay is dangerous, but they pleaded for a few more days . . . .

17 November

.... Left at 12 noon to go to Victoria to meet Chancellor Adenauer
.... [I]t was clear that Dr A had been told by his advisers to make
an effort to be polite. I think they are ashamed by the foolish things
wh he has said about me and about HMG's policy during the last
year[90] ....

18 November

After a luncheon at the German Embassy, we all went off to Chequers.
Meeting after dinner, where we got down to 'brass tacks'. I reproached Dr A for his attacks on HMG and spoke very strongly. He
seemed startled and angry. But his staff and esp von Brentano were
clearly pleased that there was plain speaking. At first, I thought he wd
break off the conversation. But all ended well in a sort of reconciliation.

19 November

Last night's row clearly produced a salutary effect. The talk this
morning – 9.30 to 12 noon – was sensible and constructive. Dr A
agreed the text of his Press Conference address, wh was moderate and
sensible. He agrees to East/West Summit at the end of April, if all the
others will conform. Anthony Eden came to luncheon and was very
helpful. I went to Victoria Station to say goodbye to the Germans,
who went by train to Gatwick. On the whole, the visit has done good.
The Germans are pleased – altho' they fear that the old man will prob
have another relapse into his suspicions and fears.[91] The trouble is that
they are all afraid of him ....

24 November

After great discussions and manoeuvres I made the statement on the
Commission for Central Africa after questions today. Last night, Mr
Gaitskell asked to see me. I saw him twice, at 7pm and at 8.30. He
told me at 7 that the Shadow Cabinet could not accept nomination to

---

90. Adenauer, in particular, feared that West Germany might be the victim of
    appeasement of the Russians, and had reacted with hostility to Macmillan's trip
    to Moscow, a hostility on which de Gaulle was skilfully to capitalise.
91. Macmillan's concerns proved well-founded. When Adenauer visited Paris at the
    start of the following month even de Gaulle remarked that he was not fair to
    the British Prime Minister.

the Commission on the basis of the letter wh I had sent him last week. It was a pity – because our positions were not really far apart. He wanted to help. I said that I could not make <u>any</u> alteration in the 'terms of reference', which had been agreed between all the Governments concerned and accepted by the 20 members already nominated. On my 'explanatory gloss' I had already done my best, at considerable risk of reaction in Salisbury.[92] So I was afraid I cd do no more. He went off to think and returned to ask whether I wd agree (as I had suggested at an earlier stage) that I might leave it open. In other words, my statement wd announce the purpose of the Commission, the terms of reference, the explanatory gloss, the names of the 20 members – and end by saying that my consultations with the Leader of the Opposition were still going on. I agreed to this readily enough. We agreed also a form of words. He then said that he wd have to ask a question, but it wd be simple and unprovocative. He wd ask whether the Commission cd consider 'other forms of association' (that is, other than federation) I wd make a simple and equally unprovocative reply. We agreed the terms of this. Then I wd refuse to answer any more questions and we wd end on this harmonious note. However, when it came to the point, Mr G (with characteristic but almost incredible duplicity) went back on this arrangement. As soon as I had sat down, he launched into a violent tirade against the Govt and all its works. At the end of 10 minutes of this stuff, he duly asked the agreed question. (Like a private schoolboy's lies, made all right, he thinks, by one little piece of truth) I thought it better, in spite of G's treachery, to keep to my side of the bargain. I therefore answered quietly and simply, as agreed. Then questions were asked – mainly by the Liberal leader – about the terms of reference, to wh I replied. I ended with an appeal to the whole House to cooperate – wh was not badly received.

. . . . Just as many people here think I did not go far enough to meet the Socialist and Liberal demands to widen the scope of the Commission's references, Welensky is very angry and thinks I have gone too far[93] . . . .

---

92. The capital of the Central African Federation (and Southern Rhodesia), now renamed Harare.
93. Gaitskell wanted the Commission to be able to consider the liquidation of the Federation whilst Welensky, who had tried to get the Commission abandoned at the end of the previous month, feared that this might happen anyway.

29 November
Motored to Chequers. For Secy, Chancellor of Exr, Sir N Brook, Sir R
Makins, Sir D Hoyer Millar. 12–1, 3–8 – Europe and the world. A
most useful talk, such as one can never have in London, with all the
interruptions of each working day. It was agreed (among other things)
that I must try to have a private talk in Paris both with President
E[isenhower] and de Gaulle separately. With the President, I must try
to win him over to the view that we cannot afford to let the Geneva
Test Conference go wrong. We must agree with the Russians on any
reasonable terms wh wd give us the beginning of control and inspection. If a moratorium is the best that can be got for 'underground'
tests, let us go for the moratorium.

With de Gaulle, I must ask questions, and try to find out what he
really wants – about NATO; about the 6 – politically and economically
about the Germans after Adenauer; above all about the Russians.
(There is much talk in diplomatic circles of a recent de G–Kruschev
understanding, with Germany and Berlin bargained against Russian
support in Algeria. I do not, myself, believe it) . . . .

30 November (St Andrew's Day)
. . . . The Labour Party Conference at Blackpool ended (as I expected)
with the roles of Gaitskell and Bevan exactly reversed. Before the
General Election, G carried B. Now B carries (indeed has saved) G.
There is a patched up truce between the nationalisers and the anti-
nationalisers. But I think the old albatross (nationalisation) is still
hung round their necks. The next stage will be interesting. Bevan made
a curious remark 'people are not discontented any more'.[94] What a
tribute to Conservative policies and themes! . . . .

2 December
. . . . The Labour Party are trying to use the problem of Africa to re-
unite their divided party. They have put down what amounts to a vote
of censure, esp with regard to my [forthcoming] visit to the Union of
S[outh] Africa.[95]

---

94. The 1959 election was already being seen as one won for the Conservatives by
    affluence.
95. Debated on 7 December, because of the apartheid policies pursued by the
    National government there since 1948.

3 December

Mr Gaitskell has now at last made up his mind. The Opposition refuse to join the Central African Commission. This is disappointing, but it is perhaps better that they shd stay out than join with merely wrecking tactics . . . .

The Italians left today. They were very pleasant and agree with us in everything. Unfortunately, the French and the Germans take very little notice of them . . . .

4 December

I am not sure how to proceed with the Parliamentary element of the Central African Commission. On the whole, I think the best course is just to appoint the 3 Conservatives and leave it at that. I saw both Herbert Morrison (of Lambeth) today and Hartley Shawcross. Ld M was very helpful and sympathetic. He thinks the Labour leaders have behaved foolishly. But he doesn't want to join himself – partly not to quarrel openly with his party (in spite of his contempt for them) and partly on health grounds. I think Ld S will help us if we wish it . . . .

11 December

. . . . Ld Shawcross will now definitely join (in spite of the efforts to dissuade him of his old Labour colleagues) . . . .

13 December

. . . . No progress at all with our European and NATO problems. The Americans, with their financial crisis,[96] are being rather 'tricky' about 'non-discrimination'. But, of course, the 6; the 7; and the European Free Trade Area are and must be to some extent 'discriminatory'. The Americans, in their desire to see Europe 'integrated' were prepared (a few years ago and until recently) to abandon the strict economic line for the political advantage. Now they are not so sure . . . .

17 December

I was led into a row with Gaitskell at question time – wh is rather a mistake for me. Nor did I come off better – it was drawn, rather in his favour. But there are moments when his false, perjured face irritates me beyond measure. (I gather from my Labour friends that he has the same effect on them) . . . .

---

96. The US budget deficit reached a peacetime record of $12 billion in 1959.

18 December

A lot of clearing up in the morning. (Parlt adjourned. I am glad to say)
I left for Paris after luncheon and dined at Embassy with Foreign
Secretary and ambassador – also Hoyer Millar, Rumbold, Dean etc.

19 December

(Paris) The so-called 'Western Summit' meeting began this morning.
We were all bidden to arrive at the Elysée at 9.30am. Chancellor
Adenauer and I were told to come at 9.20 and 9.25 respectively.
President Eisenhower came punctually at 9.30 . . . .

It was an extraordinary performance, conducted by de Gaulle with
great skill and grace, with periods both of high comedy and of farce.
The President's American slang contrasted strongly with de Gaulle's
stately – old fashioned French. However, the translator did his best. 'I
guess I'll just have to clear my s̲kedule' became 'Le calendrier diplomatique est très chargé – mais je f̲erai de mon mieux pour . . . .'

The two highlights of the talk were as follows. De Gaulle explained
that he – and he would assume all of us agreed – felt that it was now
impossible to avoid a Summit meeting of some kind with Mr Kruschev.
'Tout le monde accepte la thèse du Premier Ministre britannique'[97] etc
etc. What, when and where.

After some discussion, it appeared that I was the only person who
had been provided with a list of international events next year.
President Eisenhower suggested April 20 or 21st (the date he had been
told by his people) De G said that he wd much like to visit U.S.A.
b̲e̲f̲o̲r̲e̲ the Summit. K was coming to France on March 15. He (de G)
was having the great honour of a state visit to Her Majesty in the first
week of April. Then came Holy Week. Perhaps he might go to
Washington on Easter Tuesday (April 19th) he wd stay 3 days in
America, 1 in Canada – perhaps April 25th or 26th would do?

President gave the invitation to de G for the 19th (he could do very
little else) but his 'skedool' was beginning to look bad. There was the
King of Nepal – or Siam was it? Anyway, there was a King 'due' in
Washington about that time. Perh we could 'ring him up' and alter or
adjust the date? Anyway, about April 26th or 27th was agreed. I
objected that K wd prob want to be in Moscow on 'May Day' (May
1st) But de G and Adenauer were rather incredulous. So much for the
date.

---

97. Everyone accepts the British Prime Minister's thesis.

We next came to the place. Geneva had been regarded as inevitable. 'Ce n'est pas très gai. Le lac. L'esprit de Monsieur Calvin. Non. Ce n'est pas très gai. Tout de même . . . .'[98] So General de Gaulle. I suggested that we might have Paris. Of course, this would mean definitely accepting the idea of a series of summits – Paris must be followed by London, Washington, Moscow. If this were not accept-able, Geneva must be, for a <u>single</u> meeting. De G was pleased by the idea of Paris and consequently accepted the <u>series</u> concept without demur. Pres Eisenhower agreed quite readily, and Adenauer less willingly . . . .

. . . . On substance, the chief feature of our discussion was an angry attack on Adenauer by President Eisenhower over Berlin. This was very significant. Adenauer is trying to go back to last year's position – before the long meeting at Geneva, when (after all) some loosening of the position took place. Meanwhile, the Americans have moved from their very rigid position and are ready to consider various plans for the future of Berlin wh they were unwilling even to discuss some time ago. The Chancellor no doubt was aware of this. But the President was very firm and almost rude. He was thoroughly exasper-ated. As a result of being 'bullied' a bit, the German Chancellor collapsed and did not speak again[99] . . . .

Dec 20 (Sunday)
I got up at 7am and went off (with Foreign Secy) to breakfast with President Eisenhower at 8am at the American Embassy . . . .

The chief anxiety I have now with U.S.A. is about the Geneva H-Bomb Test conference. We put in a strong plea for a 'political' settlement, whatever the scientists may say. But the President is nervous about Congress.

I drove with the President to Rambouillet. We arrived about 10.30, and began immediately on the 'Tripartite' Conference – Eisenhower, de Gaulle, Macmillan. This lasted for two hours, after wh Adenauer arrived for luncheon. By this rather ingenious arrangement, de G in

---

98. It's not very cheerful. The lake. The spirit of Calvin. No. It's not very cheerful. All the same . . . .

99. The Geneva talks had lasted from 11 May to 5 August 1959. Adenauer, whose recollections of this meeting were very different from Macmillan's, wished to avoid repetition of the emollient proposals, including a freeze on Western troop numbers, put forward at Geneva on 28 July.

fact brought into being the 'Tripartite' system wh he has been working for during the last two years. Moreover, when he suggested that there should be regular tripartite discussions between US, UK and France on 'matters of common interest, outside and transcending NATO', the President – to my great surprise – at once accepted. Fortunately, he suggested London as the place. This leaves undisturbed the very secret discussions, on military, political and strategic matters, which we have been having for some time with the Americans in Washington. Eisenhower, of course, stipulated that the London discussions shd be 'clandestine'. De G said they wd be 'très prudents'. But naturally, since de G attaches much more importance to the <u>fact</u> of the Tripartite talks than to the <u>substance</u> of them, it will soon become known – from French sources. De G clearly thought that I had persuaded the Pres to accept what he has consistently rejected. This will do no harm – altho' it is clear that the Pres acted more or less from impulse and not on advice.[100]

After luncheon, we had a talk from Adenauer on Communism. During this discourse, I unfortunately went to sleep.

At 4.30, the Foreign Ministers arrived. The letters to Mr Kruschev (of wh they had prepared the text) were agreed. Also the instructions, in identical terms, to the 3 ambassadors in Moscow and also the communiqué. We then turned to the question of [the] economic problems of Europe. I was glad to find that the Foreign Ministers had agreed a policy (and a communiqué) on this, which was to use the next meeting of OEEC (in January) to inaugurate discussions. There was left a certain doubt as to how far these talks wd be <u>within</u> OEEC. But we got substantially what London wanted. All this is symptomatic of the new mood of French friendship towards us, wh clearly reflects instructions from de G . . . .

---

100. Talks appear never to have occurred. Whilst de Gaulle was clearly still
     disappointed when Macmillan visited him early in 1960, the subsequent
     Summit failure seems to have killed off this idea.

1960

Africa tour, 'Winds of Change' speech in Cape Town and Commonwealth crisis over South Africa – Cyprus independence – elected as Chancellor of Oxford University – cancellation of Bluestreak missile, American alternatives and the US naval base on the Clyde – continuing crisis in Central African Federation culminating in the conference on the future constitution of Northern Rhodesia – shooting down of a U-2 by Russia and the failure of the Paris Summit – civil war in Congo – the Laos crisis

1 January

. . . . 3–5.30. Commonwealth Secy, Colonial Secy, MofLabour, Sir N Brook, mostly on Africa. This absurd Labour Party plan for a 'boycott' of S. Africa may have the most grave results on employment at home, if the Union Govt are provoked to counter-measures . . . .

4 January

. . . . 12 noon. Cyprus. We decided to try to reconvene the London Conference at Foreign Minister level and bring the negotiations to a conclusion. The whole position is very tricky and I am suspicious about the good faith of the Greeks. Nor do the Turks care much about British interests any longer, for they have made an 'entente' with the Greeks . . . .

6pm. Malcolm MacDonald called. He gave a vivid account of Nehru's reaction to the Chinese aggression[1] . . . . It has been a great blow to him – but he has learned a lot from it. The two chief results are a) better feeling with Pakistan b) looking to Britain with deeper respect and confidence. Already Nehru was impressed by our Russian policy – the Moscow visit and all that. He thinks that HMG are following the right line in seeking a détente with Soviet Russia. Now, of course, he feels it all the more, because he hopes that Russia may be able to exercise a restraining influence on China . . . .

7 February (Sunday)

We sailed from Cape Town at 4pm on Friday Feb 5th after a tour of just a calendar month. (We left London airport for Accra on Jan 5th) I have <u>never</u> been quite so tired – even after the last General Election. More than 4 weeks of travelling, discussing, seeing things and people,

---

1. Sino-Indian tensions over the McMahon Line, the border between India and Tibet, had been building since the Chinese seizure of the latter and the flight of the Dalai Lama to India in 1959.

speech-making, and holding press conferences – and hardly ever more than one night in the same place . . . .

I have made no attempt to keep a diary of the tour. It would not have been possible to do so. I have the 'programmes' for each entry – Ghana, Nigeria, the Central African Federation, (S Rhodesia; N Rhodesia; Nyasaland) and S Africa. Ghana and Nigeria were the easiest intellectually; the Federation (esp with Welensky and Whitehead on one side and the Governors of N Rhodesia and Nyasaland on the other) was the trickiest, for we carry a great – if limited responsibility. In the Union . . . . I had to comfort those of British descent; inspire the Liberals; satisfy Home Opinion; and yet keep on good terms – at least outwardly – with the strange caucus of Afrikaner politicians who now control this vast country.[2]

Every night we had to deal with a considerable volume of business from home. Butler has obviously been managing very well. But my decisions have had to include an increase of 1% (4% to 5%) in Bank Rate; refusal to make any more concessions over Cyprus; and (of course) the final stages of 'The Queen's Affair'. The Cabinet agreed to the plan wh the Lord Chancellor managed to work out with Her Majesty – that is, the 'name' of the House, Family and Dynasty to be Windsor – the name of any 'de-royalised' grandson etc of the Queen, Prince Philip to be 'Mountbatten-Windsor' (like Spencer-Churchill) It sounds rather like *Alice Through the Looking Glass*, but if it gives the Queen pleasure (as it clearly does) it is right for the Govt to meet her wishes on this very modest basis . . . .

This ship (*Capetown Castle*) is very comfortable – I have an excellent cabin and sitting room. With the help of Dr Richardson's pills, I have slept for nearly 36 hours . . . .

My brother Daniel's operation (wh took place a few days after we left) has proved miraculously successful. When I saw Dr R, on the evening of Jan 5th, he warned me that the cancer was very extended and that it was unlikely that the operation cd do more than give him some comfort in the remaining months of his life. This was a terrible shock to us all. However, Dr R said there was a chance – perhaps 1 in 3 or 1 in 4 – that the cancerous growth wd be so placed or of such a character that it could all be got out and leave no fatal trace behind. Maurice – who has been excellent in this and everything else through-

---

2. Not least in giving his 'Winds of Change' address on the growth of African nationalism to the South African parliament on 3 February.

out – agreed to telegraph in code. 'Operation Successful' – if Daniel survived, 'Operation Highly Successful', if the whole cancer had been removed. This last message duly came and Dr R and Maurice have been very good – writing almost every day . . . .

On the Home side generally, the chief matter has been the concern wh the Ch of Exr feels about the economy. He fears a new inflation. I finally agreed to the Bank Rate increase, because experience has shewn that this instrument (if it is to be of any use) must be used early. Moreover, the interest rates in USA and W Germany made it necessary to protect sterling from their pressure. All the same, I wd have been for letting this happen and losing reserves, if it had not been desirable to do a little bit of squeezing internally. So I agreed. Butler was clearly doubtful; but he also yielded to the arguments deployed by the Treasury.

Apart from all this aspect of the economy, the Chancellor is alarmed at the estimates and their effect when published. Defence up by over £100m; Civil by £200m or more. (I cannot get the exact figures from the telegrams) So the Chancellor proposed an increase in the Health stamp. The Cabinet did not like this, partly because we may need a larger increase later on – with Old Age Pensions etc. Butler tells me that agreement has been reached and that the Chancellor is ready to wait a bit . . . .

. . . . [N]ew trouble is developing with Welensky and Whitehead. They are sending intemperate telegrams, threatening secession and the break-up of Federation, all because of HMG's wish to release Banda and get on with some constitutional advance in Nyasaland.[3] I expected some reaction – but not as bad as this . . . .

13 February (Saturday)

We are reaching the end of a wonderful holiday – on Monday morning we shall leave Las Palmas by Britannia aircraft, arriving in cold, sleety, shivering England the same evening. It has been hot – but not unreasonably hot. The staff (including Sir Norman [Brook]) have appeared in an extraordinary display of clothes – or rather, no clothes – wh wd seem very queer in Whitehall . . . .

Cyprus goes 'on' and 'off' – like a dish at a cheap restaurant. Julian Amery was sent out to see the Governor and the Archbp. No progress.

---

3. Macleod wanted him released so that he could give evidence to the Monckton Commission.

A complete deadlock. Then, as he was getting into the aeroplane, a message from Makarios wanting to resume. He did so – but to little effect. I think M will bargain up to the last point. But will he throw it all away on the difference between an area 11 miles by 11, or 6 miles by 6 (his own suggestion)?

The rest of the messages were about the Railway negotiations. I heard last night that a settlement was reached. 5% 'interim' increase. This is 1% more than the Cabinet hoped. But I feel sure they were right to authorise Robertson to accept. When the Guillebaud report does come out, I feel sure it will suggest at least 5%.[4] For although the Railways don't pay (and perhaps never can pay) railways workers are definitely low paid workers in comparison with other trades . . . .

No repercussions from the Union [of South Africa] except an interview with a local newspaper by Louw – (external affairs) Not bad, in form or matter – dwelling simply on the single point of the Union's right (as an independent country) to do what she likes.

I'm afraid the Cabinet have been faced with many difficult problems during my absence. The meeting of Parlt adds an extra burden and complication. Butler seems to have managed admirably . . . .

14 February (Sunday)
. . . . De Gaulle has exploded his atomic bomb, and now claims equal partnership with Britain. Yet another problem! Cuba has sold her sugar to Russia, instead of to U.S. Castro is to get $100 million credit and some fighter aircraft. What will be the American riposte?[5] . . . .

16 February
I have certainly come [home] into a great log-jam of problems. Chancellor of Exr at 10. He is worried – almost nervously so – about inflation. The additions to the estimates (£340 odd million), the Railway settlement, other wage claims etc etc . . . .

---

4. The review of pay structures on the railways, chaired by C. W. Guillebaud and set up in 1958, was due out shortly. Although the award agreed, endorsed by Guillebaud, averted a rail strike, it also added considerably to the network's financial deficit.

5. Castro had seized power in Cuba at the end of 1958. His increasing alignment with the Soviets led Eisenhower in March 1960 to authorise covert action to overthrow him.

17 February

. . . . At yesterday's Cabinet – in addition to Foreign and Colonial items – there was some rather disjointed discussion about the Railway situation. I therefore, at the Chancellor of the Exr's suggestion presided at a meeting of the Economic Policy Ctee, held in the Treasury. We made good progress, and after two hours it was decided to let the officials (Padmore and Bishop) try to draw up a paper with a set of proposals. Five ministers, PM, Chancellor of Exr, Paymaster General, Minister of Transport and M of Labour to form an 'ad hoc' committee . . . .

I have very rashly agreed to be nominated for the Chancellorship of Oxford, against a candidate[6] already nominated by nearly all the Heads of Colleges and commanding very wide support. I have everything to lose and nothing to gain – but the same is true of Foxhunting.

18 February

. . . . The Opposition tried a trick on me at questions – but it failed. Under the new plan, my PQs begin at No 40 (instead of No 45) The Opposition had wanted a definite time – 3.15. However, today they did not ask (by the MPs absenting themselves) as many as 30 to 35 of the first 40 questions (wh happened to be mostly theirs) So I came on at about 2.45. By good chance, I had gone early to my room in the House, so I got to the Front Bench in time. So the ruse failed. I then answered nearly 30 questions – from 2.45 to 3.30 and got a good-natured cheer from all sides at the end[7] . . . .

19 February

. . . . 3pm. Committee on Transport. I was so displeased by the officials' report of our talk on Wed[nesday] and their attempt to give shape to the ideas wh we floated that I got up at 7am and wrote out a new paper 'Plans for Transport' in my own hand. This was copied and distributed during the morning. We had (the committee of ministers) a good talk and broad agreement on my plan. I undertook to circulate

---

6. Sir Oliver Franks.

7. At this time questions of the Prime Minister simply formed part of a more general parliamentary question time. Following a review by the Procedure Committee a fifteen-minute slot twice a week especially for Prime Minister's questions was to be introduced in 1961.

a revised copy tomorrow morning, and Ld Mills and Mr Marples wd
see General Robertson over the week-end . . . .

20 February

10–1 and 3.30–5.30. Meeting of ministers on 'The Future of the
Deterrent' and esp 'The Future of BLUESTREAK'. The latter is a
stationary, liquid-fuel fired rocket, to carry nuclear head. We have
spent £60m on it up to date. To finish the job and get 60 of these
animals will cost £500m (at least) Ministers present, PM; CofExr;
Minister of Defence (Watkinson) Minister of Aviation (Sandys) Foreign
Secy.

The Chiefs of Staff want to abandon Blue Streak and have a mobile
rocket, prob[ably] POLARIS, to be carried on a submarine. The
arguments include question of a new American air to ground missile,
wh may increase the life of the present Bomber force by 3 years or
more.[8] I have undertaken to sum up the discussion and make my
recommendation at a meeting of the same ministers for next Tuesday . . . .

21 February (Sunday)

. . . . Iain Macleod came in after dinner to tell me that the Kenya
conference – after many difficulties – has reached a successful conclusion, everyone (except Group Captain Briggs) being in agreement.
This is certainly a great triumph for the Colonial Secy.[9]

22 February

Ctee on Transport Reorganisation. Marples and Ld Mills are working
well together. Quite a lot of progress in a) working out our plan b)
persuading General Robertson to accept it. There remains the question

---

8. The decision to abandon Blue Streak as the nuclear delivery rocket, not least
   because of its perceived vulnerability to counter-strike, effectively forced the
   government to seek American alternatives. British acquisition of Polaris had
   been informally discussed at Camp David in 1959. However, the British
   initially concentrated on the Skybolt air-to-ground missile because it could be
   used to extend the life of the existing V-Force nuclear bombers.
9. Macleod's proposed constitution, which gave the balance of the Legislative
   Council and parity in the Council of Ministers to Africans, helped by some
   inspiring Macmillan rhetoric to the conference, won the support of all except
   Briggs's United Party.

– what will NUR etc do when the Guillebaud report comes out? Strike or negotiate?

12 noon. Cabinet. I told ministers about Princess Margaret's engagement. No one was in any doubt as to what advice – shd advice be necessary – ought to be given to the Queen. I think myself that the marriage will be very popular. All our people like a 'love match' – and the *D Mirror* etc will like a commoner[10] . . . .

23 February

Alec Home has been struggling hard in Salisbury to resolve the question of Banda's release and security in Nyasaland and the Rhodesias. It is clear that the Governments (both Welensky's and Whitehead's) are deeply suspicious of London and esp of Colonial Office. His last telegrams reveal a growing sense of something like panic. Unless we are careful, the Europeans will do something rather desperate.

Telegrams arrived early this morning, shewing that he felt he had achieved as much as he could. The local Europeans would not accept that Banda should be released while the Monckton Commission were actually in Nyasaland. They thought the security risk too great. They would however agree to his coming out immediately afterwards and (if Col Secy wished) talks on constitutional advance to follow. If we would not accept this, Welensky would have an immediate General Election on the cry 'The Federation to be independent' – Whitehead wd be forced to follow suit [in Southern Rhodesia] (he has only a majority of 2 in Parlt and a minority of votes. The Dominion Party are secessionists and largely Afrikaner)

I rang up Iain Macleod to ask whether he wd like this dilemma discussed in Cabinet or in a small group. He said Cabinet. Ministers were in no doubt. They disliked yielding to pressure. But (as Colonial Secy himself said) we could not face the disruption of our Rhodesia empire for 3 weeks. The Boston tea party is a perpetual reminder to us of what English settlers can do when angry.[11] So it was decided. Suddenly – and to everyone's amazement – Col Secy announced at end

---

10. She married Antony Armstrong-Jones (later created Earl of Snowdon) on 6 May 1960.

11. The dumping of East India Company tea into the harbour by Bostonians angered by British commercial policy in their North American colonies in 1773: an important staging post on the road to the American War of Independence.

of Cabinet that altho' he thought we had taken the only possible decision, he could not possibly be associated with it and must resign. He stayed a few minutes after Cabinet and (altho' remaining firm about his intention) agreed to take a little time.

Home Sec came to luncheon alone with me. We were both puzzled. Is it a plot? (à la Thorneycroft) Is is nervous strain? (it's Iain's first problem wh entails real strain) Is it 'Bridge' (or perhaps Poker) or is it emotion? It seems hardly worth while resigning (and putting at jeopardy all that we have won for the Party and the Country by Iain's own successes and my African tour) over a question as to whether this African (who has already been eleven months in prison) is to be released 3 weeks earlier under one plan than under another . . . .

24 February

Fortunately nothing has leaked about the ministerial crisis. This comforts me a little. Iain's contacts with the press (esp popular press, like D Mirror) are very intimate. If he were playing a hand against me, he wd have used the press. I fear that he has got into an emotional, Celtic position. He certainly looks very unhappy . . . .

I am now pretty sure that he has said (or perhaps, worse still, written) some foolish things to some of these Africans. He is <u>very</u> clever and <u>very</u> keen and enthusiastic. But he is also quite inexperienced in this sort of thing. His 'honour' cannot really be involved in the question of 3 weeks less or more before Banda is let out. But it may well be engaged if he has said (or let it be known) that B <u>will be let out in Nyasaland</u>, in time to give evidence to Monckton. This is the very point at issue between us and the Rhodesian ministers. Anyway, I asked him if it wd make a difference to his attitude if B were released 3 days <u>before</u> Monckton left Nyasaland instead of 3 days <u>after</u>. He was quite excited by this, and said it wd solve the problem. So I rang up Ld Home and asked him if he thought there was any chance of getting W and W to agree. Alec Home is a really splendid fellow. He fully understood the political dangers and embarrassment wh wd follow Col Sec's resignation. He had (from the same premises) reached a similar idea . . . .

3.45–6. Defence Ctee. General agreement reached (Duncan Sandys alone dissenting) to abandon <u>Blue Streak</u> as an operational weapon. It seems sad. We have spent £60m on it. However, we wd have to spend another £500m to get 60 rockets. These are fabulous sums.

A tremendous row has started over a German plan to have 'military facilities' in Spain.[12] The Opposition here are trying to exploit this. Strauss (the Bavarian butcher-boy who is German defence minister) has already tried to put a fast one over everybody – including NATO. I am not altogether sorry about this affair. I can hold it over Adenauer, when next he reproaches me for 'defeatism' over Berlin. The new Berlin–Madrid axis, I shall say, had better defend itself! . . .

25 February

Alec Home has got Salisbury to agree. So the crisis is over – a great relief. These days have been very unpleasant, partly because I feel that I have not been told the whole truth . . . .

Iain Macleod came to supper – and told me a lot, but not the whole story. However, he seemed very grateful.

26 February

. . . . 12.30 and to luncheon. Chancellor of Exr. I foresee another row looming up. Governor of Bank and Chancellor are suddenly very pessimistic about the future – inflation, too much imports, balance of payments difficulties, loss of gold and dollar reserves etc etc – the same old story. So they want violent disinflationary measures and a fierce Budget (£100m extra taxation) It's 1955 all over again . . . .

27 February

. . . . Alec Home had got back earlier in the day. He confirmed my suspicions. Welensky's secret service knew all about Macleod's 'commitment' to Banda etc. Thus they knew the proposed 'time-schedule' for Macleod's visit to Africa and Banda's release before we even consulted them. This was the cause of their anger. This is partly due to a certain naïveté, wh Col Secy has. But it's really due to the difficulty of the same territories being under two ministries (CRO and CO) and all the confusion wh must follow. I have already been discussing with Norman Brook how we could improve matters. It's a case of 'Left Hand; Right Hand' and one not knowing what the other is doing.

29 February (Monday)

A wonderful day at home. Sat in summer house, in the sun . . . . Read Eden's *Full Circle*.[13] It is, on the whole, well done and makes a good

---

12. Then not in NATO and still ruled by the dictator General Franco.
13. The first volume of Eden's memoirs, dealing with 1951–57.

story. I think, all the same, it should not have been written so soon. He makes a very strong case against Foster Dulles's vacillations over the Suez Canal problem . . . .

5 March

. . . . About 7.30 the Registrar telephoned to say that I had been elected Chancellor of Oxford – with a majority of nearly 300 over my opponent. It was a very keen and amusing election – well over 3000 voted, wh means nearly 2000 from outside Oxford. Sir Oliver Franks was a very strong candidate. He got most of the <u>women</u> MAs and a lot of the Oxford dons. But Trevor-Roper (Professor of Modern History) ran a brilliant campaign on my behalf, and lots of friends all over the country rallied to my support. It was quite a gamble for me. There was little to gain, and much to lose. But it came off . . . .

11 March

Chancellor of Exr and other ministers on Railways. [He] agreed that we shd try to settle the wages problem at once and generously. In return, the Ry Unions must agree to work with us in the reconstruction plans. I spoke last night to almost the whole party (1922 Ctee) and found them very satisfied with the exposition of the Govt's Railway policy . . . .

The Chancellor of the Exr to luncheon. We had a good talk and I am hopeful that we shall get through the Budget and the economic problem without a row. Heathcoat Amory is a sweet man – a really charming character. But he is tired and overdone. He feels his responsibilities almost too much. Fundamentally, he lacks nerve.

For Secy came in for an hour before dinner. He is very good and sensible. He has now got nerve. But the problems are, all the same, almost insoluble.

I feel very tired. Since I got back from Africa the work has been really overwhelming. I begin to wonder how long I can stand the strain. If I could get some real rest, it wd help. But I see no chance of this until the summer holidays.

12 March

D and I left London at about noon . . . . We drove to Rambouillet, where we were welcomed by the General and Madame de Gaulle. Our talks began at 5 and lasted till 7.30. We were alone. There is no one else in the party, except Philip de Zulueta with me and his own personal aide, de Courcel . . . .

. . . . The rooms wh D and I have are in the old tower (François 1st) and are not unlike rooms in a Scottish castle. The bath-rooms etc have been made in the thickness of the wall. But a curious sort of penthouse has been put in the <u>outside</u> of the tower, as a sort of sitting room or ante-room to our two rooms (wh are one above the other) and also to provide a stair case. The furniture of this addition is 'modern' and ugly . . . . There is no comfort, and the hot water doesn't seem to work properly.

13 March (Sunday)
. . . . [H]ome in No 10 by 10.30pm.

I felt tired from the strain of talking nothing but French (he refused to have anyone else present) and trying not to fall into any major error of judgment.

Our talks were intimate, and – as far as I could judge – most friendly. I had fortunately read the last volume of memoirs,[14] and I asked de G why he continually harped on the theme of the 'Anglo-Saxons'. Apart from a general feeling that he is left out of Anglo-American talks, and jealousy of my close association with this particular President, it clearly all stems from the war. He resented – rather absurdly in the setting of Vichy and all that – the Roosevelt–Churchill hegemony. He goes back too – in his retentive mind – to all the rows about Syria; about D-Day; about the position of the French Army in the final stages of the war; about Yalta (and the betrayal of Europe) and all the rest. I reminded him of our <u>tripartite</u> discussion at Rambouillet only a few months ago, and said that I wd do all I cd to make such discussions periodic and fruitful. In addition, I wd welcome frequent Anglo-French talks and a real renewal of Anglo-French friendship. We had no Empires left – and therefore no rivalries. All these days were past. I think I did something to convince him of our real desire to work closely together, not only in Europe, but everywhere.

We next talked about Europe and Germany. He does <u>not</u> want political integration. He accepted the economic integration implied in the Treaty of Rome with regret. But it was signed, and he could not go back on it. But it <u>has</u> had a useful effect in making French industry more competitive. Politically, it keeps Germany looking to the West.

---

14. The third and final volume of de Gaulle's *Mémoires de Guerre*, *Le Salut 1944–46*, ('war memoirs, salvation') was published in 1959.

He does <u>not</u> want a united Germany; nor does he fear Germany for at least 25 years – if it can be kept in the Western group. As regards Berlin etc, his chief object is to support Adenauer because – if he is let down – more dangerous sentiments may begin to develop in Germany. At present (tho' he does not like people like Herr Strauss) he is not fearful, but rather contemptuous of the Bonn regime. Moreover, since we have all helped Germany so much since the war, he does not feel that there is the material (poverty and unemployment) for a new sort of Hitler to exploit.

On the actual Berlin issue, he wants us all to present a firm front. But he thinks a *modus vivendi* might be found at the last moment. (In this, For Secy and I agree. The Summit must not be over-prepared, but played by ear) De G thinks that Kruschev has presented himself so much as the man of peace that he will not want an absolutely barren Summit.

On the 7–6 economic split in Europe, de G says that he regards the 6 as a commercial treaty arrangement and nothing more. He thinks a treaty shd be possible between the 6 and the 7. I pressed him strongly <u>not</u> to accelerate the tariff reductions between the 6 next July (as is now being proposed) because this would increase the discrimination and might have very serious results. Altho' I came back to this several times, I cd get no firm promise from him.

On the Bomb, he wants nuclear disarmament. If not, France must have the bomb, by one means or another. If the Americans will not – or cannot – give France the information or the weapon, he will have to go ahead, whatever the cost. He said he fully realised now how great and continuous the cost wd be, both for the weapon and the means of delivery.

I told him our position and our own future problems. We were all right till the late 1960s – after that, we were not sure what to do.

As delicately as possible, I put the idea in his mind that we might be able to help him, either with American agreement or connivance. He seemed much interested. Did he want full control? Or wd he consider a NATO, a WEU, or an Anglo-French control. He would reflect on this. The first was impossible. Germany wd be the problem in the second. The third had attractions.[15]

---

15. There were certain attractions since France had just exploded its first atomic device and was looking to develop missile technology, but the McMahon Act posed difficulties in sharing technology acquired with the Americans.

He talked a good deal about Africa. He was reconciled to independence of all the former French colonies, with – at the best – a sort of Commonwealth system. As to Algeria, in spite of the Press, his policy had not really changed. There must be a political settlement. But the military situation was much improved. W Algeria was calm. Even in the East, a *de facto* end of the rebellion might be in sight.

He would then bring the Army home. That would mean that he could begin a reorganisation of NATO. He believed in NATO. But its 'set up' was absurd. Armies could not be divided. They must be organised into national units. This was particularly true of the French Army. By a NATO command structure, it was demoralised. When the Army cd be got back from Algeria, he wd raise the whole issue. Besides, except for the Church, the Army was the only stable thing in France.

The Germans shd be the advanced guard; the French the main defence; Britain shd cover the Low Countries and the sea; America shd be the grand reserve.

I asked whether he was not alarmed at the prospect of 12 German divisions on their own. He thought not. There could be 'elements' in Germany – but not the main armies. He had no objection to an allied C[ommander] in C[hief] (even an American) but it shd be like Foch at the end of the 1st war but <u>not</u> like SHAPE. I did not say much on all this, but made a mental note that this *remaniement*[16] might let us out of our 50 year treaty and our £50m a year paid across the exchanges to keep our troops in Germany.

He spoke a good deal about France and its history. He knows that she is not easily governed, but he thinks that the political parties are still unpopular and that he has the nation's support. He must use this position while he can.

He remarked at dinner that in this very room Charles X had abdicated. He went to England. Louis Philippe went off in a *fiacre* – also to England. Napoléon 3rd went to England too.[17] He paused – and said that he would no doubt be welcomed . . . .

The visit was certainly successful in revitalising our old friendship. I feel that there is just a chance that I can get him to act in this dreadful

---

16. Modification.
17. Charles X was ousted by the 1830 French revolution and his *de facto* successor Louis Philippe similarly in 1848. Napoléon III was deposed after his defeat and capture by the Prussians at Sedan in 1870.

6 v 7 economic situation, wh – if it is allowed to develop – may become really serious.

20 March (Sunday)

A bad week. T.V. (which takes nearly two days to prepare and practise. But Norman Collins helped tremendously) This took place Wed evening. A speech to 5000 people in Central Hall (and overflows) on Commonwealth. A speech at Party Central Council. A speech at Bromley. A speech (Sat) to Conservative Trade Unionists. Lunch for Ben Gurion (P.M. Israel) and 2 hours conference with him. Railways; Cyprus; the Budget; European Free Trade Area; Defence (we have clawed back £10m) I got home last night quite exhausted.

The Chancellor of the Exr (who seems rather nervy) opened a great debate on the state of the economy in full Cabinet. There was an excellent discussion, and my more confident approach got quite a lot of support, notably from Lord Mills. But the new import figures, and the estimated loss of £18[m] on the Balance of Payments a/c for the last quarter of 1959 have confirmed the Chancellor of the Exr in his more pessimistic view. I am very unhappy and very anxious about all this . . . .

The Russians have made a most exciting move at Geneva. Very unexpectedly, they have proposed the very plan for abolition of nuclear tests wh we have for months been urging on the Americans! We must now bring tremendous pressure on the Americans to agree. The President will be sympathetic; so will the State Dept. But I am not sure of the Pentagon and certain of the hostility of the Atomic Agency. There will also be complications about getting a Treaty through the Senate in an election year. Nevertheless, it's a wonderful chance. If necessary, I will go off to Washington to persuade the President . . . .

Daniel [Macmillan] arrived this afternoon, with nurse, to convalesce. It's really a miracle that he is alive. The cancer was enormous in size, but the surgeon is very confident that he has got it all out. He is very weak but cheerful. He is naturally tremendously pleased to be out of the Hospital. I have put him in my big bed-sitting room (over the dining room) with the nurse in the dressing room. He has the bathroom, all to himself and is near the lift . . . .

22 March

. . . . There has been a tragic incident in S Africa. The Union Govt's policy on 'passes' and various other forms of pressure on the Africans have produced a sort of despair. So they have started something like 'passive resistance'. This resulted in two very tragic events – one in the Transvaal and one in Cape Town. 60–100 Africans have been killed and over 200 wounded.[18] The British Press has 'gone to town' on this – with all sorts of dreadful pictures etc. Mr Gaitskell tried a Private Notice question to me wh was very properly refused by the Speaker. He then got one to CRO on the rather flimsy ground that British subjects (e.g. Basutos) might have been involved.[19] Alport (Minister of State) answered. Gaitskell, with characteristic dishonesty, cheated by asking the question 'of the Prime Minister' – wh he knew had been refused. Alport answered this and a series of other supplementaries very well and composedly. I sat by his side, but refused to be drawn . . . .

23 March
The Times has a violent attack on Gaitskell, accusing him of 'smugness', about the S African riots. With the exception of the *Daily Sketch* and the *Herald*, the rest of the Press seems conscious of the dangers to the Commonwealth of any rash or foolish action of HMG. Unfortunately, the Canadians and Indians – with somewhat different degrees of indignation – have condemned S Africa. So has U.S.A. (through a State Dept spokesman) This at least will not encourage S.A. to sell gold in New York rather than in London. But the Afro-Asians in N York are busy, and within a few days we shall be confronted with another critical decision – what to do or say at the Security Council. We must not forget that there will now be a tremendous effort to stoke up similar riots in Rhodesia and Nyasaland or Kenya, in order to put the U.K. in the dock.

The President telephoned about 4pm (our time) and made it clear that he wd like me to come over to discuss the Test agreement. He seemed very friendly. He has engagements on Sunday, but wd like to set aside Monday and Tuesday for the talks. So I will go. I'm sure it's worth it, but I do not feel very hopeful. The Americans are divided,

---

18. The previous day in Sharpeville protests led by the Pan-African Congress against the movement controls imposed in apartheid South Africa had been brutally suppressed, with an estimated 67 dead.
19. The British government and parliament was responsible for the protectorate of Basutoland (modern Lesotho), which did not become independent until 1966.

and with an administration on the way out, the Pentagon and the
Atomic groups are gaining strength.

24 March

.... The S.A. trouble is getting a little better at home, but worse
overseas. There is definitely an appeal to the Security Council. U.S. will
support the inscription of the item. If we do not 'veto' it, SA will
probably leave the Commonwealth. If we do; Ghana and Nigeria –
even India – might do so. The Opposition here have put down a
motion 'deploring the shootings' and expressing 'sympathy' with the
victims. At the Cabinet this morning, we agreed an amendment wh wd
be generally acceptable, I think. Whether the Opposition will ask for a
debate on their motion, I rather doubt.

At questions, I announced that all the Commonwealth PMs were
coming in May. This led to further questions about Verwoerd (the SA
PM) and gave me chance of a little disquisition on the Commonwealth
situation, wh seemed well received on both sides of the House.

All the afternoon with the Chancellor of the Exr. The Budget is
now agreed. 2d on tobacco; 2½% on Profits Tax. The first brings
£40m this year; the second £40–50[m] next year. The concessions in
the Budget (Entertainments Tax etc) will cost £20m. Final decision
about Bankers' Deposits (the new form of 'credit squeeze') and Hire
Purchase to be taken later – perh[aps] at end of April.[20] Increase in the
Health Stamp postponed. All this is satisfactory, so far as the actual
proposals are concerned. But I still feel that the whole mood and
presentation may result in our talking ourselves into a crisis. (Thorneycroft did this) ....

Mr Thomson .... came to see me – ostensibly about his buying
newspapers in West Africa, Ceylon and India, wh will be a good
method of 'influencing' opinion in those countries. He will openly
manage these Commonwealth papers from Canada (where he already
runs a good few) this, he believes, will avoid any 'Colonial' taint. Mr
T is vastly energetic and quite amusing. He pretends to be rather sly –
but really he is quite open. He likes money ....

25 March

10am. A long meeting of the Defence Ctee, partly with regard to next

---

20. To reduce demand in the economy Macmillan felt restricting bank lending and
     hire purchase would prove more effective than increases in taxation.

week's meeting of NATO defence ministers; partly about my visit to Washington. As well as the Test problem, we want to get SKYBOLT and perhaps POLARIS out of the Americans. This dual operation is rather a tricky one . . . .

To B.G. for the afternoon and evening. My brother Daniel is making progress, but rather slowly. D came in the evening, and we had quite a cheerful dinner. Daniel, of course, does not know what a terrible operation he has had, nor does he know that it was for cancer. He thinks it was an ulcer. So he is naturally disappointed and rather peeved by the slowness of his recovery. Actually, it's a miracle that he is alive . . . .

26 March
Left Gatwick airport at 10am. Sir N Brook; Philip de Zulueta; Con O'Neill; Sir William Penney – and two of our girls, detective etc. After two stops (Iceland and Newfoundland) we got to Washington about 5.30pm (Washington time) . . . .

27 March (Sunday)
. . . . We had a meeting of our team (including Sir W Penney) at 11am. The Americans have circulated a 'position paper' about the Geneva Test Conference – wh is, after all, the main purpose of my visit . . . .

The American paper is unexpectedly good. It obviously represents a triumph for the State Dept over the Pentagon and the Atomic Energy Authority. It is therefore the President's own decision – or so it seems to me. It accepts the principle of the moratorium for underground explosions 'below the threshold', altho' it says 1 to 2 years (the Russians proposed 4 to 5) and requires (for sound reasons, owing to the nature of the U.S. constitution) that the moratorium shd result from executive action, and not be part of the treaty.[21] (This, if the Russians can be made to understand, is the only practical way. For a treaty, even if signed in May or June could not be ratified till the Spring of next year by the next Congress. But the President can order the moratorium himself) Of course, there are a lot of difficult points in the treaty still to be negotiated – about the control system, about the

---

21. The Russians had recently accepted in Geneva the principle of banning large tests, linking this to a moratorium on tests below a threshold of 4.75 on the Richter scale. The Americans wanted a limited moratorium because of the impending end of Eisenhower's term of office.

experiments during the moratorium, about atomic explosions for peaceful purposes (e.g. building a harbour or a dam) and – most tricky of all – the number of inspections. (This is the quota idea wh I started a year ago in Moscow) But if the Russians are sincere themselves, and are convinced of our sincerity, a treaty should be negotiable . . . .

28 March
9.30. Meeting in Embassy dining room. HM; ambassador; Sir N Brook etc on our side. Herter, Dillon etc on American side . . . . I made an impassioned plea for American help in preventing the economic division of Europe, wh must involve its political and military division. U.K. simply could not afford the discrimination against our imports, wh wd produce a new crisis of sterling. We should have to take economic measures (import controls; non-convertibility of sterling; restrictionist measures of all kinds) wh were contrary to everything wh we and the American administration had been trying to achieve in the last 8 years. We should also be forced to take our troops out of Germany (to save expenditure across the exchanges) These were not threats, but facts. The Americans seemed rather taken aback by my vehemence. They tried (unsuccessfully) to question my figures as to the degree of discrimination. But Cromer, Sir Frank Lee etc had given me splendid ammunition . . . .

29 March
Yesterday's talks were encouraging and before dinner (followed by the inevitable film) we had given the Americans the text of the 'declaration' on the Nuclear Tests (wh I had dictated in the Embassy) which we propose shd be issued by the President and me. The situation is now pretty clear. The President has definitely decided to go along with me in accepting the moratorium on tests 'below the threshold'. This has been bitterly resented and violently opposed by two powerful groups – the Pentagon and the Atomic Energy Commission. The reason advanced is that the Russians will cheat and that scientists will not be able to devise a satisfactory system to distinguish the smaller test bangs from normal earthquake bangs. The real reason is that the Atomic Commission and the Pentagon are very keen to go on indefinitely with experiments (large and small) so as to keep refining weapons. This is, in a way, natural. But it means that, even when the President has reached a decision, there is a tremendous effort to hedge it around with so many 'ifs' and 'ands' as to make it ineffective . . . .

We have also got out of the Americans a very valuable exchange of notes about SKYBOLT and POLARIS. They undertake to let us have the <u>vehicles</u> (by sale or gift), we making our own nuclear heads. This allows us to abandon BLUESTREAK (rocket) without damage to our prospects of maintaining – in the late 1960s and early 1970s – our <u>independent nuclear deterrent</u> . . . .

30 March

. . . . A very busy day. The *Washington Post* publishes today what is alleged to be a true (but is in fact a garbled and exaggerated) report of my talk with Messrs Herter and Dillon on Monday [28 March]. This is a most mischievous story, calculated to make as much trouble as possible between UK and the Germans and French. Since only 4 people (of whom 2 were ministers) were present on the American side, it is clear that this is more than an ordinary State Dept leak. It looks like a calculated leak. Can hardly believe that Herter or even Dillon author-ised it.[22] Perhaps one of the two officials arranged it. We learned later that the *N York Times* had the story, in even greater detail. So it must have been given out. (It appears that it was an A.P. – agency – story) I authorised a statement for British and Foreign Press and a telegram to London. But I'm afraid the harm has been done. All through the day we got accounts of Paris and Bonn Press beginning to react. However, it may in the end do more good than harm. It may make the 6 begin to realise how seriously we feel this proposed Hallstein 'acceleration' plan[23] . . . .

31 March

We arrived at London airport at 2pm (our time) met by Selwyn Lloyd. <u>Africa</u> still seems to dominate affairs here. We had a lot of telegrams

22. Dillon, with whom Macmillan had a strong mutual antipathy, was responsible. Exasperated by the Prime Minister's apparent hostility to the Six, he leaked a summary seemingly designed to cause maximum offence to the West Germans, with veiled references to revived totalitarianism and German domination of Europe. Dillon's own critical views of the Germans were not represented.

23. Macmillan was so keen to impress upon the Americans his anxieties about the discrimination against British goods (resulting from the 20% reduction in internal tariffs amongst the Six being pushed forward by Hallstein) that he made analogous references to Napoléon's 1807 economic blockade of Britain and the need then to ally with Russia 'to break French ambitions' (DDEL: Office of Sec. of State, Box 14).

backward and forward about the 'inscription'[24] of this item on [the]
Security Council. The Afro-Asians are making a great deal of trouble
in U.N. We decided <u>not to oppose</u> inscription, but to <u>content</u> ourselves
with a protest that it is quite contrary to the Charter. Anyway,
inscription wd be carried and we cannot veto a purely procedural
question. But we now have to decide what sort of resolution we ought
to work for and what we are to do about any resolution – vote for,
abstain, or vote against (wh means veto) . . . .

Nothing more till 10pm, when I went in to HofC to vote and got
a good reception in the lobby. I have finished [Dickens's] *Bleak House*
and most of *Life of Bevin*.[25] The latter (like the former) is rather long.
But to me who knows little about the <u>creation</u> of the Trade Union
strength in the pre-war years, it is a fascinating book.

1 April
. . . . Cabinet at 11.30. The chief question was what to do about the
Security Council resolution. It is a real dilemma. The Old Common-
wealth countries (like Australia) think we should <u>veto</u> it. The New
Commonwealth (like India and Ghana) will never forgive us if we do.

I urged that we took little notice of public opinion in Britain, or in
HofCommons. Our main duty now was to keep the Commonwealth
from splitting or disintegrating. I was able to ask all ministers in turn
and find a general approval of 'abstention'. So it was decided[26] . . . .

4 April
. . . . Motored up at 2pm, so as to be in my place for the Budget at
3.30.

The Chancellor of the Exr made a speech of 1½ hours. It had one
great merit and one great fault. The merit was that there was <u>no</u> note
of despondency or alarm; reversal of engines; end of expansionist
policies, or any of the horrors which the Chancellor and the Treasury
were threatening up to a few weeks ago. I have won this battle quite

---

24. Putting Sharpeville on the agenda, a move the British deemed contrary to Art.
2(7) of the Charter, designed to protect matters of domestic jurisdiction.
25. Volume I of Alan Bullock's biography of Ernest Bevin, *Trade Union Leader 1881–1940* (London: Heinemann, 1960), had recently appeared.
26. The French supported the British abstention on the resolution condemning South Africa.

definitely. I feel, therefore, that we shall not <u>talk</u> ourselves into a crisis
– as we did with Peter Thorneycroft in 1957 . . . .

The fault was that he dwelt too long and in too great detail on all
the various 'protection of the revenue' measures. The Opposition took
the opportunity and cheered each in turn, then trying to make us out
to be 'bond-washers', 'dividend-strippers', 'golden-handshakers' and
all the rest.

The Labour Party could find little fault with the Budget, even on
1955 lines. After all, last year they had asked for <u>greater</u> reductions of
taxation than we gave. They also promised immensely increased
expenditure – far above what we have been able to absorb.

The Government benches were silent; the Conservative back-
benchers were a bit disappointed. Tobacco tax will be unpopular, but
(perhaps) soon forgotten. 8 or 10 of our chaps abstained . . . .

6 April

The family has had another blow. Christopher Holland-Martin, Anne
Cavendish's second husband,[27] died suddenly last night, aged only 49.
He had a second heart attack – the first was in January at Salisbury.
This is very sad – he was able, and very kind. It is also a great blow
for the Conservative Party. He was our Treasurer and had done a fine
job in collecting money . . . .

A long Defence Ctee. We confirmed the abandonment of BLUE-
STREAK. We have spent £65m already and I suppose, with cancel-
lations, we shan't get out of it under £100 millions. There will be
a terrible row – but it's clearly the right decision. We postponed a
decision about whether to adapt it for SPACE research, at the cost of
another £75m over the next 5 years[28] . . . .

17 April (Easter Sunday)

It has been a hard week. Two memorial services – one for Dowager
Duchess (in the Queen's chapel) and one for Christopher Holland-
Martin (in St James's Piccadilly) In both I had to read the lesson . . . .

---

27. The Dowager Duchess of Devonshire had died on 2 April 1960. Cavendish is
    the family name of the dukes of Devonshire and Anne Cavendish was Dorothy
    Macmillan's younger sister.
28. After the European Launcher Development Organisation was established in
    1964 with France, West Germany, Italy, Belgium and the Netherlands, Blue
    Streak became the first stage of its launch vehicle.

We have had all kinds of visitors, ranging from Mr and Mrs Kripalani (old friends and followers of Gandhi) who think the world can only be saved by village industries, to Mr Michael Blundell, who sees clearly and <u>may</u> be the 'chosen vessel' to solve the terrible problems awaiting Kenya . . . .

On Cyprus, Julian Amery has proved an excellent negotiator, patient and resourceful. The Archbishop Makarios is well matched. They have had 6 weeks and are progressing slowly. But the fundamental difficulty is this. The groups (Greek) on the island divide themselves into a) the Communists b) the Extreme Right – patriots of the old school c) Grivas and EOKA. <u>All</u> these groups want the settlement. But <u>all</u> of them will turn on Archbp Makarios and call him a traitor if and when he makes it. As [for] the population, they long for peace, for the prosperity wh our <u>bases</u> bring (all work is stopped meanwhile) and the money wh will flow back . . . .

I feel the Govt has lost a good deal of ground in the Press and Parliament <u>since</u> the General Election . . . . It is the usual experience. This year the unthinking people expected an easy Budget. They got a very tough one. The European economic problem is unresolved. Some industries are beginning to get worried. The internal 'boom' continues to gather momentum and we shall [have] to take some measures to restrict Bankers' Credit and Hire Purchase. (The H.P. firms – not the most reputable, of course – are beginning to offer '<u>no</u> initial payment and <u>4</u> years to pay!) . . . .

18 April (Easter Monday)
I took some of my tablets last night and slept till 11.30am. This is Dr Richardson's treatment, wh I follow every 3 months or so. The children have been amusing themselves in their various ways – 'point to point'; motor-racing; etc. Daniel and I sat in the summerhouse most of the afternoon and again after tea, two old men, musing . . . .

26 April
. . . . Sir E Whitehead to luncheon – with Lord Home. He (P.M. of S Rhodesia) is introducing a new complication into an already difficult position. He demands the 'abrogation' of the reserved powers wh U.K. Govt has on a) Land b) discrimination agst Africans. He does not seem to realise the political difficulties here, in Africa, and the connection with the Monckton Commission. We have said we are ready to consider whether an <u>equally effective</u> alternative can be devised – a

Court and a Bill of Rights, or a Second Chamber, half African. He agrees that this is reasonable, but so far has only produced the embryo of a scheme. He threatens to go home and dissolve the S Rhodesian country [sic] and go to a General Election on the cry of 'secession' – both from the Federation and from U.K. This is very treacherous towards Welensky, as well as foolish in itself. But this able, crotchety, deaf great-nephew of St John Broderick[29] is very obstinate . . . .

28 April

The Press is not too bad on Bluestreak. This rocket, wh ought to have exploded with devastating effect on the Govt, seems likely to recoil on the Opposition, for it throws another great dispute open on the whole defence question. It has (strangely enough) turned into a problem for Gaitskell rather than for me[30] . . . .

29 April

. . . . Mr Menzies came for a talk and we decided how to try to get over our first hurdle. He agrees with me as to the vital importance of trying to prevent a split in the Commonwealth Conference on 'colour' lines. The blacks and the browns versus the whites – or, to put it another way, the Old Commonwealth agst the New. I feel that I must try to get 'informal' discussion of S Africa's racial problem – among the PMs themselves – instead of a formal discussion in full conference. Even the informal talks need not be all the PMs – 5 or 6 in one group on one day; 5 or 6 in another group on another day. I will make the drawing room at No 10 available every day (morning and afternoon) for PMs to use informally . . . .

30 April

A great day! My installation as Chancellor of Oxford University. We all drove to Balliol from Chequers – Alexander [Macmillan] acted his part as page marvellously well. Fortunately, it was a glorious day, so

---

29. Secretary of State for War 1900–03, for India 1903–05.

30. By May Labour moved towards abandoning British nuclear weapons whilst leaving to the Americans the provision of the Western deterrent. Unfortunately for Gaitskell, unilateralists in the party wanted to go further, abjuring *all* nuclear weapons, which, as he put it in his unavailing attempts to defeat a motion along these lines at the Labour Party Conference later in the year, was tantamount to a declaration of intent to leave NATO.

our formal procession – from Balliol to the Sheldonian, and from the
Sheldonian to Christ Church was agreeable as well as impressive.

I will not describe the ceremony, wh was according to tradition.
My speech was half (the greater half, I think) in Latin; half in English.
Since I used the old Latin pronunciation, the wits said it was all in
English. The contested election; my references to this and my tribute
to Franks (my opponent) – together with my contrast between 18th
century elections when the candidates bought the votes and this one,
where many of the electors had to buy their votes for large sums (a
reference to MAs taken by Lord Chancellor and many others who had
never bothered to do so)[31] – all this went well. I ended with a
sentimental tribute to Oxford and all that Oxford meant to me and
countless others wh was well enough received.

Luncheon at Christ Church. Heads of Colleges (mostly supporters
of Franks) Regius Professors (mostly my supporters) not invited.
Oxford politics are splendidly bitter! Sir M. Bowra was 'all over' me –
like the Labour agent after you have won. He is always hoping for
something.

3 May

[Commonwealth Conference.] We got through (or over) the first
hurdle. Without too much difficulty either. But I sense trouble coming
all the same. It was agreed that the racial question in S.A. was,
essentially, a matter of internal policy, tho' it had its reactions on the
Commonwealth as a whole. It was agreed to discuss the problem with
Mr Louw 'upstairs' – and PMs alone. (There are 30–40 people in the
Cabinet room at formal or plenary sessions) Once this was settled, the
main business could go on. This began about 12.30 – giving me time
to open on 'world situation – Russia etc' before luncheon.

Several of PMs, wives and others to luncheon. In the afternoon,
both Nehru (India) and Ayub (Pakistan) made admirable and impressive speeches. There was then rather a battle about the 'communiqué'.
This set out the discussion and the agreement about S Africa. The
Tunku[32] talked a lot and was (I thought) rather 'brash'. Mr Louw (to

---

31. To vote in the election of the Chancellor, Oxford graduates had to have
received their MA, available seven years after graduation upon payment of a
nominal fee.

32. Tunku Abdul Rahman, first Prime Minister of Malaya. The son of the Sultan of
Kedah, he was customarily known by the courtesy title of 'Tunku'.

be fair) was objective and correct. The sad thing is that he can never be gracious . . . .

4 May
The 'Plenary' session continued – on world situation. I thought all the Prime Ministers good – esp Menzies. We adjourned at 12 noon (for the first 'informal talk' on S Africa) This, incidentally, allowed time for a meeting of a few U.K. ministers on Cyprus, where the negotiations are not going on any too well. The Archbp seems to be 'stalling' on everything. Maybe he has lost his nerve . . . .

5 May
Mr Eric Louw (S Africa) gave a Press Conference yesterday – bitter, unyielding – but very well done (so the Press say) It fills this morning's newspapers. The Tunku (Malaya) has replied by issuing an offensive (and inaccurate) attack. This appeared at lunchtime. The morning session passed off well enough (on economic situation etc) But at the end of the afternoon session there was a row between them. (Nkrumah, of Ghana, who 'joined' last year and is behaving with great restraint, is said to regard the Tunku's performances with disfavour. He thinks that a 'new boy' ought to behave better. President and Field Marshal Ayub (of Pakistan) who is like an old India Army Colonel, thinks that 'none of them come out of the top drawer, anyway' . . . . The prospects are pretty bad. If we do nothing, the Commonwealth will seem to have no faith and no purpose. If we do too much S Africa will secede and this may mean the beginning of a general break-up[33] . . . .

7 May
Chequers. A glorious day – warm and sunny. The Americans have committed a great folly. There have been going on for some time photographic flights at very high altitudes over Russia . . . . Now one of their machines has been shot down by a rocket (it is said, a few hundred miles from Moscow) What makes it so irritating is that the plane was picked up (owing to faulty flying) some days ago near the Afghan border. But it was not brought down. It seems to have started

---

33. Louw was seeking to negotiate South Africa's continuing membership of the Commonwealth if the referendum due in October endorsed the recently announced decision of the Verwoerd government to become a republic. Other members favoured expelling South Africa over apartheid.

again, had a failure (perhaps of oxygen), lost height and been shot down. Worse still, the pilot did not go by his ejection chair (wh wd have automatically blown up the machine in the air) but by parachute. He did not poison himself (as ordered) but had been taken prisoner (with his poison needle in his pocket!)[34] The Russians have got the machine; the cameras; a lot of the photographs – and the pilot. God knows what he will say when tortured! I don't know (but I greatly fear) how far he knows about what we have done. The President, State Dept, and Pentagon have all told separate and conflicting stories, and are clearly in a state of panic. Kruschev has made two very amusing and effective speeches, attacking the Americans for spying incompetently and lying incompetently too. He may declare the Summit off. Or the Americans may be stung into doing so.

Quite a pleasant Saturday – the Commonwealth in pieces and the Summit doomed. However, it was a lovely morning and I sat in the garden reading a biography of Horace Walpole[35] . . . .

Nehru came for luncheon. We were alone. He seemed in good form. On S Africa his position had hardened, I thought. He now thought that we must say something collectively, if only about the external effect of S Africa's internal policies. However, he talked almost exclusively during luncheon and afterwards about Russia, China, and Communism. He has clearly been much shaken by the Chinese aggression. His line is that they are fundamentally a more brutal and ruthless people than the Russians. He thinks their Communism is more theoretical and fervent. The Russians are 'backsliding' into bourgeoisie – not so the Chinese. He does not really think that the Chinese want to join U.N. They are better off with a grievance and freedom to do what they like. When Nehru reproved them for acting 'contrary to the Charter', they enquired blandly 'What Charter?'

By 5 o'clock we had, in addition to Nehru, Dr Nkrumah, the Tunku, P.M. Walter Nash, P.M. Menzies, and Alec Home. We tried

---

34. A U-2 flight by Gary Powers to photograph the Soviet missile installations around Sverdlovsk had been brought down on 1 May. Presuming Powers dead and his machine destroyed, the Americans had claimed that it was merely a 'weather research aircraft' until the Soviets revealed both pilot and aeroplane on 7 May.

35. Youngest son of Britain's first Prime Minister, Sir Robert Walpole (1721–42), Horace Walpole was a leading novelist and letter-writer.

to hatch out some plan for next week but did not get very far. Sir N
Brook was there too and helpful. There are two problems

1) The unfinished or adjourned row between Eric Louw and the
   Tunku, and how to handle it, and perhaps turn it to our
   advantage.
2) The S African application about becoming a Republic. My
   P.M. colleagues are very nice, and their general idea is to leave
   it all to me to find a way out! I thought Nkrumah <u>very</u> sensible.
   He is absolutely against trying to force S Africa out of the
   Commonwealth.

8 May

. . . . The Americans have now had to come clean about their airplane.
But it is still a very odd story. The pilot could <u>not</u> (say the experts)
have parachuted from 70000 feet and landed alive. Why did he not
use the ejection seat, wh wd have automatically set off a mechanism to
destroy the airplane? Why did he not shoot or poison himself? Why
did he tell his whole story and route etc? Is he perhaps a traitor? . . . .

9 May

The Soviet ambassador called at No 10 at 9.30, with a letter from Mr
Kruschev. I was relieved to find that it was all about how to conduct
the Summit most profitably. So he hasn't called it off! I don't see how
Ike [Eisenhower] can, unless the Russians shoot the unlucky pilot.
But, nowadays, they are more likely to make him appear at a Press
Conference. His letter complains of the American attitude towards the
meeting – hardly taking it seriously. He quotes some remarks by
Herter to support this contention. He regards Ike's refusal to stay more
than 7 days and then send the Vice President as insulting. He then goes
on to the American espionage flights, culminating in the aeroplane wh
was shot down near Sverdlovsk last week. He goes on to complain of
Adenauer. Part of this seems to me personally quite reasonable.
Whenever the Americans aren't frightened out of their wits, they
relapse into complacency.

10.30–12.45. Mr Louw raised a 'point of order' – a remark made
by the Tunku last week. (It was the hare wh was started but not killed
on Friday evening) Louw spoke – too long – but ably. The Malayan
P.M. replied shortly. Then everyone spoke – every single one of them
– I wound up at 12.30. Poor Mr Louw was thus hoist with his own
petard with a vengeance. He complained – but only at the end of a 2½

hour discussion on 'Apartheid' – all of which, according to him, is out
of order.[36] But he had brought it. The debate did good. All the P.M.s
can now say not merely that there have been 'informal' discussions –
there has been discussion in 'restricted session' (for, at Louw's own
request I had asked all except PMs to leave the Cabinet room) lasting
2½ hours, at which every aspect – internal and external – of S African
policy was fully debated. I thought all the PMs were pretty good.
Nkrumah was very restrained. Nehru rather sour. Welensky excellent
– wise and generous. Diefenbaker woolly. Menzies excellent. My
summing up was an attempt to be fair but decisive. After a little
wrangling, we issued an agreed communiqué, saying what had happened. There remains the last – and most difficult hurdle – the final
communiqué. Just before luncheon we voted that Nigeria (when
independent)[37] should join the Commonwealth. The PM of Nigeria
(Abubakar) was upstairs in the drawing room, waiting. We all went
up to drink his health etc. A nice little ceremony . . . .

10 May
. . . . A long and tedious meeting of Commonwealth PMs – 3.30–6. S
Africa's representative was very difficult about the Republican question. He tried to trick us into a premature decision about SA's position
if and when they had decided to go Republican. The Republics (India
and Pakistan, Ghana etc) resisted this, on the ground that it involved
us in the plebiscite. The motion was debated, critically but inconclu-
sively, for two hours. I look forward without enthusiasm to Wed and
Thursday. We shall have to reach some decisions and it will not be
easy to find a way through the maze of trouble wh S Africa is creating.
However, when Louw posed the question 'Do you want SA in the
Commonwealth or not', I was glad to find that everyone said 'yes' . . . .

12 May
We finished our regular work of the Commonwealth Conference this
morning . . . . On political, strategic and economic questions I have
sensed a greater unity than at previous meetings. Nehru (thoroughly
shaken by his Chinese experiences) has not been so pontifical as usual
about 'non-alignment'. President Ayub has been a worthy representa-

36. South Africans saw apartheid as an internal matter and therefore not a proper
    subject for Commonwealth debate.
37. On 1 October 1960.

tive of Pakistan – the first serious figure since Liaquat Ali Khan.[38] Dr Nkrumah has been sensible and moderate, even on African affairs. Of the old Commonwealth countries, Menzies has been a tower of strength – and much less provocative than last time. Nash is a nice, good-natured, well-intentioned old-fashioned Liberal – a bore, but sincere and Christian gentleman. Diefenbaker is very disappointing – deaf, ignorant, and little more than a 'tub-thumper'. He never forgets 'party' politics, and talks of little else. Incidentally, he has behaved very badly in withholding his consent – up to now – to the Queen's most gracious gesture in offering the [Order of the] garter to dear old Vincent Massey, ex Governor-General of Canada . . . .

. . . . Alec [Home] and I worked out (with Brook's help) a draft clause for the communiqué wh we thought might do. The <u>great</u> danger of no agreement is twofold. First, there may be two if not three groups formed (apart from S Africa) The extremists (brown or black) the less extreme (brown and white) the still less extreme (white – esp Australia) as well as (of course) S Africa. Curiously enough, the draft on SA becoming a Republic got through without argument. I think Louw hardly realised how far it was from what PM Verwoerd had tried to 'sell me' in Capetown and from the formula he was instructed to get. This is, at least, some relief – for the loyalists of SA will not feel let down by me.

However, the racial clause remains. We finished about midnight – there followed the usual hour on the 'box'. I felt very tired at the end of the day.

13 May

One could hardly have a worse omen for the final stages of the Commonwealth Conference than Friday the 13th. But it has all turned out well – or, at least, far beyond our expectations or even our hopes. We actually settled – by unanimous agreement – a <u>text</u> of the vital paragraph and finished the whole conference with an agreed communiqué by noon! . . . . In spite of all the newspapers, and the BBC, and the ITV, and the Labour Party and the Liberals – who all want a row and will be bitterly disappointed – we have saved the unity of the Commonwealth (at least for the time) <u>without</u> any sacrifice of principle.

While this has been going on, we have had a good deal of anxiety about the Queen Mother's trip to Rhodesia. But we decided to let it

---

38. The first Prime Minister of Pakistan, 1947–51.

go on. Governor Hone (N. Rhodesia) has asked for certain powers (to wh we have agreed) but, after talks with Macleod and Home, I decided not to allow wholesale arrests of 'agitators'. You arrest them, but what do you do with them? If you can't put them on trial, you have to let them out. We must not forget the lesson of Dr Banda. We wd have done better to throw him back earlier into the river. He has grown into a bigger fish by gorging safely in our fish-pond. In which – esp with Labour opinion – he has made a fool of himself . . . .

15 May

Left Gatwick [for Paris] . . . . at 10am. Usual reception at airport. Luncheon at Embassy. A great crowd of ministers and officials – For Secy; Hoyer Millar; Reilly (Moscow) Ld Jebb (Paris) Sir A Rumbold (F.O.) Russell (News), as well as my own staff (Bligh, Zulueta (who is excellent)) Harold Evans (News) and, in place of Norman Brook, Freddy Bishop. I am not sure what will happen next. Mr Kruschev has asked to see me at 4.30.

Meanwhile, we had a 'quadripartite' meeting at the Elysée. De Gaulle; Eisenhower; Adenauer; HM. It was pretty formal – no one got down to brass tacks. Eisenhower repeated some of his apprehensions about Berlin, but Adenauer swept them aside. De Gaulle will say nothing to upset Adenauer. I thought it wiser to say nothing at all.

We are in for trouble. Mr K[hrushchev] came, not alone or with only the interpreter (as I expected) but in full state – Gromyko (For Affairs) Marshal Malinowski (Defence) and one or two others. He made a speech, in violent terms, attacking the U.S.A.; President Eisenhower; the Pentagon; reactionary and imperialist forces generally, all (of course) in connection with the U2 aircraft shot down over Russia. He said that his friend (bitterly repeated again and again) his friend Eisenhower had betrayed him. He then proceeded with a formal declaration, actually read from a bit of paper, not left as a formal note, in terms wh we learned a little later from the French was a declaration in the same terms as he had left with de Gaulle. It wd be impossible to carry on the Summit Conference, unless President E a) condemned what had been done by air espionage b) expressed his regret c) said he wd never do it again d) punished the criminals.

I did my best to reason with Mr K (who was personally quite agreeable) but did not succeed in appeasing him. But I did not feel that he wd press his point too far. I reminded him of his letter to me delivered only a few days ago (but after the aircraft incident) in wh he discussed quite amiably <u>how</u> the Summit Conference shd be conducted and what might be the best lines of progress. K did not deny this, but was obviously incensed by the statements made by Herter and Eisenhower during last week, wh he thought aggravated their offence. President E had justified the 'espionage flights' and threatened to go on with them.

When he had gone we reported to the French and the Americans. The French view was cynical, but logical. The Conference was over. The Americans were more hopeful and thought it largely bluster. The British thought the conference might be saved if the President wd take a reasonable line – esp undertake to make no more U2 flights (this, incidentally, is no great sacrifice, because the countries involved – Turkey, Pakistan, Norway, and even U.K. – can hardly allow their bases to be used for what is, technically, agst constitutional law. In other words this particular method, however useful and important its results over the last few years – is 'blown', like an 'agent' who has been caught or gone over to the enemy)

Much coming and going between all the staffs of the three Western countries, who all seem to be on excellent terms. There was a 'tripartite' meeting at 6pm (De Gaulle; Eisenhower; HM – with only translators) We discussed the situation. No one quite knew what to do or how it wd develop. De Gaulle was pretty sure that K wd press it to the point of rupture. Eisenhower was not convinced and I refused to accept this conclusion. Anyway, we must work to prevent the conference breaking down before it even started . . . .

21 May (Sat)
I will now try to describe what happened. The <u>Summit</u> – on wh I had set high hopes and for which I worked for over 2 years – has blown up, like a volcano! It is ignominious; it is tragic; it is almost incredible. I am in bed (at Birch Grove) and will do my best to describe the story . . . .

[On] May 16 I was called at 7.15am, having slept rather badly. I got to the American Embassy, where it had been arranged that I shd have breakfast with President Eisenhower, before 8am. We had our meal alone, in a crowded sitting room upstairs, with the door open, and two French footmen, in cotton gloves, serving a series of rather improbable dishes. The President, after consuming some 'cereals' and (I think) some figs, was given a steak and some jelly. I was fortunate enough to get a boiled egg.

I thought Ike depressed and uncertain . . . . I asked him what he was going to say at 11am. He said that his people had been working late on a text. But he had not seen the last version. At 8.45 or 9 Herter came in and at last the text was produced. It was not very good and much too truculent. Nor did it make it at all clear whether the Americans still claimed the right to make these flights (contrary to international law) or whether they were going to abandon them. On this, a lot of other people began to crowd into the room and argue. There was great confusion, and some bitterness. Actually, I felt that the Americans were in considerable disarray. However, the phrase was finally agreed 'In point of fact, these flights were suspended after the recent incident and are not to be resumed'.

Selwyn Lloyd and others arrived at the American Embassy about 10am and there was a lot of talk about what wd happen at the plenary meeting. I saw the President alone for a few moments, and told him that I feared there wd be a very unpleasant scene. And so it proved. The meeting started just after 11am, opened (as if for ordinary business but with some reference to Mr K[hrushchev]'s call upon him yesterday) by de Gaulle. K – who sat on his left – with Eisenhower opposite and me on his right – then claimed the right to speak . . . . It was a most unpleasant performance. The President could scarcely contain himself, but he did. When K had finished, Ike stood up and read his declaration very quietly and with restraint. It was short and quite effective. In addition to his demands (apology; punishment of offenders; no further over-flying) K added two points – both intended to be as offensive as possible to Eisenhower. (We heard afterwards from the French that the text of these was telephoned *en clair* – i.e. in Russian[39] – from Moscow about midnight last night. This is perhaps significant and may show that K was under some pressure from the Communist Praesidium in Moscow) The two new points were a) that the Summit shd now be postponed for 6 or 8 months – i.e. till the Presidency of Eisenhower had ended, b) that Eisenhower's proposed visit to Russia (in return for K's to U.S.A.) must be cancelled. Both of these were couched in ironical and wounding terms.

After Eisenhower, I spoke. I made only a few simple points. I deplored that after a long and painful ascent towards the Summit, it shd be found to be so clouded. I understood the feelings that had been aroused, but I made this appeal. What had happened, had happened. We all knew that espionage was a fact of life, and a disagreeable one.

---

39. That is, in ordinary language, not in cipher.

Moreover, most espionage activities involved the violation of national sovereignties. I then went on to say that Mr K's whole argument had been based on statements that overflights were still American policy. That was not so. I then quoted the President's words 'and are not to be resumed'. Therefore, the conference would not be 'under threat'. I said I was glad that Mr K had not suggested the abandonment of the Summit Conference, but only its adjournment. But *ce qui est différé, est perdu* (What is postponed, is lost) The eyes of the world were on the Heads of Govts and the hopes of the peoples of the world rested on them. I hoped, after these explanations, we could proceed with our work and I appealed to them to do this.

Altho' it is not stated in the official documents, a long argument followed. K tried to make out that the President's abandonment of overflights only applied till Jan 1961 (when his period of office ended) This was explained as merely the only pledge wh a President of USA cd give constitutionally. Then K said that the pledge was not made publicly. So I proposed an agreed communiqué of our proceedings, making this public. No. K wd publish the whole text of his offensive speech. The argument went on till nearly 2pm and then we gave it up. However, it was agreed to take 24 hours to think it over and perhaps have private and bilateral talks . . . .

After luncheon, and much talk with For Secy and advisers, I determined to try to save the conference. I wd see personally, and if possible alone, de Gaulle, Eisenhower and Kruschev in that order. These discussions began at about 6pm and (with a short interval for dinner at British Embassy) lasted till midnight.

De Gaulle was charming, but 'not amused'. He thought there was no hope of saving the conference. K's brutality was deliberate. They had made the decision in Moscow, before he came, for whatever reason. However, he had no objection to my efforts.

President Eisenhower was relaxed, but talked very strongly agst K. He was a real SOB.[40] He did not see what more he cd do. He had gone a long way in his offer. He cd not 'condemn' the action wh he had authorised (and in wh we were all, in one way or another involved) The demand for punishment was absurd. What more cd he do. I said I supposed he cd say 'he was sorry' – or, preferably, a formal diplomatic apology. But I really could not press Ike much further. His staff (including Herter) obviously thought he shd have reacted more

---

40. Son of a bitch.

strongly or left the room himself. It was a terrible thing for their President to be insulted in this way.

Kruschev was polite, but quite immovable .... However, at the end of a very long talk, I got the impression that he wd not act precipitately or decisively without seeing me again.

[On 17 May] My hopes were rudely and rapidly dashed. Mr K has given an informal Press Conference (at 9.25 am) in wh he reiterated all his demands on the Americans.

However, we all 3 westerners (Heads of Govts, followed by Ministers of Foreign Affairs) met at 10am at the Elysée. It was agreed that de Gaulle shd now send out a formal invitation for the Summit Conference to start its work at 3pm. This was done. Naturally, both the US and UK will accept ....

The rest of the day was very queer. We duly met at 3pm. No Mr K. Then a series of most complicated messages arrived, one cancelling or expanding another, with almost ludicrous effect. (Small meeting – but with Foreign Ministers and one or two advisers each) Couve de Murville acted as the Mercury for these strange messages. On their general tenor, which was to ask whether the Russian requirements had been 'met', the others wanted to issue our formal declaration that the Conference was at an end. I strongly objected to this and had rather an unpleasant scene. But I said that we must not seem to be breaking up the Conference ourselves. All the world had looked forward to this day. Churches and chapels everywhere had prayed for success. We cd not 'call it a day' on a telephone message. Let him at least write a letter (Mr K) so that we had some agreed document to rely on. He ought to write anyway, as a matter of courtesy. Altho' de G thought nothing of the general argument, the last point did appeal to him. Meanwhile (after a long wrangle with the Americans on one phrase) an agreed statement was prepared, to be put out by the 3 Powers when there was no further hope. The statement is important, because it pledges us to work for Peace and says quite clearly 'they themselves remain ready to take part in such negotiations at any suitable time in the future'. I was very pleased to get this agreed text – esp the earlier part pledging ourselves to negotiations as the means to settle 'all outstanding international questions'. But this means really 'Another Summit Conference with a new President'. Can President Eisenhower and the Americans generally 'pocket their insult'. I fear it has been difficult to get agreement on the words, wh (in view of K's time-table is a direct attack on Ike.) But we got them.

The next question was 'When to issue this declaration'. My colleagues pressed for 4pm. I refused, and asked for 10am on 18th. (I intended further bilateral talks with the Russians, in a last bid for success) After a great struggle, we got agreement to meet again at Elysée at 9.30pm, and to make a final decision then . . . .

We left Elysée at 5pm (having come at 3pm) I saw the British press yesterday, before my personal talks with de G, Eisenhower, and Kruschev. The result has certainly been to help to give us a good press at home. Both Harold Evans and Russell (F.O.) have been excellent and have kept the correspondents in line by telling them, hour by hour, what is happening. At 7pm, and on our invitation, Gromyko came for a long talk with Selwyn Lloyd at the British Embassy. G made it clear that they had fully decided to break up the Conference. But he was quite hopeful about going on with the 'Test' conference at Geneva. (Indeed, it has made good progress yesterday and today!) At 9.30 we returned to the Elysée. Since no Mr K arrived, we issued our final declaration at 10pm . . . . So ended – before it had even begun – the Summit Conference.

[On 18 May] at 4pm, President E called and we had an hour's talk, alone. This was very useful. He seemed very upset at the turn of events, so I tried my best to comfort him. But I said we must now really try to get rid of divisions in the Free World – about nuclear arms, about NATO, about economic grouping (Sixes and Sevens)[41] etc etc. I thought we might revive the idea floated last autumn at Rambouillet – i.e. a sort of Anglo-Franco-American informal group. He agreed, so long as it could really be informal, and the other organisations (NATO, CENTO,[42] SEATO) not annoyed or alarmed. At 5pm, there was a long and most useful talk at the Elysée . . . . The accounts of K's 'press conference' in Paris were just coming through. It was a terrible performance, reminiscent of Hitler at his worst. He threatens, rants, uses filthy words of abuse (Germans are bastards etc!) but – if

41. A reference to the Six (Belgium, France, West Germany, Italy, Luxembourg, Netherlands) members of the EEC founded in 1957 and the Seven (Austria, Britain, Denmark, Norway, Portugal, Sweden and Switzerland) members of the European Free Trade Association formally constituted on 3 May 1960. The term seemingly dates from the dispute in 1515 between two City livery companies, Skinners and Merchant Taylors, as to which should have precedence in the Lord Mayor of London's show.

42. The Central Treaty Organisation, the successor body of the Baghdad Pact.

you analyse it clearly – he does not actually commit himself to
anything. He has a draft treaty with E Germany. He has the pen in his
hand. But he does not say just when he will sign . . . .

We discussed our line if and when Kruschev signs a peace treaty.
In itself, we cannot object. But if he says that this automatically and
unilaterally destroys our (Western) rights in W Berlin, what do we do
next?

The Foreign Ministers had been working on a very good and
simple paper – shewing all sorts of stages and possibilities – what
Americans call 'contingency planning'. I agreed, on the clear understanding that no Government is committed, in any way, to any action
until we all decide together when the time comes. Eisenhower made it
very clear that in his view we can do very little. All last year's talk
about an armoured division going down the *autobahn* to Berlin is
bunk. That is a gain. But since, in the end we shall have to negotiate,
it makes it all the more tragic that we are not doing so now, owing to
the Summit failure.

De Gaulle, in the absence of Adenauer, talked some good sense.
Berlin cannot be re-captured or defended without major war. But de G
does not believe that the Russians will force the issue . . . .

[On 19 May] I felt very tired today, with much pain in the region
of the heart. Is it thrombosis or indigestion? . . . .

I went to see M. Debré at 11.15, and had a good talk with him.
We exchanged ideas about the Tripartite plan and have (I think) hit
upon something which will work.[43] I like Debré very much. It is useful
that he really likes us. About Berlin, he was very sensible. Since we
must negotiate with Russia in the long run, Debré is in favour of
getting negotiations going at some level as soon as possible. We cd
start with ambassadors . . . .

We returned to London in the afternoon . . . .

Dr Richardson came to see me just after noon yesterday [20 May].
He says that I have not had a heart attack (he took a lot of instrumen-
tal checks) but that the symptoms of extreme exhaustion are sometimes
not dissimilar. I hope he is right.

23 May

We make no progress in Cyprus. I fear Makarios is now not so much

---

43. The idea of a clandestine Western tripartism was, however, to break down on
    American unwillingness.

unwilling as afraid to conclude the Treaty. We had a meeting of ministers concerned at 10.30, and sent some fresh instructions to Amery and Foot. The last trouble to emerge is to find a formula if we decide to leave Cyprus at any future date. To whom are we to transfer sovereignty. The Turks claim that all the powers who agreed to the London settlement must be consulted. Makarios says only the Republic of Cyprus can be the beneficiary. The Greeks agree. But if we agree to this, we are merely starting a movement to push us out. So it goes on . . . .

25 May

A very sucessful defence meeting, in the sense that everyone agreed! Watkinson leaves on Friday for Washington, with a direction wh will enable him to make a definite agreement for SKYBOLT, if U.S. authorities will sign it. He can open up the more difficult problem of allowing U.S. submarines, armed with POLARIS to make a base in Gareloch in the Clyde.

26 May

Cabinet. Routine matters for the most part. We are going to have more difficulties with the South African Govt about [the] escape route wh is developing through the High Commission territories.[44] But if we hand back 'political' figures thro' the normal machinery of the extra-dition laws, we shall have even worse trouble here . . . .

Dinner at the Other Club.[45] Before dinner, a good talk with Colin Coote, (editor D Telegraph) who was helpful. He says that the great majority of the letters he gets are anti-American. This is sad, but understandable. The French middle class were jealous of us, when we were richer and more powerful. Now the same British types are jealous of the Americans . . . .

27 May

. . . . Bob and Dame Pattie Menzies to luncheon – alone. D and I enjoyed it and I think they did. We had a good gossip on all sorts of topics and personalities. He has a great contempt for Diefenbaker and his lack of statesmanship. Bob thinks that he can never escape from

---

44. The British-administered territories of Basutoland (now Lesotho), Bechuanaland (now Botswana), and Swaziland.

45. Founded in 1911 by Churchill and F. E. Smith. See vol 1, p. 87 (19 July 1951).

party politics and is really a supreme party manager. The excuse may perhaps be made that after 20 years or more in the political wilderness, the [Canadian] Conservatives have no men of experience and few of talent . . . .

28 May

. . . . The Turks have had a military revolution. I hope it will be of a sort of Pakistan type, and the Turkish general turns out a beneficent dictator. Of course, he says he will hold free elections. But first he has to get a Professor to write a new constitution, wh must take some time! Menderes and Zorlu are in preventive arrest. I don't think it will have much effect on Cyprus, because the General [Cemal Gürsel][46] has appointed the head of the Turkish F[oreign] Office to be Foreign Minister . . . .

30 May

. . . . I went at 6.30 and stayed an hour – to the Albert Hall, for the final rally of World Refugee Year,[47] with K (Lady) Elliot in the chair. This idea, which sprang from four Young Conservatives, contributors to *Cross Bow*,[48] has touched the imagination of the country. There has sprung up an 'ad hoc' organisation to collect and organise collections. Starting with a target of £2m (to wh HMG subscribed £100,000) they have reached over £8m (HMG giving £400,000)

Gaitskell made a foolish speech, chaffing me and not praising the audience, with a style of heavy Parliamentary humour. This was not to the taste of the audience. I was short and I hope simple. I had a very good reception in consequence . . . .

31 May

. . . . 12.30. Ld Home and Ld Monckton to discuss the problem of Ld Shawcross. Ld S's unlucky illness (he had to leave the Commission just after it had started work in Africa) means that he ought to resign. But

---

46. Who made himself President of Turkey until his death in 1966.
47. This was the first UN international year, prompted by the need to tackle the persistence of refugee camps left over from the Second World War.
48. The Bow Group is a Conservative think tank founded in 1951. The idea of World Refugee Year was first put forward in the Spring 1958 issue of its journal, *Crossbow*, then edited by Timothy Raison. The other three progenitors were Christopher Chataway, Colin Jones and Trevor Philpott.

a) he doesn't much want to and has read all the evidence etc from his sick bed b) some of the Africans on Commission wd like to keep him c) some of the Rhodesians (European) are determined to use this means of getting rid of him d) it is difficult to justify his taking part in writing the report, when he has missed the work on the spot. We decided that he ought to resign, but offer his services to the Commission, wh Ld M will accept . . . .

3.30–5. Deputation of Scottish TUC and Scottish members of Parl about employment in Scotland. Since I saw the TUC a year ago, the situation has improved embarrassingly [for them], and they know it! (The figure of 3.5% is quite tolerable) But a useful talk about the future . . . .

2 June

. . . . The 'economic and financial' position causes some anxiety, altho' the actual out-turn for May (£15[m] <u>up</u> on the reserves) is better than we expected. The £ is beginning to slip a little. But perhaps the German situation will improve and that their efforts to turn away foreign money (short term) may succeed. Also, the reduction in American money rates is helpful . . . .

3 June

. . . . 10.30–12.30. A meeting on 'the state of the Economy', on all too familiar lines. Sometimes it's deflation; sometimes it's inflation. (It's just like Alice and the mushroom)[49] Chancellor of Exr; Mr Butler; Ld Home; Mr H Brooke; Sir D Eccles; Ld Mills; Sir R Hall (Treasury) Sir N Brook.

A very useful talk. No one quite knows the extent of the disease (if any) or agrees on the cure. The instruments for control are very limited – and (if it's a question of exchange) Bank Rate operates more quickly and effectively than special deposits. But if there is <u>no</u> immediate risk, I wd much prefer to use increased special deposits.

Lord Home to luncheon. I asked him whether, <u>if</u> I decided to ask Selwyn Lloyd to take the Exchequer (when D H-Amory goes) he wd take For Office.[50] He seemed rather flabber-gasted but recovered

---

49. The mushroom, when eaten, made Alice larger or smaller in Lewis Carroll's *Alice in Wonderland*. This was an analogy Macmillan used in his 1957 Bedford speech, see *HMM* IV, p. 351.

50. The reshuffle consequent on Heathcoat Amory's desire to resign.

slowly. His real trouble is not that he is a Peer (we cd get over this, I think) It's his rather delicate health . . . .

B.G. – where Daniel (looking better) has come over Whitsun. Another glorious day. Worked after dinner for an hour, after a very good and long talk with Daniel about reorganising Macmillan & Co. I think I managed to impress upon him the urgent need of getting things settled. Maurice will make a good chairman; but he has (like me) too many irons in the fire to run the whole business as managing director in addition . . . .

5 June (Sunday)

A very nice letter from Alec Home, to whom I talked on the telephone this morning before he left for Scotland. He is willing to do whatever suits me best, but he is anxious as to his qualifications; his being in the Lords; and his health. About the first, I have no doubt. He has just what a For Secy needs. About the second and third, there is more doubt. I talked to Selwyn – who is now (I think) veering towards staying at the F.O. . . . .

10 June

We left Gatwick early on Tuesday 7th and got back to Gatwick at 6pm on Friday 10th. This four day visit to Norway has been very enjoyable . . . . I had been here last when I was Foreign Secy – the Queen's State visit. The Norwegians are very staunch – they like the British and feel themselves at home with us. They fear the Russians (with whom they have a common frontier of 100 miles in the North, where infiltration cd easily take place) They hate the Germans.

The 'Socialist' or 'Labour' Govt has been in power for 25 years. If the Conservatives, Liberals, Christians, and Farmers combined, they cd put the Labour Party out. But they don't and won't. Meanwhile, there is Socialism (or egalitarianism) pretty widely applied – except in Fish, Farming, Banking and Shipping (vital for the country's life) But the 'applied Socialism' is of a fairly moderate kind and the Govt is, in many respects, not unlike our Progressive Conservative Govt here. (I think both Sweden and Norway present the policies wh Mr Gaitskell seeks vainly to impose on the British Labour Party. If he were to succeed, they too would win power and hold it for a long time)

The unattractive side of the Norwegian 'affluent society' is its increasingly Pagan character. Christianity (they have a Lutheran church) is openly despised, and a sort of vague, materialistic agnostic creed flourishes (as over a large part of British life) My speech at the Round Table dealt with this (in a passage about 'How to Fight Communism') and caused quite a sensation . . . .

There is a certain 'defeatism' and 'neutralism' growing in Norway and Dr Lange (For Minister) was quite frank about this. But he felt my visit wd do good from this point of view.

This morning we went to AFHQ, Northern Europe, at Kolsas. This is an immense 'bunker', dug into the mountain. General Murray commands – with the usual NATO integrated staff. But – alas – there are no forces to speak of! It is very thin 'on the ground'. The only real strength is Tactical Air Force – and, outside the command, the strategics in U.K. In the Schleswig area, there will soon be some German troops – but there is very little else. The Norwegians have (I think) two battalions! . . . .

11 June

Motored to Petworth.[51] Luncheon with John and Pamela Wyndham, and Selwyn Lloyd . . . . After a most frank and straightforward talk, Selwyn and I agreed that the best situation wd be himself at the Treasury and Alec Home at the Foreign Office. But we have to face the two difficulties of Alec's health and the House of Lords. Selwyn believes that both of these might be met by a Minister of State – or without Portfolio – in the Cabinet, but under the For Secy. I am not sure that this wd work, altho' I can see that (if it did) it wd help to meet both objections.

S.L. is ready and (after the shock) anxious for the change. He has had 5 years as F.S., which is an immense strain. He must realise that to go to the Home side makes him a possible rival to Butler in considering the succession. Altho' he is not ambitious in any wrong sense, he is conscious of Rab's weakness and oddness (wh seems to grow not lessen)

12 June

Minister of Defence (Watkinson) Sir Solly Zuckerman (scientific adviser) Sir Pat Dean (F.O.) and Tim Bligh (P.S.) to luncheon at B.G. We spent afternoon and evening on the SKYBOLT and the POLARIS problems. On the former, things look pretty clear and we shd be able to get a more or less formal agreement. Of course, no one yet knows whether the weapon will work or not. But we have an 'option' – and

---

51. John Wyndham's Sussex country house.

if it doesn't work, we don't buy it. Nor shall we have lost a fortune of our own money in R&D (altho' we must spend fairly substantial sums in studying the 'adaptation' problem at once). On Polaris, we have to make an immediate – and very difficult – decision. The Americans want to have a base in West Scotland, preferably the Gareloch – at the mouth of the Clyde. Apart from the difficulty of the location – so near Glasgow, etc – what will the general political reaction be here? I think it turns on whether we are just to give our allies facilities – more or less as a satellite – or whether we can make it a joint enterprise. Can we get one submarine from US and start to build another? The whole problem is full of uncertainties and dangers.

I had agreed 'in principle' at Camp David to do what we could, more or less in return for Skybolt. But Watkinson has managed to disassociate the two 'deals'.

14 June

Motored to London at lunch-time. Ld Chancellor at 2.30, to discuss the leadership of HofLords (if Ld Home is able to take the Foreign Secretaryship) He obviously wants to stay as Ld C himself. He thinks Ld Hailsham could not do it. But he thinks Ld Dundee cd.

A long meeting with Chancellor of Exr, accompanied by Sir R Hall. They depressed me, for I was not at all confident that they had any confidence in their proposed remedies for the 'over-expansion of demand': 8% Bank Rate, more special deposits, and (perhaps) stricter Hire Purchase rules . . . .

15 June

Mr Robens has been offered, and accepted, the post of Chairman of the Coal Board.[52] As he is one of the 4 or 5 leading figures on the Front Opposition bench, the Labour Party have been thrown into still further confusion. Their anger has helped to meet any criticisms from the Tory benches . . . .

17 June

. . . . I lunched with Ld Home. <u>He will take the F.O.</u> I am delighted. This settles the two chief posts. Selwyn Lloyd for the Treasury, Alec Home for the F.O. Now come the consequential problems of their

---

52. The National Coal Board managed the industry, which had been nationalised in 1947.

staffs. Alec will need a Minister of State, but of <u>Cabinet</u> rank – both to go abroad and to protect him and me in HofCommons. Selwyn will need a new FST. Ed Boyle is not his type. Then we shall need a Commonwealth Secy. This – in Africa year and with Monckton etc – is of first-class importance. Alec Home has been so good and has the confidence of all. Then the Leadership of the HofLords. Ld Hailsham came at 5 and talked about his own future for an hour or more. He thinks he might do better by going back to the Bar now. Before this, Alec and I (with the Lord Chancellor) had been discussing whether Ld Hailsham could lead the House of Lords without disaster . . . .

The Far East looks bad. The riots in Japan have prevented President Eisenhower from making his visit. This is a great triumph for the Communists, Russian and Chinese. I wd not be surprised to see Formosa and the 'off-shore' islands flare up this summer – while the Americans are occupied with their election. Japan itself may fall into extremist hands. The position in the Western Atlantic is equally bad, with Cuba under Castro – who is confiscating all the American properties and threatening to seize the oil refineries, including that belonging to Shell. The Americans are pained and uncertain. (what a pity they never understood 'Colonialism' and 'Imperialism' till too late!) . . . .

19 June (Sunday)
Another glorious day. Church at 11. Ted Heath came to luncheon. I offered him to exchange his post as Minister of Labour for Ld Privy Seal and second-in-command of Foreign Office, with full authority in the Commons. He will think about it. On the whole, I believe it wd be to his advantage. But I will not press him unduly, altho' it wd be a great convenience to me . . . .

The Labour row seems to grow in bitterness and intensity.[53] One begins to wonder whether Gaitskell will be able to survive and ride the storm. I shd be sorry if he went, for he has ability without charm. He does not appeal to the electorate, but he has a sense of patriotism and moderation. However, I can't see either Wilson or Brown as better equipped . . . .

21 June
Cabinet 10.30–1. The chief problems were a) future housing legislation b) the economic situation. On a) Mr H Brooke has put forward a most

---

53. Over the party's attitude towards nuclear weapons.

comprehensive paper, almost too much for a Cabinet to grasp fully. We decided on a small group of ministers to examine it.

On b) there was a very good discussion and a wide field of thought thrown open. Chancellor of Exr seemed rather confused. But, in general, he seemed to make out his case. It was left for him to settle later with Rab and myself.

This we did – at 6pm – <u>with</u> the Governor and Sir R Hall also present – and For Secy. We agreed to another 1% on Bank Rate (making 6%) and a further 1% 'call' for special deposits. This will <u>not</u> be popular, and I am not quite convinced that the timing is right. I shd have preferred to keep the Bank Rate in reserve, for the autumn. However, there is a lot to be said (politically) for getting the child to take the medicine <u>before</u> the new doctor takes over. Selwyn Lloyd (whom I invited to join us for the 6pm meeting) seemed to share this view . . . .

23 June

Cabinet. The Cabinet agreed to the POLARIS base, <u>if</u> at Loch Linnhe (much better than the Gareloch) and <u>if</u> it included an option for us to buy or build POLARIS submarines. The drafting will be difficult, but I made some progress this evening with a draft (wh I dictated) of a telegram to the President . . . .

24 June

Ld Hailsham came to see me at 9.30. He still cannot decide whether to leave the Govt and go back to the bar 'to make money'. He told me that he had £150,000 of his own money. But, if he became a judge with a pension, he cd in due course give this to his children. After much discussion with Alec Home, I told Ld H that, if he chose to stay, he cd become Lord President and Leader of the House of Lords. He was gratified – but undecided. I told him that he must let me know definitely as soon as he could . . . .

26 June (Sunday)

I was very tired – last week was a terrific week of difficult decisions and also <u>very</u> hot. I stayed in bed and finished the box in the morning (and so missed Church) . . . .

Ted Heath to luncheon. He <u>will</u> agree to my proposal – to be Lord Privy Seal, and chief Foreign Office representative in Hof-Commons . . . .

28 June

A day of interviews and parties! Chief Whip [Redmayne], Minister of Housing, Mr Anthony Head, Ld Hailsham. M of Housing has <u>very</u> ingenious plans for dealing with rents, rates etc.[54] The 'land shortage' seems more difficult, tho' not impossible to solve. If we maintain the 'green belt' concept rigorously, we can force redevelopment of the rotting centres (or 'twilight' areas) of some of our towns.[55]

A[nthony] Head has now accepted to be High Commissioner to Nigeria, after independence. I am very pleased. He will become a Peer. Ld Hailsham has accepted to become Ld President and Leader of HofLords.

The problem is now to get a Commonwealth Secretary. I have offered it again to Butler. (He has now been offered Chancellor of Exr – refused – Foreign Secretary – refused. So he shd feel well treated. I think he will decide to remain Home Secretary, but I should really like him to take Commonwealth. He wd be particularly good at dealing with Rhodesia etc) . . . .

30 June

. . . . The House of Commons (whips off) voted heavily against homosexuality last night. This should end the Parliamentary controversy for a time.

Defence Committee all the afternoon (4–6.30) A very difficult set of problems – future of Territorial Army, recruiting, (can we get a 'voluntary' army as we are trying or shall we be forced to 'selective service' in some form?) Air crew training (G.B. is getting too small and too full of civil airfields) German destroyers and mines . . . .

The Russians have 'walked out' of the disarmament conference. Mr K[hrushchev] has written a long, argumentative, false and curiously boring letter to me and to the other Heads of Govt. I have made a pretty good reply, published in the Press and on the whole applauded. At any rate, it is simple and sincere. We are only now beginning to realise, as the weeks go by, the full extent of the

---

54. Faced with the failure of efforts to stimulate the private rented sector Brooke proposed to encourage new housing societies with generous loans, a scheme incorporated into the 1961 Housing Act.

55. Although Macmillan was well aware of growing Labour criticism of development land shortages, limited progress was made in tackling this, and regeneration of inner cities did not seriously begin until the late 1960s.

Summit disaster in Paris. For me, it is the collapse of the work of 2 or 3 years. For Eisenhower, it means an ignominious end to his Presidency. For Kruschev, a set-back to his more conciliatory and sensible ideas. For the world, a step nearer ultimate disaster. Nor can anything be done to reverse the dangerous drift till after the American elections. If the Republicans win, one might begin some work before Christmas. If the Democrats win, nothing can be done till the Spring of 1961.

Certainly the price paid for any 'intelligence' obtained by U2 flights has been a high one.

Meanwhile, Mr Gaitskell has got a 'vote of confidence' from the Parliamentary Labour Party by a large majority. I was beginning to be anxious – for, on the whole, Mr G suits us pretty well . . . .

5 July

Cabinet reconstruction goes on. Rab does not want anything but his present position – so that is settled. Duncan Sandys will go to Commonwealth Office; John Hare to Labour (if he agrees) and then Christopher Soames to Agriculture. This still leaves the problem of Thorneycroft and Powell. On the whole, I am in favour of making them an offer, but I must carry the Cabinet and the Party with me.

PQs went very badly for me. There was a sudden storm about U2, arising from a supplementary, and I allowed myself to be taken by surprise and rattled by Brown, Healey, Silverman, Warbey, like a lot of hounds. When he saw it was a good run, Gaitskell joined in. I did not manage it at all well, but at least saved time and the big row will be next week. The trouble is how to maintain a refusal to give any information, wh is the traditional policy about what borders on intelligence and military operations . . . .

6 July

A long meeting of ministers concerned with the future of BLUE-STREAK. Shall we abandon 'rocketry' altogether? Or shall we go in for Space Research? About £15–20m a year for an unknown advantage. Much division of view. Meeting adjourned!

Another meeting in the afternoon about the Americans, General Norstad, and the nefarious plot wh the General (with or without the support of the Pentagon and the State Dept) is carrying on about the IRBMs (Polaris etc) for NATO countries. The President has not yet replied to my telegram – wh is very odd, and rather disturbing.[56]

7 July

. . . . After questions, I had to make a tribute to Aneurin Bevan, who died yesterday afternoon. It was <u>not</u> easy to get a balance between being <u>too</u> laudatory and too critical; patronising or sentimental. What I did seemed to please the House and esp Bevan's friends . . . .

. . . . Anthony Head – who had accepted the post of the first High Commissioner in Nigeria (and a Viscounty) has heard of Duncan Sandys' appointment and has now refused to go. Alec Home had an hour with him this afternoon; I had from midnight till 2am. He hates Duncan with an unreasoning and almost insane hatred (based, I suppose, on the M of Defence, and my decision to supersede Head)[57] I tried to calm him, but he was pathological . . . .

9 July

Very tired – stayed in bed – working and telephoning – most of the day. Julian and Catherine are back from Cyprus. He has really done very well indeed[58] . . . .

Walked a bit – pondered a lot . . . . Shall we be caught between a hostile (or at least less and less friendly) America and a boastful, powerful 'Empire of Charlemagne' – now under French but later bound to come under German control. Is this the real reason for 'joining the Common Market' (if we are acceptable) and for abandoning a) the Seven b) British agriculture c) the Commonwealth. It's a grim choice . . . .

10 July

. . . . In addition to other troubles, the Congo (which became independent only a few days ago)[59] has fallen into chaos; murder, rape, intertribal warfare, mass flight of Europeans etc. The Belgian Govt doesn't

---

56. Norstad had floated the idea of a European nuclear deterrent in a speech in San Francisco on 9 December 1959. Macmillan wrote to Eisenhower raising his concerns about these plans on 24 June.
57. See vol 1, pp. 614–15 (3 February 1957).
58. Cyprus became an independent republic with Makarios as president on 16 August 1960.
59. This former Belgian colony became independent on 30 June 1960.

quite know what to do. The Prime Minister (Congolese) called Lumumba (or some such name) is a Communist and probably a Russian agent; the Premier of Katanga (where the mineral wealth is) is a moderate, and wants to be independent. Sir Roy Welensky wants Katanga to be independent and would like to send in troops, by leave of U.K. Govt if we agree and without leave if we don't. I feel like Lord North[60] . . . .

17 July (Sunday)
. . . . The problem of U2 and the general agreement with the Americans on our cooperation thro' the American bases in UK, was immensely increased by a new incident, of wh we heard on Monday night. Another aeroplane (coming this time from a base in U.K.) which the U2 did not, disappeared in the sea, near the Northern shores of Russia, some 10 or 12 days ago. The Russians even joined in the search for it in the open seas. Now they claim that it violated Russian air space and was shot down over territorial waters.[61]

Question time on Tuesday was quite an ordeal. Both wings of the Labour Party joined in the hunt – altho' the Gaitskellites were a little conscious of their own weakness on defence matters. I had about ½ hour or so of it – on a private notice question by Mr G – and got through fairly well. (Actually, it was a most difficult and anxious job – the worst since Suez. For, when one is dealing with 'intelligence' matters, the ice is pretty thin) I fully expected a motion for a debate at 7pm. If it had been moved, I think the Speaker wd have accepted it. I had a private word with Mr G before questions and shewed him my main reply, about seeing whether any improvements were needed in the Anglo-American agreement. On this, he said he wd try to keep his people quiet. Anyway, it passed off all right, and a 'crisis' much heralded by the Press, never came to a head . . . .

Next, the Congo. Our decision to work through U.N.; to help Ghana;[62] and to try to keep Welensky quiet was the only way to keep

---

60. Katanga was the southern province of Congo nearest to the CAF and rich in gold, copper and uranium. Macmillan compares his dilemma of whether or not to intervene to the problems secessionist America posed for his eighteenth-century predecessor Lord North (Prime Minister 1770–82).

61. The USAF RB 47 had been shot down over the Barents Sea on 1 July.

62. Following Tshombe's declaration of Katangan independence on 11 July,

the Russians from a direct intervention. But we have not yet faced the real question of Katanga. There is still uncertainty about the Belgian attitude. Meanwhile, the Russians are making a tremendous propaganda attack on all of us – France, Belgium, U.S., U.K. etc. We are accused of destroying the independence of Congo etc etc – of 'colonisation' – or 'imperialism' in the most violent and bitter attacks, by note and radio. My statement in the House (another private notice question) seemed to satisfy all parties, but of course leaves many knotty points unresolved. We have had tremendous telegrams and telephoning about our own people – we have managed to rescue some British from Stanleyville by airlift; about UN; about Ghana troops, led by our fine General Alexander etc etc.

Then we have had the Crown Prince of Libya, (two drinks – one at No 10 and one at Embassy) M Spaak (luncheon at No 10 and European MRBMs and Germany and NATO and all that) Señor Castiella (Spanish Foreign Minister) and all that a visit from a Spanish Government representative implies (with extreme Labour people trying to whip up another row) We have had Cyprus (2nd Reading of the Independence Bill), and Socialist anger at a problem having been resolved . . . .

Among other matters wh have arisen during this wonderful week has been the reorganisation of the Govt. After much reflection, I have offered a post to Peter Thorneycroft, who left us some years ago in what was a 'little local difficulty' . . . . I saw him on Thursday and offered him Duncan Sandys' present post – Minister of Aviation. It is a great spending department, wh he obviously didn't much like. It is not one [of] the key departments – like F.O.; CRO; Col Secy, or Chancellor of Exr. To this he seemed reconciled. He is to give me his answer tomorrow. When I have this, I shd be able to complete the list. In spite of much speculation, so far no one has 'leaked' . . . .

30 July

I came to Chequers last night (Friday) arriving at 8pm and went to bed. My plan is to stay here for some days alone and try to rest . . . . I am to go on a diet (to lose some weight) and to be sure that the absence of my gall bladder doesn't result in too much strain on the

---

supported by Belgian mining interests and troops, Lumumba had appealed to the UN, Ghana and the Russians for aid.

liver etc.[63] I have had a good deal of pain in the right side of my stomach. But I don't think it is anything serious.

My mind is not working quite right. My speech Thursday last was not good. But really the last fortnight has been an absolute nightmare . . . .

We have had in

I external politics

a) note to Mr Kruschev, answering Russian note about the American aeroplane shot down in Arctic. After much thought, I decided to write an 'open letter' to Mr K – more in sorrow than in anger – and to read it out in HofC. It had a great effect, and put an end – at least temporarily – to a flood of questions about American bases in UK . . . . K has not yet answered – after about 10 days. On the whole, a good sign.

b) Congo. This is, on the whole, settling down. Hammarskjöld (U.N.) is doing a good job . . . . Meanwhile, trouble has broken out in S Rhodesia – where Sir E Whitehead (without informing Sir Roy Welensky) has precipitated riots and shooting by allowing the police to arrest a number of African politicians. The Nyasaland Conference is starting in London. Altho' Dr Banda seems a little more moderate, the Conference will prob[ably] break down and serious trouble may start in Nyasaland. Welensky is being very touchy about 'military planning' – he is obviously rattled, and raising absurd points of prestige and constitutional niceties, instead of getting on with preparations for trouble in concert with us. Ghana has boycotted all S African goods.

c) The most complicated negotiations are going on with U.S. authorities to carry out a promise I had to give in the HofC about 'reviewing' the agreement on bases. I hope we shall get something fairly sensible, but the American generals are rather sticky and add to the general dismay in U.K. by giving ridiculous press interviews of a 'sabre-rattling' kind. We are also going on with the correspondence between myself and the President on giving U.S. Navy a base for Polaris on the Clyde. (They have refused Loch Linnhe, at entrance to Caledonian Canal) This will be hard to defend here, except on some 'give and take' basis – viz. control or consultation about the use of

---

63. See vol 1, p. 244 (14 July 1953).

submarines and some kind of 'option' on the Polaris system, shd we ever want it for ourselves. The Cabinet has (Thursday night) agreed to the Gareloch or the Holy Loch on the Clyde, if we can get some fair agreement on a *quid pro quo*.[64]

d) The Iceland fishery dispute will flare up again on August 12. Our fishermen agreed not to go within 12 miles for 3 months, to allow negotiations. The 3 months end on August 12 (strangely appropriate date)[65] and our fishermen demand Admiralty protection. If we give it, Iceland may go out of NATO and the American base may be at risk. If we don't, it's a betrayal of our own men.

e) Debate on Sixes and Sevens. Selwyn Lloyd made an excellent speech – his last as For Secy. The Labour Party were cautious. The problem remains.

II on Internal Affairs

a) Rather bad papers from Treasury, on Balance of Payments and Future Govt Expenditure have alarmed the Cabinet. Once again, admirable diagnosis, no remedies!

b) Reconstruction of Cabinet .... As I expected, a great row developed about a Peer going to F.O. There was a premature leak (wh on the whole helped the Party first to get excited and then to calm down) The Opposition had a debate – and Gaitskell made the cleverest and most effective speech I have heard him make. My reply was not too good, but the Party rallied round and we won by a majority of 110 (our paper majority being 94) We had, in the end, as far as is known yet, no abstentions. I have not seen the analysed list. This was a great act of loyalty to me, and several of our chaps came from sick beds and even hospitals to vote. I have got Thorneycroft back (as Minister of Aviation) I think this is wise and he has accepted a post in the second rank, wh is good. I have given Health to Enoch Powell.

---

64. UK acquisition of Polaris, but as part of a NATO programme, had been offered to Watkinson on 6 June 1960. British hopes for a veto on the launching of the missiles within 100 miles of the UK had been deemed unacceptable by the US State Department. In the end, Cabinet approval for the base at Holy Loch was given on 15 September in return for broad American assurances about future provision of missiles to Britain.

65. The traditional start of the shooting season.

c) <u>Defence</u>. Tremendous and inconclusive arguments, about bases, weapons, air defence etc . . . .

d) <u>Blue Streak and Space Research</u>. We have put off a final decision, till we can talk to Australians and then the French. I was afraid we wd have a big row in Cabinet over this, but everyone (in spite of July) behaved sensibly.

e) <u>Cunarder</u>. We have made an agreement with Cunard Co and a new <u>Queen</u> will be built[66] . . . .

Dr Richardson (now Sir John) came to luncheon. He made a very thorough examination and seemed satisfied. He has prescribed me a course of 'rest' for the next 3 weeks, so far as this is possible while I am acting in charge of the Govt and while I have such a lot of reading etc to catch up . . . .

1 August

. . . . Sent a telegram to Welensky. He has changed right round, and now wants a British battalion at Salisbury! But it is much better to keep the strategic reserve in Kenya, so that we can send troops to Northern Rhodesia; Southern Rhodesia; or Nyasaland, as may be required . . . .

3 August

After some telephoning about various points, left Chequers by car at 11. We took our luncheon, and arrived at Chatsworth[67] about 3pm . . . . Andrew [11th Duke of Devonshire] and Debo have been angelic about it all. Really it's absurd to travel with a chauffeur, a detective, and two secretaries. I have been put into the 'Centre Room' – a splendid room, looking west. The office (scrambler telephone etc) is in the centre dressing room. This is the first time I have been to Chatsworth – to stay – since 1939. Andrew and Debo have only just moved in and they have really made a wonderful job of it. It is more beautiful than before . . . . Altho' several thousand people were milling around, one did not seem to notice them. The old drawing room (originally the dining room, in 18th century) is the dining room again. The yellow drawing room is unchanged. The old schoolroom is a most attractive general sitting room. The passages etc have been immensely improved

---

66. RMS *Queen Elizabeth* 2 launched in 1969. Macmillan had written to the Chancellor supporting this development in November 1958.

67. Family seat of the Dukes of Devonshire in Derbyshire.

.... two splendid Rembrandts remain as well as a mass of other splendid pictures. I thought the house _far_ more beautiful – much gayer, and all the lovely things admirably shewn . . . .

4 August

.... Congo is now moving to a new crisis, wh means (I feel sure) trouble in U.N. Some of our party are much worried about the Katanga. On the other hand, if Katanga is allowed to secede, the rest of the Congo may well fall to complete confusion, followed by Communism. No doubt some sort of semi-independence in a federal system (developed from the present semi-federal constitution) could be worked out if everyone were reasonable. But nobody is – at least in the Congo or the U.N. As a relief to this dark picture, the news came of the success of the Nyasaland Conference – a great triumph for Colonial Secy.[68] If this holds, it will immensely ease the whole Federation problem, on wh the Monckton Commission is shortly to report . . . .

5 August

Left Chatsworth at 9am and got to Admiralty House (where I held a meeting of ministers at 3pm) just after luncheon. There is complete confusion in the house (the move from No 10 started on Tuesday) but the office is working and the Cabinet can meet[69] . . . .

6 August

.... Congo still more confused. Hammarskjöld has 'called off' the entry of U.N. forces into Katanga and referred the matter to the Security Council, wh is to meet tomorrow night. Now the fat is properly in the fire.

I worked with the two young men [Bishop and Bligh] on our defence problems most of the morning and afternoon. They did some very good drafting after our talks – and I think we may see our way to some progress. The Chiefs of Staff's paper is interesting, but it starts

---

68. There was to be an African majority in the Legislative Council and at least three of the ten-member Executive Council were to be African.

69. In July 1957 Macmillan had appointed a committee under Lord Crawford to examine the state of 10 Downing Street – the Prime Minister's residence where the Cabinet meets – and surrounding buildings. In Spring 1958 they recommended a major programme of works. Macmillan was to move instead into Admiralty House until 1963.

from what seem to me false premises and would result in still greater expenditure. What we have above all to do is to try to economise on expenditure overseas, with its effects on the balance of payments.

.... [T]he great danger now is that the Congolese extremists (Lumumba and co) will try to defy the U.N. forces (now that Hammarskjöld has been unwilling to enter Katanga) and call in Russian or Russian satellite troops. H has himself stated that the question is now (since the Belgians have really agreed to go) an internal African dispute. This is true. It is nonetheless a very dangerous position. Civil war in Africa might be the prelude to war in the world.

Ever since the breakdown of the Summit in Paris I had felt uneasy about the summer of 1960. It has a terrible similarity to 1914. Now Congo may play the role of Serbia.[70] Except for the terror of the nuclear power on both sides, we might easily slide into the 1914 situation. I am not at all looking forward to our visit to Bonn. Dr A[denauer] has deceived me before, over a great economic issue. He promised to support the European Free Trade Area. But, under French pressure, he went back on the promises. Having a guilty conscience, he then accused me of defeatism vis-à-vis Soviet Russia .... I fear I have never succeeded in getting anything tangible out of these talks. Nevertheless, I think it wd have been wrong to refuse the invitation ....

7 August

.... Dr Nkrumah has now joined in the clamour. 'If U.N. troops do <u>not</u> enter Katanga, Ghana will conquer the rebels etc etc'. This is the impression he wants to make. But, read carefully, his statement has several reservations and lines of retreat ....

The new For Secy came to lunch here (Chequers) .... I think we worked out quite a good approach for Adenauer – to accept his pessimism about the triumphs of Mr K[hrushchev] and the increased strength and danger of Russia and then to try to point the moral – why divide Europe – first economically, and now politically? But I fear we shall waste our breath. For the Germans will agree with us (or many of them will) but A[denauer] has sold his soul to the French Faustus.[71] Only a successor can get free – and then (as I have equally warned the French) the Germans may get <u>too</u> free and get too uppish.

---

70. Austria's conflict with Serbia in 1914 acted as catalyst for the First World War.
71. Macmillan presumably meant to compare de Gaulle not to Faustus but to Mephistopheles, the demonic tempter of Faustus in the traditional German tale.

For, as Churchill said of the Germans 'They are a people who are either at your knees or at your throat'.

After Europe, Africa .... Round 'secession' will be built a great controversy (our own left-wingers, who demand secession for Nyasaland, are, characteristically, against independence of any kind for Katanga) .... If only we can get a date by wh all the Belgians are to go out, it will be clear that this has become a row between blacks and not a colonial or a black versus white dispute. This should help us. But I am frankly alarmed at possible developments. However, as long as Cabot Lodge is at U.N., the Americans are quite unreliable. For Lodge, who often even eluded or disobeyed Foster Dulles, snaps his fingers at Herter and pays little regard now to Eisenhower. Lodge is Boston – and fundamentally anti-British – not the Irish sort, wh sometimes forgets; but the 'Colonial' sort, wh has to hate England out of *snobisme* – to prove that their ancestors were at the tea-party ....

8 August

.... Motored to London after luncheon. We are pretty well installed in Admiralty House so far as the Cabinet room (in which I work) the Private Secretaries, the Press Office, messengers, telephonists etc are concerned. No sitting room or bedrooms are yet available. I think it will be quite a comfortable house ....

The U.N. Security Council start their discussion tonight. The resolution tabled by the 'neutrals' and supported by the Americans is not good, but might be worse. Shall we vote for it or abstain? The chief object of British policy must be

1. To prevent Congo turning into Korea. Therefore, however attractive in some ways the separation of Katanga may seem, the result may well be a Korean type war, following on Russian support to the rest of the Congo.

2. To support, through U.N., some kind of 'federalist' solution – by wh Katanga can have 'Home Rule' but make a contribution to the rest of this immense area (Katanga is about size of Spain, Congo of Western Europe!)

3. To stop foolish but dangerous movements by African countries alone – Ghana, Guinea, Egypt, or any other – wh may, in guise of Pan-Africanism, throw the whole continent into confusion.

4. To work as closely as we can with French and other Europeans in NATO, including Belgians

5. To get Americans to be temperate and intelligent.

9 August

There was a lot of telephoning all through the night. (I had gone from London to B.G.) Dixon told us that if <u>we abstained</u>, (wh was quite a possibility) the French, Italians wd also abstain. Then the Russians and their friends wd also abstain. So the motion wd fall to the ground. The Russians wd then move a very disagreeable motion, wh wd also be defeated or fall to the ground thro' insufficient votes. There wd then be a vacuum; Hammarskjöld wd have no authority; U.N. wd presumably withdraw. Then, the Ghanaians etc from one side, and Russians (or Russian inspired and supplied forces) on the other wd move in. The fat wd be properly in the fire. The Italians thought <u>therefore</u> they wd vote <u>for</u> the motion – wh taken <u>as a whole</u> has not worked out <u>too</u> badly – if we did.

Bob Dixon convinced us. I spoke to Foreign Secy at midnight (7pm N York time) and at about 2am (9pm NY) We authorised Dixon to vote <u>for</u>.

10 August [sic]

I heard from Philip de Z[ulueta] that the motion had been carried.[72] French abstained – and the Italians (having ascertained that we wd <u>vote for</u>) also abstained, on the calculation that even if Russians and their friends did the same, there would <u>not</u> be enough abstentions to stop the motion being carried. The French and the Italians therefore have the advantage of claiming that they 'stood by' the Belgians (and, I suppose, the European <u>Six</u>) while the British have abandoned their European friends. This they can <u>safely</u> do, relying on the British to achieve, by this vote, exactly the result the French and Italians want. It is not very distinguished – but it is very Latin . . . .

10 August[73]

Left Chequers 9.30am, with Philip de Z[ulueta]. At London airport we found Ld Home (For Secy) Sir Evelyn Shuckburgh, and Sir R Barclay. We arrived at Wahn airport – outside Cologne – at noon . . . .

The Chancellor greeted me with unexpected warmth – 'my friend'

---

72. It required the withdrawal of Belgian troops from Katanga and entry of a UN force.

73. Change of notebook, but with the same date. The previous entry was probably written on 10 August (reflecting Macmillan's tendency to date entries by the date of writing and not the date referred to), but refers to 9 August.

etc. I suppose this results from his delight at the failure of all my attempts towards a 'détente' with the Soviets. It is rather a bitter pill. But we must try to turn it to some advantage.

During the long drive in Adenauer's motor (nearly 40 minutes to Bonn) I was able to keep the conversation to generalities, but I elicited some information about the de G[aulle]–Adenauer meeting at Rambouillet. (1) A had asked for it – directly or indirectly. This was because of a number of incidents (including a speech of Prime Minister Debré) wh wounded German pride by suggesting that Germany was now only a French satellite. (2) At the meeting, both A and de G opposed the Hallstein bureaucracy in Brussels taking on too much power.[74] (3) The _political_ advance was to be on a governmental basis. Federalism must wait. De G was against a federal assembly for the 6 except on the Strasbourg model – i.e. not elected but delegated from national parliaments. (4) They did _not_ repeat _not_ 'discuss Sixes and Sevens', or the problem of U.K.'s relation to Europe . . . .

. . . . Adenauer began the meeting by a rather melancholy picture of the world today – the ever growing strength of Russia and Communism and the relative loss of authority by the forces of the Free World.[75] I responded – and underlined – this mood. According to the plan I had devised, I emphasised the seriousness of the crisis; reviewed the resources available; how they were being used; who was contributing (U.S. and U.K. enormously; France little; Germany less than nothing for she actually has a _net_ profit of £250m on military expenditure by her allies in the Federal Republic)[76] . . . .

. . . . After dinner, I told Dr A about the possibility of de G organising a meeting with me and President Eisenhower. I thought it

---

74. Walter Hallstein took office as the first president of the European Commission on 7 January 1958.
75. Reports of the enormous numbers of technologists being trained in Russia had, for instance, on 19 February 1960 led Minister for Science Hailsham to write gloomily to Macmillan, 'It is probably inevitable that the economic growth of the USSR will be greater than anything which can be matched in the West' (TNA: CAB 21/3841). For similar concerns in the mid-1950s, see TNA: CAB 124/2584 and, at the time of _Sputnik_, TNA: PREM 11/1894.
76. Aid as a means of promoting international stability was another theme. In a 30 July 1960 memorandum Macmillan had written that 'trying to make the Germans contribute to the under-developed countries would be rather a good subject for us to discuss with the old gentleman' (DWM: Ms Macmillan, dep. c. 353).

only fair to tell him. I wd not like this to reach him from other sources. Dr A was pleased at being told, but seemed not to mind, so long as any 'Tripartite' did not deal with NATO or 'upset' the NATO allies.

We then talked about the Congo. I explained to Dr A the problem presented by the vote on the resolution in the Security Council. Dr A thought we had done quite right. He was glad to know the truth, for the Belgians had already started to complain. I reminded him that the Belgians never <u>consulted</u> their NATO allies before throwing their hand in over the Congo. They merely <u>informed</u> them. Dr A agreed . . . .

11 August

. . . . We met at 11am. Dr A asked what had happened at the 'experts' meeting last night and today. Ld Home explained, <u>very simply and clearly</u> – von Brentano agreed . . . . His officials (who are clearly now alarmed and want to pull the Chancellor back) tried to make objections. Carstens (who is 'sold out' to the <u>Orthodox European</u> doctrines and has been rapidly promoted in the German Foreign Office on this account, much to Scherpenberg's disgust) tried his best. He is rather a young favourite of the Chancellor. But Dr A shut him up. I then asked Ld H to recapitulate the agreed procedure over the next few weeks – informal interchange of ideas between us both – British–German; then more detailed but still informal talks in Paris when the OEEC meets – in its new form.[77] At this point, we hope to have French experts with us . . . .

All this was very clearly set out by For Secy (who has clearly made quite an impression already) Then the communiqué was agreed and we adjourned for luncheon. This took place in the British Embassy, with the Germans as our guests. The atmosphere was good. Erhard (who had heard the accounts of the meeting this morning) was overjoyed. I thought Scherpenberg and Carstens looked pretty sour. Von Brentano was happy – but he always agrees with everyone in turn and is a nonentity. But the Germans are <u>all</u> (whichever side they're on) wondering what the French will say and in great alarm as to how firmly and brutally they will say it. For – after all – the Germans are tied up, hand and foot, by the Treaty of Rome. So we can never make progress unless we can get French good-will. This is really a matter of

---

77. Originally a purely European organisation, it was joined by the US and Canada and, in September 1961, became the OECD.

whether or not we can ever do a personal deal with de Gaulle. For – in present circumstances – what he says, counts – and nothing else . . . .

After luncheon, we left for Wahn airport. Again, I drove alone with the Chancellor. He seemed very relaxed. He liked the communiqué and had told von Eckardt to maximise, rather than minimise, its importance. Dr A regards the chief significance of what he has done to lie in an attack on 'the Professors of the Brussels bureaucracy' and an effort to get European affairs back into the hands of the Governments . . . .

12 August

. . . . The power strike situation was reported to me at intervals. The unions asked 6d per hour (the sum calculated to bring the lowest paid workers to £10 a week) The 'nationalised employers' offered 2½d. After some thought and consultation with the Ministries of Power and Labour I authorised 3d – on which a settlement was reached late tonight . . . .

13 August

. . . . The American Govt have suddenly given up trying about the H-Test conference in Geneva – or rather, it looks as if the Atomic Energy Authority have beaten the State Dept and the President has thrown his hand in. (We hear that McCone has inspired the *New York Times* to attack Herter, wh has naturally made Herter very indignant) Anyway, I have sent a telegram yesterday to the President, an urgent plea to try to save the Conference . . . .

14 August (Sunday)

Stayed in bed till luncheon. Read and worked – and dozed! The Congo situation is very bad. Still worse is the news from Accra. Nkrumah is playing with fire. He has now got Russians in considerable numbers and Russian aeroplanes, which are beginning to oust the RAF. There is talk of a 'Pan African' army – Ghana, Guinea, and now Egypt! . . . .

17 [August][78]

Great picture hanging at Admiralty House. I think it will be a very nice place to live when – if ever – the Office of Works get it ready. They have been, so far, dilatory and maddeningly incompetent – except the picture expert, who is good. Sir Norman Brook came in about some minor questions. I settled messages to the Commonwealth Prime

---

78. Macmillan actually wrote 'April'.

Ministers about admitting Nigeria. The only message wh required rather careful drafting was to South Africa.

The Turkish ambassador (Birgi) came to say goodbye. He is being transferred to Paris. I am very sorry, for he has been very helpful throughout – esp over Cyprus. He thought that the new military govt in Turkey would hold elections in 9 or 10 months. He expected Inonu to get back and Menderes and Zorlu to be forced out of politics – but probably not imprisoned. He was not so sure about the former President. Menderes made the mistake of relying entirely on the support of the peasants (which he had) and neglecting altogether the towns, the professions, the 'intellectuals' and so forth. The foreign policy would not change at all. The policy of economic expansion wd be reduced by 20% or so – nearer to what cd be managed . . . .

18 August

. . . . Left Kings Cross at 11.50 for Leeds. John Wyndham came with me. We drove to Bolton Abbey. A lovely evening – after some heavy storms. I hope, at last, to start a real holiday. Of course, I am 'in charge' – with John W. and secretaries etc. But I think they will [try] to keep from me all but really important decisions.

The people at Kings X and Leeds stations were very friendly. Outside Leeds there was an anti-H Bomb demonstration of a dozen or so youths with placards. The only good one was 'I'm not a grouse. I want to live!'

21 August (Sunday)

. . . . Congo still very confused. I have had a long letter from Nkrumah and have sent off an even longer reply. On the whole, he is trying to behave sensibly. But I fear the sinister influence of Bing. Bing lost his seat at Hornchurch. He is now Attorney General at Accra. He is a Communist or at least a fellow-traveller and hates England and English life and ways. (I think he is of a very mixed descent himself)[79] Against him, we have the useful influence of General Alexander (Chief of Staff of Ghana's army) and our High Commissioner, Snelling – who is much liked by Nkrumah . . . .

---

79. Geoffrey Bing, Labour MP for Hornchurch 1945–55, was born in Ulster. He became Nkrumah's Attorney-General in 1957 and remained as Nkrumah's adviser from 1961 until the latter's overthrow in 1966.

24 August

.... The shipping strike seems to be more or less finishing; but the temper at Liverpool is bad. Poor old Sir Thomas Yates – one of the nicest and most sensible of the TU leaders – seems to have been the real target of the rebel strikers. There is an extraordinary interview given by Cousins to a Yugoslav paper, and copied in today's *Express*, wh shd do the Labour Party a good deal of harm.

Equities are rising again – quite a boom. But I fear the base is not really sound – unless we can, by hook or crook, increase exports. I have sent Reggie Maudling a minute about this, and hope to arrange a meeting with him next week. The Treasury – or rather the Inland Revenue – are rather sticky about any relaxation of their strict rules. But I feel we must <u>encourage</u> instead of discouraging, people to go abroad on business – and even to take their wives! (This is specially frowned on by I.R. It is easier to charge a mistress than a wife to 'business expenses') ....

15 September

.... 3pm. Minister of Defence and CDS (Mountbatten). The former is learning rapidly and works hard. Poor Dickie M talks all the time and has (with all his charm) a very limited mental capacity. I fear the Americans are finding this out. The Cabinet this morning approved facilities for Polaris in the Clyde, on terms wh are (I fear) not what I originally hoped, but wh may not work out too badly ....

5.30–7.45. Selwyn Lloyd, new Chancellor of Exr. I was very glad to find him in capital form, full of confidence, buoyant, and with many practical ideas. A great contrast to the last few months of poor Don Quixote, his predecessor. Derry Amory was absolutely splendid for two years. After that, he was somehow worn out. The truth is that, unless one has the right temperament, the strain is too great for either a For Secy or a Chancellor, year after year. After all, we shall soon have had <u>ten</u> years of it – or rather the few survivors of Churchill's 1951 Govt will have had this long experience ....

16 September

.... [A] very long defence committee. We had a long wrangle about the need for a new <u>radar</u> system (£60 million odd) We agreed to the new aeroplane to replace the Canberra (90m for development over 5 years) It (TSR2, I think it is called) is said to be a wonderful aeroplane, ahead of all the world. We have heard that before. At any rate, it is

the Vickers group, in wh I have the most confidence.[80] We postponed
decision on radar till next week. I have asked for figures of possible
sales abroad, based on actual sales of our present (much less advanced)
radar systems . . . .

21 September

I came to Chequers last night, to work on a speech for U.N. if (as I
expect) I have to go . . . . The position in NY is fantastic. Mr
K[hrushchev]'s arrival in soaking rain did at least damp down the
hostile demonstrations . . . .

22 September

. . . . Cabinet at 11.30. Most of the ministers thought I shd go. But
Hare, Eccles, and one or two were doubtful. I explained my own
doubts and hesitations. I did not honestly feel that I cd achieve very
much. But Ld Home has strongly advised that I shd go – he felt it
necessary, if only to rally the West. He strongly advised making the
announcement today – before Kruschev's speech. My original plan had
been to wait to hear Mr K's line. But For Secy put (by telegram) some
very cogent arguments against this. 'If it's a fairly good speech, you
will have to say so, and it will seem as if you are trying forthwith to
negotiate. If it's a bad speech, you may not be able to go – or you can
only say that you are going to answer it. If you announce yr intention
of going to the Assembly today, you can leave it there, whatever Mr K
may say tomorrow'. So it was decided . . . .

   Henry Brooke told the Cabinet (what he told me last night at
Chequers) about rents. Ministers seemed to feel that we cd hold the
situation, but we wd be helped by some strengthening of the landlord's
duty to do repairs . . . .

24 September

Mr K[hrushchev]'s speech – 18000 words, 3 hours – has certainly not
disappointed his admirers. Unfortunately, Dr Nkrumah (Ghana)

---

80. Work on this Tactical Strike and Reconnaissance aircraft had begun in 1957
    and a government order was formally placed in October 1960. However, a
    project bedevilled with both technical and political difficulties was eventually
    cancelled by the Labour government in April 1965. Contrary to Macmillan, its
    development was jointly by Vickers and English Electric, who had come
    together to form the British Aircraft Corporation on 1 January 1960.

played into his hands with a demagogic speech about Africa. However, Dr N had the sense to support U.N. and the Secretary General.

Mr K's speech was directed to excite and inflame the Afro-Asians. He demanded immediate 'freedom' for <u>all</u> colonial territories; he attacked Eisenhower and America with extreme bitterness. He attacked Hammarskjöld and demanded the abolition of the office of the post of Secy General and the substitution of 'an executive of 3'.[81] U.N. shd leave New York. He then proposed a Summit in a few months time to 'deal primarily with Berlin' . . . .

2 October (Sunday)

It has not been possible to write every day in the diary. The pace has been too hot. We left London Airport on Sunday morning, in an RAF Comet (Sept 25th) We stopped in Iceland, where I was met by the PM of that country – a very nice man, but rather an ineffective one. We lunched alone together, and he explained at great length why it was impossible for him to make any concessions to us over the 12 mile fishing controversy. He has only a majority of 2 or 3, and a coalition govt – with the Socialists. The Communists were the strong opposition, determined to use this fishing dispute as an instrument for getting rid of the American base and Iceland out of NATO. I tried to impress on him the arguments he cd use.

a) He had got us to accept 12 miles as the final settlement. All we asked for was a 'fading out' period. Norway was going to concede us 10 years. We wd accept 5 years from Iceland. Why have a bitter conflict over this. He cd claim to have done <u>twice</u> as well as Norway.

b) We cd prob[ably] make some further concessions about particular areas <u>within</u> the band 6–12 miles, wh wd help him.

c) We cd give some economic help to his fishing and merchandising of fish.

I did not feel very encouraged by our talk. The Icelandic PM was a nice old boy, but clearly a weak man in a weak position. I hope, however, that the interview may have done some good . . . .

<u>Wednesday</u> 28 I had breakfast with Mr Nehru. I found him in a depressed and rather petulant mood. Personally charming as ever; but

---

81. His claim was that Hammarskjöld was essentially defending Western interests in Congo, and his alternative was a tripartite executive to represent the Western, Soviet and non-aligned groups.

recent events have shaken him. He blames Hammarskjöld about Congo – rather unfairly. He is very anti-Belgian.

I called on Nasser – Ld Home came with me. The talk was rather formal but friendly. N, of course, denies any responsibility for the worsening position in Middle East. But he seemed to want our relations to return to normal.

Thursday 29. Speech to U.N. Assembly. A great relief to get it over. I felt it 'went well'. The delegation seemed to like the manner of delivery, even if they did not all agree the matter. The Americans were very pleased – so were the Commonwealth (as a whole) The 'neutrals' were impressed . . . .

6 October

Arrived London airport at 2pm (GMT) Cabinet at 4pm. Apart from my account of New York to my colleagues, only two items remained from their morning meeting. The railway strike is still a danger. I had a talk with Ld Mills, Hare (Labour) and Marples (Transport) and we decided to ask Brian Robertson to try more negotiation. It seems absurd to put the whole country to the loss and trouble of a railway strike on a dispute about 2/- a week for 40,000 men.

Then long talks with Sandys and Macleod about Welensky. We finally drafted telegrams intended to meet some of his points. No doubt the Monckton Commission has gone beyond the strict terms of reference in one respect – the suggestion of a possible right to 'secede' at some future date in some undefined circumstances. But the main recommendation should please Welensky for it declares that 'Federation' must continue in everyone's interest . . . .

12 October

The Monckton Commission's report was published last night.[82] The British press gives it a very favourable reception. Welensky has fired off his protest against this going outside the terms of reference by their suggestion of 'secession' in certain future circumstances. But he has modified the terms of his original statement and I think it better that

---

82. It recommended greater representation, though not a majority of seats, for Africans in the Federal Assembly, constitutional advance in Northern Rhodesia with an African majority similar to that agreed for Nyasaland and, reflecting levels of African distrust, the right for territories to secede.

he should 'blow off steam' at once. We issued our statement, in wh we admit frankly that he has a case on this particular issue.

The Colonial Secy had a great success this morning at Scarborough (Conservative Conference) wh is gratifying.

King Hussein to luncheon. Poor man, he is brave but I fear for him. There is no doubt that his life is threatened, either directly by Egyptian agents or indirectly by Cairo stirring up trouble in Jordan . . . .

18 October

The Chancellor of the Exr and I want to appoint Sir Oliver Franks to be Governor of the Bank. Cobbold wants Ld Harcourt or Ld Cromer. But we feel sure that Franks is the best man. Cromer might well be the next – he is quite young. There is a bit of a struggle, but it will work out all right.

The foolish strike at London docks is at last over – not without my having to intervene at the end to prevent some foolish attempts by some employers to change the method of recruitment without waiting for the enquiry. This, of course, wd be reckoned as 'victimisation' and the strike wd continue or be enlarged . . . .

26 October

We had rather a difficult Cabinet yesterday morning about the whole complex of Old Age Pensions, Contributions, Health Stamps, free drugs for private patients etc. After a long discussion, at wh a great variety of different views were expressed, I thought it best to defer a decision for a day or two.

Chancellor of Exr wants to put down Bank Rate by ½% – 6% to 5½%. I have agreed. President of BofT was naturally worried about Hire Purchase restrictions. But these must stay for the present . . . .

A terrible spate of speeches has to be got ready. Cambridge on Friday; Bromley on Saturday; HofCommons on Tuesday. It takes a lot of time, and time has to be somehow found between engagements, or late at night . . . .

28 October

The Crown Prince of Morocco came at 11.30. For Secy was with me. The Prince is very plausible (in beautiful French) but I was not sure how far he was trying to put pressure on us to intervene with the French in Algeria by the obvious dangers involved in Russian or

Chinese aid to FLN (rebels, from the French point of view – a government from the Moroccans)

It looks as if Kennedy is going to win the Presidential election. He seems definitely to be gaining ground. This will mean quite a lot of readjustment of our [policy] in Washington and thinking out the best way to get on with a very different administration. On the whole, I feel that Kennedy and Johnson will be more friendly than Nixon, Cabot Lodge, Dillon etc – that is, the Republicans without Eisenhower. But it does mean new methods, and perhaps (after a short interval) a new ambassador . . . .

To Cambridge, by train, arriving about 6pm. A very pleasant dinner in Trinity, with the officers – mostly undergraduates – of the Cambridge University Conservative Association, wh seems to be flourishing. Mrs Castle (Labour: unilateralist) has a meeting of the Labour Club. She wrote to suggest a joint meeting and a debate – so that the audience could hear 'both sides of the argument'. In declining to accept this plan, I told her that I thought that in the present political situation the expression 'both sides of the argument' shewed a somewhat superficial approach. I expanded this a little in my speech. The audience (about 1000) was a splendid one – quick and attentive. We had ½ hour questions, wh was very good too . . . .

29 October

My last sitting with James Gunn, at his studio in Hampstead. He has certainly painted a very good likeness and a fine picture – in the academic style. It is for the Carlton Club. One of the bronze heads of me which Mr Nemon (who did the large head and shoulders of me for the Oxford Union) has come. He is sending another. He is certainly a very good artist.

Young Conservative meeting at Bromley at 3.45. There was a very rowdy element of Empire Loyalists – but the meeting was not broken up. It was quite interesting for me to be back with 'heckling' – but it is, in this case, of a rather stupid, repetitive kind . . . .

30 October

Stayed in bed all morning, very exhausted. Worked on yet another speech – for Parl on Tuesday. I have made too many speeches lately. Each one (because of the Press etc) needs the most careful preparation.

The new appointments to the Govt include Julian Amery (to succeed Geordie Ward as SofS Air) and Andrew Devonshire (to Under

Secy Commonwealth) At the same time, Maurice has been chosen to move the address. So there has been a little mild fun in the newspapers about 'nepotism' and 'happy families', but all in a very good tone. I think everyone recognises that Maurice has suffered, rather than gained, by being my son. A duke, of course, is always fair game . . . .

31 October

. . . . That poor creature, Oliver Franks, has finally refused the Governorship of the Bank. He has no fire in his Liberal, academic, belly. Kim Cobbold (the Governor) is, of course, triumphant. We shall now try Lord Cromer (at present in Washington) . . . .

4.30. Sir P Dixon (now ambassador in Paris) He thinks de Gaulle friendly, but living in a strange, pessimistic world – of resignation and philosophical detachment. He cannot understand our worry about 6s and 7s and will not help – except for a very big price. We can only await a new American President . . . .

1 November

The State opening by the Queen went off, as usual, without any hitch. H[er] M[ajesty] read the speech beautifully. The traditional ceremony was carried out with great dignity.

Maurice (Macmillan) moved the address, in an admirable speech. After all the talk in the newspapers about my 'family' appointments (Julian Amery, Andrew Devonshire etc) he delighted the House by his opening sentence 'as the only back bench member of the family'. Gaitskell was quite generous and even gracious. My speech was chiefly about [the] Monckton report (Central Africa) UN Assembly, disarmament, and the agreement with U.S. to possible facilities in the Clyde for Polaris submarines. The speech went off well enough, but after I had finished I found I had made a stupid mistake about my exchanges with Sir Roy Welensky. Instead of saying that my assurances to him were 'exactly in the same sense as the words I used in the House' (wh was on my notes and in a version wh I had telegraphed to Sir R W) I said 'exactly in the same words' – wh was wrong and made no sense. I telegraphed to Sir R W about this and I will put it right by a personal statement in the House tomorrow.

2 November

. . . . Harold Caccia at 5. He seems to think that Kennedy will now win, unless there is a swing back to Nixon thro' loyalty to Ike. I do not feel that K will be bad for us. He will perhaps have ideas and be attracted by ideas . . . .

A bad telegram from Welensky when I got home. He does <u>not</u> think my speech fair and will reply next week, saying that he is willing for our telegrams to be published 'to let the world judge'.[83] It is queer that Ld Salisbury asked for publication in the HofLords this afternoon.

3 November

I cannot wait to be 'challenged' by Sir R W. I have telegraphed offering to publish the relevant telegram <u>forthwith</u> (i.e. on Monday) but asking him to think again before the first breach is made in the personal and confidential telegrams between Commonwealth Prime Ministers. . . . I do not think publication will injure me. After all, <u>I</u> did not alter or extend the terms of reference. It was because I did not do so, that the Labour Party refused to be represented on the Commission. I am not responsible for what the Commission actually did or the way in wh they interpreted their terms of reference. I cd only have suppressed the report wh wd have been unthinkable . . . .

5 November

. . . . There is some trouble about Polaris (chiefly due to the folly of the State Department spokesman) but I think opinion is generally favourable to what we have done.

Gaitskell has been re-elected Leader of the Parl[iamentary Labour] Party by a 2 to 1 vote. Nevertheless, to have 81 MPs of his own party vote against him, cannot be said to be a comfortable position . . . .

7 November

. . . . Sir Roy W now does <u>not</u> want to publish the letters wh passed between us. I am glad, because I think it wd be a very bad precedent. But Ld Salisbury has revived the charge of 'bad faith' in a letter to *The Times* (if not directly at least by innuendo) wh is rather a bore, as I cannot now answer it by publishing the text . . . .

9 November

. . . . After meetings with Commonwealth and Colonial Secys (about a new department for <u>placing</u> experts and technicians in Commonwealth

---

83. Welensky threatened to publish the exchange of notes with Macmillan in 1959 agreeing the terms of reference for the Monckton Commission.

as well as Colonial countries)[84] and a lot of talk about the eternal problem of Welensky and Whitehead, D and I had 80 MPs and wives to tea . . . .

11 November

. . . . Kennedy's election to the Presidency (wh was announced on Wednesday afternoon) now seems to have been by an extraordinarily small majority of votes – about ½%. But he carried New York and one or two other states with a large number of electoral votes. I sent him a short congratulatory letter. I have for some weeks been trying to work out a method of influencing him and working with him. With Eisenhower, there was the link of memories and a long friendship. I will have to base myself now on trying to win him by <u>ideas</u>. I have started working on a memorandum wh I might send him – giving a broad survey of the problems wh face us in the world . . . .

13 November

I motored to London from Blenheim[85] last night. We had the usual cenotaph ceremony[86] – the Queen, the Duke of Edinburgh, the Duke of Gloucester, the Cabinet, the High Commissioners etc. Poor Mr Gaitskell always seems a little conscious on these occasions that he had no medals. However, he supported the war from Dr Dalton's side, in the Ministry of Economic Warfare[87] . . . .

14 November

I held a meeting in my room at HofC on the future of Nationalised Transport. We now have had the reports of Sir I Stedeford and his team.[88] Altho' they (the 4 of them) are not themselves agreed on all questions, yet their reports have proved most helpful. Marples (helped by Ld Mills) has now produced a plan and the object of this meeting

---

84. This was the Department of Technical Co-operation, established in 1961.
85. The seat of the dukes of Marlborough.
86. The annual national act of remembrance to the dead of the world wars and other conflicts at the cenotaph on Whitehall.
87. Gaitskell had tried to join the Army but had been directed into government service as an economist.
88. Following the Guillebaud Report, Macmillan had set up this inquiry under Stedeford, assisted by C. F. Kearton, Richard Beeching and Henry Benson, to review the extensive operations of the BTC.

(at wh Chancellor of Exr was present) was to get it into final shape for Cabinet. The chief point of discussion was whether the Transport Commission is to survive at all. In the end, we all came down in favour of <u>autonomous</u> groups – 1) Railway Board (with 6 semi-autonomous regions) 2) docks 3) London Passenger 4) Canals 5) Holding Company for various separate concerns – e.g. Thomas Cook. These shd (with a chairman and one or two other members, perhaps including a trade union representative) form a transport coordinating or advisory ctee. But it should have no real power. The financial proposals are drastic but sensible and will mean writing off £1200m or so as lost . . . .

15 November
The trade figures for October are alarming. £122m gap, from £76m in Sept. How far this is due to dock strike we don't yet know. But the bad trend is there. It is beginning to get really dangerous and I am considering by what machinery we can best study and grasp the situation. If it goes on (altho' obscured by the continued <u>inflow</u> of money) it will bring us into a <u>critical</u> position and might even wreck the Government. A financial crisis wd be hard to ride again – at least for me.

A great row is developing about the offer of Ford US to buy all the shares (about 30% of the whole) of Ford UK. The usual anti-Americanism is developing on the Opposition side of the House, with the usual aberration of the usual people on our side. Of course, it is absurd for us, who have such immense overseas investments and are adding to them all the time, to take this 'nationalistic' stand. Ld Beaverbrook's papers – the *Express* and the *Evening Standard* – are fanning the flames. I must admit that I wd have been very upset if Ford US had instructed Lazards to <u>sell</u> their holdings in Ford UK. But if they want to buy (to the tune of £130m) they must feel confident about the future of Britain and their British business. The argument that they will close down or reduce the output of Ford UK is rather difficult to sustain, since they can do this already, without any new investment, because they own 55% of the Ford UK shares and control in U.S. about 70%. The Chancellor of the Exr and the President of the BofT seem quite confident that they ought to allow the bid to be made. It is of course for the shareholders to decide whether they think the price high enough or not . . . .

16 November
PM of Malaya (Tunku Abdul Rahman) came at 11 and stayed an

hour. He is going to agree to Cyprus joining and S Africa remaining in the Commonwealth. I am much relieved. But John Diefenbaker is going to be troublesome about S Africa. He is taking a 'holier than thou' attitude, wh may cause us infinite trouble. For if the 'whites' take an anti-S Africa line, how can we expect the Brown and Blacks to be more tolerant.

Luncheon. National Union of Manufacturers. Speech. 800 in audience. Not a good speech, but well enough received . . . .

Voting is taking place today in a number of by-elections. I think most of them will go all right – except Bolton, about wh we are anxious. However, it is rather splendid that the Labour and Liberal attack on the Conservative candidate at Bolton is directed against him a) not having been to a public school b) on being non-u!![89] The Tory Party has certainly evolved in the last 40 years.

We are going to have some trouble in the House with the Criminal [Justice] Bill. Some (but I think not too many) of our chaps want to re-introduce Corporal Punishment. But all the 'penologists' seem to be against this.

17 November

We have won all the by-elections, by comfortable margins except Bolton East.[90] Here we expected a close fight. We held it by 500 odd votes, having lost another 500 of our own votes to an 'Independent' Conservative candidate. The Labour vote stood up well and Byers (Liberal) was well down. This is very good. In the agricultural and suburban seats, however, the Liberals took a lot of Labour votes, and finished second in 4 places. A very good result for us, by and large.

A long Cabinet. We agreed to the Ford sale (subject to certain guarantees) No one seemed in any doubt as to what it was right to do. Police pay – another £20m (half on taxes, half on rates) . . . .

Jock Whitney came and gossiped about Jack Kennedy and his character and probable ways of doing business. The father will (he

---

89. The terms 'u' and 'non-u' were coined to describe upper-class as opposed to other modes of speaking by Alan Ross in 1954 and popularised by Nancy Mitford.

90. On 16 November the Tories held Mid-Bedfordshire, Carshalton, Ludlow, Petersfield and the marginal seat of Bolton East, the former Liberal MP C. F. Byers coming third.

thinks) now come to the fore.[91] Jack K has just appointed his father's business stooge and manager to a very important place.[92] However, he has re-appointed Allen Dulles, wh is good. For A.D. is a very good friend and gives us a very good position in the intelligence field. K must be a strange character – according to J.W. obstinate, sensitive, ruthless and highly sexed.

Moroccan M[inister] of Foreign Affairs and his ambassador called. They want to take over Mauritania (wh becomes independent [from France] on Nov 28)[93] What we are expected to do about it is obscure . . . .

26 November
Sir Roy Welensky came at 6.30. We had a good talk after dinner. He was most friendly, tho' rather pessimistic. He in effect withdrew all his accusations (or imputations) of bad faith against me, altho' he still feels very bitter against Ld Monckton. He cannot answer the question 'Why did all the Europeans from Rhodesia sign the report?' . . . .

28 November
Luncheon and talk with P.M. Abubakar (of Nigeria) He is a fine man. But he will not look after Nigerian affairs. He runs all over the world, talking to people about Algeria, about Morocco, about the Congo. He also talked to us about Kenya and the need to release Kenyatta. However, he is so courteous and charming that no one can resent it.

Last Friday, I entertained to dinner (before returning to Chequers) Senators Lyndon Johnson and Fulbright. The first is Vice President Elect – a Texan, an acute and ruthless 'politician', but not (I wd judge) a man of any intellectual power. The second is very able and already a powerful figure in 'foreign affairs' . . . .

---

91. Joseph Kennedy had been US ambassador to Britain 1938–40, during which time his family made their mark in British society. In contrast to his father's pro-appeasement views, Jack had gone on to write *Why England Slept* (London: Sidgwick and Jackson, 1940), whilst his sister Kathleen (d. 1948) married Macmillan's nephew William, Lord Hartington shortly before he was killed in action in 1944.

92. Although Kennedy's father is known to have been asked to suggest nominees for Treasury Secretary and to have influenced the appointments of McNamara and Rusk, it is not clear to whom Macmillan is referring.

93. The Moroccans claimed a historic title to Mauritania, only dropped by the Crown Prince (as King Hassan II, 1961–99), in 1969.

30 November

. . . . At the Cabinet yesterday we had two hours and a half on the economic situation. It was an extremely interesting discussion, in which everyone took part. The situation is really baffling. We are borrowing short and lending long; exports are stable or falling, imports leaping up – yet the £ is strong and money – some 'hot', some genuine investment (e.g. Ford) keeps flowing in. 'Everyone believes in Britain – except the British'. The Press is lousy and does (with the exception of *D.T.* and *Yorkshire Post*) nothing but harm. *Times* is pontifical and defeatist.

The 'popular' press (tired of Gaitskell and Labour Party disputes) has started to attack me violently and 'below the belt'. Ld Beaverbrook has clearly given the order – for the *Daily* and *Sunday Express*, as well as the *Evening Standard* have started a campaign – against me and my family, against Macmillan & Co, against Dorothy and her relations etc etc! I don't think it matters very much. It is (after so much flattery) good for the soul.

I worked today on the results of the Economic Cabinet. I have asked for a number of enquiries on different aspects of the Balance of Payments problem, to see what steps we can take to reduce Imports. I will do a committee on increasing exports myself.

1 December

'Blue Streak' – shall we go on alone with space research, to the tune of £15 (fifteen) millions a year.

'Polaris' – how are [we] to scotch the ill-thought out and dangerous American plan to fill Europe with these dangerous weapons.

'Skybolt' – are the Americans going to let us down, and (if so) what can we do?[94]

All these, and other problems, fill the day. But little progress is made. The Congo gets worse and worse. Lumumba (who is a Communist stooge as well as a witch-doctor) has escaped from Leopoldville and is obviously making for Stanleyville.[95] There he has his own

---

94. Macmillan had written to Eisenhower as early as 25 October 1960 expressing concern (a) at whether Skybolt would be cancelled and (b) at the way in which the Polaris deal was being linked to an overall NATO MRBM project.

95. Now Kinshasa and Kisangani respectively. Lumumba had been dismissed as Prime Minister on 14 September after he turned to the Soviets for support against Katanga, and then held under house arrest. Stanleyville, a centre of his

clansmen. He will doubtless set up his standard there and get Russian help (we know, by secret channels, that this move has been plotted by Nkrumah and Nasser – a pretty pair!)

3 December
A tragic day! After a terribly stormy night – with an almost terrifying gale shaking the whole house and throwing down trees in the Park – we had a drenching rain _and_ wind . . . .

Lumumba has been caught by Col Mobutu's troops and brought back to Leopoldville. This is good news; but I fear that they will kill him (and perhaps eat him!) wh will bring discredit on the Congo Govt.[96]

4 December
. . . . Got back to London at 6pm and met the two Secretaries of State [Commonwealth and Colonies], to discuss the 'state of play' for the Central Africa Conference. After negotiations yesterday and today, it looks as if the Conference may _start_ tomorrow. When it will end, I cannot tell – very probably after 3 or 4 days, with an ultimatum by the Secessionists . . . .

5 December
I opened the Conference with a short formal speech (Press; Radio; T.V. etc) at Lancaster House this morning at 10.45 (having arrived at 10am for 'coffee-housing', where I saw the leading delegates, including Dr Banda) Afterwards, the Press etc left, and we settled procedural and other matters. To my surprise, all went off agreeably . . . .

6 December
Sir Hugh Foot came in this morning. I offered him a job (which I hope he will take) in the U.K. delegation to the United Nations. Now that 'Colonisation' is such a constant source of trouble and attack to us, I think he cd do some useful work. He seemed attracted.

PQs were scarcely reached – another protest and demand that my questions shd start at 3.15. I hope still to avoid having to agree. In

---

support, subsequently became the site of a Lumumbist government led by Antoine Gizenga.

96. Lumumba was sent to Katanga on 17 January 1961, where he was speedily and covertly executed.

some ways it would suit me; but I think it will only lead to fewer and fewer questions being got through and longer and longer supplementaries . . . .

7 December
We had a very long Defence Ctee this afternoon and made some real progress. But it is <u>very</u> hard to save money . . . .

8 December
10.30–1. Cabinet. A great variety of subjects. I think 8 items. As usual, every problem is more or less insoluble!

The situation in Laos is bad. The Americans are anxious to intervene overtly as well as covertly. They back a certain Phoumi – we, I don't quite know why, prefer Phouma.[97] Outside this foolish internecine war, the Communists are waiting hopefully for their chance. The Thais want intervention by the SEATO powers. It is easy to see the dangers. China must react and perhaps Russia. Yet if Laos goes, what chance is there for SE Asia? . . . .

9 December
9.45am. Cabinet. We got approval (after 1½ hours really searching work – most remarkable) for the White Paper on Transport. We hope to publish just before Xmas. It is really a bold and constructive scheme . . . .

Luncheon for <u>North</u> Rhodesian delegates (African and European) All still goes well with the Conference up to date, but I heard that later this afternoon Dr Banda stormed out in a rage (and held a 'Press Conference' – wh they all do – Europeans and Africans – on the slightest provocation) It is not thought that he will stay away altogether . . . .

I sent a message to Dr Nkrumah to try to quiet him. I also sent a vigorous telegram to President Eisenhower, to protest against the American decision to vote <u>for</u> a monstrous Afro-Asian resolution at U.N. on 'Colonialism'. Secretary Herter called it 'a most nauseating

---

97. In face of the Communist insurgency of the Pathet Lao, the CIA backed Phoumi as a right-wing strongman. Britain favoured the more conciliatory rule of Phouma, ousted by Phoumi with US support on 13 December. Phouma joined his half-brother, Prince Souphannouvong, the leader of the Pathet Lao, and, with Soviet support, escalated the civil war.

document' – and yet, to curry favour, instructed the Americans to vote for. President replied very quietly, promising to reconsider this decision . . . .

11 December

I have, in some way, strained the muscles in my right foot, wh have swollen very much and I can hardly walk. After a very bad night, I stayed in bed till the doctor came . . . .

A message has come from Chequers to say the party is still going on and they have had a long talk. 'It seems that very little can happen with the main conference until they have had the territorial conference. The three black men[98] seem to think that Federation would be all right if there were acceptable Territorial Governments . . . . This morning they are all going to Church and the Commonwealth Secretary will have a note to show you this evening explaining how things stand' . . . .

The *Sunday Express* has, as its main feature, a bitter, untruthful, and indeed almost hysterical attack on me by Lord Lambton MP. Of course, he is mad. But he is also vain and dishonest. I don't think his views matter much, but taken in conjunction with the stuff now appearing in the rest of Lord Beaverbrook's papers, including the *Evening Standard*, it looks as if he had now definitely given the order to attack me all along the line.

Lord Rothermere's papers (*Daily Mail*: *Evening News* etc) do the same – but for a different reason. Like all the Harmsworths, they only care about money. The *D Mail* and the [London] *Evening News* want to stick to all they can of the readers of the defunct *D Chronicle* and *Star* (which Rothermere has bought) Ld B (to be fair) cares more for spite and mischief than for money . . . .

Arrived at Chequers from B.G. about 6.30. Drinks etc before dinner and after dinner a few little speeches, all very sincere and in good taste. Roy Welensky and Banda both spoke well. I'm afraid Edgar Whitehead is at a disadvantage as a Prime Minister – for he cannot hear, see, or speak. Those present at this strange gathering were HM, Commonwealth Secy, Colonial Secretary, Mr Mills (P.S. to Sandys) Mr Bligh (P.S. to me) Sir Roy Welensky (PM of Federation) Winston Field (opposition leader, Federal Assembly) – a very nice man – Sir Edgar Whitehead (P.M. S Rhodesia) Mr Harper (leader of opposition S Rhodesia – rude, shallow, with Fascist tendencies) Mr

---

98. Banda, Kaunda and Nkomo.

Banda (Nyasaland) Mr Kaunda (N Rhodesia) Mr Joshua Nkomo (S
Rhodesia) Whatever may come of it, the 'week-end' has certainly been
worth while. Many of the guests had not known each other at all. Dr
Banda and Duncan Sandys read the 1st and 2nd lessons – wh was
thought quite symbolic.

12 December

. . . . After all our efforts, the 3 chief African leaders have 'done the
dirty' on us. Without any intimation of their intention, they 'walked
out' of the Federation Conference at the end of this afternoon's meeting
– this time, as they said in their respective Press Conferences and TV
interviews 'for good'. After talking over the situation with the two
Secretaries of State, I agreed to put out a statement from HMG
'postponing' the Territorial conferences until the situation is clearer.
This, of course, Dr Banda doesn't mind – for the Nyasaland constitution is agreed and elections take place in the Spring. But the N
Rhodesian and S Rhodesian Territorial conferences are much desired
by the Africans. So this move may perhaps bring them to their senses.
The real trouble is that the Africans are vain and childish. Like
children, they easily get excited. Also the Press and TV do infinite
harm in flattering their vanity.

13 December

I had a luncheon arranged for the Nyasaland group – 3 or 4 Europeans
and 6 or 7 Africans – including Dr Banda. It seemed very unlikely that
they wd turn up – but they did, and brought along another African
who had not been invited! We had a very agreeable party. At the end,
I preached them a little sermon, wh they seemed to take in good part.

The official Opposition put down a motion censuring – or at least
criticising – our defence policy. But the manoeuvre did not turn out
very well for them. The debate became one between the unilateralists
and the multilateralists in the Labour Party. Gaitskell wound up, but I
proposed not to join in, so I got Ted Heath to do it – wh he did very
well. The division is curious. Over 50 of the anti-Gaitskellites sat
defiantly in their seats below the gangway[99] (including Shinwell) and
refused to vote for the Opposition motion. It is thought that 73
'abstained', being in the House or available. This is a very large

---

99. Beyond the aisle on the opposition benches further from the Speaker's chair.

number and I remember nothing like it since the vote wh led to Neville Chamberlain's fall from power in 1940.

14 December

The Press today is concentrated on Gaitskell's position. My own feeling is that he will go on and not resign. After all, an Opposition is not like a Government.

Sandys and Macleod are trying hard to restore the position for the various conferences. But it will not be easy, and we must be careful of European opinion. Central Africa is really our Algeria, on a smaller scale.

De Gaulle's visit to Algeria has proved a bold but tragic failure. Meanwhile, Congo gets worse. The Russians are trying to set up a supporter of Lumumba in Stanleyville, and we may soon find U.N. impotent and a sort of African Korea developing. In Laos, there is confusion, and danger of civil war on an increasing scale. What a world! . . . .

15 December

Cabinet was to have been at 11am, but I put it off till noon. Sir Roy Welensky, Sir E Whitehead, and the two Secretaries of State came round at 10am and we argued at considerable length. Sir E.W. (without telling Welensky or Sandys) has sent a letter to Nkomo (the chief African figure in S Rhodesia) dismissing him from his delegation. This is because Nkomo walked out of the main conference. But it also prevents him from attending the S Rhodesian Territorial Conference – as he wd prob like to do . . . .

Dinner at the Other Club. Max Beaverbrook was in the Chair. Churchill – alas – was absent. Ld Rosebery, Ld Shawcross, Ld de la Warr, were next or opposite me. Pat Hennessy (Fords) was encouraging. He thinks the Americans mean to use the British plant to an ever-increasing extent for the world market.[100]

---

100. Sir Patrick Hennessy was chairman of Ford of Britain, 1956–68. In 1961 the US parent company bought out the minority shareholders in the British subsidiary for £119 million. The plant referred to here is probably Halewood on Merseyside. Prompted by the government's regional policy, Hennessy announced the building of a new motor-manufacturing facility there in February 1960.

I reproved Max for attacking me in all his papers! He promised to reform!

16 December

. . . . Caccia has reported the result of his interview with Kennedy. He wd very much like a meeting with me in Feb or March. I am therefore preparing a letter to be sent to him after the week-end. This _must_ interest him and put out one or two ideas – yet it must not be pompous or lecturing or _too_ radical! I spent the morning on trying my hand at various drafts.

The Governor of the Bank came at 3. He did not seem too much alarmed about the immediate future. But he is apprehensive about the pressure on sterling when the dollar recovers . . . .

17 December

10.30. Lancaster House. Roy Welensky 'wound up' the general debate in a speech wh, tho' hard-hitting, was reasonably fair. He sent me a draft last night and I had persuaded him to omit some of his attacks on the African leaders.[101] Duncan Sandys then summed up for HMG. He gave an admirably balanced account of the various views expressed. He tried to find the point of agreement, as well as of disagreement. Federation is not really objected to by Africans as such but because it is at present run exclusively by Europeans. It is therefore a political problem . . . .

I finished, giving full support to Sandys, and after a few desultory remarks (and one dangerous moment) by some delegates, I adjourned the Conference. Sir Roy W came to luncheon alone – we had a good talk. He is a very attractive man – but like so many heavy, fat, solid-looking characters, strangely mercurial. He cannot refrain from continual attacks on HMG – altho' we are, in fact, almost his only friends . . . .

19 December

. . . . Iain Macleod (Colonial Secy) to luncheon. N Rhodesian Territorial Conference met this morning and will continue this afternoon. It

---

101. Macmillan wrote: 'You make a fine statement, as follows: "I myself am entirely against the whole concept of white domination, though I am also against black domination". Do you add to the nobility of this sentiment by adding the words "which is what most of the nationalist politicians want"?' (DWM: Ms Macmillan, dep. c. 358).

will also sit tomorrow morning and afternoon. This is very good, and largely due to Sir R Welensky's help. S Rhodesian Conference will also meet, and Sir E Whitehead has withdrawn his ban on Mr Nkomo and his African friends. This is still better news . . . .

. . . . Laos is very bad. Congo bad. Iceland – a hope. The American administration has gone mad in its last few weeks – and turned nasty too . . . .

21 December

A long and difficult Cabinet. The Minister of Health wants to make what he calls 'economies' in the Service. As usual, they are not real economies – they are the old stagers – welfare milk, prescription charges, and all the rest. I do not like this 'regressive' taxation very much – nor do some of my colleagues, esp Iain Macleod. But the enormous increase in the Estimates makes one feel that something must be done. We compromised on a scheme to produce £25 million or thereabouts . . . .

Jock Whitney called for a talk. He seemed to think the new President's appointments were 'conservative' – therefore reassuring to him (but, as I did not say, correspondingly depressing to me)

25 December (Christmas Day)

A very happy day. Church at 8am and at 11am. Luncheon of 8 (including my brother Daniel, who is here for the Christmas holiday, having made a wonderful recovery) Tea – 30 in all. Dinner 18. Games etc after dinner. All the children, with wives and husbands, and all the grandchildren were present and well.

26 December

Motored to London, to see Krishna Menon, who alleged that he had been instructed by Nehru to see me. Commonwealth Secy (Sandys) was there. Krishna M was bitter, untruthful, ungenerous, and offensive – worse than usual. I think (and Mrs Pandit agrees) that he is the most evil man alive today. He certainly does this country infinite harm, in India and in New York. Yet, in spite of it all, it is a kind of a 'love hate' complex. It was nice to get home, into a healthy atmosphere, after one of the most disagreeable interviews that I can remember. Congo, Laos, Colonisation – Britain is always wrong. To get back to Birch Grove was like getting into the open air after being in a jungle full of snakes . . . .

28 December

Very interesting telegrams from Moscow. Our new ambassador, Roberts, had a long interview with Mr K[hrushchev] (at the latter's request) He seemed rather run down after his recent illness, but confident and relaxed.

1961 will be a pretty tricky year, for it is quite clear that Mr K means to press the German question.

The Yemen are turning very nasty and trying to eject our ambassador and break off relations, on some trumped-up issue. This, of course, comes from Nasser – and, of course, Saudi Arabia.

It seems pretty clear now that the revolt of the 'Praetorian Guard' agst the Emperor of Abyssinia was got up by the Russians. Happily, the legions were loyal, and the plot failed. We have earned the gratitude of the Emperor for our help in his difficulties[102] . . . .

---

102. A coup led by the Imperial Household Guard broke out on 15 December whilst Emperor Haile Selassie was in Brazil. With British help, particularly in communications, the coup was put down by loyal forces a few days later.

1961

Laos crisis – Northern Rhodesia constitution and the Central African Federation – meeting President Kennedy – sterling crisis – South Africa leaves the Commonwealth – launch of European entry negotiations – the Pay Pause – building of the Berlin wall – continuing crisis in Congo and the death of Dag Hammarskjöld – Commonwealth Immigrants Bill

1 January

. . . . I worked about 7 or 8 hours yesterday, on the memorandum about 'Problems of 1961' wh I am preparing – for my own use and perh for my closest colleagues. I feel that 1961 is going to be a dramatic year, for good or ill[1] . . . .

Trouble in Uganda – of a paradoxical kind. The Buganda want independence under their King as ruler, but <u>not</u> democracy!

The President has sent a strangely hysterical reply to my message about Laos. It looks as if Allen Dulles's policy has been accepted altogether by the State Dept and the President. This is a most dangerous situation for us. If SEATO intervenes (Thais; US; and ourselves) it will cause trouble in India, Malaya and Singapore. If we keep out, and let U.S. do a 'Suez' on their own, we split the alliance. But what is much worse, the Chiefs of Staff do not think that military intervention is really feasible, or likely to be successful . . . .

For Secy came to London tonight. Sir [Fre]Derick Hoyer Millar held a meeting today (Sunday) to consider the SE Asia situation . . . .

For Secy rang up after dinner. He has seen all the F.O. 'experts' and has prepared a draft message to Herter – who is due back in Washington tomorrow. This

1) gives warning that a military expedition may prove a difficult and hazardous enterprise, since the Communists are better placed strategically. At the best, it cd only lead to a Korean situation and partition.

2) Military intervention now will alienate much of Commonwealth and neutral nations.

---

1. This was the paper, eventually entitled 'The Grand Design', prompted by Kennedy's election. It was primarily concerned with international economic as well as military co-operation, not least against Communism. It also helped pave the way for European negotiations, concluding that 'exclusion from the strongest economic group in the civilised world <u>must</u> injure us' (TNA: PREM 11/3325).

3) We ought to try first either a 'fact-finding' ctee from U.N. or the return of the International Commission under the Geneva Treaty.[2] If these fail, we may be driven to a 6 Power Conference (awkward for US because of China)[3]

4) If all fails, we must contemplate military intervention, if we are really convinced there has been 'outside' aggression (the evidence is rather slim)

5) If this is to be an American Suez, undertaken in the last 3 weeks of President E[isenhower]'s power, we will support them. But we want to go through other motions and try other devices first. ((5) was, of course, not put like this in the message!!) . . . .

3 January

. . . . Mrs Pandit told me that she would be giving up her post as High Commissioner in April. She will have done 6½ years. It is sad – for she is a good friend, and she is very sorry to go. But she feels that her brother (Nehru) is lonely and ageing. She wants to be in Delhi to protect him from the machinations of Krishna Menon, whom she hates and fears . . . .

4 January

Foreign Secretary came from Dorneywood[4] at 10am. The Americans and also the Royal Laotian Govt now accept the Commission[5] returning – in principle. But they both suggest conditions wh – if insisted upon – will make it difficult to get the Russians to agree. We discussed and agreed on our line with all the different parties. We hope that the Assembly will today vote into power the new Govt (in effect, Phoumi's) and that perhaps when this is done, Phouma (who is in Cambodia)

---

2. The 1954 settlement of Indo-China brokered by Eden and the Soviet Union.

3. American bitterness at the 'loss' of China to the Communists in 1949 ran deep. A briefing paper for Kennedy's April 1961 meeting with Macmillan warned, 'The UK and other friendly states who speak to us of the "reality" of China must themselves keep a certain "reality" in mind, i.e. the attitudes of the American people, the Congress and the press' (JFKL: NSF 174A). Accordingly, the US continued to refuse to recognise the PRC.

4. Buckinghamshire country house gifted to the government in 1947 and, at the time, the Foreign Secretary's country residence.

5. The International Control Commission, presided over by India, Canada and Poland, which oversaw the Geneva Treaty.

will resign. This will cut away the Russian and Chinese arguments about the 'legal government'. But it is absurd to ask for 'conditions' for the Commission. The terms of reference – based on the Geneva Treaty – are quite adequate for us, and preclude partition. Given any excuse, Kruschev will retreat from the Commission (wh he has publicly asked for) and demand a large international conference. This wd not be so good for us, esp as there wd probably be no truce and the extremists and Communists might get hold of the whole country while the Conference was arguing. If the Americans accept at least an effort to get a political solution before we are driven to a military one, surely it is right not to quibble about 'pre-conditions', but get a Commission and a cease-fire with the minimum delay possible. Harold Caccia has warned us that Kennedy has no intention of getting committed to Eisenhower's plans in these next few weeks. After all, in 17 days he takes over. This rather stiff attitude of his may account for the American administration's considerable change of front in the last day or two.

A very good letter has come from Mr Kennedy. He obviously liked my letter and deals at some length with my ideas. He wd like a meeting at the end of March.

Philip de Zulueta and I worked all the afternoon on my memorandum. He has made some useful additions and amendments. We have also worked out a schedule of action for its discussion, beginning with Sir Norman and Freddy Bishop on Friday morning. It must of course be kept absolutely secret within a small circle, for much in it is dynamite[6] . . . .

5 January

. . . . Africa committee 5–7. Insoluble problems – a little progress on mechanics etc. As regards Central African Federation, the next steps are the Northern Rhodesian Conference on Jan 30 (in London) and the S Rhodesian Conference, wh resumes in Salisbury in the middle of the month. But it will not be easy to get agreement. The Africans will claim a large majority on the Legislative Council. The Europeans will be unwilling to concede even parity within the elected members (there will of course be at least 6 official members and the Governor will also be able to command a majority on the Executive Council)[7] . . . .

---

6. Not least, it envisaged exploring a new relationship with the Six.
7. Four days later Macmillan wrote to Welensky suggesting a Legislative Council

6 January

A useful morning with Sir Norman Brook and Bishop. They read my memorandum and seemed to approve (rather to my surprise) For it is a grand design to deal with the economic, political, and defence problems of the Free World! I shall have to try to get de Gaulle, Adenauer, and Kennedy to agree. But first I must get my colleagues to agree. The first stage is this – to work on the memorandum, with additions and amendments. Then Sir N B will take it to For Secy and Chancellor of Exchequer on Wednesday morning to read. There will be a covering letter from me, and a list shewing what work has been done and what needs to be done on the plan (By the way, I must give it a code name) We will then discuss it together Wednesday afternoon and evening. If they think it is, on the whole, worth going forward, they will shew it to Sir F Hoyer Millar and Sir Frank Lee. Then we will see. Now for my plans. On Jan 28–29 – visit to de Gaulle. Middle of February, visit from Adenauer. March 8–16 or so, Commonwealth Prime Ministers. End of March, visit to West Indies – partly for a little rest, partly for 'cover plan' to help Kennedy. First week in April, visit to Washington. Back April 7 or 8 for final Budget decision (rest of them, Sir F Lee says, can be made before I leave) It is a tremendous programme . . . .

15 January

. . . . I am wrestling with the problem of Dr Fisher's successor.[8] His resignation is to be announced on Tuesday. Dr F is <u>violently</u>, even <u>brutally</u> opposed to Dr Ramsay (Archbp of York) But, altho' I cannot help being influenced by his arguments, I am not altogether persuaded . . . .

16 January

I came up in the afternoon, and saw the Dean of Westminster, Lord

---

for Northern Rhodesia of 30 members, arguing that a 16:14 ratio in favour of Africans needed to be offered to save the conference. This, with nominated members 'should ensure that effective government remains in responsible hands' (DWM: Ms Macmillan dep. c. 358).

8. Until the reforms of 1977 substantially diminished their role, Prime Ministers continued to have considerable potential influence on major Church appointments, in this case to the Archbishopric of Canterbury.

Scarbrough, and the Bishop of Bradford. I am now leaning towards Dr Ramsay.

17 January
A difficult Cabinet at 11am. We are to put on (April 1st) the new Pensions Stamp (£120m) We have decided on a new Health Stamp (£48m) We accepted 2/- instead of 1/- prescription charge (£12m) We accepted the abolition of subsidy on welfare orange juice and codliver oil (£1½m) We accepted increased charges for spectacles and teeth (£2½m) But I tried to steer them off abolishing the subsidy on welfare milk. I think this will be resented both by those who care about children's health etc and by the farmers . . . .

19 January
The great Arch-Episcopal problem is resolved, not without drama, even melodrama.
    . . . . We need now a profound thinker, scholar, Christian apologist.[9] Dr Fisher has been a splendid organiser – an ecclesiastical politician. Now we need a preacher and teacher. He is a 'High' Churchman – but not an extreme Anglo-Catholic. To York, we are sending Dr Coggan (from Bradford) who is also a scholar, but an organiser as well (Dr Fisher pressed very hard for Dr C for Canterbury) Dr C is Evangelical – so we have a nice balance. I wrote to Dr R and also . . . . read him my letter, wh included a request for his view of Dr C's suitability for York (if Dr R himself accepts the move to Canterbury) The next morning, he rang up, accepting. He added that he could think of no one he wd prefer to see at York than Coggan. I then telephoned to C (who was staying at Bishopsthorpe[10] for the York Convocation) and went through the same process. He promised to answer the next morning. I also sent a letter to Dr Fisher, saying what I had done, thanking him for all his kindness and help etc etc. To my astonishment, he sent an angry reply, complaining about not having been consulted about York, as 'unfair to himself and the Church'. The real reason, of course, for his pique is that his advice was not taken on Canterbury. Since he pressed Coggan so hard for the Primacy, it never occurred to me that he wd raise doubts about

---

9. Macmillan had therefore decided to recommend the Archbishop of York, Michael Ramsay, for translation to Canterbury.

10. The seat of the Archbishop of York.

his fitness for York.[11] Anyway, this morning – no message from Dr C. Nor could he be found anywhere. He had left Bishopsthorpe. He was not in Bradford. He had disappeared. Eventually, we had a bright idea. We rang up Lambeth,[12] and discovered that Dr F had sent for Dr C. I spoke to Dr C, who promised his answer by 2pm (altho' he said that it would be favourable, but that he had promised to Dr F to wait until another letter from Dr F had been delivered to me) This arrived at 1.45, and contained a rather grudging retraction. Perhaps, as things now were, it wd be best for Dr C to go to York . . . .

20 January

We have made a small, but useful, concession on Hire Purchase. While retaining 20% and 10% down payment (according to articles) we have extended the period for repayment from 2 to 3 years. Press is favourable . . . .

I had an hour with the Lord Chancellor in the afternoon – chiefly on Africa. We both feel anxious about Kenya. In some ways this is more difficult at home even than Central Africa. People are not yet accustomed to the idea that, sooner or later, we shall have to accept independence in Kenya, and that this must mean African advancement at least to equality with Europeans. 'Sooner or later' – the Colonial Office are thinking in terms of 1964, wh seems to many of us too soon. From the party point of view, Kenya is going to create a big problem. We might even split on it. Ld Salisbury and Ld Lambton could easily rally a 'settler' lobby here of considerable power. The Kenya settlement has been aristocratic and upper middle class (much more than Rhodesia) and has strong links with the City and the clubs. The Lord Chancellor feels that the best bet is [a] Federation of East African territories and this seems also to be the view of the extreme 'European' party – Cavendish-Bentinck and his supporters[13] . . . .

---

11. Macmillan had committed a breach of protocol and, whilst he acknowledged that Fisher doubted Ramsay shared his administrative capabilities, overlooked Fisher's other concern about Ramsay's lack of interest in ecumenism.

12. Lambeth Palace, the London seat of the Archbishop of Canterbury.

13. Sir Frederick Cavendish-Bentinck, Speaker of the Kenyan Legislative Council 1955–60, had formed the Kenya Coalition to contest the reserved European seats at the upcoming first elections featuring a common electoral roll for

I am rather concerned about the condition of the Party in Scotland. The organisation is old-fashioned and semi-feudal. I have decided to call 5 or 6 ministers and Scottish notabilities together for a discussion. James Stuart will, I know, help; but he is now not well enough to be very active. He is still nominally chairman. We had originally intended Alec Home to succeed him.[14] But now that he has gone to the F.O., this plan is impossible . . . .

23 January
Left Chequers at lunch time. We had a really splendid talk – Saturday evening and all Sunday. To my surprise, my plan has won <u>general</u> support from all ministers and departments, altho' all realise its extreme difficulty in execution . . . .

27 January
. . . . Last night there flared up a tremendous row in Salisbury and Lusaka. The Commonwealth Secy arrives at Lusaka this morning, and may help to straighten it out. Sir Roy Welensky has had a bad fit of nerves. He sends me telegrams which are rude and untruthful. He agreed in London to the principles wh shd underlie constitutional advance in Northern Rhodesia – that is 'parity' or 'near-parity' on Legislative Council between Europeans and Africans, to be reached *de facto* by the nature of the franchise and constituencies,[15] and not *de jure* as a <u>racial</u> division. He said this in the drawing room at Admiralty House, just before Christmas. Macleod was present; also Tim Bligh (he has a note of the talk) Now he denies this. I'm afraid that, after all, he is a rather crooked man and he has repeated just what he did about the Monckton report. It is perhaps that he is frightened. But it is sad that he is also so stupid. He does not realise that if he forces his party delegates to boycott the Conference wh is to open in London on

---

blacks and whites. However, he was heavily defeated by Michael Blundell's more moderate New Kenya Party.

14. First discussed in June 1960 following Tory losses in Scotland at the 1959 election changes, though the reorganisation of the Scottish Party – effectively ending its autonomy – did not come until 1965. Stuart, who had effectively been chairman since 1935, remained in post until 1962.

15. By having an upper (effectively European) roll and lower (essentially African) roll, still restricted according to various qualifying criteria such as education levels.

Monday and for wh many delegates have arrived or are arriving, it will not be Northern Rhodesia wh will bust. It will be the Federation. And Whitehead (whom Welensky naively regards as a friend) will declare for the <u>secession</u> of Southern Rhodesia, supported by Harper and the Dominion Party. With <u>Africans</u> in Northern Rhodesia and Nyasaland clamouring for secession and with <u>Europeans</u> in Southern Rhodesia demanding also the end of the Federation, what hope has Welensky to maintain it. If he could only realise it, we are his only friends. Yet he pours out abusive letters and telegrams in a half mad sort of way. It is partly emotion, and partly bluff. He <u>is</u> an old T. Union leader. If he expects to settle for 5/- or 7/6, his instinct is to ask for a 20/- or 30/- wage increase . . . .

29 January (Sunday)
D and I have just got back to B.G. after 2 days and 2 nights in France . . . .

On Saturday morning we motored to Rambouillet . . . . De G was relaxed; friendly and seemed genuinely attracted by my themes – Europe to be united, politically and economically; but France and Britain to be something more than European powers, and to be so recognised by U.S. I think everything now depends on
a) whether we really can put forward a formula for 6s and 7s wh both Commonwealth and British agriculture will wear
b) whether the Americans can be got to accept France's nuclear achievements and ambitions[16] . . . .

4 February (Saturday)
I came, alone, to Chequers last night and went to bed for dinner, quite exhausted. It has been a terrible week. Apart from routine Cabinets, we have had two defence committees, as well as several ministerial meetings about the Press merger and the state of the newspaper press. First Thomson tried to buy Odhams; then [Cecil] Harmsworth King overbid him. (Of course, with shares. No one ever pays cash for

---

16. Macmillan hoped that if the Americans were willing somehow to extend nuclear secrets sharing to France – along the lines discussed with de Gaulle in March 1960 – this would encourage the latter to be more accommodating towards Macmillan's European policy. In practice the new Kennedy Administration, already recognising de Gaulle's ambitions to be the strongman of Europe, showed little enthusiasm for this.

anything nowadays) Since Odhams own the *Daily Herald*, this has excited Gaitskell and Co. G came to see me, asking for an 'enquiry'. I had Tuesday and Thursday in the House on this. I have 'stalled' so far. But I have made it plain that any enquiry cannot be into this transaction, which is perfectly legal, but into the whole economic and financial problems of the industry, including restrictive practices of all kinds.[17]

The Health charges have been announced by MofHealth (Powell) and the usual Socialist storm. At least we have given them something on wh they can agree – a vote of censure on us. Then there have been some ministerial changes to arrange – Alport (now Minister of State, Commonwealth) is to be a Peer and go to Salisbury as High Commissioner. Consequential changes to arrange. In addition, all through this horrible week there has been the Rhodesian problem. Duncan Sandys is in Salisbury, where the S Rhodesian conference is taking place. Macleod is having the N Rhodesian conference in London, boycotted by Welensky's Europeans, tho' not by Sir John Moffat's Liberals. Both seem rather hopeless. One is bogged down; the other hasn't started properly at all. Mr Greenfield (one of Sir Roy's ministers) is to come to Chequers this afternoon and stay the night. But I doubt whether I shall get anywhere with him, since he is not a plenipotentiary. Fundamentally, the problem is simple. The Europeans don't really want any African advance, but will accept something less than parity of representation for Africans in the Legislative Council of Northern Rhodesia (less in Southern) Africans demand 'one man one vote' but would accept some advance in the franchise to give parity (or, if possible, African nominal majority – to be discounted by official members) There will be no agreement. HMG must decide. If we lean too much to the European side,

1) Their confidence in HMG will be undermined
2) There will be serious disaster in N Rhodesia, perhaps spreading throughout the Federation
3) Macleod will resign
4) Our Government and Party will be split in two.

If, on the other hand, we make a decision which, without satisfying African demands goes in their general favour

1) Europeans will have no faith left in HMG
2) Sir Roy Welensky will declare Federation to be 'independent'

---

17. A Royal Commission on the Press was duly announced on 9 February.

     and will try to take over Government of N Rhodesia by force
     or bluff or both

3) If the Governor [of Northern Rhodesia] defends his position,
there will be civil war – Europeans versus British officials,
troops, and Africans.

4) Ld Home and others will resign

5) Our Government and Party will be split in two.

We must try to find a way out – by the end of next week. I confess I
do not see the way as things are.

22 February

We have had a very hectic fortnight. Apart from all the routine
Cabinets, ministerial meetings, P.Q.s etc, we have had the Archbishop
of York [Ramsey] – a long talk about the future of the Church and all
the episcopal vacancies wh are crowding on us – party at Leggatt's to
see Gunn's portrait of me; Sir Winston Churchill to luncheon, the
Greek Prime Minister and M. Averoff – the usual talks, dinners,
receptions etc; dinner with Young Conservative members, who won
seats in 1959; meeting at Stationers' Hall to celebrate 350th anniversary of Authorised Version[18] (Dr Fisher and I made speeches etc etc)
But all the time, culminating last week-end a most critical position,
internally and externally, about Northern Rhodesia. We had to chose
between two most difficult – one of my colleagues called them hideous
– choices. Iain Macleod (Col Secy) understandably has leaned over too
far towards the African view. He wanted to give them an 'African'
majority. This is not only quite intolerable to the Europeans, but
contrary to the 'multi-racial' purpose we have in mind.[19] After days of
effort (including his resignation and its withdrawal) I got him off this,
onto a much more imaginative plan,[20] designed to help the 'moderates'
of each colour.

    .... We may have a Boston tea party (Welensky declaring the
Federation independent and seizing the colony of N Rhodesia) or an

18. The King James Bible.

19. Though Macmillan was to recognise in writing to Sandys on 6 March that the
two rolls, 'with their almost certain results' (DWM: Ms Macmillan, dep. c.
358), had undermined the multi-racial principles his government had pursued
since 1958.

20. This envisaged 15 members elected on each roll and 15 who would have to win
a certain vote share on both rolls.

African blood-bath (riots all over British Africa, much accentuated if Colonial Sec were to resign) The die is now cast. Col Secy announced his plan in HofC yesterday (Ld Perth in H of Lords) The internal situation is steady. But a _very_ bad telegram has come from Salisbury. Welensky is calling his Parlt and may take some desperate action. The curious thing is that British public opinion and Press have not got hold of the true state of things. They accuse me of 'selling out to Welensky' and are all (including _Times_, _D Telegraph_ and _D Mail_) very pro-African. They don't realise yet what has been our chief anxiety – what will the Europeans in Rhodesia do? If they shd act on their own, there is nothing we can do. We cannot send British troops to fight British settlers . . . .

All through this very exhausting crisis, (about wh strangely little has leaked) I have had great help from Home, Sandys, and Kilmuir. Rab Butler has been sympathetic, but detached. Iain Macleod has been difficult and rather temperamental, but quite straightforward. (His only real fault is that he talks too freely to the Africans and is rather naïve in his faith in their integrity) It has been a very wearing time. If Col Secy had resigned, I think Govt wd have fallen. All the younger men in the Party wd have gone against us. The Chief Whip has been good, but he has had the additional worry of a period of 'filibustering' by the Opposition, with very late nights and very little business done. The Labour Party are enjoying themselves and they are more united. The 'Gallup' poll has started (at last) to move away from us – but not too seriously . . . .

All these African troubles have so absorbed my time that I have not done much other business, except for talks with Chancellor of Exr about the Budget. It is not going to be easy to have a 'popular' Budget, but I feel we must do something now for the relief of direct taxation. After the health stamp and and the prescription charges, it will not be easy to do the sur-tax changes[21] – but I think we shd do them _now_, before the Parliament gets too advanced.

23 February

A short debate yesterday – 3.30 to 7 – in HofC on Africa. Macleod opened well, I am told. Sandys ended dramatically, with an attack on Welensky (deserved, but I think unwise) I only heard Sandys, because of Dr Adenauer. Welensky threatens to 'declare' independence. He has

---

21. These raised the threshold for higher-rate income taxes.

called Parl; set up 'exchange control' and looks (from his military disposition) as if he were contemplating an attack on N Rhodesia – where he has troops and we have none.

We have had two days of Dr Adenauer and his Germans – 4 hours talk; dinner; luncheon – and little or no result . . . .

I think we shall also get German participation in Blue Streak. But the large economic issues wh face the world they affect not to understand. In other words, they are rich and selfish – and German . . . .

25 February
Rested in bed all day, working on speeches, reading, dozing. Welensky's motion in the Federal Parl (at Salisbury) is not in such violent terms as I had feared, altho' it could be used as the basis for violence. It does not demand independence, but it calls on Federal Govt to resist constitutional changes (i.e. pro African) in Northern Rhodesia 'by every means at its disposal'. That may mean war, but not necessarily. We must wait a few days, before we know the worst, but we must prepare against it . . . .

5 March (Sunday)
. . . . Sir Roy Harrod, prophet of woe. He says the £ will crash in the summer. We must restrict imports. Treasury and BofT say the opposite. What is a poor PM to do? . . . .

The Germans have today 'upgraded' the D-Mark by 5% – good, but not enough. (Incidentally, this adds £3m to our NATO costs)[22]

We have had quite a good week in Parlt. Watkinson made a sound speech introducing Defence Debate and a splendid one winding it up. Julian (Amery) was very good and cheered up our people by a counterattack. Brown was poor – he shouts too loud. We have decided to 'guillotine' the Health Charges Bills and stop the obstruction.[23] The Opposition will protest (as we did) but be secretly relieved (as we were)

I feel that the Govt stock is slipping a bit, just as mine is doing (according to the Gallup polls) But I think we can recover. The Budget cannot be popular in the short run, tho' it may be so in the longer

---

22. The stationing costs for troops in Gemany.
23. The 'guillotine' was a timetable introduced during the passage of a Bill to allow for its speedy completion.

19. Vicky's comment on the Hola Camp atrocity in the *Evening Standard*, 16 May 1959. The day before, Fenner Brockway had raised in the Commons the continuing use of detention camps in Central and East Africa despite the beatings that had led to the deaths of eleven detainees in Hola on 3 March.

20. David Low is unimpressed with Reginald Maudling's efforts to build a European Free Trade alternative with the Scandinavians to de Gaulle's Common Market in the *Manchester Guardian*, 17 June 1959.

21. Prime Minister Kwame Nkrumah of Ghana visits Macmillan at Birch Grove, his Sussex country house in the summer of 1959.

22. Labour leader Hugh Gaitskell (left) had planned to visit the Soviet bloc in March 1959, but aborted the trip when Macmillan went there himself. His eventual departure was overshadowed by Eisenhower's arrival in London and his fortnight tour had to be curtailed without visiting Poland when Macmillan announced the 1959 general election. He and Shadow Foreign Secretary Aneurin Bevan are seen here being greeted on their return to London by Barbara Castle on 11 September 1959.

23. Macmillan addresses a meeting in Rectory Grove, Clapham, in south London on 3 October 1959, during his successful general election campaign tour.

24. As party leader Macmillan is applauded as he enters the Conservative Central Office during the 1959 general election campaign. He is followed by his wife Lady Dorothy and, behind Macmillan, the then party chairman, Lord Hailsham.

25. Macmillan greets the crowds at Maseru, Basutoland, in February 1960, during his African tour.

26. Prime Minister Macmillan and President Eisenhower during talks at the president's Maryland retreat, Camp David, in March 1960.

27. Macmillan with his son Maurice in the grounds of Birch Grove, 12 April 1960.

28. Macmillan celebrating his installation as Chancellor of Oxford with students of Brasenose College, 30 April 1960.

29. Congolese Prime Minister Patrice
Lumumba meets with Dag Hammarskjöld,
Secretary-General of the UN,
in New York, July 1960.

30. Macmillan in talks with President
Nasser of Egypt at the UN,
28 September 1960.

32. Sir Roy Welensky, Prime Minister of
the Federation of Rhodesia and Nyasaland,
talking with his South African counterpart,
Hendrik Verwoerd (left), during the March
1961 Commonwealth Prime Ministers'
Conference in London.

31. Lady Dorothy Macmillan tees off
on the King's course at Gleneagles,
1 September 1960.

" Is there a psychiatrist in the house ? I've got a split image ! "

33. Michael Cummings was one of the first to suggest that there were two sides to Macmillan's character in this *Daily Express* cartoon of 15 March 1961.

34. Harold Macmillan with President Kennedy.

35. A shooting party on the Bolton Abbey estate in Yorkshire belonging to Macmillan's nephew, the Duke of Devonshire. Macmillan is accompanied here by Deborah, Duchess of Devonshire, August 1961.

36. US Vice-President Lyndon Johnson in Berlin with (right) Konrad Adenauer just after the Wall was built in August 1961.

period. I have settled its main terms with the Chancellor of the Exr . . . .

24 March

We have had 3 weeks of continuous crisis – the worst I remember since the days before Suez. For the same reason as then, I have not been able to keep this diary, day to day. There simply has not been time and the nervous strain has been too great for me to make the effort. I have had very little sleep – sometimes not more than 2 or 3 hours a night. Once or twice, under Sir John Richardson's direction, I have taken a mild sleeping pill.

There have been 4 separate crises going at once –

1) Rhodesia (first stage) involving a possible break up of the Government and/or a revolutionary movement by Sir Roy Welensky.
2) Financial crisis, threatening collapse of sterling.
3) Commonwealth crisis, with ultimate withdrawal of South Africa from Commonwealth.
4) Rhodesia – (second stage) with a fresh threat from Sir Roy Welensky and possible Cabinet crisis.

These all ended by March 21st. Now

5) The Laos crisis has blown up, with possibility of war in South East Asia.

(1) Central African Federation

Duncan Sandys succeeded well enough with Southern Rhodesia.[24] But Macleod's proposals for Northern Rhodesia produced the first stage of the African crisis. As I have recorded, we got through this with some difficulty. But it was only really postponed, until Sir Roy Welensky came to London for the Commonwealth Conference. He came a day or two early and dined with me alone. As always, he was pleasant enough – too pleasant . . . . I asked him to produce some alternative plan – if he didn't like ours, for the Northern Rhodesian constitution. He had, after all, agreed to the principles behind our plan. If our proposals did not – as they stood – carry out these principles or would

---

24. A conference in Southern Rhodesia opened on 7 February. The resulting new constitution involved a legislative assembly of 65 with a weighted system of two electoral rolls. This enfranchised some Africans (effectively giving them 15 seats), whilst retaining European predominance after it was introduced on 1 June.

work out quite differently to expectation,[25] let his officials meet with
ours to agree on a factual appreciation, and let him put in alternative
schemes. He did this on March 14 (a week after his arrival) and
proposed 3 or 4 schemes. We discussed them on March 18 and I
practically persuaded Sir R W to accept that negotiation would go on
in Lusaka, altho' we could not accept any of his plans as they stood.
Parts of his scheme 2 were quite helpful, but we could not accept a
scheme the sole purpose of wh was to ensure a 'built-in' majority for
his party. In any election there must be some element of uncertainty,
however small. (This idea seemed to shock him) However, altho' the
meeting in London on Saturday afternoon was good, by Sunday I
heard (at Chequers) that (under great pressure from Greenfield) Sir R
W had run out. Monday (20th) was a hectic day. Sir R W came to
Admiralty House (alone) and finally agreed a communiqué, wh wd
show that we had had good talks – not negotiations – that further
negotiations wd go on in Lusaka .... He went back to Greenfield,
who once more practically persuaded him out of this. I held a Cabinet
at 3.30, to make sure that they understood the position and were
prepared to support our line, whatever the consequences. At 4.15
Sandys (who had Sir Roy and his advisers in his room at the HofC
(Cabinet was in my room at House)) came in to tell us that the
communiqué was agreed. The Cabinet dispersed; Sir Roy came into
my room to say goodbye and left for the airport. So far, he has stuck
to his agreement and said nothing disagreeable either in London,
before leaving, or in Salisbury after arrival. His behaviour while in
London has been very bad. Naturally, he has sought and obtained the
help of Lords Salisbury and Lambton. The former (like his grandfather)
has proved master of 'flouts and jibes and jeers' in the H of Lords.[26]
The latter (who is ineffective as a speaker) has published a series of
rather poisonous articles in the Beaverbrook Press.

Sir Roy addressed 200 or more Conservative MPs and made a
bitter attack on Macleod and by implication on me.[27] As before, much

25. Welensky wrote on 17 February of his fears that the complicated electoral
    scheme would in practice give control not to the upper but to the lower roll
    electorate, more susceptible to intimidation from black nationalists.
26. In 1875 Disraeli in a Commons debate lambasted the 3rd Marquess of
    Salisbury as 'a great master of jibes and flouts and jeers'.
27. This was at the Commonwealth Affairs Committee on 16 March. Macmillan

of what he said was a series of lies or half-truths. But I do understand and sympathise with his difficulties. He entirely misjudged the N Rhodesian position. He should not have made his party boycott the Conference. He has made such a row (calling his Parlt together and threatening an election and a declaration of independence) that I fear he has gravely injured Whitehead's chances of winning the referendum on the S Rhodesian constitution. Nor is he sure of Whitehead's loyalty. Whitehead (if things are going badly) may himself stage a coup d'état of his own and declare Southern Rhodesia independent. Welensky knows that even the threat of this wd mean the end of Federation.

(2) Sterling Crisis

There has been, and continues still, a tremendous Bear attack on sterling. No doubt the weakness of our 'Balance of Payments' prospects has come into it. But it has been set off by the sudden revaluation of the Deutschmark – which upvalued it by 5%. This has caused wild speculation in London, New York, Paris, Amsterdam, Zurich and all the rest ever since. (a) The fact of revaluation, reminded all speculators and owners of hot money that fixed exchanges can – after all – be changed. If once, why not again? (b) The fact that the upvaluation is far too small to correspond to realities, has led everyone to think the first move in this direction may be followed by a second. Since this could only be upwards, it's an absolutely safe bet to sell dollars and sterling in order to buy reichmarks [sic]. This has been done on an absolutely unprecedented scale. We lost £67m in one day (£26[m] was the worst post-Suez day) Altogether we have lost about £187[m] of hot money from the reserves. America has had the same experience. We decided to fight and spent all this money defending the rate. We have no doubt caught out some speculators, who were borrowing at 8% and more to bear the £. All the same, it's the worst patch I have been through . . . .

The fact that this started at the beginning of the month was lucky. We need not publish the figures of the reserves till the end of March. We have had very good support from Central Banks – German and Swiss – which have put immense credits at our disposal – thereby cancelling out collectively what speculators have done individually. If the drain eases off (wh it now shows some signs of doing) we may be able to show a figure of loss at the end of the month sufficient to

received regular reports on backbench meetings from his parliamentary secretary, Knox-Cunningham.

stimulate British people to new efforts in exports, to reconcile them to a deflationary Budget, and to maintain at the same time confidence in the power of the authorities to fight back against a vicious 'Bear' attack. So matters stand today.

(3) Commonwealth Conference

This has been a most exhausting and a most painful affair. I had nourished high hopes of being able to steer the Conference into accepting the request of the S.A. Govt that S.A. should remain in the Commonwealth after she becomes a Republic on May 31st. I think I cd have achieved this except for the following difficulties, which (taken together) proved insuperable.

- a) The tremendous newspaper agitation and build-up, supported by political leaders and publicists here, against what was called 're-admitting' SA because of apartheid.
- b) The decision made by Nehru – on the day before the discussion – to urge the Afro-Asian premiers to refuse, while lying pretty low himself.
- c) The extreme rigidity of Dr Verwoerd, who never made the smallest concession to his colleagues in the Conference, even on matters strictly outside the apartheid dogma . . . .

. . . . Finally, on the Wednesday (after discussions which had lasted 2½ days) I came to the conclusion that my plan cd not succeed (acceptance of S.A. Republic on procedural basis, together with unanimous condemnation of apartheid) I think I could actually have persuaded the Prime Ministers, even Nkrumah and Abubakar (Ghana and Nigeria) to agree. But it was clear that they wd only accept it for the year – on the purely procedural ground – and begin immediately a violent campaign for expulsion. Even President Ayub (Pakistan) usually so moderate was deeply offended by some of Dr Verwoerd's remarks. Ayub (who is pure Asia[n]) is apparently regarded by S.African Govt as black. Nehru (India) and Mr Bandaranaike (Ceylon) wd equally have forced the issue. What then I had to avoid was a vote (wh I suppose Dr V might have asked for) This wd have put UK Govt into a great difficulty. We shd only have got Australia and New Zealand (Menzies and Holyoake). Canada (Diefenbaker) wd have been against us.

I had (on Monday) begun to face this danger, and devised a plan by wh Dr V shd be induced to withdraw his application if it became clear that the result of forcing the question to a vote wd be an almost overwhelming vote against.[28] He therefore, after a final talk with me on Wednesday alone, took this course.

The announcement in HofC (wh I [made] after questions) was received in a subdued silence. Debated last Wednesday, there were angry and critical speeches by some of our Conservative members, like Turton. Lord Salisbury launched another attack in the H of Lords. Among other things I have seen Salisbury and his 'Watching' Group' – rather a ragamuffin lot, without much brains or authority.[29] He is the centre and the only real figure in the revolt. I also have seen the executive ctee of the 1922 Ctee – this was a most useful meeting.

(6) [sic] <u>Laos</u>

This situation has been developing into a first class crisis during the last few days, owing to the deteriorating military position. The King and his Govt seem to be no good and the Royal Laotian Army (altho' plentifully supplied with weapons and money by the Americans) seems unwilling to fight.

We had two Cabinets yesterday – at 5 and at midnight. There was clearly a good deal of hesitation at the first Cabinet as to what line we shd take. The Americans want SEATO to intervene. If this is not agreed, they will 'go it alone' . . . . We put all the difficulties and objections to a military intervention, including U.N. and Commonwealth difficulties (the Tunku, PM of Malaya, is in London and seemed – on being consulted by the Commonwealth Sec to be unexpectedly robust) But we made it clear that, at the end of the day, whichever decision they took, we would support them. This, I am sure, is right if we are to have influence in future with the President and the new Administration.

Left London Airport at 10am, in a Comet . . . .

25 March

At 4am this morning, telegram from Washington to London, repeated to Trinidad, saying that President is very anxious to meet and talk

---

28. The suggestion was Macleod's.

29. Formed in December 1960, this was modelled on Salisbury's father's Watching Committee of 1940 set up to seek the overthrow of Neville Chamberlain. Macmillan, who had been an enthusiastic member of the earlier organisation, can have had few illusions as to the objects of the new Watching Committee.

with me about Laos before the Bangkok meeting.[30] He suggests Key
West air and naval base in Florida tomorrow (Sunday)

4am Trinidad time is 8am London time. We got off telegram at
once to try to get London's views and to collect what we could from
Butler, Heath (Ld Privy Seal and FO minister) For Secy (at Karachi on
his way to Bangkok) Sandys (to sound Tunku again and also other
Commonwealth countries).

I did not wish to <u>accept</u> meeting with President without general
approval, for I fear it may cause a scare in the world and trouble
in Parliament. However, by 11am everybody seemed in favour of
accepting and we telephoned Washington accordingly. By midnight
we had very good telegrams from Norman Brook and Philip de
Zulueta summarising view on substance; messages from Ld Privy Seal
on substance and long message (which I was particularly glad to have)
from For Secy on substance. The general view tends somewhat to
modify the original Cabinet idea that any military operation by US
[in Indo-China] should be done <u>outside</u> SEATO with its subsequent
moral and political approval. The new phrase is 'under the aegis' of
SEATO.

It is also clear that I must not commit any military support (even
more or less symbolic) without specific Cabinet approval. I have asked
Cabinet to meet on Monday morning, as early as possible . . . .

26 March

. . . . The journey is going to take 4¾ hours – not 2 hours as President
Kennedy seemed to think. He had forgotten Cuba.[31]

We touched down at Key West – the great naval station and
airport at 11.30am (Trinidad time) having gained a little on the
flight . . . .

Quite a day. I have never before been 1800 miles to luncheon –
3600 miles in all.

My first meeting with President Kennedy was quite an event for
me – and perhaps for him. He struck me as a curious mixture of
qualities – courteous, quiet, quick, decisive – and tough. Our talks

---

30. Macmillan had telegraphed Kennedy after Cabinet on 23 March suggesting not
    SEATO intervention but unilateral US action if necessary. Kennedy's desire to
    resolve this difference of opinion before the SEATO meeting in Bangkok on 27
    March led him to urge an immediate meeting.
31. Cuba would not let them overfly its airspace.

(including a sort of picnic lunch) lasted about 3 hours. The President was evidently in control of the Pentagon, not the other way round. He was clear and decisive. He was not at all anxious to undertake a military operation in Laos. If it had to be done (as a sort of political gesture) he definitely wanted it to be a SEATO exercise. He did not want to 'go it alone'. I rather objected to anything on the scale of the present SEATO plans. They were, to my mind, unrealistic . . . .

What about Plan 5/61 9.[32] Even this, as I understood it, was to involve 30,000 troops in the end – to be supplied by air, or largely by air – a ruinous undertaking.

Finally, President explained that he had in mind as a possibility a much modified plan – involving about 4 or 5 battalions – to hold Vientiane and some other bridge-heads on the river. This wd

a) preserve some Laotian territory, however small, and the authority of the King in an enclave

b) It would allow advance, if thought possible at a later date

c) It would free 7,000 Laotian troops to fight Pathet Lao, should they be inclined to do so

d) It would encourage the Thais to hold firm.

I expressed my own doubts as to the whole concept, but I did agree that it might be politically necessary to do something, in order not to be 'pushed about' by the Russians. This I thought might well be their intention at the beginning of his Presidency . . . .

Among other things which I discussed with President was whom he wd like to succeed Harold Caccia as ambassador. He was emphatic for David Gore. 'He is my brother's most intimate friend'. (And, of course, 'my brother' is thought by many to be the Grey Eminence)[33]

27 March

. . . . The Governor General [of the West Indian Federation] fears that even Sir Grantley Adams (at present Federal P.M.) is not too anxious for the day of full independence. For when that comes, he will go. Perh[aps] he cd be Governor General? . . . .

---

32. SEATO plan 5/61 and its variants – some of which involved far more troops than mentioned here by Macmillan – attempted to provide for securing the kingdom of Laos from Communist incursions from the north.

33. Bobby Kennedy and Ormsby-Gore became friends when Kennedy's father was ambassador to London 1938–40.

28 March

. . . . We left G[overnment] H[ouse] at 9am and after the usual Guard
of Honour and other ceremonies, took off about 10am.

Patrick and Diana Hailes have certainly been the most wonderful
hosts and made us all feel really welcome. GH is large, Victorian, and
comfortable. Lady H is very clever in the art of internal decoration
and everything is beautifully arranged. It's nice to find a house nowadays with 30 or 40 servants. I had an excellent valet.

Trinidad is an interesting place – rich (with oil) and lively. Incidentally, we did the island a good turn when we allowed Trinidad Oil to
be sold to a really go-ahead American company.[34] There does not seem
excessive poverty; there is an impressively large middle class; there is
as near 'multi-racialism' as you can hope to get anywhere. I have no
doubt that when the last piece of British help is withdrawn, administration will get worse and perh[aps] corrupt. But they are certainly
more advanced than many independent countries in the world today.

We got to Barbados . . . . At 4pm, after a drive through the town
(Bridgetown) [we went] to a very old, and rather pretty, Town Hall.
The Mayor in his robes; the Town Clerk in wig and gown; the
Aldermen and Councillors (of all colours and races) and about
300–400 people packed into a room that wd comfortably hold
100–200 . . . . I had to deal with a most confused series of telegrams
from For Secy (in Bangkok) Caccia (in Washington) Butler and Defence
Ministers (in London) about Laos. I'm afraid everything is in rather a
muddle, esp about the so-called military plans . . . .

29 March

. . . . Left airport at 9am. Arrived in Antigua at 10.20 . . . . Mr Bird
(Chief Minister) seemed very sensible. Nor does there seem any resentment from the Europeans about the Africans now taking the chief share
in Government. It is really a non-racial system working very well . . .

30 March

. . . . A quiet morning. I saw the Administrators and Chief Ministers
both of St Kitts and Monserrat. The smaller islands are rather afraid
of Federation.[35] At present they draw large 'grants-in-aid' from U.K.

---

34. See vol. 1, pp. 563–67 (7–20 June 1956).

35. The Federation of the West Indies, consisting of Antigua, Barbados, Dominica,
    Grenada, Jamaica, Montserrat, St Kitts-Nevis, Anguilla, St Lucia, St Vincent,

Independence and freedom are all very well. But where is the money coming from? They have more confidence in the Colonial Office than in the politicians from Jamaica and Trinidad who will dominate Federal Government. This is colonialism reversed! . . . .

A good telegram from Minister of Defence. He and Chiefs of Staff seem to understand what I want – Plan 6/51 [sic] modified – not more than <u>one</u> British battalion . . . .

We left Antigua at 12.40 – lunch on plane – arrived Jamaica at 2.45 . . . . A long talk with Manley. He is head and shoulders above any other politician in the West Indies. Federation really depends on his power

a) to persuade the other islands to be sensible at the Trinidad and London Conferences

b) to persuade Jamaica – wh has to have a referendum – to vote for Federation. (As in S Rhodesia, the referendum seems to play a dangerous part)

Bustamante (old and ruthless but the most attractive demagogue in the area) has come out strongly against Federation. He has refused to dine at GH to meet me . . . .

Manley talked about immigration – on wh he is sensible and understanding. If we could only get U.S. to accept a reasonable number of Jamaicans the problem wd be solved. In the long run he hopes that the birth rate will fall, if economic progress continues. He said that he had observed that by the merciful dispensation of Providence rich Roman Catholics had fewer children than poor ones! . . . .

1 April

Lots of telegrams. For Secy is clearly upset by the American behaviour at SEATO. Rusk (in spite of my talks with the President) has refused to allow any talks between Admiral Felt (U.S.) and General Hull (UK) He says he has received no instruction. So the full plan 5/61 holds the field – a ridiculously ambitious plan, which the President and I in fact discarded. But I think the President's reason for not sending instructions is the one he frankly gave me. 'Everything leaks from the State Dept' . . . .

Chancellor of Exr (whom I asked to send his views) is anxious about effect of any military action (with Germany, France and Italy

---

and Trinidad and Tobago (where the capital was), had been set up on 3 January 1958.

1961

standing aside) on dollars and sterling currencies. Our very bad balance of payments figures (£300[m] or more deficit) have just been published. Also, I'm afraid of Nehru, Tunku, and even F.M. Ayub getting cold feet if and when the time for action comes . . . .

4 April
. . . . Arrived at Washington about 6pm. I spent all the time on the aeroplane re-writing my speech for Massachusetts Institute of Technology on Friday . . . .

8 April (Saturday)
. . . . There was an immense audience – 4000 in the hall and more in overflow halls . . . .

The speech – wh Philip de Z[ulueta] started working on several weeks ago – went through 10 (ten) drafts. I made some final alterations in the hotel at Boston. It seemed to 'go' well with the inside audience, who listened intently. Altho' the subject matter was heavy, the phrasing etc was quite good and telling. There was a huge TV audience in US. I am told it will be on British TV today. The main theme 'Unity' came out well – military and economic unity in the Western Alliance. The economic part was divided into <u>Trade</u> (European groupings; Sixes and Sevens; Commonwealth; U.S.A on Free Trade Area) <u>Aid</u>, and <u>Credit</u> policy (imbalance and total volume of credit) This was all good and clear. The defence part was, in reality, a modified form of what I had been saying to the President – find a way of sharing the nuclear with France (and thus, in theory, at least with Europe) After much reflection we made these passages rather less 'pin-pointed' than in the earlier drafts. I did not actually mention France, apart from the allies. But my meaning will be clear to everyone, including de Gaulle . . . .

At 2.45 [on 6 April], I went to the White House, and had ¾ hour <u>alone</u> – no one present at all – with the President. . . . It was really <u>most</u> satisfactory – far better than I could have hoped.

He seemed to understand and sympathise with most of the plans wh form what I call 'The Great Design'.[36] How far he will be able to go with de Gaulle to help me, I do not know. But he will try. It was left that I should compile a secret memorandum and send it to

---

36. The ideas incorporated in Macmillan's December paper. Macmillan was here enlisting Kennedy's help in preparing the ground for the bid for European entry.

him, setting out my plan. His visit to Paris for the end of May has been announced. He will come to England after that (perh after a few days interval for another visit – not specified – wh he has in mind to pay) His excuse for coming to London will be a private visit for the christening of his sister-in-law's baby (Princess Radziwill) He will then be able to discuss the whole situation with me after seeing de G....

.... He gave me a photograph with a most generous inscription. (Rather a sell for the Socialists at home!) Some more and quite intimate talk. The President seemed to think he wd be engrossed with the <u>foreign</u> front this year, but wd get his essential measures through Congress. Next year, wd be the time for more radical things at home ....

9 April (Sunday)

.... D and I went to Cathedral, where I read the Lesson. We also had, before leaving for Ottawa, the Commonwealth High Commissioners and the Press – both (nominally) 'off the record'! ....

12 April

We left Government House Ottawa at 7.30am – took off the ground at 8am. Arrived London Airport 11.30pm (London time) A rather tedious journey ....

General and Mrs Vanier are delightful hosts and are filling the role admirably. He and I are old friends from North African days. The usual talks with PM, alone; talk with the Cabinet; reception by High Commissioner; dinner with PM; dinner with High Commissioner; luncheon and speech to Canadian Club (this was quite a good little effort – well written and rather sentimental!) D and I also saw some of the old friends who survive. The political business done was rather perfunctory – but I think they like me to go to Ottawa after Washington. It may help if and when we have to undertake a serious negotiation over Europe.

13 April

.... After questions, a long talk with the Chancellor of the Exchequer, about the remaining Budget questions to be settled. On these we reached agreement. There is trouble with the Minister of Pensions, who threatens resignation about the proposed 'pay roll' tax, as one of the two economic regulators to be entrusted to the Govt to use, <u>if</u>

<u>necessary</u>, in between Budgets.[37] The other is the power to raise or lower about £2000 a month of excise duties etc by 10%.

14 April
A rather difficult discussion in the morning – Ld Chancellor, Mr Butler, Chancellor of Exr, Mr Maudling, Mr Hare (Labour) and Mr Boyd-Carpenter (Pensions) The M of Pensions does not really object to the 'pay roll' tax. But he has strong (and not unreasonable) objections to the use of his machinery for contributory pensions for the purpose.

In the late afternoon a formula was reached. After re-writing this a bit (to help Boyd-Carpenter) I got everyone to agree . . . .

17 April
The Chancellor spoke, with greater skill and power than I have ever heard him deploy, for 1½ [hours]. The Budget has been very well received by the Party. Believe it will be understood and accepted by the Public and respected by the Foreign Bankers. £500m surplus above the line; only £60–£70[m] <u>overall</u> deficit (including the huge capital investments)[38] the two 'regulators'; additional taxes of £80m; no concessions, except some minor and consequential ones, like greater income tax allowance in view of larger contributions to Insurance funds (£12m) – all this shows a determination to defend sterling and stability by all means in our power . . . .

18 April
. . . . Cuban anti-Castro forces (obviously organised by U.S.A. people but <u>not</u> starting from U.S. territory) have landed in Cuba.[39] But I have

---

37. This envisaged taking powers to increase National Insurance by up to 4s per week per employee in order to dampen the economy. The other regulator was a power to rebate or surcharge duties or purchase tax up to a 10% variation. As Macmillan later put it, the two measures were seen as 'the stimulant and the tranquilliser' (*HMM*, VI, p. 373).

38. Capital investment in manufacturing had risen by 20% as a result of the 1960 Budget.

39. CIA planning for operations had begun the year before, Macmillan writing to Eisenhower on 22 July 1960: 'I feel sure Castro has to be got rid of, but it is a tricky operation for you to contrive and I only hope you will succeed' (*G&E*, p. 365). In the event the modified invasion launched on 15 April proved a failure.

not great hopes of their winning and if they fail it will be a blow to American prestige . . . .

. . . . [A] most tricky meeting with Colonial Secy about Kenya. A formula has been found about Kenyatta, on wh one of the African parties will agree to form a govt. But it has been made quite clear to them and to the Press by the Governor that there is <u>no</u> change in the position about Kenyatta's eventual release. This will continue to be governed by the conditions in the Governor's broadcast of March 1st. I think this will do; but of course the Party here are very suspicious. Fortunately, the African politicians are in no hurry to see K at large![40] . . . .

19 April

Mr K[hrushchev] has issued a most violent 'private message' to President Kennedy, with all sorts of threats, about Cuba. Pres K has made a most robust and spirited reply. But the counter-revolution doesn't look too good . . . .

. . . . It seems that Castro is winning. The Americans are, of course, refusing to admit responsibility in U.N. and we shall support them in a dilatory motion. But it's a bad blow for Kennedy, I fear. It may also make them feel they must do something <u>overt</u> in Laos.

20 April

Cuba is over, according to Press and I think now confirmed by Washington telegrams. There was an attempt to adjourn the HofC yesterday, wh failed.

. . . . The <u>left</u> wing was rather critical, but of course Gaitskell (who has been running for the last few months an ecstatic campaign of hero-worship for the young, starry-eyed, and progressive Kennedy in contrast with that old reactionary Macmillan) is in rather a hole . . . .

I have decided to take a hand in the 'Benn' question. This young man is refusing his father's peerage (Ld Stansgate has at last died) and

---

40. Kenyatta had been held in detention since 1952 and associated with Mau Mau by the British colonial administration. The elections in February under Macleod's new constitution had, however, seen KANU candidates pledged not to take office without Kenyatta win the lion's share of votes if not seats. Tory suspicions of Kenyatta were clear in the message Macmillan received this day from Home, which was also the day a cobbled-together KADU-led government took office in Kenya. Kenyatta was eventually released on 1 August 1961.

standing again for the vacancy in his constituency. He has a good deal of sympathy. As regards the H of Lords, we must not be stampeded by one young man. In some way, we must complete the work – or at least continue it – wh we began with the Life Peers.

21 April
Our wedding day. Sent telegram to Dorothy, who left for Scotland yesterday.

Read a little book called *Solitary Confinement* – by Christopher Burney. This has been republished by M&Co (it was originally published some years ago) It is certainly of classic quality. It is an account of 526 days solitary confinement in a French prison, the author having been an English agent dropped into France and captured by the Gestapo. It really is a wonderful little book . . . .

Left London Airport at 1.30 for Renfrew, where I was met and driven to Ayr. The Scottish Unionist Conference has been sitting. Everyone is rather depressed by the result of the Paisley by-election, where our candidate ran a bad third. It is true that the Liberal (who was second) is a distinguished and popular Scottish figure – a nationalist, and a footballer of international repute[41] . . . .

22 April
Worked on the speech all the morning. 'I am not persuaded that one Liberal swallow, even crowned with the glory of many international caps, heralds the advent of a neo-Asquithian summer'[42] – this was the phrase, about Paisley, wh seemed to please the audience. Great enthusiasm in the hall. Outside, two rival demonstrations, the anti-Polaris crowd and the Young Unionists. The latter easily imposed their will . . . .

24 April
A meeting with Chancellor of Exr, Minister of Education, SofS Scotland about Teachers' Salaries. The Scottish Teachers and the Scottish Local Authorities (which are Socialist controlled) have ganged up

---

41. The Conservative vote fell from 21,250 to 5,597. John Bannerman, the Liberal candidate, was an authority on Gaelic and had in fact been capped 37 times at rugby.
42. From 1920–24 Paisley was the constituency of Herbert Asquith, the last Liberal Prime Minister (1908–16).

together and recommended a rise in salary of 37% (about 12½%–13% both in Scotland and later in England wd be justified as a <u>three</u> year settlement) After much discussion, it was agreed that SofS Scotland should <u>impose</u> a settlement at about 13%. This ought to help the negotiations for England and Wales . . . .

25 April

Cabinet all morning – routine affairs. The chief question was about the H of Lords and the Benn case. There was a good deal of divergence of opinion as to tactics. Eventually, the plan wh I had sent down from Scotland on Sunday morning was accepted. We will announce (tomorrow) that we will move for a Joint Select Ctee on a) composition b) Peers and Peeresses <u>not</u> in either House (e.g. Peeresses in their own right or Scottish peers not elected) c) Right of Peer or Peeress in her own right to sit in H of Commons and question of 'surrender' of peerage d) Payment of Lords regularly attending[43] . . . .

26 April

10.30–1. An excellent discussion on Europe. I revealed to all the Cabinet 'The Grand Design'. On the whole, approval – tho' of course with reservation . . . .

I was very pleased with the intellectual power of the discussion, as well as the high sense of drama and responsibility. This is a fine set of men – equal in intelligence and energy to any Cabinet of the Past . . . .

27 April

10am. Meeting of ministers. I had sat up late the night before, with Ld Privy Seal, new American ambassador Bruce, two of his aides – all sitting in my bedroom from 1–2am while telephone calls were coming through from Washington about Laos. I spoke myself to the President – who seemed fairly calm. Unfortunately, there has been no effective ceasefire. The Royal Laotian Army are (so far as the wet weather and boggy roads allows) on the run. The Pathet Lao forces may occupy practically the whole of the country, including the capital, Vientiane, before the cease-fire or the arrival of the International Commission.

---

43. Benn, as a peer, was denied the right to sit in the Commons, despite winning a by-election in his seat of Bristol North East on 4 May. His Conservative opponent was declared elected instead. The matter was not resolved until July 1963, when the Peerage Act enabled renunciation of peerages.

What then happens to the International Conference in Geneva? So there is great American pressure to put in military forces (SEATO Plan 5) at once . . . .

Home Sec made the House of Lords statement yesterday. It has been very well received by our side in HofC, and in H of Lords. The Press is good. The Opposition, who had not expected this sudden move by us, seemed stunned . . . .

29 April

Slept late – with the help of Dr Richardson's mild drug (Sodium Amytal) . . . .

I was very tired, and rather depressed – so many insoluble problems, and then the shadow of the crisis in our external finances. Stayed in bed all the day – except for a little outing in the garden-house in the afternoon. A mass of papers to be read and dealt with. No Laos news as yet.

The great drama of the day has been the Revolt of the French Generals.[44] I heard about it last Sunday, on returning from Scotland. We heard de Gaulle (radio) and Debré (radio) (There is no TV at Birch Grove, except in Nanny's house at the Lodge gates) Julian Amery was here and seemed to know many of the protagonists.

It is not worth trying to record events wh are now history. De G has had a complete and overwhelming triumph. He is now supreme. The revolt broke (largely due to his moral influence with the ordinary army) in 4 days.

I decided, unlike President Kennedy, that it wd be best to send – and not publish the text of – a purely personal message. This was in these words 'My Dear Friend, I wd like you to know how much you are in my thoughts and prayers'. This seemed to please the General, rather than the published messages of support and readiness to help, wh de G thought rather patronising. I have now had (in his own hand) a charming letter from him. Is this a good augury for the Grand Design? . . . .

30 April (Sunday)

. . . . No cease-fire yet in Laos and excited telegrams arriving from

---

44. On 21 April Generals Salan, Challe, Jouhard and Zeller seized control of Algiers to oppose de Gaulle's policy in Algeria but, with only ambivalent support from the local forces, the coup collapsed.

Washington. Ld Privy Seal rang up after luncheon and we decided on the following – telegrams to Souvanna Phoumi; to Nehru; and to various others to try to get the cease-fire negotiations moving and (if possible) the Control Commission to come out without waiting for the formal cease-fire. But I am not very hopeful, and it is clear that ambassador Johnson (at Bangkok) is keeping up the pressure on the SEATO allies and on Washington in favour of immediate intervention . . . .

1 May

In addition to our other troubles, we have half London docks closed, by an unofficial strike, against the strong advice of the union, about 6 men who are employed two days in each month in some small private wharf! All this was agreed by the unions, but the Communist leaders have cooked up some grievance or other and so led 12000 good English dockers to inflict another (self-inflicted) wound on England. This at a time when we are Booming but Bankrupt. I read yesterday a most depressing Treasury paper, forecasting another very bad year on 'Balance of Payments'. Altho' the Trade Balance will be rather better, 'Invisibles' have dwindled almost to nothing and Aid and Military Expenditure overseas are more than we can afford. £350 million deficit, for the third year running! . . . . A long meeting in the morning with Minister of Labour (Hare) Minister of Transport (Marples) and Paymaster General (Ld Mills) We decided to wait another day to two before any Govt action cd be considered. Even this is very ineffective. We can put in troops to unload some foreign carrots and tomatoes. But we have not the number of troops nor have they the skill to load and unload the really important cargoes. Exports are suffering already. But at least we have half London docks working and all the provincial docks. If we put in troops, they will certainly all go on strike . . . .

6pm. Meeting on Laos. The 3 Service Ministers, (Minister of Defence was out of London) Ld Mountbatten, LP[rivy] Seal. The Americans, supported (in very silly and rather hypocritical telegrams by Australia and New Zealand) now want to take the preliminary troop movements for a military intervention . . . . Their reason is that the two sides have not yet managed to meet to discuss the cease-fire; that the Pathet Lao are obviously stalling till the whole country has fallen; that they are advancing all the time; that the Thais are getting very restless; that only U.K. and France are out of step; etc etc.

I am not persuaded that the delay in the two sides meeting to discuss the cease-fire is due to anything but incompetence, torrential rain, bad communications etc. I am also not at all clear what the military objectives now are or what forces will be necessary to achieve them . . . .

About midnight we rang Caccia in Washington. He told us that news had just come through that the two sides (Royal Laotian Govt and Pathet Lao) <u>had</u> made contact and would continue their talks tomorrow. The Americans are therefore willing to postpone the SEATO meeting . . . .

2 May

10am. Cabinet. I thought it right to summon the Cabinet and tell them the whole position about Laos. If the 'cease-fire' talks break down (as they may well do) the question of intervention will arise immediately. So the Cabinet must be fully informed and prepared.

(I fear that Phoumi – the <u>right</u> wing and theoretically <u>legal</u> Prime Minister may well – instigated by the <u>local</u> Americans – take a line intended to cause the cease-fire to fail. Equally, the Pathet Lao – instigated more by China than by Russia – may do the same) . . . .

4 May

. . . . The London dock strike is over – a silly dispute about nothing, but full of potential danger. On the other hand, the case of George Blake – a traitor – has shocked the public. The L.C.J. has passed a savage sentence – 42 years in prison! Naturally, we can say nothing. The public do not know and cannot be told that he belonged to M.I.6 – an organisation wh does not theoretically exist.[45] So I had a rather rough passage in the HofC . . . .

5 May

. . . . 11am. Colonial Policy Ctee. A long and very important discussion about Aden Colony and the Protectorates. Two schemes will be prepared for us to consider. The real problem is how to use the

---

45. Joining MI6 in 1948, Blake was a POW for three years during the Korean War. Subsequently in Berlin he betrayed many operations to the Soviets before being exposed by the Polish defector Michael Goleniewski. The existence of this British overseas intelligence service was not formally acknowledged until 1992.

influence and power of the Sultans to help us keep the colony and its essential defence facilities[46] . . . .

4.45. For Secy – back from Bangkok; Ankara; Rome. He seemed in very good form and pleased at the way Laos was working out. He said that Rusk (U.S. Secretary of State) seemed very shaken by Cuba. It seems to have been a complete muddle, and a compromise between different plans. The simple one (wh from what President said to me was what I believed they were considering) was to put 200–300 men unobtrusively ashore, to go to the mountains, and start a centre of resistance. This is what Castro himself did. Then there was a plan for a big invasion, to include American troops. It seems that the President vetoed this and gave his approval to the simple landing of some partisans. But the 'agencies' operated the full invasion plan, but without American troops, hoping no doubt to force the President's hand. He stood firm – hence the fiasco. Allen Dulles will prob go in July and President, who is thoroughly dissatisfied with the intelligence services, is to take it all in hand . . . .

8 May
10.30. Sandys (Commonwealth) and Macleod (Colonies) We agreed on the next approach to Welensky. At present, everything wh the Governor of Northern Rhodesia will agree to, does not go far enough to satisfy Welensky. Anything wh satisfies Welensky, is unacceptable to the Governor of N Rhodesia. I am more and more astonished that we ever agreed to so difficult a project as 'Federation' – wh involved two Secretaries of State being responsible for the same territories[47] . . . .

14 May (Sunday)
. . . . The President of Finland left from Gatwick yesterday, after a week's visit – wh meant for me two dinners, two receptions, and two long interviews. President Kekkonen is rather an enigmatic figure. In his own country, he is regarded by some as a most skilful political acrobat, and most successful in keeping Finland on a line of balanced neutrality wh will preserve her independence. Others regard him as

---

46. Hence the schemes aimed to preserve British influence by merging Aden in with the British-protected South Arabian Federation established in 1959 whilst retaining reserved powers over defence, foreign policy and internal security.

47. The Colonial Office had responsibility for Northern Rhodesia and Nyasaland and the Commonwealth Relations Office for Southern Rhodesia.

'sold out' to the Soviets. Naturally, his position is delicate, like that of Finland. He was elected only by <u>one</u> vote in the electoral college. 25% of the Finns vote Communist (partly from poverty; partly from anti-Swedish and governing class feelings; partly from fear of Russia) At our first talk, where he gave a very fair and very able review of Finland's recent history, I thought President K rather better than he had been painted. At the second, he seemed more discouraged and defeatist. It is not so much that he is afraid of the Russians. That is natural. But I think he also admires them and thinks that the East will win over the West . . . .

Then we have had the Blake case, and the whole question of security. The Press has been terrible, without any sense of responsibility . . . . Against this, the Local Borough elections shew a great swing to the right. We have captured Liverpool, Nottingham and several other large cities.

I had a meeting with Gaitskell, who brought old Lord Alexander of Hillsboro', Shinwell and Brown. The latter was sober (it was 11.30am) but had clearly been pretty bad the night before. I told him the facts of the Blake case and that I intended to appoint a small committee to enquire into the whole question.[48] I got G to agree to this, and with the exception of a few bad questions from bad (or mad) MPs, my statement went well . . . .

We have had long meetings of ministers (about 10 or 11) about Europe – some progress is being made. But the position is very delicate. The Commonwealth and Agricultural interests are anxious, even alarmed. The French seem more flexible. But I must wait till after the de Gaulle–Kennedy talks . . . .

. . . . Laos is better; the Foreign Secy has had a great triumph in getting the cease fire and the Geneva Conference. What will come out of it, no one can tell. Meanwhile, S Vietnam is going badly; the Communist guerrillas are doing too well . . . .

I read Christopher Soames's immense paper on Europe and the Commonwealth from the <u>Agricultural</u> standpoint. It is very long, but very well done. He and Mary came to supper. C and I had a long and useful talk about European problems and possible solutions . . . .

15 May
. . . . A luncheon for a few ambassadors and High Commissioners. I

---

48. This inquiry, under Lord Radcliffe, reported in 1962.

did this last year and have now started again. The UAR ambassador came and was very pleasant . . . .

16 May

. . . . 11–1. Colonial Policy Ctee. We argued about Aden. The line shd be to merge the Colony with the Federation of Rulers and give as much power as we can to the Sultans who are on our side. Julian Amery was a little doubtful and thought we cd go on 'stalling'. But I think on the whole we are choosing the wiser course . . . .

17 May

. . . . We had a very good talk (for two hours) this morning at the Committee of Ministers on Sixes and Sevens. It was a kind of second reading on Minister of Agriculture's paper. Butler had, naturally, anxieties and reservations about agriculture in UK; Sandys, altho' a keen European, about the Commonwealth. But all agreed that we now had a much clearer picture of what our negotiating position could be . . . .

19 May

. . . . The European problem has held the attention of Parlt, the Press, and to some extent the Public in the last few days. The Government's position is rather better understood. Some still accuse us of indecision; but more are beginning to realise the difficulties and complexities.

As far as Parlt is concerned, Ld P[rivy] Seal (E Heath) has made an excellent impression by 3 speeches – the first to the Foreign Affairs Ctee which I am told was brilliant as an objective presentation of the problem; the second and third in opening and winding up the 2 day Foreign Affairs debate.

The Minister of Agriculture went to the 1922 Ctee and was not very successful. He was in great difficulty and perhaps told them either too little or too much. But he has courage and vigour and will recover from this slight setback.

We had 5 abstentions in the division – all rather crazy (Hinching-brooke, Williams, Biggs-Davison, Fell and another) But there are many very anxious Conservatives. It is getting terribly like 1846. Anyway, none of these I have mentioned can Disraeli to my Peel.[49]

---

49. A reference to Disraeli's denunciation of then Conservative Prime Minister Sir Robert Peel's decision to repeal the Corn Laws in 1846: it took a generation for

The Press is divided. Beaverbrook's papers – *D Express*, *Sunday Express*, *Evening Standard* are already hysterical in opposition. Broadly speaking, all the rest of the Press (*Times*; *D.T. D Mail*; *D Mirror*) are sympathetic. But it is clear that we are approaching critical decisions, both for the Party and the nation. Opponents (Beaverbrook and Hinchingbrooke) are calling already for an Election, but I am not sure that they would really like one.

A Cabinet yesterday – routine business. We are having trouble about Teachers' salaries. They have put in a demand for 36% increase! . . . .

Read a very interesting book, just published by M&Co, called *Power and Policy in the USSR* by a Mr R[obert] Conquest. It is rather too detailed for the general reader, but it gives a very fascinating and I shd think fair picture of this strange system, half Orwellite and half Byzantine . . . .

President Kennedy will perhaps be able to give me some idea of de Gaulle's mind and his reaction to the proposals which (at my instance) the President will make to him. What an immense advantage de G has over me. No Parliament – and a Press that carries little influence![50] . . . .

20 May

. . . . The news from Geneva is bad in both Conferences. The Russians are now refusing any agreement unless French tests (wh they allege are done with our connivance) are brought to an end. In the Laos Conference, there is danger of a break-down owing to the breaches of the cease-fire. The Americans threaten to walk out. So it goes on. Meanwhile the British Trade Fair in Moscow has been opened with immense éclat. Mr K[hrushchev] has embraced the President of the BofT (Mr Maudling) and been in one of his most radiant moods.

The most enigmatic figure in all this is Mr K himself. He seems for the moment to have overcome all his rivals and achieved personal ascendancy about equal to Stalin. Yet there are many indications that his power is limited and that the stage may be being set for the next act in the struggle for Power . . . .

---

the Conservatives to recover from the resulting schism. The internal opponents had been prominent in the Suez Group.

50. Under Article 16 of his new Fifth Republic constitution de Gaulle had taken exceptional powers following the Generals' revolt.

22 May

.... Ld Beaverbrook's *Sunday Express* was in full cry yesterday. The leading article demands a General Election, so that the country may decide on Europe. 'Cross-bencher' says that the Home Secretary, R A Butler, has definitely decided to play the role of Disraeli – break the Government and lead the orthodox 'Country Party' to the defence of British Agriculture and the Commonwealth. I don't think this is true – as yet. But I do not hide from myself the magnitude of the decision that is soon going to face us ....

30 May

.... The Hong-Kong/Lancashire cotton agreement expires at the end of this year. So I am trying to get negotiations started for a renewed agreement. As before, the Board of Trade want to bring a lot of pressure on Hong-Kong; the Colonial Office are distressed. But if I can do so, I will try to get an agreement, for it is really vital to Lancashire to have some limitation on free imports of cheap textiles into England ....

A long Cabinet – 10.30–1 – this morning. We agreed a message to Commonwealth PMs (from me) proposing a visit from Sandys (Australia; New Zealand, and Canada) and to the others by some other minister to discuss Europe and the Common Market. I feel sure it is right to <u>consult</u> them while the Cabinet is itself trying to reach a conclusion and <u>not</u> afterwards – for that is not really consultation. Moreover, only a Cabinet minister can develop the whole argument, political as well as economic.

A long discussion on West Indian immigration into UK, wh is now becoming rather a serious problem. There seemed to be general agreement that we shall have to legislate in the autumn.[51] Colonial Secretary (rather surprisingly) concurred. But we must keep a final decision till then and meanwhile ask Ld Chancellor and his Committee (who have already done a lot of work) to go on preparing the necessary measures. There are a great many complications – not the least of wh is Irish immigration ....

Anthony and Clarissa Eden came to supper. He came at 7 and we had a good talk. I thought him much better and rather fatter (a good

---

51. The relevant Cabinet committee under Lord Kilmuir had just concluded that the numbers of immigrants were increasing and their quality falling. Rejecting controls via housing or health policy, they suggested immigration control instead, in what became the 1962 Commonwealth Immigrants Act.

sign) . . . . He was very useful and helpful about some of our problems. His meeting with de Gaulle and M Debré (a few weeks ago in Paris) had been useful. It seems clear that there has been a change in French opinion. They now seem really to want us in Europe – but will they pay our price?

The internal political situation about Europe is interesting. In both Government and opposition parties there are 3 groups – the keen partisans of our joining the Six; the keen opponents; and the doubtfuls. Of course, the Opposition has an easier hand to play; they can just wait and criticise whatever we may do.

31 May

. . . . There is a so-called settlement of the English Teachers 'pay' claim wh is going to lead to a lot of trouble. The SofS for Scotland has been firm, and refused more than 12%, facing strikes and all sorts of trouble – but successfully. A month later, the English Minister of Education wants to pay 16% . . . .

There is a good story going round about F.M. Earl Alexander. He went to Rome with the Queen on her recent visit. A young Italian official said to him 'Have you ever been to Rome before, General?' Slightly taken aback, Alex replied 'Oh yes! You know, I conquered it.'[52]

1 June

. . . . Laos; Berlin; the economic situation; Sir Roy Welensky; 'Sixes and Sevens' – now (with Finland) eights;[53] France and nuclear power; a new 'Security' case;[54] an unpopular and difficult Finance Bill; a growing sense of Russian pride and intransigeance – altogether, quite a pocketful of trouble. Will 1961 be the end? Who can tell? War in Laos and/or war over Berlin are both possible. The first wd not necessarily lead to general war; the second must do so, once serious military operations are launched . . . .

2 June

. . . . Colonial Policy Ctee 10.45–12. A most difficult situation is developing in the Cameroons. No decision, but some special studies to

---

52. His forces captured Rome on 4–5 June 1944.

53. Finland became an Associate Member of EFTA on 27 March 1961.

54. The discovery of the Soviet spy ring at the Admiralty Underwater Weapons Establishment in Portland.

be put in hand urgently. Our 'mandate' ends in October. It now looks as if, when we leave, the Communists will take over. Can anything be done to avoid this?[55]

12 noon. Harold Caccia – some useful gossip from Washington, in addition to some more serious discussion. The rather 'raffish' life of the President and his circle will be overlooked and even enjoyed by the American public if he has any luck or any success. So far, with Cuba, Laos, and now the Dominican Republic,[56] he has had nothing to show except failures. On the other hand, the American economy is recovering rather more rapidly than expected.

In the afternoon, a visit from Ben Gurion, PM of Israel. He was robust and active, in spite of his years. His chief plea was to be allowed to buy Thunderbird (our ground to air missile) His reason is the great superiority wh Nasser now has over Israel in the air. They have MIG Bombers, which Israel fighters cannot deal with. The Russians are (he says) training and probably operating the crews. On the ground, altho' the Egyptian army is improving under Russian instructors, Ben Gurion is confident that the Israelites can defeat the Egyptians. But in the air, they cd easily be overwhelmed at the very start. I replied that of course we wd think it over, but we really didn't want to start a missile race in the M East. It is true that 'Thunderbird' is defensive – or at least designed for a purely defensive role . . . .

Sandys, Iain Macleod and I met at 6. A long talk about Rhodesia. On S Rhodesia, according to Duncan Sandys, all the work is done. Nothing remains but to put the last touches to the White Paper and publish it. The Africans have now 'run out' (at least Nkomo) but this is largely a political gesture. Whitehead means to hold the referendum at the end of July, and believes that he will win, unless there is too much trouble about Northern Rhodesia. Altho' there is no settlement, or even grudging acquiescence, Governor Hone is now prepared to put forward to the parties in Lusaka important modifications wh shd help Welensky.[57] What the other parties will say, the Governor cannot tell . . . .

---

55. A guerrilla war against the Cameroon People's Union had been ongoing since 1955 and continued after the French part of Cameroon became independent on 1 January 1960.

56. Presumably a reference to the assassination of the US-backed dictator Rafael Trujillo on 30 May 1961.

57. Hone had suggested increasing the predominance of the Upper Roll to please

3 June

Commonwealth Sec; Colonial Sec; Mr Trend (Cabinet Office) came at
11.30 to decide what instructions shd now be sent to Governor Hone
and what message to Welensky. We adjourned for luncheon and
resumed at 2.45. Iain Macleod is clearly worried by the turn things
have taken. But altho' he seems to feel that Sandys has been 'appeasing'
Welensky at the expense of the White Paper scheme to wh the Govt is
honourably committed, I feel that Sandys has behaved absolutely
correctly and has done a superb job in getting W into a better frame
of mind and at least to face realities. What has upset the Colonial
Secretary is that the Governor, on his own, and without any prompting
from London, has put forward a compromise plan wh is not altogether
within the White Paper concept.[58] We were all surprised at this.
Eventually at about 5, we separated and I fear the Col Secy is in
unhappy mood. We seem to be back in an atmosphere of crisis and
'resignation'.

4 June (Sunday)

Last night, just before dinner, we got agreement on telegram to
Governor Hone (N Rhodesia) approving his attempt to get 'acquiescence' in his new plan from the African parties in Lusaka. We also
approved telegram from Sandys to Welensky telling him that we wd
try to get 'acquiescence' but that if we failed, 'all bets were off'. We
also told him that we cd not accept his (W's) proposed amendments to
the Governor's plan.

So our internal situation goes on, for the present. But Colonial Sec
(altho' a brilliant and most likeable man) is not an easy colleague. He
is a Highlander – wh means that he is easily worked up into an
emotional mood; it also means that he is proud and ambitious. But he
has great qualities – a soaring spirit and a real mastery of Parliamentary speaking. I wish he were not so fond of the Press. Every politician
who has cultivated them has injured his position, in the long run.

Welensky, whilst also changing the qualification so that more Africans were on
it.
58. In an attempt to try and force candidates to appeal to both European and
African constituents, the White Paper had envisaged a Middle Roll (the Upper
Roll plus the top third of the Lower Roll) electing reserved National seats.
Welensky had never liked this and Hone's suggestion was an attempt at an
alternative.

Before Radio and Television, it was perhaps excusable for politicians to fear them – and run after them. Now, with the loss of their monopoly, they have lost their power.

Sandys is a great contrast to Macleod. As cool as a cucumber; methodical; very strong in character; has gradually mastered the art of Parly speaking; tremendously hard-working; not easily shaken from his course – ambitious, and rather cruel (e.g. his treatment of his wife) The Press (Sunday) as futile as usual. It gets worse every week – but I find the gutter press at least more amusing than the Astor press. The *Observer* (David Astor) is more pretentious and more dangerous than *The Times* (John Astor) wh is just silly . . . .

Dorothy came to London from B.G. in the afternoon. We drove to London airport together, to meet President and Mrs Kennedy. They arrived about 8.20 – 50 minutes after the scheduled time. The reason was that the last talk with Kruschev at Vienna lasted rather longer than had been expected.

. . . . The President and I drove in an open car; Mrs K and D behind us, in a closed one. There was a <u>very</u> large crowd, almost – but not quite – as big as for President Eisenhower last year . . . .

11 June (Sunday)

I got to Birch Grove last evening, after one of the most exhausting weeks wh I care to remember. Everything is going wrong – and some things badly wrong. However, I have had it almost as bad – esp just after Suez.

The President's visit was a success from the point of view of our personal relations. He was kind, intelligent, and <u>very</u> friendly. I find my <u>personal</u> friendship beginning to grow into something like that wh I got with Eisenhower after a few months in Algiers. <u>Intellectual</u> relationship (to put it rather pompously) is, of course, much easier. Eisenhower was an American soldier, trained as a soldier and talking that language. He had no other experience at that time. He did not find it easy to <u>discuss</u> a problem, altho' his instincts about how to handle it were generally right. Kennedy, with an entirely different mental background, is quick; well-informed; subtle; but also – in appearance at any rate – modest, and proceeds more by asking questions than by answering them. Ike was surrounded by 'tycoons' and 'blockheads'. K is surrounded by university dons and 'egg-heads'. Ike was my friend and Britain's friend. Some of those round him had the old Republican animosity towards us. K looks like being a good friend to me. He has <u>some</u> old prejudices (perhaps a little of the Irish tradition) about us – but he lives in the modern world – even in the rather selfish modern world. His friends are intelligent or at least amusing. Ike's friends were not by any means all hostile. George Humphrey, for instance, helped a lot <u>after</u> Suez. But I think a Democrat administration wd have been more sympathetic <u>about</u> Suez and wd have helped us more in the earlier stages, after the seizure of the Canal. Foster Dulles took too hesitating and legalistic a view.

The greater part of our talk consisted of the President giving us his impressions of de Gaulle and of Mr Kruschev – what they said or did not say. Naturally, he was full of Mr K (having just left Vienna) and he was obviously much concerned and even surprised by the almost brutal frankness and confidence of the Soviet leader. The Russians are (or affect to be) 'on the top of the world'. They are now no longer frightened by aggression. They have at least as powerful 'nuclear' forces as the West.[59] They have interior lines. They have a buoyant economy, and will out-match capitalist society in the race for materialist wealth. It follows that they will make no concessions (unless these suit them) and will not be afraid of our reaction to what they may choose to do – in Germany or elsewhere . . . .

On Berlin, K delivered to the President a long aide-memoire – clearly intended for publication – it was pretty plausible and will be difficult to answer effectively. Kruschev is determined to bring the issue to a head in the autumn – perh <u>after</u> the German elections.[60]

Faced with all this, and by no means encouraged by the reality (apart from the superficial success) of his visit to Paris, the President seemed rather stunned – baffled, wd perhaps be fairer. This was the real reason for his wish for a <u>private</u> talk – the presence of even the leading experts and trusted civil servants on both sides prevents talk from being absolutely frank. I welcomed this. For I did not wish, if I called attention to some of the underlying realities of the Berlin problem, to be reported verbally and then misreported by hearsay, so that Americans wd think we were 'yellow' and French and Germans (who <u>talk</u> 'tough' but have no intention of <u>doing</u> anything about

59. This was not in fact the case, but was widely believed in London and
     Washington at the time, as were exaggerated views of the advance of Russian
     technology.
60. He threatened to sign a separate peace with East Germany, and that this would
     end existing Allied access rights to West Berlin.

Berlin) could ride out on us. (This has happened before, and I was determined not to let it happen again) . . . .

However, it was clear that the President (with the exception of the actual delivery of nuclear information or nuclear weapons) carried out most loyally our arrangement and really did do everything I had asked him to do both in Washington and in the memorandum which I sent him recently. De Gaulle was very avuncular, very gracious, very oracular, and very unyielding. He would take all the plums – tripartism, new arrangements in NATO, and help with the technique of missiles and bombs (other than the actual nuclear content) with cavalier profligacy. But when it came to <u>giving</u> anything in return – e.g. Britain's desire to enter Europe on reasonable terms, having regard to Commonwealth and British agricultural structures – then the General was in his most austere and Puritan mood. So far as I can see (unless the General was just playing the hand <u>very</u> close to his chest) my great plan has failed – or, at least, failed up to now. But we have at least got a completely new American attitude to our efforts and a new understanding. So Dillon (as a leading Democrat minister) is hardly on speaking terms with that Dillon (who was a leading Republican minister a few months ago and treated me so badly in Washington by giving our private talks almost verbatim to the Press) . . . .

At 8pm a very pleasant party at <u>Buckingham Palace</u> . . . . The Queen very kindly invited those of my leading colleagues whom I cd not have at luncheon – (Butler and Ted Heath) . . . .

The rest of this week has been very heavy going. The President of Mali (about 4 million people in Africa, formerly French Soudan) and his court. He was very amicable and very intelligent – obviously rather left wing and much impressed by Soviet achievements. Nevertheless, I think he is ready to learn and will probably moderate his views. We gave him full treatment – dinners, receptions, Guildhall and Palace – very tiring for Dorothy and me and very time consuming . . . .

. . . . Above all, looms a new economic and financial crisis. This has been a bad week in the market. Partly because of our bad 'balance of payments' position; partly because of widespread rumours that the Swiss franc is to be 'upvalued'; partly because of [a] sense of the worsening foreign situation – there has been a great loss (£100m or more) in the reserves . . . .

On Thursday, D and I went to Cambridge and I was given a degree

(Hon DL)[61] and it was amusing to see the differences between the ceremonies – as well as the similarities – at the two universities. The Public Orator was excellent (Mr Wilkinson) and both the Latin and English versions were admirable. Curiously, my old friend Jean Monnet was given a degree at the same time. Is this a happy omen for European unity? . . . .

There are lots more telegrams from Rhodesia. I fear that there is very little hope of reaching any settlement of N Rhodesia out there. So we shall have to reach our own decisions. This will put a great strain on the political situation here, as well as in Rhodesia. It's very sad, for though there are great issues at stake, the dispute is one wh it shd be possible to adjust. But Welensky hates Macleod and vice versa, and each hopes to destroy the other. Unfortunately, Sandys (Commonwealth Secy) will be going off on his visits to Australia, New Zealand etc (about Europe and the Common Market) about the critical time.

13 June
Cabinet – long and difficult. We decided not to get drawn into the Cameroons but to get out on October 1st, when our mandate ends[62] . . . .

14 June
Sir W Haley came to see me. *The Times* had (for once) a very sensible leading article on the Common Market problem . . . .

15 June
I could not speak or move this morning. Telephoned to Sir John Richardson who sent me some medicine and came at 7pm to see me. Nothing wrong but exhaustion. I stayed in bed all day, except from 2.45 to 3.30. I managed to get to HofC and answer my questions. This is important. If I am ill for a day (wh by God's grace I have not been since I kissed hands as P.M.) the press will put me down as on the way out.

I lay in bed counting my blessings!

---

61. Actually an LL D (Doctor of Laws).
62. A former German colony, Cameroon had been governed under a League of Nations mandate by the British and French after the First World War. It was reunited when the British withdrew.

1. <u>Economic problem</u>	Trade balance (prob[ably] insoluble)
	Loss of invisibles
	overstrain in Economy
2. <u>Europe</u>	Sixes and Sevens (obviously insoluble)
3. <u>Laos</u>	(no settlement in sight. Communists now breaking cease fire)
4. <u>Central Africa</u>	Political crisis certain – at home and in Welensky etc
	Federation
5. <u>Berlin</u>	(No solution possible; if anyone tries to talk sense, he is at once called a coward and traitor)
6. <u>Security</u>	(Troublesome, but I think manageable – Opposition will try to get a ministerial resignation)
7. <u>Recruiting Regular Forces</u>	(target will <u>not</u> be reached. So what do we do? 'Selective Service' or what) . . . .

I am writing this in bed, after taking some of the doctor's drugs, so perhaps the mood is blacker than it ought to be. But the trade figures are really awful . . . .

18 June (Sunday)

A great number of officials arrived. I think we were 25 or 26 at luncheon. We got <u>somewhere</u> – but not very far really. Like all great issues, it will (in the end) be decided by some quite small events. At any rate, we agreed enough to allow the 'peripatetic' ministers (or perhaps one shd say the St John the Baptists)[63] to set out on their tour of Commonwealth countries. This is really quite a good plan. Duncan Sandys will go [to] Australia, N.Z., and Canada. Heath will go to Cyprus. Ld Perth to W Indies. Peter Thorneycroft to India, Pakistan, Malaya, Ceylon. John Hare to Ghana, Nigeria, Sierra Leone etc . . . .

A <u>terrible</u> message from Sir Roy W arrived tonight. Rude, blackmailing, coarse and silly. He will come to London – rally his friends in the Press and the Conservative Party (Lords Salisbury and Lambton,

---

63. Presumably Macmillan meant that they were to prepare the way for the European entry bid, as John the Baptist had prepared the way for Jesus.

as well as Turton, Grimston etc) He will have Ld Beaverbrook's press.
He will denounce ministers as crooks and double-crossers. He will
dissolve his Parlt and ask for a 'doctor's mandate'. He will ruin
altogether Whitehead's chances of holding <u>Southern</u> Rhodesia steady
(the referendum about the new (and fairly liberal) constitution
wouldn't have a chance) He will publish all our private and personal
messages (choosing of course, passages out of their context to prove
his favourite point that he 'has been let down', and omitting all the
passages wh give a fair or impartial picture) He will publish (alleged)
interception of telephonic and other communications between British
ministers. He will pose again as the injured innocent, whose true
character is only understood by Lords Salisbury and Beaverbrook. If
the result of all this is a) the defeat of Whitehead's plebiscite on the
new constitution b) the consequent retirement of Whitehead and the
coming to office of the Dominion Party – ignorant, narrow, and almost
Nazi c) the end of Federation since not even the S Rhodesian Parlt will
now be its friend d) violent outbreaks of disappointed Africans in N
Rhodesia, with serious conflicts between both races and the police e)
an increasing economic slump, leading to something like disaster – if
this is the result, R.W. doesn't care. It's the fault of HMG . . . .

19 June
. . . . (Africa Committee) This meeting includes wise old birds like Ld
Chancellor with his great experience, and some very able and sensitive
characters like Foreign Sec (Home) We all agreed – tho' with some
hesitation – to stand firm on a 'package' deal with Welensky, based on
a fair interpretation of the White Paper. The real issue, in N Rhodesia,
turns on 'Upper Roll Predominance'. Sir RW and his friends demand
this; Sir John Moffat (Liberal) and the Africans, while in theory
demanding 'democracy' or 'one man one vote', will accept equality of
strength between upper and lower roll in electing the national seats. In
other words, it is 50–50 (as the White Paper says) or 60–40, as Sir
RW demands. There are, however, points where we can fairly meet the
Federal Party. The White Paper says national candidates must be made
to appeal to <u>both rolls</u> and to <u>both races</u>. (The minimum percentage is
to do this. But certain flaws have been shewn to exist in our minimum
percentage scheme, as drawn, and we will alter it. There are 4 or 5
other points of varying importance where we can help)[64] . . . .

---

64. Under Welensky's pressure the scheme was amended so that candidates had to

4–6. Cabinet. Ministers have been very good about letting a few of us try to manage this tiresome Central African affair. But I felt that we had now reached a point at which they must be properly informed .... I was much impressed by the quality and tone. Against this background the Commonwealth Secy shews to great advantage. *'vir gravissimus et ornatissimus'*.[65] The Colonial Secy does not always do himself full justice, as he seems to change his ground too often (this particularly upsets the For Secretary)

The Cabinet decided 1) to stick to 'equal' voting between the 2 rolls 2) to make the qualifying percentage on a <u>racial</u> not a <u>roll</u> basis. (This is right, because owing to there being 2000–3000 Africans on the upper roll, an African could, in theory, get the qualifying number without getting any European support, while the opposite is not true) ....

Dined with For Sec (Alec Home) at Bucks, to talk over various insoluble problems. He was very distressed about Rhodesia. But he admitted that the Cabinet had decided with its eyes open. I had made no attempt to minimise – I even exaggerated – the likelihood of Sir Roy Welensky 'going off the deep-end' and the effects of such action. Whitehead would be sunk. Harper (the horrid little S Rhodesian 'pocket Hitler') wd triumph (on his policy of taking away from the Africans the few privileges which they have got) Sir R.W. wd be in open rebellion and HMG put in a ludicrous as well as impossible position: at the same time, Central Africa might be the scene of strife and conflict on a terrible scale, white versus white, black v black, all against all ....

21 June

.... Sir John Richardson has been to see me. I have no more *élan vital*![66] I am finished! In other words, I ought to have a month's holiday. As it is, I am to have four days, starting tomorrow evening.

---

attain a percentage of votes from both races rather than both rolls, fixed at whichever was less out of 12.5% or 400 votes. This favoured Europeans since 400 votes equated to 12.5% of European but only 4% of African votes. Candidates were also required to obtain at least 20% of their votes from either roll and an Asian seat was introduced. These changes were intended to ensure cross-racial and pro-federal electoral success.

65. This appears to be a misquotation of Cicero's *'gravissimus vir et ornatissimus civis'* – a most dignified man and excellent citizen.
66. Life force.

22 June

. . . . The Cabinet is being very steadfast on Rhodesia, in spite of
immense pressure exerted by Sir RW on his agents here (Lords Salisbury, and Lambton operate in one sphere; Rt Hon Turton and Mr
Grimston in another; [John] Hall MP and some smaller fry, in a third;
Fell, Williams and others of the lunatic fringe in a fourth, finally, in a
fifth, a number of MPs on both sides of the House, who are not exactly
'bought' but have received some favours . . . .

My 'rest cure' failed – for on Friday afternoon I had to come down
and preside over a number of ministers who spent nearly all Friday –
morning, afternoon, and evening, in the Cabinet Room. Rumours kept
changing – Sir R Welensky would come to London after all. He would
not. No: he would. And so this threat (or promise) was played,
backwards and forwards, like a ping-pong ball. Sandys kept his head;
Macleod overplayed his hand; Alec Home was so disgusted by Macleod's tactics that he nearly resigned himself; Ld Chancellor tried to
keep the peace; then they sent for me – practically in pyjamas! . . . .
The culminating scene was at Salisbury – Welensky, waiting to board
the London Comet, to bring him here, and urged to do so by
Greenfield's persistent telephone calls. Another aeroplane, smaller but
more seductive, was also awaiting his will – he could go to N Rhodesia,
to rest and fish. Finally, he was called to the telephone box in Salisbury
airport and solemnly adjured by Duncan Sandys (who has a noble
'organ') not to come. If he came, all our concessions wd be back in the
melting pot. 'That sounds like a threat' said Welensky. 'It is' said
Sandys . . . .

Saturday morning, Sir John R[ichardson] came and was encouraging – if I can rest. But when and how can I rest? I am beginning (at
last) to feel old and depressed . . . .

Then the telephone began. Welensky presses for more concessions.
I have said no . . . . It is now absolutely vital to make the announcement and stop further argument.

At last, this seems to have been achieved and at 7pm tonight I was
told that everything was settled and the Colonial Secy wd make the
statement tomorrow. I sent a final telegram to Sir Roy W of rather
insincere 'good wishes' . . . . The ministers are all 'on edge'. In spite of
all the threatened resignations (a daily event with Macleod) no resignation has actually become effective. Macleod, with many faults, has
been persistent, imaginative, and ingenious. Sandys has been most
loyal to me and absolutely tireless. Nor have we, in making some

concessions to Welensky, surrendered any principle. We have <u>not</u> conceded 'Upper Roll Control' – and that was the real point. All these are comforting reflections, but they may all be proved wrong in a few days! . . . .

Alec Home has sent me a host of minutes – but they are clear and well argued. I agree with him, and yet I don't! I feel 'in my bones' that President K[ennedy] is going to fail to produce any real leadership. The American Press and Public are beginning to feel the same. In a few weeks they may turn to us. We must be ready. Otherwise we may drift to disaster over Berlin – a terrible diplomatic defeat or (out of sheer incompetence) a nuclear war.

8 July (Saturday)

The stream of visitors – each involving a luncheon, a dinner, a reception, a cocktail party – makes work almost impossible during the last 6 weeks of the summer. Moreover, as a new State is born almost every month, the flow increases . . . .

In addition, I have had a number of speeches. A large rally last Saturday at Bowood Park – the day our troops entered Kuwait.[67] This was a very successful affair – 6000–7000 people – I had not been since George Lansdowne pulled down the later and larger house [in 1955]. It has certainly revealed the earlier and smaller house in its true beauty . . . .

<u>Problems</u> . . . .

1. <u>Security</u> – we have got through the immediate Parliamentary row and I have been able to save the First Lord [of the Admiralty].[68]

2. <u>Berlin</u>. We have played this rather cannily, I think. By agreeing to all that the Americans propose, even the absurd 'contingency planning' we have, I think, rather turned the tables on the *Washington Post*, *Chicago Tribune* and other anti-British forces in and outside the administration and Congress. They have been accusing us of 'dragging our feet' – but Ld Home and I have been making such firm statements in Parliament and

---

67. Kuwait became independent on 19 June 1961. Following reported Iraqi threats, British forces were deployed there at the end of the month, being replaced by Arab League forces later in the summer.

68. This followed the publication on 13 June 1961 of the Romer report into the Portland spy ring.

outside . . . . Anyway, after some weeks of this manoeuvring, the President has changed his tune, and has let it be known that he favours 'negotiations'. The regular methods of attuning public opinion to this change are being applied. Even the columnists have to change their tune . . . .

3. <u>Laos</u>. Worse again. Here the warlike party in Washington seems to be forcing the pace . . . .

4. <u>Europe</u>. The situation is unchanged. Sandys, Thorneycroft, and Hare are touring the Commonwealth . . . .

5. <u>Central Africa</u>. By a miracle, we have achieved a solution of the immediate crisis . . . . Even Kenya seems a bit easier.

6. <u>Economic</u> situation at home has not improved, but has not got spectacularly worse. The Chancellor of the Exr is here [Chequers] this week-end and we will work out our plans. The real trouble is how to cut down <u>military expenditure</u> and <u>Overseas Aid</u>. These together are costing us nearly £500[m] across the exchanges. With the virtual disappearance of the 'invisibles' (£200m sunk to £20[m]) the task is well-nigh impossible for us. Something must go. Internally, expenditure is too high. But (with a few noble exceptions) individual ministers are not very cooperative.

Meanwhile, as if all these difficulties were insufficient, the <u>Kuwait</u> crisis blew up. The Cabinet left the whole management of this affair to me. I got the For Secy and the Minister of Defence to work side by side with me, wh they did with admirable loyalty and skill. But, remembering Suez, I was careful throughout to have meetings of ministers (including Chancellor of Exr; Ld Chancellor; and Home Secretary) and also – before the final decision to launch the forces – of the whole Cabinet.

We had good support from C.D.S. (Ld Mountbatten) and the Chiefs of Staff. The plan (in spite of inescapable difficulties, chiefly due to 'overflying' problems) worked out pretty well. We worked through some long and anxious nights, esp when we thought Kassem [Qasim] wd seize Kuwait City and territory virtually unopposed. Now our worry is the opposite. Since the Iraqi attack has <u>not</u> in fact developed, all the pressure will be turned on us. It is going to be difficult and expensive to stay; hard to get out. The Opposition in Parlt have behaved pretty well – so far . . . .

All this concentration of work on special problems, combined with the usual Parliamentary routine (PQ etc) speeches, as well as the calls of hospitality, have tired me greatly. It is quite an effort now to make an effort. But I cannot leave the ship now. I must try to get her into calmer waters before I do so.

I have been reading Toynbee quite steadily.[69] It is soothing, in a curious way, to learn about so many civilisations wh have 'risen and fallen' . . . .

15 July (Saturday)

. . . . From the internal political point of view I think the 1922 Committee, wh I addressed on Thursday, was the most important. I was rather nervous about it, having heard talk about great discontent in the Party. But in fact it went off very well. I made a serious and carefully prepared speech. The questions were not hostile (except from Ld Hinchingbrooke who is <u>mad</u> – but not <u>bad</u>, like Lord Lambton) One piece of good news came out yesterday, in the shape of the trade figures, showing a much reduced 'gap' – down to £20m. Of course, it may be a flash in the pan – but it may be a beginning of better things. The worst feature of the situation is the <u>utter irresponsibility</u> of labour in some of the <u>new</u> industries (motor-cars: aviation and the like) and the <u>hopeless conservatism</u> of labour in some of the <u>old</u> industries (shipbuilding etc) So what with 'wild-cat' in one and 'restrictive practices' in the other group, our poor economy suffers grievously . . . .

22 July

Chequers. I came last night, after a Cabinet meeting at HofC. At this meeting, which was fully attended (except C of Exr who sent Economic Secy) and at which <u>every</u> member of the Cabinet took part, there was a <u>unanimous</u> decision in principle that I shd announce on Monday next that HMG wd <u>apply to enter the Common Market</u>. Whether or not, having taken this momentous decision and communicated it to the Governments of the Six, we shall reach agreement on the vital points of a) Commonwealth b) British agriculture, I cannot tell. I shd judge that the chances are <u>against</u> an agreement, unless – on political grounds – de Gaulle changes his mind. For I feel that he is still hostile and jealous . . . .

. . . . [T]he HofC has become rather restless. I have agreed to answer at 3.15 – which means a quarter of an hour grilling at Question

---

69. Macmillan was working his way through Arnold Toynbee's twelve-volume analysis of the rise and fall of civilisations, *A Study of History* (1934–61).

Time twice a week. Under the old system, my questions were often only partially reached or not at all . . . .

. . . . The economic situation gets worse in the short term. It looks as if another £100[m] will go from the reserves in July. I only hope the export figures will be good. I fear that now sterling (being the weakest world currency) is taking all the strain of the rapidly worsening international situation . . . .

23 July
I have read a 'first novel' by a Mr Vincent Cronin – *The Letter after Z.* Not ill written; adventurous; readable; but too much sex, in the sense of descriptions not of love but of coupling. If the Victorian novelists were too prudish, the Elizabethan are being too anatomical – almost medical – in their descriptions. . . . I seldom read novels – at least new ones – but I could not sleep . . . .

Selwyn [Lloyd] has made good progress with his statement, but we are not very happy about the Government expenditure aspect. If we are to get our 'drawings' from the International Monetary Fund, we shall have to make – or pretend to make – large savings on Govt expenditure. This is (in the short as well as in the long run) more difficult than extra taxation . . . . But if the package is not good enough, the international usurers – bankers – will turn us down. Then sterling will go. (Whether this matters as much as we all think or not, I am not sure. It matters politically, because sterling has become a symbol. What really matters is that we should not add to demand by wage increases) . . . .

24 July
The Cabinet met at 11 and agreed the Chancellor of the Exr's proposals.[70] There was general support for not using the second regulator (payroll tax) and for not altering Hire Purchase terms. We must now 'wait and see' the result on sterling . . . .

26 July
The Press is hostile – but of course has nothing to suggest. Sterling

---

70. Announced the following day and including the Pay Pause, a seven-month freeze on public sector wages to contain inflationary pressures, increases in purchase tax and interest rates and cuts in government spending.

made a recovery yesterday evening, as one would expect. But will it hold? . . . .

29 July

. . . . Worked all morning on the speech for Wednesday – the Common Market. This will be a most important debate – not easy to handle. But at least I shall not (I wd expect) be howled down by Gaitskell and the Labour Party . . . . Maurice [Macmillan] came and we had a drive round the estate. At Pooks[71] I found all the family, except Joshua. Alex was in tremendous form. He has just left Eton and is hoping to be taken at Balliol next term. Joshua (aged 16) has become a rabid Marxist and wears a 'Ban the Bomb' [badge]. 'Terribly conventional' says his brother, contemptuously . . . .

5 August

. . . . It has indeed been an extraordinary week. . . . In the Financial and Economic struggle, we have – it seems – won the <u>first round</u>. The measures wh we discussed at such length with the Governor and others have been successful, at least in the short run. The pressure on sterling has stopped – the rate has risen – and some money is coming back to the reserves. We have also paid back some of the loans from the Central Banks. The large drawing from IMF has been satisfactorily arranged.[72] So the speculators will feel that whatever may happen in the long run, sterling will not be devalued in the short run. In addition, the rise in the 90 days Bill rate to 6½% or above, shd alter the 'leads and lags' position, and make ordinary business men more ready to hold sterling or sterling Bills against their future needs. I hope the 'forward' position will now begin to improve. But, of course, all this is preliminary to the <u>second round</u> – that is, whether we can restrain personal incomes to a level justified by productivity. If we can do that, exports shd begin to rise and imports fall. The short term measures, including the use of the first regulator, the Bank 'squeeze' etc should have some impact on demand – perhaps, as months pass, to the tune of several hundred millions. But this will all be nullified if we put up personal incomes by £1000m in the next twelve months, as we have in the last twelve months. The Cabinet discussed the very difficult

---

71. Maurice Macmillan's house, where he lived with wife Katie, daughter Rachel and sons Alexander, Joshua, Adam and David.

72. $1.5 billion was borrowed.

question of the Government's <u>own</u> employees – civil servants, industrial and non-industrial; health service employees; police etc. Here we
have <u>compulsory arbitration</u> agreements, binding on both sides, and
going back to 1925. Are we to honour them? If we do, in one or two
'disputes' outstanding the arbitrator will be sure to give anything
between 6%–8%. Then private industry will despise the Government
and throw up the sponge. This means devaluation next spring. (The
only ministers seriously in favour of this course were Butler and to
some extent Macleod) Are we to 'suspend' them – as an Act of State?
For this, Lord Mills, Attorney General, and some other. Or are we to
give notice that while the machinery of negotiation, including arbitration, is to go on, we must reserve the right of when and in what stages
to implement any decision. This is really the 'pause'. Minister of
Labour – fortified by his officials – was strongly in favour of this third
course. Chancellor of Exr, on the whole, preferred [this]. (I cd see that
Sir Norman Brook favoured it) So it was settled, at a Cabinet held
yesterday (Friday) morning. I suggested that it might be helpful for this
decision to be conveyed to the Civil Service T. Union leaders, representing the various bodies, at an <u>oral</u> interview and not just shot at
them by a cold official letter. We shd make some <u>appeal</u> to them, as
well as confront them with [a] <u>firm decision</u>. This too was agreed.

The other great question wh has filled the week has been 'The
Common Market' . . . . On Monday, I made the statement wh the
Cabinet has agreed, announcing the intention of HMG to make a
formal application for membership of the EEC under Article 237 of
the Treaty of Rome[73] with a view to a negotiation on our obligations,
internal and external (British agriculture and Commonwealth Trade)
There were a lot of supplementaries, wh I answered as well as I could
and the general effect was fairly good. But the Conservative Party is,
naturally, anxious and rather jumpy . . . .

On Wednesday morning, the 3 or 4 weeks Press campaign against
me – carried on in almost every paper – as being tired, failing, losing
grip etc, culminated in a report in the luncheon editions of the *Evening
Standard* and the *Evening News* that I had had a 'heart attack'. Harold
Evans was rung up all the day by every conceivable paper, news agency

---

73. This allowed any European state to apply to join. In making his statement on
    31 July Macmillan stressed the risk of European isolationism and that the
    object of British entry was to prevent this and to promote 'greater unity of the
    free world'.

etc in every country in the world. All he could say is 'wait and see. The P.M. introduces the debate on the Common Market at 3.30 this afternoon'. So much depended on the speech. At the audience on Tuesday evening the Queen expressed concern at these reports of my health. I cd only remind her of what Mark Twain said of the reports of his death[74] .... By a piece of good luck (aided by an excellent mildly stimulant pill wh Sir John Richardson had given me) the speech was a tremendous success, both in matter and manner. Everyone, on both sides, listened to it without interruption. Many of my friends thought it the best speech I had ever made. The late evening papers (perhaps a little repentant of all their whispering campaign culminating in the heart attack [rumour]) switched right round. *Evening Standard* heading was 'Premier Rebounds – Back to Top Form' wh (in view of Max Beaverbrook's position on Common Market etc) was generous. Anyway, it was lucky – for a failure or only a moderately good speech at this point might have been fatal. Gaitskell made what was meant to be a 'balancing' speech, but the result was that he lost all the ground he had made in the last few weeks. His speech (in Churchill's favourite phrase) did not 'match the level of events' ....

Maudling wound up in an adequate speech, but not one of his best. On the second day (Thursday) Wilson made a brilliant speech, attacking the Common Market but more intent on attacking HMG. It was mean – as is his character – but admirably done. Ted Heath (Ld P[rivy] Seal) answered in a speech mainly addressed to the Conservative doubtfuls (Commonwealth interests; sovereignty etc) and tried to undo the harm done by a very clever and very hostile speech made on the day before by Sir Derek Walker-Smith. This he did well – quietly and simply. Shinwell made a wild speech; [Michael] Foot a bitter one (admirably dealt with by a crushing quotation by Sandys later) Maurice made one of the best speeches of the debate and enormously increased his reputation. He has come on tremendously, in vigour of thought and power of details. Ld Hinchingbrooke, Sir P Smithers, Miss Jenny Lee – all spoke. Our new alliance between the extreme Right and the extreme Left was very queer. It was ridiculed by someone who said he had lived to see 'Butskell' replaced by 'Silverbrooke'[75] ....

---

74. 'The report of my death is an exaggeration', said by the American novelist to a reporter in 1897.

75. Mr Butskell was invented by *The Economist* in 1954 to describe the apparent continuity in economic policy from Labour's Gaitskell to the Tory Butler.

The official Labour amendment was fatuous and was so like the Govt motion in essentials that a strong Speaker (like Fitzroy)[76] would have refused to call it. However, it was voted on and by some miracle we won by well over 100 .... When it came to the Government motion, the Opposition abstained. A division was forced by the extreme Left – 5 voted against us, including 1 Tory .... About 20–22 Conservatives abstained. We expected 30 – so the whips have done well. They abstained in both divisions. The Conservative abstainers are of two kinds – earnest Imperialists, like Biggs-Davison, Russell and others. This disgusted group (who oppose the Govt in every trouble, whatever the subject) [are] led by 3 ex-ministers. 2 of them I had to dismiss for incompetence or idleness – Turton and Walker-Smith. 1 was dropped by either Churchill or Eden – and he is angry with me for not having made him Speaker, a post held by a former Grimston in the 17th or 18th century.[77] The others [are] the usual grumblers, like Paul Williams, Jenkins, etc. But I see no Disraeli among them; not even a Lord George Bentinck[78] ....

.... In the afternoon I recorded a T.V. broadcast. In the interval of other things, we have been trying to prepare for this and in the end we got quite a good script. But how to 'perform' a 12 minute 'solo' is quite another thing. I have learned to do the interviews or discussions adequately. But the 'solo' (wh is thought to suit when one speaks as P.M. to the nation – and other nations) is much more difficult. We had 3 times and finally chose the last. (Certainly, this 'recording' technique is much less nerve-wracking and produces better results) ....

I spoke on August 4th – the 47th anniversary of the outbreak of the First World War – from which fatal date spring all our troubles – the beginning of the end of Europe's supremacy, and the predominance of the white man in the world. From this date began the end of the old British Empire and the capture of the greatest Euro/Asian country –

Silverbrooke was presumably a Eurosceptic compound of the left-wing Labour MP Sydney Silverman and the Tory right-winger Lord Hinchingbrooke. The term does not appear in the record of this Commons debate, so it is unclear who said it. Jenny Lee, widow of Aneurin Bevan, was another left-wing Labour MP.

76. Edward Fitzroy, Speaker 1928–43.

77. Sir Robert Grimston, MP for Westbury. Sir Harbottle Grimston was Speaker in 1660.

78. Disraeli's principal collaborator in the backbench revolt against Sir Robert Peel in 1846.

China – by the strange doctrines of a German Jew intellectual – Karl Marx. Happily, we did not realise all this when we were young.

6 August (Sunday)

A quiet day yesterday. I slept badly, but stayed in bed, dozing and reading till luncheon. A good deal of rain in the morning. The Macmillans and Fabers are all around, which is very pleasant. They are all such nice children – considerate, amusing, and apparently fond of the grandparents. The little ones, of course, adore Dorothy – who has a magical way of treating children. The older ones like arguing with me. It reminds me very much of my youth and how we all argued then . . . .

The Press (Sunday) is puzzled and rather annoyed by my 'come-back'. I have always had a bad, or at the best a grudging Press – I think because I do not cultivate sufficiently their rather unpleasant proprietors (Beaverbrook; Rothermere; Roy Thomson; David Astor) The only exception to the general deterioration of all the Press into treating politics, economics, finance, literature with a sort of 'servants hall gossip' technique is *The Times*. It is sometimes very silly; often intellectually patronising; but it is not corrupt . . . .

7 August

The Russians have put another man in orbit round and round the Earth and brought him safely back. He seems to have gone round 17 times. It is a wonderful feat of science and technology, altho' I shd have thought it rather dull for the man . . . .

The Lord Chancellor and Lady K[ilmuir] to dinner. I had a long talk about the future of the Ministry and the problems ahead. David K is absolutely loyal, and without being brilliant, very sensible. It is, I think, important to have some changes in the Government. But it will not be easy to get any vacancies without some painful decisions.

8 August

. . . . The Americans have made a complete *volte-face*. They now want to prepare immediately a 'negotiation' with Soviet Russia to be held in October (that is, after the German elections and before Mr K[hrushchev]'s Party Conference). This is remarkable, because up to now they have been taking a 'tough' line and opposed to negotiation, exc[ept] in the last resort thro' UNO. We have always been in favour of negotiation at some point, preferably before the Soviet signature of a Treaty with the DDR, but, if necessary, at a later stage if any pressure is in fact put on access to Berlin. The French and the Germans are shocked by the new American policy and want to wait. They accept the need for negotiation, but think that it wd be taken as a sign of weakness if we offer it now, and wd negative, in Russian minds, any effect which the military preparations may have. The For Secy took a middle position, shewing sympathy with the French and German view (this is important from the 'European' standpoint) but suggesting that we might postpone the offer of negotiation until the first week of September or thereabouts . . . .

9 August

. . . . There was quite a lot going on, including the draft of a letter from me to Prof Erhard (President for the month) making Britain's formal application to join the European Community. This was not too easy to draft and everyone had different views. Ld P[rivy] Seal (Heath) was acting for F.O. Eventually, a text was agreed. I signed it; it was sent to London and will go by bag to Bonn tonight. This is quite an historic affair! 6 months after I concocted the Grand Design at Chequers after Christmas.

The other subject was the military and political command structure for NATO etc. It is really urgent to get this settled, esp in view of all the nuclear weapons there are lying about in Europe, which some idiot may decide to use . . . .

Another day of complete rest, as ordered by the doctor! . . . .

On the short term economic front, the situation seems in hand. Sterling is strong and being supported by foreign buying. We must now face up to the wage battle. This will be decisive, one way or the other. Then there will be Govt expenditure and the 1962–3 estimates. We are bound to have trouble with the ministers in the spending departments – esp with Minister of Education. Nor will the Minister of Defence find it easy to make the economies – esp the overseas economies – wh we must have. At the same time, what is the use of our scraping and scrounging to get £50–150m of 'economies', if the extra wage and salary bill of £1000m or more is presented again? If this happens, sterling must be devalued. Yet, if this is not to happen, there are bound to be one or more serious strikes . . . .

11 August

. . . . A very busy day, with 2 boxes, both large and difficult! Most of the decisions to be taken can wait till Monday, when I shall be in London and can see Sir N Brook and others. All my colleagues, after wishing me a good holiday, have gone away, leaving me in charge of all the Departments of State! . . . .

12 August

. . . . I had a little walk in the woods with [gamekeeper] Blake. The tame pheasants have done pretty well. The wild birds nested and hatched well, but have suffered from foxes and cats. The foolish laws wh we passed against traps have made it more difficult to deal with vermin. Rabbits are coming back and the new 'humane' traps don't catch them . . . .

19 August

. . . . A lot of telephoning, morning and evening, to Alec Home about the 'Berlin Crisis'. The East German authorities have shut down on all movement from East to West Berlin.[79] The flood of refugees had reached such proportions – over 3000 a day – that they were probably almost compelled to take this course. Partly because the West German elections are going on, and partly because the Americans have got very excited, the situation is tense and may become dangerous . . . .

. . . . The President sent me a message about sending more troops into Berlin. Militarily, this is nonsense. But I have agreed to send in a few armoured cars etc, as a gesture. I still feel that from Kruschev's point of view, the Eastern German internal situation was beginning to crumble and something had to be done . . . .

25 August

I left Bolton Abbey after a most delightful week and went by train from York to Edinburgh, where Dorothy met me in her car and we drove together to Gleneagles Hotel . . . .

. . . . I suppose the newspapers will criticise us for being on holiday during the Berlin crisis, but actually this is nonsense. The situation has got considerably worse, however, during the week. The Russian and East German pressure on Berlin is growing apace. East Berliners are literally 'sealed off' and the crossing places are few and well guarded. There is, actually, nothing illegal in the East Germans stopping the flow of refugees and putting themselves behind a still more rigid iron

---

79. The Berlin Wall went up on 13 August.

curtain. It certainly is not a very good advertisement for the benefits of Communism – but it is not (I believe) a breach of any of our agreements. However, there is now a new note, attacking us for our misuse (as they call it) of our military air route to West Berlin. The Russians accuse us of using this route – intended for Western military purposes – for taking 'revanchists and saboteurs' (that means Adenauer and Co) in and out of W Berlin and of taking East German refugees out. The legal issue is rather obscure. The Americans have been very active (sending more troops and their Vice-President to Berlin) but have kept their heads. The French (which means de Gaulle) have been very extreme, and seem to contemplate war with equanimity. The West Germans have behaved pretty sensibly, in spite of the election . . . .

26 August
D and I played from 9–12, on the King's course. We were rather harried by photographers, but played rather well. Neither of us has touched a club for 12 months . . . .

31 August (Thursday)
. . . . The 'approach' to Russia over Berlin is not yet settled, but it looks as if the French will agree in the end. Congo bad – the U.N. having seized Katanga, agst wh Sir Roy Welensky has spoken violently. N Rhodesia unsettled, and the problem will arise as to whether we are to modify the constitutional plan. (I fear we shall have a conflict again between the two Secretaries of State) Kuwait is settled in principle, but the Arab League is finding great difficulty in producing a force to replace our troops. The market is unsettled and we have lost some sterling, altho' the rate has held up fairly well. The T Unions are angry with the Govt over the wage pause, but it is too soon to see what will actually happen . . . .

4 September
. . . . The President and I have issued a joint declaration calling on the Russians to cease all atmospheric tests and offering to do the same.[80] This agreement to be without control or supervision. The World Press has received this declaration very well indeed. Even the Conference of Neutral Countries in Belgrade has been impressed.

---

80. The Russians had just done a series of 16 tests.

5 September

.... There is more trouble in N Rhodesia. Col Sec has been urged by Moffat (Liberal) and Kaunda to make some changes in the constitution proposals. But if we do, it will (a) seem a concession to violence (b) set off Welensky in full cry, with consequential results at home[81] ....

6 September

.... After luncheon, Sir P Dixon (our ambassador in Paris) called. He has agreed to my proposal that he shd take on the leadership of the officials who are to do the Common Market negotiation. But this must be fixed with de Gaulle. I am hoping that he will be pleased with the idea .... If de G agrees, he wd not give up the Embassy in Paris, but of course Rumbold (minister) wd have to do the routine work. In much the same way Chauvel (French ambassador in London) is the chief French delegate at the Laos conference in Geneva ....

.... At 5pm to 6pm a meeting on various 'Intelligence' problems – chiefly reconnaissance flights, submarine intelligence etc. All these involve some risk (remember always U2) but great gains. It is a question of balance of the two ....

Altho' the joint declaration of President and Prime Minister, with offer to Mr K[hrushchev], had an excellent reception all over the world, the only reply of the Russians was to explode another atmospheric bomb. Unfortunately, this caused the Americans to get very excited, and much pressure to be exerted from the Pentagon and from the Hill[82] on the White House. The President gave in and has announced his decision to resume underground tests, not repeat not atmospheric tests. Altho' the British Press has not been altogether sympathetic, this hurried decision, of which we were given only 1½ hours notice, has taken the gilt off the gingerbread, and relieved the Russians of some part of their presentational difficulties. (It is interesting that the President/PM offer has been censored from all Russian press and radio) ....

9 September

.... Messages about a possible Russian attempt to stop our aircraft, civil and military, going into Berlin. For some reason, this is now thought likely. I rather doubt it. A most elaborate procedure has been worked out, with a view to avoiding an armed clash as long as

---

81. A reconsideration was promised on 13 September, if violence ceased.
82. Capitol Hill, the seat of Congress.

possible. In the last resort, our <u>military</u> aircraft are to have 'fighter' escort, who are to defend them. But since any attack is more likely to be by ground-to-air missile, I do not think this will be very efficacious. However, there is <u>not</u> repeat <u>not</u> to be any attack on the missile bases, in such an event, but an immediate recourse to the Security Council and then the Assembly of U.N. . . . .

15 September
. . . . The U.N. authorities have tried to conquer Katanga province on behalf of the Central Govt by brute force. Tshombe has resisted. There have been a good many casualties. Hammerskjöld has either blundered, or his agents have acted without his authority – or (wh I fear is the most likely) he has deliberately deceived us . . . .

What is more dangerous, Ginzenga (a Russian stooge) is getting powerful in the Central Govt. A communist African has been sent as 'agent' to 'govern' the Katanga province. Unless we and the Americans act quickly and resolutely, we shall have undone in a week all we have done – at huge expense – in a year. Congo will be handed to Russia on a plate . . . .

. . . . The Turkish trials are over, and poor M. Menderes and M. Zorlu are condemned to death. This is really a brutal sentence. These men no doubt did some very rough things, but they certainly behaved well to us over the Cyprus settlement . . . .

16 September
I decided last night to send a message to the Head of the Turkish Govt pleading for mercy for Menderes and Zorlu. Sir Winston Churchill has also sent a message. But it's no good, I fear . . . .

In the evening. I dictated the first draft of the speech for the Conservative Conference in October. We have now begun to go rather badly <u>down</u> in the Gallup poll. This was bound to happen at some point during this Parliament and I wd prefer to have it now rather than later. It is due to <u>three</u> main causes

(1) Mr Gaitskell's very patriotic and successful stand against 'unilateralism' has undoubtedly increased his national stature

(2) Our economic troubles are attributed to the Govt – the 'stop and go' policy, as they call it. Some critics say we ought to have <u>more</u> planning. Others say that we have never given the 'liberal' economy a chance, because of our excessive fear of unemployment. The ordinary public are puzzled, and blame us.

(3) The Foreign and Colonial problems have frightened people.
They have not full confidence that we can handle them . . . .

. . . . I have had a talk with <u>Butler</u> about all this and I have persuaded
him to give up the <u>Chairmanship</u> of the Party to a younger man (if I
can find the right one) who could devote his <u>whole</u> time to thinking,
organising, and speaking. We agreed that the right man for the job (if
he can be persuaded to do it) is Iain Macleod, now Colonial Secretary.
He could help me to increase a sense of purpose – a movement –
almost a crusade . . . .

17 September (Sunday)

Telegrams and telephones all last night and this morning. Hammarskjöld has agreed – indeed has himself proposed – a meeting with
Tshombe to try to arrange a cease-fire and then a negotiation for some
settlement. This is <u>very</u> good news. Lansdowne has done well. The
meeting is to be this evening, or more probably tomorrow, at a place
called Ndola, just inside N Rhodesia. Both Welensky and the Governor
have agreed. Ld Alport will go up and meet H[ammarskjöld] and
L[ansdowne] . . . .

Meanwhile, Ld [Bertrand] Russell, Canon Collins and a crowd of
4000 (with 6000 onlookers) made a demonstration in and around
Trafalgar Square wh lasted till midnight. They protest against the
Atom Bomb by sitting on the ground (like Orientals) The police seem
to have managed it very well, but they had to arrest some 400 when
Home Secy spoke to me (about midnight)[83]

18 September

A very confused day, beginning with uncertainty and ending with
tragedy. Although Ld Lansdowne's plane arrived safely at Ndola,
Hammarskjöld's crashed . . . .

There was a request for Ethiopian planes (on Saturday) to be flown
across Kenya and Uganda to help U.N. We asked for explanations of
their purpose before granting permission. Hammarskjöld yesterday
(before leaving Leopoldville) undertook that they would <u>not</u> repeat <u>not</u>
be used in general 'strafing' of Katanga ground positions or personnel,

---

83. CND had been founded in November 1957 with Collins as Chairman and
Russell as President. The more militant Committee of 100 was founded in
1960, to campaign through civil disobedience, such as the sit-ins of 17
September in London and at Holy Loch.

but only to deal with 2 fighters which the Katanga forces have got and wh have been attacking the U.N. troops. On this, we sent a telegram this morning, agreeing. It will, of course, be very awkward if it turns out that one of these 'pirate' planes attacked H on his peaceful mission. But it seems impossible, and does not fit with their safe arrival and circling round the airfield about midnight last night . . . .

I had a long talk last night with Macleod about the future of the Party, and the idea of his taking on as Chairman. He is attracted by it; but I think he fears that he will be said to have been got rid of from the Colonial Office. This may be said by some; but of course, for me to appoint him Chairman is a mark of complete confidence. I did not press the issue too far but asked him to reflect and talk to the Chief Whip. I saw the Chief Whip this morning (who is keen on the idea and goes further in thinking that Iain might perhaps lead the House as well, Rab becoming in fact, if not in name, 'Deputy Prime Minister'.) Chief Whip and Iain will have a talk. Then Rab must be seen again. This is a very delicate affair and must not be rushed . . . .

19 September
. . . . [I]t now seems clear that Hammerskjöld's plane was destroyed by an accident and not by an attack or by sabotage. It was only 4 miles from the airfield and in a direct line with the run-way. The pilot must have miscalculated and hit the trees[84] . . . .

20 September
. . . . Mr Gaitskell asked to see me and as I cd not refuse, he came to Chequers at 4 and stayed till 5.30. Of course his 'Shadow Cabinet' is urging him on and he wants to appear energetic. We had a useful talk and he seemed (as always) very understanding of all our difficulties. What he will say is quite another thing, when he speaks in public! The Opposition are pressing (but I think rather formally, for the record) for the immediate recall of Parlt. Nothing cd be more foolish. It wd create a panic . . . .

21 September
. . . . Cabinet at 11. We discussed the Chancellor of the Exchequer's letter on 'Planning', wh is to go to employers and T. Unions. This was adjourned from Tuesday. A rather interesting and quite deep diver-

---

84. This incident remains shrouded in conspiracy theories.

gence of view between ministers, really corresponding to whether they had old Whig, Liberal, laisser-faire traditions, or Tory opinions, paternalists and not afraid of a little *dirigisme*[85] . . . .

22 September

. . . . Sir Solly Zuckerman in the morning. He told me about the US/USSR/UK meeting of scientists wh took place recently at Vermont. It followed the earlier, so-called Pugwash, meetings.[86] The subject is 'disarmament'. The meetings are, naturally, known to and approved by Governments, but they are unofficial and without commitment. The fact that Governments (including the Soviet Govt) take them seriously is about the only hopeful thing on the international horizon . . . .

I am sending a personal message to Adoula (P.M. of Congo) who . . . . seems to have got it into his head that we are working for a secession of Katanga under Tshombe, for colonialist and materialist reasons. Lansdowne has done some good in trying to show him that we want a united and peaceful Congo and are doing all we can to get Tshombe to a negotiation with Adoula. At least, a cease-fire between U.N. and Katanga troops has been arranged. But I fear that the Central Govt may try to take over Katanga with its own forces . . .

23 September

. . . . George Lansdowne was uncommonly lucky not be killed. He had been invited by Hammarskjöld to go to Ndola with him from Leopoldville in the same aeroplane and this was arranged. At the last moment, L and H agreed that it might look better (from U.N. and H's point of view) if they went separately. Another aeroplane was provided. George left first and arrived safely. H's left a few minutes later and crashed just outside Ndola airfield.

The 'popular' press today excelled itself. Hardly a word about U.N. crisis, Congo crisis; Berlin crisis or even general home affairs. The whole front page of these papers is devoted to a murder case. Some time ago (a month, I think) a motorist on the new A6 road was found shot – dead. Another woman was injured. Last night a man

---

85. A reference to the economic planning and state direction pursued in post-war France. Its apparent relative success in delivering economic growth led to growing interest in trying to apply similar techniques in Britain amongst both major political parties in the 1960s.

86. Because the first meeting was held in July 1957 at Pugwash, Nova Scotia.

whom the police – 'wanted to get in touch with' (presumably the murderer) came to Scotland Yard – about midnight – to be interviewed – and, I suppose, detained. What is fun is the rival headlines – *D Express* has 'Dramatic phone call to *D Express*'. The *Mirror* has 'He phoned the *Mirror*'. The <u>whole page</u> of the *D Mail* (not apparently rung up by the man Alphon) is devoted to 2am drama, Alphon at Yard.[87] Well, I suppose it helps to keep the public calm amidst all the real troubles of the world. Murder trials have perhaps their contribution to make to 'unflappability'.

I read quite a good book on Modern Turkey . . . . I very much fear that, since the Revolution, the new regime is beginning to swing away from the West. No doubt Menderes and Zorlu had many faults, but they at least stuck firmly by the Western alliance . . . .

25 September

. . . . Ld Hailes to luncheon. He seemed very distressed at the result of the Jamaican referendum, wh seems to put an end to the years of work for the West Indian Federation.[88] All the Premiers are arriving here next week. Nobody knows what to do next.

Butler and Chief Whip after luncheon. 'Rab' agrees to yield the Leadership of the House and the Chairmanship of the Party to Iain Macleod. He will remain Home Secretary, and will help me in various committees, including the Ministerial Group to guide the Common Market negotiations. I am very pleased with this. We discussed at some length the consequential changes wh will be needed.

F.O. have agreed my plan about Congo, to consult Western Govts <u>and</u> the Industrial organisations (Tanganyika Holdings and Union Minière) to try to bring pressure on Tshombe to be reasonable . . . .

26 September

. . . . The President's speech at U.N. reads very well and has had a good press here.[89] It is simple and noble. But, of course, he is in a great

---

87. Peter Alphon was released four days later and James Hanratty was later hanged for the crime. Doubts about the validity of this conviction fuelled the subsequent successful campaign against the death penalty.

88. Jamaican rejection led to the formal dissolution of the Federation in April 1962, followed by independence for Jamaica and Trinidad and Tobago in August.

89. Kennedy had challenged the USSR to a disarmament race, indicating his

political difficulty, wh the Republicans, led – I am sorry to think – by Eisenhower, are trying to exploit. Having now been convinced by the steady pressure of our diplomacy <u>and</u> by an honest re-appraisal of the strategic situation, Pres K has realised that the slogan 'be tough on Berlin' is not, by itself, a policy. In this conversion, the close friendship wh has developed between Rusk and Ld Home has played a notable part. But Kennedy got elected by attacking Eisenhower as 'weak' and on the slogan 'Wake up, America!' So, elected on the Churchill ticket, he will now be accused of following a Chamberlain policy. Yet he – and all thinking people – know that we must have a negotiation and (with the cards we have) we cannot play the game too high.

Another problem is that of German psychology. For 15 years, Adenauer has been telling the German people that the Western powers wd, in the long run, secure for them the re-unification of Germany. Now it is becoming clear (General Clay's indiscretion has merely let the cat out of a transparent bag) that Germany is not going to be re-united and that *de facto* recognition of E. Germany will be inevitable. This *déception* may be dangerous, and another German myth may grow up of an Anglo-Saxon (US/UK) 'sell-out', (from wh France disassociated herself, thereby getting 'Peace with Honour' at our expense) and this may, in years to come, lead to a sort of new NAZISM and perh even a neutral or pro-Russian Germany. All these fears are rather distant, but not necessarily unreal. For this reason, I hope that the Germans will now form an '<u>All Party</u>' Govt, to carry the burden of whatever finally emerges equally between them[90] . . . .

I had a talk with Henry Brooke. I rather think he will accept my proposal. I want him to leave Ministry of Housing and go to help Selwyn at the Treasury, as 2nd in Command. It is a step <u>down</u> in protocol, but not in <u>power</u>.

A good meeting of ministers on the Common Market. We approved the Agricultural brief and postponed the Commonwealth

---

willingness to sign a test-ban treaty, stop the production of fissile material and run down existing weapon stocks.

90. Lucius Clay, a hero of the Berlin airlift and now Kennedy's special envoy to Berlin, arrived in the city on 19 September and three days later hinted that the time was coming to accept the reality of two German states. *Die Welt* claimed that their failure to face this reality helped to explain the CDU losses in the West German elections of 17 September, though these were not sufficient, as Macmillan clearly hoped, to force a grand coalition on Adenauer.

brief till next week. We heard very satisfactory news about the
reception by the Six of our application and about the method of
negotiation to be followed . . . .

28 September
. . . . Cabinet at 11am. We decided to stand firm on Civil Service
wages, in spite of arbitration etc. The Wages Battle is now on.
Everything depends on what happens during the next few months.
Reggie Maudling has accepted Colonial Secy, in succession to Mac-
leod. I am very pleased . . . .

30 September
Worked on speech (George Christ helping) 10–12. This is for the Party
Conference. Senator Fulbright 12–1. He talked all the time, so I did
not have to express any views.

Ld Mills in the afternoon. He has placed his office unreservedly in
my hands, with a view to Cabinet changes. All the same, he will be
very sad to leave and I shall be sorry to lose him. Perhaps I can find
some solution. I have offered John Boyd-Carpenter a peerage and head
of the Assistance Board (£5000 for 7 years) but I don't think he will
want to leave HofC. These personnel problems are very trying . . . .

1 October (Sunday)
. . . . Worked on boxes and on speech. John B-Carpenter has refused –
a great bore. The Chief Whip is disappointed. We have still <u>two</u> major
offices to fill – Board of Trade and Ministry of Housing . . . .

The Syrian coup looks as if it had been (for the moment, at any
rate) successful.[91] No one seems to know, however, whether they are
'Right Wing' or 'Communist'. By a strange turn of the wheel, the F.O.
have become rather pro-Nasser and seem to feel that the break up of
the U.A.R. will cause still more trouble in M. East, help Qasim to be
still more troublesome in Iraq, and put Kuwait in jeopardy . . . .

3 October
. . . . There has been a lot of talk with Chief Whip, and I have now got
the following firm decisions (with agreement of ministers concerned)
for submission to the Queen.

---

91. This led to the end of the union with Egypt.

Butler	Home Secy
Macleod	Chancellor of Duchy (he will also be Leader of the House and Chairman of Conservative Party. Neither of these, of course, require the Queen's approval)
Maudling	Colonial Secretary
Brooke	Chief Secretary of Treasury and Paymaster General
C Hill	Minister of Housing
Erroll	Board of Trade

This leaves the question of John Boyd-Carpenter till he returns. It also leaves no place for Lord Mills, wh I much regret. I am still trying to contrive a way of keeping him as a useful friend and counsellor.

8 October (Sunday)

The Cabinet list is complete and will be published tomorrow at 4pm. There are some consequential changes, wh allow one or two new young men to come forward. Keith Joseph becomes Minister of State, Board of Trade. Ld Dundee becomes Minister of State, Foreign Office, which makes an office available (Minister without Portfolio) for Ld Mills. I fear Ld Lansdowne will be rather hurt, but I can make him Minister of State Colonial Office next Easter in place of Ld Perth, who wants to go back to the City. Mrs Thatcher, a clever young woman MP, and Monty Woodhouse are the newcomers.

On public affairs, we are making very slow progress – but very slow – with the Russians. The difficulty is now with the French and Germans . . . . The Americans must bring pressure on the Germans. We will support them – but of course the Germans attach chief weight to what the Americans, so long their patrons and protectors, say. President K seemed thoroughly 'fed up' with both Adenauer and de Gaulle.

It is curious how all American statesmen begin by trying to treat Britain as just one of many foreign or NATO countries. They soon find themselves relying on our advice and experience . . . .

The Labour Party Conference at Blackpool reversed last year's 'unilateral' vote by a large majority. When analysed, however, what has happened is that 2 or 3 unions, controlling 2 or 3 million votes, have turned round. The constituency parties are as 'pacifist' and 'extreme left' as ever. However, it is a great and deserved triumph for Gaitskell and will increase his stature in the country. He has been very persistent and courageous. Curiously enough, having voted for 'multi-lateralism' at 4 o'clock, at 4.30 they voted against the executive on the means to implement the policy wh they had just approved – viz. against POLARIS submarines at Holy Loch and against German troops training in England . . . .

The position in the motor industry is curious. Fords have not yet struck (over the tea-break) The unions are trying to get the men back at Rootes' Acton plant. This strike of 1000 men is causing a complete hold up of all Rootes' factories, involving all their car production and thousands of men.

In the Building industry (including Mowlem's, who are doing No 10 Downing St) there are sporadic strikes, also about the Tea Break in the morning.[92] Meanwhile, our French, German, and other European competitors are hard at work . . . .

Jean Monnet came to luncheon on Friday – full of vigour as ever. He is very hopeful about the Common Market negotiations and thinks that de Gaulle has changed his view about the question. Up to now, he has been hostile and this has been reflected all through the French bureaucratic hierarchy. But (so says Monnet) the mood has changed. I had to tell Monnet that I thought the difficulties here were growing – pressure from Canada and Australia; anxiety of farmers; Trade Union fear of 'competition' etc etc. I therefore hoped that we could have a quick negotiation and get it over. If it dragged, opposition and pressure groups wd grow in strength. Monnet agreed with this . . . .

I went yesterday (Saturday) afternoon to Pont Street, to see poor Harry Crookshank. I sat with him for about ¾ hour, holding his hand. He is very weak, and I shd think cd not live more than a few days now. The cancer is in the liver – as in poor Ronnie's case (Knox) He talks a little and seems to have no pain . . . .

9 October

. . . . Went with Maurice to the Fortune Theatre. A revue called *Beyond the Fringe* – by four young men.[93] Very amusing and satirical, tho' not

---

92. A fortnight-long strike by the 400 workers involved in the reconstruction of 10 Downing Street only ended on 17 October. The issue was whether or not the new work agreement in the building trade, which came into force on 1 October, included paid tea breaks, a matter only resolved by a decision to leave the issue to local arrangements. Paid tea breaks, which had crept in during the Second World War, remained the norm.

93. This celebrated satirical revue by Alan Bennett, Peter Cook, Jonathan Miller and Dudley Moore opened on 10 May 1961.

malevolent. There were two skits of me and my presence to enjoy them drew applause from the audience.

10 October

The [Cabinet]changes have had an <u>excellent</u> and on the whole favourable Press. The significance of Macleod becoming Chairman is well understood. It means 'Progressive Toryism'. The 'double-banking' of the Treasury is approved by the serious critics . . . .

13 October

The Brighton [Conservative Party] Conference has gone very well so far. Yesterday the 'Common Market' received 'overwhelming' support. Only 30 or 40 voted against, in a huge assembly of 4000 or more. Similarly, Butler defeated his 'flogging' critics with the same ease. This is certainly a reward for firm leadership. Rab (Butler) has always 'hedged' on crime, as on everything else. He has brought much of his trouble on himself by an appearance of vacillation. This is not really fair to him. Like Arthur Balfour, he has a fine, academic mind, wh I personally admire but is out of tune with a modern style.

The Press today is very interesting. The Beaverbrook press subdued; the *Guardian*, with typical Liberal meanness, chagrined at the disappearance of Colonel Blimp.[94] The *Herald* is more generous, esp about the Common Market. *The Times* has a leader on Butler and crime, written in its most 'auntie' mood. The *D.T.* (for once) is fairly polite to the Govt. The *Mirror* is very good, praising HMG and the Conservative Party about the Common Market. What particularly pleases me is a) the <u>image</u> of the Party – as liberal (with small l) progressive, modern, efficient – is noted b) its catholicity is emphasised – aristocrat – Ld Home; academic and civil service tradition – Butler; the new managerial type – Heath; the strong political character – Sandys; the progressive intellectual – Macleod; <u>all</u> have had equal success. I am particularly happy about <u>Butler</u>. He was rather depressed and this will cheer him up.

The only trouble is that my speech (always difficult to make) must be a <u>flop</u>. I can only repeat what my colleagues have said and try to give a little new turn of thought and expression . . . .

---

94. The reactionary moustachioed figure created by the cartoonist Sir David Low in the inter-war years.

14 October

.... I am amused at the way legends grow or are created. Butler is now putting about that it was he (not I) who suggested Macleod's appointment to Leader of House and Chairman of Party. He practically said so in his 'winding up' speech to 4000 representatives yesterday afternoon. Altho' this bears no relation to historic truth, it may be a useful myth ....

19 October

The two day debate on Foreign Affairs ended last night. The Opposition did not divide. The only result of the debate from the p[oin]t of view of <u>internal</u> politics has been to reveal again the deep rift in the Labour Party, wh was nominally healed in their Blackpool Conference. When Gaitskell spoke, he was loudly applauded by his own side <u>above</u> the gangway. <u>Below</u> the gangway, they sat in stony silence. His speech was good and very helpful. Healey on the second day seemed to try to restore the balance, and made a mischievous speech. He argued in favour of a United and <u>Neutral</u> Germany. Alternatively, for 'disengagement' – as we know a most sensitive subject with the Germans wh needs the most careful handling. Whereas Gaitskell was strangely sympathetic to de Gaulle, Healey was anti-French ....

Altho' the debate went well, the situation is still obscure. Kruschev, in the course of a 6 hour speech at the Communist Party Congress threatened to blow up a 50 megaton and even a 100 megaton bomb. <u>But</u>, he said there was now no fixed date for the unilateral treaty with DDR. He was ready for negotiation. But the French and Germans are still unwilling to take part ....

Poor Harry Crookshank – my oldest friend – died on Tuesday. I had intended to go to Scotland tonight to shoot for 2 days with Alec Home. But I must go to the funeral tomorrow. I have sent a little piece about him to *The Times*. We went to Summerfields together nearly 60 years ago. We got scholarships at Eton in the same election. We went to Oxford in the same year (1912) and into the Army – Grenadiers – together in 1914. We were both seriously wounded in the same battle – the Somme. We were in HofCommons together from 1924. I shall miss him very much ....

At 12, Sir T Williamson and Mr Cousins – to protest about the effect of the wages 'pause' on certain Government industrial employees. They made quite a good case, <u>if</u> you ignore the economic position as a whole ....

A curious debate followed, a 'prayer' agst an Order in Council concerning compensation paid to British subjects for losses of property in Germany. 35 Tory members (not Whigs or 'Commonwealth men') voted to benefit Prince Ernst of Hanover, a grandson of Kaiser Wilhelm 2nd. He claimed British nationality under a legal judgement wh interpreted the Act of Settlement![95] The Govt had 100 [majority]. So the administration was not brought down by the Hanoverian interest! (As this Prince married a daughter of Lord Iveagh, I wd have thought he cd have had sufficient provision for his needs from the vast Guinness fortunes) Mr Channon, member for Southend, whose mother was [a] Guinness and is an amiable young man, very foolishly canvassed strongly for the Prince. Fortunately, all this happened so late at night, that it is hardly mentioned in the Press . . . .

24 October
. . . . The bursting of a new and vicious series of bombs by the Russians culminated in the 30 megaton bomb exploded yesterday. We held a meeting of experts at 10.30 to agree a statement to be made by Minister of Defence at 12 noon. My PQs were few and not very difficult. The 'bomb' statement went off well. We have a complete scheme for dried milk for infants, if the iodine contamination from fall-out shd become serious.

By a ridiculous contrast with all this ultra-modern horror, I turned for ¾ hour to considering the fate of the Doric Arch at Euston. The President of the [Royal] Academy led a deputation of architects, artists, critics, and noblemen who all said this was a splendid – indeed a wonderful – work of art. It must not be lost, whatever the cost[96] . . . .

25 October
Polish ministers for foreign trade and planning at 10.45. The new President of the Board of Trade was with me. The usual insincerities.

11.30–12.30. Talks with President of Senegal – these, on the contrary, were sincere and valuable . . . .

---

95. The 1701 Act which brought the Hanoverian dynasty to the throne.
96. Macmillan obviously did not agree, asking no questions of the deputation. Nor did he mention the issue again. The government decided not to intervene and in 1962 this emblematic piece of nineteenth-century classicism was destroyed in the redevelopment of the station, becoming a *cause célèbre* for the nascent architectural heritage movement in the process.

26 October

I have started a cold, with a very bad throat. Sir J[ohn] R[ichardson] came in the morning, and gave me some remedies. Cabinet at 11. Long and difficult. One of the most complicated items was whether or not to agree with Lord Robens and the Coal Board, who want to raise the price of Scottish coal by 15/- a ton. Scottish coal is run at a heavy loss, year after year. Ld R wants to <u>reduce</u> demand and so help in closing the worst pits. But how do we reconcile this with (say) putting ½ the new steel plant with Colville's, in Scotland – for social reasons – instead of in S Wales, for economic reasons?

The likelihood of a strike in the Power Stations is growing. Ffoulkes (the Electrical T.U. leader – a tough and able Communist) has asked for £2 immediately. This is intolerable, both as to amount and date. But these 150000 have the whole country in pawn. Owing to the greater interlocking and greater complication of these plants, we cannot do what we did in the General Strike of 1926. We cd produce little or quite insufficient power to meet the needs of a nation now wholly geared, industrially and domestically, to electricity . . . .

27 October

I have been very anxious for some days to find some way of seeing the President for a talk on the way things are going, esp in Europe. When all the fuss about the recent Russian explosions came to a head, I thought this might act as a 'cover plan'. I cd go to U.S. as head of the other Western nuclear power. This cd hardly offend de Gaulle and/or Adenauer. But I cd also discuss the Berlin situation and the approaching stalemate.

Alec Home (prompted by Hoyer Millar) put up all the usual objections. (all foreign ministers hate any sign of acting by Heads of Government) However, I sent a telegram to the President, suggesting the possibility of a talk and proposing (if he liked the idea) a quick visit. As a result, we had a long telephone conversation this morning (on the special Atlantic 'super scrambler') . . . .

We finally agreed

a) what I shd say and what the President shd say on Tests – subject to confirmation

b) that [ambassadors] Thompson and Roberts must now really get on with the probe in Moscow, getting on to some discussion of 'substantial' questions

c) that – in view of all the trouble going on now in Berlin, with

Western and Russian tanks facing each other – it wd perh[aps] be thought rather 'panicky' to have a meeting. We must aim at Bermuda in December.

29 October (Sunday)

My throat is worse and I don't know how I shall manage on Tuesday. I worked practically all today on the speech. This is always a difficult speech to make, covering a very wide field . . . .

Two 'young ladies' here to work on the speech. We finished the 3rd draft tonight. I must await the criticisms of the 'departments'. This gives us a day and a half to get it into final shape.

We are having trouble with the plan to go on with 'Blue Streak' as a launcher for a European space experiment. The Australians are making trouble about the terms on wh Woomera range is to be made available. Mr Menzies (who is anyway in a bad mood over S Africa; Ghana; European Common Market etc) is being very difficult. The Italians are also running out.

The news about the power plant workers is confusing. I still hope we may be able to settle this, on payment of not too much 'Danegeld'.[97] It's no use, in a general campaign, getting bogged down in a battle on a sector of the front where you are bound to lose . . . .

30 October

. . . . Ministerial meeting on Nuclear Tests. We agreed to making an underground test, with American cooperation, for a warhead for 'Skybolt' . . . .

31 October

A bad day. Opening of Parlt by the Queen – a fine show, as usual. I had to speak in the House, and made rather a mess of it. The Opposition have now decided to counter the command of the House wh I have had up to now, by 'barracking'. This makes a serious speech very difficult. They listened well enough to the first half (on Russia; Berlin; nuclear tests etc) When I got to the Home front they started (obviously organised and led by a Mr Brown – deputy leader) jeers, shouts, catcalls etc. I got them round a bit at the end. But I must clearly think out a new tactic to deal with this . . . .

---

97. Money to bribe them to go away, as used by the Anglo-Saxon King Ethelred II in the tenth century AD to buy off Viking marauders.

1 November

We decided to reduce Bank Rate by ½% – wh makes it now 6%.

General Norstad (SACEUR) called to see me. I thought him in a very neurotic state – unfit to command at such a time. Fortunately we have a sensible British deputy . . . .

2 November

Cabinet 10.30–1.30. Two hours excellent discussion of the German crisis – Berlin etc. I thought it wise to put all the Cabinet in the picture. They don't know what to do – nor do I. But I feel sure that they will support me if and when I decide to take a prominent part in the drama.

The news from Ghana is very bad. It is now thought that Nkrumah will <u>leave</u> the Commonwealth immediately after the Queen's visit. This will put us in a ludicrous position. But I don't quite know how to circumvent this . . . .

4 November

Nehru to luncheon – with Duncan Sandys. He looked much aged and very tired (having arrived by air from Delhi – without stopping, except for refuelling – only 2 hours before, this is not to be wondered at) At luncheon, he talked fairly freely about Russia and China. He was on the defensive about Belgrade, and the 'double standard' applied by the neutrals to Russia and to the West. Sandys left after luncheon – I tried to get Nehru to open up on the various issues where we are in disagreement, to a greater or lesser degree – Congo, SE Asia etc. He seemed reluctant, partly from fatigue and partly because his good manners make him unwilling to say jarring things when he is your guest – so I did not press him. We talked about Berlin and Germany and he seemed sympathetic, recognising my difficulties. The curious thing about N is that all his pro-African ideas are purely theoretical. He looks down on most Asians from the proud position of a high-caste Indian aristocrat. Africans he regards with contempt. The very phrase 'Afro-Asian' must offend him. But it is, of course, a political position. Nor must we forget that the Communist threat in India is very real.

The news of 'explosions' in Accra came through just before luncheon. I had some talk with Sandys . . . .

5 November (Sunday)

. . . . We decided just before luncheon that (if Nkrumah agreed) Sandys shd leave tonight – Sunday – for Accra to report to us. The Queen is by way of leaving on Thursday morning . . . .

6 November

A lot of telephoning. The Press has clearly approved the Sandys visit to Accra. In spite [of] all the talk in Parlt and in spite of a hostile, even malignant, Press, both the Conservative and my own percentage in the Gallup poll show a considerable recovery since July and August. It's a strange country!

I don't like the news from Bonn. The 'right wing' elements seem to have forced a promise – even a written agreement – from Adenauer about foreign policy. This will make negotiation over Berlin more difficult and de Gaulle will become more intransigeant. There is little news from our ambassador yet. Everyone in Bonn is being very 'cagey'.

13 November (Monday)

This has been a very hectic period . . . . The Chief Whip warned me – on Monday night – that there was a growing feeling in the Conservative Party against the Queen going to Ghana. Altho' on Tuesday afternoon (when the first Press reports began to come through about the drive in an open car wh Duncan Sandys had persuaded Nkrumah to make with him over the royal route) there was some amelioration, the Chief Whip was not sure what wd result. If (after my statement, which must be on Wednesday, since the Queen was to leave Thursday morning) the Cabinet decide to advise the Queen to go, there wd certainly be a motion for the adjournment. If the Labour Party saw their chance and voted agst us (on the grounds of the Queen's security) at least 80–100 Conservatives wd be in the same lobby and the Govt wd be beaten. This naturally worried me, altho' I felt the danger exaggerated. However, I thought it my duty to warn the Queen. For (if we were beaten) I cd not repeat not alter my advice. I wd resign – at (say) 11pm. The Queen (who was to leave at 9am for London Airport) wd no doubt have retired early. But she wd no doubt see me. She cd refuse my resignation, and ask me to carry on. I could agree, but I could not alter my advice. So the Queen wd leave, with a hostile vote from HofC, and flouting their advice . . . .

All this we discussed, at considerable length, during these anxious days, with a sort of mock seriousness. It all seemed too absurd to be true . . . .

. . . . All the 'security' authorities regard the risks as no greater than India, Pakistan, Iran; or Belfast!

Fortunately, the instigators of this revolt in the Conservative ranks were very good men – worthy men, and only caring about the Queen's safety. It was led by John Morrison, Spencer Summers and others of the same kind. J.M. is, of course, very influential as Chairman of 1922. None of these are of the self-advertising or embittered type (like Lords Lambton or Hinchingbrooke and Mr Turton) so nothing at all got into the Press up to the end. The Socialists never realised their opportunity and our danger[98] . . . .

. . . . [T]he European position is stagnant (or was so till late in the week) The President had (at his request) a long telephone conversation . . . . (It was interesting and impressive how simply he declared himself baffled and uncertain what to do next) Pres K suggested that if I wanted him to come over to England while de Gaulle is here (next week) and join the discussion, he wd sure come. Whether Birch Grove House could hold them all, I rather doubt.

However, after much reflection on Friday and Saturday, and long talks with For Secy, Sir N Brook, and others, I compiled a message wh went yesterday. These telegrams set out in full what President Kennedy asked for a) What he shd say to Adenauer b) What we wd do if both Adenauer and de Gaulle remained intransigeant.

Under b) I proposed a Western 'Summit' in Paris in Dec, to be followed (if necessary) by a NATO Summit. President K is still very anxious that we shd meet. Since he seems to like the idea of Bermuda, I have invited him for end of December or beginning of January. This is apart from any meetings we may need to force the hand of de G and Dr A on negotiation with the Russians . . . .

19 November

Motored to Birch Grove, where I found Dorothy very busy with the preparations for de Gaulle's visit . . . .

Yesterday was very fine – just a little wind – a perfect shooting day. We got 320 pheasants – all very high, many birds were really out of shot. It was wonderful sport. Duke of Roxburghe; Duke of Marlborough; Ld Sefton; Col W Sterling; Ld Carnarvon; Ld Porchester made together as fine a team of guns as you cd get together in this island. I cannot now (and never could, except for perh[aps] a few years

---

98. The visit passed off successfully and without incident.

when I shot so much with Evan Baillie) get anywhere near that class. However, I enjoyed myself enormously. One bird (a hen) was the highest pheasant I have ever shot . . . .

20 November

Mr Fleming (Canadian Finance Minister) came at 10.30. It was not clear what his purpose was. He <u>said</u> it was to express his regret about the misunderstandings over George Drew (Canadian High Commissioner in London) who is said to have refused to go to a meeting of High Commissioners on Common Market. Also about the alleged insult to Derry Amory, because no Canadian Ministers attended his [Heathcoat] Canadian Club luncheon in Ottawa. All this is part of the natural nervosity of Canada over the Common Market negotiations. I am not sure how far the French are stimulating this, in the hope of making the negotiations abortive. They are playing a funny game . . . .

There has been the first serious breach in the Wages Pause. This is due partly to the weakness of the Electricity Board and partly to the incompetence of the Minister, Richard Wood. The negotiators, after eleven hours argument, rang up R Wood late on Thursday night, and told him that they cd see no alternative to a settlement on terms <u>far</u> worse than the Board had – informally but firmly – agreed with Ministers. This settlement gave 2d instead of 1d increase (per hour) and agreed to Jan 28th instead of April 1st. Poor Richard Wood protested over the telephone but <u>did nothing</u>. He shd have urged the negotiators to break off the talks or adjourn them. He shd have at once informed me, or the Chancellor of the Exr, or Ld Mills. He did nothing, or worse than nothing. He went off to Yorkshire by the night train on Thursday, and did not even inform his colleagues of this catastrophe. There has been a great row in the Party wh began to assume dangerous proportions. So I took control, and decided to make [a] statement in the House tomorrow, after Questions. I have had long discussions with Macleod and Chief Whip over the question of the resignation of the Minister. I am afraid poor Richard (though a charming character) is not very clever. He does not seem to realise the harm he has done. All the same, I want to minimise it if I can. This makes me instinctively against dismissing him. If he resigns, that's another thing.

22 November

I have decided definitely <u>against</u> dismissing Wood. But I fear [he] is not very quick. However, Ld Robens likes him, and is (I think) more likely to stand firm if I leave Richard W. than if I get rid of him. The question of miners wages will be the real test. That, and the railways. If we can get delay here, till say April, we shall have had a reasonable success.

Meeting with Tunku and the Malayans, to sign the agreement wh has been reached about <u>Greater Malaysia</u> and the <u>Singapore Base</u>. The defence part of the agreement is quite satisfactory (wh is better than we expected)[99] . . . .

As I was going out to dinner with the Press Club, I was given a letter from Gaitskell, in wh he attacked our lack of 'consultation' with the West Indies, quoted a telegram from Sir Grantley Adams, and asked me to make a statement in the HofC. Gaitskell said that he was publishing his letter. This was the repetition of the technique he tried with me over the 'Off-Shore' islands some years ago . . . . I beat him then and I beat him again today. I got a reply prepared in my office; agreed with Colonial Office; delivered to him at Hampstead; and sent to Press – all by 10am . . . . Gaitskell is the kind of cad that only a gentleman can be . . . .

23 November
. . . . Long discussion on Berlin. The Cabinet are <u>very</u> anxious and very unwilling to be dragged into [a] dangerous situation by our Allies . . . .

Dined at 'The Other Club'. Churchill was there. I thought him rather stronger. He quite enjoyed the evening. It is a pity he is obstinate about using his hearing aid.

24 November
. . . . I worked all the morning on various papers and memoranda for the French visit. There were also a lot of other things to tie up. The French have now given the 'Heath' memorandum or opening speech (wh it was agreed should be kept as a <u>secret</u> document among the 6) to the Americans. As we have sternly resisted giving copies to Canada and other Commonwealth countries, this puts us in great difficulty. It looks as [if] this is a definite effort of the French to wreck the Common

---

99. This extended the Anglo-Malayan Defence Agreement negotiated at independence in 1957 to cover Singapore, Sarawak and British North Borneo, which were now being considered for incorporation with Malaya. A key point was continued British use of the Singapore base.

Market negotiation. But they don't want to refuse us; they want to create such pressure against us at home and in the Commonwealth that we shall be forced to withdraw our application. We must not fall into this trap.

We certainly have a host of problems, at home and overseas. The Press, including the so-called Conservative Press, is more and more critical of all our policies, home and foreign. The 'gossip' writers, and the 'angry young men' (Fairlie; Worsthorne and co) are very much against me personally. *The Economist*, wh thinks the only cure of all evils is to keep money permanently at 7%, is angry at our recent reductions. The curious thing is that the people seem still to be on our side. Dorothy has been making a series of 'tours' lately in different parts of the country, and gets an impression of great friendliness and sympathy . . . .

25 November

I left London yesterday afternoon at 2pm. Gen de Gaulle and Madame de G arrived punctually at 3.30 . . . .

The local interest is, of course, intense, mixed with a certain pride. The house is looking lovely and the servants are reinforced by 3 Government 'butlers'. Carol [Faber]'s cook is here to help Mrs Bell. All sorts of other women, old or returned servants etc, seem to have appeared. Every room in the house is full . . . . We have taken 5 rooms at the Roebuck, for his doctors etc. Blood plasma is in a special refrigerator in the coach house.[100] Outside the gates, the Press swarm. The Red Lion is selling beer in hogsheads. Police (with and without alsatian dogs) are in the garden and the woods (one alsatian happily bit the *Daily Mail* man in the behind) Altogether, a most enjoyable show . . . .

29 November (Wed)

. . . . I must now try to give some impressions of the de Gaulle talks on Berlin. Perhaps the easiest way is to repeat here the telegram wh we compiled for Washington, for the information of the ambassador and for him to pass on to President Kennedy . . . .

'President de G explained that France was concerned above all,

---

100. This was because de Gaulle was subjected to numerous assassination attempts – most recently on 8 September 1961 – not least from those opposed to his policy of self-determination in Algeria.

and perhaps even more than her British and American allies, to ensure
that Germany was tied in to the West . . . . In the circumstances he
saw no advantage in embarking on negotiations at the present time.
Even if the Federal German Govt of the day accepted the concessions
wh wd be asked of them, the German people wd be left with a sense
of betrayal. Whatever the U.S. and the UK might do, France, altho'
not proposing to fight a war with the Russians on her own, wd not be
party to such an arrangement. The Germans wd then in the future feel
that at least they had one friend left in the West . . . .

'He agreed that the division of Germany and the Oder-Neisse
frontier were facts which cd not be altered at least for the time being
and about wh an agreement cd perhaps one day be reached with the
Russians. But these facts were all more or less favourable to the
Russians and there was no need to accept them unless at the same time
the Russians wd accept the situation in Berlin as it had existed since
the war; this was a fact favourable to the West. However to raise all
these questions wd mean embarking on a very wide negotiation in the
present situation when the Russians were building their wall in Berlin,
threatening to sign a peace treaty with East Germany, menacing
Finland and generally behaving in an aggressive way. It was quite
arguable that the West might offer the Russians a wide negotiation on
condition that they first changed their aggressive attitude but the West
shd at the same time make clear that if the Russians refused, they wd
not negotiate at all . . . .

'We asked Pres de G how one cd be sure what the Soviet attitude
was if one was not prepared to discuss the matter with them. He
replied that he wd not object to further soundings of the Soviet position
being carried out by British or American officials in order to verify the
basis on wh negotiations could begin . . . . He added that this procedure shd not be too inconvenient for the Americans and ourselves
since we were already negotiating with the Russians about nuclear
tests and disarmament without French participation . . . .'

. . . . The rest of the talks – Friday evening and Saturday morning
– with de Gaulle alone were about the Common Market. But I saw no
reason to tell the Americans about these, equally discouraging,
conversations! . . . .

Of course, de G's policy is clear and has never changed. He does
not want war. He does not believe there will be war. But he wants to
pretend to the French and the Germans that he (de G) is the strong,
loyal man. He will not 'do a Munich'. But he only dares take this line,

devoutly praying that the British and Americans will get him out. He really admitted this to me. He said it was not perhaps anything but a rather <u>cynical</u> policy. Yet it was justified, for we must at all costs prevent another German 'myth', such as had made Hitler's rise to power possible. But naturally his main purpose is to see that France gets the credit for loyalty, and that the Anglo-Americans are made responsible for the betrayal of Germany . . . . (It wd be, of course, a complete collapse of de G's plan if the Americans suddenly turned tough . . . . If de G thought there was real danger of war, he wd be in a panic) . . . .

De Gaulle now hears nothing and listens to nothing. Couve de Murville (a functionary, not a politician and a cold Protestant fish) sees him but rarely. Debré is a <u>good</u> man, and in many ways a sensible man. But he is loyalty personified. His Minister of Finance is the former Governor of the Bank of France (Baumgartner) – a good man, but without influence. Joxe is about the only one who dares speak to him. De Courcel is nothing . . . .

The tragedy of it all is that we agree with de G on almost everything. We like the political Europe (*union de patries* or *union d'Etats*)[101] that de G likes. We are anti-federalists; so is he. We are pragmatists in our economic planning; so is he. We fear a German revival and have no desire to see a reunited Germany. These are de G's thoughts too. We agree; but his pride, his inherited hatred of England, (since Joan of Arc)[102] his bitter memories of the last war; above all, his intense 'vanity' for France – she must dominate – make him half welcome, half repel us, with a strange 'love-hate' complex. Sometimes, when I am with him, I feel I have overcome it. But he goes back to his distrust and dislike, like a dog to his vomit. I still feel that he has <u>not</u> absolutely decided about our admission to the Economic Community. I am inclined to think he will be more likely to yield to pressure than persuasion . . . .

30 November

Chief Whip in the morning. The situation about the Immigration Bill is no better. Ministers concerned are working on an 'Irish' plan – but it will be pretty thin, and I fear may not satisfy our critics. It will be a strange irony if Ireland once again brings down a British

---

101. Union of countries or states.
102. Burnt at the stake by the English in Rouen in 1431.

Government[103] – and this time over a Bill which (according to Gallup) over 90% of the people support.[104] The trouble is that after 10 years the Conservative Party has got pretty restive. There are too many ex-ministers who had to be got rid of for incompetence (like Turton, Aubrey Jones, Walker-Smith) and too many young men still disappointed. Fortunately, I have got most of the ex-ministers to the Lords, but those that are still with us are very critical and dangerous. Aubrey Jones (the most incompetent Minister of Supply I can recall) has now become a great authority on defence. Another in this category is Walker-Smith. He was a really bad Minister of Health. Now (with Lord Beaverbrook's help) he defends the Empire against Europe. Finally, Turton (useless in the FO; incapable at Ministry of Health) is now a bitter, old-maidish critic on everything. He is Lord Salisbury's representative in HofC, without Lord S's personal charm . . . .

4 December

I have read Iain Macleod's [recently published] *Neville Chamberlain*. It is a very slender affair. In dealing with his social legislation etc it is quite good. The defence of 'appeasement' and of his conduct of foreign affairs is very weak and goes against the evidence. I shall await Anthony Eden's volume with renewed interest.[105] He sent me 3 chapters to read regarding his [1938] resignation wh give a very different account to Neville's 'diary'. But I don't suppose either are consciously giving a false picture. It's really that Neville, having started on the completely false premise that Mussolini and Hitler told the truth, followed a course wh was doomed from the start. I then began to read again Wheeler-Bennett's *Munich*. There is real history – well documented, well-written, and authoritative. What worries me all the time

---

103. As effectively occurred with Salisbury's first and Gladstone's third governments in 1886.

104. Two days earlier this had been a major concern in the Macmillan-chaired Cabinet committee on the Bill. Henry Brooke however wrote to Macmillan: 'Private Members . . . . have not yet reached the point of realising that a certain amount of illogicality has to be included if we are to achieve the objective of giving control over coloured immigration into this country' (TNA: CAB 130/ 180 and PREM 11/4682) – the illogicality being that Ireland, despite being outside the Commonwealth since 1948, was not to be affected by the legislation because of the perceived need for Irish labour.

105. *Facing the Dictators*, the second volume of Eden's memoirs, was published in 1962.

is the possible parallel. Are we 'appeasing' Soviet Russia? Ought we to risk war? Is Kruschev another Hitler? Myself, I am pretty happy about the answers to all these questions. Still, they pose themselves . . . .

18 December

As usual in a period of 'crisis' I have been too busy or too exhausted to 'write up' the diary. There has been an internal political crisis, wh has been both acute and dangerous. It arose out of a decision of the Cabinet, taken at 10.30pm on Thursday, Dec 7th, to supply 24 1000lb bombs to U.N. for their operation in the Congo, against the attacks of the Katanga forces.[106] The Foreign Secy – and F.O. – had been resisting this demand for some weeks, but it came to a head because of the damage wh (it was claimed) the 'pirate' aircraft working for Tshombe were doing to U.N. troops. These, of course, comprise troops from 4 Commonwealth countries. Eventually, after grave doubts expressed by many ministers, esp Ld Hailsham, the Cabinet agreed to supply the bombs, with the clear restriction that they would only be used against air-craft on the ground or air-strips and airfield. The next day, I heard (with some relief) that U.N. HQ had refused the restrictions and asked us to reconsider this. We refused. Then (unhappily) U.N. agreed.

This was on the Friday (Dec 8th) I went to Portsmouth that night, for a day's shooting – 260 pheasants, and a lovely day. By the evening, and during Sunday, there was a lot of telephoning and I realised that we were in for a row. The official announcement that we were supplying the bombs came out on Friday night. By Monday morning both Conservative MPs and Conservative Peers were in full cry. Meanwhile (perhaps luckily) the U.N. officials on the spot were giving some very indiscreet interviews to the Press, suggesting an interpretation of their objectives as something amounting to 'imposing a political settlement' by conquering the Katanga forces . . . .

After a meeting of all the ministers who cd be got together, Heath (Ld Privy Seal) made a statement saying that in view of all the uncertainty, we wd hold up delivery of the bombs. It was a long statement, very well done, but led to a tremendous pressure of questioning from both sides of the House . . . .

After much discussion as to what shd be done about the Congo, with the Chief Whip calm but anxious, we decided not to appeal to

---

106. Following the British-supported Security Council Resolution 169 on 24 November.

the Security Council but to make a direct appeal to the Sec General, asking for a 'cease-fire' and for negotiation between the various Congo personalities . . . .

The position in the Party was very tense on Monday and Tuesday. My 'supplementaries' at question time on Tuesday helped – this was a tactical error of Gaitskell and Wilson. They shd have let a formal question and reply go without further ado. But they asked a lot of supplementaries wh gave me the chance of a little speech – or series of speeches – comforting to my own side.

On Wed. I saw the Executive Ctee [of the 1922] and on Thursday the debate. For some reason (I suppose, age and infirmity) I have felt this 'crisis' far more than I shd have done – have worried, and slept badly and so on. All the same forces are being mobilised as were at Suez. *The Times*, good; the *Observer*, awful; The *Manchester Guardian*, infuriating and superior. The *D. Mirror* 'Macmillan betrays U.N.' – *D. Express*, good; *D Mail*, fair.

The trouble in the Party is that in addition to the small group of people who really hate me – Lords Hinchingbrooke and Lambton; Nigel Birch; Mr Turton and about 10 others – the anxiety about U.N.'s performance in the Congo had spread to the whole centre of the party. Nor do I blame them. For U Thant, under Afro-Asian pressure, and through the incredible folly and weakness (mixed with vanity) of Adlai Stevenson (U.S. representative at U.N.) has gone on relentlessly (or, rather, allowed the U.N. military command in Congo to go on) with an attack on Elizabethville,[107] regardless of civilian lives or material damage. They do not seem to realise that if they 'win' the battle, they will be in the same position as Britain and other colonial powers have often had to face – they will be forced to 'take over' and administer the Katanga. At the same time Adoula (who is a Kerensky type) will fall, and Gizenga (Communist-trained agent) will take over[108] . . . .

The debate on Thursday 14th was crucial. The Press had talked of up to 60, or even 100 Tories abstaining – wh wd have meant the end of the Government. Heath (Ld P[rivy] Seal) opened, with a quiet, well-constructed, and effective speech. Wilson (his first effort as 'Shadow'

---

107. The capital of Katanga province, now Lubumbashi. Britain called for a
     ceasefire, the subject of the 14 December debate, and on 18 December
     inconclusive talks about reuniting Katanga with Congo began with Tshombe.
108. Gizenga's government in Stanleyville had been recognised by several
     Communist states. It was overrun the following month.

For Secy instead of 'Shadow' Chancellor of the Exr) made a bad speech
– offensive, vulgar, poisonous. It made the Opposition laugh, but with
the laughter one has at salacious jokes in an improper play. They were
really ashamed. Gaitskell wound up well – the first part academic, the
second part rhetorical – both good. I wound up (in my new style, with
<u>no</u> set speech but a few notes) The majority for us was <u>94</u>. It ought to
have been 96 – but 2 chaps were 'locked out'.[109] We had 10 or so
'abstentions' – and the Socialists had about the same number absent
unpaired. A good result. But I fear we only got through the first stage
of this trouble. We worked hard on the Americans (U Thant is useless)
and so did the President on UN authorities. As I write, while the
fighting in Elizabethville continues, there seems just a chance of some
negotiations starting . . . .

19 December (Tuesday)
The news from the Congo is better. We have managed to get the two
negro gentleman to confer in some neutral spot. Mr Adoula and Mr
Tshombe will no doubt fail to agree – partly because Adoula . . . .
thinks he has the US and the U.N. behind him, with limitless amount[s]
of money. However, the meeting of the two men and a 'sort of' cease-
fire in Elizabethville have certainly helped me politically . . . .

The United Nations army consists (with the exception of the
Swedes, who have not fought anybody for 200 years) and of the Irish
(who will fight anybody) of a queer lot. The chances of being a
survivor if you are wounded in this war are said to be slender. You are
likely to be killed and eaten either by the backward races of Congolese
or by the advance guard of civilisation represented in the U.N.
army . . . .

PQs – only 3. The House seemed very jumpy . . . . Then a talk with
Chancellor of Exr till 8.30 – about the problem of Railway wages.
These men really <u>do</u> deserve a small increase. But how can we prevent
a small stream becoming a flood? Selwyn L[loyd] had talked with Dr
Beeching (the new Railway boss) and with Lord Mills. They expected
to have some plan ready for me when I return.

Left London airport at midnight – in a BOAC Britannia. For Secy;
Sir N Brook, Sir W Penney, Sir E Shuckburgh and Philip de Zulueta

---

109. MPs have only eight minutes after a division is called in which to get into the
     lobbies to cast their votes before the lobby doors are 'locked'.

made up the main party – also Samuel (PS to Ld Home) and Russell (For Office news dept) Sir John Richardson (my doctor) also came.

20 December

.... The recent political crisis in HofC has been interesting. The Conservative Party in Parliament has been much shaken. The real reason is that members (who have up to now shut their eyes to the realities of the modern world) have been rudely awakened. Britain (or France, or Germany, or any European power) can no longer exert a <u>decisive</u> influence on these world events. U.N., driven on by the Afro-Asians and the 'unaligned', with their bitter 'anti-colonial' complex, and supported spiritually and financially by the U.S. can do what they like. Of course, Britain can resign (as many Conservatives wd prefer) But then we lose all influence. What we <u>can</u> do (and did very successfully in the last few days) is to try to get the President and the Secretary of State to exert themselves, instead of leaving the direction to the Adlai Stevensons and other half-baked 'Liberals', whom they commonly employ (for internal political reasons) at U.N. ....

But apart from the actual occasion for this revolt (wh at one time seemed to be likely to destroy the Govt) there was revealed a hard core – 10 to 20 MPs on our side – who are so bitter agst me and my 'progressive' colleagues that they will use every difficulty or every critical situation to work up a large-scale revolt. They cannot normally attract the 'respectable' or 'middle' opinion in the party. But they can get some of them in on a special issue – e.g. Queen's visit to Ghana; Congo; breach of Pay Pause by electricity settlement; Immigration Bill; Loans to Coal industry etc . . . .

Meanwhile, except for Butler (who seems in low spirits) and Eccles (who is going to resign over his educational estimates)[110] the Cabinet and the Government as a whole seem in good heart.

23 December

.... We got back to London airport at 12 noon (London time) having left Bermuda at 10pm last night (local time) . . . .

The meeting with the President was interesting, and on the whole successful . . . .

    (1) We are determined to negotiate with the Russians about Berlin and get a solution if it is humanly possible . . . .

---

110. He did not.

(2) On Tests. The last Russian tests are rather alarming. We know
    that they are working very hard on an 'anti-missile' missile.
    They have built a town of 20,000 people wholly devoted to
    scientific work in this sphere. In addition, the 100 megaton is
    not just a stunt. At 25 miles up, it wd be immune from anti-
    missile attack. It would scorch with fire half France or England
    if dropped. What then shd we do. I made a tremendous appeal
    to the Pres[iden]t that we shd make another effort – in spite of
    the Russian trickery, and bad faith – to put a stop to all this
    folly. We have agreed only now to make some preparation for
    renewed tests – prob at Christmas Island – on this anti-missile
    development. But we will hold our hand – to see whether in
    the next few months we can make some progress, both on
    Berlin and in Disarmament.

(3) On Congo, Americans support Adoula, but recognise that U.N.
    leadership, civilian and military, has made great mistakes . . . .

(4) On Common Market, and freeing of World Trade, we are
    absolutely agreed . . . .

In general, our talks, sometimes alone, sometimes with the two Secretaries of State (Rusk and Ld Home) sometimes with other experts,
according to the subject, were easy and open. I found Pres[iden]t
apparently <u>very</u> friendly and rather humble. He is courteous, amusing,
and likes a joke or a neat turn of a phrase. He is <u>very</u> sensitive. He
seemed particularly pleased by the present wh I brought him (a copy
of the William and Mary ink stand on the Cabinet table) and by Debo
Devonshire's present (silver buttons – of the footmen's coats – with
ducal coronet and crest)

In health, I thought the President <u>not</u> in good shape. His back was
hurting. He could not sit long without pain. He cannot bend down to
pick up a book or a paper off the floor . . . .

These journeys tire me more each time and these discussions take
a tremendous lot 'out of one'. The London Press continues critical of
the Govt. *The Times* is particularly smug and irritating. Happily, I
think the Press, with its gossip and sneering and pomposity and
pettiness – as well as its downright lies – is losing influence every day.
TV, ITV, Radio – these are the instruments. Kennedy told me that he
was using the T.V. to appeal to the people over the heads of a broadly
hostile Press. I wonder whether a monthly Press Conference on American lines would be a good thing for me to try.

It seems now agreed that I shd go to Bonn on 8th or 9th Jan. to see Adenauer. This is really quite unnecessary and may even introduce complications. But since everyone else has visited every one (with this exception) in the last few weeks, this visit will complete the international quadrille . . . .

Christmas Day

I woke at 6am with the cold on my chest; laryngitis; acute pain, no temperature – or rather, abnormally low. Could not go to Church, wh is sad. Stayed in bed till tea, when I got up for an hour, to see all the children and all the in-door and out-door servants get their presents at Xmas tree . . . .

Another glorious day – cold and sunny. Dr Somerwell came to see me and reassured me about my throat. From the acute pain I felt sure I had cancer! . . . .

28 December

. . . . I pondered and brooded in bed and produced by last night a new plan for trying to get a general détente between the West and Communism, in wh all the questions wh seem insoluble by themselves might be subsumed into a new and general approach – a return to the Summit concept, before the breakdown of May 1960 . . . .

1962

Continuing crisis over Northern Rhodesia and Congo – Common Market negotiations – the Orpington by-election defeat – security breaches and spy scandals – incomes policy and the reconstruction of the government in the 'Night of the Long Knives' – revolution in Yemen and the undermining of the South Arabian Federation – the Commonwealth Conference – the 'Modernisation of Britain' – Cuban missile crisis – securing Polaris missiles at Nassau

2 January

. . . . A new row is starting about N Rhodesia. Mr Maudling (the new Colonial Sec) is being more 'African' than Mr Macleod (the old one) So he wants us to go back radically on the June plan, which was 'agreed' with Sir R.W. after immense labour then . . . .

The Lord Chancellor came to see me about this. Once more, he will help me in this new (and unexpected crisis) At the same time, Minister of Education (Eccles) and his Parl Sec (K Thompson) are clearly preparing for a dramatic exit from the Govt, wh Eccles is clever enough to see in great difficulties and slowly breaking up. However, I don't think everyone, however disgruntled, will turn to him . . . .

5 January

. . . . Congo a little better. Urquhart (the new U.N. official) seems sensible, altho' tired out, without a staff, or any real base to support him. The Swedes are said to be 'trigger-happy'. If so, it's the first time since Charles XII.[1] The Ethiopian troops are believed to be under better control, and less raping and murder. It is even reported that U.N. military and civil forces are returning some of the cars and other equipment wh they had stolen in Elizabethville from Europeans, esp British citizens. This is thought to be a great advance . . . .

The shipbuilding employers, like the engineering employers, have refused any wage increase. The Post Office workers are 'working to rule' and this (with the ice and snow) has produced a rather bad situation. Everything turns on a) holding on to the wage pause for 2 or 3 more months b) being able to slide into 'wage restraint' c) getting started the machinery for a long term policy. (Of course, too much strain on us by resigning ministers in other spheres of policy, may make our position untenable. But we will have a good try!)

---

1. A great soldier who reigned 1697–1718.

In bed all day, writing, read[ing], dozing. Read Meredith's *Victoria* – an old favourite. I suppose few people read Meredith nowadays. I read this book (wh I had not looked at for a long time) with pleasure – partly, perhaps, nostalgic pleasure – for it reminded me all the time of Sligger and Humphrey Sumner,[2] and Italy in 1913, and Oxford, and the old dead world, into which I had just begun to live and move before it crashed . . . .

10 January

We got back from Bonn last night, after a good day's talk and some useful agreements (at least in principle) about British costs in Germany. The Germans seemed for the first time to realise the very serious character of this exchange problem and to be ready to place substantial orders . . . .

A very long meeting about Northern Rhodesia – 10.30–1.15, and no progress. The new Colonial Secretary (Maudling) is 'plus noire que les nègres'[3] – that is, more difficult and intransigeant than his predecessor (Macleod) He threatens resignation . . . .

. . . . If Maudling resigns, with Ld Perth and Hugh Fraser, he may force Macleod to do the same. Yet we cannot do as he demands and tear up altogether the agreement we made with Welensky. But if these ministers go, it will be very hard (with all our other difficulties) to prevent the break-up of the Government . . . .

15 January

. . . . We are now faced with the wage demands of the Coal Miners and the Railwaymen (as well as Gas; Bus, and some other public employees) The 'go-slow' in the Civil Service is 'off'. (It had produced a great many bitter jests. How <u>could</u> the Civil Service go any slower? Etc etc)

Lord Robens is cooperating well. Dr Beeching (Railways) is a more difficult character . . . .

One of the strange results of an outbreak of small-pox, traced to

---

2. F. F. 'Sligger' Urquhart, the first Catholic college fellow in Oxford since the Reformation, was at the centre of Balliol social life in Macmillan's time. Macmillan was amongst those invited to his villa near Chamonix. Sumner – later Warden of All Souls College, Oxford – was alone amongst Macmillan's close Oxford friends in surviving the Great War.

3. More black than the blacks.

Pakistani immigrants, has been to make the ordinary people more in favour than ever of the Immigration Bill[4] . . . .

18 January

Yesterday was an all Italian day. Meetings in morning and afternoon. Luncheon at Italian Embassy for us; dinner at Admiralty House for them. The talks were useful but not dramatic. Both ministers (Fanfani and Segni) are able, courteous, and well-informed. Their chief anxiety is as NATO members. They don't want to be exposed to dangerous courses over Berlin. They were critical of the French. On Europe, they will be helpful – but they have rather 'federationist' ideas . . . .

Cabinet at 11. Railway wages. Then the great question of Nuclear Tests. I shewed the Cabinet my latest correspondence with President Kennedy and we agreed (after much helpful discussion) a final reply. We agree to make Christmas Island available for Tests; he agrees to my new initiative to try to bring them to an end . . . .

19 January

. . . . Chancellor of Exr at 11.30. We agreed a statement on Railway wages, to be issued by the Treasury to which Dr Beeching has at last been induced (by the combined efforts of Ld Mills, John Hare and Ernest Marples) to agree. We hope this will lead to arbitration. But it is not a binding arbitration on either side . . . .

A rather disappointing message from Ld Alport, in Salisbury. He thinks the security situation in N. Rhodesia very threatening, and no compromise possible. Even if we make the major changes which Maudling proposes in the June plan, there is no reason to believe that the Africans will accept anything on these lines. They are really going back to the pre-March 1961 position, and demanding 'one man, one vote' and a secure African majority in the Legislative Council. It is certain[ly] difficult to know what to do. There really seems no way out from a civil war or an African revolution. All this results from Welensky's intransigeance on the one hand and (I fear) our own hesitations on the other. Meanwhile a complicated, and

---

4. A girl arriving from Karachi, where a smallpox outbreak was raging, was hospitalised in Bradford on 23 December, dying a few days later. Primary infections peaked in Bradford with five deaths on 11–13 January. With the end of fatalities came the search for scapegoats. The headline in the *Yorkshire Post* on 15 January, for instance, was 'Pakistanis blamed in the Smallpox City'.

potentially dangerous, situation is developing over the request of U.N. (thro' U Thant) for authority to station 'observers' in N. Rhodesia to stop the arms traffic [into Congo] wh they allege has been going on. This raises the question of responsibility? Is it U.K. Govt? Is it Govt of Federation? The legal position is obscure. The actual position is that, whatever our <u>legal</u> powers, HMG cannot in fact enforce them. The U.N. still correspond with us about all this. We have <u>not</u> passed on U Thant's last reply, for we thought it ill-judged and offensive . . . .

20 January

. . . . I cannot feel much confidence in the immediate future, but the fault lies partly in ourselves, not our stars.[5] Departmental ministers seem to take an increasingly narrow view of things. When we discuss great issues, they are sensible and constructive. But that doesn't seem to prevent them forcing the particular views of their own departments, whether Home or Overseas, in such a way as to threaten the disruption of the Government. Eccles now is taking this line, and all about a few million pounds, up or down, in the school building programme. I fear Minister of Housing will do the same.

24 January

Cabinet at 10am. The Railway wages decision which we have taken has caused a storm of protest. This is the contrary to what we expected. We thought we shd be attacked for weakness. We are being attacked for strength! . . . .

25 January

. . . . A rather depressing and sterile argument about the Estimates. Everything is agreed on the Government <u>investment</u> side, except schools and houses. David Eccles was very argumentative. I think he is looking for an opportunity to leave a ship of whose buoyancy he is not quite sure. But perh this does him an injustice . . . .

In the evening, Cabinet discussed U.N. (resolutions about Portuguese Africa – Angola) The usual dilemma. If we vote <u>for</u> these resolutions (wh contain absurd and impossible paragraphs) because we

---

5. An application in a rather different context of Shakespeare's *Julius Caesar*, Act I, Scene ii, lines 141–42: 'The fault, dear Brutus, is not in our stars, / But in ourselves, that we are underlings.'

can give a <u>general</u> consent to their purpose, we are guilty of a breach
of strict logic and even honour. If we vote <u>against</u> (or <u>abstain</u>, wh is
now thought tantamount to a negative vote) we are pilloried (with
Portugal and S. Africa) as one of a minority of 3. The Americans never
help. They just blindly vote for 'anti-colonialism'. They get no thanks
from anyone. But their influence in the U.N. is large – chiefly because
they are U.N.O.'s 'sugar-daddy'.[6]

Cabinet went on to discuss the finances of U.N.O. In spite of the
gross mismanagement of the Secretariat, the organisation is really
suffering from a) default of subscribers b) huge military costs of Congo
etc. The Cabinet was with difficulty persuaded by the For Secy
(Chancellor of Exr) to offer to buy $12m <u>bonds</u>, if certain conditions
were met. This decision will be very unpopular in the party, but I think
it is right and on the whole in British interests.

PQs quiet – only 5 asked. Some MPs don't come or take off their
question at [the] last minute.

Debate on guillotine motion [on the Commonwealth's Immigrants
Bill]. The Opposition 'flapped' – they had great difficulty in keeping
the debate going till 10pm. M[ichael] Foot made a fine anarchic speech
– attacking everybody. He is a strange character – an undergraduate
still. He writes well; speaks well; talks well. But he has not the charm
which Bevan had. In our politics, rebels must have charm – it's best
for them to be Celts.

26 January

. . . . The Civil Service unions are poisoned with Communism. 25% of
their paid officials are Communists. What a state of affairs, and how
repugnant to the real views of the masses of respectable civil servants.
It is the Electrical T.U. story all over again.

Dr Erhard called – happy Germany, rich – incredibly rich – with
no problems, exc[luding] Berlin.

29 January

. . . . I had a long talk this evening with Reggie Maudling, Colonial
Secretary. He got back today from West Indies. I thought his attitude
to the N. Rhodesian problem much more relaxed. No threats; no talk
of resignation . . . .

---

6. On 30 January Britain voted in the UN General Assembly for the resolution
censuring Portugal for not promoting democracy in Angola.

30 January

11–1. Meeting on Northern Rhodesia. Lord Home, Ld Kilmuir, Mr Butler, Mr Sandys, Mr Maudling. After 2 hours, we <u>all</u> agreed on the plan wh we wd <u>all</u> agree to recommend to the Cabinet. Ld Chancellor took charge of drafting the various documents, telegrams to Alport – for talk with Welensky etc . . . .

I am still waiting to hear from General de Gaulle whether he will join in our appeal to Mr Kruschev on the Nuclear Tests. We hear (privately and secretly) that he is rather attracted, but (since he cannot bear to agree with anyone) will raise all kinds of minor difficulties . . . .

2 February

. . . . Yesterday was a difficult day, with a long Cabinet, wh approved the first stage in the Rhodesian affair. Also, a great discussion on Railways Wages and the next step in the Incomes Policy after the first stage of the Pay Pause ends on April 1.[7] The Post Office workers have given up their 'working to rule' – after a month. It is satisfactory that the PMG has made <u>no</u> concession to obtain this.

It looks as if the unofficial 'one day' strike or go slow on the railways and tubes will be abandoned. So we <u>are</u> gaining some ground.

I went to the 1922 Ctee yesterday and was well received by the party. They are, of course, anxious and many have no nerve. The newspapers today published long and very tendentious accounts of this 'private' meeting. Chief Whip is naturally upset.

. . . . Today, Colonial Policy Ctee in the morning. West Indies – sad but not dangerous. Kenya – insoluble, we are faced with terrible decisions here. It is our little Algeria.

An amusing meeting at Oxford. It was organised by the University Conservative Association and took place in the Union. The hall was packed, with a good sprinkling of Liberals and Socialists. Outside, there were 500 or 600 more – who had come to listen. There were loud-speakers. Mixed with them was a band of 'Anti-Bomb' demonstrators. I had some difficulty in getting into the hall, but once in it was a splendid meeting. I abandoned most of my prepared speech and I had a very good and attractive audience, with plenty of heckling and

---

7. Published as *Incomes Policy: The Next Step*, this envisaged pay not increasing faster than national income. Rail, however, was widely seen as a special case. Although Marples initially resisted anything more than the 2.5% increase in national output, the final settlement was a 3% rise in rail wages.

interruption. Of course the Press today completely misrepresent what happened. To add to the general 'rag', my bust (by Nemon) wh is in the Oxford Union was removed the day before the meeting, but found by the police and put back in its place . . . .

3 February

. . . . An agreeable, but somewhat crazy MP (Legge-Bourke, Ely) has made a speech, full of praise of me, but saying I should retire, exhausted, in favour of a younger P.M. The Press has naturally made much of this. However, I am better treated by my party than Gaitskell . . . .

4 February

. . . . Julian, Catherine and I went to luncheon with Michael and Pamela Berry. They have got a very nice house. The Berrys are hostile to me politically – in *Daily Telegraph* and *Sunday Telegraph*. All the Sunday Press (except curiously enough Max Beaverbrook's paper) is full of gossip about the attacks on me by Tory back-benchers . . . .

6 February

On the whole, yesterday was a good day. The Press (as usual) with the exception of the *Manchester Guardian*, makes no attempt at an objective account of the debate.[8] The *Daily Mirror*'s headline is MAC FLOPS (4½ million) The *Daily Express* is 'MAC TRIUMPHS' (also 4½ million circulation) The *Daily Telegraph* is peevish (because Lady Pamela is in a peevish mood) *The Times* is 'wet' (because the Astors – who are physically brave take no part, and Sir William Haley – well, you could wring the water out of him). And so on. But one can always tell. I know that the HofCommons thought my speech was good – not a triumph, not rhetoric, but good, persuasive debating. The party were satisfied, and more – almost enthusiastic. There are the malignant opponents – like Lambton, Fell, Turton etc who will never be satisfied. There are the true cranks, like Legge-Bourke, who now tells everyone that he did not see my broadcast or hear my speech to the 1922 Ctee, yet has made these two incidents the ground for his attack on me. But he was smashed on TV by Nabarro.

Gaitskell opened, with a good speech. I followed. H. Wilson

---

8. The occasion was a censure motion moved by Gaitskell against the Foreign Secretary over critical remarks he had recently made about the UN.

wound up for Opposition in his usual style 'the long smear'. Ted Heath wound up for us, with a good slashing reply. Majority 98 (4 of our chaps, coming from Yorkshire, were 2 hours late – or we wd have had 102) Churchill came and sat on the front bench by my side while the division was being announced, and we walked out slowly together (he leaning heavily on my arm) amid applause.

7 February

. . . . De Gaulle has sent a very friendly reply, but turns down the 'joint approach', chiefly because it is linked with the Disarmament Ctee 'a demogogic machine'. I am rather relieved, for the French will make nothing but trouble. But I think it was right to give him the chance.

Ted Heath came to luncheon and gave me his impression of the Common Market negotiations, their difficulties and their prospects. The hope is to finish by the end of July – but I doubt it. If it does, we shd have to aim at Commonwealth Prime Ministers in late September or early October. This cd be followed by Party Conference and then Parlt. But I fear that the negotiations may drift on. However, it all opens up a fascinating autumn . . . .

16 February

A very busy period, ending with a quiet day (stayed in bed till luncheon) The chief events have been

(1) <u>H Bomb Tests</u>. This includes my statement in HofC, which went very well. The 'two-pronged approach' made the whole difference. If I had merely announced the agreement to provide Christmas Island for the American atmospheric tests, if shewn to be necessary, without the joint letter from President K[ennedy] and myself to Kruschev urging a new and urgent approach to the disarmament question,[9] it wd have been much more difficult. I 'got away' with the announcement of our own underground test at Nevada, and I was not cross-examined too closely on the point wh had caused so much concern to the

---

9. A few days later, on 21 February, at a dinner for the Association of American Correspondents, Macmillan told his audience 'that the perfection of an anti-missile missile, by the estimate of British experts would take the entire British gross national product for the next ten years. Even then, the experts could not be sure that it would work. This was compelling reason to get together with the Russians and try to avert such an expenditure' (JFKL: Ms Estabrook).

Cabinet – that of who had the veto.[10] The emphasis on close consultation was accepted. This affair has certainly caused more trouble to Gaitskell, for it reopens the old wound between the unilateralists and the multilateralists. I think the Govt got credit from the handling of a difficult problem. However, Mr Kruschev is now also trying to get ahead of us, by proposing an immediate 'Summit' meeting of 18 'Heads of Government' in Geneva, without any preparation or any experts. This of course is pure propaganda, but we have to deal with it cautiously, or we shall be accused of 'dragging our feet' . . . .

(2) <u>Berlin</u>. The situation is worse, and is rapidly becoming dangerous. I don't know what to do. The diplomatic 'probe' in Moscow has made no progress at all . . . .

(3) <u>Central African Federation</u>. Sandys is still in Salisbury. He is having good talks about the 'future' of the Federation. W[elensky] is at last beginning to face realities, 2 or 3 years too late. He recognises that Nyasaland cannot be kept in. He still hopes that the Rhodesias might hold together. Whitehead (Southern Rhodesian Premier) is clearly beginning to doubt this. The problem of the Northern Rhodesian constitution is <u>not</u> yet resolved . . . .

(4) <u>Kenya</u>. We have had long Cabinet discussions . . . . The truth is that Kenya is at the moment bankrupt (deficit is £30m) and (with self-government followed in a few months by independence) may become a bloody shambles.

(5) <u>Congo</u>. Worse again. The U.N. authorities are threatening 'military' action in N. Katanga. This means another period of murder and rapine by these savage and undisciplined troops. I doubt if we can continue to 'support' the Congo enterprise if this happens.

(6) <u>Costs of British in Germany</u>. We are promised £33m a year for two years; but we want £60m. What are we to do? We <u>ought</u> to reduce our forces in Germany, but if we do at this moment we shall be much criticised by all the NATO countries. The Americans, who have filched some of the German orders wh we were expecting by acts of ruthless and brutal salesmanship,

---

10. Discussed at length on 3 January, 18 January and 1 February, the Cabinet's concern was the political difficulty of conceding American tests on British territory, not least in light of the new 18-power disarmament talks in Geneva.

have the insolence to criticise us, covertly not yet overtly, for 'falling down on NATO commitments'.

(7) <u>British Economy</u>. A very disappointing month (January) Exports level; imports a great deal up. Trade gap £67m. No increase in production. However, some experts prophesy an improvement soon. If only all the people who write, lecture, broadcast, and even preach about economic growth did some useful work, the increase in man-power wd perhaps enable us to achieve it.[11] Meanwhile, difficult Cabinet discussions, adjourned from day to day (but <u>no</u> resignations as yet) about the expenditure on current and on capital a/c for next year. It will be £111m <u>above</u> the Chancellor's target. The Minister of Education's figures are still in dispute . . . .

(8) <u>Railway strike</u>. The leaders of the 3 unions appealed to see me – so I accepted. We had a good deal of discussion amongst Cabinet colleagues and Treasury experts about what I was to say. Finally, a document was agreed, from wh I did <u>not</u> repeat <u>not</u> depart . . . . 3 hours talk; much consumption of whisky; etc etc. It was announced yesterday that there would be no strike. This was a great relief. The Press is very kind. 'Mac's Triumph' etc etc. How quickly it changes. Up till the debate in the House; the 'bomb' initiative; and the settled railway strike, it has been the ageing and feeble Premier.

(9) <u>Security</u>. The Radcliffe report has now been delivered to me.[12] A rather complicated negotiation followed, with Gaitskell and his Privy Counsellors.[13] Mr G is always affable. But he is weak and gives no lead to his own people. George Brown was so rude that I could have kicked him out of the room. But it is

---

11. Calculation of relative economic performance internationally took off in the late 1950s and helped to prompt a spate of soul-searching, most notably in Penguin specials such as Andrew Shonfield, *British Economic Policy since the War* (Harmondsworth: Penguin, 1956) or Michael Shanks, *The Stagnant Society* (Harmondsworth: Penguin, 1961). To try to build support for growth from both labour and industry the National Economic Development Council was established – unrecorded by Macmillan – in March.

12. Set up after the George Blake case, it made various recommendations on improving security and combating Communist penetration within government services.

13. A confidential briefing for senior members of the Opposition sworn of the Privy Council.

not malice. He is just common and so ill-bred as not to be conscious of his boorish behaviour. He is one of those few men who is more disagreeable sober than drunk . . . .

Yesterday I came into the smoking room and found myself at a table with Sir H Legge-Bourke. The poor man was very embarrassed and tried to move away. But I got him talking; bought him a drink; and got a lot of friends to gather round. The news of the settlement of the Railway question had just been announced and there were many congratulations, from Labour as much as from Conservatives. Poor Harry seemed to be wondering whether the poor old Prime Minister was really past it after all, only fit to be put out to grass or sent to the knackers . . . .

21 February

Defence Ctee 11–1.15. Some difficult questions, chiefly on 1) size of British element in army 2) future of Gurkhas. We agreed on 171,000 all British. This wd entail gradual reduction of Gurkhas. But since these are not acceptable in Europe or Africa, their use is really limited to Hong-Kong and Singapore.

Mr Tyerman, editor of the *Economist*, to luncheon. Also Edward Boyle. As usual, the editor was full of praise for our economic policy in private, altho' in public his paper attacks us every week . . . .

22 February

. . . . PQs went well – even merrily. As I left at 3.30, the Tory back-benchers cheered. I have never known this before. If only we can prevent this foolish split on Rhodesia, our general position is improving . . . .

23 February

. . . . Talk with For Secy . . . . about Mr K[hrushchev]'s reply. Being young, impulsive and imaginative, I wd like to invite him at once to a meeting with President Kennedy and myself. But the President is slow and cautious, old in experience if young in years! It is strangely unlike the popular idea of the situation . . . .

24 February

. . . . The President has sent off a reply to Mr K[hrushchev], without proper consultation with us. I have made a fuss about this and it has been stopped in Moscow. It will give us a chance of getting it made a little less stiff . . . .

25 February

. . . . The Central African situation is getting more and more confused.
Welensky now threatens to come here. This wd be fatal (from his point
of view) and make it almost impossible for us to make any concessions. The <u>real</u> problem is now emerging – not the <u>details</u> of the N.
Rhodesian constitution, but the certainty that (in view of their hatred
of all Welensky stands for) the secession first of Nyasaland then of
N. Rhodesia from Federation. Welensky may (as he threatened last
March) have resort to force. Nor can we stop him. But will Whitehead,
the P.M. of Southern Rhodesia, stand with him? W is a downy old
bird, brought up in the English political tradition, not an emotional
Lithuanian Jew. I like and in many ways admire Welensky – but he
has – by a tragedy of errors – given a quite false picture or 'image' (as
they say nowadays) of himself, both in Africa and at home . . . .

26 February

. . . . From our sources of information we know that Welensky and his
High Commissioner (Robinson) give every private document and all
private discussions to Ld Salisbury and his group. Robinson spent
all Saturday with Ld S at Hatfield (or Cranborne)[14] This makes it
dangerous to talk to him or to send messages to Welensky with any
real confidence or frankness. These gentlemen also (quite naturally)
try to play off one Secretary of State against another. What is amusing
is how naïve they are! They talk blandly to us what are absolute lies
without realising that we have sources of information wh make us
fully aware of the truth.

I decided to see Reggie Maudling at 3, and I told him <u>how</u> I
proposed to conduct the vital Cabinet. This took place from 4.30–7.
It was an <u>excellent</u> discussion, in tone and content. We began with a
general review of the whole situation in the Central African Federation
and the grim future ahead. Nyasaland was already demanding 'secession'. As soon as N. Rhodesia got any kind of right of self-expression,
the Legislative Council there wd do the same. 'Partition' (that is of
N. Rhodesia) wh wd enable the Copper Belt to be a multi-racial area,
working with S. Rhodesia, and shedding the rest to become <u>purely</u>

14. Hatfield House in Hertfordshire is the seat of the Marquesses of Salisbury, and
    Cranborne in Dorset that of the heir to the title, Lord Cranborne. Sir Albert
    Robinson was the last High Commissioner for the Central African Federation
    to Britain (1961–63).

African territories, <u>might</u> have been a way out – but it seems now too late. The world wd of course say that the Europeans were seizing the only part of N. Rhodesia that was any good, and throwing the rest away, to be poor, backward, and non-viable states. (This wd not be quite true but it wd be what all Afro/Asian states wd say) On the other hand, if the Federation is to collapse, will it or can it do so peacefully. May not Welensky be forced to use force and seize the Copper Belt. He knows that we cannot send British soldiers to stop him . . . .

Dined in HofC with Chief Whip. We did some soundings. I feel that Ld Perth is pushing on Maudling to abolish the Asian seat or resign. I think M is hesitating. It is a narrow point on wh to resign (he is 44 years old) and in a few weeks no one will know or remember what it was all about. On the other hand, he is very conscientious and the Governor and Colonial Office are of course pressing him hard . . . .

27 February

The Cabinet met at 10.30 . . . . everyone being in favour of some early announcement on the N. Rhodesian constitution and everyone accepting the abolition of the numerical alternative and the equalisation of the percentages for Europeans and Africans. Several members took part – mostly in favour of retaining the Asian seat, but some against. In order to be quite fair, I read out a paper wh I had prepared overnight, giving a way in which I thought the 'paying back' of the 500 additional Africans on the Upper Roll <u>could</u> perhaps be presented. The atmosphere was tense but very dignified. From the human point of view, it was the most dramatic Cabinet since Thorneycroft's resignation – with this difference. There was more sympathy with Maudling, both in substance and on the way in which he presented his case. Also Welensky's threats had their effect in creating resentment agst him . . . . Everyone agreed that we must reach a decision and <u>announce</u> it before Welensky could get to London.

After some ¾ hour discussion, Colonial Secretary said – very quietly – that he felt the Govt and the country were faced with such great problems in every field that – whatever it might be – he wd <u>accept</u> the decision of his colleagues. This was a dramatic moment – certainly for me. But I felt it all the more necessary to go on with the discussion on <u>merits</u>, as a matter of courtesy and good feeling. Finally, it was agreed to fix the percentage at 10% and to retain the Asian seat.[15]

---

15. The suggested percentage of votes required from both races had previously been

Telegrams were then sent to Alport and Welensky. These had to deal with Sandys' report to the Cabinet on the broad problem of the future of the Federation as well as on the N. Rhodesian constitution. The first was important in order to make it quite clear – and to have it on record that the Govt is not in any way committed to the ideas discussed at Salisbury concerning the future federation, esp. as regards the partition schemes which Whitehead is promoting.

The second was to give the Federal Govt the final decision of HMG on the Northern Rhodesian constitution. Unfortunately, owing to various delays, these telegrams did not reach Sir Roy Welensky until just before his aeroplane was due to take off. As a result, he took off for London at 5pm (our time) 7pm (local time) . . . .

Maudling and I dined at Bucks. We had quite a relaxed evening, and went to HofC at 10.30 to vote on the 3rd Reading of the Commonwealth Immigrants Bill. After all the threats of opposition from our side and of abstention, we got a majority of 107.

Lord Perth has written to resign about N. Rhodesia, wh is pretty silly in view of his chief's decision . . . .

28 February

In the morning, a whole sheaf of telegrams from Washington. The President wants to start Nuclear Tests – at Christmas Island – almost at once, without waiting for the Geneva conference. This is a blow, for I thought he was in a mood to delay. I arranged a meeting for 5pm with For Secy; Minister of Defence; Sir Solly Zuckerman, Sir William Penney etc. At this meeting we decided on our course, and sent appropriate messages to Washington. The President wants to announce this decision tomorrow (Thursday) But Friday or Saturday wd be better for me from HofC point of view. I have urged him most strongly to give at least a reasonable time during wh we might urge Russia to agree to a Test Ban agreement. Otherwise, the American attitude will be called brutal and provocative – in spite of past history of Russia's duplicity . . . .

Lord Perth in the morning. He has 'unresigned' – so that is satisfactory. Welensky arrived this morning, but I arranged for him to be met

---

12.5%. Although Asians in Northern Rhodesia were unenthusiastic about a reserved seat it was retained to please Welensky, who saw it as helping to balance African representation. The alternative of a minimum of 400 votes from the other race had already been dropped by Cabinet on 1 February.

by a Parl Sec, and instructed Sandys and Maudling to refuse to see him until <u>after</u> the statement. This was made (very effectively and briefly) by Colonial Sec at 3.30. It was <u>well</u> received by all sides of the House. The famous Asian seat was hardly mentioned! The <u>left</u> (Opposition and Conservative) seemed pleased by the <u>equalisation</u> of percentages and the removal of this discriminatory plan. The right (Conservative) were quiet (I wish they had made some protest, for this always helps with the Africans) Denis Healey (for Labour) did <u>very</u> badly. He made a violent attack on Welensky (who certainly said some very foolish things at the airport) but, apart from this, his manner and matter was poor. By contrast, Maudling was calm and statesmanlike . . . .

I had a small, but quite successful luncheon party today. Mr Cecil King (Daily Mirror) Lord Monckton, Mr Heath (Ld P[rivy] Seal) Andrew Devonshire, and Sir Frank Lee. Cecil King (who is a nephew of Lord Northcliffe) is a true Harmsworth – eccentric, cynical, power-loving, but quite amusing. He was very merry at the expense of Roy Thomson – his rival. He was hopeful that Ld Shawcross, in his report to the Press, wd show up some of the iniquities of the Printers' Trade Unions.[16]

1 March

. . . . Dinner for President Elect of Costa Rica. According to him, his is a happy little country. The divergences between rich and poor are less marked than elsewhere in Central and S. America. Communism does not exist. There is no Army, Navy, or Air Force, and therefore no revolutions and no dictators.

2 March

10.30 Ld Hailsham, Ld St Aldwyn (Chief Whip) – on new Life Peers. Mr Gaitskell has again agreed to nominate 5. There is a problem about one, who is said to be disreputable. Whether that matters much in the H of Lords is doubtful . . . .

Dorothy and I went by train to Oxford, to dine at Somerville College,[17] of which I am Visitor. These distinguished ladies were very pleasant and it was a most successful evening. The 'dons' (if that is the right word for them) range from extreme left to extreme right in

---

16. Instead the Royal Commission report, appearing in May, was concerned more with press ownership.

17. Then a women-only college.

their opinions. Their charms are mainly, tho' not in every case, intellectual . . . .

4 March (Sunday)
. . . . Sir Edgar Whitehead (P.M. of Southern Rhodesia) came to luncheon and stayed till 4pm. He gave me an outline of his plan for remodelling the areas of the Central African Federation. It is certainly imaginative, but there are grave objections to it. He was very interesting indeed about the 'liberalising' movement wh he has got going and the progress he has made. He certainly knows a great deal about Africa and Africans. Unlike poor Welensky, he has a first class brain . . . .

Motored to London. Chancellor of Exr at 7, who stayed to supper. He gave me the outline of his Budget – wh will be in effect a 'standstill' Budget, still restraining and deflationary. The most interesting item will be the legislation in the Finance Bill to bring short-term profits on stocks and shares and on <u>land</u> transactions into income for tax purposes. This should help with wage restraint.

5 March
I was rung up early by the For Secy, who told me that Kruschev had now agreed to the procedure wh we and the Americans had proposed for the Geneva Conference, including the prior meeting of the three Foreign Ministers to discuss in particular the nuclear test problem. This helped very much with my statement in the HofC on the American resumption of tests and the use of Christmas Island. The statement, on wh we worked all the morning, went off very quietly. Mr Gaitskell (who seems to have been nobbled by the President) was very helpful, and even shot down Grimond for me. Supplementaries were few. The left wingers and fellow travellers seemed stunned by the news of Kruschev's acceptance . . . . There was no attempt to adjourn the House, so I was able to catch the 5pm train to Leicester. Here we had a splendid meeting – 4000 in hall, with many standing. A good amount of opposition – some quiet, some vocal. The speech proved very successful and was very much applauded at the end. The jokes went well. (But beware of oratorical questions! I was caught out by one. 'What is the obstacle to progress?' 'You are' – this floored me) . . . .

6 March
Back in London by noon. I left Rab to do a largely routine Cabinet.

P.Q.s (<u>not</u> very successful) Met Persian P.M. (Dr Armini)[18] at airport at 5. I took him back in my car. He seemed friendly and intelligent. Iran has great difficulties and so has Dr Armini. Inefficient and corrupt administration and too great a gulf between rich and poor are the chief. I think he is making some headway. But the Shah is easily discouraged; is surrounded by an intriguing court; and does not seem to back any P.M. long enough to get results. The land reform, agreed in principle, is a slow business in practice . . . .

7 March

10am. I had a talk with Norman Brook and Chief Whip about forming a new dept (from C.R.O. and C.O.) to deal with Central African affairs. Both Secretaries of State have agreed in principle. I am going to try to persuade Butler to take it on . . . .

8 March

. . . . The Americans (whether President himself or not, I am not sure) seem to have put a lot of pressure on Gaitskell about abandoning the independent British nuclear force. I shall have to face President K[ennedy] with this when I see him.

The doctors have come out with a tremendous report on the dangers of smoking – esp. cigarettes. This puts us in rather a fix. For how are we to get £800m indirect revenue from any other source?

Colonial Secy gave rather a dismal account of Kenya Conference and of the future. The only cheerful thing is that there is no suggestion now of early 'independence'. The stage of 'full internal self-government' must be gone through . . . .

A long and useful talk with Lord Swinton this afternoon . . . . Swinton thought we had got the North Rhodesian constitution just right. To have gone further and abolished the Asian seat agst Welensky's wishes wd have given him a real grievance and the accusations of bad faith wd have been irresistible. Ld Salisbury wd at last have had a real case. I told him my plan for putting the whole territory of the Federation out of CRO and CO and into the hands of a single minister. He approved – but only if it was under a minister with some other employment, e.g. Home Secy. Otherwise, it looks rather panicky and a

---

18. The name of the Iranian prime minister was actually Ali Amini, who served from May 1961 to July 1962.

minister specially appointed wd be expected to pull some rabbits quickly out of the hat . . . .

9 March

The election result at Lincoln is bad;[19] we have lost 3000 votes to the Liberals. Labour has done well. But until the series – nine by-elections in all – is completed, it will not be possible to draw any conclusions. Naturally, with the 'pay pause' etc, our stock is not very high. Nevertheless, I think we are relatively stronger than in 1957 and 1958. The chief difficulty at the next General Election will be the cry 'Time for a Change!' However, what happens in the European Common Market negotiations will probably dominate the political scene and may even lead to a break up of present political alignments . . . .

Rab came at 11. He has accepted the new post – SofS for Central African Federation, combining what is now under CRO and what is now under CO. I am very pleased. He is certainly much better in health and spirit since he gave up the Chairmanship of the Party and the Leadership of the HofCommons. He will, of course, remain Home Secretary. This is a far better plan than finding another minister. For Butler is recognised as my deputy and his appointment to this African work will not excite the jealousy of the other ministers concerned . . . .

12 March

. . . . 4pm. Treasury ministers; MofDefence; Ld Privy Seal, on result of Mr Brooke's negotiations in Germany. I think we may get orders to the tune of 600m deutschmarks for 2 years. This goes some way to help – but by no means all the way. Nevertheless, I don't think we can go below seven brigades in Germany at present . . . .

24 March

. . . . I sent Solly Zuckerman and William Penney to Washington. They were cordially received, but found that the American scientists had made no progress in the field of seismology at all comparable with our work. Unfortunately, altho' they were impressed, they were not wholly convinced that <u>national</u> instruments cd detect underground tests in Soviet territory with any certainty. This is a pity – and worse. For if we cd have offered to do without the <u>stations</u> in Russia, and only ask

---

19. Easily retained by Labour with 19,038 votes to the Conservatives' 11,386 and Liberals' 6,856.

for <u>occasional visits</u> by teams wh cd be neutral, we wd really be in a
position to shew up the hollowness of the Russian fear of espionage
. . . . There seems therefore no way of preventing the starting of the
American tests at Christmas Island after Easter . . . .

. . . . Butler's acceptance of the new office (Central African Office)
to cover all the territories of the Federation now divided between
Commonwealth and Colonial Offices has been well received – after an
initial burst of derision in HofC – by the Press and by thinking people.
Fortunately Welensky, Whitehead, Banda, and even Kaunda seem
pleased.

Greater <u>Malaysia</u> is in trouble. I foresee a situation like that in
Central Africa. The two departments will quarrel and we shall get
nowhere. I am considering putting Borneo, Brunei, etc under the
Commonwealth Secy. But I must await the report of the Cobbold
Ctee.[20]

The great problem, wh looms ahead, is how to arrange for the
meeting of Commonwealth PMs on Europe. The negotiations for
Britain's entry into the Common Market are going on well in Brussels.
Altho' they are at present of a preliminary character, they will come to
the crunch during the summer. We may expect to know by the end of
July on what sort of terms, as regards EFTA countries, British agriculture, and the Commonwealth, we can join the Six. In fact, we
are having the closest consultation all the time with Commonwealth
officials. We have had visits from and to individual ministers. But
everyone will pretend the opposite (if it suits them) and nothing will
be regarded as constituting 'consultation' except a meeting of Prime
Ministers. So the question arises, when? . . . .

But, of course, the whole political situation has been dominated
by a series of by-election results which seem to indicate a dramatic
change (for the worse) in the fortunes of our party. These bad results
(in Middlesboro' – where we were at the bottom of the poll and in
Blackpool – normally a safe seat, we only scraped in) culminated in an
overwhelming defeat in Orpington.[21] Here we had, in a seat adjacent

---

20. Set up under Lord Cobbold in February, reporting on 4 July in favour of the
    incorporation of the colonies of North Borneo (now Sabah) and Sarawak with
    Malaya into a new federation of Malaysia.
21. In Middlesbrough East (14 March) and Blackpool North (13 March) the Tory
    vote fell by 20% or more. As in Orpington, this was largely because of
    defections to the Liberals.

to and similar to Bromley,[22] a majority of 12000 or more. We lost by 6000! This has not been due to the <u>Socialists</u>. They have held their own seats, without change. But we have been swept off our feet by a <u>Liberal</u> revival. Some say that this phenomenon is similar to what happened in 1957 [sic] – Tonbridge and Torrington. But it is far more pronounced and seems to indicate a real movement, representing or expressing real grievances or emotions. On the grievances, it is the revolt of the middle classes or lower middle classes, who resent the vastly improved condition of the working classes, and are envious of the apparent prosperity and luxury of the 'rich' – whether they live on office expenses, capital gains, or capital. These white collar 'little men' – clerks, civil servants etc have voted Conservative 'to keep Labour out'. Now (especially at by-elections) they are voting Liberal to 'give the Govt a smack in the eye' . . . .

Then there is fashion. It is getting dull to be a young Conservative. It is not at all smart to go Labour. Liberal is not in establishment; has a flavour of 'something different'.

Most of all, it is a revolt against all the unsolved problems. The Bomb (it favours the abolition of the British independent deterrent) Relations with Russia. NATO. Berlin. Rhodesia (it is violently anti-white) But it springs most from the Govt's inability to keep the economy on an even course of continuous progress. It deplores 'Stop and Go' or 'acceleration and brake'. It wants enormously <u>increased</u> expenditure, and <u>reduced</u> taxation. It wants a larger army, without conscription. It wants wage stability, without any restraint. In a word, it wants what we all want and know we can't have.

The Pay Pause – the Govt's policy – has offended dons, schoolmasters, school-teachers, civil servants, clerks, nurses, public utility workers, railwaymen, and all the rest. But perhaps it is most resented by the doctors, dons, nurses etc who feel that they are <u>relatively</u> ill paid, compared to the high wages wh they hear about coming in to the ordinary artisan's household.

Anyway, it is a portent. And the Tories are very worried. Naturally, their disappointment must find an outlet. This must, in the long run, mean an attack on the Leadership of the Party . . . .

I had to go on March 15 and 16 to Liverpool and Manchester – two speeches, (nominally non-party gatherings but largely Conserva-

---

22. Macmillan's seat. The Orpington result (14 March) was Liberal 22,846; Conservative 14,991; Labour 5,350.

tives) and they seemed steady enough. Tory MPs are divided into different groups. But the enemies of the Leadership, already numerous, have undoubtedly been strengthened. And Lord Salisbury is working hard, with growing power. He genuinely believes that the loss of our Conservative voters to the Liberals is due to our having followed too 'Liberal' policies! He thinks reaction is the cure, and he regards me as the arch-enemy of reaction . . . .

In addition to everything else, I have had long talks with Selwyn Lloyd (Chancellor of the Exr) about the Budget. It cannot be popular. It will keep taxation about the same (with some increases and some decreases) The proposed tax on speculative gain – stock exchange or land – will in theory please those who don't indulge, but will be violently opposed by those rich men in our party who keep their standard of living by dabbling in the market, without income tax. Our plan is right – but there will be trouble. Lord Ritchie – Chairman of the Stock Exchange – has already denounced it, on the basis of rumour . . . .

25 March (Sunday)

I got to B.G. yesterday, after luncheon, in a state of great exhaustion. D and I are alone. I have something wrong with my left leg, and can scarcely walk. (I must see Richardson. It may be gout. I have given up alcohol for Lent, and this is apt to produce an attack of gout) My eyes, esp. the right eye, are weaker. (I was warned that this wd happen and sooner or later cataracts wd develop) So I felt bad. The weather is cold, but the sun warm. I sat in the summerhouse, well wrapped up, like an old invalid on the deck of a ship. All these ailments are tiresome, but they cannot surely all be due to the revival of Liberalism! . . . .

The political situation at home will certainly get worse from our p[oin]t of view in the next series of elections. It will also show in some fairly startling national Gallup polls, wh will prob. shew us at the bottom of the three. I am going myself to Stockton (my old seat) but I hear very discouraging accounts. Really the Liberal revival is not a revival of Liberalism. They have no policy and no principles. They are purely opportunist. It is an anti-party movement. 'A plague on both yr houses' is the real slogan. This is understandable, perhaps healthy. But it is not easy to deal with. If only something cd go right on the foreign front! (But when it is, it's forgotten – like Cyprus) . . . .

The more I reflect on the political situation, the more perplexed I am. We must not abandon our economic policies, which will perhaps bring their results. But we must, even if we can 'expand' again with more vigour, try to improve our 'incomes policy'. Otherwise we shall merely fall into another sterling crisis . . . . I fear the truth is that after ten years of unparalleled prosperity, the people are bored. Or perhaps the truth is that we have killed the class war and the fear of Socialism. So, by removing their fear, we have made it possible for people to gratify their exasperation at minor difficulties by voting against the Government. In a word, we have made England safe for Liberalism! . . . .

28 March

. . . . D and I had luncheon at Buckingham Palace today. The Queen gave this party (quite small) for Mrs Kennedy and her sister Princess (sic) Radziwill. Mrs K is on her way back to U.S., after a trip to India, Pakistan etc. I sat next to her. She was very agreeable, and flattering. She assured me of the President's devotion to me! Mrs Bruce (ambassador Bruce's wife – second wife) was on my other side. I found her rather intense. She understands Modern Art and has theories about the Ballet . . . .

31 March

We have had a heavy week – Cabinet; interviews; P.Q.; luncheon for Mrs Pandit (who is passing through London) Mrs P was very critical of Mrs K[ennedy] in India. She wd not 'do' hospitals, schools, and all the other chores. After the formal dinners, she and the 'Princess' wanted only to go to night-clubs. Mrs P contrasted this with the Queen's devotion to duty . . . .

Worked on speech for Stockton. I do not get any reassuring news from there. The 'Liberal' tide is still flowing, and I fear we shall be at the bottom of the poll. It is hard luck on our candidate who, without a Liberal, very nearly won the seat in 1959 . . . .

7 April

. . . . The whole of Monday was occupied by an electioneering tour – from 10.30am to 10.30pm. The speech, in the Palais de Danse, seemed well received by a large audience. The general view was that the Liberal would be second and that we shd be a bad third. However, much to my relief we were second – by a short head.[23] The news came through at midnight on Thursday and was certainly a great relief . . . .

Budget Cabinet met today. Ministers were rather taken aback by

---

23. Labour 19,694; Conservative 12,112; Liberal 11,722.

the extremely bleak proposals – some increased taxation and no reductions. As we had already discussed and agreed the so-called Capital Gains Tax (wh I prefer to call Tax on Short Term Speculative Profits) discussion was really concentrated on particular features. The Purchase Tax changes, reducing 50% to 45% and raising 5% to 10% are logical. But the increase on clothing and furniture from 5% to 10% will be very unpopular, and people will forget the many items, from motor-cars to cosmetics wh come down by 5%. There is to be a Tax on Sweets – 15%, and soft drinks, wh will bring in £40m. There is no relief except some minor adjustments in the lowest scales of unearned income, to help old people living on investment income. The Budget approved (rather grudgingly) the Cabinet discussed the economic situation and prospects. According to the Treasury, these are good. The political question is how to hold on till the light appears at the end of the tunnel. I fear that the real trouble is psychological. The younger men, in politics and industry, have not had much to contend with. They are too easily discouraged. And Selwyn, tho' an admirable minister and splendid colleague, somehow fails to 'put it across'. He has not the appearance of having 'Fire in his belly' . . . .

9 April
Budget. The usual scenes in the HofC. Members mustered 3 top-hats – 2 on our side, 1 Labour. Selwyn's speech was excellent in form and delivery – well arranged and clear . . . . The tax on sweets will be attacked hysterically, but after a week or two will be forgotten . . . .

10 April
Not too bad a Press, altho' not enthusiastic. *The Times* silly – in the governess mood which Haley has carried on from Geoffrey Dawson.[24] The *Telegraph* rather superior (which is Lady Pamela's line nowadays) The Beaverbrook Press enthusiastic! The *Financial Times* very good, and really friendly and understanding. Most of the journalists have asked for an expansionist or reflationary Budget, without realising that the best weapons for this (when required) are non-Budgetary – Bank Rate; Special Deposits; and Regulator.

After questions (of which I had about 12) I made a statement about nuclear tests. I read out the joint statement, issued by President K[ennedy] and myself. I also read out text of my own letter to Kruschev. The

---

24. Editor of *The Times* 1912–19 and 1922–41.

House was very quiet and dignified. There were a good many questions, starting with Gaitskell, who was helpful. Grimond rather silly. What will happen if Kruschev responds to my letter, I don't know! But I fear he is stubborn about 'international verification' – and that must be the key of any treaty to ban tests. But the real reason is prob[ably] that the Russians have another series ready. It suits them well enough that the Americans shd start and give them the excuse to follow . . . .

12 April
. . . . At noon, Minister of Defence and For Secy. Two new papers on Berlin, for discussion in the ambassadorial group. The first seemed to me foolish, and even dangerous. The second was more constructive. Somehow or other we must try to get a meeting with K[hrushchev] and settle Berlin . . . .

16 April (Monday)
In spite of four days more or less in bed, my throat is no better. I have spoken to Sir John Richardson, who has prescribed some more remedies. I think I must have had laryngitis all this time. I feel very weak in body, but not in brain . . . .

21 April (Easter Saturday)
I got to B.G. late on Thursday, having left Chequers on Wed. evening for London where I spent one rather full day. The HofCommons met at 11am. I answered PQs about Tests, and made it clear that short of a last minute change of heart by the Russians, this must go on. Except for the extremists below the gangway, this was accepted . . . .

After questions, I made a statement announcing Sept 10 for Commonwealth PMs meeting. This was well received. Mr G was calm; Mr Harold Wilson heavily facetious; the Conservative 'Right' had gone home for the holidays. There was more trouble about Heath's speech on the 'political' aspects of EEC. Harold Wilson, by quoting a phrase or two out of my speech last July tried to make the accusation of bad faith. But his attack recoiled on him. He is 'too clever by half'. In some ways I prefer his drunken colleague Brown, who is the 'Pistol' of the Labour front bench. His loud and alcoholic boastings are in true Shakespearian character.[25]

---

25. Brown, whose drinking was notorious, is being compared to one of Falstaff's dishonest and drunken companions in Shakespeare's *Henry IV Part 2*.

We had a bad electoral reverse in Derby [North] by-election – we were third – the Liberals being a few hundred ahead (the reverse of Stockton) Our General Election vote of 20,000 dwindled to 10,000.[26] In other words, the same emotion is all over the country . . . .

Meanwhile, in spite of the obvious unpopularity of the medicine, it is working. The pay pause, with all its unfairness, has given us a precious advantage. German and French costs are beginning to rise. Altho' exports have not risen in any spectacular way, the prospects are good and there is a steady improvement. Imports are down. The Balance of Payments results for 1961 are far better than we cd have hoped. The prospects for 1962 are very good. Bank Rate is down from 7% to 5%. I have agreed to another ½% reduction on Thursday next. There will be another 'boom' at the end of this year or the beginning of next. As long as we can prevent a ridiculous increase in wages, we should be in a good position. But will the public realise? . . . .

I feel rather overwhelmed by the responsibility on me and rather lonely. The sudden change of political fortune is at once reflected in the ordinary intercourse of life. 'It was roses, roses all the way . . . .' (I read Browning still, in the little book of selections wh we did with the Reverend Henry Bowlby in *Sunday Private* in 1906)[27] If I were not so old, I wd be very cynical. But it is the young who are cynical – or at least believe themselves to be so . . . .

25 April
. . . . Telegrams to PMs of Canada, Australia, and New Zealand, warning them that owing to the Russian refusal even to accept the principle of international verification, (quite apart from its application in practice) the Tests at Christmas Island must begin . . . .

This morning For Secy called. I asked him if there was any news. 'Yes – very bad news indeed'. 'Oh dear! What's happened?' 'There's no cover at all, owing to the late spring. The wild pheasants are nesting practically in the open, and as soon as an egg is laid it's taken by a crow or a jay'. I found this comforting . . . .

Denzil Freeth (Parl Sec for Science) has been arrested for being drunk – and I suppose disorderly – in the Strand. The Chief Whip

---

26. The Conservative vote fell by 25% and Labour easily retained the seat.
27. The quotation is the opening line of Robert Browning's 'The Patriot'.

agrees with the poor young man that he shd resign.[28] I am very much against this – assuming that this is the only charge. There are worse things can happen. There is nothing unmanly about being drunk, and very good precedents among my great predecessors. (In the street is perhaps a pity.)

After luncheon, drove to London Airport. We left at 4.30pm (our time) on a BOAC Boeing and arrived New York at 5.30pm (their time) This resulted in our not going to bed till 6am (our time) after a very pleasant dinner wh Jock Whitney gave for us. Mr Blough .... was there – a quiet, modest, and intelligent man. He seemed somewhat dazed by a row which he has had with President K[ennedy] on steel prices. The companies tried to raise prices (wh in a free society seems reasonable enough) but the President by threats and a certain amount of blackmail got a breach in the line. One of the smaller and weaker companies gave in, and was followed by Mr Blough (U.S. Steel) and the rest. The companies have a case. They say that, at present prices, they have insufficient margin for ploughing back profits. The general view is that they will obtain larger investment allowances in the Bill on this subject now before Congress. Meanwhile the NY Stock Market is having a fit of jitters . . . .

26 April

.... Called on U Thant (acting Secretary General) who was very pleasant and seemed sensible enough. He is anxious to get U.N. out of the Congo commitment if he can. But these particular Africans seem really impossible to deal with – Tshombe and Adoula are equally difficult . . . .

27 April

.... [A]rrived at MATS Terminal Washington at about 5pm, just as President Kennedy flew in from Florida, where he had been on holiday . . . .

The evening was spent in a very curious entertainment. The President and I were guests of the White House correspondents and news photographers at the Sheraton Hotel. This meant drinking with various groups before the dinner; an enormous gathering – about 1000 – for dinner. Speeches. An 'all star' entertainment (including Peter

---

28. He remained in post until October 1963 but resigned from Parliament at the next election.

Sellers and the world's best jazz players) a 'take off' of me; a 'take off' of the President; a reply by the President doing a 'take off' of himself – altogether a most uproarious and amusing evening. For some reason, I was presented with a silver cigar box. The speeches, the dinner, and the entertainment all went on in a continuous flow. It was a very American scene – with all the American humour and good-nature, and a sort of hilarious school-boy crudity which was engaging . . . .

3 May
Arrived in London at 8.30 (our time) . . . .

6 May
Spent yesterday in bed. I felt utterly exhausted. I suppose the strain of the N. American trip was greater than I thought. The pace was certainly terrific – two major speeches and almost continuous conference, with two statesmen, interlarded with the luncheons and dinners wh are so fatiguing.

I must now try to sum it up.

U.S.A.   (i)   The most striking thing seems to be a greater friendliness to U.K. than I remember before, pervading every aspect of our relations. The dinner in N. York was an example. The newspaper publishers and their staffs are pretty 'tough guys'. It is – traditionally – a very unresponsive audience. It is supposed to be very hard to get more than a perfunctory murmur of applause. Yet I got a really remarkable tribute at the end of my speech, including a 'standing ovation'. It was more like a party gathering after a successful election.

(ii)   The President went out of his way to do me honour. He met me at the airport; he put in a very impressive guard of honour; he took me to the White House in his helicopter; he came to dinner at the British Embassy on the Saturday night – all these are really a breach of protocol for anyone not a head of state . . . .

(iii)   The President likes these private and confidential talks. He seems to want advice – or at least comfort. At the same time, it's all very vague. And when we come down to brass tacks, we don't make much headway. Tariffs on glass and carpets go up 40%. American policy is <u>very</u> hostile on shipping and gets worse not better. Mr Ball (of the State Dept) is allowed to go on with his intrigues agst us in Europe and the Common Market negotiations[29] . . . .

(iv) The position of our ambassador – David [Ormsby-] Gore – is unique. He is <u>very</u> close to the President and yet gets on well with the State Dept.

(v) On future policy – Nuclear Tests, disarmament, 'détente' with Russia etc, the President is in agreement with us. But he is <u>very</u> secretive and very suspicious of leaks, in the State Dept or Pentagon, which are intended to frustrate his policy. He is all the time conscious of this, as well as of the difficulties with Congress. He looks to us for help – and this means not going too far ahead of him.

(vi) The economic situation – rather like at home – is obscure. It does <u>not</u> improve quite as fast as they wd like.

(vii) The Administration are angry with the French <u>and</u> with the Germans. This is rather dangerous for us and our European negotiations. They are angry with de Gaulle for being so rude to them (and Americans are still very touchy) as well as for being so cynical in his policy – e.g. about Berlin, where he pretends to a firmness wh he wd never display in fact. In the same way they feel that the Germans are wanting to be betrayed, so as to have both security and a grievance. All this is too subtle for the Americans and irritates them . . . .

<u>Canada</u>   (i) The Toronto speech was as successful as the New York speech. Yet it was much more 'tricky' to get it right. For the General Election has started and Prime

---

29. Ball was a great Europhile, but very concerned about the Commonwealth and EFTA dimension of the British negotiations because, as he wrote on 25 April 1962, of the need 'to resist any increase in the number of nations that have preferential access to the Common Market as against US producers' (JFKL: NSF 175). Whereas Macmillan had a broad concept of European unity, it was much more narrowly conceived in the State Department.

Minister Diefenbaker is ready to pounce on any error or slip.

(ii) The references to Britain's double duty – to the Commonwealth <u>and</u> to Europe – were well understood and well received.

(iii) Prime Minister <u>Diefenbaker</u> has a strong position, politically. He is a skilful operator – some wd say a pure demagogue. Nobody likes him, but many fear him. The result of the Election is uncertain. But if D wins again, he will be in a very strong position to make trouble in September.[30]

(iv) The Cabinet is weak. The only figure that counts at all is the P.M.

(v) It is no good trying to deal with them by courtesy or sweet reason – tho' it is right to show both. D will only yield to facts.

(vi) The extreme and demagogic Diefenbaker view about Europe is <u>not</u> repeat <u>not</u> shared by the <u>serious</u> people in Canada, from the Governor General downwards. I was particularly struck by the broad views of the bankers and business men whom I met in Toronto . . . .

14 May

. . . . Last week was quiet enough, in its opening. We knew that the local government elections wd be bad for us. They have proved disastrous. We have even lost nearly all our seats in Bromley – chiefly to Liberals.[31] The Liberal 'revival' is now beginning to 'snowball'. The *Daily Mail* is in full support . . . . The chief attack of the more serious Press (*Times, Manchester Guardian, Yorkshire Post*) is on the failure of the Government to make its 'incomes policy' effective. It accuses us all the time of temporising or retreat. Yet <u>no</u> newspaper has even published the fact of the 10% increase in wages to wh the newspapers proprietors have just agreed for journalists. They have gone further –

---

30. Diefenbaker's massive majority won in 1958 evaporated in the 18 June election, but he was able to retain power as a minority administration.

31. In the Bromley Borough Council elections the Tories lost three seats to the Liberals (and held only one by a mere 12 votes), one to Labour and one to the Ratepayers' Association.

in shame, they have jointly conspired to try to hide the truth. There is absolutely no justification today for this increase of all up to £2000 p.a. It is just the Press Lords yielding to blackmail. Yet Sir W Haley (who is the arch-humbug) writes pompous articles about the Govt's lack of courage!

All the week the trouble in the docks has been boiling up. The employers (a very weak lot) promised us that they would offer either a 3% rise or a 42 hour week. On Tuesday they offered both. So they started with too high a bid and were ignominiously pushed on further still . . . . I got to Admiralty House for luncheon on Saturday. I had invited Chancellor of Exr, Ld Chancellor, Ld Mills, Mr Hare (Labour) Mr Macleod was in Wales, for a by-election. We discussed the situation on the basis that nothing cd now avert the strike, and that the Minister of Labour shd not bring any pressure on the employers to improve their offer. On the contrary, as a member of the Govt he had already told them that they had gone too far.

However, they were already on the run and after 8 hours' strike, they capitulated at 11pm to Cousins. This is a great blow to our incomes policy, and makes it difficult to see where we go now[32] . . . . The situation in Laos has got suddenly worse. After months of arguing and no result (owing to the intransigeance of the American stooge, Phoumi, who has turned out a rebellious stooge) the Pathet Lao – the Communists – have broken the truce and made a considerable advance, at one point to the Mekong river and the Thai border. The Royalist Laotians all ran away, as fast as their legs wd carry them, and leaving their equipment (American) for the Communists to collect. The President has started to move a fleet and to land the Marines. But (so far) this is on the basis of the bilateral undertakings between U.S.A. and Thailand. But, of course, if there is not a fairly rapid negotiation, I fear SEATO will be brought in and this means the Commonwealth Brigade and more British troops . . . .

15 May
. . . . After PQs, a large deputation from the Cotton Board, demanding the exclusion of foreign textiles. (It is paradoxical to find the descendants of Bright and Cobden as extreme protectionists.[33] The wheel has

---

32. In effect a 9% increase was conceded.

33. Nineteenth-century cotton manufacturers were enthusiastic supporters of John Bright and Richard Cobden's campaign for free trade.

come full circle!)[34] I was <u>not</u> able to tell them, but we have a good hope of negotiating the continuance for another 3 or 5 years of the <u>voluntary</u> agreement wh I made in 1958–9 with Hong-Kong, India and Pakistan . . . .

16 May

<u>English</u> people (I underline English) are either great hypocrites or have a wonderful power of self-deception. All the press attack the Govt for 'giving in to the dockers'. A great row is being fomented in the rank and file. Another great Liberal triumph (this time in the Montgomery-shire parliamentary by-election)[35] At the same time, <u>everyone</u> – from the barber to the City tycoon – is <u>absolutely delighted</u> that there is to be no strike . . . .

17 May

A long Cabinet. We agreed to send a more or less token force into Thailand, shd we be asked to do so by the Thai Govt. A squadron of 'Hunters' of the RAF cd go back. They have recently been in Thailand on an exercise. But I have my doubts as to whether the Thais really want us, now that they have beguiled the Americans to send substantial ground forces in. Anyway, the Cabinet agreed and the Australian and NZ Govts have done the same . . . .

19 May

. . . . A critical position has been created in Hong-Kong area by a <u>mass</u> movement of refugees from Communist China. It is impossible to take in any more. But they press forward in thousands. We have built a fence; it is trampled down. A stronger and higher fence; it yields to human pressure. Are we to use 'gas' or bullets to keep them back? It [is] said that it will soon be a matter not of thousands, but of hundreds of thousands. I have authorised the Governor to take (as emergency measures) gas or tear shells[36] . . . .

The strange feature of the present situation is the paradox that de

---

34. A quotation from Shakespeare's *King Lear*, Act V, Scene iii, line 165.

35. The Liberals easily held the seat with a positive swing of about 10%, whilst the Tories only just retained second place over Labour.

36. About 1 million had flooded in, following the failure of Mao's 'Great Leap Forward'.

Gaulle wants the kind of Europe we wd be able readily to join, but he doesn't want us in it. (*L'Europe à l'anglaise sans les Anglais*)[37]

Sir Pierson Dixon, who has the most subtle mind in Whitehall, thinks that de Gaulle has now definitely decided to exclude us .... Others (and I am one) do not feel so sure that de G has definitely made up his mind. I think he may still be torn between emotion and reason. He <u>hates</u> England – still more America – because of the war, because of France's shame, because of Churchill and Roosevelt, because of the nuclear weapon. Yet it is a sort of 'love–hate' complex ....

23 May

.... So far, the Women Conservatives seem to have given rather a cool reception to the platform – all except Dorothy, who got a tremendous amount of applause for a little speech.

I stayed in my bedroom – reading the papers, reading [Jane Austen's] *Sense and Sensibility* and lounging – and working on various little interpolations wh might improve the speech as a performance. A sandwich; some barley-water, and a pill wh Sir J. Richardson has given me. (I took two, actually) This is <u>much</u> better for me (and my race) than alcohol, wh makes us truculent and prosy. The speech went off very well. I had (as I expected) a less enthusiastic reception when I came in than last year. The hostile Press could call it 'cool' without too much bias. At the end, I had a <u>very</u> great cheer and this continued till my departure through the Hall, which was better (as regards applause etc) than last year. It will be amusing to see what the Press will make of it. D had great applause. She has not spared herself since I became P.M. She has been <u>all over</u> the country, to simple and friendly meetings of women of all types. Now (when they come together at their conference) very many of them know her personally. Neither Mrs N. Chamberlain, nor Lady Churchill, nor Clarissa Eden, attempted anything of the kind. In her own way, Lucy Baldwin achieved the respect and affection of the women workers.[38] But in those days women played a smaller role ....

27 May (Sunday)

.... Worked all the morning on the two great issues

---

37. An English-style Europe without the English.
38. Wife of Stanley Baldwin, Leader of the Conservative Party 1923–37 and Prime Minister 1923–24, 1924–29, 1935–37.

1) <u>Britain and Europe</u>, in the light of my visit to de Gaulle next Saturday and Sunday.
2) <u>British Economy and an Incomes Policy</u>.

Both intractable, obscure, and baffling problems. On 1) there seems an increasing impression that de Gaulle does <u>not</u> repeat <u>not</u> want us in Europe (altho' it seems as if Couve de Murville accepts our adhesion as 'an historical fatality') But the General may feel unable or unwilling to oppose our application <u>openly</u> and <u>directly</u>. His instructions to the negotiations are likely to be obstruct, waste time, try to make everybody – including the British – lose heart. Alternatively, if this fails, the French will insist on terms so harsh for our farmers and for the Commonwealth that we shall be forced to withdraw. This, of course, is a dangerous game. French hegemony in Europe (or a part of Europe) may be maintained for a time. But the future will be insecure. What will Germany do after Adenauer? What will France be, <u>after</u> de Gaulle?

On 2) our Incomes Policy, the colleagues are all confused – so is the Party in the House. We must try to work out something rather more imaginative than we have done so far[39] . . . .

Motored to London. Ld Home, Ted Heath, Sir H Caccia, Sir P Dixon, Sir Frank Lee and Philip de Zulueta to supper. We had a most useful discussion on

a) General de Gaulle's present attitude towards Britain's entry into Europe
b) How best to argue with him.

Sir P Dixon (our ambassador in Paris) feels that recent events – the set-back to his European political plans; the resignation of the 5 MRP ministers after his Press Conference;[40] the failure of his specially chosen Court to condemn General Salan to death;[41] the continued disorders in Algeria – have shaken the General's position. Now we have the familiar charges of disloyalty and bribery. So we <u>may</u> be approaching the end of the regime. On the other hand, no one man and no group

---

39. Macmillan's notes for the Cabinet discussion, for instance, envisaged getting the working classes to accept incomes policy by offering schemes such as redundancy, retraining and sick pay.
40. Following de Gaulle's dismissive attack on supranationalism on 15 May. His attempts at a more intergovernmental approach through the Fouchet Plan had, however, been rebuffed.
41. Salan, the military commander in Algiers in 1958, had joined the OAS settler terrorist opposition to the abandonment of French Algeria in 1961.

of politicians wants to displace him with Algeria really unresolved. All this may make him more difficult to deal with. The General seems now to have turned definitely <u>against</u> Britain. Yet no one can be sure. The ambassador feels that *folie de grandeur* – the familiar disease of dictators – is beginning to be more marked. He simply cannot believe that any other view than his own cd be arguable, much less tenable. He pontificates more and thinks less . . . .

29 May
. . . . D and I attended service at St Paul's to celebrate the tercentenary of the 1662 Prayer Book. The Archbishop of Canterbury preached a <u>very</u> good sermon – fair, scholarly, and noble. It is a pity that his delivery is in the 'sing-song' style, so often parodied and ridiculed . . . .

30 May
. . . . 12 noon. Butler to talk about Africa. He thinks that Nyasaland must 'secede' but that it ought to and can be done 'decently'. He thinks we shd work for <u>some</u> association (but not the present Federation) between N and S Rhodesia . . . .

1 June
A quiet morning – working, writing, reading. A young man called Mr Rees-Mogg (of the *Sunday Times*) called to see me. I suppose it helps, but I am beginning to doubt it. The Press continues to sneer at me daily. The Berrys (*D.T.* and *Sunday T.*) are the most wounding (if one were capable of being wounded) The *Mirror* Group are naturally offensive. Except for the Common Market, Ld Beaverbrook remains friendly . . . .

2 June
. . . . Bob Menzies and Marshall (N.Z.) have issued a statement about the Common Market which has hit the headlines.[42] I thought Bob seemed rather ashamed today and he pretended that he had no idea it wd have such publicity. This is, of course, absurd, since Bob is an old hand. What the effect will be, it's too early to tell. Fortunately, they have concentrated on their weakest point – free entry of <u>manufactured</u> goods under the Ottawa agreement. No mention is made, in their self-righteous declaration, of how the British preferences have been

---

42. It warned of drastic consequences for their economies if there were not adequate safeguards negotiated by Britain with the EEC.

whittled away over the years, and the many discriminatory means taken – esp. by Canada – agst British trade.

D and I left London at 2pm. Philip de Z[ulueta] came with us. We were met by M de Courcel, Sir P Dixon etc and drove from the airport .... to Château des Champs. This is a very beautiful early 18th century house, wh belonged to Madame de Pompadour and was bought, restored, and presented to the state by a rich Jew. It has a wonderful garden ....

3 June (Sunday)

On reflecting on the talk, I felt reasonably satisfied. The General did not show the rather brutal attitude wh had been attributed to him, and predicted as likely. On the other hand, it is clear that he is <u>not</u> really keen on having us in Europe for two main reasons.

(1) It will <u>alter the character</u> of the Community, both in the economic and the political field. Now it is a nice little club, not too big, not too small, under French hegemony. With us, and the Norwegians, and the Danes etc it will change its character. Is this to France's advantage?

(2) He thinks that, apart from our loyalty to the Commonwealth, we shall always be too intimately tied up with the Americans. De G regards [the] American alliance as essential, but he feels that America wants to make Europe into a number of satellite states ....

After tea, we left for the airport and got to London airport about 7.45.

I find it difficult to be sure about de Gaulle's attitude. My talks with him have certainly convinced him that HMG regard it as, on the whole, a British interest that we shd enter the European Community, if reasonable terms can be made, esp. for the old Commonwealth countries. I think he is persuaded also that we put as much, perhaps even more, weight on the political as on the economic arguments. He was impressed by my review of this unhappy century, and how a close Anglo-French alliance, really effectively managed from day to day, would have avoided both wars and all that has flowed from them. Nevertheless, I am not at all sure how far de Gaulle and the French really feel it to be in France's interest to have us in. It cannot be done without much discussion and negotiation and without disturbing some of the agreements so painfully arrived at by very hard bargaining between the Six. Moreover, it means the end of the French hegemony.

6 June

. . . . A new worry is that the collapse in the N.Y. Stock Market is beginning to affect sterling. I suppose Americans are selling their British investments to pay for their losses on Wall St.

The Common Market controversy is working up. Ld Beaverbrook has now got Ld Montgomery, whose views are being disseminated in large paid advertisements in all the newspapers. The Conservative opposition (led by Sir D. Walker-Smith; Mr Turton; Ld Hinchingbrooke; etc) is getting under way. The Labour Party is uncertain – a new battle against Gaitskell, who has been deserted by Healey and (probably) Harold Wilson. Meanwhile, the political battle in the constituencies goes on without much regard to these great issues . . . .

11 June (Whit Monday)

. . . . We had rather an amusing family dinner for Ld Hinchingbrooke and Anne Cavendish (Holland-Martin) after their wedding on Thursday. It was the second day of the Common Market debate; so Hinch. cd not speak or vote against the Govt! . . . .

12 June

. . . . Sir Milton Margai came after luncheon. He is PM of Sierra Leone.[43] He wants affection, still more, he wants money. The cost of losing an Empire is frightful. Winning it was cheaper.

Sir Roy Harrod thinks the economy is on the decline and shd be expanded, but without increasing wages (wh merely increases costs) There seemed no answer as to how this was to be done, except by increasing enormously the salaries of dons and professors, whose wages do not enter into costs, since they produce nothing.

Meetings of ministers on a) India's threatened purchase of Russian MIGs – fighter aircraft b) Greater Malaysia. On a) the President of U.S. is getting very excited and we are interchanging messages. I don't really see what we can do unless we threaten to reduce our aid to India. U.S. and U.K. are providing more than either of us can afford for India's grandiose 5 years plan. Then Krishna Menon, having got millions out of us on civil account – wh will never really be repaid – turns to Moscow for military aircraft. These will really be a gift too . . . .

Australian Club Dinner, chief guest, Mr Menzies. I had to propose

---

43. It had become independent on 27 April 1961.

the toast and did so quite effectively, I think. 'Bob' was in great form
– but much more reasonable than I had expected about the 'Common
Market'. He was obviously trying hard to play the game and his talks
with all of us have helped.

13 June
Naturally, the *Express* has completely misrepresented both my speech
and Bob's. Sentences are taken out of their context and printed in
heavy type. The qualifying sentences are suppressed. Jokes are turned
into serious points and vice versa. If anyone really thought the British
Press had any decency or honour, to read today's paper wd disabuse
him. A disgraceful 'leader' in *The Times*, on the Incomes Policy. The
reports of Bob's speech and mine, equally distorted by the Papers wh
are <u>for</u> as by those wh are <u>against</u> the Common Market. Sensational
attacks on the British Army in Germany. (Nobody seems to realise
that a 'regular' army will naturally drink far more than a 'conscript'
army. But no one reads Kipling nowadays) . . . .

17 June
Back from Birch Grove to Chequers, for a talk with some of my colleagues – Ld Hailsham, Mr Macleod, Selwyn Lloyd. Also I had Michael
Fraser (of [Conservative] Research Dept) and Tim Bligh. We had 3 or
4 hours of useful talk. I have finished the draft paper for the Cabinet
on an Incomes Policy. It is very bold; but if the Cabinet accepts my
plans (based on my broad proposals to them before Whitsun) it will at
least give us back some initiative. I thought the Chancellor of the Exr
rather chilly. The others seemed strongly in favour . . . .

18 June
. . . . The Chief Whip came at 7pm and stayed to dinner. We discussed
Parliamentary tactics, on the basis of Cabinet approval to my scheme.
Perhaps a debate towards the end of the session, on a motion of
confidence, in wh the broad outline of the plan wd be unfolded. This
would be followed by a T.V. Broadcast the next night (Gaitskell wd
claim a right to reply, but I don't think that wd matter) The chief
difficulty I feel is that the Cabinet may take a cool view of my plan –
as too bold and too revolutionary. But at a time like this, we shd
follow Danton's famous words '*de l'audace*' etc'.[44] Chief Whip was

---

44. Georges Danton in the revolutionary Legislative Assembly urged in 1792 that

robust over this. Anyone who disagrees should resign. Nothing wd be better for me and the party!

19 June

At Chequers. Worked in bed till luncheon. A complicated exchange of messages between me and President Kennedy and Duncan Sandys (in Delhi) about the proposed purchase of Russian fighters (MIGs) by Nehru. This is being pressed hard by Krishna Menon, and opposed by Desai. The trouble is that we cannot afford to give the Indians £5m worth of our fighters – with more to follow. Nor can they pay, because they have no money. Apart from massive 'aid' (in the form of capital goods) we have just had to give them cash (£5m last week) for ordinary day to day purchases. The Americans wd pay (or lend) half. But even so we cannot really do it. Moreover, a gift to India of this kind will enrage the Pakistanis. The last telegram from Duncan [Sandys] gives some hope that the Indian Govt (if Nehru stands up to Menon for once) will agree to postpone the whole question for some months.[45]

McNamara's foolish speech about nuclear arms has enraged the French and put us in a difficulty, wh the Opposition here will try to exploit.[46] I shall have a chance to tell Rusk on Sunday what terrible damage the Americans are doing in every field in Europe. In NATO, all the allies are angry with the American proposal that we should buy rockets to the tune of umpteen million dollars, the warheads to be under American control. It's a racket of the American industry. So far as the Common Market is concerned, the Americans are (with the best intentions) doing our cause great harm. The more they tell the Germans, French etc that they (U.S.A.) want Britain to be in, the more they incline these countries to keep us out. Finally, at a time when the dollar is weak and may, in due course, drag down the pound and bring

---

to save France from her enemies *'il faut de l'audace, encore de l'audace, toujours de l'audace'* – we must dare, dare again and always dare.

45. The British tried to persuade the Americans to help finance an Indian purchase of British-made Lightnings instead. American concern about how Pakistan, already heavily dependent upon the US for arms, would react was just one reason why this was unsuccessful.

46. On 18 June McNamara had observed that the US now knew enough about Soviet nuclear deployments, but that the French disrupted calculations of nuclear balance, and described additional nuclear forces (including, by implication, the British) as 'dangerous, expensive, prone to obsolescence and lacking credibility as a deterrent'.

all Western Capitalism into confusion, they go round the European capitals explaining their weakness and asking for help. So gold price (and gold shares) go up. It's rather sad, because the Americans (who are naïve and inexperienced) are up against centuries of diplomatic skill and finesse . . . .

20 June

Woke early and worked on routine papers. The final draft of my Cabinet paper has gone to the printers and should be distributed today. I am seeing Butler (for luncheon) and Lord Mills at 3. I fear they will both be against me. Ld Mills will in the end support me (I think) but from friendship and loyalty not (I fear) from conviction.

A long talk with Governor of Bank (Ld Cromer) He is very intelligent. He agrees with me! But, in reality, altho' 'sound' Ld C has a nose. He is not a Baring for nothing – a long business and financial tradition. He realises that the new danger to the world is not world inflation but competitive deflation. (The impending collapse of the Canadian dollar is symptomatic. We are trying to get up an American/ British/European consortium to lend Canada $750,000) But all this makes (*pace* Ld Mills) an effective 'incomes policy' more important. At present we dare not re-inflate, because our system is open at both ends – wages, and imports. Increased wages mean (without increased productivity) more imports and less exports . . . .

21 June

Butler was helpful at luncheon yesterday. He feels that the present grave political position is due entirely to the bad handling of the economic problem (or rather its bad presentation) by the Chancellor of the Exr and the Treasury. He felt that drastic action was necessary to save the situation. This means the problem (an immense human, political problem) of replacing the Chancellor of the Exr . . . .

22 June

. . . . The Cabinet was largely taken up with the 'Incomes Policy' Paper – which I had produced with the help of Tim Bligh and some of the back-room boys. A very good but very critical discussion. We shall have to do a lot more work on it. This makes me all the more angry with the Treasury and the Chancellor for their delay and lack of initiative. A whole year gone, and then the P.M. has to do it himself, at the last minute.

SofS Scotland at 3 – for a talk. The economic situation in Scotland is rather difficult.[47] But, more serious, the Scots are losing their nerve and engaging in a spasm of self-pity . . . .

29 June

. . . . The Cabinet yesterday was chiefly concerned with the Pilkington report on Television. Happily for us, the tone and temper of the report is deplorable. Such spleen and bias are shewn in every sentence, that the recommendations (wh might be <u>very</u> troublesome) are weakened in force and persuasiveness.[48] There will be a splendid political row over this – for, unlike economics, here is something on which everyone can have an opinion – highbrow and low-brow, rich and poor . . . .

3 July

. . . . Poor John Hare has got into a mess with a speech in his constituency on Saturday, picked up by the Press. He made some justified but, at the moment, unwise criticisms of some Commonwealth countries in regard to the Common Market. All the papers took it up – Lord Beaverbrook heading the pack. Mr Gaitskell was not unhelpful in the House yesterday, where the absent Hare (who had gone to Wimbledon!)[49] was abused by Left and Right anti-Common Market-eers. He suggested a personal statement. Hare, of course, talked of resigning but I want to help him and told him so . . . .

I motored up (leaving at 1pm) for PQs, voting later. Worked on further sections of the speech and brooded about Cabinet reconstruction. I have not yet made up my mind what to do . . . .

7 July

The *Daily Express* – as part of its campaign against the Common Market – is now suggesting that there <u>will</u> be an Election about it in

---

47. The Toothill Committee, set up in November 1959 by the Scottish Council of Development and Industry, had reported in 1961 and argued that regional policy needed to shift focus from tackling unemployment to combating low productivity.
48. Presumably Macmillan objected to the imbalance in the report between praise for the BBC and criticism of ITV. The report recommended a third television channel, to be given to the BBC, and an overhaul of the ITV regulatory system.
49. For the annual Lawn Tennis Championships.

the autumn. The next stage, of course, will be to claim that there must be an Election about it.

Lunched at Lords, in a very Harrovian box – the Moncktons! Poor Eton had to follow on, and started badly. Michael Faber[50] (who virtually opened the innings) stayed in a long time and made 25. Eventually, Eton made a fine recovery and drew the match . . . .

8 July

. . . . I am sure it is necessary to make the vital change at the Treasury. Selwyn – of whom I am very fond and who has been a true and loyal friend since I became P.M. seems to me to have lost grip. He is, by nature, more of a staff officer than a commander. But lately, he seems hardly to function in some vital matters – e.g. this Incomes Policy affair. The Pay Pause started a year ago, exactly. By the end of the year, it was clear that it was to be succeeded by a more permanent policy. In spite of continual pressure from me, nothing at all was done, except long and fruitless discussions in Economic Policy Ctee and in Cabinet. There I brought [it] to a head and in despair wrote the new policy myself during the Whitsun holidays, with the help of two young men from the Cabinet Secretariat and Tim Bligh.[51] I am still doing all this, and naturally enough there are a lot of questions and details to be settled. But the Chancellor of the Exr ought to have got going at least after the turn of the year (that is after 6 months of Pay Pause – Phase One) Had we done so, the Incomes Policy plan wd be now in better shape. Again, in the vital matter of getting our gold obligations reduced (repayment to the IMF of our borrowings) nothing has been done until I sent for the Governor myself (rather improperly) and found that he agreed with my apprehensions. If Cripps (who was a rigid moralist) thought it right to deny over and over again his intention to devalue[52] (an observation solemnly repeated when the decision had actually been taken) why shd he suppose that an Irish-American President shd shrink from the same process (wh is indeed, in a sense, necessary to prevent wild speculation)? But whereas the dollar and sterling, and prob[ably] other currencies, wd move together, we have gold debts (and debts in

---

50. Macmillan's grandson.
51. This was to lead to the creation of the National Incomes Commission as a non-binding body to judge pay claims according to the 'guiding light' – that is that personal incomes should rise in line with, not in advance of, national wealth.
52. As Chancellor of the Exchequer in the run-up to the 1949 devaluation.

terms of gold) which wd become twice as onerous.[53] So we ought to pay them off in dollars as soon as we can. I have now persuaded the Treasury to concert with the Governor and prepare a plan.

The real trouble about the Chancellor's policy is that (altho' we have all tried to help) he has not been able to 'put it over'. Whether anyone can, may be doubted. But whether at Foreign Office or at Treasury, Selwyn (altho' an excellent operator in many ways) has never spoken 'as one with authority'.[54] Nevertheless, if (as I must) I decide that he must go, when and how? It will be personally terrible and I shrink from it. It will be said to be a 'panic' measure. I will be accused of gross 'disloyalty'. Yet all those I trust – Alec Home, Norman Brook, Chief Whip, agreed that it is right. I am to talk with him on Thursday, and try to give him fore-warning in a nice way, with a view to the changes (which shd be on a large scale) being announced at the end of the session (August 3rd)

10 July
I went back to Chequers last night, after a light day's work in London. The chief thing was a difficult Defence Committee meeting. But we got agreement on the number of Skybolt rockets to be ordered and the number of warheads to be manufactured in England . . . .

2.30. Queen, Queen Mother and all the Royals at Victoria Station, to greet President Tubman of Liberia. (At least this got me out of P.Q.s) . . . .

State Banquet – all the usual pomp, wh is very impressive. I was lucky, and placed between two white ladies! (Mrs Archbp of Canterbury and Duchess of Beaufort)

14 July (Saturday)
I am writing in bed at Birch Grove, feeling exhausted, almost shattered by the events of the last two days. On Thursday morning, we had a Cabinet, the chief item on the agenda being a paper of mine (the result of many recent meetings and talks) on the Incomes Policy problem. It was a most unhappy morning. Whether Selwyn had heard rumours, or whether it was an advanced form of the strange kind of apathy which has overcome him recently, I cannot tell. There was a good discussion, esp. good points were raised by Macleod, Hare, Maudling and Hail-

---

53. Because gold was priced in dollars.
54. A Biblical quotation from Matthew 7:29; Mark 1:22.

sham. Selwyn took little part. Brooke (Chief Secy) seemed embarrassed, but was – of course – useful and sensible. After P.Q.s; visit from Nigerian Minister – Mr Njoku – meeting on Greater Malaysia – the fatal hour of 6pm, fixed for my interview with Selwyn, came.

I did my best – but it was a terribly difficult and emotional scene. It lasted ¾ hour. Naturally, I tried to persuade him of the need for a radical reconstruction on political grounds; that he had filled with distinction the two highest posts – Foreign Secy and Chancellor of Exr – and that (unless he aspired to leading the party, wh he had often told me that he had not) now seemed the time for him to start that third career in business about which he had often talked to me. But it was of no avail. I'm afraid the truth is that these events are always very bad and perhaps the worst of all the duties of a P.M. Selwyn refused a peerage; said he wd stay in the House and support his financial policy (or, I suppose, criticise any deviation from it) After he had left, I got Henry Brooke (Chief Secy) to see me. Henry is a man of great probity. He told me that he had no doubt at all that Selwyn had lost grip. He even said that he (Brooke) had felt torn between conflicting loyalties. He ought to have told me his feelings. Yet how could he speak to me against his own Chief? (This assessment gave me great comfort, after the distressing interview with Selwyn) I asked Brooke to be Home Secy (in place of Butler, who is to become Secy of State for Central Africa and 'Deputy' Prime Minister) He said frankly that his ambition was to be Chancellor of Exr, but of course he wd serve loyally wherever he was needed . . . .

Chief Whip came about 11pm. Having looked carefully at today's morning Press (where there were stories ranging from <u>hints</u> of changes to headline and detailed <u>accounts</u> of what these wd be);[55] having studied today's <u>evening</u> papers (with <u>very</u> circumstantial accounts of major changes) and having seen early editions of some of <u>tomorrow</u>'s papers, I decided to get on with the reconstruction without <u>any</u> delay. Chief Whip and I worked till late into the night on various plans.

The next day (July 13th) I was rung early by Alec Home, who told me that Hare (Minister of Labour) had reported to him that Selwyn had told him that he (Hare) ought to resign in sympathy with Selwyn and his rough treatment – or, at least, should demand that the policy (Pay

---

55. Walter Terry in the *Daily Mail* scooped the story. His source was his
    proprietor, Lord Rothermere, who had gleaned the details over lunch with
    Butler on 11 July.

Pause etc) with wh Hare had been so clearly associated, shd not be abandoned. All this confirmed me in the need for speed. Could we complete a list and get it to the Queen for her signature by 6pm (for publication at 7pm)? This would stop intrigues in the House and the Party over the week-end, fostered by the speculations of the week-end press. If we could not act, the whole Government and Party might be split from top to bottom, and (in the present circumstances – bad by-elections etc) the Govt wd fall. So we set to. In the end, things worked out pretty well. David Kilmuir, Harold Watkinson, Maclay, Percy Mills, as one wd expect, did not think of themselves but only of me and the best course for the country.[56] I got an Earldom for David; a Viscountcy for Mills, and CHs for Watkinson and Maclay. I told Tim Bligh to ring up Selwyn and say that in the emotion of our talk, I had forgotten to offer him a C.H. Wd he like it? I was glad to hear that he accepted.

Poor Dr Hill was very upset – it was painful. But he is really not up to it. David Eccles, to whom I offered the B of Trade, preferred (not being Chancellor of Exr) to go altogether (with a Peerage) I was glad about this solution, which enabled me to bring in Sir E Boyle (a very clever young man) to Education. Another clever young man – Sir K. Joseph – is to go to Housing and Local Govt. Deedes (never in office) is to be Minister Without Portfolio and do 'public relations'. Maudling becomes CofExr; Reggie Manningham-Buller becomes Ld Chancellor. Thorneycroft goes to Defence, vice Watkinson. (I have not filled Aviation, wh need not now be in the Cabinet. Thorneycroft naturally sat in Cabinet as an ex-Chancellor of Exr) John Boyd-Carpenter becomes Chief Secy; Powell (Health) enters Cabinet.

It was a dreadful day (I think I saw 20 people – some twice) but we got the list to the Queen .... by 6.10pm – with all the various changes, peerages, decorations etc, and these went to the Press in time for 7pm news. Selwyn thought fit to write a letter (rather stiff) to which I replied. These also were given to the Press. No other letters – I really thought seven or eight wd be rather absurd ....

This morning's Press is varied. D. Mirror is very violent against me. Times similar, D.T. good. D. Express bad in headlines, good in leader. D. Mail silly headlines but good leader and political column.

---

56. This was wishful thinking on Macmillan's part, with Kilmuir particularly angry.

Sketch puerile and vulgar. I have not seen *Guardian*, *Y. Post*, and *Financial Times*. The dangers are

(a) A rally of extreme restrictionists to Selwyn. This has already started with a bitter letter to *Times* from Nigel Birch.

(b) Sense of 'panic' measures. It was unfortunate that [North East] Leicester by-election – where we were third, beaten by Liberal – was announced on Thursday night.[57]

(c) Accusation agst me of 'disloyalty'. I have saved my skin by throwing my colleagues to the wolves.[58] This will be pressed in spite of 6 years during wh I have been accused of just the opposite.

(d) More serious. Effect on market and sterling if the idea gets about that we are going to reverse engines and go in for a dangerously 'expansionist' policy. After discussion with Governor of Bank, I got Maudling to issue a statement last night, to reassure in particular foreigners etc. Here the continued weakness of the dollar does not hurt us, at least temporarily.

Well, it's all over. I am in bed, in mother's old bedroom, looking out into the garden and the woods. It is all very peaceful. Dorothy is here with me – otherwise we are alone. D is very robust over all this – but it's very sad. I was particularly sorry to have to ask David Kilmuir to make way. Of course, he was splendid about it. But he is one of [the] oldest, staunchest, and most loyal friends, and I shall miss him very much.

I have spoken to Norman Brook and Tim Bligh on the telephone. We shall have to have a Cabinet on Tuesday (wh had not been planned) and there is a frightening amount of work to be done. The Tunku arrives on Monday and our talks begin on Tuesday morning. Then there is the Incomes Policy, and discussions with T. Unions and Employers – and the speech. Then there is a new war starting (owing to the folly of all concerned) in the Congo. Then there are some rather alarming secret news about an impending Russian action of some kind

---

57. Labour retained the seat with 11,274 votes to the Liberals' 9,326 and the Tories' 6,578.

58. As the Liberal MP Jeremy Thorpe famously put it, 'Greater love hath no man than this, that he lay down his friends for his life', neatly reversing Christ's injunction in John 15: 13. The whole event has gone down in history as the 'Night of the Long Knives'.

in Berlin . . . . It is curious that (except the *Daily Mirror* and the gutter press) Ld Home is praised by all. Two years ago, I was thought crazy for appointing him . . . .

15 July (Sunday)
The Chief Whip and Tim Bligh (Private Secy) came in the afternoon. Maurice came to help – for he has good knowledge of the younger men. We made quite a good start in filling up vacant offices – Julian Amery to Aviation, Hugh Fraser to be SofS Air. The law officers present no difficulty. Solicitor-General [Hobson] will go up to A.G. and Rawlinson will be Solicitor . . . . I think the new team of junior ministers will make a good impression. One or two were sad to go (but it was necessary) We have altogether 10 new faces in the administration by this means . . . .

17 July
Short session of the new Cabinet 10.15–11. A curious feeling. It is very sad not to see David Kilmuir sitting opposite me, as for so long. Ld Home (For Secy) has taken his place. But there <u>was</u> a sense of freshness and interest . . . .

I entered the HofC at 3.10 for my questions. No applause from our side, jeers from Opposition.[59] During my answers, a lot of laughter and barracking from Opposition. Our side quiet, except for one or two who tried to come to my help but did (as so often) more harm than good. It was clear to me that the storm is going to be quite hard to ride. Curiously enough, those most vociferous for change seem now to be the chief critics . . . .

Dinner with Macleod and a group of his research friends – some in and some out of the House. All these, being 'progressives' were keen on the changes.

18 July
Luncheon with Independent Peers Ctee followed by speech to members. This had been arranged a long time back. Naturally, in the circumstances the room was crowded. The Press in morning was very bad. My reception in the House (which was, I think, due to the somewhat 'dazed' condition of members) was represented as so bad as to be a real challenge to my leadership. So this speech to the Lords

---

59. In contrast to the cheers which greeted Selwyn Lloyd.

(since everything gets about in Westminster) was important. Also John Morrison (Chairman of 1922 Ctee in Commons to wh this gathering of Peers corresponds) was present. I felt rather exhausted in the morning and managed to be fairly quiet. As a result, I made (without a note) what was regarded as a first-class speech – on policy, on the future of the party and so forth . . . .

19 July

. . . . After questions, I saw the 1922 Executive and explained the whole position to them as much as I could – both on economic policy and on personalities. My real trouble is that I cannot give the real reason for getting rid of Selwyn – that he had lost all grip on the situation. Nevertheless, this is gradually getting known in Westminster. It has long been known in Whitehall . . . .

. . . . There were 250 members present. I spoke quietly and simply – chiefly on the personal aspect of the changes. There was no 'panic'. A radical reconstruction was necessary and I had decided on it in principle some time ago. The problem was timing. There were arguments for now – before outcome of Brussels negotiations; before Party Conference; and before shape of departmental estimates and therefore next year's Budget was fixed. I paid tributes to Selwyn and other colleagues. One or two questions (not hostile) and I returned to Admiralty House, where we had a party for 190 constituents. I felt very satisfied. I had a good and sympathetic reception. I felt that feeling was now moving definitely towards me and my action. (If the letters wh MPs are receiving are anything like those wh we are getting at No 10, this may have affected them. Ours are 10–1 in favour)

20 July

The Press had obviously got very different accounts of the 1922 meeting from different MPs. *The Times* (who must have either a tape recorder or <u>pay</u> directly an MP to give a <u>true</u> report) gave my speech and other remarks and incidents absolutely correctly. The *Daily Express* got an account from someone hostile (either Lambton or Nabarro, I wd think) and was both incorrect and damaging. They also had a long story of the whole 'crisis' last week – not very inaccurate but very twisted. *D.T.* fair and friendly. So was *Guardian*. Indeed if anyone read more than one paper, he wd be puzzled. The meeting was a triumph and a humiliation, as recorded by reporters who were not there.

Later in the day, orders from Ld Beaverbrook must have come. The humiliation in the *Express* became <u>almost</u> a triumph in the *Evening Standard* . . . .

29 July (Sunday)

. . . . [T]he new crisis is the failure to reach any agreement at Brussels about the Commonwealth problem on temperate foodstuffs. The French were successful in forcing a rather negative attitude on the other 5. After 3 days' talk, the meeting was adjourned till next Wednesday . . . .

Heath and Bob Dixon came to Chequers at 5pm on Saturday (direct from Brussels) Alec Home stayed on from luncheon, and we had a talk about the next steps. The situation is very complicated, and I fear that all this intransigeance will harden opinion here. All the same, the Europeans point out that we are asking [for] guarantees for the Old Commonwealth countries which we have never been willing to give them ourselves! . . . .

30 July

The 'serious' Press is pretty good, and states the issues between us and the Six quite fairly. The 'popular' press is pretty hysterical. 'Mac's New Crisis'. The suggestion is that a) if we reach agreement in Brussels, Butler will lead a revolt in the Party, on the cry of 'selling out the Commonwealth'.[60] b) If we fail, the P.M.'s Common Market policy, of wh he is the chief partisan in the Govt, will be humiliated and he must resign. I think this rather crude view may, in fact, be true. But I think it is premature . . . .

. . . . I am trying to think out how to handle this 'crisis' in Europe. The weaker brethren will want us to play for a final break. That might be popular – in the short run – but it would be very wrong and (rightly) do us great damage as a Party in the long run. I wd prefer to leave that job – if it has to be done – to someone else to do.

31 July

Cabinet; P.Qs; Defence Ctee. The Defence Ctee could <u>not</u> reach

---

60. Macmillan clearly took this threat seriously, apparently telling Selwyn Lloyd two days later that 'Butler had been plotting to divide the Party on the Common Market and bring him down'. He may have suspected Butler of planting the story.

agreement on a paper by CofExr and MofDefence. The usual story – BLUE-WATER (on which £25m odd has been spent and on which another £70m–100m is due to be spent is now to be abandoned. The MofDefence agrees; the SofS War and CIGS reacted violently.[61]

2 August

Morning and afternoon were taken up with long discussions with Sir Solly Zuckerman and Ld Mountbatten and various ministers. CDS and Chief Scientific Adviser (Solly and Dickie) have really convinced us that the whole concept of a soldiers' battle (30 days or more) with conventional forces aided by so-called 'tactical nuclear weapons' is an absurdity. There are already many thousands of such weapons in NATO, amounting to many series of megatons. Once these were used, it is the equivalent of the strategic nuclear battle. But the trouble is that we have not yet convinced our NATO allies. But we believe that the President is seriously alarmed about the situation and that he has lost faith in General Norstad. (I have always liked him, but thought him stupid) . . . .

5 August (Sunday)

. . . . Ld Home came at 7pm, to talk about the proposed Nuclear Test Ban and the draft Treaty wh the Americans are to put forward at Geneva. I'm afraid they have got themselves into rather a mess. From fear of Congress, the Administration is unable to put forward a plan wh might attract the Russians.[62] So we are back with 'internationally controlled control posts' and an unstated number of 'on-site' inspections. While the Russians (as Mr K[hrushchev] indicated to me in Moscow) might accept a small number of annual inspections, they will

---

61. The Cabinet agreed to cancel Bluewater, a short-range surface-to-surface missile, on 3 August 1962. Macmillan felt its viability had been undermined by the aggressive marketing of rival American systems.

62. Macmillan wrote to Kennedy on 1 August 1962, 'As you know, my own view is that all nuclear tests should be abolished and as I explained in Bermuda last year I do not believe that we should be worse off if this were to happen. Whatever your and our scientists may say, I believe that we could really detect any significant series of Soviet tests if they tried to cheat.' As a further message from Kennedy two days later made clear, however, the Americans remained sceptical about the prospect of detecting Russian tests from home-based seismic control posts. Therefore on-site inspection remained key for them and 'We could not get five votes for any other position in the Senate' (JFKL: NSF 173).

argue that the new American proposals are not an advance but a retrogression.

Congo has quietened down a bit. The reason is that the Advisory Committee (wh U Thant and the U.N. staff have to consult) represents the nations wh have troops in the U.N. forces in Congo – Indians, Irish, Swedes, Ethiopians etc. A year ago they were all for firm action. But having got a bloody nose, they have not (happily) stomach for any more fighting. So now the Americans want 'economic sanctions' agst Tshombe – i.e. refusing to allow the export of copper. Cynics observe that (since most of the world's copper wh is not in Africa, is in American hands) the effect of such a boycott will benefit the Americans and American shareholders. (They have little or no holding in Union Minière) Our real concern is that Welensky might be driven by United Nations folly to some folly of his own. He might reach a merger or armed alliance with Tshombe. It wd be tempting. The Katanga and the N. Rhodesian copper belt really form a single system . . . .

At 8pm the heroes of Brussels (Ld P[rivy] Seal and Sir P. Dixon) arrived, with Sir Frank Lee. They told us the full story of the 4 days. Altho' it is disappointing that there was not a final picture for us to give to the Commonwealth PMs, yet there has been a great deal of progress. Indeed, it may be argued that [it] is just as well not to have everything too cut and dried on Commonwealth issues. The Africans and West Indians are really taken care of; India and Pakistan pretty good, and Ceylon too. (The nil tariff on Tea opens the whole European market for exploitation) On temperate foodstuffs, there has been a good deal of progress on principles. But the French opposition prevented a final agreement. The French attempt to get a new interpretation of the financial agreement through the whole body at 4am this morning, was resisted by Heath and also (when the swindle involved had been explained to them by their own civil servants) by the other Six [sic]. After hearing all the explanations, I felt not too depressed. It is an adjournment, not a breakdown. It upsets our time-table – but perhaps this will work out to our advantage.[63] The real danger is that

63. Joining the EEC, with its Common External Tariff, meant adjusting Britain's existing trade preferences with the Commonwealth. The tenth ministerial meeting in Brussels on the entry negotiations, however, was adjourned that morning, having failed to resolve differences on Commonwealth exports of temperate foodstuffs. Blaming the French (whose financial proposals whilst disadvantageous to the British were neither new nor as unsupported by the rest

while the <u>Anti</u> Europe movements are able to go all out agst us, we are still hampered by the need for further negotiation from launching an all out campaign in favour . . . .

10 August

. . . . 3.30 Chancellor of Exr. I liked Maudling's general approach. He agrees with me that the British economy requires some 'stimulation', but wd prefer to wait till after September. To my great pleasure (and surprise) the Treasury are now adopting my views about the need for increasing world 'liquidity'. This after 18 months – nearly 2 years – of battling with them and the former Chancellor. The Bank of England have also come round to this view. Since it is clear that the President still refuses (or is unable) to raise the price of gold,[64] the Bank have devised a scheme of their own. Of course the real problem is to get public opinion to recognise that there is nothing more 'immoral' in an international Bank creating credit – or money – out of nothing than a national bank doing so. Internationally we are still in the early 19th century . . . .

Read *The Second Empire* by Philip Guedalla.[65] Forty years ago, I thought it brilliant. Now, in spite of great learning and even depth of feeling, it is almost unreadable. The style wh fascinated us at Balliol and the Union before the First World War is intolerable now. But what a tragic story! And how brutally cynical are the Prussians! (Does anyone really deplore the partition of Germany, whether Russian, French or British – or even, perhaps, Catholic and Rhineland Germany?) . . . .

21 August

. . . . On Friday, after dinner, motored to Bolton Abbey. Shot Saturday

---

of the Six as Macmillan implies here) may have been politically useful for him. So was the breakdown, as it meant an agreement was not reached before the tricky Commonwealth summit in September.

64. Gold was fixed at $35.20 an ounce at Bretton Woods in 1944. As surplus dollars to fund US trade deficits accumulated around the world, their convertibility into gold ran down US gold reserves. An alternative means of managing this market was the London Gold Pool established in 1961–62, though this only lasted until a combination of sterling's 1967 devaluation and the Vietnam war led to its disbandment in 1968.

65. An account of France under Napoléon III until defeat by the Prussians in 1870.

and Monday – glorious weather and lots of grouse. (300 and 200 brace days)

David Gore was in the party, wh allowed a good talk on Sunday over the whole range of affairs. The President wants to <u>do</u> something big; but doesn't know how to do it. On Berlin, Tests etc – he can make little progress. On the economic front, he is equally constricted by the political situation internally and the American dread of unorthodox policies . . . .

I got to London about 2.15pm from Leeds. A lot of routine work filled the afternoon, but also a good talk with Duncan Sandys. Malaysia and Aden have succeeded (at least at this stage)[66] Malta is stuck. The <u>frightful</u> cost of independence to old colonies is staggering. Malta (with some ¼ million people) wants £25m in cash!

Dined with Butler. This was at Bucks, to wh he invited me to come as his guest. The engagement was made in July. It was clearly to be an occasion. And it was. He told me that in spite of a) the farmers b) the Commonwealth c) the probable break-up of the Conservative Party he had decided to support our joining the Common Market. It was too late to turn back now. It was too big a chance to miss, for Britain's wealth and strength. But we must face the fact that we might share the fate of Sir Robert Peel and his supporters.

22 August

Cabinet – fully attended – 10.30–1.15. All (except for a short discussion on Congo and on Berlin) was devoted to a report by Butler's Committee on Common Market, wh had been in session on Monday and Tuesday. The views of the ministers on the Ctee (including Commonwealth Sec and Min of Agriculture) were unanimous. The Cabinet accepted their decisions, after a long, clause by clause, discussion of Ld P[rivy] Seal's paper. (I was much struck by modest but impressive contributions of some of the new members – Boyle, Keith Joseph etc) . . . . Rab was firm, if rather gloomy. This gloom was shared to the full by Soames (Min. of Agriculture) who prophesies great trouble from our farmers . . . .

6pm. Ld Poole. He seemed more hopeful about Britain's economy, but very gloomy about the future of capitalist society in the Western

---

66. In Aden British pressure for merger with surrounding monarchical protectorates in a new South Arabian Federation culminated in a controversial vote in favour in the Legislative Council on 24 September.

world. This was partly the result of a visit to U.S.A., where he was overcome with dismay at the reactionary views of American businessmen. Oliver Poole feels that unless the Western world can devise better monetary and other measures to help <u>all</u> the world, the underdeveloped and neutral countries will turn more and more to Communism – not because they really like Communism, but because Capitalism will have been tried and found wanting . . . .

30 August

. . . . There was quite a turmoil about a ridiculous T.V. performance by Dr Adenauer, rather critical of me and referring to my private letters to him, the attack has recoiled on the German Chancellor and I think the air is cleared. The German officials and public are obviously incensed by his indiscretions.[67] Even the *Express* seemed to take my side . . . .

2 September

The Dock Strike is over. The Press is more friendly than usual. Dr Adenauer's foolish and undignified statements are favourably contrasted with our dignified attitude. The German Press and politicians are turning more and more against the 87 year old Chancellor. Much speculation on the result (and effect on the other 4 countries of EEC) of the Adenauer–de Gaulle meeting. Our F.O. feel it likely to be <u>less</u> dangerous than before Adenauer's 'gaffe'.

The TUC Congress is due to start – the [General] Council has been meeting last week. The Press has started an absurd rumour (begun, maliciously I think, in the *Guardian* and taken up by the others) that the Govt are going to give up NIC and any attempt at an 'Incomes Policy'. This is due to the delay in announcing the Chairman.[68] I am

---

67. Adenauer was increasingly concerned both economically (because of Commonwealth ties) and politically (because of Berlin) about the British entry negotiations and implied from Macmillan's letters that the British saw economic and political unity as different issues, prompting Labour to request publication of Macmillan's correspondence with him. Adenauer was primarily slapping down his foreign minister, Schröder, who had just told *Sonntagsblatt* that British entry would strengthen Europe both politically and economically. Realising the gaffe of quoting private correspondence, German officials tried to get the offending passages removed but the broadcaster refused.

68. The NIC was not formally inaugurated until November under Sir Geoffrey Lawrence.

urging Maudling to get on as quickly as he can, so as to scotch these stories . . . .

3 September

. . . . Duncan Sandys came for dinner and we had a good talk afterwards. The [Commonwealth] conference is going to be terrible – not only all the PMs but most of the Opposition leaders. No real discussion; mostly posturing – at least this is what I fear.

Read 3 volume *Life of Peel* by Fowler (published in 1889) Being almost entirely composed of <u>letters</u> and <u>documents</u>, it is really fascinating to read. I much prefer the sources of history to the facile comments of clever young men. From letters, memoranda, and other documents you can form your own judgment . . . .

5 September

. . . . 8.15. Mr Menzies to dinner (alone) We had a very frank talk and a very useful one. I formed the impression that he is going to try to take a constructive line – not break up the conference or appeal to the British people over our heads. I told him that I thought he had the <u>power</u> to prevent Britain joining Europe. But I thought it a terrible responsibility before history . . . .

8 September

. . . . Went to bed at 6 and worked and read. Having read Peel and the destruction of the Tory Party in 1846 (wh I may be about to repeat) I re-read volume 2 of Disraeli's *Life*,[69] covering these exciting years.

I have received a letter from John Morrison (Chairman of 1922 Ctee) demanding a change in the Chairmanship of the Party.[70] I will merely acknowledge it, I think for the present . . . .

9 September

Gaitskell, with the support of or after conferences with Commonwealth Labour leaders has issued a statement <u>against</u> entering Common Market on present terms and demanding a second conference. The effect of this cannot yet be assessed. He also demands a General Election on the issue if the parties are not agreed.

Heath made some progress yesterday with Australians and New

---

69. By W. F. Monypenny and G. E. Buckle, published in six volumes, 1910–20.

70. Morrison had been complaining about Macleod's arrogance back in February.

Zealanders, but not in any detail. I stayed in bed in the morning. Finished Disraeli vol 2 – painfully relevant! . . . .

Mr Diefenbaker came to luncheon – alone. He kept his cards very close to his chest and gave me no indication of what he proposed to say in the great debate. He was <u>very</u> pleasant; talked chiefly of internal politics, from the Taper and Tadpole point of view from which he seldom if ever escapes.[71] He is incapable of large ideas. On the other hand, I thought him somewhat subdued by his electoral reverses and financial crisis.[72] But this may easily result in his trying to recover ground by a great Commonwealth demonstration at the Conference, on Beaverbrook lines.

Later in the afternoon came Bustamante (PM of Jamaica) and Dr Williams (PM of Trinidad) The first is a genial rascal, of Tammany Hall type.[73] The second is a clever man, with culture, education and ideas – but also, in his own way, a rather sinister politician . . . .

10 September

The first day of the great [Commonwealth] Conference is over. The morning was occupied by procedural and other matters. Nehru and Ld Home to luncheon. N. looked old and tired – with little to say. In the afternoon, we had an hour and ten minutes from me, followed by an hour and a half from Heath. This left them exhausted – and I hope impressed. We had taken a lot of trouble with my speech and I think it made a good effect. The debate begins tomorrow and we shall see what will be the general tone . . . .

The Press today is <u>very</u> critical of Gaitskell. *The Times*, the *Guardian*, the *Daily Mail* are all very scornful of his 'political' manoeuvre. The *Daily Mirror* wh is <u>pro</u> Common Market but violently <u>anti</u> Government, tries to explain it away. The *Daily Telegraph* is good. The *D. Herald* (wh being under *D. Mirror* control is <u>pro</u> Common Market) is hard put to it and confused. Of course, he may have struck a timely and fatal blow. Only time will show. I'm afraid

---

71. Taper and Tadpole were Tory political fixers in Disraeli's novels of the 1840s.
72. Unusually, whereas most exchange rates were fixed at this time, Canada had floated its dollar since 1950. Various factors combined in speculative pressure on the currency from the late 1950s.
73. The political machine which controlled New York city politics from the 1790s to the 1930s.

he is a poor creature, without any real breadth of view or sense of values. Or perhaps he has them and is consciously false to them . . . .

12 September
We have now had <u>two</u> days of Commonwealth speeches. It has been a broadside attack upon us, led by Diefenbaker on the first day, in a false and vicious speech. Menzies wound up the first day with a very able and <u>very</u> damaging speech. Holyoake said N. Zealand wd be ruined. Nehru (who seemed painfully weak physically) was peevish. Ayub Khan was forceful but ill-informed. The Africans, who got everything they cd want by 'association' are too proud and too anti-white man to ask for it.

Actually, the second day was better – Trinidad (with Dr Eric Williams) talked good sense – at great length and Malaya was friendly . . . .

. . . . It is ironical to hear countries wh have abused us for years now beseeching us not to abandon them. The thought that U.K. might declare herself independent seems so novel as to be quite alarming.

Mrs Diefenbaker is said to have 'gone religious'. But she is a nice woman – without humour but I think honourable. Mr D is a very crooked man. He is so self-centred as to be a sort of caricature of Mr Gladstone.[74] He can persuade himself that the only test of any question is the political advantage of himself and his party. But he has had a shaking in Canada.

Bob Menzies made a deplorable speech, of wh he is clearly now ashamed. Butler (who has been sitting by me all through) was disgusted. Poor Ted Heath – who is only accustomed to Europeans, who are courteous and well-informed even if hard bargainers, was astounded at the ignorance, ill-manners, and conceit of the Commonwealth. Also – the mixture of great and important nations and small islands makes it all rather unusual.

Holyoake was, by contrast, courteous but unconstructive. Moreover he (like the others) seemed to think that we were deciding whether or not the E.E.C. shd be formed, not accepting its existence. It does exist and the only question is 'What are we going to do about it'. I confess to being a bit shaken – but we must try not to 'flap' . . . .

---

74. The great nineteenth-century Liberal leader was famously racked by his conscience.

17 September

Conference at 10.30 . . . . The situation is fluid, but I get the impression that in the case of India and Pakistan, they know they are doing pretty well. Indians always bargain up to the last rupee. Pakistan, well led by President Ayub, cannot appear to ask for less than India. But Ayub has behaved very well. He went to Paris on Saturday morning, to lunch with de Gaulle. The French found him impressive.

. . . . Australia is anxious, but Bob [Menzies] (hard pressed by McEwen) is playing politics. All the same, they have some ground for anxiety.[75] New Zealand merely say that they trust us to get them something special . . . . 5 or 6 others spoke – but I was able to begin my final speech at about 12 noon and finish before 1. I think it was pretty good. They seemed really impressed by the figure I gave about our acceptance of Commonwealth Cotton imports. 40% of our home consumption is imported from Commonwealth countries. Nearly ½ million operatives have left the textile industry. How can our market (alone in the world) remain a free market for Commonwealth goods.

The afternoon meeting was devoted to a debate on the world situation, opened by Ld Home, as UK Foreign Secretary. There was a wrangle between Ghana and Sierra Leone, wh was quite significant. The latter accused the former of sending semi-communist agents to subvert his people . . . .

18 September

. . . . Sir R Welensky and Mr Butler to luncheon. The outlook for the Rhodesias is bad. One of the African PMs in this morning's discussion declared ominously that they wd prove Britain's Algeria.[76]

After luncheon, the first session on the draft communiqué. This lasted from 3.30–5pm. By then, it was clear that the communiqué (altho' broadly agreed by officials last night) was going to prove a real difficulty . . . . The text wh was put forward was based on that which I prepared myself a week or more ago. It set out the 4 general principles which had been the main theme of my winding-up speech and which had been well taken up by the Press. But each P.M. wanted to add his particular illustration to the general principle – so that the communiqué wd be a sort of 'shopping list' . . . . I felt it useless to go on, but proposed

---

75. In 1960–61 Australia had total exports valued at £A929m, of which £A232m went to Britain.

76. Algeria had finally achieved independence from France on 5 July 1962.

that the officials might meet in the evening and prepare two drafts – one the original draft with some of the major amendments of principle wh had been mentioned in the discussion; the other, a draft with all the particular reservations etc affecting their own countries wh delegations sent in. So we adjourned. I was very depressed and so was poor Ted Heath. However, my scheme (really suggested to me by the incomparable Norman Brook) may work out. When they see the <u>long</u> draft, with a reference to every country's demands, they may realise its absurdity . . . .

19 September
The Press very gloomy. Mac's failure. Mac's collapse. Mac's Test. The Conference in ruin. The best was the *D.T.* and *Times* who said that there was still hope of an agreement.

This was, in fact, reached in 1½ hours and the Brook–Macmillan tactics succeeded. The 'long' draft was rejected at once; we worked methodically and amicably thro' the 'short' draft. There were one or two difficulties, but a wholly different atmosphere to yesterday . . . .

The communiqué was issued at 2.15. I was so exhausted that I went to bed at 5pm and slept for 2 hours! . . . .

20 September
Cabinet at 10am. The chief discussion was naturally on the Conference and the next steps. The colleagues seemed very steady. All the afternoon and evening were taken up with preparing a broadcast, wh I recorded at Admiralty House. I think it was quite good. Dorothy, Carol, and I watched it at 9.30. Gaitskell immediately demanded the right to reply, which he is to do tomorrow. I think BBC were rather feeble in granting this so quickly. He will no doubt make an effective reply (for he is a very good arguer and has a very agile brain) But it may accentuate the divisions in his party. He has the same problems in this respect as I have.

21 September
D. Express is violent to a degree hardly believable – quite like the press of the early 19th century. The Liberals (who seemed to be hedging) have come down in their conference quite firmly <u>for</u> the Common Market. Poor Roy Harrod and Juliet Rhys-Williams (dear, trusted, loyal friends) who used to be strong 'Europeans' have now changed round, and become <u>violent</u> opponents. This saddened me, for I am devoted to them both.

The *Manchester Guardian* still hedges – it represents the kind of attitude wh Ld John Russell[77] spent his life in promoting – always willing to wound and afraid to strike – and always essentially priggish and slightly dishonest. The *D. Mail* is good. *The Times* and *D.T.* remain firm. *Yorkshire Post* good. *D. Mirror* attacks me personally but supports my policy. *D. Herald* (supporting Gaitskell but owned by *D. Mirror*) is in trouble. On the whole, last night's broadcast has been well received. Macleod and Central Office are enthusiastic . . . . The controversy is now beginning to crack the old Party alignments. Where it will end, no one can tell. Of course, it all really depends on the final terms wh we can get at Brussels. The Tory Party will be under a double attack – on the Commonwealth issue – sentiment; on the agricultural issue – money, i.e. profits for farmers and rents for landlords. Rab remains firm and confident . . . .

22 September

(Birch Grove) Severe crisis – political, or personal, makes [Sir Walter] Scott a necessity. I have read *Woodstock*, *Kenilworth*, *The Abbot*, and am now started on *Waverley*.

Gaitskell's reply was very clever.[78] (I did not see it, but read it this morning) Whether he was right to move so definitely anti Common Market, time will prove. He went much further than before. He criticised the terms, but he also seemed now to [be] agst going in on any terms. England he declared, wd be like Texas. (Yet he wishes us to abandon the nuclear deterrent and throw ourselves altogether into American arms!) . . . .

23 September

. . . . Motored to London, for talk with Oliver Poole and Ted Heath. Oliver is ready to help in every way and has ideas for organising the pro Common Market forces. He does not feel that it is necessary to form a new institution but rather to use what we have got. He is to talk over plans with Deedes and Macleod and (in the first instance) Beddington-Behrens, whose European Ctee is already doing good work . . . .

---

77. The principal author of the 1832 Reform Act and Whig Prime Minister 1846–52 and 1865–66.
78. To Macmillan's broadcast.

25 September
10.30–1 and 2–3.30 with Mr Streatfield. Altho' I do not now own an
acre of ground in Sussex (or elsewhere) or a share in the Birch Grove
Estates Co, and am not a director of the Co (as Daniel and Maurice
are) I take a great interest in being shown from time to time by the
excellent agent (Streatfield) the progress that is being made – in farm
building, farm improvements, and forestry. It was a most glorious day
– sun all day – and quite hot . . . .

27 September
. . . . 11. Colonial Secy (Sandys) Sir N Brook and others. The problem
– British Guiana. This colony is now 'ripe for independence'. But
this means 'ripe for Communism'. Jagan is half-Communist; his wife
is [a] full-blooded and dangerous Communist. He is now 'Premier' –
under a British Governor. If 'independence' comes he will be a second
Castro. This naturally concerns us and fills the Americans with intense
alarm (They are ready to attack us as Colonialists when it suits
them. They are the first to squeal when 'decolonialisation' takes place
uncomfortably near to them.) However, we have some ideas as to
how this situation might possibly be retrieved. B.G. is half India[n];
half negro. Jagan only commands the Indians; the negroes oppose
him[79] . . . .

6pm. Marples, Hare, Brooke (Home Sec) about the 1 day Railway
Strike, called for next Wednesday, to protest against the reduction of
the railway workshops. It seems that all this blew up while Greene (the
moderate leader of NUR) was away and he has lost control. Woodcock
(T.U.C.) is behaving in a foolish and excited manner. The unions have
a right to be consulted as to terms of retirement and redundancy and
the Transport Commission a duty to work closely with the unions on
these matters. But the unions are trying to oppose the whole policy –
in other words, continue to build wagons which are not wanted and
steam locomotives which are not required. (Ry workshops cannot
build electric or diesel engines) This is fantastic and everyone knows it.
The Ry Clerks and ASLEF (footplate men) are not striking. But that
won't help us much.

---

79. This tactic succeeded when the People's National Congress of Forbes Burnham
    narrowly won the 1964 elections and took what is now Guyana to
    independence two years later.

28 September

10.15. Thorneycroft (Defence) and Carrington (First Lord) – also Norman Brook. There has been another 'espionage' case – and a very bad one in the Admiralty. An executive officer, homosexual, entrapped by the Russian embassy spies and giving away material (of varying value) for 5 or 6 years. He was only caught by the help of a Russian 'defector'.[80] There will be another big row, worked up by the Press, over this . . . .

30 September (Sunday)

. . . . Mr Gaitskell produced last night (with the help of the Labour Executive) yet another (but I suppose more authoritative) statement on Europe and the Common Market. It goes back on 'Kansas' and '1000 years of history' which were the features of Mr G's broadcast – that is, against Europe in principle. Now the line is that there's a lot to be said both ways; that 'on the whole' Europe is a good idea for us if we get much better terms than seems likely[81] . . . .

2 October

Mr Marples seems to have made a 'dramatic' effort on the television, in a debate with Mr Greene (Gen Sec NUR) to call off the 1 day strike. But I don't think he will succeed, and he may make himself look rather silly . . . .

3 October

The 'one day' Ry strike is on. It will, of course, because of the complicated character of railway operations, have effects over 2 or 3 days more. The newspapers (happily) are half the usual size. The *D. Mirror* is angry with the TUnion and especially attacks the Labour Party Conference (wh is being almost put into the shade by all these events) Marples (who acted, I suppose, on the spur of the moment) is much criticised by the *D. Mail* and the *D. Express*. Both these papers urge his resignation or dismissal. He did not inform me of his proposal,

---

80. After he defected to the US in 1961 Soviet agent Anatoliy Golitsyn denounced John Vassall, who had been entrapped by the KGB when naval attaché at the Moscow embassy in the mid-1950s.

81. Gaitskell, however, told the American journalist Robert Estabrook two days later that the entry terms were very bad and that his opposition to the Six had been apparent since his 1957 Godkin lectures at Harvard.

but I feel sure he did not mean to make it when he went in to the studio. Anyway, I must support him . . . .

Telephoning and minuting from 9am to noon – when I got up. Chief Whip is, as usual, calm. M of Labour is a bit upset, but as long as Marples will now shut up (wh I have told him) this particular episode will die out, leaving us winners on points . . . .

Ld Home to supper, to report on New York and Washington. Altho' there is a certain lull, we are in a great tangle in every part of the world. The Russians are clearly using <u>Cuba</u> as a counter-irritant to <u>Berlin</u>. The President is angry with us for not being willing to join in a boycott or blockade. He is either unwilling or unable to understand that we cannot give orders to British shipping, esp. ships on charter, to avoid going to Cuba without legislation. (In war, of course, it's different. But we are <u>not</u> at war with Cuba) Nor does he realise the violence of the feeling of British shipowners against American government and their discrimination, subsidies and other methods of injuring British shipping.

Things in Congo are no better, and here again the Americans are angry with us for not being willing to join in boycotting Congolese copper. (We cannot help remarking that the Americans own most of the rest of world copper supplies and the market is dull) Finally, we have now found out that they have lied to us over the Israeli missiles and are still lying to us.[82] This makes them sore. The President has found (like other bright young men) that it's easier to criticise than to act. The economy has not expanded; he has yielded to Dillon and the orthodox bankers, who have therefore not been very helpful to Maudling's excellent plans – altogether we are in rather a bad period with U.S. This is sad and may do us both harm. Fortunately, <u>personal</u> relations with President and Secretary Rusk are good. David Gore is absolutely invaluable.

4 October

. . . . Philip Swinton to luncheon – alone. We discussed Gaitskell's Brighton speech and its political implications. It is generally taken as having thrown over the agreement reached on the previous Sunday and therefore definitely <u>against</u> the Common Market <u>in principle</u>. (Of

---

82. Contrary to Anglo-American agreements, in August 1962 the US had offered to let Israel purchase Hawk missiles, a decision which clearly still rankled with Macmillan months later.

course, there are plenty of saving clauses, but this is the broad effect) Since it happens that the right (Sam Watson – Miners Union – Bill Carron – Engineers – and all the MP 'moderates') are pro Common Market and the Left (including the Shinwells, Mikados, Dribergs and Cousins – Transport workers) are violently anti, the result is that Mr G[aitskell] has now thrown himself into the arms of the men he has been fighting for three years, and has abandoned the friends on whose loyalty he has depended.[83] There is said to be much anger about this.

Oliver Chandos and Alan Lennox-Boyd came at 3.15. Oliver is pro Common Market; of Alan, I am not so sure. But both came to warn me of the trouble which the 'sovereignty' argument was going to cause in the Party. It is being put about that I am determined to abandon the Queen and promote a federal Europe at the expense of the national identity. This is absurd – but may be dangerous and I am glad to be warned.

6.30–1.30. Macleod; Chief Whip; Rab Butler; Ted Heath. A long discussion, including supper, about political situation and the possible courses open to us. We discussed the possibility of an immediate election. But Mr G[aitskell] has not really gone far enough to justify such a course. If he had declared his determination to repudiate, after a General Election wh Labour might win, any Treaty made in this Parliament, then I think the only reply possible (if the negotiation is to continue) wd have been to seek a definite mandate to go forward. But in all the circumstances, we must – I feel – go forward . . . .

5 October

. . . . All the afternoon and evening on the situation in the Yemen, wh is developing very badly for us.[84] If the new revolutionary Govt is established, the pressure on the Aden Protectorate and then on the Aden Colony and Base will be very dangerous . . . .

8 October

. . . . Much telephoning – chiefly about the Yemen situation. We are hoping to get into better relations with the Saudi Govt,[85] wh is much

---

83. As Gaitskell's wife Dora noted, 'all the wrong people are cheering'.

84. The (anti-British) monarchy had been overthrown in a coup backed by Nasser on 26 September, with immediate consequences for radical nationalist opinion in the neighbouring British-controlled Aden Protectorate.

85. Diplomatic relations were restored on 17 January 1963.

alarmed. Owing to the defection of some of their airplanes to Cairo, their whole air force is grounded (they are also short of spares) . . . . The rebel Govt clearly holds the towns. The tribes are beginning to move in the north, and perh. in the west.

Read Asquith's *Biography* (volume 2) and also the volume of Lloyd George's *War Memoirs* about the end of the Coalition. Also the passages in Owen's *Life of L. George* about this episode. I have lost Ld Beaverbrook's History.[86] I must get these volumes again to read. This whole affair is still subject to much dispute – as, I suppose, will be the story of my recent Govt changes. But, in my experience at any rate, there is nothing like the number of people involved or the atmosphere of intrigue. This is partly due to the practice of Cabinet minutes and agenda; partly to the end of country-house week-ends (where these plots were mostly hatched) . . . .

9 October

. . . . [A] long talk with Butler about Central Africa. He has certainly succeeded in giving us a quiet 6 months. But with the Nyasaland conference in November, and the Northern Rhodesia elections, things will begin to move towards a new crisis. Rab is wise and wily – both useful qualities in this tangled problem. He is to speak on Thursday at the Conservative Conference. The opponents of the Common Market have put forward a very ingenious amendment, equally hard to oppose or accept (as the words stand) But I hope our speakers will be able to get the Conference to the simple concept of 'For' or 'Against' the general idea of Europe . . . .

10 October

. . . . I worked a great part of the day on the speech for Saturday. The trouble is that I have to prepare it without knowing the outcome of the debate tomorrow (Thursday) on the Common Market. I spoke on the telephone to Ted Heath in the afternoon. He is a little anxious about the amendment, which will confuse the audience. But he says that the general spirit seems favourable. It is odd that the only person

---

86. Presumably a reference to Beaverbrook's somewhat tendentious account of Lloyd George's wartime coalition and his own part in its history, entitled *Men and Power 1917–1918* (London: Hutchinson, 1956). Macmillan appears unaware that it was this government (1916–22) which introduced Cabinet minutes and agenda.

not able to take part in this critical discussion (which, if it went wrong, wd be fatal to the Government of wh I am the head) is myself! . . . .

Anthony Eden (Ld Avon) came to luncheon. We were alone. He was pleasant and relaxed. He is doubtful but (I think) resigned about Europe. He felt N. Zealand must be safeguarded, and to some extent Australia. Canada is little affected, he thinks. For the rest, he is not much concerned. But he cannot really accept the new world and the new balance of power in the world. His mind goes back to his days (as For Secretary, before and during the war) when Britain's position was quite different in a different world . . . .

The Governor of the Bank called. He is <u>not</u> very hopeful of increased <u>private</u> investment until the Common Market issue is settled. This means (and he accepts it) that we can only re-stimulate the economy by public investment. But, of course, the haunting fear of another 'balance of payments' crisis remains. I do not see how we can handle this effectively so long as sterling remains (with inadequate reserves) a reserve currency for the world[87] . . . .

11 October

Went for final sitting to James Gunn.[88] He is finishing the Balliol portrait. There is now one at the Carlton Club; one at Eton; and one is for Balliol. The last is, I think, the best.

The news reached me at lunchtime that the Conservative Conference had rejected the Turton/Walker-Smith amendment on the Common Market by an overwhelming majority – only 50 or so out of 400 voting for it. Butler and Heath seem to have made excellent speeches . . . .

15 October

. . . . Everyone seems very pleased with the Tory Conference and with

---

87. Balance of payments crises had recently occurred in 1957 and 1961. The Sterling Area created in the 1930s linked the currencies of a considerable number of mainly Commonwealth countries to sterling. As the terms of world trade moved away from primary products in the 1950s, the tendency of these countries to incur dollar deficits, hitting the sterling balances, increased. Sterling's reserve function was effectively ended with the 1967 devaluation.

88. Society portrait painter Sir James Gunn began work on the Carlton Club portrait in June 1960. It was unveiled in February 1961, and he began on the other two in May 1962.

my speech. We now have to face a long and difficult resumed negotiation in Brussels. Mr Gaitskell seems now to have 'sold out' to Lord
Beaverbrook and [to be] going more and more against 'European
entanglements'. But some of his party are obviously distressed . . . .

16 October
<u>Edinburgh</u>. I came up last night by train. The King of Norway arrived
at Princes St Station at noon. He had come to Leith by yacht. The
ceremony was very fine, with the advantage of more colour than we
get in a state visit to London (due to kilts, plaids etc) and the wonderful
'drop-scene' of Edinburgh Castle, instead of the sordid yellow-brick
depository wh is the background at Victoria Station. Fortunately, it
was a lovely day – with bright sun . . . .
    I spent the afternoon
1) at the new Forth Bridge. It is making good progress and they
   hope to finish at the end of next year.
2) BMC [truck] Factory at Bathgate. This is an entirely new
   effort and (together with Rootes' factory)[89] will open a new
   chapter in Scottish industrial life. I was much impressed by the
   management. The shop-stewards were friendly – or, at least,
   courteous . . . . it

18 October
. . . . There are some very interesting reports of the Cabinet Committees on 'Population' and what another 6m people will mean in form
of houses, schools etc. Also on 'Location of Industry'.[90] Ministers are
divided as to what we ought to do or not do. I am getting Cary
(Cabinet Office) and Bligh (P.S.) to luncheon today for a talk on all
these questions.
    Meanwhile, more trouble in the motor-car industry – at Fords and

89. Rootes developed a new car-manufacturing plant at Linwood in the late 1950s,
    encouraged by the new steel plant approved by the government. It was never a
    success. Rootes was taken over by Chrysler in 1967 and Linwood closed in
    1981.
90. These were the two Cabinet memoranda on regional policy produced two days
    earlier by Henry Brooke's Cabinet Committee on Population and Employment,
    established earlier in the year in response to the 1961 Toothill Report on the
    Scottish economy and the subsequent official committee under Sir Thomas
    Padmore.

(very unusual) at Vauxhalls. The Communists are pretty active in these great factories. But the real difficulty is the irresponsible attitude of the shop stewards and the increasing powerlessness of the unions.

19 October
We had a good day yesterday. After a quiet morning, Bligh (my P.S.) and Cary (Cabinet Office) came to luncheon. We worked till 6.30 – on what I am now going to call 'The Modernisation of Britain' question, in all its aspects.[91] I hope to be able to get out some kind of a plan of action within a few days, for a preliminary discussion with one or two colleagues.

Chancellor of Exr (Maudling) to dinner. We had quite a useful talk, on same lines. The immediate problem is how to boost up our own economy. Like the Governor, the Chancellor seems against lowering the Bank Rate – at any rate for the present. But he will concentrate on trying to reduce the long term rate of interest. This is made possible by the rise in gilts. (Unfortunately, I feel that the rise in gilts is only the reflection of the recession) But even here, we must try to bring more pressure on Building Societies to lower their rates. Another measure (wh I think shd have a quick effect) to which I agreed, was an immediate cut (to be announced when Parlt returns) of Purchase Tax on Motor Cars from 45% to 33⅓%. It will 'cost' the Revenue £30m. But I believe it will have a good effect all round . . . .

We have also discussed methods of
a) <u>funding</u> part of the sterling balances
b) paying higher Bank Rate for external money than for internal.
If we cd do one or both of these, we cd 'reflate' much more safely . . . .

No more news of the Yemen. But I am not very hopeful. Our 'covert' plans have worked well, in their limited field. But the 'rebel

---

91. Four days later in this internal paper Macmillan wrote, 'The challenge of Europe is exciting, but negotiations are going to take longer than people think, and there will be a let down'. Instead there was a need to 'direct development, to plan growth, to use the instruments of the Government to influence and determine private decisions . . . . [the] Forces at work now [are] too complicated, risks of set back too great to leave to market forces and laisser-faire' (TNA: CAB 129/111, C(62) 201).

Govt' is strongly and overtly supported by U.A.R. and the internal position in Saudi Arabia seems confused and weak[92] . . . .

20 October

. . . . I talked with Ld P[rivy] Seal (Heath) He is harassed, but not depressed. He had 5 hours with Couve de Murville 'going over the ground', but not really getting to any firm positions. But Heath feels that France cannot now <u>openly</u> oppose our entry or be seen to be asking quite impossible terms . . . .

21 October (Sunday)

Slept rather badly again – wh is unusual for me . . . .

About 10pm I got a message from President Kennedy, giving a short account of the serious situation wh. was developing between US and USSR, over Cuba . . . .

22 October

The first day of the World Crisis! Ambassador Bruce called at noon. He brought a long letter from President Kennedy, as well as a great dossier to prove that (contrary to <u>specific</u> assurances given by the Russian Govt and by Gromyko in particular) there had now been secretly deployed in Cuba a formidable armoury of MRBMs and IRBMs (short and moderate range missiles) which were a pistol pointed at America (and Canada and S.America) and wh. cd not be tolerated . . . .

Ambassador Bruce, in his detached and quiet manner, did not attempt to conceal the excited, almost chaotic, atmosphere in Washington. The photographs revealing the full extent of the offensive missile deployment in Cuba had only become available about Oct 17. The President had hurriedly cancelled his [midterm] election tour, and returned to Washington on Sat 20th. All the decisions had been taken on Sat and Sunday. He felt sure that the decisions were not yet final – hence the delay in getting me copy of speech. The ambassador thought that the President's proposed action (wh. seemed to be to impose a 'quarantine' or blockade on all ships, Russian or neutral, carrying arms to Cuba, and to threaten a more complete blockade if necessary) wd not satisfy the 'war' party in U.S., and yet wd have

---

92. Britain and the Saudis were covertly supporting the royalists in Yemen via the South Arabian state of Bayhan.

great dangers of precipitating a clash. We speculated a little about the likely response by Mr Kruschev. Wd it be words or deeds? In the Caribbean or in Europe?

After a hurried luncheon with Alec Home, I had a talk with the Governor of Aden, (Home and Sandys present) about the Yemen situation. It seemed generally agreed that (altho' Hassan, *père et fils*)[93] and Badr might be able to raise enough of the tribes to incommode the new revolutionary Govt, it was unlikely that they wd be able to overthrow it. The Governor recognised this as a sound assessment and agreed that it followed that early recognition was inevitable. But he pleaded for a little more time, in order a) to give Hassan and co a last chance to see what they cd do b) to make it apparent to the rulers of the Protectorate that the Royalists had really had a chance and good support from us c) to get our friends to realise that recognition was unavoidable and gave us at least a chance of getting on some working basis with the new republican Govt. About a week seemed the time to be allowed.

. . . . In spite of all the promises, no copy of the President's speech. This finally arrived about 5pm. Alec Home came over and together we worked out a reply to the President. I think it was a pretty good document. While we said that we wd support him in his determination to prevent the Russians 'get away' with this new act of aggression, we must put forward some points for thought. (In my first draft, I had thought of advising him to seize Cuba and have done with it. But I felt this would be wrong a) because it wd be dangerous in writing – on the record b) because such a risk wd be justifiable, if effective. Since President had evidently determined on his line, it seemed a risk that shd not be taken. All the same, the Suez analogy is on my mind.) If K[ennedy] 'misses the bus' – he may never get rid of Cuban rockets except by trading them for Turkish, Italian or other bases. Thus Kruschev will have won his point. He may even be able to force the frightened Americans to trade Berlin for Cuba. The blockade is to be of 'arms'. That will prevent more rockets reaching Cuba. But only an intensifed and complete blockade can bring down Castro's Govt. But this will be long (at least 3 months) and will (since it is patently

---

93. Father and son. Badr succeeded his father Ahmad (reigned 1948–62) as ruler of the Imamate of Yemen on 19 September, but was initially believed killed in the coup on 26 September. Unlike Ahmad or Badr, Ahmad's brother Hassan and his son Muhammad had not dallied with the Russians or Egyptians.

'illegal') cause a great deal of trouble with neutral and even with friendly countries. I sent for Chancellor of Exr and put him in the picture. His advice was sensible. He wd see Governor of Bank. There wd be heavy buying of gold and a general fall of all stocks and shares – but no panic.

Talked with President on the telephone at 7.30pm (Washington time) 11.30pm (GMT) He seemed rather excited, but very clear. He had just finished his broadcast. He was grateful for my messages and for David Gore's help. He cd not tell what Kruschev wd do. He was rather vague about the blockade (it is clear that all kinds of plan have been all day under discussion.) He is building up his forces for a *coup de main*[94] to seize Cuba, shd that become necessary.

I gave a large dinner for General Norstad, which lasted from 8–11 . . . . Washington, in rather a panicky way, have been urging a NATO 'alert', with all that this implies (in our case, Royal Proclamation and call-up of Reservists) I told him that we wd not repeat not agree at this stage. N. agreed with this, and said he thought NATO powers wd take the same view. I said that 'mobilisation' had sometimes caused war. Here it was absurd, since the additional forces made available by 'Alert' had no military significance.

I took Gaitskell (who was at the dinner) to Cabinet room and showed him all the documents, and the President's speech. He did not take a very robust attitude. He thought his party 'would not like it'. I doubt if they would like any decision – firm decision – on any subject. Late to bed.

23 October

Cabinet 10.30–1. I explained the whole Cuba situation, and read out aloud (but did not circulate) the vital documents . . . . Ministers seemed rather shaken, but satisfied.

Hailsham, Keith Joseph, Carrington, Michael Fraser, and John Wyndham to luncheon. A merry party. John was very funny about the occasion when he was 'positively vetted' by M.I.5. One of the dangers of a young man getting into enemy hands is being in debt. So the security people say 'Do you owe any money?' It's a routine question. 'Yes' says John. 'How much?' says M.I.5 officer. 'Oh, about a million pounds', says John. (It was just after Ld Leconfield's death, when John

---

94. A direct assault.

rejoined me) 'Collapse of inspector' (as they used to say in the old *Punch*es)[95]

2.45. General Norstad. He had little to say, except the good news that he had persuaded Washington to be more reasonable . . . .

One of the tasks wh. occupied us late into the night was the sending of appropriate messages to various friends. All need careful and separate drafting. De Gaulle, Adenauer, Fanfani in Europe. Diefenbaker (Canada has already got cold feet) Menzies, Holyoake – and then Nehru and Pres[iden]t Ayub. (I also sent a warm personal message to Nehru about his troubles. The Chinese are pressing on victoriously all along the front. We are giving India lots of ammunition, light arms etc.)[96] . . . .

24 October

Woke early – 6.30am and 'did the box', wh. I had left unfinished last night. A very confusing morning, with Ld Home; Harold Caccia and much sending and receiving of telegrams. An anxious day, too. For the first clash will soon begin, if the Russian ships sail on. Not much from Russia yet, except words. No reaction in the Caribbean area, but not yet possible till the Russian ships, the first 14 of which are said to be carrying rockets etc, reach 500–300 miles from Cuban waters. The President has so far kept the blockade narrow, only rockets etc, not even minor arms are included . . . .

A talk with the President at 11pm. (Home and Caccia present) . . . . Rather unexpectedly, President asked me straight out the 64 thousand dollar question 'Should he take out Cuba'. I said I wd like to think about this and send an answer (it's just like a revue called *Beyond the Fringe* wh. takes off the leading politicians) Then the news. Nothing has happened very definitely yet, except an intervention by U Thant. This will be awkward, but I hope will not be published till tomorrow. I told President that U Thant was giving the show away. Kruschev cd accept the truce, (unpoliced) Kennedy cd not. Now that Russians have been proved blatant liars, no unpoliced agreement with

---

95. A reference to the Victorian phrase, 'collapse of stout party', popularised in the captions of cartoons pricking pomposity in the satirical London magazine *Punch* (1841–1992).

96. Border clashes around Dhola had escalated into a full-scale war on 20 October. The month-long conflict ended with China having successfully seized Aksai Chin, abutting Tibet, from India.

them is possible. President will think carefully about his reply. Meanwhile the 'guilty' ships seem to be turning away. At least 3 or 4 have
done so. We also know (from British intelligence) that a number of
Russian ships not so far on in the queue are returning via Baltic to
Polish or Russian ports.

25 October

Up early, to hear news and meet at 9.30 with Home and Caccia to
finish statement for Parliament. I altered the draft and got in some new
points about U Thant's move. I also got some good 'supplementaries'
ready. House met at 11am. The Conservative benches were packed.
Opposition party full, esp. <u>below</u> the gangway. Statement well received
on all sides. Gaitskell, as usual, said he wd ask 2 questions and
proceeded to ask 10. But his tone was helpful. He was most damaging
about 'consultation'. His memories are, of course, of Suez.[97] Wade
(Liberal deputy leader) was weak and futile. Shinwell asked a lot of
questions but was not effective . . . .

2.45–5.15 Cabinet. A very good discussion arising from some
papers by a Ctee of the Home Secy.[98] These covered the whole field of
the future pattern of Britain – industrial location, housing, office
building, transport etc. It was a fascinating discussion, where there
was a clear division between the 'Liberal' survivors (Erroll; Ld Chancellor: Minister of Health) the keen 'Dirigists' (Brooke; Keith Joseph;
SofS Scotland etc) with some 'pragmatic' dirigists. I reserved my
summing up till next Monday.

I told the Cabinet about Cuba (wh. they seem quite happy to leave
to me and Alec Home) We also had a talk about Railway Wages and
how to handle both Beeching and the Ry Unions. This time they are
'ganging up' together to screw more out of the Taxpayer.

6.30–8.30. Lobby correspondents at Admiralty House. The consumption of alcoholic refreshment was extraordinary . . . .

President came on at 11pm. There was a much clearer picture now.
U Thant had made his proposal of a 'cease fire'. Of course, the
Russians accepted, for they had everything to gain. Kennedy's answer
was very ingenious. He referred to the major question – how to get rid
of the rockets. But he wd agree to ambassador Stevenson discussing it
with U Thant in N. York. 14 ships have turned round. 1 oil tanker

97. When Gaitskell complained that he had not been consulted.
98. The Cabinet Committee on Population and Employment.

stopped, and was allowed to proceed. But the difference (at present hardly revealed) is this. The Americans will <u>not</u> agree to call off the blockade on the unsupported word of the Russians . . . .

26 October

No early news from America. A bad report from Brussels. Heath has had no success with the 6 on British farming needs. But, of course, this is only the first stage in the bargaining. We shall know more after the next two days of talk.

Unemployment is now just over 500,000. 2.1% and of course 4% or 5% in some areas. There is still a shortage of skilled men. The economy is clearly more relaxed than the Treasury experts told us. At the same time, we have to guard agst a rise in wages and prices . . . . Employers, who clung on to labour – good or bad, needed or unneeded – during the boom, are now letting them go. This is healthy. At the same time, it is not good enough (as some of the experts wd advise – Spearman, Nigel Birch etc) to sit tight and do nothing. What is needed now is a stimulus not to <u>all</u> consumption (such as use of regulator wd do – including whisky and tobacco) but to <u>selected consumption</u>, wh. a) has wide effect on other industry b) good export history.

Chancellor of Exr came at noon today, to settle final plans for a little scheme wh. we have been talking about and minuting each other about for some weeks . . . . We agreed to a) quite considerable changes in various investment allowances[99] b) – more important – immediate reduction of motor car purchase tax from 45% to 25%. Since the motor industry is so wide-spread, this shd have a good general effect on the economy . . . .

28 October (Sunday)

I am writing this in a state of exhaustion, after being up all Friday and Saturday nights – to about 4am. (The difference of hours in America and England is the cause)

It is impossible to describe what has been happening in this hour by hour battle – in many ways rather like a battle. The <u>Turkey</u> offer of Kruschev (to swap Cuban missile bases for Turkish) was very dangerous. *The Times* and *Manchester Guardian* were particularly gullible. The Press today – *Observer* and *Sunday Times* esp – were awful. It

---

99. Firms were allowed to write off the first year of investment in a development area or in scientific research.

was like Munich. The *Sunday Telegraph* was very good and firm. All through Saturday night, the strain continued. This morning, I decided (Butler, Home, Thorneycroft, and Heath agreeing) to send a message to Kruschev. We <u>supported</u> the American demand that the missiles shd be taken out of Cuba. I appealed to him to do this, and then turn to more constructive work – disarmament and the like. Our message was sent off at 12 noon. As we were finishing luncheon together, the news came (by radio) that the Russians had given in! First, they admit to the ballistic missiles (hitherto denied by Communists <u>and</u> doubted by all good fellow-travellers in every country) Then they said they wd be 'packed up, crated, and taken away' – a complete climb-down (<u>if</u> they keep their word)

4 November (Sunday)

. . . . All this week, life has gone on. Two or more Cabinets. The Parliamentary dinner. A speech on the opening day. An audience. Yemen (always with us) The Royal Society, of wh. I have been elected a member. Other Club dinner, with an almost complete turn-out for Churchill. A day's shooting (yesterday) at Broadlands. The reform of the defence structure – talk with Mountbatten. Sir Norman Brook's serious illness . . . .

Nevertheless, the week has seemed rather unreal, compared to the week before – with all those messages and telephone calls, and the frightful desire to <u>do</u> something, with the knowledge that <u>not</u> to do anything (except to talk to the President and keep Europe and the Commonwealth calm and firm) was prob. the right answer. I still feel (with all the other work of the week) tired out. One longs for some days of continued rest, wh. is impossible. At 68 I am <u>not</u> as resilient as when I was a young officer. Yet this <u>has</u> been a battle, in which everything was at stake . . . . The only unlucky thing was that we decided to send our message to Kruschev through <u>diplomatic</u> channels. This meant that it was not published till the very moment when the Russian <u>radio</u> message of 'climb-down' came through. It almost seemed as if we had sent the telegram backing the horse <u>after</u> the race. Otherwise, I think we played our part perfectly. We were 'in on' and took full part in (and almost responsibility for) every American move.[100] Our complete calm helped to keep the Europeans calm (The

---

100. The British certainly had plenty of discussions with their American counterparts

French were anyway contemptuous; the Germans <u>very</u> frightened, tho'
pretending to want firmness; the Italians windy; the Scandinavians
rather sour as well as windy.) But they <u>said</u> and <u>did</u> nothing to spoil
the American playing of the hand.

The following seem to be the main questions and thoughts that
occur to me.

(1) <u>Why did Kruschev do the Cuban missiles?</u>
The general view is that he thought he wd be able to complete the job
without being found out, or by denying the facts (as he did, followed
by all the other Communist states, as well as by the *Tribune*,[101] the
Manchester Guardian. Even *The Times* was rather sceptical at first.)

He hoped to finish the job; go to United Nations at end of
November; threaten about <u>Berlin</u>, and then reveal his Cuban strength,
pointing at the 'soft under-belly' of U.S.A., 3 minutes warning instead
of 15. (Of course, to us who face nearly 500 of these missiles in Russia
trained on Europe, there is something slightly ironical about these
20–30 in Cuba. But, as I told the President, when one lives on
Vesuvius, one takes little account of the risk of eruptions.) This
explanation of Mr K's motives wd seem to account for his continued
references to making no trouble about anything till after the American
elections (early November) He meant, till after the missiles were safely
installed in Cuba.

(2) <u>What did it cost K[hrushchev]?</u>
Quite a lot – prob[ably] £300–400m. Over 100 ships had to be
chartered or made available. We think there are some 10000 Russian
military personnel on the island. Besides the <u>offensive</u> weapons, there
are a lot of ground to air missiles (SAMs) wh. of course could not be
managed by any but Russians. There is also a great deal of other
military material – tanks, guns, etc.

(3) <u>Why did he make the offer to swap Turkey (American base)[102]</u>
    <u>for Cuba (Russian base) on Saturday?</u>
.... Of course, there is no comparison between the NATO and
Warsaw Pact forces, which have faced each other for 15 years or more
in Europe, and the <u>sudden</u> introduction of missile threat into the

---

during the crisis, though whether they directly influenced decisions is much
more doubtful.

101. The weekly journal of the left of the Labour party, founded in the late 1930s.
102. Only established in 1961, to the Russians this base was as offensive as the
Americans found theirs in Cuba.

Western hemisphere. But the *Manchester Guardian* and all that ilk fell for it like nine-pins. K must have been aware that he could get a lot of this sort of support. It did involve <u>admitting</u> the existence of the ballistic missiles – hitherto denied. But the American photographic air reconnaissance was too good and too persistent to be laughed off altogether. The Turkey–Cuba deal wd have [of] course been greatly to the advantage of U.S. The Turkey base is useful, but not vital. Cuba was vital. I suggested to [the] President that if anything of the kind was to be done, it wd be better done with our Thors. For British opinion could stand up; the Turks wd feel betrayed. (This offer, tho' it was not necessary, was useful) However, it became clear on Saturday that anything like this deal wd do great injury to NATO.[103]

(4) <u>Why did he suddenly abandon the Turkey–Cuba deal, and send the telegram of Sunday, in effect throwing in his hand?</u>

This is the crucial question and on the answer, much depends. Why did he not make some counter-move, for instance, on Berlin? Will he make it quite soon? Or on Turkey, or Persia? This is, of course, still a mystery and every ambassador and F.O. expert has a different theory. The general view is that he realised that the Americans were serious and wd invade Cuba and capture it. (This they intended to do on Monday morning. The invasion was always timed for the Monday 29th. The President told me earlier in the week about 23rd or 24th that the 'build up' wd take a week from the day he made his speech – Monday 22nd) <u>This American invasion could not be stopped by conventional means.</u> Therefore the Russians wd have [had] to use nuclear, in a 'fire first' attack. This they would not face – and rightly. But if the Americans attacked, they wd do three things (i) destroy Castro and the Communist regime (ii) deal a great blow to Russian prestige (iii) capture the missiles. So, by his apparent 'cave-in', Kruschev at least avoided all these disadvantages . . . .

(5) <u>What are the strategic lessons?</u>

May they not be that, under the cover of the terrible nuclear war, which nobody dares start, you can get away with anything you can do

---

103. Macmillan offered to immobilise Britain's 60 Thor missiles, under UN supervision, in a letter to Kennedy of 26 October 1962. In the event, unbeknownst to Macmillan and despite Turkish opposition, the President had agreed to the removal of the Jupiter missiles in Turkey. Meanwhile, on 1 November 1962 Thorneycroft told Robert Estabrook that Britain's Thors were already being decommissioned.

by <u>conventional</u> means. You can take Cuba. The enemy can only reply by all-out nuclear war. But this applies to Berlin. The Russians <u>can</u> take Berlin by conventional means. The Allies <u>cannot defend</u> or <u>recapture</u> it by any conventional means. (The conclusion to be drawn is rather sinister)

(6) <u>What is going to happen in Cuba etc?</u>

U.N. (U Thant and co) and USA are going to find it quite difficult to deal with Castro . . . . The other <u>defensive</u> weapons will remain in situ (SAMs etc) and Cuba will remain as the base for Communist propaganda throughout Central and S. America.

(7) <u>Conduct of Crisis</u>

President Kennedy conducted his affair with great skill, energy, resourcefulness and courage . . . .

   (a) He played a firm <u>military</u> game throughout – acting quickly and being ready to act <u>as soon as</u> mobilised. This was Eden's <u>fatal</u> mistake – in which we all share the responsibility. You cannot keep an 'army of invasion' hanging about. It must invade or disperse. President K did not bluster – but everyone knew that (if no other solution was found) there wd be an invasion.

   (b) He played the <u>diplomatic</u> card excellently. The European and other allies had no real grievance about non-consultation. The flying visit of Dean Acheson to Europe and the information to NATO Council was more than correctness demanded.

   (c) He played the <u>United Nations</u> admirably. Eden tried to use U.N. (but Foster Dulles really wrecked us there) Kennedy mobilised a lot of U.N. opinion and used <u>Stevenson</u> (a regular smarmy, Hugh Footy, Liberal type) to keep UN quiet. If it had come to the point, U.S.A. wd <u>not</u> have had majority support in the Assembly. So they wisely never let it get out of the Security Council. In S. Council the Russians made the fatal mistake of bare-faced lying. Zorin was still denying the existence of the missiles in Cuba, when Kruschev's message was published offering to swap them for those in Turkey! . . . .

(8) <u>Anglo-American Relations</u>

In the debate on Tuesday (when Gaitskell took this line) and on Wednesday (when it was developed by Harold Wilson) the Opposition (supported by some of the press – esp. the 'columnists' and gossip writers) have been making out that the Americans not only failed to consult us, but have treated us with contempt; that the 'special relationship' no longer applies; that we have gained nothing from our position as a nuclear power; that America risked total war in a US/USSR quarrel without bothering about us or Europe. The reasons for this attitude are (a) ignorance of what really happened (b) desire to injure and denigrate me personally (c) argument agst deterrent (d) annoyance at the success – or comparative success of Cuba enterprise (e) shame – for they let it be known that they wd oppose force, or threat of force. In fact, of course, the President and Rusk (and, above all, the President's *chef de Cabinet*,[104] McGeorge Bundy) were in continuous touch with Alec Home and me. David Gore was all the time in and out of the White House . . . .

5 November

. . . . The Vassall case is getting more embarrassing . . . . I feel that the people really to blame were the ambassador and head and chancery in Moscow. One ought to know the private life of a staff in Moscow in a way which is quite impossible in London. What seems odd is that this man can write his memoirs and sell them to the Press for an immense sum after conviction and this must be due to the connivance of the Police . . . .

I had a long talk on Friday with Sir Burke Trend. It is (I'm afraid) pretty clear that Sir Norman Brook will not function any more. I hope he will be well enough to come back before the end of the year, (so that we can make our farewells appropriately) when he retires . . . .

I feel that Sir N. Brook has not been able to give me full time. Under the new arrangement,[105] Trend will really only have the Cabinet Office and will be able to become my *chef de Cabinet* . . . .

15 November

The last week has been very heavy work. Apart from Cabinet; dinners and talks with Japanese Prime Minister; Queen's diplomatic reception; PQs; Cuba; Yemen etc, we have wasted all the rest of the time on the Vassall spy case. On this there has been a continual running crisis – involving (rightly or wrongly) Mr Galbraith's resignation (he having written some foolish if innocuous letters to Vassall when both were in

---

104. Head of office.
105. Sir Norman Brook had combined the offices of Cabinet Secretary and head of the Home Civil Service since 1956, an arrangement ended with his retirement in 1963.

the Admiralty), and a sort of mass hysteria worked up by the Press and the less reputable members of the Opposition like Brown and Crossman and Gordon-Walker. When this culminated in an accusation of treachery against both Galbraith and Ld Carrington (First Lord) and against the Board of Admiralty etc, I had to admit to myself that a Committee of Civil Servants wd not do[106] and propose a Tribunal under the 1921 Act, over wh Ld Radcliffe has agreed to preside . . . .

I do not remember a more worrying time – and so wasteful of effort. I suppose I wd have done better to have had a judicial enquiry of some kind at the start. Had I known that all this mud wd be thrown about, I wd have done so. But we cannot have a Tribunal every time we catch a spy. Now that the net is closing, we shall probably have some more cases. The public does not regard catching a spy as a success, but as a failure. Unhappily, you can't bury him out of sight, as keepers do with foxes. Maurice has been a great help all through, and knows the feelings of the Party very well. In a curious way, I may have gained by this incident, as it has helped to re-establish my ascendancy over the HofC . . . .

Kruschev is still making difficulties about Cuba. He seems really to have moved away the missiles but is arguing about the bombers.

16 November

Another long talk [to Kennedy] on the telephone last night. The new machine is (a) better – you talk as in an ordinary telephone (b) safer – it wd take 90 years to break the code (c) British. A score for us! We discussed Yemen, Cuba, Laos, and Berlin. On Yemen, the President was trying to help and sent me a written message wh goes a long way[107] . . . . On Cuba, I urged him to be quite firm on the bombers and said that I wd back him up publicly.[108] On Laos, we will try to get Malcolm MacDonald (now travelling in SE Asia as a private citizen) to go to Laos and try to get some spunk into Souvanna Phouma. This is the 'moderate' leader, who is the key to the whole settlement. He is said to be losing heart and threatening to return to Paris where his

---

106. Though this was Macmillan's first resort to manage the affair.
107. It outlined plans to secure withdrawal both of Saudi and Jordanian support for the royalists, and Egyptian support for the republicans.
108. Kennedy was threatening to reimpose the quarantine around Cuba unless the USSR withdrew its IL-28 bombers from the island, which Khrushchev agreed to do on 20 November 1962.

treasure is – and his heart (in the shape of his daughters) These characters always seem to collect a fortune in their few years of political activity. On Berlin, President said he had said very little to Chancellor Adenauer (whom he did not trust) Till Cuba was settled, he cd not open up a negotiation on Berlin and to talk prematurely to Adenauer wd be dangerous.

10.30. [Sir Charles] Cunningham (Home Office) and Hollis, with Trend. We discussed some <u>regular</u> procedure wh we might invent in case more spies are caught (as they will be) . . . .

17 November
. . . . The Pakistanis are getting rather unreasonable about our <u>help</u> to India, wh. is very limited. But one wonders whether the time may not soon be ripe for an attempt at conciliation. There is certainly a better feeling in India among quite a number of influential people . . . .

25 November (Sunday)
. . . . I am making a little progress with my 'Modernisation of Britain' Committee. Unhappily, owing to the difficulties of some of the heavy industries – shipbuilding, heavy steel, etc – the unemployment figure (all over) has risen to 2.4%, with some black spots in Scotland, N.W., NE, and of course N.Ireland. The attraction of the South (where employment is good) continues in spite of all our efforts to guide and bribe industries to go to the old areas. We shall have to do more still.

The 5 by-elections have gone badly. We lost a seat in Glasgow and we also lost S. Dorset (where we had Lord Sandwich – formerly Hinchingbrooke – against us in support of a popular local man who ran as an 'Anti-Common Market' Conservative and took 5000 votes). This put Labour in by 700. The other three seats we kept, but by sadly reduced majorities.[109] The Press on Saturday and today have been quite hysterical and prophesy a revolt against me in the Parly Party. The only thing to do is to remain calm and go on with our work.

26 November
Butler came to see me, bringing Dr Banda with him. The Nyasaland

---

109. In the by-elections on 22 November the Tory poll fell by 15–20% and they lost Glasgow Woodside and South Dorset to Labour, only retaining Norfolk Central by 200 votes and Northampton South by 900. In Chippenham the majority was still well down on 1959 at 1,588.

Conference has gone off well. But there will be a row from Welensky when we announce that we are prepared to give Nyasaland the right of secession . . . .

27 November

. . . . Eden's book is interesting.[110] I have been looking again at certain passages, and wondering how far the pre-war analogy applies today. Kruschev and Hitler are very different characters. Hitler <u>had</u> to act with frantic haste. He could not wait, for he was putting on Germany strains which such a country cd not stand for more than a short time. Moreover, since we <u>have</u> 'stood up' to the Russians for 15 years; since Cuba represents a success; since Kruschev may be the best type of Russian leader we are likely to get, there <u>is</u> a strong argument for trying now to negotiate either some limited agreements or over a wider field . . . .

29 November

. . . . Both Chancellor of Exr and Home Secy (as heads of the respective committees)[111] have agreed to my 'Modernisation of Britain' plans for work and decision. This is a great relief, for I feared that Treasury might be hostile . . . .

1 December (Saturday)

. . . . Ted Heath came about 6.30 and we had a good talk before and after dinner. The <u>French</u> are opposing us by every means, fair and foul. They are absolutely ruthless. For some reason, they <u>terrify</u> the Six – by their intellectual superiority, spiritual arrogance, and shameless disregard of truth and honour. (This, of course, is France throughout all history) <u>But</u> they are afraid of being pilloried as the destroyers of European unity. The crunch will come in Jan or Feb. It will be a trial of nerve and will. We must threaten to show up the French before the world.

---

110. Eden's inter-war memoirs, *Facing the Dictators* (London: Cassell, 1962), had recently been published.

111. The Economic Policy and Population & Employment Cabinet Committees. Maudling and Brooke, with Macmillan, formed an informal steering group to explore increasing productivity and ways of rectifying imbalances between rich and poor regions.

A very useful talk, and we agreed <u>on – of midnight</u>[112] on a very revolutionary scheme.[113] Whether we shall be able to carry it out, I don't know.

3 December

C.I.G.S. (General Hull) for an hour in the morning. He gave me a most interesting account of the military situation in India, from wh. he has just returned. The <u>Army</u> according to him fought well enough and in some instances with great gallantry. The Command was feeble.

Commonwealth Secretary came later in day, after a successful statement in Parl. He has certainly done a good job and has <u>forced</u> Nehru and Ayub at least to meet. Whether any child will ever be conceived and born after this shotgun wedding, I rather doubt . . . .

6 December

. . . . A very bad poll for Conservatives and esp. for me in *D. Mail* Gallup poll.[114] This is partly the result of the really hysterical talk about unemployment both in Press and on Radio and TV.

1922 Executive after questions. Not too bad. I made it clear that I wd be happy to resign the leadership of the Party if it wd help. It is significant of our bad position that this is the first time I have had to use this weapon . . . .

7 December

A great furore about a speech by Dean Acheson, wh. seems to indicate the view that Britain's role is played out.[115] Of course, Dean

---

112. This was Macmillan's way of expressing that agreement occurred on the stroke of midnight.

113. This seems to have involved drawing on American support to pressurise Hallstein.

114. Actually by National Opinion Polls, it put Labour on 43.3%, Conservatives on 35.5% and Liberals on 18.9%. Macmillan had a satisfaction rating of 47.9% and a dissatisfaction rating of 50.7%. Most worryingly, Gaitskell (23.8%) was well ahead of Macmillan (17.2%) on who would make the best prime minister, whilst 44.3% said Macmillan should retire immediately, slightly more than the 43.1% who said he should lead the party in the next election.

115. On 5 December at West Point military academy Acheson's speech on 'Our Atlantic Alliance' contained an incendiary paragraph starting, 'Great Britain has lost an empire and has not yet found a role'. It might be noted that a similar line had appeared in 'The Commonwealth: Passage to Europe' in *Time*, 21 September 1962.

Acheson was always a conceited ass, but I don't really think he meant
to be offensive. However, (not a good sign, for we ought to be strong
enough to laugh off this kind of thing) public opinion (if you trust
the Press) is upset. (Altho' some of the papers – *D. Mirror*, *D. Mail*
and even *Times* – quite reasonable) Lord Chandos, Sir Louis Spears
and others from the Institute of Directors have written me a formal
letter of protest, wh. they have put on BBC news, T.V., and published
in Press last night and this morning. So I thought it best to use this
as a peg for a reply. This I compiled early this morning, and after
getting Sir H. Caccia's approval on behalf of For Secy, I had it put
out. I think it will please the Conservative Party and the 'patriotic'
elements in the country. But it sticks firmly to the principle wh. I have
been preaching all these post-war years – that is, the doctrine of
'interdependence' . . . .

9 December

. . . . The Sunday Press is hysterical about Europe, about Skybolt,
about the Tory Party, about Miss Fell (given 2 years for giving secret
papers to her Yugoslav lover),[116] about my resignation, about Dr
Adenauer, about Welensky, about David Ormsby Gore, about Acheson. (Most of the Press take the view that Britain is no good anyway)
The Press are even more inaccurate than usual, alleging that President
and I talked twice on telephone last week, wh. is not true. Nevertheless,
(in spite of the Press exaggerations and misrepresentations) I do not
recall a time when there are so many difficult problems to resolve and
awkward decisions to be made . . . .

There is trouble in Brunei. Some 2000 to 5000 rebels have seized
the Shell refinery and tried to throw out the Sultan. No doubt this is
fomented from Indonesia by Sukarno. I always feared that once the
West New Guinea question was settled and the Dutch 'ousted',[117] he
wd start in Borneo.

I came to London in the afternoon and had a meeting at Admiralty
House. Minister of Defence (Thorneycroft) CDS (Mountbatten) and
[Sir Robert] Scott.[118] I think we are sending enough reinforcements to

---

116. Barbara Fell in 1959–60 passed documents to the Yugoslav embassy press
attaché, Smiljan Pecjak.
117. The Dutch left what is now called West Irian in October and Indonesia took
over in January 1963.
118. The permanent secretary to the Ministry of Defence 1961–64.

get <u>military</u> control of Brunei.[119] But I fear there will be a lot of political reaction. It will be represented as against 'Greater Malaysia', when it is really an Indonesian expansionist plot. (The Shell Co's oil installations etc in Brunei are of very great value)

We then discussed further 'defence organisation' and completed the first minute and annexe for me to circulate. It is a bold scheme[120] . . . .

10 December

. . . . Lunch for three Federal ministers from Central Africa, who have come here (at Welensky's request) to bring pressure on us about Nyasaland and about N and S. Rhodesia. On the first, we can give them no satisfaction. The Cabinet has decided that if Nyasaland wants to leave the Federation (as Dr Banda and his party certainly desire) she must be allowed to do so. This announcement will be made on Dec 17, <u>after</u> the elections in N. Rhodesia and in S. Rhodesia have been concluded. As for the future of the two Rhodesias, we can assure them that we mean to work for some association. But we cannot pledge ourselves (as Welensky wants us to do) to any precise form. It is all very sad. The Federation <u>was</u> a good idea. But it has been wrecked by two things

a) The 'wind of change' which has swept through Africa with unexpected force (unexpected, at least, ten years ago)

b) The policies first of Huggins – now Lord Malvern[121] – and secondly of Welensky, which have made the Federation, in the minds of Africans, a symbol of white domination. Poor Sir Edgar Whitehead (Premier of S. Rhodesia) has been the victim of their illiberalism.

Meetings on 'Skybolt' (wh. the Americans are clearly now going to abandon) on Yemen; and on aid to India . . . .

---

119. Military control was rapidly reasserted, though the rebellion was not crushed until April 1963. Subsequently Brunei did not participate in the proposed Malaysian Federation.

120. The plan was to integrate the armed forces and the historic departments of the Admiralty, War Office and Air Ministry into a single Defence Ministry, with a junior minister responsible for each service. This was implemented in 1964.

121. Prime Minister of Southern Rhodesia 1933–53, of the Central African Federation 1953–56.

11 December

Cabinet at 11. 1½ hours on Congo. A very good discussion, in which all joined in. We decided that we cd not agree to impose physical sanctions on Tshombe, by preventing the transport of copper from Katanga mines through N. Rhodesia (it is very doubtful if we have the legal right to do so. It rests with the Federal Govt.) We also decided that, if other governments decided to boycott the purchase of copper from Katanga (in order to break Tshombe's power) we would not join the boycott but we would limit our purchases to the average rate of the last 3 years (Actually, U.K. purchases are small – only some 3000 tons out of a total of 250,000 tons.) In other words, we wd make a market in UK in order to break the boycott. On the next point – if U Thant asks for a new resolution from Security Council, to give him power to conquer Tshombe by force – shall we veto or not, opinions were divided. We left it that a decision wd be taken when we know all the circumstances.[122]

Maudling (Chancellor of Ex) to lunch. We agreed to abolish all the 45% range of Purchase Tax and bring them to 25% (like the motorcars) This is to be done immediately after Christmas. At the same time he will say that there will be no changes in purchase tax in the Budget. This will stop people holding off from buying. We also agreed to reduce Bank Rate from 4½% to 4% at beginning of January.

We discussed special measures for NE Coast. We need not a Committee or a Board but a man, who can do in NEast what Ld Brecon did so successfully in S. Wales and N. Wales[123] . . . .

Thorneycroft came in at 5pm to report his talk with McNamara, American Minister of Defence. It seems clear that Americans mean to drop 'Skybolt'. There will be a great row in both countries. And it means a great battle with President Kennedy next week . . . .

14 December

Left Northolt at 2.30, arriving Orly airport at 5.15 (French time) Dorothy came with me. Philip de Z[ulueta] acted as my chief adviser and secretary. We were met by guard of honour etc and drove straight

122. The UN had negotiated a federal settlement, inaugurated in October, but Tshombe repudiated it. In December, without a further resolution, the UN conquered Katanga.
123. Lord Brecon, Minister of State for Wales 1957–64, in 1958 established a development corporation for Wales.

to Embassy, where we dined quietly with ambassador and Lady Dixon. Alexander Macmillan (now at Sorbonne) came to dinner and seemed very well. Peter Thorneycroft and Alec Home came in at different times, to report on NATO matters. In spite of all the rumours in the Press, things seem fairly quiet. Mr McNamara (U.S. Defence Minister) made his offer to sell nuclear rockets (without war-heads) to the Europeans. They did not seem much attracted . . . .

16 December (Sunday)

. . . . We got back to London – rather delayed by wind – about 6.30pm after long talks 3.30–7pm on Saturday (alone with de Gaulle) 10–11.30am on Sunday (also alone) 11.45–1pm (with For. Secy, British ambassador, M. Pompidou (Prime Minister) Couve de Murville; Courcel . . . .

On foreign and defence policy, the talks were satisfactory. The General and I were broadly in agreement about the immediate policy towards Moscow. We also agreed the need for a wide détente at the right time. On NATO and on the nuclear we also agreed. The General was as sceptical as we are about the great battle to be fought with conventional forces in Germany. He thinks (as we do) that it wd last 3 hours, or at the most 3 days . . . .

I thought the discussions about as bad as they cd be from the European point of view. The only glimmer of hope lies in the French unwillingness to be held up to all the world as having openly wrecked our entry and having never really tried to negotiate seriously. The agricultural interest is, of course, very great. But I think jealousy of Britain is an even stronger motive. The French (or rather de G. and his friends)[124] want the Six, dominated by France. They do not want a Europe of 8, 9, or 10 states, with an equilibrium of power. This is (I think) very short-sighted. They underrate the German danger in the future. But their pride and natural isolationism makes them afraid of larger concepts. It was a very depressing experience, the brutal truth, of course, cleverly concealed by all the courtesy and good manners which surrounded the visit in all its details.

I got back to a meeting on Skybolt and Polaris, wh. lasted till late in the evening. We shall have a difficult time with the Americans in Nassau.

---

124. De Gaulle had recently been strengthened by success in the Assembly elections in October.

23 December

We got back to London airport [from Nassau] about 9am this morning (Sunday) absolutely exhausted. We have had a tremendous week – three days hard negotiation – nearly four days in reality. The Americans pushed us very hard and may have 'out-smarted' us altogether. It is very hard to judge whether they speak the truth or not. But McNamara struck me as a man of integrity – much more reliable than President Kennedy, who makes the facts fit his arguments – or so it often seems. One of the unknown factors was, all through, how far the Americans were speaking the truth about Skybolt. A very successful test was made on the day after our conference ended. Did the President and McNamara know about this or did they expect another failure? But, whatever the test may have shewn, it is clear that the American defence minister and the White House have decided – on wider grounds – to concentrate on Minuteman (the Intercontinental Rocket) and Polaris (the submarine weapon). It is also clear to me that they are determined to kill Skybolt on good general grounds – not merely to annoy us or to drive G. Britain out of the nuclear business. But, of course, they have handled things in such a way as to make many of us very suspicious. Nor do we yet know what will be the effect of the successful test of Skybolt in American politics. The President is clearly alarmed. The Air Force 'lobby' in Washington, as well as the 'Douglas' lobby,[125] will be much strengthened. All this may have repercussions on the general agreement wh. we reached and published at Nassau on Friday, Dec 21st . . . .

. . . . Whether Parlt and the country will think we have done well or badly I cannot tell yet. Yesterday's Press was quite good (except of course Lord Beaverbrook's) Today's (Sunday) is very bad. The Opposition will attack our whole record on defence (and with some reason, for we have chopped and changed in this baffling sphere) The 'Patriots' (led by Beaverbrook and the isolationists) will accuse us of 'selling out Britain'.[126] No one will find it profitable to take a fair and balanced

---

125. Douglas Aircraft had won the contract to develop this missile in 1959.

126. In the US the furore surrounding this meeting concerned the somewhat synthetic outrage the British expressed over the Skybolt cancellation. This, and the agreement allowing US use of Holy Loch, enabled them instead to acquire submarine-based Polaris missiles (coming into service in 1968) as a means of delivering British-manufactured nuclear warheads. In the UK the furore concerned the American linkage of the agreement with the development of a

view. As usual, *The Times* is <u>very</u> bad. The *Telegraph* (*Daily* and *Sunday*) is much better. *S. Times* not too bad . . . .

Broadly, I have agreed to make our present Bomber force (or part of it) <u>and</u> our Polaris force (when it comes) a NATO force for general purposes. But I have reserved absolutely the right of HMG to use it <u>indefinitely</u> 'for supreme national interest'. These phrases will be argued and counter-argued. But they represent a genuine attempt (wh. Americans finally accepted) to make a proper contribution to <u>interdependent</u> defence, while retaining the ultimate rights of a sovereign state. This accepts the facts of life as they are. But I do not conceal from myself that the whole concept will be much knocked about by controversy at home. The Cabinet (wh. met on the Friday morning and was kept fully informed throughout) did not much like it, altho' they backed us up loyally . . . .

26 December

. . . . The election in S. Rhodesia (ejecting Sir Edgar Whitehead and substituting Winston Field) is <u>on the face</u> of it, a retrograde and reactionary vote.[127] But it may really simplify the situation for Butler since <u>none</u> of the 3 Provincial Governments is now in favour of the Federation. But, of course, the <u>real</u> danger is increased. We may see S. Rhodesia <u>forced</u> to join S. Africa. So, multi-racialism will have failed. The white man will be driven to extremism everywhere in Africa, in order to fight African extremism. The future in Kenya will be still more threatening and depressing . . . .

. . . . I feel very sad now about Selwyn Lloyd and David Kilmuir. I fear that I shall never regain their friendship, altho' I am sure that what I did was right in the national interest . . . .

30 December (Sunday)

We were going to have a shoot on Thursday, but there was a blizzard and a heavy fall of snow. This continued on Friday. Yesterday there was at least a foot of snow everywhere. The children enjoyed them-

---

multilateral NATO force, undermining British independence. It, however, still gave Britain the nuclear status necessary, as Macmillan put it in Nassau, to show they were 'keeping up with the Joneses'.

127. The Rhodesia Front won all its 35 seats in the essentially white constituencies. Whitehead's United Federal Party picked up 29 seats and there was one Independent.

selves tobogganing etc. Last night, another blizzard. I felt very tired, and slept a great deal . . . .

In the afternoon, with a police car in front (armed with shovels) and chains on my car, managed to get to London. It took over 2 hours – very few cars, but the roads very bad . . . .

31 December
Home Secretary and Chancellor of Exr all the morning. We discussed various <u>general</u> measures for the economy. The Treasury are now quite in expansionist mood. The reduction from 45% to 25% Purchase Tax of <u>all</u> remaining items in the 45% category will be announced tomorrow. Another ½% reduction (from 4½% to 4%) in Bank Rate on Thursday. We discussed plans for N.W. and NEast and some special measures. All the afternoon was busy. 2.45–5pm with Service Ministers, who are putting up a strong reactionary fight (aided by Chiefs of Staff) <u>against</u> reform of service and defence organisation . . . .

1963

*More spy cases – Gaitskell dies and Wilson becomes Labour
leader – breakdown of the Common Market entry negotiations –
Nigeria and the Enahoro affair – Southern Rhodesia and the break-up
of the Central African Federation – the Profumo scandal – signing of
the Test Ban Treaty – 'Confrontation' with Indonesia – Macmillan's
resignation and the struggle for the succession – death of Kennedy*

1 January
1962 is over. It has been a <u>bad</u> year, both in Home and Foreign politics. The Govt's position is weak and there is a general view that the Socialists will win the General Election. The country is in a dissatisfied and petulant mood. My own popularity has gone down a lot. There is a wave of anti-European, <u>and</u> anti-American feeling. There is trouble about growing unemployment. The Press is, with scarcely an exception, hostile. The TV is critical. Altogether, we are at a low ebb. Can we recover in 1963 or 1964? I don't know. But I mean to have a good try . . . .

6 January (Sunday)
. . . . The Sunday Press is very hostile and prophesies my early departure and the fall of the Government! Happily, since I was not unduly elated by the extravagant praise of 2 years ago, I am not unduly depressed by this change of mood. The trouble is that [the] Gallup poll will reflect all this criticism and our party, in and out of HofC, will be affected . . . .

11 January (Friday)
I am resting in bed this morning, after a very heavy week. Apart from Congo, where U.N. forces – aided and abetted by U.S. forces – have defeated Tshombe and produced an internal crisis in the Tory party, there has been a lot of routine work, ministerial meetings etc . . . .

The T.V. programme *Panorama* (25 minutes of my life from school to now) was quite good and seems to have had a good effect. It was sufficiently critical to be clearly composed and produced by active Socialists.

We have been arguing backwards and forwards about a 'special Commissioner' or some such a character to help NE Coast, where quite a radical approach seems now to be required. After a lot of thought, I decided on a <u>Minister</u> (not a Ministry) and on a Minister of first rank (not an Under Secretary or Minister of State as had been proposed and generally agreed) I chose Hailsham, who at once accepted. I was delighted and the reception when it came out on Wednesday was pretty good. Anyway, the Opposition are very angry, so they must be afraid that he may do some good . . . .

The 150th annual dinner of the Birmingham Chamber of Commerce at 7.30 (600 or more present) White tie; decoration; started late, got later, with a long, pompous and uneatable dinner. Speeches – 3 before me – included a reactionary, witty, Liberal 'laisser-faire' kind of speech, attacking the Local Development Act [sic] and the attempts to help the North etc etc[1] . . . . I discarded a great part of my speech, and plunged into a fierce reply, sometimes indignant, sometimes sentimental. By the end, I got all these Brummagem types to a standing ovation, lasting several minutes. I was proud of this; they quickly seemed a bit ashamed . . . .

We have in our prison a Russian spy, Lonsdale, sentenced to 20 years[2] imprisonment by the L.C.J. He suborned a number of minor characters (British subjects) who (as such) are guilty of treachery to their country. L. is said to be a good 'professional' intelligent officer, of 20 years standing, agreeable, clever, and of good character. If he wd talk, he cd give us information of real value. But he won't talk. We have offered substantial reductions (of 5 years or so) but he is not tempted. If he has heard of the capture by the Russians of one of our men – Wynne – he may be hoping for an exchange. Of course, in value there is no comparison between the pieces – one is a pawn (ours) the other a knight or bishop (the Russian) But public opinion might force us to a disadvantageous swap. If L. talks, it wd be worth reducing his sentence to the end of (say) 1963 or 1964. But will he talk? The best thing is that he talks (in exchange for promise of early release) and afterwards in exchange for Wynne. This wd enable him to go back to Russia. If he talks and is released, he cannot[3] . . . .

---

1. W. E. Kenrick, the President of the Chamber of Commerce, had made this attack on the Local Employment Act 1960.

2. In fact 25 years.

3. Posing as Canadian Gordon Lonsdale, the Soviet spy Konon Molody established a spy ring in the Underwater Research Establishment which was broken and brought to trial in 1961. Greville Wynne was an intermediary for the key western source, Oleg Penkovsky, arrested by the Soviets on 22 October 1962. Whilst Penkovsky was executed, Wynne was sentenced to eight years' imprisonment in May 1963, before being exchanged for Lonsdale/Molody in 1964.

12 January

.... The Brussels negotiations are about to be resumed in rather a tense atmosphere. French propaganda agst us, both about Brussels and about the Nassau agreement is developing on familiar lines. I am not discouraged. They often do this as a prelude to an agreement. M. Pisani (French Minister of Agriculture) said this to Christopher Soames (our Minister) 'Mon cher. C'est très simple. Maintenant, avec les six, il y a cinq poules et un coq. Si vous vous joignez, (avec des autres pays) il y aura peut-être sept ou huit poules. Mais il [y] aura <u>deux</u> coqs. Alors – c'est pas aussi agréable'[4] ....

28 January (Monday)

I am at Chequers, where I came last Friday – with Philip de Zulueta to work. The weather is still cold; the last fortnight has been a nightmare on this account alone. The snow and ice have dislocated all our life – there has been nothing like it since 1947. In my view, the authorities, of all kinds, have done remarkably well. The streets and roads have been cleared and in spite of delays, trains and buses have kept on running pretty well. The public, (who are in a very peevish mood – or at least the Press) do not take this view and seem to criticise everyone very sourly. Anyway, we managed to settle the Electricity dispute <u>without a defeat</u>. (Indeed, the extreme T. Unions and the shop stewards complained bitterly about the agreement reached – 3 year agreement, and about 4% rise a year – <u>very</u> good from the Incomes Policy point of view ....

The effect of the 'go-slow', together with the tremendous load on electricity owing to the weather has been trying – 'cuts' 'blackouts' etc. (On Friday night we had a breakdown from midnight till 4pm Saturday, owing to the peculiar effect of frost and fog on the insulators, wh. upset the grid from Birmingham to Buckinghamshire. However, except for baths and central heating, it was not bad – we cook on coal at Chequers and there are good fires in the rooms) However, the thaw looks like coming and the strike has been foiled ....

The result of the cold weather has been to add an immense figure (perhaps 150–170 thousand) to the registered unemployed. The total

---

4. 'My dear. It's very simple. Now, with the Six, there are five hens and one cock. If you join (with some other countries) there will be perhaps seven or eight hens. But there will be <u>two</u> cocks. This is not as pleasant ....' Macmillan passed on this explanation of French behaviour to Kennedy on 15 January.

is now about 800,000 – the largest since 1947. Naturally, the Opposition are jubilant and we are to have a 'vote of censure' next week.

Apart from the cold weather and the electricity dispute (which have taken up much of my time, with seeing ministers, Emergency Ctee etc.) I have not been able to write in the diary for more than a fortnight because of the crowding pressure of events.

(1) On the <u>Brussels</u> front everything has been reduced to chaos by the extraordinary behaviour of de Gaulle. He gave a 'Press Conference' (with all the Corps Diplomatique present) to denounce Britain and oppose – on principle – her entry into the Common Market.[5] Following the Conference .... the 'Goebbels'[6] (M. Peyrefitte – Minister of Information) was putting round every kind of lie about us and about me. The reasons given for de G's sudden decision (of wh. not even Couve de Murville had been informed) are so diverse as to be ridiculous. The General's *démarche* to the world, was followed by Couve de Murville going to Brussels to demand that the negotiations must now stop. This caused anger (but, alas, impotent anger) among the 5, who were just beginning to realise the real inwardness of French policy. De Gaulle is trying to <u>dominate</u> Europe. His idea is not a partnership, but a Napoleonic or a Louis XIV hegemony . . . .

To illustrate the impudence of the French, Couve de Murville tried to give 'orders' from the General to the Dutch and Belgian Foreign Ministers. If it were not for the fatal survival of Dr Adenauer (the Pétain of Germany)[7] we cd hope for a firm stand by the Germans. But they will, I fear, give way in the end. The Brussels meetings start again today. Couve de Murville's motion that the negotiations be brought to an end (wh. he moved ten days ago) will now be further discussed. Our difficulty will be to retain the moral leadership wh. we have established abroad, without yielding to any merely delaying compromise, wh. our public at home will not tolerate. It is, I fear, very hard

---

5. On 14 January. His grounds were differing economic structures, the impact on the EEC of new members and Britain's unwillingness to comply with the organisation.

6. Joseph Goebbels was Hitler's propaganda minister.

7. Hopes that the Germans might put pressure on de Gaulle were dashed when the aged Chancellor (compared here to the elderly General who led France's puppet government after defeat by Germany in 1940) went to Paris and on 22 January signed the Elysée Treaty of friendship.

on Ted Heath (Ld P[rivy] Seal) who has been a wonderful ambassador and negotiator throughout.

(2) On the <u>Polaris</u> front we have had an agitating time . . . . There has been great difficulty in settling the financial terms (wh. were left for a later agreement when we finished at Nassau) and the American defence minister has been very grasping. I have refused to agree to his demands and have been forced to appeal to the President direct. I heard yesterday that he accepted my proposals. The trouble has been about a possible contribution by us to <u>future</u> marks of the Polaris missile (not A1 or A2, wh. is in service, but A3, wh. is under development) I have refused to make an open-ended contribution to an unknown bill for R&D. But I have offered, in lieu, to add 5% to the retail cost. So, if we bought £50m of missiles, we wd pay £52½[m]. Not a bad bargain. But it has caused me some sleepless nights.

(3) <u>Mr Gaitskell</u>. Poor Hugh G. who has been ill for some weeks with a mysterious germ or virus, died on the night of Friday 18th. It was apparent from the bulletins that he was unlikely to survive both the disease and the treatment. It is very sad – for altho' I did not find him a sympathetic character – he was a man of <u>high</u> quality and his death is a real loss to the nation. His successor is to be chosen soon. The candidates are Harold Wilson, Brown, and Callaghan. The first is able but dangerous. The second is a buffoon. The third is pretty good and wd be a respectable leader.

I did a broadcast tribute on Saturday 19th as P.M. I took a lot of trouble with it and it seems to have been liked. On Tues. 23rd I had to do the same in the HofC. Altho' we normally only <u>adjourn</u> on the death of a PM or ex-PM, I thought it right to make an exception in this case. The Labour Party were pleased by this.

It is not easy to estimate the effect of Gaitskell's death. (So far as the Gallup poll is concerned, it seems to have <u>increased</u> the Labour majority!!) Of course, he had become both experienced and respected. Wilson is the first, but not the second. Brown neither. He was the sort of upper-middle class leader which a party of the Left requires in <u>normal</u> times – Asquith or Attlee. He moved in many circles, and attracted the academic, the literary and artistic, and (through his friendship with Ann Fleming)[8] some of the 'smart' society of London. He was thought much of abroad in 'progressive' circles – both in

---

8. The wife of 'James Bond' author Ian Fleming, with whom Gaitskell had an affair.

America and (to a less extent since his anti-European market attitude) in Europe. He was a distinguished man, with considerable political courage – or at least, skill. He held his party together. His successor (with an election approaching) shd be able to do this easily.

(4) <u>Unemployment</u>. The economy is not <u>yet</u> responding to the Chancellor of the Exr's measures. The pound is strong; exports not bad; imports lower and so balance of payments good; production increasing slowly. But, there are bad prospects for <u>shipbuilding</u>; for <u>heavy steel</u> and engineering – that is, for Scotland, NE Coast etc. The aircraft industry is in great trouble.

I have had conferences with Scottish T.U.C. (wh. went off well) and lots of ministerial meetings. Ld Hailsham's appointment for NE Coast has been well received. I spoke in Liverpool last Monday – a very good meeting, but not enthusiastic as in the periods of boom. Nevertheless, the atmosphere was sound. I was able to announce the re-scheduling of Mersey-side under the Local Employment Act.[9] I also had 20 minutes on Europe etc, which has received great praise from many quarters – including a public statement by Spaak.

(5) <u>Yemen</u>. We have brought back Gandy (our minister) for consultation, but as he at once went down with influenza, we have not made any progress. There is still a <u>violent</u> division of opinion about recognition between Colonial Office and Foreign Office – M of Defence siding with C.O.[10]

(6) <u>Brunei and Malaysia</u>. We have had very alarming reports of Indonesian schemes agst Borneo. They seem about to 'hot up' the Brunei rebellion again; to infiltrate across the Borneo borders in <u>large</u> numbers (it's all jungle country) and perhaps to attack openly by sea. We have alerted some more troops and aircraft and let it be known as publicly as possible that we are doing so[11] . . . .

I have had to spend several hours being reproached (and almost

---

9. Promised in the 1959 election, this 1960 piece of legislation offered industry a mixture of inducements and disincentives to settle not in wealthy areas but instead in areas where unemployment exceeded 4.5%.

10. The Colonial Office led opposition to recognition, whilst the Foreign Office essentially shared the American view that little could be gained and much lost by opposing Nasser here. Macmillan disagreed, noting on 25 February, 'For Nasser put Hitler and it all rings familiar' (TNA: PREM 11/4173).

11. On 20 January the Indonesian foreign minister had announced a policy of confrontation (*Konfrontasi*) against the accession of Sarawak and North Borneo to Malaysia.

insulted) by two very unprepossessing characters Mr Kawawa and Mr Obote, of Tanganyika and Uganda (also luncheon for them and their retinues) However, it all ended amicably and they accepted a very harmless communiqué. They were complaining about the slow march of events in Kenya – wh. is only their affair to the extent that they are all three in the East African organisation.[12] I must say that Duncan Sandys handles these people with extraordinary patience. After one evening's talk, they sulked and at the last minute refused to dine and go to the ballet with the Commonwealth Secy. (The High Commissioners and their staff were bitterly disappointed) Duncan said and did nothing, but went himself, with his wife and daughter. Altogether, this has been a shattering time ever since Christmas.

All our policies at home and abroad are in ruins. Our defence plans have been radically changed, from air to sea. European unity is no more; French domination of Europe is the new and alarming feature; our popularity as a Govt is rapidly declining. We have lost everything, except our courage and determination . . . .

4 February (Monday)

Last week was very hectic. The Brussels negotiations came finally to an end in a <u>brutal</u> way[13] – Couve de Murville (who is a pretty cold fish, anyway) behaved with a rudeness which was unbelievable. The 'Five' rallied round, but in the end were powerless. Poor Heath. No one cd have been a better negotiator and ambassador – but French duplicity has defeated us all . . . . There is the fear of immediate political and economic injury to us, as the French plans unfold. (They began an attack on Sterling, by selling heavily in Paris – but I think this has been staved off) . . . .

I decided that it was a time to try to rally the country and the party. So I both <u>opened</u> and <u>wound up</u> the Polaris debate, with vigorous speeches . . . . The Opposition pretended to be angry because I quoted from a speech of Gaitskell's in 1960. 'On this day, of all days' etc. Actually, I had been provoked into this quotation (wh. is the *locus*

---

12. Tanganyika had become independent in December 1961 and Uganda in October 1962. Kenya, which was relatively wealthy but did not achieve independence until December 1963, was linked with them through the East African Common Services Organisation, though contemporary hopes of a more thoroughgoing East African Federation were to prove stillborn.

13. On 29 January.

classicus[14] of the defence of the British independent deterrent) by Gordon-Walker. It was rather a fake protest. Even a saint may be quoted. But the movement to 'beatify' (as a preliminary to sanctification) of Gaitskell is very strange. The Socialists are really doing themselves a great injury by this exaggerated attitude. No subsequent leader will have a chance . . . .

I did a short broadcast on Wednesday, (recording it after very long defence speech etc was over) on the breakdown of Brussels. It seems to have been very well received. Indeed, on Thursday night, I felt a little of the 'post-Suez' spirit returning to the Party – and perhaps later to the country. At any rate, my personal position has been strengthened – both at Westminster and in the country generally . . . .

On Friday morning, Heath and I left early for Rome and we got back on Sunday evening (Feb 3rd) The visit had been planned for some time – the Italian PM having visited us in Jan 1962 . . . . The Italians are angry and alarmed. They hate the French, esp. de Gaulle . . . . But the Italians are also weak, and it is good to keep them up to the mark by all possible means. They hope that the Germans will remain firm, but fear Adenauer. The idea is a) to demand a meeting of Western European Union[15] b) to block developments – esp. those wh. the French want – in the Community c) to use NATO more effectively, and perh. stimulate an early meeting of Heads of Government. All this is good – but I rather fear that the French calculation is right. All this indignation, they believe, will blow over and they will be left undisputed masters of the field . . . .

The Tory party is (I think) in rather better shape since last week's debate. But a new Conservative group (called, I think, the Monday Club and founded by Lords Salisbury and Boyd)[16] is demanding my resignation . . . .

17 February
. . . . The Yemen problem (like so many) has settled itself! The 'Repub-

---

14. Classic place or example. The debate was on 31 January, the date of Gaitskell's funeral.
15. The Ministerial Council of WEU was seen as the best means of keeping channels open following the breakdown of the European negotiations.
16. In fact the Monday Club was founded in January 1961, on the right-wing fringes of the Tories, by four young Conservative activists, not least to oppose Macmillan's African policies. Lord Boyd of Merton (the former Alan Lennox-Boyd) and Lord Salisbury became joint patrons in 1962.

licans' have got tired of waiting for 'recognition' and have closed the Embassy. The F.O. and F.S. are rather upset. The Col. Secy is triumphant – so is M of Defence. I think it's the best thing 'in the short term', for we have lost the confidence of all our friends in the new Aden Federation.[17] In the long run, it may bring us trouble . . . . Qasim in Iraq has been brutally killed (as he killed the King and Nuri Pasha)[18] His body has been thrown to the dogs (duly televised – such is the strange mixture of old cruelties and new refinements) and a new regime has taken power. No one quite knows its character . . . .

Wilson got in fairly easily over poor Brown. I'm afraid Brown lost the Welsh and Scottish Labour MPs who (tho' his natural supporters) are mostly 'teetotal' and wd not vote for a drunkard. Wilson is an able man – far more able than Brown. He is good in the House and in the country – and, I am told, on T.V. But he is a fundamentally dishonest – even 'crooked' man – almost of the '3 Card Trick' kind. This may, sooner or later, find him out – or, rather, be found out. (There was a terrible attack on him last night by the satirical sketch of the BBC – *That Was The Week That Was*)[19]

The Gallup Poll has been very bad – 15% against the Party; as much against me. The collapse in Europe; the Polaris problem; above all, the economic setback and the frightful weather (still snow and frost and unemployment!) have caused a wave of depression in the Party in the HofCommons . . . . 'Macmillan must go' is the cry. Faced with Wilson (47 or so) we must have a young man (Heath or Maudling) This line of approach leaves out poor Butler as well as me. Of course, there's something in it. We have had a run of bad luck. Once this starts everything seems to go wrong. Really, everything that wd have been passed over as a minor contretemps when things are good is elevated into a major crisis when things are bad. Nevertheless, apart from spite, this is mostly defeatism. If I were to resign now, it could be of no benefit to anyone. We must go on at least till May, perhaps to Oct, 1964, in the hope that our economic measures will have produced their results . . . .

---

17. The Cabinet had, in any case, endorsed non-recognition on 14 February.

18. The CIA-backed Iraqi coup started on 8 February. Qasim was summarily tried and shot the following day.

19. Macmillan's comment on his treatment on *That Was The Week That Was*, in a note to Reginald Bevins on 10 December 1962, was 'It is a good thing to be laughed over. It is better than to be ignored' (TNA: PREM 11/3668).

19 February

. . . . More trouble with the 'spy' problem. We think we have at last
solved the mystery of who 'tipped' off Burgess and Maclean.[20] It was
a man, much suspected at the time, but agst whom nothing cd be
proved – one Philby. He was dismissed in 1951 from the service and
has lived since in the M. East, chiefly in the Lebanon, where he writes
for the *Observer* and the *Economist*! In a drunken fit, he confessed
everything to one of our men, so the whole thing is now clear. Maclean
and Burgess were worse than mere <u>defectors</u> – they were spies, paid by
Russians, over quite a number of years. This man Philby seduced them
and recruited them to the Russian service. He has now disappeared
from Beirut, leaving £2000 in cash for his wife . . . .

Read *Mr Hamish Gleave* – a novel by Richard Llewellyn, based on
Burgess and Maclean and trying to give the intellectual and moral
explanation for a man of Maclean's type turning traitor. Readable, but
fundamentally weak and rather naïve . . . .

21 February

. . . . More snow, ice on roads, and no sign yet of a real thaw. We
were lucky that unemployment figure has remained under 900,000 –
for all work on roads, building etc has stopped for over 2 months.

. . . . I have had to deal with a sad case of Fletcher-Cooke (Under
Sec. Home Office) who has got into trouble.[21] I fear he will have to
resign.

. . . . Saw 1922 Executive and told them firmly that I had no
intention of resigning or of having election till 1964. Of course, if
Govt were defeated in HofC, we wd resign; the Queen wd send for
Wilson, who wd form a Govt and dissolve – and win. We must stick
together and hold on. I think this lecture had a salutary effect . . . .

---

20. Having come under suspicion, Maclean, with Burgess, fled to Moscow in May
    1951. On 7 November 1955 Macmillan, as Foreign Secretary, told the
    Commons somewhat disingenuously that he had no reason to believe Philby – a
    Cambridge colleague of Burgess, who had been staying with him in Washington
    – was connected with their flight. Philby had in fact been recruited by the
    Soviets in 1936.
21. A juvenile delinquent he had been persuaded to try and help go straight was
    apprehended speeding in Charles Fletcher-Cooke's car without licence or
    insurance. Amidst press speculation Fletcher-Cooke (Conservative MP for
    Darwen 1951–83) resigned his ministerial post.

27 February

.... I had a good talk with Chancellor of Exr. I think he is moving on towards my idea of 'The National Plan'[22] .... Last evening, I saw 3 service ministers and 3 Chiefs of Staff about the new plan for Defence Organisation, which Ld Ismay and Sir Ian Jacob have helped to prepare.[23]

28 February

.... A difficult meeting on Yemen. The invaders have been cleared off our ground.[24] But what are we to do next? The Egyptians are heavily committed and will be difficult to dislodge by diplomatic means, altho' the Americans are trying to do so. Saudi Arabian Govt is very wobbly ....

4 March

.... David Bruce, (American ambassador) in London came at 5 and stayed 2 hours. He has been a week in Washington, from where he had little to report except talk, more talk, and still more talk. Some of the 'new frontiersmen'[25] can walk (indeed this is test of devotion to the White House and since no American ever walks, is thought a miracle of ascetism) but they can all talk ....

5 March

I woke to find a tremendous row wh. had been set off by a T.V. interview with M. Bidault on B.B.C. The story is a fantastic one. Bidault arrived (illegally) in England in January. He gave a TV interview to BBC, wh. was recorded and then (presumably) left this country. The BBC told the F.O. that they were going to give the broadcast [on] TV just <u>before</u> the last Brussels talks. Ted Heath (Ld Privy Seal) asked the producer (on a personal basis) <u>not</u> to do so. The

---

22. The first NEDC report on 6 February, setting a target of 4% annual growth, led Macmillan to urge Maudling that they needed a national plan of expansion (including various tax concessions) to achieve this.

23. Ismay was military secretary to the prime minister, and Jacob his deputy, during the Second World War. Their report led to the consolidation of the Ministry of Defence into a single organisation.

24. There had been border incursions into Bayhan, part of the South Arabian Federation.

25. A collective term to describe those around Kennedy. He had, in his 1960 acceptance speech, used the idea of exploring beyond a 'new frontier' to express the aspirations of his administration.

F.O. made the same request through normal channels. The recorded programme was <u>not</u> shewn, and F.O. apparently assumed that it wd be permanently suppressed. Suddenly, last night, without any warning, the BBC produced it on *Panorama*[26] . . . .

7 March

The position in the Yemen is deteriorating rapidly. There are now 28,000 Egyptians (one third of all Egyptian active forces) in the Yemen. It is getting pretty clear that the Egyptians mean to use Yemen as a jumping off ground for Saudi Arabia – a great prize. They are dropping arms <u>inside</u> S.A., and obviously are in touch with subversive elements there. What is ironical is that the Americans, who accepted the threat to Aden and the Federation with some equanimity (only an old colony!) are now tremendously excited and alarmed about Nasser going for S.A. and all the vast American oil interests involved. I fear that there is little more that we can do to help the so-called 'Royalists' more than we have already done by 'covert' methods . . . .

8 March

M East news is bad – very bad . . . . In Syria, the right-wing <u>anti-Nasser</u> Govt, has been overthrown by a *coup d'état* and the new regime looks like being pro-Nasser.[27] So the squeeze will begin, both on our Aden Protectorate and on Saudi Arabia . . . .

I spoke (30 minutes) to National Union [of Conservative and Unionist Associations] at Church House . . . . D remarked that when I came in there was quite good applause – not dramatic – out of loyalty. When I sat down there was tremendous applause – wh. meant that I had given them what they wanted! Actually, it was quite a good speech, with some amusing passages. The theme really was 'Modernisation of Britain' and was the first launching of these ideas . . . .

A very difficult question arose in yesterday's Cabinet about sending back a Nigerian notable, accused of treachery and subversion, whom Abubakar and the Nigerian Central Govt want to put on trial. He

---

26. Georges Bidault, a former French foreign minister, had very much opposed Algerian independence. The nominal leader of the terrorist OAS, he had been in hiding outside France since his role in the assassination attempt on de Gaulle of 22 August 1962.

27. As in Iraq earlier in the year, this marked the advent of a Ba'athist Arab nationalist regime.

(Enahoro) escaped to England; applied for writ of Habeas Corpus; lost in all the English courts; but this was a conditional undertaking about his being allowed to have British lawyers (in certain circumstances) to defend him. The Cabinet was much divided, but it [is] really a very serious issue, for Nigeria is the most friendly of all the African ex-colonies and I shd be sorry to have a quarrel with Abubakar (the P.M.) about this if it can honourably be avoided. The Ld Chancellor, the Attorney General, and the Home Secy have agreed a formula, which I have sent with instructions to Ld Head (High Commissioner in Lagos) to try with Abubakar[28] . . . .

9 March

. . . . Another 'spy' case – but (like the housemaid's baby) a very little one. A transport officer in Moscow, who manages the embassy cars etc, was caught by Russian police sleeping with a Russian woman – I imagine a decoy. He is a married man. The Russians tried to blackmail him, but he wisely informed the ambassador who sent him straight home[29] . . . .

The Gallup poll continues unfavourable. It seems that nearly half the Conservatives think that I should retire in favour of another leader. But it was rather a loaded question and I think the poll probably reflects the general discouragement of ordinary Conservatives . . . . [I]t is sobering to reflect how little gratitude there is in politics.

10 March (Sunday)

. . . . Read again (after reading Mr Young's biography) Blanche Dug-dale's 2 vol Life of A.Balfour. Altho' in reviewing the new biography the *Times Lit. Supp.* is very scornful of the old, I am bound to say that

---

28. Access to a British lawyer if Chief Anthony Enahoro was deported back to Nigeria was controversial in light of Nigeria's exclusion of E. F. N. Gratiaen and Sir Dingle Foot – the latter Labour MP for Ipswich – the previous year during a similar case. The deal then sought was that any British lawyers entitled to appear in Nigeria except these two could defend Enahoro before the Nigerian courts. Enahoro was a leading member of the Nigerian opposition who fled to the UK in 1962 when faced with trial for treason over an alleged coup attempt.

29. It is a sign of heightened sensitivities following Vassall that the Prime Minister noticed this. Ivor Rowsell was an MI6 officer who went on to run intelligence stations in Africa.

the new one draws very freely on its predecessor, adding (of course) to suit modern taste a lot of sex and scandal . . . .

11 March

. . . . We have a troublesome problem in Kenya, quite apart from the internal difficulties – KADU, KANU, and the Europeans.[30] The great Northern province consists of Somalis. Quite naturally, if British rule is to end, the Somalis want to join Somaliland. But the Kenya Africans object to this. In their view, nationalism is not for export. The Ethiopians object equally, as the Northern neighbours of a Somalia of wh. they are ancient and jealous enemies.[31] If the conquering Europeans brought a lot of problems to Africa, they are certainly destined to leave a lot behind. I am beginning to think that we ought to try to get the United Nations in on this problem before we hand over to an independent Kenya. If we do not, and war follows, either between Africans in Kenya, or Ethiopians, against the Somalis, we shall be accused of leaving as great a mess in E Africa as the Belgians left in the Congo . . . .

12 March

. . . . Sterling was weak yesterday and again this morning. A total loss of $100m in 2 days. But we must not take the orthodox methods. We must stand quite firm. Naturally, loss of confidence is bound to follow from an open correspondence in *The Times* and articles in all other papers about the advantages of 'floating' or 'devaluing'. How incredibly naïve the economists are! . . . .

Sterling was a little firmer at the close of the day, with some buying from New York. The rate ended at 2.80,[32] so one hopes that some of the 'spot' speculation got caught. The 'forward' rate is bad; the dollar

---

30. Apart from the political complication of a large settler population in Kenya, suspicion that the main nationalist party, KANU, was dominated by the Kikuyu and Luo tribes led to the formation of KADU.

31. British Somaliland had become independent on 26 June 1960 and on 1 July 1960 it united with newly independent Italian Somaliland. In the event irredentist Somali aspirations were decisively rejected by KANU.

32. Since 1949 the formal exchange rate had been £1 = $2.80, though in practice it could move a little around this peg level in daily quotations on the foreign markets. The day before, sterling had closed below par for the first time in months, though with some Bank of England intervention this was swiftly rectified.

premium increased. The Bank has spent £60m or so. What will happen tomorrow is anyone's guess, but the Bank hope that things will quieten down. There is no reason for all this – no technical reason. It is due to the economists – Harrod, Juliet Rhys Williams, [George] Schwar[t]z, Harold Wincott, [Nicholas] Kaldor, and all the rest of this motley crew.[33] Up to now the 64 thousand dollar question has been 'How to Boom without Busting'. With the help of the experts and *The Times* newspaper it seems that our immediate future may be to Bust without Booming.

D and I dined with the Churchills. I thought him much better than last time and his mind much clearer. He said of Lawrence (of Arabia) 'He was a remarkable man – and very conscious of it'. I asked him which office of all those he had held he preferred (other than PM) He said at once 'First Lord of the Admiralty'. He had read Beaverbrook's book on Lloyd George's fall and enjoyed the style and content. Clemmy Churchill (who hates Beaverbrook) thought it a horrible book. In spite of a terrible letter from Asquith to Beaverbrook (after L.G.'s fall) which ought not to have been printed, Lady Violet and Co are ecstatic about the book. So lasting is the feud.[34]

Lady Churchill talked about Mr [Kenneth] Young's new biography of Balfour. She did <u>not</u> believe that AJB lived in adultery with Lady Elcho. She did not think him capable of a 'grande passion'. She called AJB 'a cold fish' . . . .

13 March
Yesterday I saw Mr Merchant (State Dept) and Mr Finletter ([US ambassador to] NATO) – two serious but pleasant enough Americans.

---

33. Kaldor, an economic adviser to the Labour Party, had published a letter in *The Times* at the start of the month suggesting devaluation or floating sterling as a means to promote expansion. Maudling had made a similar argument to Macmillan at a meeting on 21 February. Macmillan had then countered that this could be seen as a gimmicky move towards monetary indiscipline. Contrary to Macmillan's implications here, Rhys Williams and Harrod (and Ralph Harris of the Institute of Economic Affairs) responded to Kaldor with letters to *The Times* on 4 March, arguing against devaluation on not dissimilar grounds. Schwartz was the senior City writer for the *Sunday Times*, and Wincott the editor-in-chief of *Investors Chronicle*.

34. Violet Bonham Carter's father Herbert Asquith was ousted from the premiership in December 1916 by fellow Liberal David Lloyd George. Beaverbrook had recently published *The Decline and Fall of Lloyd George*.

They came with ambassador Bruce about the 'multilateral NATO nuclear force'. The State Dept and the New Frontiersmen are very keen on this, chiefly to satisfy Germany and to depress the power of Britain.[35] (They have not forgiven me for my victory over the President at Nassau. They confidently hoped that by abandoning Skybolt they cd drive Britain out of the nuclear game. But Kennedy was really swayed both by argument and emotion) Happily, McNamara and the Defence Dept dislike both the State Dept (Rusk) and the New Frontiersmen (Rostow and Co) . . . .

14 March
. . . . 10.30–1.15. Cabinet. A long agenda, but the 'one Cabinet a week' certainly gets <u>more</u> not less business done,[36] and leads to more inter-departmental agreements, without reference to the Cabinet . . . .

15 March
A silly story about Vassall excited the House of Commons last night and the Press this morning. It was alleged that Vassall has given (to somebody) new and startling evidence – 'sensational'. Even papers like the *Yorkshire Post* gave front page headlines and long leading article to the nonsense. Of course, it was found on enquiry a) that Governor of Prison has reported Vassall's statement to Home Office b) H.O. to Attorney General c) A.G. to Lord Radcliffe. And all this <u>had</u> happened 6 weeks ago. We have put out the facts – but I have no doubt that the Press will ignore it (or print it small) and the BBC (who played it up high this morning) will ignore it. So low have the Press and the BBC sunk.

    After this episode, I was forced to spend a great deal of today over a silly scrape (women this time, thank God, not boys) into which one

---

35. Kennedy sent Merchant to Europe to promote this scheme in January. He wrote to Macmillan on 27 May, that it 'was primarily to respond to the pressure for MRBM deployment [especially from Germany] in a way that would avoid national manning and ownership of these strategic delivery systems that the MLF concept was first developed' (JFKL: NSF 174). The Pentagon did not share the State Department's enthusiasm for mixed-manned, nuclear-armed surface ships.

36. Prompted by a note from Hailsham on streamlining government in October 1962, the Cabinet agreed on 6 December 1962 to move to one Cabinet meeting a week, concentrating routine business instead into the main Cabinet committees.

of the ministers has got himself. It's Jack Profumo – SofS War.[37] It wd not matter so much if it was just an affair of morality. But unfortunately among the frequenters of this raffish and disreputable set which centres round Lord Astor (Bill Astor) was the Russian military attaché![38] This is the new Cliveden set![39] Jack Profumo was warned off this particular 'call girl' by MI[5], and laid off.[40] Unfortunately, some months later, the girl got into a criminal case. A negro tried to murder her, on the ground that she had given him a venereal disease! She disappeared, after selling her life story, all about the Russian military attaché and the British Secretary of State for War to the *Sunday Pictorial* for £1000![41] What adds a certain spice of humour to this degrading story is that I think our people (M.I.5) were hoping to use the lady to get intelligence out of the Russian.[42] Anyhow, the Russian officer has been recalled as a security risk, no doubt, from their angle . . . .

I have been for some time meditating a direct approach to President Kennedy about the Nuclear Test Ban negotiation wh has got hopelessly bogged down at Geneva . . . .

---

37. This is Macmillan's first mention of this affair in the diaries, the day the *Daily Express* suggested Profumo was about to resign. However, he knew of the rumours but accepted Profumo's denials when quizzed by the government law officers and Tim Bligh in early February.

38. In fact the assistant naval attaché, Yevgeny Ivanov, who was recalled to Moscow in January.

39. The society osteopath, Stephen Ward, was a tenant on Lord Astor's Cliveden estate. He brought Christine Keeler and her lover Ivanov there on the weekend of 8–9 July 1961. Profumo, a house guest at Cliveden, began his brief affair with Keeler then. Cliveden also gave its name to a group of aristocratic pro-appeasers before the Second World War.

40. Ward introduced Keeler to Ivanov and nursed hopes that she would acquire for him secrets about nuclear deals with West Germany to sell to the Soviets. Astor wrote to the Foreign Office about Ward's Russian connections on 2 August 1961. MI5 also were concerned and alerted Sir Norman Brook who – unbeknownst to Macmillan – warned Profumo on 8 August 1961 not to associate with Ward.

41. A jealous former lover, John Edgecombe, had shot at Keeler at the flat belonging to Stephen Ward she shared with Mandy Rice-Davies at 17 Wimpole Mews, Marylebone. Edgecombe was gaoled for seven years on 15 March. Keeler, meanwhile, sold her story to the *Sunday Pictorial*. They, fearing libel action, did not initially publish, but the substance of the story appeared on 8 March in Andrew Roth's *Westminster Confidential*.

42. They hoped he might defect.

20 March

.... Monday was an Irish day – Mr Lemass (P.M.) and Mr Aiken (Foreign Minister) at noon (for talk and luncheon) followed by dinner with them ....

The Irish story is a very queer one – perhaps one shd learn from it. Hundreds of years of bitter quarrels; a rather remarkable Anglo-Irish civilisation; British politics dominated (off and on) by Ireland for nearly a century; a bitter rebellion; partition (the only immediate solution to the Ulster problem) civil war among the natives following the complete surrender of the British – and now, peace – perfect peace. No one ever speaks or cares about Ireland. The Anglo-Irish gentry fish and hunt and play no role in the country. The English go to fish and hunt. The Irish 'rebels' now enjoy the most Conservative, clericalist, and reactionary Govt in Europe. The population has sunk to under 3 million. The Irish aren't even amusing any more (not a joke or an anecdote from any of the ministers or officials) The Prime Minister is a Jew;[43] the Foreign Minister (who was a distinguished gunman and is supposed to have shot more British officers and civilians – in the back – than anyone in the 'bad times') is a monetary expert, and discourses at length on everything from Keynes to Triffin. It is a queer evolution, from which no very clear moral can be drawn except perhaps that it [is] still more exciting and better for one's moral and intellectual health to travel than to arrive ....

Our political position (according to the Gallup poll) gets rather worse. We are 15 points behind the Socialists. The Liberals are losing to them and to us – but more to Labour, alas. However, there is still some time to go.

Among other meetings we had (on Monday after luncheon) a useful meeting of the 'steering committee'[44] of the Party. I see quite an attractive policy developing round the main theme 'modernising Britain' or 'Britain in Top Gear'. This must start with the Budget and the economic expansion. We are still aiming at about £260m new money, and the £90m or more wh. we have already put in. This will be by remission of taxation. £40m – Schedule A; £30m halving the Stamp Duty; £180m – reduction of Income Tax thro' revision of Allowances etc. This, with up to £30–£50[m] of new expenditure in Scotland, N.

---

43. Why Macmillan thought this is unclear. Lemass was in fact a somewhat unorthodox Catholic.

44. To prepare a manifesto for the next General Election.

East etc, added to what we have done since the autumn it gets fairly near to the £400m demanded by the National Economic group of something or other – experts [NEDC]!

Maurice M[acmillan] came to supper last night. We had a good talk about M&Co. He is just back from New York, where the St Martin's Press[45] has been in need of reorganisation. We have invested a lot of money in this venture and Maurice thinks that, with his new arrangements, we may be able to turn it into a sound concern. Then we talked about the organisation of the English business – Australia – India etc. Also about my brother Daniel. He is 77 and it is rather a problem for Maurice. Daniel ought really to retire.[46]

The 'Press' continue to be very hostile to the Govt. This is largely due to the Vassall case; the Tribunal; and the anxiety about what Lord Radcliffe will say. The imprisonment of the two reporters for contempt of court, for refusing to disclose to the Tribunal the source of their information (they clearly had none) has been treated by the Press (or most of it, with the honourable exception of the *Guardian* and to some extent *The Times*) as if these men were martyrs[47] . . . .

22 March
In the debate last night on the Nigerian Chief [Enahoro], both Brown (for Opposition) and Brooke made excellent speeches. Some of our party (those normally out for trouble with some conscientious souls as well) are worried and spoke against us. The A.G. wound up in an excellent speech. But the House seemed to avert its eyes from the true facts. If the Home Sec were to refuse to return this man under the 1881 [Fugitive Offenders] Act, Nigeria wd at once repudiate the Queen and the Commonwealth. Yet the Nigerian Lord Chief Justice has just been asked (and accepted) to join the Judicial Ctee of the Privy Council!

The Opposition had asked for the debate to take place on the 2nd Reading of the Consolidated Fund Bill, on which there can be no vote. I had assumed that this was because they realised the Commonwealth problem and wished to wound only. However, when they saw the

---

45. The American subsidiary.
46. The following month Maurice succeeded him as Chairman of M&Co.
47. On 7 March Brendan Mulholland (*Daily Mail*) and Reg Foster (*Daily Sketch*) were gaoled for refusing to reveal their sources for articles about Vassall's private life.

attitude of some Tory members, their hopes were excited and they demanded a continuation of the debate in conditions where a vote could be taken. So there will be a short debate – and a vote – on a quasi-'vote of censure' on Tuesday night. I think we shall just scrape through, but it may be a near thing.

Later in the debate (the Consolidated Fund Bill is 'excepted' business) attacks were made on a minister (unnamed) alleged to [be] mixed up in a rather squalid criminal case, about a black man who shot a 'model'.[48] 'Model' is the word wh. is nowadays used to describe a rather better class prostitute, usually (like Harriette Wilson) under the protection of one patron, but sometimes willing to distribute her favours more widely. It has been widely rumoured for some time that a Mr Ward (an osteopath, suspected of being a pimp) had this girl in his string, and that Bill Astor was mixed up with the affair (having given this Mr Ward a cottage at Cliveden) . . . . The girl, who should have appeared in the trial of the black man – another lover – for attempted murder, has disappeared. Bill Astor has also left the country. The old 'Cliveden' set was disastrous politically. The new 'Cliveden' set is said to be equally disastrous morally.

All this gossip, grossly exaggerated no doubt if not altogether untrue, has been circulating in the lobbies and the clubs for some months.

. . . . Conferences were held in the middle of last night and early this morning I was asked to approve a 'personal' statement after the House met (at 11am) today. I went thro' text with Attorney General and Chief Whip and went to the House to give Profumo my support. His statement was clear and pretty convincing . . . .

Profumo has behaved foolishly and indiscreetly, but not wickedly. His wife (Valerie Hobson) is very nice and sensible. Of course, these people live in a raffish, theatrical, bohemian society where no one really knows anyone and everyone is 'darling'.[49] But Profumo does not

---

48. Using parliamentary privilege Labour MP George Wigg raised this matter, alleging that the imprisonment of journalists deterred press reporting. This led Macmillan to the decision that Profumo should make a personal statement to the House on 22 March in which he denied any impropriety.

49. This was the excuse Profumo used for the appearance of this word in his letter to Keeler of 9 August 1961. At this time he ended the affair. Profumo's wife was an ex-actress.

seem to have realised that we have – in public life – to observe different standards from those prevalent today in many circles.

Luncheon for Winston Field, new P.M. of S. Rhodesia .... Winston Field defeated Sir Edgar Whitehead in December and so the party of Sir Roy Welensky. But he says he gets on well enough with Roy. Field says that the Federation can't go on – but I fancy that he is trying to avoid saying this openly himself and is trying to make us (HMG) say it for him .... I warned Field that Welensky might try a 'referendum' of his own (Federal) constituents, who are – in effect – the constituents of the S. Rhodesian Parlt. If the question were loaded, he might win a great majority and claim a success for himself and a defeat for Field. The S. Rhodesian P.M. seemed sceptical about this, tho' I thought he was somewhat alarmed. Of course, as Winston Field frankly said to me after luncheon, the S. Rhodesians want 'independence'. But when? Before Harold Wilson and Co are in power in UK, is (naturally enough) Mr Field's demand ....

24 March

.... Michael and Pamela Berry; Oliver and Lady Poole to luncheon. A very pleasant party – the Berrys outwardly very pleasant and very loyal!

Oliver stayed on (his wife had her own car) till 6pm, talking about politics, the Party and future prospects .... We talked about the Chairmanship of the Party. He thinks Iain Macleod good and representative of the right ideas .... He feels he shd either go on till the General Election, or perhaps have a change in mid-summer. He liked my idea for a change to someone not a politician; not in the Cabinet; not a rival for the throne when it becomes vacant. He accepted that this might mean him. If I want him, he will serve. This is very satisfactory.

Finished Wheeler-Bennett's *Nemesis of Power*.[50] It is a terrifying book and everyone in politics or F.O. ought to read it again every year. Will the Germans be democrats for long? .... My fear is that unless we can satisfy them by a general Test Ban Treaty with a treaty against the spreading [of] nuclear weapons (a non-dissemination treaty) the Germans are bound to become a nuclear power sooner or later. The 'multilateral force' agreed at Nassau will perhaps do something to satisfy them. Or may it only whet their appetite?

---

50. A history of the German army 1918–45, published by M&Co in 1954.

How vast these problems are, compared with all the minor issues on which elections are won or lost!

25 March

.... Mr Kaunda and Mr Nkumbula to luncheon – African leaders of the two parties which form a coalition Govt in Northern Rhodesia[51] .... After luncheon poor Rab had his meeting with them. They demanded immediate acceptance of 'secession'. When he demurred to this, they walked out ....

Read a [newly published] little book on theology by the Bishop of Woolwich called *Honest to God*. Orthodox people think it heretical. Bp of Southwark (who sent it to me) thinks it 'sincere and "challenging"' (which it is) Archbp of Canterbury is disturbed. Will it be another Bishop Colenso case?[52] I reserve judgment till I have perhaps read it again. I liked the opening chapters, but was repelled by some of the looseness of thought as the book went on.

We have the final debate and vote on Chief Enahoro (the Nigerian who is to be sent back for trial) tomorrow night. Much to my disgust, the Nigerians have chosen this moment to give notice that [they] will become a Republic in October.

27 March

Yesterday afternoon certainly proved a very bad day. It started well. My PQs were not embarrassing. Ted Heath's statement on NATO went well enough. I was very nervous about the F.O. draft, wh. I insisted on altering to make it quite clear that we had no commitment of any kind – esp. financial – to the so-called 'multi-manned' nuclear force. However, neither Wilson or Brown knew the first thing about Nassau and its implications and Brown floundered badly ....

At 5 a difficult discussion with ministers and officials about Govt

---

51. Kaunda split from Harry Nkumbula's African National Congress in 1958 and the following year the United National Independent Party was formed. The latter formed a coalition with Nkumbula's smaller party following the 1962 elections until their triumph in the January 1964 pre-independence poll.

52. In his 1860s writings John Colenso, first Bishop of Natal, questioned the historical accuracy of the Bible and doctrines such as eternal punishment, provoking ecclesiastical conflict in both Britain and South Africa. The furore over Bishop Robinson's calls for a new image of God a century later was relatively short-lived. Mervyn Stockwood, the Socialist Bishop of Southwark who sent Macmillan the book, was both Robinson's boss and supporter.

offices. The F.O. ought to be pulled down and rebuilt. But in what style? Conventional (and bad) or modern (and a risk – perh bad, perhaps v. good) I want a glass tower; but no one agrees.

At 10.10pm .... the adjourned debate was resumed about Ena-horo. I need not describe (for it is in all the Press this morning) the scene of confusion wh. arose from a sudden new hare started – without notice – by George Brown. It was a very complicated and subtle legal point wh. somebody on the Opposition side had thought up, wh. suggested that a charge under a clause in the Penal Code wh. allowed 7 years imprisonment, by some cross-reference or twist of words cd be held to imply or allow a death penalty. Naturally, when Brown produced this, neither Home Secy nor Attorney General cd give a definite opinion as to the validity or otherwise of this legal point. After some wrangling, I felt the only thing to do was to move the adjourn-ment and say that we had no intention of returning this man to stand trial on a capital offence nor had Nigerian Govt any wish to try him on this basis. It was a bad result for us and seemed a success for Opposition ....

After the adjournment of the House, a long meeting in my room .... What sufferings we go thro' to try to keep the Commonwealth together ....

28 March
Cabinet. The Rhodesian problem was the chief item. Things are mov-ing to a climax. It is an extraordinarily complex situation. The Northern Rhodesian situation is fairly simple. They want the 'right to secede' to be granted. On that basis, they are willing to come to a conference to discuss the links between the territories, chiefly economic, which shd follow the dissolution of the Federation. They recognise that the process of disentanglement will take perhaps a year ....

The Southern Rhodesia position is more complex. They have had independence – in effect – for 40 years, except for defence and Foreign Policy .... As a result, they have had no African representatives in their Parliament up till a year ago, when Whitehead – under great pressure from Sandys – agreed to 15 Africans, elected on a very restricted franchise .... Whitehead was pledged to remove discrimi-nation, even – vital test – in land. He had begun the process. Field and his party are reversing all this. For the moment there is a strange kind of alliance between Field and Kaunda (or Banda) They want to end

Federation. But there is, now that the die is cast, likely to be an alliance between Welensky and Field. Southern Rhodesia demands (with a certain show of reason) that if the Federation is to break up, S. Rhodesia also must be independent, and Welensky will support this claim. Actually, HMG have no physical power to take any part in the affair. But we have a legal position and some moral influence. S. Rhodesia is a Government of several million Africans by 200000 whites, among whom the planter interest predominates. Are we to give this country, with this constitution and now under Field (a reactionary, almost a fascist) instead of Whitehead (a gentleman and a liberal) formal independence (and, presumably, financial help) If we do, we shall be blamed by all progressive and even moderate opinion. If we do not, we shall do no benefit to the Africans and we shall force S[outhern] R[hodesia] into the hands of S. Africa. This will mean a 'bloc' of white power from the Cape to the Zambesi . . . .

. . . . At 4pm Rab came, with his chief assistant Mr Tennant. We worked away at . . . . a great number of possible drafts. Finally we came to the simplest, embodying the principle that no country or territory can be kept in any association 'against its will'. (This means 'the right of secession') On this formula, Kaunda (N. Rhodesia) will come to the Conference; Winston Field will only come if independence of S. Rhodesia is granted or at least accepted now. Welensky will get in a rage and refuse everything.

Cabinet at 10pm in HofC. For two hours the Central African question was discussed. There was universal approval for accepting 'the right to secede', in spite of what must follow. There was a very strong disinclination to accept independence at this stage, either for Northern or for Southern Rhodesia. I felt that the Cabinet in this were slightly ostrich-like. They think that the question can be postponed for a year or more. I doubt this.

30 March

. . . . [D]raft telegrams to President K[ennedy] about the Test Ban agreement. I have had a reply (rather a disappointing one) about this, altho' we know (from certain sources) that the Russians may be ready to move from 3 inspections to 5.[53] The Americans want 7 (originally 20) I fear that the political forces which restrain the President are again centred in reactionary Democratic Senators . . . .

---

53. The Russians had on 19 December 1962 offered three inspections per year.

. . . . [T]elegrams to and from Nigeria about Enahoro. The Nigerians are deeply offended by attitude of HofC, and I fear a breach. They threaten (<u>not</u> Abubakar but unofficially) either to leave the Commonwealth or to break off diplomatic relations with U.K. . . . . The Opposition are behaving quite irresponsibly . . . .

1 April

Defence Committee at 11. We decided that we cd not now get out of the NATO commitment to keep 55,000 men in Germany. We decided to give our 'support' to the President's 'multi-manned' nuclear ships (while secretly hoping the scheme wd fall through!) But we wd argue with McNamara about his absurd idea of <u>doubling</u> the continental forces (another 30 divisions!) We can do this safely, because it has no real connection with the Nassau agreement. I am very anxious to get the 'technical' agreement signed, before bringing too much pressure on Washington on other issues . . . .

6–8pm. Cabinet on Southern Rhodesia's request for 'Independence' . . . . The younger men are shocked at the idea of agreeing to independence in view of the lack of representation of Africans. Curiously, I don't think the electorate are much interested. Broadly, the lower classes dislike the 'blacks' – the intellectuals etc like them. But there is a sort of guilty conscience (slavery; colonialism etc) all through the country . . . .

10 April

. . . . [T]here was the annual 1922 Committee luncheon, at the Savoy. It was an occasion of special importance for me, for <u>two</u> reasons. 1) After all the rough weather of the last year or more, can I claim that we are moving into better weather conditions. Shall I put all doubts at rest, and announce my determination to continue as P.M. and to lead the Party in the next General Election. 2) The luncheon was to be the occasion for presenting me with a picture of quite remarkable interest and importance. It represents (the artist Mr Thompson RA) the interior of the HofC on the debate on the Address in 1960 – I am speaking; Maurice [Macmillan] (who moved the Address) is behind me. Sir Winston in his corner; Gaitskell rising slightly to intervene . . . . After discussion earlier with Chief Whip, I announced my intention (D.V.) of leading the Party in the next Election.

At 4pm I rose to speak on the Enahoro debate. The speech as it stood on Tuesday evening did <u>not</u> satisfy me. Too many lawyers and

officials had had a hand in it . . . . At 3am, I decided how the speech
shd be rearranged and re-developed. I finished at about 5am. The boys
finished it (with some more dictation) in the morning and the 'young
ladies' copied it all out with great skill and speed. In a House wh. was
on the whole hostile, and where even our most loyal members (on our
side) needed strengthening and their doubts removed, it was an exercise
such as is only too rare in our debates. One had to try to persuade the
waverers.

The speech was thought to be very good by all – opponents,
doubtful and supporters. Some said it was the most effective speech
wh. I had ever made in the HofC. Anyway, I think it did some good.
It was a worthy debate. Brown followed me – the second half of his
speech was excellent. A Tory M.P. (Dudley Smith) made an eloquent
plea to release the Chief whom he claimed as a constituent (This
seemed rather obscure – I think he meant was arrested in his constituency – his bird, as it were) and voted against us. We had 40 abstentions
(20 or so abstaining from voting, about 20 by absence) We had a 2
line, not a 3 line 'Whip', wh. was wise. By this means we got our
normal majority (56). With a 3 line whip we shd not have got more –
perhaps less – and the injurious effect wd have been worse. Henry
Brooke wound up effectively, with a dignified, firm, and impressive
speech. John Strachey (who wound up for Opposition) was persuasive
and damaging to our cause. However, considering what we expected
only a day or two ago – a negligible majority or a defeat – I am much
relieved. The Whips did a wonderful job. All 'reliable' people (including ministers) were treated as if it had been a 3 line whip. Otherwise,
we wd have fallen to a very low figure.

Had the worst happened, I don't think we cd have got away with
a 'Vote of Confidence' the next day. After all, this was a vote of
censure,[54] not a defeat on some amendment or other or a chance vote.
I should have had to resign as P.M. (and, of course, Henry Brooke as
Home Secy) Whether the Queen wd have sent at once for Wilson, I am
not sure. She might perhaps have thought it within her rights to try
another Conservative. But this wd have put her in a difficult decision,
and the Opposition might have had good ground to resent her
action . . . .

---

54. On a motion by Brown protesting against the refusal of political asylum to
    Enahoro.

11 April

.... The negotiation with Ld Poole about becoming joint Chairman of the Party with Iain Macleod is almost reaching finality. The question of agreeing their respective functions was discussed at some length – I finally got away from London about 10pm ....

16 April

Motored to London, arriving 10.15. A talk with Home Secy about this tiresome 'leak' on Civil Defence, and the printing of the pamphlet by CND and the Ctee of 100, wh. purports to reveal the various Civil Defence measures, including the Regional HQs. It is not very serious from a practical point of view, but it's another security failure of the Govt, and the Press – smarting under Vassall – has grasped eagerly at a new chance of attacking me and the Home Secy ....

Ernest Marples, Minister of Transport, came at 3 and stayed till 5. He is really a remarkable figure and I only wish we had more ministers with his imagination and thoroughness. We talked about Railways, Roads, Ports and Docks, and whole plans for Transport in the future. In 10 years, we have gone from 2 million to 6 million motor cars. In another 10 years, we may [go] to twelve and eventually to 18 million cars! What must we do now to prepare not so much the roads between the towns, but the towns themselves to prepare for these developments.[55]

Next – Shipping and Shipbuilding. Our plans are rather stuck – and we must decide – yes or no – whether we are going to have a plan for scrapping and building, involving a temporary subsidy. The Treasury; the Bd of Trade; and Minister of Labour (for some queer reason) are trying to 'stall' on this. I sent round minutes demanding early decision. Ernest observed to me how queer it was that I spent my time urging ministers forward. He wd have thought I wd be restraining them. So it wd be – if they were 'sword men' and not 'gown men'.

We discussed how the Beeching principle might be applied to Government as a whole![56] It is, of course, true that we have not adapted the ministry, Parliament, and the Civil Service to the new

---

55. This was addressed in the 1963 report *Traffic in Towns*, which also pointed out there were already 10.5 million cars in Britain.

56. Beeching's report *The Reshaping of British Railways*, published on 27 March, proposed rationalisation of the network – including controversial line closures – to establish the railways on a sounder financial basis.

situation – when any Government – Socialist or Conservative – is
forced to take a hand in almost every aspect of commercial and
industrial life . . . .

17 April
. . . . The Civil Defence affair looks like developing to a disagreeable
position for the Govt. Unluckily, it is the Home Office who are made
to look ridiculous and poor Henry Brooke, for all his many virtues,
can be 'guyed' rather easily. It seems that the 'leak' was due to one of
the 'pacifists' posing as a *Daily Mail* reporter, [who] got all this
information (wh. in any case the Press shd not have been given) out of
the Home Office officials themselves . . . .

19 April
. . . . At 4.30, Sir Laurence Helsby to see me. We have caught a spy (or
rather a man 'getting ready to spy' – buying equipment etc) He is an
employee of Euratom, doing 'liaison' with the Atomic Energy Authority. I hope an arrest can be made next week, when the man is expected
to return from a trip abroad. It will be rather delicate with the Euratom
authorities but rather a triumph for the security service. For once, we
have 'got' a man <u>before</u> he has done us any injury . . . .

23 April
. . . . A very interesting talk with Harriman, who arrived yesterday,
on his way to Moscow. Ostensibly going about Laos, he shd be able
to get Kruschev talking about Test Ban. Averell Harriman is <u>anti-
Pentagon</u> and an enthusiastic supporter of my view about both the
feasibility and vital importance of an early agreement. The President is
nervous about the Senate. Averell thinks that the overwhelming enthusiasm of the American <u>people</u> wd force the hands of the <u>politicians</u>. It
is very encouraging to have people like Harriman around – liberal,
enthusiastic, a good negotiator, and very youthful for his age . . . .

24 April
I slept very badly – rare with me, but for some reason not quite so rare
as formerly. The weather is good and shd be fine for Princess Alexandra's
wedding. She is – and deservedly – a great favourite of the people. The
streets are full – and many have been up all night to secure a good place.
This loyalty is always forthcoming towards any members of the Royal
Family who 'give' as well as 'take'. Hence the Queen Mother's popularity.

The Press today gives a good account of question time yesterday on 'Spies for Peace'.[57] *Daily Telegraph* said 'Composure unshaken. Damaging Counter-attack. Twenty minutes of cross-examination in wh. Mr Harold Wilson came to the assistance of Mr George Brown, deputy leader and laid himself open to damaging counter-attack, failed to shake the PM's composure'. This is significant. Some weeks ago, however well I had handled a question or a debate, the *D.T.* wd not have admitted it. I notice a change in the Press generally, beginning to show itself. The *Daily Express* may start to come round as the Election gets nearer. The *Daily Mail* is very angry about the Vassall case (where its reporter was revealed to be a pretty poor type and is now languishing in prison) Also, the *D. Mail* is in a managerial crisis. The editor, Hardcastle, has been dismissed – circulation is falling. This is a pity, for [George] Murray (the leader-writer) is one of the ablest journalists in Fleet Street. I hope he will remain . . . .

6 May

. . . . Motored up this morning to Victoria Station, to meet President of Cameroons and his party. They did not appear very gracious – the glum, not the smiling type of African. The Pres[iden]t has already made trouble about his rooms at the Dorchester. They were not grand enough and the protocol dept of the F.O. committed the cardinal error of putting his wife, and not his mistress, in the adjoining bedroom. The wife has been sent to the floor above . . . .

Mr McEwen, Australian Minister, and second in command to Bob Menzies came to luncheon. He is a tough bargainer (as we found during the Commonwealth Conference last summer and throughout the Brussels negotiations) But he is able and has learnt something in recent years. He explained that Australia wanted all that she cd get on the agricultural front. Australia was not an exporter of industrial goods. But she must increase – under high protection tariffs – her industrial population and production. An increase in her population (and an increase was vital for political and defence reasons) must be absorbed in the factories and not on the land. He proposed further (apart from special arrangements during the Kennedy round for Australia)[58] that the chief industrial exporting nations, rather than let the

---

57. The civil defence disclosures.
58. The US Trade Expansion Act 1962 paved the way for a new 'Kennedy' round of GATT negotiations to cut most tariffs in half, break farm-trade restrictions,

Kennedy round be held up by the intransigeance of the European 6, or break down on the agricultural issue, should get together and negotiate a 50% tariff cut to each other, leaving others to come along later. He admitted that this wd really be contrary to GATT principle and practice. But he cd see no other way out. He is to talk further with Pres[iden]t of B of Trade this afternoon and during the next few days, before GATT starts . . . .

For Secy at 3pm. Jordan seems a trifle calmer, but we agreed a directive for our talks in Washington. What I fear most is the fall of King Hussein (by treason, murder, or subversion) followed by an immediate move by Israel to seize Jerusalem and advance to the left bank of the Jordan.

We discussed the Wynne case and how to handle it. The Russians are throughly alarmed at the degree to which their system has been penetrated by the British and American intelligence.

Dinner and reception for the 'Cameroonians' – on familiar lines. They were not very gracious, but as they are hardly civilised one must be patient. I thought the President himself held moderate and sensible views about Africa and 'Freedom' . . . .

7 May

. . . . Speech on Vassall – 37 minutes – quiet but (I think) dignified. The House listened very well and seemed – on all sides – to like it. Wilson failed – too clever and too cheap. Ian Gilmour made a brilliant maiden speech . . . .

Long discussions with my secretaries and Chief Whip about another 'scandal' wh. threatens to 'break'. I trust it may not, but it is well to be prepared[59] . . . .

9 May

. . . . 5–7.30. Talk with Foreign Secy and Defence Minister on a number of very tricky problems with wh. the Americans are presenting us. They are trying to force us to contribute to the 'multi-lateral' force of surface ships with Polaris missiles. But we are already spending an immense sum on our own Polaris submarines. Nor does anyone (except

---

reduce non-tariff barriers and aid developing countries. Negotiations did not formally start until 1964 and concluded in 1967.

59. Stephen Ward had that day been to see Tim Bligh, saying that Profumo's denials were untrue.

the Germans) really want this force, its 'control' is unsettled, including the vital question 'who controls the missile war-heads'. The German General Staff no doubt sees in this plan a way to get into the nuclear business. I agreed, at Nassau, to this plan in principle. But I never undertook to contribute to it.

There has been rather a 'dusty' answer' from Mr Kruschev on the Test Ban. But I don't want the Americans to take his long letter as a definite rejection. We must consider the next step most carefully in the light of it and whatever interpretation we may put on it. I have sent a message to the President urging him to say nothing about the reply at present. When it becomes known that we have received it, we shd say that we are studying it . . . .

10 May

We have had a great defeat in the Local Elections, losing over 500 seats in the boroughs. Even in Bromley, we did badly. However, it is too soon to analyse what it means electorally. I fear it shews that (in spite of improving Gallup polls) we are still in a low position. The rise of the Liberals seems to be checked (except in Bromley, where they now control my two best Conservative wards.) How far this wd affect a General Election, one cannot tell. But it is all rather depressing.

The usual sort of day. We work away, with unsparing efforts, at insoluble problems, and get no thanks from the great British public! . . . . 11.45. Ld Carrington; Mr Galbraith; Chief Whip; Attorney General. Lord Poole. Shall the ministers sue the offending newspapers or not. The result of the Tribunal and the debate on Vassall had to be awaited.[60] It was agreed that the ministers who had been libelled did <u>not</u> want damages. But they should demand an apology and payment of the expenses they had incurred – something between £6000 and £8000 a piece . . . .

3.30. Ld Dalhousie – on retirement as Governor General of Federation.[61] He gave a tragic account of the failure of the Federation, chiefly due to the wave of African nationalism which cannot be resisted or stemmed . . . .

---

60. The Radcliffe Tribunal exonerated both Carrington and Galbraith in the Vassall case, and the latter was restored to the government on 3 May.
61. Lord Dalhousie had been Governor-General of the Federation of Rhodesia and Nyasaland since 1957.

20 May

The last few days have been even more hectic than usual. First, we have had the Belgian Royal visit – Victoria Station; Royal Banquet at Belgian embassy. The more unlucky of my colleagues got stuck for 3 hours at Mansion House and Guildhall in addition. D. went to the Ballet at Covent Garden, in Royal box. I was prevented by yet another flare up about the Nigerian Chief in the H of Commons – an adjournment motion, weakly granted by our weak Speaker . . . .

The King and Queen were very well received and seemed to enjoy themselves. Dear Ld Mountbatten was torn between his royal and his defence duties. He is awfully nice and very intelligent – but he is really rather silly sometimes. He is very interested in genealogy, and has written a long book to prove all his own. He claims descent from most of the great figures of mediaeval chivalry, including the Black Prince. This has caused much amusement. The Dowager [Duchess of] Devonshire told me that a saying was current in Court circles to the effect that 'the origin of the Battenburg family is lost in the mist of the early nineteenth century'.

Dicky sent a copy of his book to John Wyndham, calling attention to a common ancestor in the 14th century. John characteristically replied that there must be some mistake, since his own great-grandfather had been a bastard.

In addition to the usual engagements, luncheons, interviews, speech-writing etc etc, we have had 3 days of really concentrated work . . . . The two great questions have been 1) Kruschev's reply to President/P.M. letter on nuclear tests. 2) U.S. proposal for so-called 'multi-manned' force . . . .

. . . . David Gore has been quite invaluable. He has established a remarkable position with Kennedy, an intimate and trusted friend. It is most fortunate – and almost unprecedented – for a British ambassador to have this position and is based on old pre-war friendships between various Kennedys and Cavendishes and Gores . . . .

By Sunday night, I was able to compose two replies to the President's two letters. On the first, I have strongly urged him not be discouraged by the rather negative side of Kruschev's reply to our letter. It does not, in spite of all the rather specious and irritating arguments, reject our main proposal – viz. To send two high-powered emissaries, known to be in our special confidence, to Moscow to carry on the talk and see whether we can somehow get closer together. The

Americans will not like this – but David Gore is confident that the Pres[iden]t will agree – if only to please me. (Incidentally, this makes rather nonsense of the mischievious line taken by the *Times* correspondent and exploited vilely by the *Sunday Mirror* yesterday. [Louis] Heren, *The Times* man, is a <u>very</u> bad man. He was mischievous in Singapore and in Bonn and now in Washington. The story is that the President has 'snubbed' me – cannot get on with an old Edwardian like me, and longs for Harold Wilson.[62] Incidentally, *The Times* withdraws today – after Heren had been sent for by the White House and reprimanded. But Crossman's story in the *Mirror* will never be disbelieved and will do great harm. Perhaps when Pres[iden]t actually announces his invitation to stay a day at Birch Grove, the truth will be believed. (Altho' mischievous people will say that he has yielded to my entreaties.)

On the 'multi-manned' fleet of 25 ships, with 200 Polaris missiles, to which we are asked to contribute 20% of [the] cost, the other chief subscribers being the Germans, the Italians, and the Americans, I have told the President frankly that I cannot do more than discuss it fully with Cabinet as a whole when Ld Home gets back – tomorrow week – from Ottawa, where the NATO meeting is taking place. I have every hope that <u>our</u> plan – the inter-allied nuclear force, to consist of what each of us has now or is likely to get – will be accepted at NATO. This will carry out our undertakings at Nassau – and, of course, we have now the full Polaris agreement with the Americans duly signed and sealed.[63]

Apart from the money – which in view of our tremendous commitments for overseas defence we cannot afford – our own defence advisers regard the surface fleet as a ridiculous idea. The ships are to be unarmed. What then about escorts? Or if they are to be armed, the cost will be increased enormously. They will be vulnerable. They add nothing useful to the power of the West. It is purely a <u>political</u> idea to try to keep the Germans from the temptation to break their Treaty and go in for their own nuclear arm or join the French in one. It must be judged on this basis. Yet, it will be difficult to defend in Parlt if all the

---

62. In contrast, Ormsby-Gore wrote to Macmillan on 22 March about Wilson's impending visit to Washington: 'I have noted a marked lack of enthusiasm for the visit among the Administration. Unfortunately those who have already met him dislike him, and those that have not distrust him' (TNA: PREM 11/4331).

63. Completed on 6 April 1963.

defence experts are known to be agst the plan. The only thing to do now, I have decided, is to play for time. The Cabinet has not yet discussed this, but the senior ministers are divided. For Secy, mildly in favour; Ld Privy Seal strongly in favour; M of Defence and Chancellor of Exr strongly against.

. . . . In the afternoon and early evening, the Rhodesias. We are soon going to move to a crisis on this. Butler (and to a lesser extent Home) wd favour giving independence to S. Rhodesia in return for an almost formal bow towards the principle of African advance. Sandys and Macleod will oppose this violently, as destructive of the Commonwealth (Australia, N. Zealand and Canada will be almost as critical of S. Rhodesians as the new Commonwealth countries) Ld Chancellor will take a middle position. But apart from our internal political differences, in the Cabinet and in the Party, the reality is that we shall either keep S. Rhodesia in the Commonwealth or lose at least all the African countries . . . .

The Indonesians are going to seize Shell.[64] £50m gone in a day. There is, it seems, no remedy, except war. The Americans don't mind. [The] American Administration cannot face a 'Suez' and American (local) oil companies will be quite pleased. What will happen when Venezuela goes Communist and seizes all the American plants and concessions? . . . .

It is sometimes strange to contrast the popular idea (as set out in the Press) of my life and work, my hopes and fears, with the reality. The British public seems to be becoming more and more cynical and satirical. I read a most depressing account, based on question and answer, of what the young intelligensia are supposed to be thinking. The number questioned was 7000 or so; the questions very detailed and very well devised. Religion, morality, patriotism, honour, all these are at a discount. Envy (altho' concealed) is a strong emotion, and a rather doleful highbrow concept of a good time. How to appeal to this type is not an easy problem to resolve. I have meanwhile worked further on a rather dull speech to the Conservative women for Thursday, on what the 'intellectuals' will, I fear, regard as very orthodox lines . . . .

---

64. Foreign oil companies, including the Anglo-Dutch Shell and (as Macmillan subsequently realised) American firms, were required to replace their concessions with production-sharing contracts.

22 May

I gave an interview a few weeks ago to Jocelyn Stephens, of the *Queen* magazine. This weekly illustrated journal has made considerable progress, and has taken the place of the *Tatler* and *Bystander* and *Sketch* on one side, but on another has gone in for being representative of 'Bright Young People' of the intelligensia and not merely of the rich. It is satirical, destructive, and often offensive. Lately, however, it has swung back to a more friendly tone. This article is appearing in this week's issue of the *Queen* (which has of course only a limited circulation) but has been used extensively (without my permission but greatly to Mr Stephens' pecuniary and my political profit) in today's *Daily Mirror*. It is <u>really</u> friendly – tho' rather 'shy-making'. The Central Office wd have had to pay a lot to get anything of the kind! So, altho' it is rather against the grain to have all these personal matters published, I think that there is great gain . . . .

23 May

. . . . Another row has boiled up in the House about Chief Enahoro and the refusal of the Nigerian Govt to allow Dingle Foot to go to Nigeria. Home Secy (Brooke) is accused of 'duplicity' and a vote of censure on him has been put down. It will be debated on Monday and we shall have a rough time. He has not (to tell the truth) managed this affair very well. But the Opposition has behaved disgracefully, without any regard to Nigerian susceptibilities or Commonwealth interests . . . .

25 May

Dress rehearsal of Trooping [the Colour] – I watched it from the drawing room window at Admiralty House. A very pretty sight – a sort of military ballet.

In the evening, I went to and spoke at the Grenadier Guards Old Comrades Ass[ociation] Jubilee Dinner. The Colonel of the Regt (General Adair) and lots of officers, warrant officers, NCO[s] and guardsmen. Lot of old Guardsmen of all ranks. The 'Connaught Rooms' packed to overflowing. The Band. Cornet solo. Everything splendidly done, in a most Grenadierly way. One man, in Chelsea Pensioner uniform, was in my platoon at Loos! . . . .

27 May

. . . . An hour with Dr Hallstein (of the European Commission) – as pleasant, and (I wd think) as fundamentally unreliable as ever.

Henry Brooke came at noon for a talk about the [Enahoro] debate. I think his speech is a good one. His case is intrinsically sound, but very easy to attack in a plausible way. For there are niceties and even subtleties in our case; these can be made to seem intentional exceptions. However, as it turned out, Harold Wilson (who moved the motion at 7pm) made a mess of it. He got his vital facts completely wrong, and cd as easily be accused of 'misleading' the House as the Home Secy. Henry Brooke's speech was good, and received reasonably quietly. I thought the Opposition knew in their hearts that poor Henry wd never try to deceive any one. He is a man of patent honesty and sincerity, not for nothing a grandson of Stopford Brooke.[65]

Fortunately for me, instead of putting up Soskice to wind up (who wd have made a quiet and persuasive speech, difficult to answer in detail and understating rather than exaggerating the case) they put up Brown (who ranted) Brown's speech was so outrageous and vulgar that it enabled me to throw away my speech, and make a sort of rabble-rousing wind-up in the old style. Our chaps were delighted, and as a result we got a majority of 88! We had one abstention (Legge-Bourke, who is honest but touched in the head) and one against (Jenkins, who is a rascal)

28 May
. . . . Cabinet at 11.30. We agreed to accept a compromise with the President about 'The Air Umbrella' for India.[66] It will be a 'training' scheme, to help train the Indian Air Force and to acclimatise our own visiting squadrons to the terrain. It will <u>not</u> be played up. But it <u>will</u> lead the Indians away from 'non-alignment' and the Chinese <u>will</u> notice what is happening. There will be <u>no commitment</u> on either side, of any kind and this will be made clear. With some reluctance, Cabinet agreed and I have sent a message to President K[ennedy] accordingly. I am rather glad to have something on wh. to <u>agree</u> with the Americans, as we are bound to have trouble about the multi-lateral nuclear fleet . . . .

---

65. Stopford Brooke was a notable nineteenth-century clergyman who left the Church of England in 1880 and drifted towards Unitarianism. His grandson was much more conventionally Anglican.

66. An idea Macmillan broached with Kennedy in January, to take advantage of Indian concerns following the recent Indo-Chinese war to extend air defence to India.

29 May

. . . . I have now agreed with Pres[iden]t Kennedy the terms of our joint reply to Mr K[hrushchev]. We are rebutting some of his arguments, but (I hope) not in an arrogant or provocative way. But we <u>are</u> welcoming his willingness to receive our 'two emissaries' to discuss the Test Ban with him. The letter will be delivered on Friday, but I will announce our agreement to send the joint reply at Question Time tomorrow.

30 May

I have two 'security' troubles. The first is not too bad but may become a nuisance. It concerns Philby, once employed by F.O. (in war and immediately after) who was suspected of being the 'Third Man' who gave the tip-off to Burgess and Maclean . . . . Some months ago he disappeared, leaving his wife and children. She has now come to England and we hope (since she is American by birth) that we can persuade her to return to U.S. His disappearance caused a flurry but the Press (since dog does not eat dog) kept fairly quiet. We now know that he (Philby) is in Russia. When this news comes out (if it does) there will be a new row.

The second matter is more serious. The case of Mr Ward (who got Profumo into trouble) is being pursued actively by Harold Wilson, Wigg and one or two of that ilk. Wilson has sent me some so-called evidence that Ward was a spy or agent of the Russians. (The security people do not believe this, but believe that he was a pimp, not a spy) Wilson came to see me on a fishing expedition on Monday. He is clearly not going to leave this alone. He hopes, under pretence of security, to rake up a 'sex' scandal, and to involve ministers, and members of 'the upper classes' in a tremendous row, wh. will injure the 'establishment'.[67] Wilson, himself a blackmailing type, is <u>absolutely</u> untrustworthy. No one has ever trusted him without being betrayed (This is the line of Gaitskell's friends, including his widow) I have asked the Lord Chancellor to look into all the available evidence about the Ward case and advise me about what, if anything, should be done.

5–6. Mr Krishnamachari (Indian Minister of Defence.) I explained

---

67. A term popularised and generalised following its initial use by Henry Fairlie in 1955 to describe the closing of ranks by social and political elites following the defection to Russia of Burgess and Maclean.

to him the US/UK scheme for sending squadrons to India and to train
Indian pilots. He quite understood the reasons for the plan and the
wisdom (from his point of view as well as from ours) of 'playing' it
publicly in the way I had suggested. There wd be <u>no</u> commitment on
either side as a result. Mr K. cd not resist a long denunciation both of
the Pakistanis and of the Chinese. He classed them together, more or
less, in his mind as dangerous. But of the Pakistanis he spoke contemptuously; of the Chinese, with real fear. Actually, as he began to cool
down, he admitted that there was now a growing body of opinion in
India in favour of a settlement of their differences with Pakistan. But
he hinted that no progress cd be made now and that the best hope was
to keep negotiations strung out as long as possible, with the hope of
tensions being reduced. The settlement wh. Pakistan has made about
their frontier with China has been bitterly resented in India.[68] Mr K.
thought Burma very weak. The 2nd in command to the Marshal who
now governs Burma is 'sold out' to China and is a Communist. The
whole position in SE Asia is very bad. Indonesia will make trouble,
and the other states are weak.

4 June (Tuesday)

.... We have had 4 lovely days – perfect weather, sunshine all the
time, and the long evenings still and warm. A little golf .... a drive to
the ski-lift in the Cairngorms and a ride up in the 'chair', with a
marvellous view at the top; a lucky visit to see the (very rare) osprey's
nest, guarded day and night by the bird-watchers .... no messages,
except about the poor Pope [John XXIII], who died last night. He
has gone very quickly, since my last talk with him – in February.
He has done a fine piece of work in 4 years, both for the Roman
Church and for the Christian world ....

Today we motored to Oban, from Nairn, taking pic-nic luncheon. We stayed with Colonel and Mrs Campbell Preston (she being a
sister of Lord Cowdray) We arrived about tea-time to their house –
Ardchattan Priory, Connel ....

7 July

One of the difficulties of keeping a diary is that during a real crisis, it

---

68. In March Pakistan ceded Kashmiri land claimed by India, the Shaksam valley,
    to China.

37. The newly-knighted Sir David Ormsby-Gore leaving Victoria Station, London with wife Sylvia and children (from left) Alice, Francis and Jane to take up his post as British ambassador to the USA in October 1961.

38. Outside Birch Grove (from left) Macmillan and Charles de Gaulle take a break from Anglo-French talks on 25 November 1961 with their wives Yvonne de Gaulle and Lady Dorothy.

39. Celebrating the Lancaster House
conference agreement on Jamaican
independence in February 1962 are
(from right) Jamaican Chief Minister
Norman Manley, Colonial Secretary
Reginald Maudling, his junior
minister Hugh Fraser and the leader
of the Jamaican opposition
Sir Alexander Bustamante.

40. Mac the axe: Macmillan pictured
on 16 July 1962 shortly after the
'Night of the Long Knives'
Cabinet reshuffle.

41. Leaving the first Cabinet meeting following the 'Night of the Long Knives' on 17 July 1962 are (from left) Enoch Powell (Minister of Health), Christopher Soames (Minister of Agriculture), Iain Macleod (Chancellor of the Duchy of Lancaster) with (in background) Lord Hailsham (Lord President of the Council).

42. A demonstrator is led away by police during the general strike that started in Aden on 24 September 1962.

"What makes you so damned sure they're on our side?"

43. December 1962 was a difficult month in the Anglo-American relationship, what with Dean Acheson's comments at West Point and the problems with Skybolt. William Papas here comments in the *Guardian* (10 December 1962) on Macmillan's difficulties in securing a credible missile from the Americans for Britain's nuclear warheads at the forthcoming Nassau conference.

44. Chairman of the British Railways Board Dr Richard Beeching (left) discusses his 1963 plans for reducing the rail network with Minister of Transport, Ernest Marples.

45. John Jensen in the *Sunday Telegraph* (10 March 1963) captures the dilemma of Brendan Mulholland (depicted) of the *Daily Mail* and Reginald Foster of the *Daily Sketch*, who were both gaoled for refusing to reveal their sources for reports about the Vassall scandal.

46. The man of the moment: having given his statement in the Commons claiming that 'There was no impropriety whatsoever in my acquaintanceship with Miss Keeler' Secretary of State for War John Profumo went with his wife, the actress Valerie Hobson, to relax at the races at Sandown Park on 22 March 1963.

47. Stephen Ward had access to Lord Astor's pool, which is where he and his friends would mingle with Astor's house-guests. One such, John Profumo, met Ward's tenant Christine Keeler there on the weekend of 8–9 July 1961 and began a brief affair which was to have far-reaching consequences. Ward is pictured here with (right) Christine Keeler, (left) Mandy Rice-Davies and (bottom) Paula Hamilton-Marshall.

48. CND demonstrators outside Birch Grove during Macmillan's talks with President Kennedy, 30 June 1963.

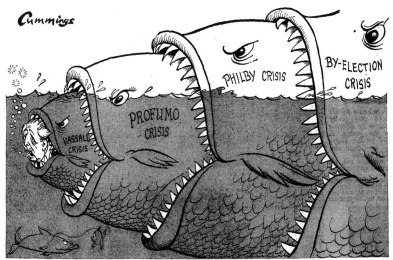

"That fellow Jonah had all the luck—he was only swallowed once . . ."

49. Michael Cummings in the *Daily Express* (6 July 1963) illustrates the various crises then engulfing Macmillan's government.

50. Moving back into 10 Downing Street, 3 October 1963.

51. Sir Alec Douglas-Home takes up office as Prime Minister, 19 October 1963.

52. New Prime Minister Harold Wilson with his Chancellor James Callaghan during Labour's victory conference in Brighton, 12–13 December 1964.

breaks down.[69] This happened to me during the Suez crisis. It has happened during what I may call the Profumo crisis. When I was at Oban, I was told by telephone that Profumo had admitted that he had lied to me, to the House, and to the courts.[70] Altho' we managed to finish our Scottish holiday and go to Iona and Gleneagles as planned, from the day I got back till now (when there is a slight pause) there has been a serious and at times dangerous crisis, wh. seemed likely to involve the fall of the Govt as well as my resignation[71] . . . .

I got back to London on June 10th. Parliament was to meet on the 16th, but M.P.s were already in London, holding meetings etc. Every part of the Profumo story . . . . was used agst the Govt by an exultant Press, getting its own back for Vassall. *The Times* was awful – what has since been called a 'Haylier than thou'[72] attitude which was really nauseating . . . . Day after day the attack developed, chiefly on me – old, incompetent, worn out. In the debate (on June 17) I had to tell the whole story – from Feb 1st[73] (when Profumo denied and continued to deny any but the most perfunctory acquaintance with Ward and Miss Keeler) to his confession. I had to defend the police, the security service, and Civil Service, and myself. Meanwhile, the Parliamentary Party were undergoing one of those attacks of hysteria wh. seize men from time to time. In the end, 27 of our Conservatives 'abstained' – that is, not only the usual malcontents, like Birch, Ld Lambton etc, but a lot of worthy people, who had been swept away by the wave of emotion and indignation[74] . . . .

---

69. There is no missing volume. This entry appears at the end of series 2, vol 22 of the manuscript diaries.

70. On 4 June. Impending Labour parliamentary questions prompted by Ward as well as the Lord Chancellor's inquiries led Profumo that morning to confess and resign both as a minister and MP.

71. This is the only diary hint that four ministers (Powell, Boyle, Brooke and Joseph) had contemplated resignation, countered by Macmillan's point that the government would then have to resign as well. It is also the only hint at Sandys's offer in Cabinet on 20 June to resign over allegations that he was the 'headless man' in compromising photographs publicised during the recent and scandalous Duchess of Argyll divorce case, in which some 200 co-respondents were cited.

72. A play on the sanctimonious attitudes of the then editor, Sir William Haley.

73. When Profumo was questioned both by Tim Bligh and by the government law officers.

74. Another dozen absented themselves whilst others were only persuaded to

In the debate, I set out to prove 3 propositions. First, that I had acted honourably; second, that I had acted justly; third, with reasonable prudence. One comfort to me was that the first two were accepted by all the House and even by the Press . . . .

This week, June 17th–22nd was the second week of the crisis – the first Parliamentary week . . . . Altogether, partly by the blackmailing statements of the 'call girls', partly by the stories started by or given to the Press, and partly (I have no doubt) by Soviet agents exploiting the position, more than half the Cabinet were being accused of perversion, homosexuality and the like . . . .

The third week of the crisis began on Monday June 24th. I had announced the appointment of Lord Denning[75] to hold a judicial enquiry into matters arising from the Ward case and any security risks involved.[76] I hope (the report is not yet ready and cannot be, I wd judge, for some weeks) that this will clear the ministers and make people a little ashamed of their behaviour . . . .

During this week (also very busy with ordinary business and other engagements) the massive reaction began. I have had telegrams, letters, messages etc on a scale never equalled (I am told) in the history of No 10. This has come from people in all walks of life and who have either had some association with me (e.g. a Platoon Segt at Loos) or who knew me only by reputation . . . . It was very moving and encouraging . . . .

I am writing this after what I might call the fourth week of the crisis, and the end of the first stage. The second stage may be set off by something unpleasant about this or that minister being revealed by Lord Denning. Or it may simply revert to the Feb/March situation – the desire of the Party for a change and for a younger man to lead them in the Election. To this, of course, I can have no objection in principle. I have not yet decided what wd be best and I don't think anyone is yet sure . . . .

----

support on the promise that Macmillan would go in the autumn. The Conservative majority fell to 57.

75. As Macmillan later explained in the Commons on 22 December, neither of the alternative methods of inquiry – by select committee because of the risk of partisanship or by judicial tribunal in light of recent press experience – recommended themselves.

76. Ward had been arrested on 8 June and charged with living off immoral earnings, committing suicide during the trial.

Now that I can sit back a bit (I am writing in bed – very tired, but not broken) there are some interesting deductions or reflections.

(1) <u>Dorothy</u>, <u>Maurice</u> and the <u>family</u> generally have been wonderful. D. has helped by her contempt and by her calm . . . .

(2) <u>Cabinet</u> – after some wavering by some of the younger men – has stood firm agst intrigue. Maudling (the new heir, according to MPs) has behaved correctly and wisely. Alec Home has wavered a little on what he called 'my power to establish my authority' but they have both been sympathetic and kind . . . .

(3) <u>Party in Country</u> – from Ld Poole to the humblest sub-agent – solid. Constituency workers, wonderful and moving in their support. To attack Dorothy and me as loose and degenerate (as *The Times* does) infuriates them.

(4) <u>Public</u>. *The Times* has had the most spectacular failure. They could scarcely find a letter on their side to print and (in very shame) they have had to print some, at least, of the many letters in my support.

(5) <u>Press</u> – all bad, except lately Lord Beaverbrook's. (I saw Lord B. on Friday July 5th. He asked me to luncheon and I went. We were alone. He urged me to fight it out and thought that I was the most likely leader to beat Labour. His papers will, from now on, begin to support) The *D.T.* and *Sunday T.* bad. Lady Pamela Berry (who fancies herself as another Lady Londonderry)[77] has turned against us and means to make Maudling my successor. *Sunday Times* – good. *D.Mail* – weak and sensational. *Mirror* and *Sketch* – the gutter press, in every sense of the word. The Public read the press. The *News of the World* is said to have added 120,000 to its circulation by the memoirs of one of the leading prostitutes.[78] But are they influenced by the Press? . . . .

(6) <u>House of Lords</u>. Good . . . . Ld Salisbury very good. Altho' he disapproves of my politics, he is too much of a gentleman to use this means of attack.

(7) <u>House of Commons</u>. Naturally, in the last year of a Parl[iamen]t, there is a certain disintegration. This is more than usual, after 12 years of office. Various groups are

---

77. The leading inter-war political salon hostess.
78. They allegedly paid £24,000 for the 'Confessions of Christine'.

a) MPs who do <u>not</u> intend to stand again – and, if they have already received their knighthoods – have nothing to gain!

b) MPs who <u>have</u> been ministers, and (for one reason or another) have not 'made the grade'. Birch; Vaughan-Morgan; Turton etc

c) MPs who have <u>not</u> been promoted and have now lost hope

d) Difficult characters, with personal dislike of me – Turton etc

e) Natural gossipers and trouble-makers, with weak heads and hearts.

<u>But</u> – and this is the wonderful thing, these did not amount to more than 10%. 90% are fine . . . .

The President's Visit

The Cabinet had two long – and excellent – discussions on the 'Multi Manned Surface Ships Polaris Fleet'. There has been a great deal of nonsense talked about this project, from all sides. The protagonists of the idea (the President and afterwards, more vigorously, the State Dept) originally talked about a multi-manned Polaris <u>submarine</u> fleet. This was indeed talked about (not at any great length) at Nassau. But the American Polaris experts and naval experts were a) unwilling to let their complicated communication system come under such wide control b) shared the doubts of our naval experts as to whether multi-racial crews cd be subjected to the strains of submarine life for the long periods required. So they switched on to the idea of a fleet of surface ships . . . .

 . . . . The Cabinet was rather divided here. Some felt it wrong and wasteful; others thought that if it came about we <u>must</u> be in it. On the whole, everyone agreed that it wd be best to postpone a decision until <u>after</u> the Moscow talks on a possible Test Ban agreement.

The President flew in from Ireland (where he had made a sentimental journey to 'the home of the Kennedys' and a rather foolish speech about Liberty) With a characteristic change of plan, he decided to stop in Derbyshire; go to Chatsworth; and see his sister (Lady Hartington's) grave. (By a strange irony she is buried next to Lord Frederick Cavendish, murdered by the Irish)[79] . . . .

---

79. Murdered by nationalists in Phoenix Park, Dublin on 6 May 1882, the day he took office as Chief Secretary for Ireland.

Altogether, it was a <u>great</u> success from our point of view – altho' I'm afraid Dean Rusk and the State Dept were a bit sour. We got <u>all</u> we wanted.

1) Full steam ahead with Moscow talks – Test Ban to be no. 1 priority

2) Go slow on Multi-Manned . . . .

Today's Sunday Press carries Maudling's speech as a challenge to me.[80] It was (I feel sure) not meant to be so. (Max Beaverbrook thinks Heath much better than Maudling) But Butler (who has had a great success in Central Africa) will be back in a day or two. His reputation will certainly be enhanced by his preliminary agreements and his handling of the situation in Central Africa.[81]

I find it still difficult to make up my mind. Of course, if things go badly with the Denning Report, there will be no choice. I shall have been destroyed by the vices of some of my colleagues, wh. were (naturally) unknown to me. But if we can get the House up, there will be time to take stock of the position and make my decision calmly and quietly . . . .

11 July

. . . . I had an hour with Harold Wilson and tried to explain to him how the so-called 'Security' services really worked. It seemed to me right to do so and he took it quite well. (He had never heard of C)[82] . . . .

12 July

Gallup Poll worse again, after the recent recovery. We are 17% behind Labour – an immense and unprecedented gap. Liberals have shrunk to 7%, but it looks as if these Liberals (they were 14% or more at one

---

80. As the potential young pretender, Maudling's speech in Cambridgeshire criticised the failure of the (ageing) party leadership to engage with the ideals and interests of younger voters.

81. Butler had at the Victoria Falls Conference (28 June–4 July) successfully negotiated the dissolution of the Central African Federation, providing independence and black majority rule in Nyasaland and Northern Rhodesia, whilst avoiding conceding it to white-ruled Southern Rhodesia.

82. The head of the Secret Intelligence Service (MI6), so-called because this is how its first head, Sir George Smith-Cumming (1909–23), habitually signed himself. The then 'C' was Sir Richard White (1956–68).

time) have gone to Labour. However, at this moment in time, British politics are very confused. An amusing question time in the House yesterday allowed me to score a lot of runs. But underlying a greater sense of calm, I feel a growing desire in the Parl[iamentar]y Party for a change in the Leadership – not sudden or dramatic, but in the right time and in the right way. This is quite different from the hysteria of a few weeks ago. But it is probably more important because more serious. I gave an interview to Henry Fairlie, wh. fills most of today's *Daily Express*. On the whole, it is good – but perh. gives rather too much the impression that I have decided not to go on to the Election. Nevertheless, for the next few weeks, uncertainty is the best position for me. Then, in the holiday season, I can make up my mind without undue pressure. I am very anxious to get the Defence Reorganisation launched. I have <u>tried</u> for many years and have at last succeeded in getting general agreement . . . .

The Press (wh. in this country is both irresponsible and unpatriotic) has got a story today about a Russian <u>defector</u> and blown it up into a scandal! Actually, this man got to USA over 18 months ago. He helped the American intelligence authorities a lot, since he had himself been a member of the Russian espionage system. His statements indeed led to the pinning of certain leakages on to Vassall. He has been in England for 4 months. We have given him a new name and a new life, and so long as he is let alone, he can be both happy in himself and useful to us. Now the Press (in spite of our appeal to them to let him alone) have come out with a story which may lead to his identification. This means

a) The Russians may 'bump him off' here – by a railway or motor-car accident or some other means
b) He will sulk – and be no more use to us
c) Other possible 'defectors' may be deterred.

All this, because Michael and Lady Pamela Berry and Colin Coote put a good 'scoop' ahead of the national interest.[83]

Averell Harriman came to luncheon and I had a good talk with him alone afterwards. He is certainly 'on our side' and will do all he can to get a Test Ban agreement of some kind with the Russians.[84] He was <u>very</u> sound about Germany and France, and how to handle them.

---

83. After this exposure Golitsyn left Britain.
84. The talks opened in Moscow on 15 July, with Harriman representing the US and Hailsham the UK.

I had a special message from the President, wh. encourages me. But what will Mr Kruschev do? We do <u>not</u> know the answer. Does he want an agreement or not?

The situation is dramatic and vital for me. If there is any chance of an agreement and a Summit meeting afterwards, I will fight on in home politics. If not, I shall feel inclined to throw in my hand . . . .

15 July

Lord Rothermere to luncheon alone. He was very agreeable and promised support. He urged me to stay as P.M. The trouble is that he doesn't <u>control</u> his papers as Ld Beaverbrook does.

Cecil King (of *D. Mirror*) came in afternoon. I asked his advice as [to] how to revive the European concept. He is still as keen as ever, and wd support us again on this one issue . . . .

17 July

There is a good deal of difference of opinion between the F.Office (esp. Ld Privy Seal) and Ministers of Defence (Thorneycroft) and Aviation (Julian Amery)[85] Alec Home is moderate – but Ld P[rivy] Seal (Ted Heath) is so bitterly anti-French as to be (quite understandably) almost unbalanced in his hatred of de Gaulle, Couve de Murville etc. This does not reflect itself in any immediate dissensions on actual policy, tho' it does in the day to day courtesies of life. Starting from the Princess Margaret episode (cancellation of her trip to Paris)[86] the F.O. and ambassador Dixon are taking a very detached attitude, even in meetings at luncheon, dinner etc. But Thorneycroft and Amery have friendly relations with their opposite number, Messmer – French Minister of Defence. The French ambassador here has been rather foolish in trying to build up an anti-Foreign Office party, and too obviously showering Thorneycroft, Amery, and Philip de Zulueta with persistent invitations to luncheon, tea, and dinner. Yet he never bothers to call at F.O. This has led to Heath making a row in connection with Messmer's visit to London this week. However, all this has now been subsumed in the situation wh. may develop from Moscow. If we got a Test Ban Treaty, even <u>without</u> underground, the question of trying to

---

85. The issue was Kennedy's offer the day before to share nuclear secrets with the French if de Gaulle would support the test-ban agreement. Macmillan supported this but de Gaulle did not.

86. In the aftermath of the breakdown of the European negotiations.

get France to join and of using the occasion to open up new vistas of European policy becomes real . . . .

D. Sandys is back from British Guiana. As usual, he has acted firmly and with vision. I have sent a message to President Kennedy wh. ought to comfort him. We shall not give B. Guiana 'independence' only to create a Cuba on the mainland. It is, however, rather fun making the Americans repeat over and over again their passionate plea to us to stick to 'Colonialism' and 'Imperialism' at all costs . . . .

18 July

. . . . Dinner for British Nigeria Assn . . . . A very large number of Nigerians present (including the Chief Justice, who answered the toast) It was clear that, although they were grateful to me for standing so firm about the Chief Enahoro incident,[87] the attitude of the whole Labour Party, some of the Conservatives and nearly all the London Press has made a very deep wound . . . .

The Board of Trade have made fools of themselves in Dundee about Jute. It is really quite serious. I fear that it has always been rather a 'messy' department, without political judgment and dominated by extreme Cobdenite ideas.[88] Freddy Erroll is an excellent export salesman and in this field has done a fine job. But he has not got <u>tact</u> at home, or judgment. But I can't change him now, without starting a general post. This wd be dangerous.

The position in the race to succeed me is quite amusing. Macleod is (for the moment) hardly a starter. There wd be long odds against Ted Heath. Rab (Butler) is coming up and gaining on the favourite, Maudling. But his speech was thought to be in bad taste and has done him harm. (His hat had been put firmly in the ring by his supporters.) There was no need to throw it in again himself, and in rather an ungracious way towards me. Moreover, with all eyes now on Moscow,

---

87. Back in Nigeria Enahoro was imprisoned for treason until his release following the 1966 coup.

88. Macmillan suggests the Board of Trade were free-trade zealots following the doctrines of the nineteenth-century Liberal MP and thinker Richard Cobden. Macmillan, in contrast, had been a keen protectionist in the inter-war years. The Board's suggestion of substantially lifting restrictions on jute imports from India and Pakistan was to be modified in light of concern about the impact on employment in Dundee, where jute processing had long been a key local industry.

people are wondering whether M[audling] has enough experience over the whole field to be P.M.

Hailsham, who had been a well placed horse, then dropped behind, is coming up again. All this diversity of view, wh. is spreading in the Parliamentary Party and in the Party in the country, does me no harm! . . . .

21 July

. . . . For Sec discussed security and I went over to dine later at Dorneywood. 'C' came to dinner and we had a long and valuable talk. I am terribly worried about certain possible developments, wh. will have a shattering effect[89] . . . .

22 July

. . . . Motored to London Airport, to meet M. Adoula (PM of Congo) He speaks good French . . . . The situation is quiet – wh. means that the great provincial wars (with Tshombe, for instance) are over, at least for the time. But since there are no police (who have mutinied and become armed bandits) there is no order. Except for a few cities, the Govt's writ does not really run in this vast area . . . .

A debate on Housing in North and East London was led off by Wilson[90] – a fine style of invective. He attacked me for not being present (I was in fact at London Airport) He was said to have not made a good speech. We won by 97 and 90 in the two divisions, wh. was good . . . .

23 July

The Denning enquiry continues. It is clear that there can be no report till September. Ld D. is going to find it rather difficult to draw the line between becoming a censor of morals and a protector of national security.

---

89. Presumably a reference to suspicions recently reactivated by Michael Straight to the CIA that Sir Anthony Blunt, Surveyor of the Queen's Pictures, had been both a Soviet spy and recruiter of Burgess and Maclean. Blunt confessed on 23 April 1964, but was not unmasked until 1979.
90. He was attempting to associate the 1957 Rent Act with shameless profiteering by reference to one of the bit-players in the Profumo scandal, the shady landlord and sometime lover of Mandy Rice-Davies, Perec Rachman (d. 29 November 1962).

The other 'security' enquiries are proceeding. I am beginning to wonder whether all this game of espionage and counter-espionage is worth the candle . . . .

The whole day was spent in messages to and from Moscow and Washington. No one seems to know the exact position. The text of the [Partial Test Ban] Treaty is certainly agreed. But they are now arguing about the form in which reference is to be made to the 'non-aggression pact' wh. Soviet Govt have proposed. The Germans (encouraged by the French) are beginning to panic. Since the Germans have defaulted on their financial agreement with us, we shd really be justified in reducing or removing altogether our troops in Germany. Public opinion here wd be deeply stirred – to real indignation – if this Test Ban Treaty were to be wrecked by any of the NATO allies, big or small . . . .

25 July

A very long and tiring – but historic day. Messages from [Ormsby-] Gore in the night and telephone conversation between him and Ld Home shewed that the President had decided to accept Ld Hailsham's compromise words to be put in the communiqué (not the Treaty) about the Russian proposal for a 'non-aggression pact'. It seemed therefore in the morning that (since the Americans had not come back in open session on the 'depository' clause in the Treaty, that all wd be all right. Telegrams from Moscow indicated a probable 'initialling' ceremony at 4pm or so (Moscow time) so I wd be able to make a statement at 3.30 in the House . . . .

Telegrams from Moscow seem slow. I think they have not got 'machine' cyphering – it is too dangerous. But from 2–3 came dramatic calls for help. The whole treaty wd be jeopardised by two new demands – one about the famous 'depository' clause and the other quite new. The significance of the 'depository' clause is, in reality, negligible. But it amounts to this. If Formosa – or China as the Americans recognise the govt of Chiang to be – asks to adhere to the treaty, what happens. Russia will refuse to register a country whose government they do not recognise. Similarly, if East Germany wants to accede, U.S. and prob[ably] UK will refuse. The absurd thing is that neither of these two countries cd, by any stretch of imagination, develop the capacity to make a nuclear explosion. The new American clause seemed to go back on the compromise already agreed wh. was quite sensible and said that no country need accept formal adherence from a country with wh. they were not in relations . . . .

The other American clause was that nothing in the Treaty could be taken to prevent the use of nuclear weapons in war! This was so absurd as to be hardly credible. The title of the Treaty was 'Test Ban Treaty'. How cd this amendment or new clause be in order? . . . .

I went to Admiralty House, and after a lot of messages, I at last got a talk with the President at 5.30. He told me that he had abandoned the American position and had told Harriman not to insist. Indeed, he said that the Treaty was just being initialled! (He might have told us before and saved us a lot of anxiety!) He said some lawyer had thought all this up! . . . . I had time to tell Dorothy the news and go to HofC to 'face' the 1922 Ctee. This much advertised meeting turned out very strangely. I was received with great applause and banging of desks. I spoke for 40 minutes, on broad policy, home and abroad. I had thought out the speech on Sunday and (except for one page of notes) spoke extempore . . . . Of course, the news of the Test Ban Treaty was known to members and mentioned by John Morrison, chairman. But I hardly mentioned it, except in its natural context in East/West problems. When I sat down, after simply saying about myself that my sole purpose was to serve the Party and the Nation and to secure a victory at the Election, there was great applause. There may have been a few abstainers at the end of the room (but very few) Spencer Summers moved that the Ctee adjourn without questions. Loyally meant, but a bad idea. I told Morrison I wd prefer questions. There were few, and about the normal policy matters – the naval carrier, the burden of rates etc. Ld Lambton got up and made a rather obscure speech, but was listened to with great impatience. Altogether, it was a triumphal vote of confidence . . . .

26 July

A very good Press on the Treaty, except *The Times* wh. is mean and niggling. The Press gives an account of the 1922 according to the views of the editor and with no regard to the truth. (*Daily Telegraph* absolutely false) But for the most part, they find it hard to conceal the truth coming out . . . .

27 July

Woke early, but after a good night. I feel a strange reaction. We have worked so hard and so long for the Test Ban and it has (until a few weeks ago) seemed so hopeless, that I can hardly yet realise what has

happened. When the President gave me (on the telephone) the news
wh. we had not yet got, I had to go out of the room. I went to tell D.
and burst into tears. I have prayed hard too for this, night after
night . . . .

30 July
Cabinet at 11.30. Lasted 30 minutes. The new 'carrier' for the Navy
approved. This is right and will be liked by our party.[91] The cost will
be high, but spread over nearly 10 years . . . .

1 August
. . . . I was glad to be able to get BofTrade to accept SofS Scotland's
wishes on Jute. BofT are <u>very</u> heavy handed when it comes to dealing
with industries with special problems. The officials are ruthless
Cobdenites.

A good discussion about School Meals. The pundits want to put
up the price (to save £6m) The politicians know that this would be
folly. More important – the U.N. resolution about arms embargo for
S. Africa. The difficulty of a) trying to get sensible amendments to
extreme resolutions or b) letting them be as extreme as possible, in
the hope that there will be enough abstentions to block them c) doing
all this in the middle of the night . . . . and no text except read over
the telephone d) of weighing the African feeling agst common-sense
and the real interests of the Free World – since S.A. is essential, for
our communication to India etc e) finding a compromise which will
get support at home f) dealing with Governor Stevenson and the
Americans – who will vote for an arms embargo because they sell
none now to S. Africa and want the negro vote in the North for the
Presidential election – all the Southern states are lost to the Democrats
anyway.

So the world is governed and these great ideals and principles rule
the Security Council and the Assembly of the United Nations! . . . .

2 August
. . . . The *D. Mail*'s 'Gallup Poll' has shewn a tremendous swing back
towards us. Only 6% or so behind Labour (instead of 18–20%) and I

---

91. This was the CVA-01, a scheme for a new 50,000-ton-plus carrier,
   subsequently cancelled in 1966.

have risen equally or more in public favour.[92] How strange it all is. If only we can avoid more ministerial scandal. But, alas! I fear that Ld Denning's report (from rumours we hear) will condemn one important and one unimportant minister (or rather fail to clear him of scandalous conduct)[93] This will be another great shock and may make my position impossible. However, all this is pure rumour and may be wrong. Naturally, I have been careful <u>not</u> to try to see or get anything out of Ld D. I think he will, in fact, seek the unofficial help of the Ld Chancellor before he actually sends in his report.

Saw 'C' this morning. There is certainly a strong Russian effort to penetrate MI5. 'C' is collaborating closely with head of M.I.5 (Hollis) in tremendous effort to find where the leak is (if indeed there is a leak) If they succeed, it will help the Service but probably bring down the Govt![94] . . . .

4 August (Sunday)
49th anniversary of outbreak of war. It seems an incredible time . . . .

. . . . Governor Stevenson (U.S.A.) has made a statement of nauseating hypocrisy, wh. we must try (I suppose) to follow (I hope a little more honestly) We all agree to <u>no arms for S.Africa for internal oppression</u>. We want to sell arms (such as submarines, warships, aeroplanes) against external aggression. But that's where the big money is. While Governor Stevenson was pontificating at U.N., American arms interests – with full support of State Dept and Pentagon – were making a desperate bid against our exporters for some

---

92. Concern about the effects this might have on crucial decisions Macmillan had to make about his future were meanwhile being voiced. The same day Ormsby-Gore wrote to Kennedy, 'The Prime Minister is in such a state of euphoria after the Test Ban agreement that Alec [Douglas-Home] doubts whether he now has any intention of resigning. This may lead to trouble as an overwhelming majority of the Conservatives in Parliament are convinced he should make way for a younger man in the shape of Reggie Maudling this autumn' (JFKL: President's Office files, special correspondence, Box 31).

93. Denning cleared Sandys of being the 'headless man', though doubt has since been cast upon this finding. The unimportant minister Macmillan refers to was Marples.

94. This followed the Blunt revelations and (domestic security service) MI5's mishandling of the Profumo Affair. Hollis was himself suspected within the service of being a Soviet agent.

huge contracts. The 'New Frontier' is often only the old battlements writ large.

5 August

A stream of telegrams about the Security Council of UN and the S. African resolution .... The French system in U.N. has certain attractions. It is not to resign, but to abstain on everything![95] ....

6 August

We left London Airport (Dorothy came with me) at 10.45, and arrived at Helsinki at 4pm (local time) It is over 23 years since I went to Finland (in Feb 1940) with Ld Davies [of Llandinam] – to try to help the Finnish Govt by a) volunteers b) munitions. They were then fighting the Russians, who had made a sudden and quite unprovoked attack ....

7 August

9.30–11. Talks with President Kekkonen and Prime Minister Karjalainen. Not very satisfactory. Pres[iden]t K. plays his cards pretty close to his chest. He wd not answer any question without a good deal of prevarication – esp. about the quotas etc and the very unfavourable balance of trade wh. we have with Finland. He was equally cagey about Russian oil. His Govt is refusing increased licences to Shell (wh. they are bound by their undertaking at the time Finland was admitted to EFTA to do) We suspect that the Russian pipe line will be extended to Leningrad and then to Helsinki and that all the Scandinavian states will gradually turn over to Russian supplies. This is bad commercially and <u>very</u> dangerous strategically ....

8 August

Alone with President Kekkonen. He spoke a little more freely and almost sincerely. It is clear that <u>he</u> is the boss. The Prime Minister was party secretary; the foreign minister (Merikoski) is a 'Liberal' professor – a nonentity and rather a fellow traveller. President K runs a coalition of Agrarians; Conservatives; Liberals, and Trade Unionists. He has split the Social Democratic (or Labour) party (wh. annoys the Swedes) but <u>has</u> succeeded in keeping out the Communists. The danger lies in the difficulty of seeing an alternative Govt (except Communists) This,

---

95. A voluntary arms embargo to South Africa was adopted by the Security Council on 7 August, with Britain and France abstaining.

at least, is the Swedish and Norwegian 'Social Democrat' argument. But I am not persuaded that it is sound. The Finns have a difficult hand to play. But considering that they only came into existence as a country in 1917 – that before that they were (till 1809) a province of Sweden; then a Russian province, and considering that they were dismembered by loss of Karelia in 1940, it is really wonderful what progress and stability they have achieved . . . .

9 August
Press Conference – the usual questions from British and American correspondents. I <u>very</u> much doubt the value of these conferences. The local press are always polite and shy; the visiting press are rude and offensive . . . .

We arrived at Stockholm about an hour after leaving Helsinki. I was sorry not to have seen more of Finland, but we had very little time. There is something rather fascinating and endearing about this gallant people. Sweden is a very different affair – a popular monarchy, an aristocracy still owning large estates, an industrial and banking system among the strongest in Europe, a strongly supported Govt – nominally Social Democrat, in fact anti-Socialist and 'conservative', cooperative Trade Unions, a highly developed educational system, good army and air force, and a wonderfully efficient shipping and shipbuilding business and a long history, with fine buildings and public monuments. A large dinner at the Foreign Office, followed by a reception in the fine suite of rooms. P.M. Erlander made a welcoming speech – in good enough English. I had a prepared speech, but discarded it and spoke 'off the cuff'. I think our hosts liked this . . . .

13 August
. . . . Left airport at 11am for England . . . .

In the airplane we read telegrams wh. arrived late last night or early this morning. Rusk seems to have done pretty well in Bonn, altho' the Germans (led by old Adenauer) tried to make difficulties. However, they have now promised to adhere to the Test Ban Treaty.

The Senators (including Fulbright) whom Rusk brought with him for the signature in Moscow have been 'shooting a big line' against EEC and French protectionism. They threaten removal of American troops from Europe. (I don't think de Gaulle will mind this at all)

16 August

I came to B.G. last night, after two heavy days in London – chiefly on Foreign Office affairs. The Germans are being thoroughly sticky and seem utterly unaware of their guilt. All they expect is automatic support from their allies. I think Herr Schroeder came to see me Wednesday evening at 6pm, with German ambassador. Ld Home and Sir F. Roberts were there too. The Anglo-German talks had lasted all day. The Germans will, I believe, <u>sign</u> the Test Ban Treaty, in spite of Chancellor Adenauer's double-faced attitude. According to Schroeder he had the greatest difficulty with the Cabinet. A. was very pessimistic, oracular, and Erhard hardly knew what to do. However, with Rusk's assurances about East Germany etc, and what we have said about this, S. thinks the German Cabinet will agree to <u>sign</u>. Decision to be taken August 16th (today) Then there will be the question of ratification by Parlt. This will be in October or November. Adenauer is supposed to resign in October. Obviously, all his colleagues are terrified lest he make the 'German crisis' the excuse for staying on!

I judge from all this that the Germans (lined up partially – but only partially – with the French) will try to prevent any further <u>advance</u> in trying to work for some détente with Russia. They will put up an impossible demand on 're-unification' as a condition precedent. This, of course, means an end to negotiation with Kruschev. The question is, will the Americans stand for this? State Department? Yes. President Kennedy? I still hope, no . . . .

The delay on Malaysia is <u>very</u> bad and there is a danger that the U.N. team may report unfavourably.[96] What terrible troubles are caused by U.N. Yet, in some cases, I suppose it is useful. It is strongly <u>anti-white</u> in bias. For instance, Nasser is bombing Yemen and Saudi Arabia <u>day and night</u> with powerful Russian bombers, <u>and</u> is using poison gas. Nothing happens. No protest. No Afro-Asian resolution in Security Council or Assembly. Imagine what wd happen if we were doing one twentieth of this from (say) Aden . . . .

I am now beginning to think seriously, and serenely, out of the turmoil of HofCommons and all the rest, about my own future. I can do this quietly for the next few days (at B.G.) and then during my

---

96. Agreement on Malaysia had been formally signed on 8 July, but implementation was delayed whilst a UN survey was carried out. When referendums confirmed support for Malaysia in Sabah and Sarawak on 14 September formal inauguration of Malaysia followed two days later.

fortnight's holiday in Yorkshire. I shall come south at the end of August. It seems to me at present that the question of the leadership of the party cannot be left uncertain beyond October. (Conference is October 13th) . . . .

I don't particularly want a tiresome 8 weeks from Nov. to Christmas, with party in HofC making trouble and then resigning at Christmas. Unless there was some great <u>international</u> prize, the extra two months are not worth the trouble. So it is the choice between finishing my political life at end of October, or going right through to and including the Election . . . .

Rab Butler rang up from Mull last night. He had nothing to say. I think his purpose was just to be friendly. It seems strange to reflect that all this turmoil and strain may suddenly cease in a couple of months. It will be a relief – but I dare say life will seem very empty.

The Stratford poll has just come in. Maude wins by 3500. This is bad.[97] The optimists hoped for 7000. The Central Office estimated 5000. The Labour poll is constant at 12000. But Liberals have polled 7000 (they did not contest this seat at the General Election) I think the Liberals must have taken our votes. I fear this result will be thought <u>bad</u> for us, both by our friends and by our enemies.[98] I spoke to Ld Poole, who takes the same view, but thinks it has not much relevance to the personal issue wh. I have to decide.

Read again Life of Bonar Law – by Blake – (well written and some parts quite valuable for precedents of how a party crisis can be dealt with and a P.M. and party leader resign or resist)[99] . . . .

19 August (Monday)
At Bolton Abbey. I came here yesterday afternoon . . . .

. . . . It is comforting that something remains constant. I think I started coming here in 1923, and have been every year (except the war

---

97. The Stratford-upon-Avon by-election was triggered by Profumo's resignation. The Tory vote fell some 25%.

98. Poole later wrote (28 August) to Macmillan that this result showed that successes like the Test Ban Treaty 'are no electoral alternative to economic affluence and security' (DWM: Ms Macmillan, dep. c. 355).

99. What interested Macmillan in Robert Blake's life of Andrew Bonar Law was presumably the crisis in the Conservative Party at the end of Lloyd George's government, resulting in Bonar Law succeeding as Prime Minister from 23 October 1922 until his resignation due to ill health on 22 May 1923.

years) The Abbey Church; the house (with the furniture and the beds); the river; the stepping stones; the Deer Park Hill; – all remains and I hope will remain. The motor-cars are kept <u>out</u> of the Abbey grounds. As I lie in bed in the King's room, reading and writing there is no sound, but of running water and a gentle sighing wind in the cedars and yews outside the windows.

In this atmosphere, I try to meditate about what I am to do – to stay and fight the next General Election, or to resign the leadership <u>before</u> the Election. If the latter is right, then comes the question when? In October, before the Party Conference; or at end of October, before Parlt meets; or in January, when Parlt is again in recess? These seem the possible alternatives – not an easy choice.

29 August

I came to Swinton[100] on Sunday, after a very pleasant week at Bolton Abbey. Unfortunately we had nothing but rainstorms and tremendous winds. This is very tiring and makes shooting very difficult. I shot well the first day and each successive day steadily worse.

. . . . Much as I love Bolton Abbey, I fear I am really too old for this sort of shooting now . . . .

. . . . Everywhere in the world there are troubles . . . . In Germany, there is nothing to be done until Adenauer has gone – and, I wd suspect, little even then. France, under de G[aulle], remains in sullen isolation. In U.S.A. it is the President's last year, and he is (I think) anxious to move on, but doesn't know how. At home, the economy is good. The building strike is settled on very reasonable terms (4%) But it has been a bad summer, and I feel that my power and even my influence is slipping away. How long is it worth staying on and for what purpose. I must try to study all this next week. The real issue is simple. Can I get the <u>next</u> move in the détente with Russia under way or will Franco/German opposition be too great? If there has to be substantial delay, I cannot wait and had better rest content with what has been achieved.

I rather shrink from going back, out of the clean Yorkshire air, into Whitehall and its fog. Naturally, what I decide must depend partly on the date of publication and the content of the Denning report . . . .

---

100. The Yorkshire home of Lord Swinton.

2 September

A full day in London – chiefly trying to deal with a problem which has arisen in connection with Ld Denning's report. It ought to be published in a manner wh. will obtain full 'privilege' – otherwise, press and others will hesitate to print it in full, for fear of actions for libel. But to obtain this privilege the report must be a 'parliamentary paper' or 'ordered to be printed' (by either Lords or Commons) A 'command' paper, published by direction of a minister, does not have this privilege or pass it on to others. Since Parlt is not sitting, it seems that it must either be recalled for the sole purpose of ordering the Denning report to be printed, or we must wait till the end of October (when Parlt reassembles) wh. wd be a great nuisance and keep the whole affair hanging on . . . .

I saw two American 'publishers' Mr Pulliam (of Indianapolis) and Mr Maxwell (*Chicago Tribune*) Both were agreeable; rather prosy; very friendly, and said much the same thing (except that they differed about whether Rockefeller or Goldwater wd get the Republican nomination) Both thought that Kennedy wd win, unless the Black v White row develops too far.[101] Curiously enough, both had interviewed leading Labour characters here and both agreed as to what they said. They are confident that they cd win an early election. But if delayed till October 1964, they are not so sure. They also say that they wd prefer me to have been driven out of office by the Conservatives. They feel that they cd beat any other leader more easily than me. This is why they have not attacked me very violently, but left this to the Tory dissidents to do . . . .

5 September

. . . . My mind is beginning to be clearer about my own position. I must stay to deal with Ld Denning's report and the debate in Parl. – say early November. But I cannot go on to an election and lead in it.[102] I am beginning to feel that I haven't the strength and that perhaps

101. Barry Goldwater won the Republican nomination for the 1964 presidential election, but lost by a big margin despite picking up five formerly Democrat states as white Southern voters reacted against the black civil rights movement.

102. A note from Dilhorne the day before suggested after soundings that all but three of the Cabinet wanted Macmillan to lead into the next election, not least because of the lack of agreement on alternatives. The alternatives mentioned

another leader cd do what I did after Eden left. But it cannot be done by a pedestrian politician. It needs a man with vision and moral strength – Hailsham, not Maudling. Yet the 'back-benchers' (poor fools) do not seem to have any idea, except 'a young man'.[103] Admirable as Maudling is, I doubt if he cd revive our fortunes as well as Hailsham. (I sent H. to Moscow on purpose, to test his powers of negotiation etc. He did <u>very</u> well) . . . .

8 September (Sunday)

. . . . President K[ennedy] has answered my message; he, like me, is anxious to get on with talks with the Russians. But we both agree that we must wait till the Rusk–Gromyko talks in N.Y. or Washington in a few weeks time . . . .

Reading Evelyn Ashley's 2 volume *Life of Palmerston* (published 1879) one realises how <u>bad</u> a biography can be as art, and yet how interesting. The truth is that the two long volumes are just extracts from letters, despatches, memoranda, and speeches. These are strung together by some rather banal but mercifully short passages. Altho' the details of each particular foreign problem are different – and different, alas, Britain's physical power, tho' not altogether her influence – the situations are just like those wh. we have had to deal with. Do you go to help Portugal? Not, <u>of course</u>, to interfere in Portuguese politics. That's for the people themselves. But to protect them from outside aggression, yes. So we go not to help King Hussein agst trouble in Jordan, but agst threat to Jordan from Iraqis, whether in formal attacks or by guerrilla warfare. This doctrine (as in Kuwait) can cover <u>internal</u> revolution <u>externally</u> supported by subversion on any large scale. This was exactly the doctrine in Portugal, Spain, Naples or Sicily. Of course, it's better if you have a treaty. What, of course, we have got no longer is the <u>moral</u> basis wh. has passed (temporarily, I hope) from the white races to Negroes, Indians, Chinese etc (wh. means, Afro-Asian group at U.N.) . . . .

Maurice [Macmillan] came about 6. He has had rather a heavy time, with visits to New York and Toronto on business. We had the evening alone and a very good talk together, about politics, business,

---

were Butler, Heath, Maudling and Hailsham, with a slight preference for the last.

103. Maudling was slightly younger than the Leader of the Opposition, Harold Wilson.

and family affairs. He is really a wonderful son and a tremendous help to me. He approves (on the whole) the conclusion to which I am now inclining – resignation after Christmas . . . .

10 September
. . . . Motored to London at 1pm. Meeting with Ld Hailsham, Ld Chancellor, Mr Butler, Mr Macleod, Attorney General and Deedes. The subject was how to deal with the publication of the Denning Report. I expect to receive it on 16th. I must submit it to the Security Ctee (for any excisions on security) I must discuss it with my legal advisers (for any excisions on the ground of 'contempt of court', in view of trial of Miss Keeler for perjury)[104] I must discuss it with Wilson, on these two aspects. It will take 10 days to print. There is then the question of 'privilege'. This could be done (if Opposition agree), by recall of H of Lords. But they probably will not agree. We cannot recall House of Commons, because of the 2 party conferences. So it may not be possible to get the necessary Parliamentary immunity until Parlt meets on Oct 24, for the Prorogation . . . .

11 September
I had rather an amusing luncheon party at Chequers today, wh. has caught the public imagination and come out very well on T.V. The captains of the English and West Indian elevens, who have just concluded a very interesting and sometimes exciting series of Test matches. W.I. won. The English captain (Mr Dexter) is a very nice young chap, and is Conservative Candidate for Cardiff East. The W. Indian (Mr Worrell) is charming – quiet and good manners. I had as guests – Sir Learie Constantine (High Commissioner of Jamaica) who [is] a most charming and genial character. He was a great Test match cricketer. Also came Iain Macleod, Minister of Works, Duke of Norfolk and Tim Bligh. I took them to the Long Gallery for coffee after luncheon. As it was raining, we broke the rule and had photographs in the Hall.

Christopher Soames at 3. He talked about the new agricultural plan, wh. requires careful negotiation with countries involved. We also had a talk on the general political situation. He wants me to go on,

---

104. She was later gaoled for nine months for perjuring herself earlier that year when giving evidence at the trial of another of her lovers, Aloysius 'Lucky' Gordon.

but realises that it is not likely that we can win again. If I cannot go on (wh. S. thinks a lot to ask, since it is not really in my interest) he is either for Butler or Hailsham.

Butler came at 6.45 and we had long talks about the pos[itio]n before and after dinner. I was rather careful not to give him any idea about wh. of several alternatives I wd choose, for he is not discreet. But I got a good idea of his own position. He wd naturally (if I resign) accept the Premiership if there was a general consensus of opinion for him. But he doesn't want another unsuccessful bid. He wd not go in for a ballot of the Party or backbenchers. But he wd serve in this Parlt and the next, in office or in opposition. He is 60. He likes politics. He doesn't want to go into business, for he has enough money. It is clear that in his heart he does not expect any real demand for him. He wd prefer to be Warwick,[105] (wh. he cd be) and not try to be King (wh. he can't be) On the whole, he is for Hailsham. I have never seen him so well (his holiday has done him good) or so relaxed.

12 September

. . . . Sir Milton Margai (Sierra Leone) came with D of Devonshire. He is on a visit to England for a few days, after a short visit to Paris. (He has a wife in England – white – who is not allowed to come to Africa. He married her when he was a medical student many years ago in Newcastle. So in Newcastle she stays, except to go to a house in Marlow – on the Thames – wh. HMG got for her and her husband for this visit. Racial prejudice, I suppose? But a queer story)

There was supposed to be a serious discussion of economic aid, contracts for a bridge etc. But Sir M.M. was so heavily drugged that he did nothing but giggle. It seems that he takes a drug wh. makes you not sleep but giggle . . . .

M of Defence and some of his staff about Indonesia and Malaysia. I wanted to be assured that we have enough units in the area and are in a position to reinforce them rapidly[106] . . . .

---

105. Richard Neville, 16th Earl of Warwick, was a powerful fifteenth-century magnate whose role in deposing and making kings during the Wars of the Roses led to him later becoming known as 'Warwick the Kingmaker'.

106. In view of Indonesian hostility to North Borneo and Sarawak joining Malaysia on 16 September. A military 'Confrontation' (as this undeclared war came to be known) began along the border later that month and lasted until August 1966.

13 September

Yesterday was the first fine day for weeks, and <u>some</u> harvesting has started round here. Today has begun well. Worked in bed all the morning – rather a heavy box and many problems, involving minutes to several ministers. Without continual drive and effort it is almost impossible to get anything done. If ministers wd think more about pushing their Permanent Secretaries than (like Stalky) about their 'careers',[107] we would make more progress.

Read *Catch 22* – an American novel, about the American airforce in the 2nd war – very bitter, but very amusing . . . .

John and Pamela Wyndham came to luncheon. In afternoon, we drove to Coventry and spent a most interesting hour being shewn the new Cathedral by the Provost (Mr Williams) I thought it splendid – far finer than the pictures shew. Also, the spirit of it all was remarkable. It has certainly caught the imagination of the public. 2000 people came <u>every hour</u> to see the Cathedral. The community spirit; the international spirit; the Christian Church in action – these are the themes which the genius of Basil Spence, and the other artists who have helped has brought into the understanding of the ordinary public . . . .

17 September

. . . . 5pm. Senior colleagues – about 6 – to discuss Denning's report – just received. There is nothing sensational. All the libellous 'rumours' agst various ministers are dismissed. The rest of the story is told as I told it in the HofC. The only troublesome thing is para. 286 which puts the blame on us for having been deceived by Profumo. But that's an old story. Some of the ministers were worried, but Rab and Hailsham and the Lord Chancellor were quite robust.

Motored back to Chequers. Ld Home came to dinner and stay the night. We had a talk on a number of outstanding matters – Yemen and Egypt; multilateral force; France etc. I told him that I thought we ought to have a change at the Paris Embassy. For no fault of his own, Bob Dixon can have no influence. While de Gaulle remains in power, there is little to be done. Since we are so weak at the moment in the higher ranks of the Foreign Service, perh. an amateur might do.

---

107. A reference to Rudyard Kipling's collection of school stories, *Stalky & Co.*

18 September

. . . . I fear that the Indonesian Govt will react against us, perh. by confiscating our valuable investments. (Shell; Unilever etc) But I doubt if they will risk war agst Malaysia. They will, no doubt, try subversion etc, esp. in Sarawak and Borneo.

When Ld Home was here on Tuesday night, I talked to him about my own position and about a possible successor. He was very distressed to think that I had any idea of retiring, but cd well understand my reasons and thought them sound.[108] As for a successor, he favours Hailsham, but fears that there will be complete disunity in the Party and that great troubles will follow. I may be forced to stay. I replied 'In that case I shall be "drafted" – not a "limpet". I don't want it to be thought that I am just clinging on' . . . .

19 September

Motored early to London. Cabinet met at 10.30. A long discussion about the problem of publication of the Denning report. All members of the Cabinet have now read the report, but there was little discussion of its contents. This was partly because we were considering the question of privilege[109] – absolute or qualified – the need to recall one or both Houses of Parlt – the drawbacks and even dangers of this course – the worse alternative of waiting till October 24th. After a bit, the idea emerged of 'Publish and be damned'.[110] Why not? What cd happen to anyone? After all, newspapers and others reproducing the text of the report only get 'qualified' privilege anyway. (They are secure unless 'malice' can be proved, and obviously 'malice' can't be proved agst a newspaper that usually reproduces a command Govt paper) Who then gains from 'absolute' privilege and what is the gain? Prime Minister and Stationery Office gain (Lord Denning has, it is thought, absolute privilege anyway) What is the gain? Well, with 'absolute', a writ cannot even be issued or an *ex parte mandamus*[111] brought. With 'qualified' a writ can be issued, and be used to delay

---

108. This differs from Home's account, which was that he advised Macmillan to retire.
109. From prosecution for libel, which could be made absolute if Parliament was recalled.
110. Quoting the Duke of Wellington regarding the intentions of the courtesan Harriette Wilson to publish her memoirs.
111. A common law writ, in this case to prevent publication.

things or even prevent further publication, tho' it is <u>very</u> doubtful if any court wd sustain it. So, it was left to me to decide, if I wished, for 'publish and be damned'.

As regards omissions, there were one or two minor points which on 'Security' grounds wd be desirable. The chief were references to the possibility of winning over Captain Ivanov (of the Russian Embassy) to be a defector and the possible use of Mr Profumo for this purpose. There was also the question of Miss Keeler, who is about to be summoned and prob[ably] go to trial for perjury and attempt[ing] to hold up course of justice. Has Ld Denning said things wh. wd prevent her having a fair trial. The Law Officers gave later in the day a written opinion that there was really nothing about Miss Keeler in the Report wh. had not already been published <u>by</u> her or <u>about</u> her . . . .

At 2.45 Wilson came, with his Chief Whip. He had read the report on Tuesday and commented rather sadly to Bligh that there wasn't much in it. I suppose he meant 'not much for me'.

I told him . . . . of the only omissions on security grounds wh. seemed at all desirable. I explained to him the position about Miss Keeler. We had a short talk about this, but he said he wd leave decision to me and support publicly whatever I decided. Then about publication, I explained about privilege, and said my inclination was to publish immediately it cd be printed. He seemed very startled and said 'and not call Parlt to get absolute privilege?' I said I thought it almost impossible (because of our two Party Conferences) to call H of Commons. There wd be difficulties about the Lords, I said, smiling sweetly! (He was hoping, of course, that we shd go for the Lords and get into a great morass of trouble, from all sides, with Lord Salisbury sniping from the side) Then he said it wd be a pity to discuss Denning on Queen's speech. Why not get it out of the way by a discussion <u>after</u> the Conservative Party Conference (Parlt to meet on October 14th) or alternatively just before Prorogation (Parlt to meet Oct 22nd) I tried to ignore this. When he came back to it, I said I wd consider it, but it seemed not a very good plan to me.

A few ministers met at 4.30. I decided to publish <u>in full</u> (with no omissions) and to publish <u>as soon as possible</u>. As for Parliament's recall, it was quite out of the question.

Cabinet met again at 5, and went on till 7.15 – chiefly on the multilateral or multi-manned nuclear force. There was great and even bitter discussion between Heath (L P[rivy] Seal) and Thorneycroft (Defence) Most of the Cabinet were torn between the feeling that the

force was absurd and unnecessary as a military force, with corresponding difficulty of getting any political support here, and the equal danger
of U.S.A. forcing the pace without us, and a complete rift in the alliance,
leaving U.K. <u>out</u> of Europe, and <u>out</u> of American-German axis.[112]

Chief Whip dined with me. Wilson has put out his demand for recall
of Parl. but not sent me any formal request. We will put out that if a
formal request is sent, it will be refused. All precedent is against such a
recall. I think Labour are upset at the course events have taken . . . .

20 September
. . . . Ld Home began by reporting on Indonesia. At least the Govt has
apologised for the attack on our Embassy (which was destroyed by
fire.) Since the Govt obviously organised the attack,[113] I suppose they
had a right to apologise, as well as a duty! About British properties
(Shell; Unilever; Dunlop – some £150m or so) the position is very
obscure. I fear the worst . . . .

21 September
. . . . I ought to record a most <u>extraordinary</u> incident in the security
field. The Russian defector who came to England from US, and whose
identity was disclosed by the *Daily Telegraph* (disregarding the D
notice wh. <u>all</u> the other newspapers accepted)[114] has now gone back to
US (where he can be more easily protected from Russian vengeance)
He has produced a story, supported by a good deal of evidence over
the last 10 years, which he has given to the American authorities. It is
that Harold Wilson has been, from 1951 for a number of years,
working for USSR and in effect, an agent! McCone – head of American
security, has (through our security people) asked for our 'assessment'
of these allegations. I don't suppose, in all the history of this country –
at least in modern history – a P.M. has had such an extraordinary
question asked by an ally about the Leader of the Opposition. At first,
I told For Secy that I thought we cd just reply that it was absurd. But
yesterday afternoon, I thought that – this official paper being 'on the

---

112. In the event, with West Germany the only European state to respond with
     much enthusiasm, the idea was later quietly buried by the Johnson
     administration.

113. On 18 September to protest against the creation of Malaysia.

114. Dating from 1912, D-notices provided a non-binding way of urging the press
     not to publish certain information in the national interest.

record' – we must <u>do</u> something about it, and I have accordingly asked the F.S. to have a talk with 'C' and report to me what action he thinks we ought to take. I can then discuss it with Home Secy and Hollis. It's an odd world![115] . . . .

Worked on speech for Blackpool[116] – completed about 3000 words. I have now reached the definite decision to announce that 1) there will not be a General Election this year – 1963, 2) that I will <u>not</u> lead the party at the next General Election, but following Sir W.S.C[hurchill]'s precedent in 1955, retire in time for a new P.M. to have a proper time and some freedom of manoeuvre for the dissolution. But I will <u>not</u> inform anyone of this except Lord Home, Ld Poole, Chief Whip and Tim Bligh (of course, Dorothy and Maurice) I shall tell the Cabinet on Tuesday morning before Blackpool Conference and make my speech on Saturday October 12th.

I hope the Party will act sensibly and calmly, so as to enable me both to preserve the Queen's prerogative and enable her to exercise it in a way wh. gets general support in the Party. This will not be easy. Lord Poole and Bligh came to luncheon and we discussed a lot of plans arising out of all this. Meanwhile, we hope to get the Denning report published on Thursday next. The Press will, of course, concentrate their attack on me, as well as the Attorney General and the Chief Whip. The A.G. has offered to resign, but I have got him to agree to stay on and (like Mr Britling) 'see it through'[117] . . . .

25 September

I went to see Churchill at Chartwell. I found him much better than I expected. Christopher [Soames] had told me that since the last seizure (wh affected his legs) he was failing very rapidly. He doubted whether he wd even know me. But since then his astonishing constitution has served him well. Actually, today was a good day. Montague Browne told me that it was an exceptionally good day. He has some <u>very</u> bad days, when he is very moody and speaks to nobody. Fundamentally, I fear, he is very unhappy. He said to M.B. the other day 'I am unhappy.

---

115. Golitsyn also alleged that Gaitskell had been killed so that Wilson could become Labour leader. Hollis told McCone that there was nothing to the allegations.
116. The impending Conservative Party Conference.
117. A reference to H. G. Wells's novel set during the First World War, *Mr Britling Sees It Through*.

I wd like to go to sleep and not wake up'. Lady C. has had a sort of collapse and is staying with Mary Soames – not far – ½ hour or ¾ hour drive. In some ways I think her being away from time to time relieves the tension in this strange situation – 88, 80, – husband and wife both ill and really waiting for the end.

He talked about the films of his life; about *The River War*,[118] and the tents where he slept with the Spanish officer, with bullets going by just overhead.[119] About the First War, and his life in Admiralty House. (He was interested in the move back to No 10) He talked a lot about old friends – Jumbo Wilson, Alex, Monty.[120] Altogether it was rather wonderful. He remarked that he made me Minister of Housing. 'You were disappointed at the time; but it made you P.M.' . . . .

26 September

The Press are so disappointed by the lack of scandals in Denning, that they all turn on me . . . .

A very good talk in the afternoon with Ld Hailsham (who has been working for North East Coast) and Keith Joseph (Local Govt) I am very anxious to launch a scheme for 'Regionalising' the country. In Scotland, we have a SofS and a satisfactory organisation. Wales works well enough, with M of State and Cardiff office. NE Coast has got going, with Ld Hailsham supervising. We want now an organisation for N[orth] West (wh. shd be fairly easy) and for S[outh] East. I hope to get something for Queen's speech and organised during the next few months.

Meeting with Ld P[rivy] Seal and Harold Caccia. We agreed on a reply to President Kennedy's message about de Gaulle. President K wants to offer him something on nuclear knowledge (only of underground techniques) if he will sign the Test Ban Treaty. But of course he won't.

We had, I think a splendid counter-attack on Profumo case. Hailsham and Macleod were excellent on T.V. My broadcast on sound radio was said to be good. Ld Shawcross was very effective – and a very friendly neutral! . . . .

---

118. Churchill's account of the Anglo-Egyptian campaign to recapture Sudan in 1898.
119. During the Spanish war against rebels in Cuba in 1895.
120. Three Second World War Field Marshals, Lords Wilson, Alexander of Tunis and Montgomery.

27 September

.... [I]t [is] clear that what Lord Shawcross said in refuting the criticism of ministers wh. Ld Denning made in para. 286 of his report has had a great effect. All day long came messages of congratulation. I feel somehow that the tide is turning and that the people as a whole will support me. The American Press headlines (curiously enough) are 'Macmillan vindicated'. Maurice rang up, very cheerful. Ted Heath and Julian Amery came to luncheon, and were also jubilant . . . .

Governor Rockefeller (New York State) came to luncheon, with Dr Kissinger (who is by way of being an expert on military strategy) I like R – who was simple, intelligent, and restrained. He is a Liberal Republican (just as Kennedy is a Liberal Democrat) It will be a strange fight if R. gets the nomination, between two Liberal multi-millionaires. R. was critical of the administration's foreign policy, wh. he thought erratic and presumptuous. He said that the administration were determined to prevent Britain being a nuclear power and that my success with the President at Nassau had upset them very much. He himself sympathised with us and with the French. It wd be equally bad for Europe <u>and</u> for America if U.S.A. became the only nuclear power in the West . . . .

30 September

. . . . Lord Swinton to luncheon – a useful talk about the whole political situation. He is – on the whole – in favour of the plan for my resignation in January; but <u>only</u> if we can get <u>Hailsham</u>. Altho' an old and devoted friend of <u>Butler</u>, S. thinks he wd lose the election disastrously. Maudling wd be worse, electorally. S. thinks that Butler wd be prepared to stand down for Hailsham, but he is not sure. If H. cannot be got by agreement, I ought to stay on, at whatever inconvenience to myself . . . .

2 October

Came to London – to <u>No 10 Downing St</u>, instead of Admiralty House, after 3 years absence. I am very glad to be back, and architect and builders have certainly done a good job.

Wilson has made a very brilliant and effective 'key-note' speech at the Labour Party Conference,[121] which will have a wide appeal and be

---

121. It promised a compelling but unspecified modernisation through the 'white

difficult to answer. All the difficulties are swept under the carpet, and a 'new vision' is developed in a Jack Kennedy sort of style. It was excellently done, if fundamentally dishonest . . . .

Slept in No 10, for first time for 3 years. My own room is very pleasant, tho', of course, much smaller than the one I had in Admiralty House . . . .

3 October

Cabinet at 10.30. A large number of rather difficult questions. Indonesia: Horticulture: Rating Reform: Service Pensions: etc. By 1.15 there were still 4 more items, and we shall have to resume on Tuesday morning, before everyone goes off to Blackpool [for the Party Conference]. This was the first Cabinet meeting for 3 years to be held in No 10 Downing St. The house is really very nice – not so fine a house or with such noble rooms as in Admiralty House. I think the work has been very well done, on the whole . . . .

4 October

Maurice [Macmillan] came in at 12 noon and we had some further talk about my position and the leadership. He (like Dorothy) is now persuaded that my decision to retire before the General Election is right. The problem is how exactly to announce it and how to get the right successor. Butler wd be fatal. Maudling uninspiring. Hailsham, with Maudling and the others in loyal support, might still win.

The Labour Party Conference is, on the face of it, a great 'boost' for Labour. But since all the cracks were papered over, I see trouble ahead if the Election is not till Oct. 1964. Already the newspapers are putting some awkward questions . . . .

6 October

. . . . I did not sleep at all last night. I tried to read Wolfgang Michael on George 1st but I kept reverting to the problems of Queen Elizabeth 1st [sic]. There are so many factors – the chief one being that there is no clear successor. But there is also a growing wave of emotion in my favour, throughout the party, esp. the party in the provinces. This will be evidenced at Blackpool. I have written the actual speech – leaving 6 or 7 minutes at the end for the personal bit – to go or to stay? I hate

heat' of scientific and technological revolution as a means of sidestepping party conflicts over issues like nationalisation.

the feeling that I shall be letting down all these loyal people, from highest to lowest, if I give up. On the other hand, I shall prob[ably] be humiliated if I stay and everyone will say that failure has been due to the old limpet . . . .

All the afternoon till 6pm we discussed the problem (MVM[acmillan], JA[mery] and I) I am beginning to move (at the last minute) towards staying on – for another 2 or 3 years. Maurice says that, altho' it wd be difficult to win, for the 4th time, yet it might be done, by a sort of emotional wave of feeling – partly materialist (if you like) but partly sincere. After all, we have brought them both Prosperity and Peace.

Alec Home came . . . . Everyone else went away, so that Home and I were alone for dinner. We had a good talk before and after. We began with a discussion of whether or not there was any real chance of a good forward step in the East/West situation. He is not too hopeful; but reminds me of the situation last year, on the Test Ban. The French are of course, against a détente, (unless initiated and led by de Gaulle) The Germans under Schroeder are rather better – although Adenauer – even in retirement and von Brentano will certainly cause trouble.[122] The real difficulties are (a) my power in G.B. is waning, as Parlt draws to its close (b) President's ditto. Worse still, policies wh. are popular here (Test Ban etc) are not so very popular in U.S.A. The President has been very good about following behind our lead. But as his Election approaches, he will worry more and more about the electoral effects of his policies . . . .

Alec Home was, on the whole, in favour of the plan wh. I had outlined – Plan A when we met last. But he (and I) have begun to wonder whether it can, in fact, be worked. It wd mean from October 12 to (say) first week in January (3 months) during which I am to be P.M. under (self-imposed) sentence of death. Would not the whole situation disintegrate? We felt that if I announced on Saturday that I wd not fight the Election, it would be impossible to prevent the search for a leader from beginning at once, to the exclusion of everything else.

On the other hand, if I announced my determination to go on, it would be accepted – and welcomed by a great majority. But there wd still be a substantial and very vocal minority. It wd be a great moral

---

122. Adenauer resigned on 15 October and was succeeded the following day as Chancellor of West Germany not by Schröder but by Erhard.

and physical strain to overcome them – and 2 or 3 months bitter struggle. Then the Election. I might have a really humiliating defeat. At least a change might be better and cd hardly be worse than the present 'Gallup' polls indicate.

7 October

Motored to London in morning. I had first a talk with Bligh, who tells me that the Cabinet are rallying to me with great enthusiasm. Only one or two exceptions. In the course of the morning, I saw Butler – who wd clearly prefer me to go on, for – in his heart – he does not expect the succession <u>and</u> fears it.[123] Then came Ld Chancellor (Dilhorne) <u>all</u> for going on – 'the call to battle'. Then Chief Whip – very ready to fight, if he is given the order. Then Duncan Sandys – unhesitating and loyal.

.... At 5.30, came Oliver Poole – who has been wonderfully helpful and resourceful throughout. I told him that I was now beginning to think that I had no option but to see it through ....

Oliver Poole, who was deeply moved and almost in tears, told me that he thought it was his duty, as Chairman of the Party but still more as a personal friend, with a very great affection for me, to warn me against this course. He thought we shd lose the Election anyhow. This was almost inevitable, tho' we wd have a good try. But a collapse (wh. was likely) while bad for my successor wd be humiliating for me. Why shd I endure it? ....

At 6pm, we were joined by Ld Chancellor (Manningham-Buller) Butler, Home, and Sandys. A long discussion brought out all the same points again. Duncan was <u>very</u> strong for me going on. Alec Home was balanced, but on the whole adverse. Duncan stayed to dinner, and Chief Whip came in afterwards. It was clear that I wd get <u>full support</u> of Cabinet if I decided to go on, but that several wd be rather unhappy, partly for my sake, partly for that of the party.

8 October

A dramatic day – at least for me. I went to bed last night determined to inform the Cabinet that I had now decided to stay on and fight the

---

123. Butler's own notes of this meeting speak of advising Macmillan 'that it would be wiser for him to go'. He was, however, also aware that his own support within the parliamentary party was slim.

General Election[124] and to ask for the full support of my colleagues.
I wd say that I fully realised the difficulties but that I felt they cd be
overcome.

In the middle of the night (or rather earlier in the evening while
our agitated discussions were going on) I found it impossible to pass
water and an excruciating pain when I attempted to do so. I was seized
of terrible spasms – but no water emerged. Dorothy came to my help
and got a doctor – Dr King-Lewis. (Sir John Richardson was on
holiday in Windermere) He finally arrived about 4am and managed to
give me relief by inserting an instrument to draw the water out of the
bladder. Unfortunately, the bladder kept filling up and by about 8am
it was worse. Dr K-L came again and helped. He promised me that he
wd get Mr Badenoch, the greatest surgeon in this line of business, by
1pm.

Cabinet at 10. A large number of items – rating relief, Robbins
educational report etc etc.[125] At noon, I stopped further items; asked
Cabinet Secretariat to leave (except Sir B. Trend) and explained shortly
the problem to the Cabinet and announced my plan. Since I realised
(I said) that there cd be no free discussion of this in my presence, I
withdrew. (The 'plan', of course, was to announce at Blackpool that
I wd lead in the General Election) At this point, I had no reason to
think (from what Dr King-Lewis had said) that my trouble wd be very
serious. He hoped that normal passing of water might be re-established
in a few hours. Any treatment of a more radical character cd be
perhaps avoided or postponed. Of course, Dr K-L was quite right to
keep me quiet at the time and had no idea of the issues involved.
He thought it only a question of going to Blackpool for the speech
on Saturday. But during the Cabinet, I had to go out twice with the
spasms, and felt pretty bad.[126]

At 12.45 Mr Badenoch came. He re-inserted the instrument and
drained the bladder. After consultation with Dr K-L, he told me that
the cause was inflammation of the prostate gland (by either a benign
or malignant tumour) and that it wd have to be dealt with. Sir

124. Indeed, Macmillan telephoned the Queen's assistant private secretary, Sir
     Edward Ford, that morning with this news.
125. The only diary mention of the Robbins Report, outlining plans for further
     expansion of higher education.
126. Whilst Macmillan was out of the room Home told colleagues he would not
     contend the succession.

J.R[ichardson] had been told by telephone and wd be in London by 4pm or so. It was agreed that there shd be a meeting at 6pm to decide on a course of action. Meanwhile, I heard (at about 1.30) from Chief Whip that the Cabinet had (with one exception) agreed to back me to the full if I decided to go on through the General Election (The exception was 'Aristides' – Enoch Powell, who thought I ought to resign.)[127]

The afternoon went on, with coming and going, some pain and some moments of relief. We were giving a party to our staff, to celebrate the return to No 10, at 6.30–8. I managed to appear at this, after the doctors' conference and verdict. The decision was to go to hospital at once, for the operation. The rest of the evening was rather confused. I telephoned to Ld Poole (at Blackpool) Butler came in to see me. I had talks with Maurice and my daughters. At 9pm I went to the Hospital (King Edward's Hospital for Officers) in excruciating pain[128] . . . .

9 October

Before I left No 10 last night, Harold Evans quite rightly insisted that the true story shd be given to the Press. So this morning it is headline news. In the day, Ld Home, Bligh (with Jane Parsons for dictating) both Philips (Zulueta and Woodfield) and Ld Chancellor have been to see me and we have got a lot of work done.

1) Letter for Alec to read out on Friday,[129] wh makes it clear that altho' I had decided to go on through the Election, this is now impossible.
2) Approval of this letter by the Queen.

---

127. Powell, a former Professor of Greek, is here compared to the Athenian statesman Aristides, nicknamed 'the Just' because of his personal integrity. Deedes's contemporary notes, in contrast to Macmillan's diary, were: 'Majority view clearly a decision is urgent, and seems to be in favour of change', though Powell appears the only one prepared explicitly to voice this.

128. Meanwhile, that evening at the party conference in Blackpool, news of Macmillan's condition was beginning to filter out to his newly arrived Cabinet colleagues.

129. Home was to present this in his capacity as President of the National Union of Conservative Associations. He stayed in London and met with Macmillan that morning, not travelling up to Blackpool until Thursday 10 October, by which time he was thinking and the press were talking of him as a possible leadership candidate.

3) Letter in general terms about situation to the Queen.
4) I have had – before getting ill – a wonderful letter from the President about my part in getting the Test Ban. Cd it be read to the Conference? Or published in some other way? David Gore will ask Pres[iden]t (It was read. HM. 15.10)
5) Some general plans about date of my retirement and successor taking over. If Hailsham is to be a competitor, he must at once give up his peerage and find a constituency[130] ....

Wrote up the diary. Read Bible (Samuel 1) ....

(The Press has been very sympathetic, on the whole)

10 October[131]

Operation performed successfully.[132] I did not remember having been taken from my room and the operating theatre.

It was all over by 1pm.

But I remember little about the rest of the day, or the next day ....

12 October

A horrible day – with perpetual 'spasms' wh. were very painful but happily not dangerous.

The public events of these days – Oct 11th onwards, are quite beyond my control. I decided nothing about myself, and gave no instructions about anything or anybody. The conduct of the Govt I have handed over to Butler but I shall take this back as soon as I am able to do so. But I fear that all kind of intrigues and battles are going on about the leadership of the Party. Perhaps those who were so anxious to get me out will now see the disadvantages. What I do

---

130. This was conveyed to Hailsham by Amery and Maurice Macmillan when they arrived in Blackpool that afternoon.

131. That afternoon Lord Home read out to Conference Macmillan's valedictory address. Harold Evans in his diary suggested that this being brought forward to Thursday was designed to aid Hailsham, who later announced his intention to resign his peerage and stand for the Commons. If this was the intention, the over-exuberance of Hailsham and his supporters ensured an opposite effect was achieved.

132. This rectified a swollen prostate. Macmillan was aware that his condition was not cancerous, but seems to have regarded it, according to the distinguished urologist who treated him, A. W. Badenoch, as 'an act of God' determining his resignation.

profoundly hope is that the image of the party is not injured by all this
public disputing . . . .

14 October

I had rather a better night, but very confused dreams and ideas. It
seemed to me that everyone was trying to destroy me and were all
marching on the Palace, with that purpose. The Queens were protect-
ing me.

The night was not quite so painful as the night before and I slept
quite a lot. But I am writing this without seeing the paper properly
and knowing quite what words I am using.

D. tells me that the messages etc have been quite overwhelming
and very kind. I feel as if I were dead. I suppose, in a way, I am.

Actually, things began to get sorted out a bit today. The Lord
Chancellor came this afternoon; the Chief Whip this morning. Both
these are, in principle, 'Hoggites' but they feel rather upset at the
rather undignified behaviour of Hogg and his supporters at Blackpool.
It wasn't easy for him, since whenever he appeared he was surrounded
by mobs of enthusiastic supporters. But it was thought that he need
not have paraded the baby and the babyfood in the hotel quite so
blatantly or talked so much at large. This is said (by both L.C. and
C[hief] Whip) to be turning 'respectable' people away from Hogg. Nor
need he have talked so much about his giving up his peerage and going
into the H of Commons at this stage.[133] After all, I was not yet
politically dead – certainly not buried. So Hogg (who really had the
game in his hand) had almost thrown it away. But the movement agst
Hogg (on this account) had not gone to Butler or Maudling, but to
Home. The 'draft' Home movement was in reality a 'Keep out' Butler
movement. I was struck by the fact that both Ld C and C. Whip agreed
on this analysis and that both are, or were, supporters of the Hogg
succession. Both are agst the Butler succession on the ground that the
party in the country will find it depressing. One thing stands out clearly
– Julian Amery and Maurice [Macmillan] were right all along when
they told me that I could sweep the board at Blackpool. Had I not
been struck down on last Monday night by this filthy disease, I cd

133. A move only made feasible as a result of the Peerage Act, which received the
      Royal Assent on 31 July 1963. Peers were now allowed, in light of the Benn
      case, to resign their peerages, a development from which Home was also to
      benefit.

have reduced to nothing all the Lambtons, Nigel Birches etc in the Party – at least temporarily – we would have had a battle – or running fight till February – then we wd have all got together for the Election. Now we are in disarray.

I feel almost tempted to step back into the ring, but I know it wd be folly. I have lost the great moment 'Blackpool'. 'The Spirit was willing but the Body was weak'.[134]

What worries me in all this is the underlying struggle. It is really the old one, I feel Hogg (with all his absurdities and posturings and emotions) represents what Stanley, and John Loder, and Boothby, and Noel Skelton and I tried to represent from 1924 onwards.[135] Those who clamour for Butler and Home are really <u>not</u> so much shocked by Hogg's oddities as by his <u>honesty</u>. He belongs <u>both</u> to this strange modern age of space and science <u>and</u> to the great past – of classical learning and Christian life. This is what they instinctively dislike. (Religion is not so bad when it is patrician – reading the lessons as long as you own the advowson etc)

<u>Poole</u> and <u>Maurice</u> [Macmillan] came at 6pm. They were both calm and firm. The unlucky coincidence of my physical breakdown with Blackpool conference had created rather a shambles. But the basic situation was the same – the party in the Country wants Hogg; the Parl[iamentar]y Party wants Maudling or Butler; the Cabinet wants Butler. The last 10 days have not altered this fundamental fact.

15 October

. . . . Tim Bligh at 10am. Then Butler. I shewed Butler the minute of instructions which I wished him to read to the Cabinet.[136] He seemed to acquiesce willingly enough. The Kenya problem (wh. is becoming

---

134. A paraphrase of Matthew 26:41 (and Mark 14:38).

135. Skelton had published a pamphlet entitled *Constructive Conservatism* in 1924 and acted as a kind of informal leader to a group of progressive young Tory MPs, including Macmillan, first elected that year. See *HMM* I, pp. 177–78.

136. This set out a process whereby the preferences for future leader would be canvassed by the Lord Chancellor consulting the Cabinet, the Chief Whip the other ministers and MPs, his equivalent in the Lords – Lord St Aldwyn – the peers, whilst Lord Poole was to talk to Lord Chelmer and Mrs Shepherd as representatives of the National Union of Conservative Associations, and the Conservative Women's Organisation. It is, however, dubious to say the least to suppose that such a survey in such a space of time could be particularly rigorous, and Dilhorne and Redmayne certainly exaggerated Home's support.

very acute)[137] will occupy Cabinet this morning and perh. this afternoon as well. Otherwise, Butler was friendly, but seemed in rather a
daze.

. . . . In the afternoon, I saw Alec Home, Iain Macleod, Ted Heath,
Reggie Maudling, Quintin Hailsham. I have made records of what
they all said. The situation is certainly very confused . . . .

16 October

Woke late – 8am – after rather a restless night. The whole burden of
the Premiership has fallen on – or been assumed by me. But it is a
terrible tangle and no one seems to know what is to be done. The Press
this morning is less excited – except the *D. Mirror*, wh. is vile. It is a
comfort to feel that they insulted Churchill even more grossly.

I saw this morning Philip de Zulueta. He has decided to go into
the City instead of returning to the F.O. Thorneycroft and Edward
Boyle came 10.30 onwards – the first a Hoggite, the second a Butlerite
– neither extreme. Then Agriculture (Christopher Soames) who was
very sensible. Then Selwyn Lloyd – dapper, agreeable, and sensible.
On the whole, he preferred Home. Butler was much disliked by the
Party Organisation, esp. the women. Why this is so, no one seems to
know. Slept for an hour after luncheon.

After luncheon, Minister of Labour (Hare) – he is for Hogg. Then
Home Secy (Brooke) he is for Butler. Then Housing (Keith Joseph) He
is for 1. Maudling, 2. Butler. He is fearful of Hogg's eccentricities, esp.
in foreign affairs.[138] Practically all of these ministers, however, whether
Hoggites or Butlerites or Maudlingites, agreed that if Ld Home wd
undertake the task of P.M. the whole Cabinet and the whole Party wd
cheerfully unite under him. Sandys (Commonwealth Secy) feels this
specially strongly.[139]

---

137. There were already tensions in the recently convened conference on Kenya over
     KANU's desire to reduce the regional safeguards built into the 1962
     constitution, when KADU's general secretary arrived in London on 13 October
     with news of attempted arrests of his colleagues by the KANU government and
     pressing for partition. The Home government subsequently decided to support
     KANU and KADU backed down.

138. This is Macmillan's only hint, reported to him from Ormsby-Gore via Home, at
     the American disquiet at the prospect of Hailsham as Prime Minister.

139. The diary is silent on Macmillan's final visitors that day, Macleod, Hailsham
     and Heath, the last of whom came out strongly for Home.

17 October

In the morning I saw (separately) the following
1) Ld Chancellor[140]
2) Chief Whip and John Morrison – the latter I saw alone for
   some minutes[141]
3) Ld St Aldwyn[142] – Chief Whip in Lords
4) Lord Poole; Mrs Shepherd, (Chairman, National Union) Ld
   Chelmer.[143]

This was in accordance with the minute which I had sent to Cabinet
and was approved by them.

After luncheon (3pm onwards) I saw Ld Chancellor; Chief Whip;
Ld St Aldwyn; Lord Poole together.[144]

---

140. At 11am. He found that without Home the Cabinet split with 8 for Butler, 7
     for Maudling and 5 for Hailsham. With Home the vote became: Home 10 (plus
     Home himself), Maudling 5, Butler 3, Hailsham 2. He also reported that of the
     junior ministers consulted by Redmayne, 28 supported Home and 14 Butler.
     There appeared to be no obvious left/right split in support. Macleod, in his
     subsequent *Spectator* article, claimed only two of the Cabinet positively
     supported Home, though it seems (as Nigel Lawson pointed out in the *Sunday
     Telegraph*, 3 October 2004) that Dilhorne correctly recorded him as supporting
     Home, albeit for tactical reasons, in the hope that a resulting impasse would
     enable him to become Premier.

141. According to Knox-Cunningham's minutes at 11.33 a.m. (Morrison) and 11.42
     a.m. (Redmayne) respectively. Morrison – who had been quietly campaigning
     for Home before the crisis broke – advised that the 1922 Executive had been
     for Maudling at Blackpool, but that now most backbench support would go to
     Home and 'There are strong blocks against all the others' (DWM: Ms
     Macmillan, dep. c. 355). Redmayne advised similarly, and that Hailsham and
     Butler could be mollified, the latter by an offer of the Foreign Office.

142. At 12.07 p.m. Although Salisbury and Eden were apparently for Hailsham, St
     Aldwyn's view was that the Conservative peers were two to one for Home,
     with support for the rest equally divided.

143. Macmillan actually saw them first, at 10.28 a.m. Chelmer later told me that he
     advised that the ideal would be Hailsham as a front man and Heath to keep
     everyone in order. This is only obliquely confirmed by Knox-Cunningham's
     contemporary notes, in which Chelmer is recorded as observing that
     Hailsham's support had declined since Blackpool, but that he was still ahead in
     the South East. Poole argued that the North was also strongly for Hailsham
     though Mrs Shepherd did comment that 'A great many said that if Lord Home
     could be persuaded that would be the answer' (DWM: Ms Macmillan, dep. c.
     355).

144. Poole observed at the start of this meeting that the Young Conservatives were

All this tired me very much. It took 2½ hours in morning and 2 hours in afternoon . . . . But after 6, the work began and I dictated memorandum for the Queen (shd she ask my advice) and also signed formal letter of resignation. We finished at midnight! Tim Bligh has set up an office in the hospital and two typists from No 10 have been here all day.

The remarkable and to me unexpected result of all these 4 groups of people asked to give their views was (rather contrary to what I expected) a <u>preponderant first</u> choice for Ld Home (except in the constituencies, who hardly knew he was a serious candidate but agreed that he wd be universally acceptable if <u>drafted</u>) and an almost universal <u>second</u> choice. There were <u>strong</u> pro-Butlerites; but equally violent <u>anti</u>. There were strong – very strong – pro Hailsham – but very violent anti. On Maudling the feelings were not so strong in either direction[145] . . . .

18 October

A terrible day and very bad for me. The doctors protest, but I cd see no way of shuffling out of my duty. At the end of the day, I can hardly hold a pen.

At 7.30am Bligh rang up to say that a critical situation had developed and that he and Chief Whip wd be round at hospital at 8.30am to consult me. It seems that the news that the general choice favoured Home got out last night (leaked by some one)[146] Meetings

---

80–90% for Hailsham, who was also better supported in the suburbs. Although surprised by how little the Foreign Secretary was known throughout the party, he felt Home would have been second if constituency associations had known he was a runner.

145. The Chief Whip in the afternoon meeting in fact advised that Home led on MPs' second choices, with a split on first preferences with Butler. Maudling apparently drew his support almost exclusively from younger MPs. Macmillan was clearly aware of the risks of plumping for Home, commenting at the meeting on the need for the 14th Earl of Home to 'spread out into a Palmerston figure' able, as any Prime Minister must, to dominate the Commons. However, he was reassured by the thought that Home 'dominated our party committees more than anyone I know' (DWM: Ms Macmillan, dep. c. 355), an observation clearly borne out by Knox-Cunningham's minutes for him of various backbench committees over the previous years.

146. Macleod was telephoned by William Rees-Mogg of the *Sunday Times*, whose

were organised by Powell, who got Macleod to help him. Erroll and Maudling were brought in. Hailsham came too.[147] Also Butler was approached. The idea was an organised revolt by all the <u>unsuccessful</u> candidates – Butler, Hailsham, Maudling and Macleod – against Home.[148] Considering their intense rivalry with each other during recent weeks, there was something rather 18th century about this (Fox–North Coalition perhaps)[149] and somewhat distasteful. Home rang up and felt somewhat aggrieved. He had only been asked to come forward as a compromise candidate, for unity. He felt like withdrawing. I urged him not to do so. If we give in to this intrigue, there wd be chaos. Butler wd fail to form a Govt; even if given another chance (for Queen might then send for Wilson) no one else wd succeed. We shd have a Wilson Govt; a dissolution; and our Party without even a nominal leader. Chief Whip (and Tim) took same view. This was a most critical moment, but I decided to go on. My letter of resignation was sent and delivered to Palace at 9.30am . . . .

So ended my premiership – Jan 11 [sic], 1957 – Oct 18, 1963.

. . . . Alec Home was sent for and accepted the charge of seeing whether he cd form a Govt.

He rang me up at lunch time – rather agitated, but I urged him to try to pin down Butler and Maudling. If he cd get Butler to take F.O. and Maudling the Treasury, the game wd be in his hands. During the rest of the day I only got news from time to time – at 5pm from Bligh and at 8pm from Elizabeth Home. I did my best to encourage him to

---

source was apparently Butler. Maudling found out from his Private Secretary, Derek Mitchell, who allegedly heard in turn from de Zulueta.

147. Aldington, not Hailsham (who was only contacted by telephone), was at the meeting on the evening of 17 October at Powell's house. The Chief Whip was, however, summoned and told that second preferences were not the same as supporting Home for leader. Instead, he was told that, with Hailsham and Maudling now supporting Butler, the latter should be regarded as the acknowledged successor. Redmayne's report of this to Macmillan no doubt informed his following remarks, but contrary to some claims there is no evidence that this event altered Macmillan's resignation timetable as, on the morning of 17 October, he had already arranged to see the Queen the following day.

148. Butler was to chair a meeting that morning with Maudling and Hailsham, at which they agreed to serve under him.

149. The unlikely coalition government of long-term political enemies Charles James Fox and Lord North and their supporting factions in 1783.

stand firm. He wisely saw every member of the Cabinet alone and asked them the simple question 'did they want him or not'. The rather unholy alliance between Butler, Maudling, and Hailsham, but really got up by Macleod and Powell, began to crack. Perhaps Butler realised that he was merely being used as a 'stooge' and that the young men wd desert him as soon as they had broken Ld Home (I think Hailsham – who has been apparently in a highly emotional state since Blackpool – realised this and being a straight and honest man began to break away)

At night, I knew no more than that it looked as if Butler and Maudling wd agree to serve. I slept well, considering . . . .

19 October

I heard at about 11.30am from Bligh that Butler, Maudling and Hailsham had agreed to serve and that Home was leaving for the Palace to kiss hands. This is splendid. It seems that Macleod and Powell are still standing out – apparently on the ground that H[ome] is a Peer. But, of course, that ground is anathema to the supporters of Hailsham. Or is there something worse about the 14th Earl than the 2nd Viscount? All this inverted snobbery is absurd. Press today much more guarded. It is clearly not so easy to denigrate Home's character.

D. came in at 6pm and Reggie Buller [Dilhorne] at about 9.30pm. It seems as if Cabinet making is now going on all night. I am much relieved. I have been very unfairly attacked about this, but that doesn't matter. I feel that if I had not acted there might have been complete disaster. It is quite untrue that I was determined to 'down' Rab. It is true that of the three I wd have preferred Hailsham, as a better election figure. All this pretence about Rab's 'progressive' views is rather shallow. His real trouble is his vacillation in any difficult situation. He has no strength of character or purpose and for this reasons shd not be P.M.

20 October

Holy Communion was brought to me at 8am – a nice little service. Alec and Elizabeth are now established – and, of course, very grateful. I feel sure that he is the right choice, both as PM and as likely to fight a good election.

The Press not too bad. Rees-Mogg (who acted as Rab's 'election agent') has a bitter attack on me in *Sunday Times*. *Observer* curiously fair. *S. Telegraph* not too bad. *S. Express* turning towards Home. The *Sunday Mirror* hysterical. Dorothy tells me that on TV and Broadcast the discussions have been fair and tended to favour Home. I'm sure the mass of the people will respond to his natural, firm, sincere leadership . . . .

The more I reflect on the events of the last week the more astonished I am at the failure of Rab, who was Deputy P.M. and put in charge when I went to hospital, to <u>do</u> anything about the crisis. I had made it clear that I cd not go on and he shd have at least tried to get some method of testing opinion organised. He may have thought that the thing cd just drag on – but this was clearly impossible. He cd have asked the Ld Chancellor (who was clearly <u>not</u> a potential P.M.) to take charge – and he cd have asked someone else who was also obviously not a candidate to work with him (if he had any doubts about the Ld Cr) I, of course, cd have merely resigned on entering the hospital and when asked for advice by the Queen, said I was too ill to give it. This wd have got me out of all this trouble, but it wd have been very wrong both as regards the Queen and the party. The truth is that with the 3 main 'hats' in the ring (Butler, Maudling, and Hailsham) and the very strong feelings both <u>for</u> and <u>against</u> wh. were excited by their candidature, the only way out (short of a total failure to form a Conservative Govt) was a 'compromise' candidate. Ld Home was the only compromise candidate possible. Incidentally, he was the best candidate of the 4 – but that is another argument . . . . Meanwhile, one can only hope that the Conservative party in the HofC will at last have the sense to start attacking the Socialists and not their own leaders. I feel that there is a good chance of this. Throughout the country, I feel sure that the constituency organisations will rally round the new leader. Of course, Macleod and Powell (if they stay out)[150] will do a good deal of harm. But this trouble must be worn. Fortunately, neither of them are popular figures. The first is thought to be too ambitious, the second too rigid . . . .

21 October

Ralph Allen, Chairman of the Bromley Conservative Association, came at 11am, full of kind and loyal messages from the constituency. I told him that I wd <u>not</u> inflict a by-election on the constituency but remain member at least till the end of the Parlt. About the General Election, I wd let them have my decision soon after the New Year . . . .

Oliver Poole came at 12.30. To my great joy, he has agreed to remain at Central Office to help John Hare, the new chairman. Iain Macleod and Powell have definitely refused to serve . . . .

---

150. They were the only Cabinet ministers to refuse to serve under Home.

22 October

I have started on the heavy task of going through all the letters, telegrams, cards with flowers, etc etc wh. I have received in the last fortnight. They have all been acknowledged, but I am now picking some of them out for personal letters. They have been very well arranged in different folders – ambassadors, churchmen, MP[s], Peers, constituents etc etc. People have certainly been very kind. Today's announcement of Maurice [Macmillan]'s appointment as Economic Secy to Treasury is a great joy to me. In the only two papers wh I read now (wonderful liberation) – *Times* and *D. Telegraph* it has been welcomed very generously . . . .

24 October

Went out for drive (Dorothy driving) in Regent's Park from 11–12. I had a little walk. The 'outing' (my first) did me good. The pain is less acute . . . .

Some nice photographs in the evening papers of Dorothy and me sitting in Regent's Park – but rather pathetic, with a distinctively old age pensioner look about us . . . .

29 October

. . . . Tim Bligh came to luncheon and gave a most spirited account of the critical days – Thursday, Friday, and Saturday – before Ld Home was able to form his govt. He confirmed that only my telephone messages to Lord H and to his wife had sustained him through the critical moments. Finally, a telegram from the National Union convinced Butler that he must fall into line. This was on the Saturday morning. Of course, the Macleod, Powell, Maudling, Erroll intrigue on the Thursday night was not really intended to make Butler PM. He wd fail, after Home's failure. Then Maudling or Macleod wd be sent for.[151] This altogether left out of account the danger that the Queen, after two Conservative failures, might send for Wilson . . . .

31 October

I went to M&Co at 11am this morning. It was the day of the monthly Board meeting, and I chose it accordingly, to make contact with the

---

151. Home told Maudling that if the latter refused to serve, the Queen would send for him, not Rab.

directors – all known to me as young men in different jobs 12 years ago. I did not stay for more than a few minutes, to tell them of my plans to start active work in a month's time. They all seemed pleased. A gold watch was to be presented to a Mr Woods (who is retiring after 46 years) and for some extraordinary reason the TV insisted on taking this for the News . . . .

Philip Swinton to luncheon. He is a very dear and very old friend of Butler's. But he was _wholly_ in agreement with the choice of Alec Home. He had himself taken some part, in the decisive week, in persuading Alec to undertake the task. Lord S. is really extraordinary. He is nearly 80, but he is as spry as ever.

According to Ld Carnarvon this story is going round. Ld Stuart (of Findhorn) after seeing me in the hospital went, by agreement with me, to see Churchill, to warn him that I intended to resign in a day or two. Churchill then observed 'I suppose that means that we shall have Lloyd George!' . . . .

5 November
More and more correspondence – it is becoming a serious problem with so little staff. Knox-Cunningham goes on, in a most devoted way, acting as PPS and hon. Secretary – otherwise, I shd be lost . . . .

10 November
I went out yesterday to watch the shoot. I stayed too long and was very tired at the end of the day. Of course, I did not try to fire a gun . . . .

Maurice [Macmillan] is enjoying his new life, as a Minister. I hope I shall enjoy my old life, as a publisher; but I feel diffident about being much use after all these years.

11 November
. . . . The political situation is interesting. On the face of it, the loss of Luton by-election last week by 4000 (from a majority of 5000) makes it appear that the Socialists _must_ win a substantial and perhaps a smashing victory _if_ 400 Liberal candidates really appear in the field. In Luton (where Charles Hill had originally been a Liberal) the Liberal candidate took only 5000 votes.[152] But obviously they were people who

---

152. Labour 21,108; Conservative 17,359; Liberal 5,001; Communist 490.

had voted for Hill in 1959. Repeated all over the country (so write the pollsters and the pundits) this must lead to 1906 or 1945.[153]

On the other hand, Alec Home had a considerable triumph in his election in Scotland. His majority was 9000.[154] Many experts had predicted that he wd just scrape home or even that the Liberal wd win. Today the Conservative Party meets to elect a leader. My letter of resignation will be read and Ld Carrington will propose Alec Home. I hope Butler will second the motion.[155]

Much will depend on the opening days of the Session. If the new P.M. can hold his own against Wilson and can make effective his control of the HofC (as I did after Suez) then things may change and a new mood be created. I certainly could <u>not</u> have done this after 12 years. A new P.M. has at least a chance.

I spoke to Whitehead (M&Co) about various business things on the telephone. My new life is beginning – or rather my old life is being revived. I am still <u>weak</u> and very depressed – what nannies used to call 'low' . . . .

17 November (Sunday)

. . . . Maurice [Macmillan] 'wound up' for the Govt on Thursday – his first speech from the 'box', and by all accounts did very well. Randolph Churchill came to luncheon yesterday – to talk about a 'paper-back' wh. he is preparing for publication about the Tory leadership.[156] After consultation with the Chief Whip I thought he might as well have the true story of those last few days from me, rather than publish a lot of inaccuracies.

. . . . Read a *Life of Adenauer* by Charles Wighton, wh. struck me as remarkably accurate. The account of A's relationship with me, oscillating from occasional friendliness to deep suspicion, based on his fundamental Anglophobia, is – if I remember right – pretty good . . . .

18 November

Miss Birch (one of the Central Office secretaries) came by train. I got through a lot of letters – private, constituency, M&Co, etc – which

153. Both huge electoral landslides against the Conservative Party.
154. He held Kinross and West Perthshire with 14,147 votes. The other votes were: Liberal 4,819; Labour 3,752; SNP 1,801.
155. He did.
156. Published as *The Fight for the Tory Leadership* (London: Heinemann, 1964).

have been piling up here and causing me distress. It seems strange no longer to be able to ring the bell for a 'young lady' at any time, day or night. Certainly, the No 10 service is so good that you are quite spoilt . . . .

One of my great 'releases' is from reading the papers. Just a glance at the headline – the deaths, births, and marriages in *The Times* – and that is all. No Sunday papers! I feel a wonderful gain from not having to wallow through all that gossip and dirt – and the time saved allows one to read books.

22 November

I have read Macaulay's *Essays*. It [is] extraordinary how readable they still are, but how very thin the Whiggish complacency has worn by now, esp. when it is mixed with Liberal laisser-faire economics. But they are readable. I also have read a book I had never read before – Macaulay's *Life and Letters* by Trevelyan (his nephew) wh. gives a charming picture of the man, with all his fundamental simplicity and kindness. The nearest man in my life time to Macaulay is Sir Edward Boyle, (who was Minister of Education in my Cabinet) He knows everything and is a large, boisterous, and rather attractive bachelor – or, shd I say?, maiden aunt.[157]

We went to Petworth. A nice party – Sir Anthony and Lady Rumbold; Sir Martyn Beckett, Lord Plunket, Diana Norwich.[158] Just before dinner, we heard the stunning news – overpowering, incredible – of President Kennedy's assassination in Dallas City, Texas.

26 November

All Saturday and Sunday; the Press, the Radio, and the TV has been devoted to the details of this terrible event. It has been a staggering blow. To the causes which he and I tried to work for, it is a grievous blow. For Jack Kennedy's acceptance – of Test Ban and of policy of détente with Russia were really his own – I mean, were <u>not</u> shared by any except his most intimate advisers. He took great risks for them – as he did with the policy of ending negro inferiority. I was pestered all the week-end to appear on Radio or TV but refused. It seemed to me

---

157. The Whig politician, essayist and historian Thomas Babington Macaulay (1800–1859) was also a bachelor.

158. Respectively, a diplomat and his wife; an architect; a courtier; and the famed beauty of the inter-war years, Lady Diana Cooper.

better to speak in the HofCommons, wh. I did yesterday. I motored from Petworth to London; lunched with Katie Macmillan; spoke for 5 minutes (after the 3 official spokesmen – Barber, Gordon Walker, Wade) and motored back to B.G. I was very exhausted but I got through without a break-down. Of course, the whole thing only took ½ hour, wh. made it easier. The Press today is <u>very</u> complimentary about my speech and I have heard that Ambassador Bruce and his colleagues at the Embassy were very pleased . . . .

. . . . I was represented at the funeral by Andrew Devonshire. It must have been a wonderful gathering in Washington. The loss to the Anglo-American system is enormous. Poor David Gore will now no longer have the privileged position wh. he has enjoyed so long and used so well.

30 November (St Andrew's Day)

. . . . It is wonderful <u>not</u> to read the newspapers – except a rapid glance thro' *The Times*. It makes such a difference. One feels better, mentally and morally, not to be absorbing, unconsciously, all that steady stream of falsehood, innuendo, poison wh. makes up the Press today, apart from the purely informative sections. 'Gossip', in one form or another, is the main theme and mainstay of modern journalism. Altho' there are nowadays no servants, we are all regarded as making up a vast 'servants' hall' . . . .

6 December

The by-elections are bad. Quintin got in – but only by 5000. A Lancashire seat shows an increased majority for Labour. Suffolk (John Hare's seat) came out today.[159]

I spent 3 days at M&Co – lunching there each day with one or other of the directors . . . . There are a lot of problems to be dealt with at M&Co and I shall be <u>fully</u> employed. David Gore (ambassador in Washington) is over for 2 days. He came to see me yesterday afternoon. What we do not realise here is the bitterness and hatred which many Americans – some Republican businessmen, some Southern 'diehards' felt for Kennedy . . . .

---

159. On 5 December there were by-elections in London St Marylebone (retained for the Conservatives by Hailsham), Sudbury and Woodbridge (also held by the Tories) and Manchester Openshaw (easily held by Labour).

22 December

I went to London on Monday, for the debate on Ld Denning's report etc. Alec Home opened – with a short, sensible speech, and Wilson followed with 50 minutes of spleen, wit, sarcasm – very well done, but not – I thought – altogether to the taste of the House. I spoke at 6pm – 20 minutes. It was a good speech and was well received. It, in effect, killed the debate. Members of both sides were very nice about it, both in the debate and in speaking to me in the lobby.

I went to M&Co on Tuesday, Wed, and Thurs. I am beginning to delve into its affairs. There's a lot to be done. My brother Daniel came to luncheon one day. I fear the last years of his lonely reign have left (and created) a lot of problems . . . .

1964

Controversy over Home's succession to the Premiership – back to publishing – views on Resale Price Maintenance – starting work on the memoirs – the 1964 General Election and the advent of the Wilson government

5 January (Sunday)

I have had 4 working days in London and found it very tiring. I stay in the Carlton Club, (wh. is comfortable) and manage to walk to the office (wh. is good for me) But I find getting about London difficult and exhausting (without a motor-car and a detective) telephoning complicated and defeating (without a private exchange) and the opportunities for work immensely curtailed by no private secretaries and lady typists etc at call. All the same, I am comforted by my physical conditions for my decision. I could not have gone on. I feel very weak and easily tired, even now. I do not feel able to apply my mind, except for short periods . . . .

12 January (Sunday)

. . . . I read the papers hardly at all – Cyprus,[1] riots in Panama, Steel Strike, etc etc. Nor do I hear anything of home politics and the prospects for the General Election. I am to dine with Alec Home alone on Tuesday, so I shall hear something. The truth is that I am still in a kind of daze – like a man who has had concussion. I can just manage to concentrate on a limited range of problems (e.g. those of M&Co) but all the flexibility and resilience of my mind (wh. I think was considerable) has gone. However, I suppose this is the result partly of the operation but partly (and perhaps principally) of 10 years and more of tremendous work at tremendous pressure . . . .

18 January (Saturday)

. . . . Read a book on Archbp Laud – by Duncan-Jones. Laud was not really quite a 'big' enough man for the job he tried to do. But it is

---

1. Civil conflict broke out between Greek and Turkish Cypriots in December 1963, leading to UN deployment from March 1964. A ceasefire was not brokered until August 1964.

1964

curious that his side has really won the battle in the Church of England.[2] The sad thing is that the CofE has lost the nation.

Last Sunday all the newspapers were full of Randolph Churchill's book on *The Fight for the Tory Leadership*. It was, of course, a great pity that he wrote this little book at all. It wd have been far better for us all to have left it to 'History'. However, since no one has ever been able to dissuade R[andolph] C. from doing anything he has decided to do, I thought it wiser that, at least so far as I was involved, his account of the facts shd be correct . . . .

As a result, R.C.'s book was well reviewed – on the whole – but was clearly a disappointment to that part of the Press (practically the whole press) which only wants sensational stories, whether true or untrue, wh. can inflict the maximum pain on individuals and do the maximum damage to established institutions. So the Sunday Press – and the dailies – took a rather sober line and accepted RC's interpretation as well as his presentation of the facts. (Of course, in many parts of the book wh. did not affect me, I did not advise him. The views expressed were his own and I certainly wd not accept them all. But on the two or three chapters about what I did just before, during, and after my illness, the facts are more or less right)

Now – when the mild but not unhealthy interest caused by Churchill's book seemed to be dying down, Iain Macleod has weighed in with a 4000 word article in the *Spectator* (of wh. he is now the Editor) and has fairly put the 'cat among the pigeons'.[3] His article is very cleverly written; on the whole, the Press on Friday and Saturday did not swallow his account either of facts or motives. He alleges that I was all along determined not to have Butler as P.M., but he does not altogether dissent from this decision. He says that the Lord Chancellor's account to me of [the] view in the Cabinet was incorrect, whether from malice or incompetence. But the really damaging part of his attack is on the alleged determination of the small inner ring (Macmillan; Redmayne; Manningham-Buller etc) to have an Etonian! This, of

2. William Laud, Archbishop of Canterbury 1633–45, whose high church views and persecution of puritans led to his execution during the English Civil War. The Anglo-Catholics Macmillan sees as dominant in the Church of England in the early 1960s were not directly Laud's doctrinal descendants.

3. 'The Tory Leadership', *The Spectator*, 17 January 1964. Macleod seems to have felt a need to respond to the way, as he saw it, Macmillan had used Randolph Churchill's book to put his side of the leadership struggle.

course, just suits the Press today, most of which loves to attack Eton and the 'aristocracy'. It's all great nonsense, but it touches off the curious 'inverted snobbery' emotion wh. is very strong today . . . .

19 January (Sunday)

Macleod's article in the *Spectator* is published in full in the *Sunday Mirror*, with a tremendous splash of 'anti-Establishment' sentiment. Macleod, who sent his son to Harrow, is described as 'middle class'. Martin Redmayne, who is a shop-keeper, is elevated to the old aristocracy. Hogg and I . . . . are attacked as typical Etonian 'upper-class'. It's all quite crazy. Butler (because he was not selected by the Cabinet, the HofC, the HofL, or the organised Party, is represented as the victim of my malign conspiracy. (all this is supposed to have happened as the result of long manoeuvring and careful planning. But, in fact, had it not been for my illness, I shd now be Prime Minister myself)

The rest of the Press have joined in. *Sunday Telegraph* is very malignant (representing Lady Pamela [Berry] – the woman scorned) The *Observer* silly (typically Astor) But *News of [the] World* good. *Sunday Times* is level-headed. What harm this will do is hard to say. Our Electoral prospects are not good – for natural and normal reasons, 13 years of power. But I'm afraid Macleod['s] 'blow below the belt' will do some damage. (His statements are, in many respects, just not true. But who cares? Or how can it be shewn?)

Alec (P.M.) rang up this morning and asked for advice as to how he shd treat it. (He has to speak tomorrow in Wales) I thought he wd be wise to ignore the whole thing. Controversies of this kind (not principles but gossip and personalities) are like fires. They must be fanned if they are to burn . . . .

25 January

. . . . Macleod's article has made a great stir . . . . I fear it is another blow at an already weakened Govt, and there is great indignation with Macleod throughout the Party. His chief argument agst Home's appoinment as PM was the implication that among 360 Tory MPs there was none fit to be P.M. It was pointed out that Macleod's appointment to be Editor of *Spectator* might equally be said to be an insult to thousands of 'working' journalists . . . .

7 February

Life has gone on quietly. I do 3 nights in London, 4 at home. This

gives me nearly 4 working days in London. The problems at M&Co
are serious. The last years of my brother's regime have been rather
bad. Poor Maurice had not the authority to interfere or the power to
impose his will.[4] I hope we can save the business from disaster. So far,
I have been trying to reduce the 'overheads' – wh. are ridiculously
high.

All the questions about Randolph's book to the P.M. have been
dealt with firmly and effectively by him. 'How did Randolph know
what advice Mr M. had given the Queen? Who told him?' – this sort
of folly was not thought beneath them by even Wilson and Grimond.
Nobody <u>told</u> R.C. But since he and the whole world knew that the
Queen left the Hospital at 11.30am on that Friday morning and that
Lord Home arrived at the Palace at 12.30pm (having been summoned
at noon) it was not difficult for R.C. or anyone else to hazard a
guess! . . . .

10 February
The letter to the Chairman of Bromley, announcing my decision <u>not</u> to
stand again is published today, my 70th birthday. Also, Dorothy's
honour – Dame Grand Cross of British Empire. Telegrams, plain and
coloured; letters; presents are pouring in . . . .

12 February
. . . . Read a *Life of Spencer Perceval* by a Mr Gray. Shall we all be as
forgotten in 100 years as this rather dim P.M. Even assassination cd
not make him a compelling figure[5] . . . .

13 February
A very good morning at M&Co – a conference of all the educational
staff (editorial) Naturally, they all want more staff and more overheads.

Lunched with Churchill. He is very weak – but still an occasional
flash. He insisted on me going with him to HofCommons, and we
made quite a sensation walking in together. He comes in a wheeled
chair to the door and then somehow (leaning heavily on my and
another's arm) gets to his place – the corner seat below the gangway

---

4. Maurice Macmillan had tried to introduce cost controls when his uncle was
   incapacitated with cancer in 1960, without success.
5. The only Prime Minister (1809–12) to thus die.

on the Govt side. We sat through the last half hour of questions and then went to the smoking room. Wilson was pert. Selwyn Lloyd very effective. Brown was just plain stupid and very properly treated by Sandys with contempt . . . .

22 February (Saturday)

. . . . I work from 10am to 4.30 or 5 at the office. I cannot manage more. Then I read, dine quietly – alone – or not at all, and go early to bed. This last week I have been at Carlton Club; the week before at 12 Catherine Place.

The very bad figure of Imports and Exports – the widest ever – has created a panic which *The Times* and the Labour Party are trying to exploit. Either there will be (they both hope) a collapse or another 'Stop'.[6] Haley is the chief criminal in this as in everything else – a defeatist in war and peace. I have sometimes wondered about his loyalty to anything or anybody. However, I hope Maudling will remain calm and borrow from the IMF . . . .

I have had a lot of argument with the Vice-Chancellor of Oxford [Sir Walter Fraser Oakeshott], but he has given in gracefully. I think he was himself (being rather a naïve man) the victim of a plot. There was a letter to *The Times* drafted, wh. was just Labour Party propaganda attacking the Govt for not giving enough money to universities. But the second draft (wh. is published this morning) is quite irreproachable. It was lucky that I got in on this . . . .

1 March (Sunday)

. . . . I follow the news in rather a detached and desultory way. Everything is held up by the British and American elections, and till these have taken place, there can be no real negotiation with Russia. Africa is having growing pains everywhere, as was to be expected. S. Rhodesia is a problem, because I fear that Field will want to bring the independence issue to a crisis before the British election. Cyprus is insoluble and the Archbishop [Makarios] weak and crooked.

As regards our own affairs, the boom is strong and last month's import and export figures rather alarming. But I think it shd be possible

---

6. A reference to 'stop-go' economic conditions. Whenever expansion was attempted, as then under Maudling's 'dash for growth' launched in the 1963 Budget, capacity constraints tended to lead to soaring balance of payments deficits and inflation, forcing the 'stop' through higher interest rates.

to get through this time without such drastic measures as were necessary in 1961–2. Wages have not gone up so often or so much as then. We have more borrowing power. We can do an import control to save £200–300m if necessary. European inflation, esp. Belgium and Italy, is going ahead faster than ours.

I cannot judge what will be the 'political' effect of the 'Resale Price Maintenance' legislation.[7] I am sceptical of its economic effect – perhaps 1% on cost of living. Whether the Net Book Agreement will survive,[8] no one knows. I doubt if it was worth while bringing it on so late in the Parliament, when fears are at their maximum and yet there has not been time to disprove them. Ld Mills, whom I saw the other day, is strongly of this view . . . .

10 March

. . . . Dined at the HofC and <u>voted</u> for Govt on 2nd Reading of Retail [sic] Price Maintenance Bill. This was a curious day. The Opposition, in a tactical desire to allow Conservatives to vote against or abstain, did <u>not</u> vote at all on the 2nd Reading. Whether this was a good strategic position, I am not sure.[9] We shd say 'What? Do you have no view at all on this important issue? Yet you aspire to manage our Economic Life'.

20 Conservatives (the usual gang) voted agst; 20 or so abstained. (The Press exaggerates the abstainers, because naturally no pairs were obtainable from an Opposition who were Total Abstainers.) . . . .

15 March (Sunday)

. . . . The Govt have got into a great mess over the abolition of Retail

----

7. Resale price maintenance enabled manufacturers to stipulate the prices at which goods were sold. A recent Labour private member's bill prompted Heath to introduce legislation to tackle this anti-competitive practice. Macmillan had contemplated abolition in 1962. However, there was now much opposition in Conservative ranks fearful of alienating small business supporters. These fears proved exaggerated, as did Macmillan's concerns that the effects would be inflationary.

8. As a publisher Macmillan clearly had an interest in the Net Book Agreement. Introduced in 1900, it was a price-fixing agreement between publishers. On the grounds that it assisted the production and distribution of works of limited interest, it was however deemed acceptable when reviewed by the Restrictive Practices Court in 1962, and was not to be abolished until 1997.

9. It did facilitate the biggest Conservative parliamentary revolt since 1940.

[sic] Price Maintenance. What upsets the country is to see the Labour Party united and the Conservatives quarrelling. It was <u>too late</u> in the Parlt to embark on a matter wh a) is not vital b) will not affect cost of living – at least for some time c) affects all the small shop-keepers d) gives opportunity to all the disaffected MPs – who really have been out of sympathy with the leadership of the Party for a long time as too progressive – to have their last fling (most of the rebels are <u>not</u> going to stand again) . . . .

The only encouraging sign is that Harold Wilson is beginning to abuse Alec Home in very offensive terms. This is good . . . .

19 March

Luncheon in my honour by the Jesuits of Farm St – with Father Corbishley presiding – a very kind thought and some amusing talk, chiefly very critical of the Curia and enthusiastically in favour of Pope John.[10] Reggie Maudling asked me to see him for a talk. I went at 5.20 and stayed an hour . . . . The Chancellor of the Exr was as calm and sensible as ever. The Treasury are (with their usual stop-go mentality) getting a bit alarmed about 'over-heating' the Economy. As usual, they want to increase taxation (but by a petty amount – some £100m in relation to the national income) As usual (like Butler's 'pots and pans' Budget)[11] they want to tax drink, tobacco, and betting. Reggie asked me for my views, wh. I shall do over the week-end . . . .

25 March

D and I had luncheon with the Maudlings at No 11.[12] No guests. Quite a good talk. I gave him (as he had asked) a memorandum about the Budget and the Economy. Maudling was concerned about the Retail [sic] Price Maintenance Bill. The Govt only escaped defeat on an amendment by 1 vote last night![13] I think all this points to October for the Election . . . .

---

10. The central decision-making body of the Catholic Church, the Curia was to be gradually reformed by the new Pope, Paul VI.

11. The post-election Budget of October 1955 which, amongst various tax rises, increased purchase tax on kitchenware.

12. 11 Downing Street, traditionally the official home of the Chancellor of the Exchequer.

13. This aimed to exempt various medical products from the legislation. Macmillan did not vote.

29 March (Easter Sunday)

.... The Sunday Press is very hostile to the Govt and very critical of the Party in the HofC. They are almost beginning to praise me! I fear the effect on the workers and voters of all these divisions among Conservative MPs. Rather embarrassingly, it has now become known that I refused to allow RPM to proceed in the last year of the Parlt while I was in charge. Maudling and Heath (so P.M. told me) threatened to resign if the Bill was not introduced. It was therefore drafted hurriedly and the Party taken by surprise. I am annoyed at this 'leak' about my attitude, because it does harm to Alec.

The Greater London elections (on April 9th) will be a test and an indication. For some reason, Central Office are fairly hopeful. But I am not too sanguine. London is affected by the *Express* etc, in a way that the provinces are not.[14]

Owing to the bad weather and my gout (which still hangs about in the left foot) I have not had any walks, except in the garden. The season is very late. No sun. No warmth. 'The leaden sky of an English spring'.[15]

Our Macmillan affairs are still very complicated. We are still waiting for LCC and Fine Arts [Commission] permission to build on our site in St Martin's Street.[16] Until we get this, we cannot sell and get some reduction of our huge overdraft. Otherwise, except for some staff difficulties, I think there is some improvement in sales and therefore in the weight of the overhead ....

30 March

.... Some days I feel so well – for a short period – that I regret my resignation. Other days, I feel good for nothing – low, deflated, and terribly tired. I don't want to see 'company' and am tired by luncheons

---

14. These were the first elections to the Greater London Council. This body formally replaced the London County Council in 1965 and extended London's boundaries into suburbia. Conservative hopes that this would aid them electorally were not immediately realised, the 1964 vote returning 64 Labour and 36 Conservative councillors.
15. Derivation unknown.
16. The decision to sell the historic M&Co head offices in St Martin's Street (which joins Leicester and Trafalgar Squares) and use the proceeds, in part, to finance a new warehouse/offices in Basingstoke had been taken by Maurice in 1963.

and dinners. I fear people think I am avoiding them; but it is better so. In due course, I hope to get better and the periods when I feel as well as ever give me encouragement . . . .

1 April
. . . . Read a *Life of Bismarck*[17] (Heroes of Nations series) by Headlam. Quite interesting – but much too favourable to a wicked, unprincipled man – fore-runner of all the German follies, of 1914 and 1939.

2 April
. . . . I have sent a further memorandum to Alec Home, urging him to have the Election in October and to announce this <u>immediately</u> – <u>before</u> the London elections. Oliver Poole agrees with this.

Lunched at the Carlton Club, where I saw a number of my old colleagues. I had a long talk with the Chief Whip after luncheon. He was, of course, opposed to the R.P.M. Bill at this time. It has thrown the whole Party in Parlt into confusion, and done damage in the constituencies. So he agrees that we ought to postpone the General Election until the dust has settled a bit.

The Times is publishing a series of 3 articles on 'Conservatism since the War'. Two have appeared and one is to be published tomorrow. They are vicious and defeatist, written by an old-fashioned Liberal. The general view is that the author is Enoch Powell.[18] I don't think they will do great damage, but it is all part of Sir W. Haley's rancour against us all . . . .

5 April
. . . . The *Sunday Times* published in its supplement a long extract from David Kilmuir's book of Reminiscences. I only glanced through it, but I fear it will do a good deal of harm. The account of the Cabinet changes in the summer of 1963 [sic] is querulous. He obviously thought all the changes right, except his own. It's a pity he has thought fit to write so soon about such intimate personal relations. Some of the remarks attributed to me are quite incorrect . . . .

---

17. Chancellor of imperial Germany 1871–90.
18. The articles were indeed written by Powell at Haley's suggestion, criticising foreign policy and the 'farce' of the Commonwealth and, in the final article of 3 April, presenting a free market critique of government policy.

12 April (Sunday)
We left Lismore yesterday,[19] after a most delightful week. I have killed
3 (three) fish, wh feat has delighted everyone, including the Press and
the Television. Fishing and Hunting (including steeple-chasing) are still
the way to an Irishman's heart . . . .

18 April
. . . . The P.M. (whether because of my advice or not, I do not know)
has made a statement definitely saying that the General Election wd
not be till the autumn. He <u>did</u> take my advice and make this statement
<u>before</u> (just before!) the London local election results were known.
(These were <u>bad</u>) As to the Budget, it is just the old Treasury 'pots and
pans'. £100m from Tobacco and Drink – including Beer and muddling
about with the tax on Pool Betting, Fixed Odds etc. Since the Election
is postponed, I do <u>not</u> think these rather piffling changes in taxation
will have much <u>political</u> effect. The theory that they have some
<u>economic</u> effect (reduction of purchasing power – which is vast – by
an odd £100m) is a bit weak. Perhaps, however, they have some effect
on the 'Zurich Banker'[20] (that austere figure who dominates Treasury
thinking still) Anyway, the London Elections, the General Election
announcement, and the Budget have now all happened. There is still
the R.P.M. Bill to get through Parliament. But when that is over, there
is a fair chance for the Conservative party to rally.
      D. and I are both surprised at the interest [with] wh. our move-
ments are still reported. It seems rather strange . . . . But we are
interviewed, photographed, televised almost as in old days . . . .
      I have heard from Knox-Cunningham (who sends me a daily
report when the House is sitting) of the general disgust in the Party
with Ld Kilmuir's book. The fact that he criticised <u>all</u> his colleagues
so freely and so soon (there is a decent interval to be observed in
memoirs of this kind) has angered the Party. From my point of view
the generality of his criticism makes his account of the changes in the
Govt in 1962 less credible and less effective. What makes it so sad is
that I am told he sold the rights of his book (or at least the serial
rights) for a very modest sum – £2000 or so – hardly enough to jus-

---

19. Lismore Castle in County Waterford, Ireland, one of the Duke of Devonshire's
      estates.
20. Better known, in Harold Wilson's phrase, as the 'gnomes of Zürich', these were
      international financiers felt to be speculating against sterling.

tify such a breach of decorum. I am very sorry indeed about all this, for I have had a long and happy relationship and real friendship with David Kilmuir. I fear it will be difficult to re-build it. The truth is, that I think he is not at all well and has lost all his old sense of reality and sound perspective.

25 April

Ld Kilmuir's book has now been published. Except for *The Times* (which praises it as part of Haley's almost insane hatred of Tory Party) it has been ridiculed by the Press. Michael Foot's article in the *Evening Standard* is quite in Macaulay's style.

The political situation is <u>not</u> good. Altho' the ending of R.P.M. Ctee stage is helpful. Heath has managed this very well. I was in the House a good deal this week, and I have been worried by the defeatism of our people. Everyone seems to assume a Labour victory. This idea is, naturally, spreading in the Country. But Alec is doing awfully well – making fine speeches and giving a splendid lead . . . .

The Govt have quite rightly decided on holding all the outstanding by-elections, and take a chance. This is a necessary consequence of the October decision. I have, rather rashly, agreed to speak at Devizes . . . .

. . . . Dined at HofC on Wednesday, with Selwyn Lloyd and Boyd-Carpenter. The former has perked up a lot and seems to have no grievance . . . .

6 May

UDC elections shew some swing to Labour, but not so marked in the North.

The Cyprus position is aggravating and dangerous. The Aden situation is very dangerous.[21] The Americans (without the Eisenhower or the Kennedy link) are hopeless. The State Dept is (as in the Great War) anti-British by tradition and sentiment. Even de Gaulle's insults have not cured them. Good relations with U.S. must be <u>at the top</u> and at the <u>bottom</u> – the White House and the people. Went with Dorothy to memorial service for Cuthbert Headlam – one of my oldest political friends, starting our work together in Co Durham in 1923 . . . .

15 May

This has been quite an exciting week, politically. 4 by-elections, all in

---

21. The SAS were currently involved in heavy fighting in Radfan.

Govt held seats, and all thought to be in some danger. The Glasgow
seat, Rutherglen, was lost.[22] The other 3 were kept. The key seat was
Devizes, where Charles Morrison (John M's son) was engaged. As
John M. has always been a very loyal friend and has done a fine job
as Chairman of the 1922 Ctee, I agreed to go to speak. Knox
C[unningham] drove me there (from B.G.) on Monday afternoon
(11th) and the meeting was held that night. It was a fine meeting –
1000 to 1100 – and I made a good speech. The reception was
tremendous – quite moving. We spent over an hour afterwards with
the workers. The news of this election came through late on Thursday
(14th) after I had been dining with John Hare and Oliver Poole.[23]

The other two seats, Winchester and Bury [St Edmunds], came out
today. We did well in both.[24] This turn of events shd make quite a
difference . . . .

20 May

. . . . Read poor David Kilmuir's autobiography – terribly egotistical
and rather naïve. I am told that Ld Shawcross is much annoyed about
the Nuremburg trial as described by K.[25] As in everything else, K. takes
all the credit to himself, and represents S. as having played no part of
any consequence. K. is very critical of us all – Butler, Eden, Selwyn
Lloyd. The attack on me for the Govt changes of 1962 (wh. led to K's
retirement) is not too bad. He admits that he kept telling me that his
office was at my disposal whenever it might suit. What annoyed him
was being taken at his word . . . .

30 May

A very heavy week – mostly at M&Co (including Thursday with the
Board meetings) Altho' I see some improvement, I fear our situation is
very difficult. We have too high overheads; too high cost of production;

22. Labour 18,885; Conservative 15,138.
23. Conservative 19,554; Labour 17,884; Liberal 4,281.
24. Winchester: Conservative 18,032; Labour 11,968; Liberal 4,567. There was a
    bigger swing to Labour in Bury St Edmunds, where the result was Conservative
    21,271; Labour 11,295; Liberal 10,588.
25. The trials of Nazi leaders for crimes against humanity during the Second World
    War held in Nuremburg from November 1945 to October 1946. David
    Maxwell-Fyfe, as he then was, served there as one of the British prosecutors
    under Shawcross.

and too low sales. The only encouraging thing is that sales for first quarter are about 30% up on the same quarter last year. The African business has big possibilities. Longman and Oxford Press are entrenched – but with the European inspectors. These are now leaving, and we have a chance of getting in well with their African successors. I find work at St Martin's St very tiring – esp. getting there and back. The bus is quite nice, but crowded. The taxies shake horribly . . . .

Senator Edward Kennedy called to see me; not, I thought, as impressive as the others. Last night, I took part in a T.V. [programme] with Mrs Kennedy, Mr Lemass, Burgomaster Brandt, Ed. Kennedy, and Bobby K[ennedy] – through *Telstar*,[26] each speaking from our own countries and continents. I was amused that *Telstar* didn't work for about half the time, and we had recourse to other, more orthodox, methods. But before I came on, *Telstar* recovered! How odd it wd all have seemed 60 years ago. I remember my excitement at hearing a gramophone record . . . .

7 June (Sunday)

. . . . Nehru's death (a few days ago) was not unexpected – but a great shock. His long tenure of power (17 years) has covered the whole period of independence India. What will happen now? Shastri has been elected his successor – a better choice than seemed likely had he died some years ago.[27] Krishna Menon's star was eclipsed by the Chinese attack on a very unprepared India. If Mrs Pandit (N's sister) becomes For Secy, this will be good from our point of view. The funeral scenes – with many foreign dignitaries – have been quite a sensation. Nobody took the slightest notice of N's wishes. In spite of his scepticism and dislike of priests, he was 'given the whole Hindu works'. Procession; uncovered coffin; Hindu priests; funeral pyre; etc. There is to be a tribute to him on Monday (tomorrow) at the Albert Hall, to wh. I must go . . . .

14 June

. . . . The election spirit is more or less loose now, and rather absurd speeches and allegations from all sides fill the Press and (I think) bore

---

26. The first international communications satellite was launched in 1962 and this one, actually *Telstar 2*, replaced it the following year.
27. Lal Bahadur Shastri served as India's prime minister until his death in 1966. Macmillan is presumably referring to Shastri's resignation as Minister of Railways and Transport following a horrendous rail accident in 1956.

the public. I feel that Alec (P.M.) shd keep out of all this 'mud-slinging'. Mud shd perhaps be slung, but <u>not</u> by the principals . . . .

19 June
Bill Deakin (St Antony's College Oxford) and Mr Dilks[28] (L[ondon] S[chool] of Ec[onomics]) came to luncheon. We discussed my prospected book, for wh. contract with *Sunday Times* is now being negotiated. If I can get Mr Dilks to help me, I shall be very lucky . . . .

24 June
The Parliament drags on. I still feel sure that the P.M. was right to wait till October.

I had a good talk with him last week, and I felt that he was growing in confidence and strength. But I hope he will <u>not</u> let 'speech-writers' put in rather school-boy attacks on Wilson. He shd never mention Wilson. I never mentioned Gaitskell. Then when G. made a stupid mistake (about taxes and expenditure) in the middle of the General El[ection] of 1959, I was able to turn and rend him with effect . . . .

3 July
A very heavy week – most difficult problems at M&Co – Ghana; Nigeria; the LCC and our building; the financial situation etc etc. I wd rather be Prime Minister! I begin to appreciate Gladstone's saying 'no man shd ever lie awake at night over any <u>public</u> disaster' . . . .

5 July
. . . . Mr Dilks finished his preliminary task. We have had long talks about how to approach the problem of the book. I am beginning to be rather concerned as to whether I can do this or shall have to fall back (like Eden) on allowing someone else – not Dilks, who is too busy, to write it for me . . . .

19 July (Sunday)
Yesterday morning there was a tremendous thunderstorm. No damage here that I have heard of. All afternoon and evening in Bromley, for our Conservative Fete. This <u>was</u> positively our last appearance and

---

28. David Dilks was recommended by Eden, on whose memoirs he had also worked.

there was a corresponding amount of drinking etc before we got home (by about 8.30pm) A long day – and a rather melancholy one. The <u>last</u> constituency engagement, after 41 years as candidate or member.

I spent most of this evening, and Dorothy spent most of the night in getting the house ready for today's opening of house and garden. I am writing in bed, in the morning, instead of going to Church. For D. has so much to do and cannot drive me. Last year, I had a fast car and chauffeur! . . . .

Trade figures for June bad – a widening gap. *The Times* is gloomy and talks of an increase in Bank Rate. I hope Chancellor of Exr will not yield to this. He must take some risks, at least till after the Election. It is, I fear, true that the 'boom' has gone rather too far. But the real trouble, once again, is the waste of labour, esp. in the South. Manufacturers keep more labour than they really require, for fear of not being able to replace any men or women if once they leave. The whole labour force works below its capacity, if pushed. The resulting purchasing power adds to the already excessive demand for consumer goods, often <u>imported</u> consumer goods.

Governor Goldwater has got the nomination and has delivered quite a remarkable 'acceptance speech' in terms wh. wd be welcome to Mr Martell, the British Fascists or the Empire Loyalists.[29] But just as Goldwater was 'written off' too lightly six months ago, so there is a danger that he may not be taken seriously enough now.

21 July
Went to Basingstoke, to the Macmillan building there. It is a splendid place, and well designed. I wish it had not cost quite so much! . . . .

22 July
I went to see Churchill at 6pm. He was very bad – a tragic figure. I think he was bored, because he had been to the HofC.

23 July
. . . . Goldwater's securing of the Republican nomination is having a great effect on European opinion. De Gaulle has taken instant

---

29. Goldwater's call for a 'cold war offensive on all fronts' was certainly associated with fascism by his Democrat opponents, whilst his line that 'extremism in defence of liberty is no vice' would have appealed to the English populist libertarian Edward Martell.

advantage by a 'Press Conference' in which he attacks America and reproves Germany for her loyalty to U.S.A. instead of submitting to the French hegemony . . . .

26 July (Sunday)
. . . . Composed a short speech for the 'Motion on Retirement of Sir Winston Churchill'. It is not easy to think of anything suitable to a man who is, after all, still alive . . . .

28 July
. . . . Made my speech and the last I shall ever make [in the Commons] . . . . I think it went well . . . .

30 July
A very hot day. Macmillan Board all morning. Lunch with P.M., who seemed very cheerful. I gave a dinner at HofC to my own 'staff', who have been so loyal. Ld Poole; Ld Egremont; Sir T Bligh; Sir Philip de Zulueta; Ld Normanbrook; Freddy Bishop; Sir A Rumbold; Ted Heath and Martin Redmayne (my Chief Whip) Knox-Cunningham and Maurice. I voted twice – the last votes I shall ever give. The second was for the Church of England vestments measure. It seemed strange to be in the Chamber for the last time.

The party was agreeable but rather sad. I have certainly been wonderfully served . . . .

6 August
. . . . On August 4 I began preparing the synopsis of my memoirs. I do 2 to 2½ hours dictating . . . . I chose August 4th because of its being the anniversary of the outbreak of World War I.

John Egremont (Wyndham) came to luncheon from Petworth. He is going to accompany me on my election speeches. I am to make 4 (Nottingham: Preston: Doncaster: Halifax) and 1 in Bromley . . . .

The Americans have taken a strong line in SE Asia. They were attacked by North Vietnamese motor-boats and have reacted strongly, both against the boats and the bases. The Russians have grumbled out threatening warnings. I do not anticipate serious danger, but the Chinese will prob[ably] react in Laos, wh. is virtually indefensible . . . .

27 August
. . . . I have been reading some of the inter-war books and pamphlets

wh. I published, either in my own name or in collaboration. *The Middle Way, Reconstruction* etc. Also *The Next 5 Years*.[30] Really rather good! . . . .

. . . . I am worried about M&Co's difficulties, but the 1963 accounts (wh. I have just got in a provisional form) are a little better than 1962, tho' below – far below – previous years. The journals are making a good profit. But the book publishing business is just about breaking even. Then we have the Basingstoke building to finance, and we have not yet got our plans for St Martin's St approved,[31] altho' this looks more hopeful. However, I hope 1964 will be better and the Pan Co (which we own to 60%) is doing very well.[32] So is Canada. The St Martin's Press is at least not asking for more capital . . . .

12 September
Dictated in the morning. I have finished the Battle of Loos (Sept. 1915) Read Ll George's *War Memoirs* – some useful stuff. Left at 1.45 for Hove, where there was a meeting of S.E. Area Conservatives. It was one of a series of similar meetings throughout the country, each addressed by a Cabinet minister. Keith Joseph spoke well – good matter but rather dully delivered, in a monotonous way . . . . The meeting began with a relay (for 10 minutes) of the Prime Minister's speech in London. I spoke at the end – rather well and very pleasing to the audience, with some of the old tricks! I had a wonderful reception on entering the Hall and a great ovation after my speech . . . .

13 September
I have read the Labour manifesto. It is rather cleverly directed to a) the young b) the moderate vote. There is very little 'Socialism' in it. If Baldwin were alive he wd be gratified to see how both parties have moved to the Centre. But I suspect Wilson. He covers up a lot of

---

30. *Reconstruction* (1933) called for a Central Economic Council to plan recovery from the depression that hit at the start of the decade, developed by the cross-party Next Five Years Group in 1935, of which Macmillan was a leading light, and given fullest detailed expression in *The Middle Way* (1938).

31. Fearing that it would affect the skyline behind the National Gallery, the LCC forced M&Co to scale back plans for the replacement building on the site.

32. Leading paperback publisher Pan had been owned by a consortium of London publishers until 1962 when Macmillan and Collins bought out their partners. In fact M&Co owned 51%.

dangerous proposals with smooth ambiguities. Our manifesto comes out this week . . . .

29 September
. . . . My political efforts for the Election are at present confined to my speeches at Hove, and a speech at Bromley, on the adoption of my successor. This got a good press, at any rate from the news angle. It was about the nuclear problem and the independent deterrent. I start my little campaign tomorrow. So far, it is hard to judge what is the 'state of play'. Wilson is making a tremendous effort and fills the papers, radio, TV with his personality. He may bring it off with a triumphant success, and he may still end by boring the electors. He is utterly untrustworthy and quite unscrupulous . . . .

4 October
John Egremont and I set out for the North and got back yesterday. Speeches at Nottingham (Rushcliffe division) SE Derbyshire, and Preston . . . . I did not much like the atmosphere. There was no hostility, but no enthusiasm . . . .

5 October
. . . . The Gallup Poll (after moving to us) has been a disappointment. It shews 4% for Labour. Last week, it shewed ½% for Conservatives. The *Daily Mail* Poll, wh. comes out on Wednesday, will be important. Unluckily, these Polls have a political effect, for many people – it seems – tend to back the winning side at the end of an Election. Central Office still believe in a small majority for us. I'm afraid this all means that Maurice [Macmillan] cannot hold Halifax, unless his personality and all the work he has done pulls in 500–1000 votes on these grounds . . . .

6 October
. . . . *The Times* is now openly announcing a certain Labour victory and exulting in it. All their news is 'slanted'. The *Observer* is, of course, a 'Left Wing' paper. What terrible harm the Astors have done to their adopted country. Some of them are vicious and degenerate (like Bill and David) others incredibly stupid (like Gavin)[33] The old

---

33. Macmillan had been close to the Astors in the inter-war years. This may have contributed to his resentment as he felt their press turning against him towards

641

vulgarian who bought his viscounty left America in anger because he was beaten in an election in New York. Poor Waldorf and Nancy 'meant well' and Nancy was a good and loyal friend to many. But she was not an Astor, by birth or temperament. Now it is rumoured that in the last few days of the Election, Sir W. Haley – the Editor – is to come out with an open and violent demand for Wilson instead of Home. Gavin, of course, will do nothing. However, Haley may overdo it and produce the opposite effect. After all, it was his attack on me in the Oxford election that won me the Chancellorship.

Meanwhile, the 'polls' are bad. There is a feeling that after starting well in the first week, things have begun to slide . . . .

My book makes progress. I have now written a prologue (of 50000 words, to be shortened to 20,000) and introductory chapters amounting to over 30000 words. I have got to the year 1920. Whether it is readable or not, I can't judge . . . .

21 October
The General Election has resulted in a Labour Govt. But the majority – which I expected to be 50 or 60 overall – is only 4.[34] But it is enough to bring about a change of Govt – wh. is what the people wanted and shewed by voting Liberal. The Socialist poll is not increased. Our 'dissatisfied' or 'floating' voters (who supported me in 1959) have voted Liberal, regardless of the effect. The distinct Socialist gains are very small. The seats wh. they have won are mostly like Halifax, wh. poor Maurice lost by 1000. But he had this time a Liberal opponent, who took 7000 votes.

Altogether last week was rather sad. I grieve over Alec (who I like so much) and very much over Maurice. I have had long talks with him about his future plans. It is too soon yet to make any decision about Halifax other than to be careful not to make a decision.

My meeting at Doncaster (for Tony Barber) was rather rough. At

---

the end of his premiership. Meanwhile, Bill Astor's inability to shake the lurid rumours prompted by his essentially tangential involvement in the Profumo scandal even led to him being denied entry to the British embassy in Washington in 1964. Macmillan's animus against him might also have been fuelled by his brief second marriage to Macmillan's niece, Philippa Hunloke, and her involvement, by bringing Stephen Ward on to Astor's estate, in the scandal.

34. Labour 317 seats, Conservative 304 and Liberal 9.

Halifax it was quiet. At Liverpool, where I visited 9 Committee rooms and made a speech in the evening, things were ominously quiet . . . .

Maurice seems in quite good form, Julian Amery had better luck, since he scraped in by 14 votes, after 3 recounts.

I lunched yesterday with Alec, and we discussed the future. I urged him to take no decision about himself till Christmas. After that, we must act quickly, both as regards leadership and organisation. Wilson may well ask for a dissolution in March or more prob. May (after a rich-soaking Budget) Alec has done as well as anyone could have done. But he has not quite the 'modern' outlook wh. politicians nowadays must feel or simulate.

I had a talk also with Oliver Poole – who is imaginative and wise. The trouble is still a lack of unity, wh. I cd (up till the last year – 1963) usually command. The rivalry goes on between Maudling, Heath, and Macleod . . . .

25 October

Mr Wilson is forming a very large and spectacular Govt. He is trying to emulate Jack Kennedy. But he forgets that what made Jack irresistible was his charm, his vitality, his generosity, his faith – not his team of 'high-brow' dons. He also forgets that, in fact, poor Jack achieved nothing positive. His triumph over Cuba was his courageous reaction to a crisis imposed upon him. In spite of all the talk, on defence, on monetary policy, on tariffs – nothing really happened. Had he been spared, I believe he would have had a much more fruitful second term.

I go now Tuesdays and Thursdays to the office. The rest of the time, D and I are here, alone. It is very peaceful; the weather has been wonderful – sunny and dry. I am getting on, slowly but surely, with the book . . . . I am working on a scheme which Dilks and I drew up and it seems about right as to scale . . . .

Poor Rab. Quite rightly, Alec has made a reorganisation of the Central Office, and this will involve Rab's giving up the Research Dept, over which he has nominally presided for many years. After his 'interview' during the most critical days of the General Election, I think Alec wd have been justified in never speaking to him again.[35] But

---

35. In his interview with George Gale, which appeared in the *Daily Express* on 9 October, Butler admitted that the election might slip away from the Conservatives.

– as I have always suspected and now know – poor Rab is more or less 'mad' . . . .

27 October

. . . . The new Govt measures have been announced. It is not stop and go, we are told. But it amounts to 15%, on all imported goods, exc[luding] Food.[36] (What a curious reflection on the great Free Trade and Protection controversies of the past) This is supposed to damp down imports and must do so to some extent. I had agreed a scheme of physical control of imports (to the tune of some £200m) which must be ready for the need (as there clearly is now) But the Socialists are not prepared to exert the classical remedies (Bank Rate: Bank squeeze: incomes policy etc) so they trust to additional protection or revenue tariffs and to 'subsidies on exports' . . . .

Wilson presents all this with great skill, like Kennedy, whom he is trying to imitate. Govt announcements on TV (not in Parl) 'the fireside chat' etc. And the vast number of new ministries etc give a sense of urgency. Ll.G. after Asquith; Churchill after Chamberlain; Kennedy after Eisenhower – this is the picture wh. he presents with no little skill. Motored home with Dorothy in the evening. I find a day in London tires me terribly; but I must manage at least 2 days a week . . . .

6 November

. . . . We had a shock this week by the Govt's sudden decision to stop all office building in London. The contract of sale for St Martin's St (at a price of £835,000) was signed 3 weeks ago. Will it hold?

With some relief, I heard today that it will, and the purchasers have signed a building contract already – wh. should let them through the net.

The Govt are shewing great activity, Wilson in particular. His 'leper' speech will not do him much harm, I wd say.[37] His general bustling arrogance will be regarded as a contrast to the 'tired, supine,

---

36. These import surcharges were to tackle a ballooning current account deficit.
37. In an election in which both parties played the race card in Smethwick, the Conservative candidate Peter Griffiths had unexpectedly unseated the new Labour Foreign Secretary Patrick Gordon Walker, largely because of a fall in the latter's vote. In light of Griffiths's alleged racism, Wilson called him a 'parliamentary leper' during the debate on the Address.

lazy Tories'. The autumn Budget, to be introduced on Wed, will 'soak the rich' in order to finance more Old Age Pensions etc. This will be popular. It looks like a May election, wh. the Socialists should be able to win if the tide is still running their way. But the electoral system is very uncertain. If the Liberal vote recedes, or fewer candidates are run, then Conservatives may well win back a fair number of seats. Meanwhile, I have a feeling that we are once again working hard to stop a boom wh. is about to fade out anyway . . . .

13 November
The Budget on Wed seemed rather fierce – 6d on Petrol (now) 6d on income tax (as from April '65) 5/- about on insurance stamps. None of this is in any way related to the 'balance of payments'. It is just to bribe the electorate (pensioners etc) Now there is to be a reintroduction of rent control (wh. will reduce the accommodation available) It seems all rather old fashioned. We must wait a bit, I suppose, for the theme of 'modernisation' etc to unfold itself . . . .

16 November (Monday)
. . . . The Govt now threaten us with a Capital Gains Tax;[38] higher income tax; higher sur-tax; increased death duties and new rules about handing over property; attack on family trusts; interference with private business. They have refused to supply the aeroplanes ordered by S.Africa, thus losing an export order of some £30m, to wh. Verwoerd retaliates by denouncing the Simonstown agreement.[39] De Gaulle, incensed by the decision (or semi-decision) to abandon Concord, has ordered the French technicians to hold no more talks with their English counterparts.[40] The nuclear policy of Britain is in shreds,

---

38. A limited form of taxation of short-term capital gains had been introduced by Macmillan's government in 1962, but Labour had promised a strengthened version in its 1964 manifesto.

39. Macmillan's government had agreed to supply South Africa with Buccaneers (naval aircraft) before the 1962 UN arms embargo was announced. Labour eventually honoured this contract, whilst announcing an arms embargo on all new orders on 17 November. The South Africans did not retaliate against the 1955 Simonstown agreement, whereby the Royal Navy retained access to this naval base.

40. This was the first time Macmillan mentioned this Anglo-French supersonic airliner project, negotiated in 1962. Not least because of the penalty clauses for

and we are neither to have our own weapon or join MLF.[41] However, the Govt is 'active' and 'dynamic' and the ministry has more members than ever before in history. The P.M. is to raise his salary to £15,000 a year, announcing at the same time that he does not intend to 'entertain'. MPs are to get £3000 a year. The great advantages gained by Labour Govts are fully enjoyed by their successors . . . .

28 November
The last week, in HofC and City has certainly been remarkable. The Govt naturally lay the financial crisis to the door of the Conservatives. In fact, it is they who have destroyed the national credit, a) by wild talk b) by insulting every country in the world, one after the other c) by the breach of our agreements – the 15% customs tax being contrary to EFTA, GATT, and all the rest. In a few weeks Wilson and his friends have destroyed our credit all over the world. Their popularity at home, however, increases daily . . . .

8 December
A long day at St Martin's St. We are making progress, but what with 7% Bank Rate on our overdraft and 6% additional to Printing Costs, and one thing and another, I am not too happy about our profit margins . . . .

10 December
A nice day. Dictated for an hour – corrected for an hour or two – we are now in Chapter 6 – the 1924–9 Parlt . . . .

I signed my contract with S. Times today. They signed theirs with my Trustees. The M&Co Book contract was also settled and signed, with one minor point reserved. The price is £360,000 – of which £34,000 is to be paid to me in 4 annual instalments to write the book and pay the assistants etc.[42]

---

cancellation insisted upon by Macmillan's government, Labour decided not to drop Concorde.

41. Labour had never been any more enamoured of the MLF idea than the Tories. In the face of Washington's indifference to their Atlantic nuclear force alternative, they rapidly decided to keep Polaris.

42. This was the fee from the Thomson Organisation (then owners of The Times and Sunday Times) for the British and Commonwealth rights, whilst the family firm contracted the book rights for a relatively modest sum.

.... Stocks and shares are falling rapidly. I hope all the owners of unit trusts and beneficiaries of Pension Funds and left-wing clergymen, living on the equity investments of Queen Anne's Bounty and the Church Commissioners realise what is happening.[43] The real test is whether unemployment will follow the financial slump. This isn't Stop and Go; it's just loss of control, and crash into the wall at the end of the garden ....

20 December

.... Two days in London at M&Co. A lot of rather difficult problems – esp. about educational films and how far we should go into this new aspect of educational business. Maurice [Macmillan] is back and a great help. He tried for Salisbury seat, but did not get it. I'm afraid he is so modest that these selection ctees do not realise his worth. He has, (I am glad of this) refused to allow his name to go forward for East Grinstead Div[isio]n. It wd not be a good idea, for many reasons. In any case, he wd fail and that wd not be good. The constituency is too big and too demanding for anyone who is really in politics. It has never had such a member ....

The economy (esp financially) is shaken by the Govt's extraordinary antics. The threat of taxation, imprecise, uncertain, and menacing, is much worse than anything else. It seems odd to adopt this procedure instead of awaiting a Budget and Finance Bill with definite proposals. The Govt now has to support the gilt-edged market as well as sterling. This is entirely due to the uncertainty of the application of Capital Gains Tax to redeemed Govt securities ....

Christmas Day

8am H[oly] C[ommunion] 11 Matins. Church very full each time. We supplied the full complement, save only the very youngest grandchildren, I think we were (counting D and me) 23 in all at Matins. The rest of the day seemed to pass quickly – eating and drinking, Xmas presents, games etc. It was altogether delightful – one of the nicest that I can remember ....

30 December

The Times is now in full support of the Govt. They hardly criticise the

---

43. Set up in 1704 for the maintenance of poor clergy, Queen Anne's Bounty was merged into the new body of the Church Commissioners in 1948.

tremendous wage rises and vast increases in Govt expenditure. If it had happened in our time, Haley wd have gone mad with rage. It is said that Gavin Astor voted 'Labour' at the last Election and his paper is certainly now nothing but a dearer edition of the old *Daily Herald*. The sinister thing behind this is, of course, the American determination to reduce us to a mere satellite. What the Astors and Haley really approve in Wilson is his readiness to abandon Britain's strength, independence (of the right kind) and honourable partnership with U.S.A., for which all his predecessors (even Attlee) fought . . . .

1965

*Churchill's death – expanding publishing operations in Africa –
reactions to Labour's Capital Gains Tax – Rhodesia's unilateral
declaration of independence*

5 January

. . . . I scarcely read the papers, but I judge that the Govt is still popular and that Wilson has succeeded in impressing his 'image' on the mass of the people. It seems strange that a man who claimed exemption (as a civil servant or the like) at 23 and took no part in the 6 years war, can be P.M. We are certainly a forgiving people . . . .

11 January

. . . . I see that Reg Bevins (whom I promoted and preserved) is writing his memoirs for the *Sunday Express*. They are advertised as a violent – and as regards Butler and the Premiership – an untruthful attack on me. I suppose he is hard up . . . .

13 January

. . . . The TSR2 is now to be abandoned, according to the newspapers. This is a great tragedy for the Aircraft industry. We are to buy American! They must have worked on Wilson at Washington to good purpose[1] . . . .

15 January

The news of Churchill's stroke and grave illness reached me this afternoon. At the request, very urgently pressed, of the T.V., I went to London to do a short tribute, to be ready if needed . . . .

19 January

Churchill is still alive, but in a sort of coma. The stroke was a week

---

1. This Tactical, Strike and Reconnaissance supersonic aircraft had been in development since 1956. Ironically, Macmillan's own decision in July 1962 to limit the payload of tactical nuclear weapons to 10 kilotons helped undermine the rationale for the project. American F-111s were to be purchased instead, but when their costs in turn escalated the RAF was supplied with American F-4 Phantoms and British Buccaneers.

ago, but was not announced till last Friday, when the newspapermen got hold of it. He may last some time. I did not go to London, as usual, today. Randolph and young Winston came in the morning. There is really no hope of any 'recovery'. Churchill sleeps and has no pain. He does not seem to recognise anyone in particular; it is a great strain for them all, esp. Clemmy . . . .

21 January
. . . . Churchill's condition is just the same. Wilson is behaving rather foolishly in holding up all public business – his trip to Bonn; CIGS to Nigeria etc. This is quite wrong and quite unnecessary.

22 January
We sat up late last night to hear the by-election results. They are quite extraordinary. [Patrick] Gordon Walker, the Foreign Secy, (who lost his seat at Smethwick in the General Election) was sent to Leyton (in Essex) which old Sorensen was forced to give up to make room for him. Sorensen was rather a sweet old man – a radical pacifist, a philanthropist, and a devout man – of what sect, I forget.[2] He was a survivor of a type wh. has now almost died out – the old preacher, the heirs to Bunyan and all that. I should think he was loved by his supporters and respected by his [opponents]. I used to have good talks with him and always found him sincere as well as earnest. He was indeed 'A Reluctant Peer', but Wilson bullied him into it. G.W. came down to be elected, without charm, without sincerity, with a certain sour superiority which Socialist dons affect . . . . The majority was 7000. The constituency reacted. Many abstained, and some Labour men must have voted for the Conservative, Old Etonian, business man – Buxton. (Buxton actually increased his vote over his General Election figure on a 60% poll. So he must have got some Labour or Liberal votes) As a result, the Foreign Secretary lost by 200 votes. But Leyton did not stand alone. The loss of Leyton may well be due to personal rather than political reasons – the resentment of the constituency at being used for the convenience of the Govt and the fact that Sorensen's extreme reluctance to give up was well known; the arrogance of Gordon Walker, who clearly treats voters as merely the instrument of his ambition, and has no human interest in them; the rise in all prices, including house mortgages; some even say the patriotic reaction

---

2. Reg Sorensen was a Unitarian minister.

caused by Churchill lying on his death bed. In a way, therefore, a
by-election held at Nuneaton the same day was perhaps more significant. The great Cousins stood – the dictator of the Trade Unions.
Again, the Trade Unionists abstained or voted Tory. A vast majority was cut in half. The swing was nearly 5%.[3] So ended Wilson's
'Hundred Days'. I shd think he will be known in future as Waterloo
Wilson.[4] Walker has resigned. He could scarcely hold his place
and go to the Lords, after all the fuss they made about Alec Home
being made For Secy by me. The press today is staggered. Actually,
the Election results were rather late for comment. But the headlines
are certainly sensational . . . .

24 January (Sunday)
Churchill died at 8am today. Altho' the end has been inevitable since
the stroke a fortnight ago, yet the shock is great. England without
Winston! It seems impossible. Not even the oldest of us can remember
England without him as a considerable figure. Church at 11. I read
Ecclesiasticus and Corinthians instead of the regular lessons.

Fog and drizzle. All the snow has gone. A dark, dreary, cheerless
day. D and I alone. A lot of telephoning, but I had to refuse the Press
etc. At 8am the tributes Wilson, Home, Grimond and myself – in that
order. Wilson was excellent, a masterly performance, giving a review
of Churchill's life and achievement – apparently learnt by heart, for he
never looked at his notes. It was really a very fine piece of work, altho'
rather too professional. This was nevertheless one of the best things
I have ever heard on this medium. Home looked ill and seemed very
thin after Wilson. Grimond was very bad and in bad taste, bringing in
Liberal politics. I think mine was adequate, or perh. a little more. It
was very short.

. . . . Brooded late over Churchill. Talked with Normanbrook on
the telephone, who is very cast down. Slept very badly, only an hour
or two during the whole night. It is the end of an era, and in this sense

---

3. Leyton: Conservative 16,544; Labour 16,339; Liberal 5,382. As a result Patrick
   Gordon Walker stood down as Foreign Secretary. Nuneaton: Labour 18,325;
   Conservative 13,084; Liberal 6,047.
4. The idea of a new government making its mark in its first hundred days
   originated with FDR in 1933. Macmillan instead ironically compares it to the
   hundred-day return of the Emperor Napoléon ended by the battle of Waterloo
   in 1815, though his prediction was inaccurate.

like Queen Victoria's death. No one quite brought out what tremendous fun Churchill was – a puckish humour, and a boyish enjoyment of life – these were captivating and irresistible. It has been announced that the Queen has ordered a State funeral, which will be on Saturday, preceded by 3 days lying in State in Westminster Hall. Parliament will pay its tribute tomorrow . . . .

28 January
Early to London. D and I went to Fred Woolton's memorial service in the Abbey. It was fine, but not very personal. Afterwards, Knox-C[unningham] took us into Westminster Hall. It was a very wonderful sight. The people wait for hours in the queue, and pass reverently by the coffin. Clem Attlee came with us . . . .

29 January
To London again – went to Abbey for memorial service for FM Lord Wilson (Jumbo) I served with him in Mediterranean. He became SAC after Eisenhower went to 'Overlord'.[5] He was a shrewd but kindly man – a good general up to a point. He went to Washington to succeed [Sir John] Dill and this allowed Alex[ander of Tunis] to become SAC. The service was fine – somehow more impressive than yesterday's. We had the Rifle Brigade band and Last Post and Reveille, wh. are always moving. Lunched with Wyndhams. Then at 2.30, rehearsal of pall-bearers at St Pauls. It was terribly cold and if this weather goes on there will be a lot of sickness following tomorrow's event. D and I dined with Moucher [Devonshire]. Maud Baillie and David Cecil were there.[6] Pleasant reminiscences, wh. is all we have to live on now.

30 January
Cold – bitter cold – but happily dry. No rain, sleet, or snow, as had been foretold. There will be so many accurate and full descriptions of this wonderful ceremony that I need not try to write more than a few words. The pall-bearers were his friends and comrades in war – Eden, Menzies, Attlee, Normanbrook, Bridges and myself among civilians; of the military, Portal (the only survivor of the great Chiefs of Staff) Slim, Mountbatten, Ismay, Alexander. It was a great honour

---

5. The codename for the invasion of Normandy in 1944.
6. Maud was Dorothy's eldest sister whilst Cecil was Salisbury's younger brother, Professor of English Literature at Oxford and a Macmillan author.

to be of this remnant. Our part in the ceremony was simple but dignified. As usual, everything was perfectly arranged and the complicated ceremonial for Royal arrivals etc and the foreign visitors – all this was admirably done. We waited in St Dunstan's Chapel (NW corner of Cathedral) watching the procession on TV, until the time came for us to take up our position on the steps outside, to meet and escort the coffin. Here it was bitterly cold, with a piercing wind. Our seats, after the coffin had been put on the catafalque, were on each side of it – under the dome . . . . The service was short, but very moving. We led the procession out and then waited till it moved off, with the coffin, to the Tower.

The most trying time for us then came. We had to wait about 20–30 minutes in the frightful cold, until the Royalties, Heads of State, ambassadors etc had got away. I thought both Attlee and Pug Ismay wd die. Somebody got some chairs at last – but what we needed was a brazier.

After luncheon at the Carlton, to which I had Lady Normanbrook, Ld Amory, and the Egremonts, D. and I motored home. I was an icicle – chilled right through. I had a hot bath and went to bed, with a streaming cold, neuralgia (acute) and threatenings of gout. But I wd not have missed it. It was really wonderful . . . .

3 February

. . . . Read again Anthony Eden's first volume – I mean first in sequence. 1931–1938. It is written by Dilks, with some suggestions by Eden. It is, therefore, scholarly and correct and well planned. But it does <u>not</u> hold you. This alarms me. I really don't see how one can make a book of memoirs readable, unless it is indiscreet or pugnacious – like L[loyd] G[eorge]. However, I must plod on . . . .

6 February

. . . . David Kilmuir and his wife to dinner. Both seem to have now recovered and were as pleasant as ever, Sylvia went out of her way to please . . . .

A lot of telephoning and a good many papers to deal with this last week from M&Co. We are searching for a new office, in place of St Martin's St, which we must soon evacuate. There are also great problems likely to arise from the next Budget – the threatened Capital Gains Tax and the probable attack on family trusts. All this is very worrying . . . .

28 February

The Government seems to threaten us with some new idea every day.
Taxes must go up in the Budget, for expenditure will be very high.
Wages continue to rise and the inflation grows. The Conservative
Opposition has settled its internal dispute,[7] but is not very effective.
Wilson is <u>very</u> able and makes (I am told) a fine impression on the
Television. He trying to elevate the Premiership into a Presidency
modelled on poor Jack Kennedy. We have quarrelled with Spain, S.
Africa and now Roumania (very impartial) and lost large export orders
in consequence. The aircraft industry is in ruins. Defence is handed
over to the Americans. But nobody cares, I mean among ordinary folk.
There is over-full employment and rising wage-packets . . . .

2 March

Very cold – a bitter NE wind. I went to London and spent a useful
morning at M&Co with Brooks and Kay on African Affairs. Up till
lately, Oxford Press and Longmans have had it all their own way. But
they worked with and through the European directors of education
and the like. But they appear not to have foreseen the 'wind of change'.
We have come in late – too late. In ordinary times we shd not have
had a chance. But Kay's friends are the Africans (nor is my name
unknown to them) and we are now beginning to get under the new
African administrations some share of this growing market. Of course,
nationalism is all the thing – so we are starting companies in Uganda,
Nigeria etc. We are to have a share in the Ghana State Publishing Co.
It's all rather hazardous, but rather exciting.

I lunched with Alec Home at Bucks. I got the impression that he
was tired and rather depressed. He is <u>excellent</u> in the HofCommons;
quite good on the platform; no good at all on T.V. This last is the vital
qualification for a statesman today! What wd Lord Beaconsfield have
thought, who regarded even the platform with some suspicion[8] . . . .

4 March

Deep snow. I had meetings in London but did not venture up by an
early train. Lunched with Knox-Cunningham at Carlton Club. He is

---

7. Presumably a reference to the establishment in February 1965 of a new means
   of selecting the party leader by ballot of Conservative MPs.
8. Disraeli was created Earl of Beaconsfield during his second Premiership
   (1874–80) in 1876.

rather alarmed at the line the new Ulster P.M. (O'Neill) is taking towards Dublin.[9] Knox is a true Orangeman, and fears the Southerner's wiles . . . .

7 March (Sunday)

Cold; sunny; no wind – a glorious day. 'Biddy' Monckton is one of the few remaining friends of the Duke and Duchess of Windsor, for Walter was his close adviser. She gives a pathetic account of the Duke. He had a very serious operation in America some months ago, and is very weak. Now he has had another operation on his eye. He is in the London clinic. The Royal Family have sent enquiries, but no more. Public opinion, without knowing the various difficulties, is becoming rather critical of the Queen. People feel that after 30 years there ought to be at least a 'family reconciliation'[10] and that she shd visit her uncle – who is now over 70 and may not live long. This worries me, for I cannot bear to see the Queen in a difficult position. I don't want to interfere, but perhaps I will try to see Michael Adeane. No doubt the Queen Mother is still adamant . . . .

A good deal of work done on the book. I have finished a long chapter on the 1931–5 Parliament – called Reconstruction. I have found it very difficult to write. There is too much material and yet it's all rather small beer. I was a private member, of no importance, airing my views! . . . .

11 March

. . . . The Queen's desire to visit her uncle has been put out this morning. The Press is good and I feel sure this will do the Queen's general 'image' benefit. The announcement from the Palace was well expressed – dignified and simple . . . .

16 March

. . . . Luncheon at Pan, for annual a/cs. It has been a good year, the profit being initialled at £230,000. M&Co and Collins are equal

---

9. Terence O'Neill (Prime Minister of Northern Ireland 1963–69) had responded to the riots in Belfast during the 1964 general election by inviting the Irish Prime Minister Seán Lemass to visit in January, reciprocating by himself visiting Dublin in February, moves which troubled loyal Unionists like Knox-Cunningham.

10. Following the Duke of Windsor's abdication (as Edward VIII) from the throne in 1936.

partners in this enterprise, which (through Maurice) we acquired from Alan Bott's executors. We payed [sic] about £250,000 for 51% interest – and it has proved a good investment . . . .

Afternoon at M&Co – a lot of trouble is taking place in connection with the appointment of a Production Manager. This ends the reorganisation wh. I undertook when I came back to M&Co 18 months ago. Sales; Production; Accounts – these are the three <u>service</u> departments, which must be organised on efficient business lines to serve publishing. Here the editors (general; educational; etc) are the real creators of the business. They must do the really constructive work. They need a touch of genius. They shd be able to look to efficient <u>service</u> depts and not have to worry about these aspects. Chairman and Managing Director shd preside over the whole . . . .

17 March

I do not follow the political moves very closely, altho' Knox[-Cunningham] keeps me informed. I shd say that the Government has gained since the Election – or, perhaps, that the Conservatives have lost ground. Alec and his colleagues do not seem to make much impact. I seem to remember that we had this experience in 1945 – but then we had a huge majority agst us. The Tories ought to do better in the present situation – but there seems little punch and no new ideas. On the other hand, Alec is prob. right in not trying to force the issue prematurely. Wilson might like an excuse to dissolve . . . .

18 March

. . . . The Russians have performed the incredible feat of firing a rocket about 100 miles up, to travel 17000 miles an hour, with a man getting out on a guide rope, doing some acrobatics, then getting back into the vehicle. This is supposed to be preliminary to a landing on the Moon in a few years' time. The Americans are terribly jealous and worried. Europe is hopelessly behind . . . .

19 March

I am always very tired after London. Slept poorly and felt quite exhausted. It is a nuisance, for I must go at least 2 days a week to keep a proper control of M&Co . . . .

23 March

. . . . René Massigli (ambassadeur de France) – my old friend – called.

He was amusing about de G[aulle]. He does not think Pompidou cd follow him – or indeed anybody. Meanwhile, France is prosperous enough and enjoying being strongly governed. But it will break out when the Emperor dies!

He thought the Chinese wd never let go Vietnam and SE Asia. They can use it to prevent a reconciliation, or at least a détente, between America and Russia – the thing they fear the most. This is very shrewd. Wise Westerners (beginning with Arthur Balfour) have always wanted to draw Russia to Europe. China, by inflaming the SE Asia tribes, can prevent, or at least delay, this . . . .

24 March

. . . . The Americans have been dropping 'gas' (really a form of tear-gas) bombs in Vietnam. This has upset the Government benches – at least below the Gangway. What Wilson wd have said had Alec been in power, I can certainly imagine! But Wilson and the For Secy ([Michael] Stewart) are giving the Americans 'unswerving support'. Do they remember Suez? Happily, the U. Nations is now prevented from any action because of the great dispute about 'subscriptions', and voting[11] . . . .

25 March (Lady Day)

. . . . Dined at The Other Club – a long and rather desultory discussion about the future of the club. For a long time it has departed from its original concept – as indeed has Grillions[12] – of a place where leading men of both political parties shd meet. It has been dominated by Churchill and consists now of his friends. The possible courses are 1) to wind it up 2) to try gradually to bring it back to the first idea, which FE [Smith], L[loyd] George and Winston had when they started it in 1912 – all young men 3) to go on as we are, as an agreeable dining club, of Winston's friends. It might soon be re-named The Churchill Club (like the Pitt Club)[13]

---

11. Countries in arrears on their UN subscriptions, under Article 19, were not allowed to vote in the General Assembly. At this time so many were in arrears, with the deficit on peace-keeping alone being at least £80 million, that the General Assembly was ineffective.

12. A dining club founded in 1812, initially at Grillions Hotel, Albermarle Street.

13. The Other Club was actually founded in 1911. No name change occurred.

26 March

.... Philip de Zulueta and his wife came to supper. We had a good talk. He has been on a tour in Africa and Australia, and also to Israel – on behalf of his firm. He is gloomy about the pos[itio]n of Britain at the moment. The policy of applying a nominal brake (7% Bank Rate) and the accelerator (wage increases; large Govt expenditure; etc) at the same time is intended to deceive the foreign investor. But it doesn't. He may go on leaving money here, tempted by Bank Rate. But the French policy of selling dollars and sterling and buying gold (wh. is how the French started the 1931 collapse) is very dangerous to us.[14] Philip feels unhappy at the lack of any contact between the City and the Politicians. Meanwhile, the HofCommons is getting quite rowdy and excited scenes take place. It all seems very remote and rather silly when one is not a member . . . .

30 March

Memorial service for Herbert Morrison to which I felt I must go, as I had served him as Parl Sec in the Ministry of Supply in 1940. He was one of the last of Churchill's War Government. The new fashion is a sermon or allocation in praise of the departed. This was done by Mervyn Stockwood (Bp of Southwark) and quite well done. But I don't much like the plan – and the more distinguished the dead man is and the more that has already been said and written about him, the less necessary is the funeral oration . . . .

31 March

To London again. Lunch with the Salisburys – Bobbety in good form, and Betty very gracious and friendly. We had a talk about Alec Home's position, wh. seems to be rather weakening. But we recalled that this always happens when we lose an Election – c.f. Baldwin, or Balfour[15]

7 April

.... Yesterday Callaghan introduced his Budget in what seems to have been a very competent speech. Everything is taxed – £215 million more.

---

14. On 4 February, arguing that inflation was being imported from the US, de Gaulle called for a return to the gold standard and started converting surplus dollars and sterling into gold.

15. A reference to infighting within the Conservative party following electoral defeat in 1923, 1929, or 1906.

Capital Gains Tax; Corporation Tax;[16] and taxes on almost all things like drink, tobacco, cars etc. Except for Capital Gains Tax (30%) not very original.[17] The process of giving excessive wages and then trying to claw back the increase of taxation goes on. The papers are hostile. Even *The Times*, wh. is run by Socialists and Radicals, is critical. The actual conditions of the new Capital and Corporation Taxes are so obscure as to be incomprehensible until the Finance Bill is published . . . .

31 May

I have not had the heart to write for many weeks. D and I left England on April 14th for our cruise, wh. was very agreeable and made us feel much rested and younger in spirit. We started from Venice – and our visits were to Delphi, Athens, Delos, etc. It was a most delightful tour, with some agreeable people on the ship and some good lecturers – esp. Sir John Wolfenden. Then, in the last two days, came the blow. We were at Olympia, in the museum, when a man came to tell us that there was a telephone call from England. It was poor Maurice [Macmillan], and his news was grievous. It was to tell us of his son, Joshua's death – at Balliol. We had to go on with the ship to Corfu and then with great difficulty we got a plane to Athens and home. I cannot write of this terrible business – the Press, the Inquest and all the rest. The funeral service and burial was at Danehill (Pooks is in this parish) and the grave looks out over the Weald. Maurice has gone off abroad with Katie. Alexander is in Glasgow, on the *Glasgow Herald*. Adam, much affected, is back at Eton. Life has gone on. But it is the first loss of this kind we have had in the family and all the circumstances were so distressing as to make it a sad shock to us all. Had it not been for the folly of the Balliol Dean he wd be alive today. The boy took a sleeping pill on the top of alcohol.[18] Four times during the next day a friend, finding him sleeping heavily, called the Dean. He did nothing. At last, the friend got an ambulance. Even then he was still alive.

---

16. Hitherto companies had paid 15% profits tax and income tax only on undistributed dividends. This new tax was levied at 40% on total profits and companies were also required to pass on income tax due on dividends.

17. The new CGT was levied at 30% on gains on all assets over £1,000 in value except owner-occupied property.

18. Joshua had already been treated for addiction to heroin earlier that year. On this occasion he mixed alcohol and valium and choked on his own vomit.

The Press, with the name of an ex-P.M. and Chancellor of Oxford to exploit, and with a story of drugs etc and pompous leading articles to cover their wallowing in sensation have been particularly nauseating. The younger children in all the families are recovering. Maurice and Katie have been very good and I am glad that they are still abroad for a time.

Life has gone on. The chief public event wh. I had to do (in great sorrow) was at Runnymede, for the Kennedy memorial. It was happily a lovely day and the ceremony went off well. I spoke first; then Wilson; then the Queen. Dean Rusk replied. The T.V. audiences in UK and USA were said to have reached a prodigious total. I took a lot of trouble with my speech and it was good. All the Kennedys – Mrs Jack (or Jacqueline) Bobby etc, with Moucher Devonshire and the Harlechs came on the Sunday to Birch Grove. It was good to see them – a tempestuous, lively, gallant family, who have had sad losses – two brothers and a sister – but drive on, with courage and gaiety, treating life as a great adventure . . . .

Everything goes on, but for me rather sadly. I think so much of poor Joshua, who was so young and so charming. It seems dreadful to have been taken, just as his life was starting, while Daniel and I go on, between 70 and 80 years old . . . .

The political situation is strange. Never before have Governments tried to carry major (and even revolutionary) changes with so slender a majority. They succeeded at first, because they had public opinion with them and the almost certainty of an increased majority if they were defeated in Parlt and forced to dissolve. I am not so sure that this is now true. The local elections (not of course more than a modest guide) have swung violently away from Labour. The alarm caused by the Budget taxes – esp. the Capital Gains and Corporation taxes – and the general sense that with all Wilson's clever talk on the T.V. and all his showmanship nothing much is happening except to make people more uncomfortable – all this is having a considerable effect. Of course, the Govt may get through this bad patch and hold on through the winter. Most people feel this, wh. means a General Election in the autumn of 1966. Meanwhile, Alec Home's position improves and Macleod has ostentatiously accepted his leadership . . . .

4 June

. . . . As a kind of 'tranquilliser', I am taking a course of Henry James! What a world – how quiet and peaceful and happy it was for the 'upper and upper-middle classes'. Now it's a nightmare. Happily, it's a much better world for the masses, as has been brought home to me most forcibly in writing the history of the inter-war years . . . .

5 June

. . . . I have definitely finished Chapter 14 today. I have now 2 more to do – 'Munich' and 'The Phoney War' and that will bring me to the formation of the National Govt in 1940. These will be difficult chapters, esp. the first. It is hard to be <u>fair</u> and <u>judicial</u> about Munich; people had the most bitter feelings then and have still . . . .

8 June

London. I find the problems of M&Co more and more difficult. The truth is I am too old to bother about <u>new</u> problems. I prefer reading and writing about old ones. All this morning 'in conference' (as they say) with Brooks and Kay about Nigeria. It seems we now have to start a special company for Northern Nigeria if we are to get the business . . . .

9 June

. . . . Dorothy seems happy enough with her garden, but she too is (at last) shewing signs of getting older. Yet she gardens and rushes about on the family errands with undiminished intensity . . . .

. . . . The American policy in Vietnam is being a good deal criticised in 'progressive' and 'intellectual' circles in America. I see that Bobby Kennedy has spoken not altogether favourably of what the President is doing. Yet I think Wilson is right to support U.S.A. Govt. There is always a danger of America getting tired of world affairs. We had quite enough trouble trying to tempt her to take an interest in the old days . . . .

13 June

. . . . An absurd Honours List, including 'The Beatles' – also 6 more Life Peers. Is Wilson trying to swamp the House of Lords by these massive creations. <u>No</u> hereditary titles, peerages or baronetcies.

The Gallup Poll shows a sudden and decisive swing <u>against</u> Labour, largely by Liberals coming over to the Conservatives. I have no faith in the public opinion polls except when they favour us! . . . .

16 June

London again. Saw Obote (Uganda) and Kaunda (N. Rhodesia) and

Nyerere (Tanzania). They are all very pleasant and courteous to me, whom they seem to regard as the Founding Father of modern Africa! . . . .

15 July

Luncheon with Oliver Poole. He takes a very gloomy view of the future. No one (Labour or Tory) in his mind is really up to the job that has got to be done.

Wedding at St Margaret's of Nicholas Hunloke (Dorothy's nephew) to a daughter of Ld Hinchingbrooke. The situation was complicated, almost farcical. Anne Cavendish (D's sister) is the boy's mother. Henry H. (her divorced husband) was there. Anne then married Ld H. She is about to divorce him – a terrible story of wickedness and folly . . . .

23 July

Alec Home rang me up last night . . . . to tell that he had decided to resign the Leadership of the Conservative Party. I am <u>very</u> sorry.[19]

24 July

Great excitement about Alec's decision, resulting in telephone calls from the Press (to whom I refuse all statements) and from some of my old colleagues. The choice seems to lie between Maudling and Heath – about even money on each. Christopher Soames consulted me as to whether he should stand. I advised him not to do so . . . .

27 July

Knox-C[unningham] rang me up after luncheon to say that Ted Heath, rather unexpectedly, had a small majority over Maudling – but not sufficient, under the rules, to avoid a second ballot. Enoch Powell only got 15 votes. He rang later to say that Maudling had decided to withdraw, so Ted will be elected unanimously, as no one else is likely to come forward. I feel sure that Ted is the best choice. He is a stronger character than Maudling . . . .

---

19. Three days later Macmillan wrote to Home: 'You made a wonderful recovery for the Party and only by a bit of bad luck . . . . were prevented from getting a majority. Had this happened, there would have been no questioning of your leadership.'

2 August

Great pressure was brought upon me by the Chief Whip and the Central Office to attend the formal meeting at Church House – where MPs, candidates, and peers confirm the new leader of the party. Accordingly, I went up early to London and after an hour or so at the office, arrived at the Hall at 11.50. When I went in, just after Alec, they all stood up and clapped as in old days. The business was rather long – an hour – but very dignified. There were tributes to Alec, moved by Lord Carrington and seconded and supported. The motion of confidence in Heath was again moved by Carrington and seconded (in an excellent speech) by Maudling. Heath spoke briefly but well in reply. I remembered January 1957, when I was elected.

The debate in the House (vote of censure)[20] took place later this day. Heath was good; but not quite up to the absurd expectations of the Press, who regard the whole thing as a gladiatorial sport. The economic situation gets worse. A loss of gold last month, wh. the authorities put at £50[m] and everyone believes (apart from juggling with the figures) to be £150m . . . .

16 August

. . . . The Malaysian Federation, wh. we made in 1963 with such difficulty, has collapsed, with the secession (or expulsion) of Singapore. I fear the Chinese and the Malays could not get along together, after all our hopes and their protestations.

Rather better trade figures last month, with record exports. The Americans will lend more money and Wilson will scrape through – or so it seems now . . . .

29 August (Sunday)

. . . . I have received, but refused, an invitation to speak at New York in October at a great dinner in honour of Eisenhower's 75th birthday. Had this been a national affair I would have gone. But I don't like the idea of a dinner 'sponsored' by the Republican party and probably intended to collect funds . . . .

26 September (Sunday)

. . . . The public news has been dramatic and sad. India and Pakistan have been at war but after a fortnight have agreed to a ceasefire. Each

---

20. A motion of no confidence in the government moved by Heath.

side has fought with tanks, guns, aeroplanes etc wh. have been given
to them by the Americans and ourselves to defend Asia from Communism. They have used them in this fratricidal war. It looks as if they
have only agreed to the cease-fire (organised by U.N.O.) because they
have used up most of their weapons – esp. aeroplanes and tanks. In
this field it has been a battle between British and American types!
China entered the game (whether by a new sort of Ribbentrop–
Molotov pact[21] with Pakistan or not is obscure) and started to send
threatening ultimata to India about the Sikkim frontier line. The
interesting thing is that Russia protested strongly, and joined with U.K.
and USA at the Security Council in united action to stop the war. (This
unity has not happened for 20 years)

We have had a terrible shock yesterday, Ann Macpherson (one of
my secretaries) went to meet David Dilks at the station and on the way
back managed to overturn her car on the Horsted Keynes road, about
a mile from B.G. She has escaped with a bit of bruising, some shock
and a few cuts. David had to go to East Grinstead hospital, with bad
facial cuts (which needed quite long and difficult surgical repair) and
will (I'm afraid) have a shock reaction of a fairly serious kind.

I got Mrs Dilks down in [the] afternoon and she is staying at B.G.
It was a terrible blow to me, for I feel responsible. What folly! These
'young ladies' always drive too fast. What makes it so infuriating is
that I had ordered a taxi for him. But she was going to H[aywards]
Heath for shopping and said she wd bring him back with her. As she
has motored many miles and for many years, I thought nothing of it.
Dorothy (who was going over to Sarah [Heath, their youngest daugh-
ter]) had fortunately not left and was very efficient. She got Dr
Somerwell and the ambulance here within ½ hour and the hospital
warned. There are, happily, at East Grinstead hospital admirable face
surgeons, in the McIndoe tradition[22] . . . .

The Govt are now well ahead in the Gallup poll and there is
growing support for Wilson. There is certainly a feeling that they have
tried to grapple with the problems, whether their methods have been
good or bad. In fact, we have been shewn that the new international

---

21. The German/Russian pact of August 1939 which facilitated the dismemberment
    of Poland at the outbreak of the Second World War.

22. Archibald McIndoe pioneered plastic surgery at East Grinstead to treat the
    terrible burns suffered by airmen during the Second World War.

plans for supporting a weak currency do work.[23] But of course borrowing from the bank does not make one's business solvent *per se*. The latest thing is a proposed measure of semi-nationalisation and heavy taxation of land values. Of the equity of the latter I do not doubt. I dabbled with it in theory and rejected it. The difficulty is that unless you have complete nationalisation, and retain a free market, the price is likely to rise to meet the taxation. Lloyd George discovered this in the 1909 Budget[24] . . . .

29 September

London. The chief work at the office was routine. But I also saw one of Kay's friends, the Minister of Education for N. Rhodesia (Zambia) who was most friendly . . . . All the afternoon with John Brooks, who has just returned from Malaysia – Kuala Lumpur and Singapore – with a quite hopeful picture. Longman and OUP are strong; also a Chinese firm; also a 'semi-nationalised' Malay firm. But he thinks we can nevertheless increase our sales . . . .

7 October

. . . . The political situation at home is unchanged. The Government are in a good position, either for continuing or going to the Country. The apparent solution of the sterling crisis (by vast borrowing wh. will have to be repaid) and Wilson's general sense of timing and political skill give Labour a better position than seemed likely in the summer. However, a Govt always gains when Parl is 'up'. What Heath will do remains to be seen. A kind of Tory 'restatement of Faith' has come out today,[25] but I have not had time to study it. From the general press account, it seems quite good . . . .

---

23. These included a stabilisation loan from the IMF and American support in securing a $1-billion bank aid package in September, as well as a number of domestic economies.

24. One controversial aspect of the 1909 Budget was Lloyd George's duty of 20% on the increase in land value not directly attributable to the work of the owner on its sale or transfer. Labour's Land Commission Act, eventually passed in 1967, introduced a levy of 40% on land's development value, and a Land Commission to direct development. As Macmillan predicts here, this had the perverse effect of disincentivising the market, drying up development land and driving up prices.

25. Highlights of *Putting Britain Right Ahead* included strengthened monopolies law, registration of trade unions and employers' associations, a more flexible

10 October (Sunday)

. . . . Finished <u>Bodley's</u> <u>France</u>.[26] It is good and very well written. His prophecy that the Republic regime would not last but be replaced by a new Caesarism has proved true. Caesarism has re-emerged with de Gaulle, as he thought it would and the instrument is the plebiscite. But the Republic lasted longer than Bodley expected. Nevertheless, it was pretty shaky even <u>before</u> the second war . . . .

12 October

Bobbety Salisbury has the whole *Daily Express* this morning. He has an article calling 'the Wind of Change' the 'Bugle for Retreat' but otherwise he has nothing practical to suggest. Heath has got alarmed and slightly altered his emphasis. There may be trouble at the [Party] Conference at Brighton. Went to London. A good many difficulties, as is natural. In India, for instance, we are going again to accumulate money wh. cannot be got back to England . . . . I spent the afternoon (with Kay) calling on some Uganda ministers. I hope we shall be able to arrange a joint company for Uganda, on Nigerian lines.

In Western Nigeria there has been an election. Our friends – or rather Kay's friends – got re-elected by the simple but effective device of kidnapping some 20 of the Opposition candidates on their way to nomination, thus securing an equal number of unopposed returns . . . .

14 October

The Conservative Conference at Brighton has been overshadowed by the Rhodesian problem.[27] In spite of this, Heath seems to have opened with a good speech . . . .

---

labour market, streamlining of planning and the development of leisure facilities.

26. John Bodley's acclaimed *France* was published in two volumes by Macmillan & Co. in 1898. Bodley was the father of Macmillan's close friend, Ava Waverley.

27. Southern Rhodesia had unilaterally changed its name to Rhodesia in October 1964, just before Northern Rhodesia gained independence as Zambia. Meanwhile, Winston Field had been ousted as Prime Minister by Ian Smith in April 1964, not least because of his failure to press for independence. British unwillingness to grant this without black majority rule led Smith unilaterally to declare independence on 11 November 1965. Heath was meanwhile embarrassed by the support for Smith from some elements in his party.

15 October

Still glorious weather – cold, but warm in the sun. The Conservative conference, about to quarrel over Rhodesia or to be swayed by Ld Salisbury, was restored by Alec Home, who saved the day.[28] This is rather ironical . . . .

30 October

. . . . The 'financial and economic' position of the country is improving, at least temporarily. Exports are up; imports down – the trade gap not more than £28[m]. The pound is firm, no doubt because with the vast borrowing or reserve currency to defend the £, foreign money (short term) is coming in to get advantage of the high Bank Rate. I am not sure that the fundamental situation is really improved. However, all this goes to help the Govt, with 11% lead in the Gallup (reduced to 6% this week) I wd have thought the Socialists ought to take the plunge. But I doubt if Wilson will do so – and he may perh. be right. The people (who do not want another election so soon) might resent it . . . .

11 November

. . . . The Rhodesia dispute continues. Wilson has been to Nairobi, and a procedure – a Royal Commission – seemed agreed. But Smith accuses Wilson of cheating him and being 'too clever by half'. So he is. The Govt stock remains high, but not quite as high as it was. The Conservatives now do not enjoy the respect of the people. To have got rid of Alec Home at this time was folly. The people regard Edward Heath as a sort of 'rich man's Wilson'. They admire him, but do not trust him – as yet. This shd come in time, for he is a man of good character.

I went to see my brother Daniel, just back at Grosvenor Square from some weeks in St Thomas's Hospital. He is better and has no pain (he has gall-stones) but he is very weak and frail. We have got 2 nurses, day and night, to be with him. He now reads very little, wh. is not a good sign with him – for ordinarily he is a voracious reader.

I have had to go to London a lot during these last weeks; there is much going on at M&Co and altho' the new management idea is taking shape, yet they all need a guiding and a firm hand to keep the

---

28. Home succeeded in getting Salisbury to withdraw his amendment deploring any kind of sanctions against Rhodesia.

balance. As usual, we are trading beyond our means, and suffering from difficulties of transferring money. We have, for instance, at the moment £¼m in India, which sum is useless to us.[29] Meanwhile, we have a similar overdraft in London.

Parlt has been prorogued and opened. It seems odd not even to bother to read the Queen's speech. It all seems very remote from me now.

David Dilks has been reading the proofs of Lord Moran's Diary of his life with Churchill. I fear it will cause a terrible row. D.D. is not sure that the diary is genuine. He thinks he can prove (in some places) that it has been 'doctored'. I think it will sell, like Greville, but he thought [it] in even worse taste than Greville.[30] Personally, I think historians give far too much weight to diaries or the reports of chance conversations.

Wilson is an able man and a very astute politician. He has run for a year on a very small majority. He has cleverly made it out (and the Press has helped him) to be smaller than it really is. It is 3 <u>overall</u>; but, with the Liberals, it is 20. The Liberals will never turn him out, so long as he avoids extreme measures. He is playing for the centre – a sort of Socialist Baldwin. He can disregard his left (just as I cd more or less disregard my right) This puts the Tories in difficulties. Heath has to complain because the Govt do <u>not</u> introduce a Bill to nationalise steel! Of course, something may arise suddenly to make Wilson's position impossible – but, so far, he has shewn a great authority and sense of timing and the Govt are gaining ground. It's perhaps a little <u>too</u> clever; but it <u>is</u> clever.

We had a dinner (with champagne) for the 3 'young ladies', to celebrate the final completion of vol. 1.

We heard this afternoon that Mr Smith had declared the independence of Rhodesia. This is sad news, full of dangers and problems ahead. Apart from local reactions, it will let in the UN; China; Russia; USA, and everyone else to try to create another Congo. Unless <u>very</u> carefully and wisely handled by HMG I foresee terrible and disastrous developments. If everyone keeps their heads, these may perhaps be avoided. Sad to happen on Armistice Day.

---

29. Because of Indian exchange controls.
30. Charles Greville's diaries of political activity and gossip 1817–60 were one of Macmillan's favourites. Between 1950 and 1966 he read them five times. Moran was Churchill's physician.

12 November

Tories are <u>up</u> 2% at the Erith by-election. The Labour vote has dropped 1000. The Liberal vote <u>down</u> by 4000.[31] Not very different from Westminster – altho' rather better for the Tories. The encouraging thing is the Liberal collapse . . . .

6 December

We get messages about Daniel each day – just the same and I rang up on Sunday night (last night) The nurse said he was no worse. But he slipped away peacefully at 4am this morning. It is a terrible blow.

9 December

Daniel's funeral was today. He wanted to be cremated and his ashes scattered, so we had to do what he wished. The ceremony was dignified and in a way beautiful, but terribly sad.

15 December

We are to have the memorial service tomorrow (at St Martin's) I have had a very large number of letters. Daniel's kindness and generosity made him loved.

. . . . I have read *Pride and Prejudice* and *Emma* and am now in *Mansfield Park*. Jane Austen soothes me, for I am tired and nervous. I think all this time about Dan and our childhood and all the memories which there is no one now to share with. Arthur is better but [his wife] Peggy ill.[32] D and the children have been very kind. Maurice had a deep affection for his uncle and <u>all</u> the children loved him . . . .

19 December

A terrible night of rain and storm. Since we live on the top of a hill, our position is not too bad. But half the county is flooded.

Ghana and Tanzania have broken off relations with U.K. – also Egypt.[33] Wilson went to speak at the United Nations, for no purpose except to force President Johnson to see him in Washington later. All the African states boycotted him. He seems, by his duplicity, to be

---

31. Labour 21,835; Conservative 14,763; Liberal 2,823.
32. Daniel was the eldest and Arthur the second of Macmillan's brothers.
33. On 3 December the Organisation of African Unity agreed that its members should break diplomatic relations with Britain if it failed to tackle Rhodesia by 15 December. Many subsequently did so.

equally hateful both to Whites and Blacks. Sterling is under pressure again. The economic structure of UK is very fragile, and the continual attacks on industry by the Socialists do not improve confidence. The sole benefit of a Socialist Govt ought to be to have some control on Labour and the T. Unions. But they have none. Brown's policy of 'incomes control' is a complete flop and he has become a joke . . . .

21 December
. . . . The inflation is growing more rapidly than (I think) in any post-war year. Yet the Tory Party is weak, divided, and not held in any great esteem in the country. The 'dismissal' of Alec Home was worse than a crime. It was a blunder . . . .

1966

Coups in Nigeria and Ghana – argument with Wilson about nuclear diplomacy with the French and Americans in 1962 – Labour triumphs in the General Election

2 January (Sunday)

.... A busy week, with two visits to London, chiefly about our publishing efforts in Africa. The Rhodesia trouble has made everybody very jumpy – also, most of the African states are more or less bankrupt ....

9 January (Sunday)

I scarcely read the newspapers now, but the Rhodesia news looks as if the 'economic sanctions' will disrupt the life of the settlers; create wide-spread unemployment, esp. among the Africans, and generally create a chaotic situation. If this is the purpose of the British P.M. and Govt, they must be ready to take immediate advantage of it at the critical moment. Short of 'the use of force', this will not be easy ....

I have spent 3 days – Wed., Thurs., and Friday – preparing a TV talk or interview, which is to be released about the time of publication of my first volume. A vast quantity of engineers, 'technicians', secretaries, producers etc arrived and for 3 days were the delight of the Amery and Heath children. Those taking part were Mr [John] Grist (BBC) Mr N[igel] Lawson (late BBC and now Editor of the *Spectator*) Mr [Charles] Collingwood (distinguished American journalist, who works for Columbia Broadcasting) There was one long session (practice) on Wed; 3 of 1½ to 2 hours each on Thurs; and one of 1½ hours on Friday. They all left on Friday about tea-time and I retired to bed, absolutely exhausted. With their technique, picture and words are on the same film or reel. Out of all this, 50 minutes or so are selected. I have received a modest fee for all this, but have really submitted to it in order to help my publishers ....

27 January

There has been a lot of business and a lot of worry. The 'coup' in Nigeria,[1] by which two or more P.M.s have been assassinated, including

---

1. A military coup took place on 15 January.

the Sardauna of Sokoto (the Duke of Omnium)[2] and my dear friend Abubakar, the Federal P.M. Our Mr Kay was at Kaduna when all this happened. He is back now, but in a very poor state of health. All this has meant a lot of time at the office. We have many other troubles, with the India situation, already bad, likely to be made much worse by Shastri's death.[3] The black market value of the rupee is about <u>half</u> the nominal value and everyone seems to expect devaluation. We have £150,000 which we cannot get at.

The Exchange Control want us to force the M&Co of Canada to pay out excessive dividends. Mr Brown threatens us if we do. Mr Callaghan wants us to do so, not for exchange reasons, but to collect more tax.[4] Altogether, it is a difficult time . . . .

I have written 4 chapters of volume 2. Volume 1 has gone to press. [US publishers] Harpers want me to shorten volume 1, by leaving out all the part of English political and economic questions between the wars – or at least, by shortening it very much. We have thought a lot about this – but Alan Maclean, [Tim] Farmiloe etc are <u>much</u> against this. They say it would destroy the balance of the book and its character. I expect Harpers (Cass Canfield) are right from the commercial angle and I dare say it wd be better also for selling the book in England. But I don't like to try to re-write it now, altho' I am ready to do so if the M&Co advisers want it – which they don't . . . .

28 January
Everyone expected a close fight at the Hull by-election. Actually,

---

2. Omnium was a powerful magnate and political figure in Anthony Trollope's Barchester and Pallister novels. Sir Ahmadu Bello, the Premier of Northern Nigeria, occupied a similar position in the region through his role in the Muslim emirate of Sokoto until his assassination in the coup.
3. Indian Prime Minister Lal Bahadur Shastri died on 11 January.
4. The then exchange control system was established in 1939 to manage Britain's balance of payments. Excess dividends from Canada, following two years of exceptional profits, would both benefit the exchanges and allow Callaghan's Treasury to take more tax from the British parent company. Brown's Department of Economic Affairs was, however, by this stage increasingly in favour of devaluation rather than the austerity with which the Treasury also tried to shore up the currency. Eventually M&Co Canada agreed to declare a small increase in dividends, well short of that demanded by the Treasury.

Labour won by over 5000 (against 1100 at General Election)[5] This is a <u>great</u> triumph for Wilson. The tide is clearly flowing for the Government. This is partly because it always does (it did with us for the first year or two) and partly because of the antics of the Tory party in Parliament. The tragedy was that Alec Home had not the guts to stick it out. He would have won through. The <u>working</u> class (as opposed to the middle class) are not [to] be attracted by the Heath-Maudling type. If they are going to vote Tory, they want to vote for the <u>officer</u>, not the <u>warrant officer</u>. They have plenty of them in their own ranks . . . .

6 March

. . . . After the Revolution in Nigeria, there has been one in Ghana, and Nkrumah has been deposed in his absence. This latter is a good thing, as N. was prodigal to the extreme, as well as tyrannical. But it's a bit tricky for us, for we have between £200,000 and £250,000 worth of books to be paid for. They are waiting to be shipped if and when a letter of credit arrives . . . .

Wilson has declared that Parlt will soon be dissolved, with polling on March 31st. The signs are (according to the pollsters) that there will be a 'walkover' victory, as in 1906 or 1945. I am not quite so sure, but I do not doubt that Labour will get a good majority. The Tory Party have behaved in the HofC with such egregious folly that they deserve defeat . . . .

19 March

. . . . Philip de Zulueta rang up. It seems that Harold Wilson, speaking at Bristol, has made a lying attack on me. He said that I <u>deceived</u> General de Gaulle at Rambouillet in 1962 (Dec) by <u>not</u> telling him that, if <u>Skybolt</u> failed, I intended to get a substitute, prob[ably] <u>Polaris</u> at my meeting with President Kennedy at <u>Nassau</u>. He alleged that it was because de Gaulle was so incensed by my perfidy, that he put his veto on Britain joining the Common Market. Happily, only a few months ago, de Gaulle told Heath that this story (which had been put about at the time by the lower types in Paris and London, and had been repeated by some Labour politicians – tho' not openly) was completely untrue. My memory is fairly good, and I recall a long talk about all this at Rambouillet and de G's reasonable attitude. But

---

5. In a seat narrowly gained by Labour from the Tories in the general election they picked up votes from the Liberals whilst the Conservative poll was static.

fortunately, we found in the papers the complete printed text of all the conversations. Philip came down for luncheon, and by 3pm we had sent a statement to the Press[6] . . . .

20 March
Splendid coverage in all the (Sunday) Press. *S. Times* had sent a photographer: *S. Telegraph* made it the news story. Even the *Observer* was good . . . .

21 March
My attack (or rather protest) at Wilson's lies about me has very good coverage in today's Press – wh. is unusual, after a Sunday display. Tory speakers are taking it up . . . .

24 March
. . . . No answer at all by Wilson. Callaghan (C of Ex) made a silly reply (to a persistent Tory heckler) He said that perh. there had been some mistake and de G. may not have understood my French!

I shall wait a little longer and then perhaps (if Wilson makes no move) send another communication to the Press. Unhappily, altho' everyone seems to regard Wilson as a liar and a crook, they all mean to vote Labour.

Heath has put on a very good show, but he is not making headway. The trouble is that he looks too professional (like Disraeli) The people still like an amateur, if he is in the professional class. But I feel that the result may be a little better than the 'polls' (Gallup etc) wd indicate . . . .

27 March
. . . . Maurice, Katie and family came back last night from Farnham, for a day's rest. Long talk with Maurice. He is most interesting about the decay of Conservatism among the middle-classes. They are going Liberal and he is seriously worried that the nominal Conservative

---

6. There was misunderstanding at Rambouillet, and a discrepancy between the British and French records, although this seems to reflect that Macmillan thought in terms of Anglo-French co-operation after acquiring missiles from the Americans (who did after Nassau offer Polaris to the French on the same terms as the British) whilst de Gaulle wished to avoid an American interloper. Nassau then provided a convenient occasion for de Gaulle's veto but it was not, as Wilson implied, its cause.

majority may almost fade away. But, of course, if he is elected at Farnham, it shd be possible to get things right, with a new approach. The reason for the Liberal rise is social, not political. It is a protest agst the old Admirals, Generals, and 2nd or 3rd generation gentry who run the Conservative Associations as a pleasant social club for themselves . . . .

I talked with Julian Amery, at Preston. He seemed cheerful – tho' with a majority of 14 (or 13) and the polls showing the swing to Labour, he has an almost impossible task . . . .

28 March
Since Wilson has not replied – has neither justified nor withdrawn his false statement about me, I issued another challenge, wh. appeared in all the papers this morning. At his Press Conference, he was forced to say something, but it was a wicked, shuffling, wriggling statement. So, with [the] help of Philip de Z[ulueta], I drafted and sent out within one hour, a final reply. I shall say no more.

29 March
Even *The Times* has a leader supporting me agst Wilson. All the Press takes the same line. It will do no good politically, I fear. But it will at least get the record right . . . .

30 March
Both Heath and Wilson made good final broadcasts – at least, so people say. I have not looked at any T.V. Happily, we have not got the instrument at B.G. (except in the Servants' Hall) I fear a 'landslide' to Labour. My guess is that they will have a majority of 160–180 in HofC . . . .

2 April (Palm Sunday)
The General Election is over. We lost about 50 seats, giving Wilson about 100 majority (the same as I had in 1959) This is by no means a landslide – the actual turnover being much less than one wd have thought from the various polls. (In 1945 we lost 213 seats) Unhappily, Julian Amery lost Preston – but only by 2000. Since last year [sic] his majority was only 13,[7] this means that he has only lost 1000 votes

---

7. Actually 14 – the Conservative vote fell from 20,566 in 1964 to 19,121, whilst Labour's rose from 20,552 to 21,539.

turned over – a very fine result. Maurice got in at Farnham by nearly 9000 – a very good result. Henry Brooke, Thorneycroft, Soames and a few other leaders are out, wh. is a pity . . . .

28 April–12 May

D and I have had a wonderful holiday together. She told her sister Maud that she had enjoyed it enormously. So did I. Turnberry; Arran; Strachur; Gleneagles. D. drove the car everywhere and we stayed with the Fitzroy Macleans at Strachur – otherwise hotels. It was the most delightful weather all the time.

Read Moran's *Churchill* – interesting, but very unfair to everyone and Moran did not really understand WSC . . . .

20 May

D. had agreed to open the house and garden on this day for the Sussex Historic Churches Fund. She worked hard at home and garden as usual. £400 made for the fund. Olaf Caroe and Kitty were here and seemed delighted, as he runs the appeal.[8]

---

8. This is the final entry in volume three of the third (post-premiership) series of Macmillan's manuscript diaries. The day after this entry Lady Dorothy suddenly died of a heart attack, and Macmillan never started another volume of diaries.

Biographical Notes

Sir Abubakar Tafawa Balewa – Nigerian Chief Minister 1957–60 and Prime Minister 1960–66.

Dean Acheson – US Secretary of State 1949–53 and unofficial foreign policy adviser to the Kennedy and Johnson administrations.

Sir Grantley Adams – Prime Minister of Barbados 1954–58. Only Prime Minister of the West Indies 1958–62.

Sherman Adams – White House Chief of Staff 1953–58

Sir Michael Adeane – Private secretary to Queen Elizabeth II 1953–72.

Konrad Adenauer – West German Chancellor 1949–63.

Cyrille Adoula – Prime Minister of Congo 1961–64.

Frank Aiken – A senior IRA commander during the 1919–21 Anglo-Irish war. Irish Minister of Defence 1932–45, of Finance 1945–48, of External Affairs 1951–54 and 1957–69, Deputy Prime Minister 1965–69.

A. R. W. (Toby) Low, 1st Baron Aldington – Conservative MP for Blackpool North 1945–62. Deputy Chairman of the Conservative Party 1959–63.

Albert, 1st Earl Alexander of Hillsborough – Labour MP 1922–31, 1935–50. First Lord of the Admiralty 1929–31, 1940–45, 1945–46, Minister of Defence 1946–50, Chancellor of the Duchy of Lancaster 1950–51. Labour leader in the House of Lords 1955–64.

Harold, 1st Viscount Alexander of Tunis – Macmillan worked with him during the Second World War, which Alexander ended as Supreme Allied Commander in the Mediterranean. Governor-General of Canada 1946–52, Minister of Defence 1952–54.

Henry Alexander – Chief of Defence Staff, Ghana 1960–61.

Cuthbert (Cub), Lord Alport – Conservative MP for Colchester 1950–61.

Created life peer in 1961. Assistant Postmaster-General 1955–57, PS (1957–59) and Minister of State (1959–61), Commonwealth Relations Office. High Commissioner to Central African Federation 1961–63.

Julian Amery – Married to Macmillan's daughter Catherine. Conservative MP for Preston 1950–66, for Brighton Pavilion 1969–92. Under-Secretary, War Office 1957–58; Colonial Office 1958–60. Air Secretary 1960–62, Minister of Aviation 1962–64, of Public Building and Works 1970, of Housing and Construction 1970–72, of State at FCO 1972–74. Active in the Suez Group and later the Monday Club and well connected in French right-wing circles and the Middle East.

Robert Bernard Anderson – US Navy Secretary 1953–54, US Treasury Secretary 1957–61.

David Astor – 3rd Viscount's brother. Editor of the *Observer* 1948–75.

Gavin, 2nd Baron Astor of Hever – Chairman, The Times Publishing Co Ltd 1959–66, President, Times Newspapers Ltd 1967–81.

William Waldorf (Bill), 3rd Viscount Astor – Son of Waldorf (2nd Viscount) and Nancy Astor. Conservative MP 1935–45 and 1951 until inheriting the title in 1952. His second wife (1955–60), Macmillan's niece Philippa, in 1956 suggested renting a cottage on his Cliveden estate to Stephen Ward, helping to create the setting for the Profumo affair.

Clement, 1st Earl Attlee – Labour MP 1922–55, Prime Minister 1945–51, Leader of the Opposition 1951–55.

Evangelos Averoff – Foreign Minister of Greece 1956–63.

Muhammad Ayub Khan – Commander-in-Chief of the Pakistan Army from 1951 and, after leading a military coup, President 1958–69.

George Ball – Befriended Jean Monnet when with the US Strategic Bombing Survey in London 1944–45, becoming a passionate supporter of European integration. US Under-Secretary of State for Economic Affairs 1961, Under Secretary of State 1961–66.

Hastings Banda – Nyasaland nationalist leader who effectively became Prime Minister from 1961 and, after independence (as Malawi) in 1964, President 1966–94.

S. W. R. D. Bandaranaike – Prime Minister of Ceylon 1956–59.

Anthony Barber – Conservative MP for Doncaster 1951–64, for Altrincham and Sale 1965–74 and Party Chairman 1967–70. PPS to Macmillan 1958–59, EST 1959–62, FST 1962–63, Minister of Health 1963–64, Chancellor of the Exchequer 1970–74.

Sir Roderick Barclay – Ambassador to Denmark 1956–60, adviser on European questions, Foreign Office 1960–63, Ambassador to Belgium 1963–69.

Sir Evelyn Baring – Governor of Kenya 1952–59.

Max Aitken, 1st Baron Beaverbrook – Press baron (proprietor of the *Daily Express* and *Evening Standard*), imperialist of Canadian origin, former minister in Lloyd George and Churchill's wartime governments and maverick Tory.

Sir Edward Beddington-Behrens – Founding member of the British European Movement and, with Macmillan, of what became the Central and Eastern European Commission.

Richard Beeching – After a distinguished business career with ICI he became Chairman of British Railways 1961–65.

David Ben-Gurion – Prime Minister of Israel 1948–53, 1955–63.

Anthony Wedgwood Benn – Labour MP for Bristol South East 1950–61, when he succeeded as 2nd Viscount Stansgate. His fight to renounce the title led to the 1963 Peerage Act. He re-took the seat 1963–83, then sat for Chesterfield 1984–2001. Postmaster-General 1964–66, Minister of Technology 1966–70, Secretary of State for Industry 1974–75, for Energy 1975–79.

Sir Isaiah Berlin – Oxford philosopher and intellectual historian.

Michael Berry – Chairman and editor-in-chief, *Daily Telegraph* 1954–87 and husband of Lady Pamela.

Aneurin Bevan – Labour MP for Ebbw Vale 1929–60 and Deputy Leader 1959–60. Minister of Health 1945–51, of Labour and National Service 1951, Shadow Foreign Secretary 1956–60.

Reginald Bevins – Conservative MP for Liverpool Toxteth 1950–64. PPS to Macmillan 1951–53, PS to Ministry of Works 1953–57, of Housing and Local Government 1957–59, Postmaster-General 1959–64.

John Biggs-Davison – Right-wing Conservative MP 1955–88. Leading member of the Suez Group and the Monday Club.

Nigel Birch – Conservative MP 1945–70. Secretary of State for Air 1955–57, EST 1957–58.

Freddy Bishop – Principal Private Secretary to Prime Minister 1956–59, deputy secretary to Cabinet 1959–61, then at the Ministry of Agriculture, Fisheries and Food 1961–64, of Land and Natural Resources 1964–65.

Tim Bligh – Private Secretary to Sir Edward Bridges (head of the Treasury) 1949–54, Assistant Secretary (1954–59), Under-Secretary (1959) at the Treasury. Principal Private Secretary to Prime Minister 1959–64.

Michael Blundell – Leader of New Kenya Group 1959–63 and Kenyan Minister of Agriculture 1955–59 and 1961–63.

Lady Violet Bonham Carter – Daughter of Liberal Prime Minister, H. H. Asquith, mother of Mark Bonham Carter (Liberal MP for Torrington 1958–59), mother-in-law of Jo Grimond, and leading Liberal figure.

Robert Boothby – Conservative MP for East Aberdeenshire 1924–58. From 1929 he had a long-term affair with Macmillan's wife, Dorothy.

John Boyd-Carpenter – Conservative MP for Kingston-upon-Thames 1945–72. Minister of Transport and Civil Aviation 1954–55, of Pensions and National Insurance 1955–62, Chief Secretary to the Treasury and Paymaster-General 1962–64.

Edward Boyle – Conservative MP for Birmingham Handsworth 1950–70. Junior education minister 1957–59, FST 1959–62, Minister of Education 1962–64.

Willy Brandt – Mayor of West Berlin 1957–66, West German Vice-Chancellor and Foreign Minister 1966–69, Chancellor 1969–74.

Heinrich von Brentano – West German Foreign Minister 1955–61.

Sir Norman Brook, 1st Baron Normanbrook – Cabinet Secretary 1947–62, Joint Secretary to the Treasury and head of the Home Civil Service 1956–62. Chairman, BBC Governors 1964–67.

Henry Brooke – Conservative MP 1938–45, 1950–66. FST 1954–57, Minister of Housing and Local Government and for Welsh Affairs 1957–61, Chief Secretary to the Treasury and Paymaster-General 1961–62, Home Secretary 1962–64.

Alfred B. (John) Brooks – Joined M&Co in 1919, becoming head of the Overseas Department before retirement in 1967.

George Brown – Labour MP for Belper 1945–70 and Deputy Leader 1960–70. Secretary of State for Economic Affairs 1964–66, Foreign Secretary 1966–68.

Anthony Montague Browne – Churchill's private secretary 1952–65.

David Bruce – US Ambassador to France 1949–52, to West Germany 1957–59, to the UK 1961–69.

Nikolai Bulganin – Chairman of Council of Ministers of the USSR 1955–58.

McGeorge Bundy – US National Security Advisor 1961–66.

Alexander Bustamante – Chief Minister (1953–55), Prime Minister (1962–67) of Jamaica.

Richard Austen (Rab) Butler – Conservative MP for Saffron Walden 1929–65 and Party Chairman 1959–61. Minister of Education 1941–45, of Labour 1945, Chancellor of the Exchequer 1951–55, Leader of the Commons 1955–61, Lord Privy Seal 1955–59, Home Secretary 1957–62, First Secretary of State with responsibility for Central Africa 1962–63, Foreign Secretary 1963–64, Shadow Foreign Secretary 1964–65.

Sir Harold Caccia – With Macmillan in North Africa. High Commissioner to Austria 1950–54, Deputy Under-Secretary, Foreign Office 1954–56, ambassador to the US 1956–61, Permanent Secretary, Foreign Office 1962–65.

James Callaghan – Labour MP 1945–87. Shadow Colonial Secretary 1956–61, Shadow Chancellor 1961–64, Chancellor of the Exchequer 1964–67, Home Secretary 1967–70, Foreign Secretary 1974–76, Prime Minister 1976–79.

Augustus Cass Canfield – Chairman of US publishers Harpers, 1955–67.

Sir Olaf Caroe – Secretary of India's foreign affairs department during the Second World War and Governor of North West Frontier province 1946–47.

Peter, 6th Baron Carrington – High Commissioner to Australia 1956–59, First Lord of the Admiralty 1959–63, Leader of the Lords 1963–64, Defence Secretary 1970–74, Energy Secretary 1974, Foreign Secretary 1979–82. Conservative Party Chairman 1972–74.

Richard Casey – Australian liaison officer with the Cabinet Office

1924–31. Served as UK Minister of State Resident in the Middle East 1942–43 and Governor of Bengal 1943–46. Australian Minister of External Affairs 1951–60, Governor-General of Australia 1965–70.

Barbara Castle – Labour MP in Blackburn 1945–79. Minister of Overseas Development 1964–65, of Transport 1965–68, for Employment and Productivity 1968–70, for Social Services 1974–76.

Fidel Castro – Seized control of Cuba in 1959 closely aligning it with the Soviet Union and remaining in power until 2008.

Oliver Lyttelton, 1st Viscount Chandos – Conservative MP 1940–54. Colonial Secretary 1951–54. Chairman of AEI Ltd 1945–51, 1954–63, President of Institute of Directors 1954–63.

Jean Chauvel – French Ambassador to Britain 1955–62.

Eric Edwards, Lord Chelmer – Chairman of the National Union of Conservative and Unionist Associations 1957–65.

Chiang Kai-Shek – Head of Chinese Nationalist government 1928–49 and, after expulsion from the mainland by the Communists, President of the Republic of China (Formosa/Taiwan) 1949–75.

George Christ – Conservative party parliamentary liaison officer 1945–65.

Randolph Churchill – Conservative MP 1940–45, son of Sir Winston, journalist.

Sir Winston Churchill – Prominent member of Asquith's Liberal (1908–16) and Lloyd George's coalition (1916–22) governments, then Conservative MP for Epping 1924–45 and Woodford 1945–65. Chancellor of the Exchequer 1924–29, Prime Minister 1940–45, 1951–55.

Sir Cuthbert Clegg – Industrialist. Leader of UK cotton industry mission to India, Hong Kong and Pakistan 1957. President, UK Textile Manufacturers' Association 1960–69.

Cameron, 1st Baron Cobbold – Governor of the Bank of England 1949–61. Chairman, Commission on Malaysia 1962. Lord Chamberlain 1963–71.

Donald Coggan – Bishop of Bradford 1956–61, Archbishop of York 1961–74, Archbishop of Canterbury 1974–80.

Canon John Collins – Founded Christian Action in 1946, Defence and Aid Fund for South Africa in 1956, and founding chairman of CND 1958–64.

Colin Coote – Oxford contemporary of Holland. Liberal MP 1917–22. Foreign correspondent with *The Times* 1922–42. Deputy editor (1945–50) and editor of the *Daily Telegraph* 1950–64.

Geoffroy de Courcel – French Ambassador to Britain 1962–72.

Frank Cousins – General Secretary, T&GWU 1956–69. Labour MP for Nuneaton 1965–66. Minister of Technology 1964–66. A leading Labour opponent of nuclear weapons.

Maurice Couve de Murville – With Macmillan in North Africa. French Ambassador to Italy 1945, Egypt 1950–54, NATO 1954–55, the US 1955–56 and West Germany 1956–58. French Foreign Minister 1958–68, Economic and Finance Minister 1968, Prime Minister 1968–69.

George Baring, 3rd Earl of Cromer – Governor of the Bank of England 1961–66, Ambassador to the US 1971–74.

Harry Crookshank – A friend of Macmillan from Eton and Oxford and fellow Conservative MP from 1924–56. Secretary for Mines 1935–39, FST 1939–43, Postmaster-General 1943–45, Minister of Health 1951–52, Leader of the Commons 1951–55, Lord Privy Seal 1952–55.

Richard Crossman – Worked for Macmillan in North Africa. Labour MP 1945–74, Minister of Housing and Local Government 1964–66, Leader of the Commons and Lord President of the Council 1966–68, Social Services Secretary 1968–70.

Hugh Cudlipp – Editor of *Sunday Pictorial* 1937–40, 1946–49, of *Daily Express* 1950–52, editorial director of *Sunday Pictorial* and *Daily Mirror* 1952–63, Chairman of Daily Mirror Newspapers 1963–68.

Sir Patrick Dean – Assistant Secretary (1953–56), Deputy Under-Secretary (1956–60), Foreign Office. UK representative to UN 1960–64, Ambassador to the US 1965–69.

Michel Debré – French Minister of Justice 1958–59, Prime Minister 1959–62, Economic and Finance Minister 1966–68, Foreign Minister 1968–69, Defence Minister 1969–73.

Bill Deedes – Journalist with the *Daily Telegraph* 1937–2007. Conservative MP for Ashford 1950–74. Minister without Portfolio 1962–64. Editor of *Daily Telegraph* 1974–86.

Alfred (Tom), Lord Denning – Master of the Rolls 1962–82.

Moraji Desai – Indian Finance Minister 1959–64, 1967–70, Prime Minister 1977–79.

Andrew Cavendish, 11th Duke of Devonshire – Succeeded 1950. Macmillan's nephew. Married Deborah (Debo) Mitford in 1941. Minister of State, Commonwealth Relations Office 1962–63, Colonial Office 1963–64.

Mary (Moucher), Dowager Duchess of Devonshire – Macmillan's sister-in-law and widow of the 10th Duke. Bobbety Salisbury's sister. Mistress of the Robes to the Queen 1953–67.

Sir William Dickson – CAS 1953–55, Chairman, Chiefs of Staff Committee 1956–59, first CDS 1959.

John Diefenbaker – Canadian Prime Minister 1957–63, Leader of the Progressive Conservative party 1956–67.

Sir Reginald Manningham-Buller, 1st Viscount Dilhorne – Conservative MP for Daventry 1943–50, for Northampton North 1950–62. Solicitor-General 1951–54, Attorney-General 1954–62, Lord Chancellor 1962–64.

Douglas Dillon – US Ambassador to France 1953–57, Deputy Under-Secretary of State for Economic Affairs 1957–58, Under-Secretary of State 1959–61, Secretary of the Treasury 1961–65.

Sir Pierson (Bob) Dixon – With Macmillan in North Africa. Ambassador to Czechoslovakia 1948–50, to UN 1954–60, to France 1960–64, Deputy Under-Secretary, Foreign Office 1950–54.

Allen Dulles – Younger brother of John. Director of the CIA 1953–61.

John Foster Dulles – US Secretary of State 1953–59.

Henry Scrymgeour-Wedderburn, 11th Earl of Dundee – Conservative MP 1931–45. Minister without Portfolio 1958–61, Minister of State, Foreign Office 1961–64.

David, 1st Viscount Eccles – Conservative MP for Chippenham 1943–62. Minister of Works 1951–54, of Education 1954–57 and 1959–62, President of the Board of Trade 1957–59, Paymaster-General 1970–73.

Felix von Eckardt – West German government press officer from 1952, from 1958–65 State Secretary in the Chancellor's office.

Sir Anthony Eden, 1st Earl of Avon – Conservative MP for Warwick and

Leamington 1923–57. Foreign Secretary 1935–38, 1940–45, 1951–55, Dominions Secretary 1939–40, War Secretary 1940, Prime Minister 1955–57.

Dwight D. Eisenhower – With Macmillan in North Africa. Supreme Commander, Allied Expeditionary Force in Western Europe 1944–45, SACEUR 1950–52, US President 1953–61.

Sir John Elliot – The son of R. D. Blumenfeld (editor of the *Daily Express* 1909–29). Chairman of London Transport 1953–59.

Ludwig Erhard – West German Economics Minister 1949–63, Vice-Chancellor 1957–63, Chancellor 1963–66.

Tage Erlander – Prime Minister of Sweden 1946–69.

Frederick Erroll – Conservative MP for Altrincham and Sale 1945–64. PS to Ministry of Supply 1955–56, to Board of Trade 1956–58, EST 1958–59, Minister of State for Trade 1959–61, President of the Board of Trade 1961–63, Minister of Power 1963–64.

Franz Etzel – West German Finance Minister 1957–61.

Harold Evans – Macmillan's press secretary 1957–63.

Amintore Fanfani – Italian Prime Minister 1954, 1958–59, 1960–63, 1982–83, 1987, Foreign Minister 1958–59, 1962, 1966–68.

Anthony Fell – Conservative MP for Yarmouth 1951–66, 1970–83. Member of the Suez Group and the Monday Club.

Winston Field – Elected to the Central African Federation Assembly for the Dominion Party in 1957, he became the first Rhodesia Front Prime Minister of Southern Rhodesia in 1962–64.

Geoffrey Fisher – Bishop of Chester 1932–39, of London 1939–45, Archbishop of Canterbury 1945–61.

Dingle Foot – Brother of Hugh and Michael. Liberal MP 1931–45, Labour MP 1957–70. A distinguished lawyer who was Solicitor-General 1964–67.

Sir Hugh Foot – Brother of Michael and Dingle. Governor of Jamaica 1951–57, of Cyprus 1957–60. UK representative to UN Trusteeship Council 1961–62. Minister of State, Foreign Office 1964–70.

Michael Foot – Brother of Dingle and Hugh. Labour MP for Plymouth Devonport 1945–55. Succeeded Nye Bevan as Labour MP for Ebbw Vale

1960–92. Deputy (1976–80) and Party Leader (1980–83). Editor of *Tribune* 1948–52, 1955–60. Employment Secretary 1974–76, Leader of the Commons and Lord President of the Council 1976–79.

Sir John Forster – Chairman of National Arbitration Tribunal 1944–72.

Sir Oliver Franks – Worked with Macmillan at Ministry of Supply during the Second World War. Ambassador to the US 1946–52, Chairman of Lloyds Bank 1954–62, Provost of Worcester College, Oxford 1962–76.

Hugh Fraser – Conservative MP for Stafford and Stone 1945–84. Under-Secretary, War Office 1958–60, Colonial Office 1960–62, Air Secretary 1962–64.

Michael Fraser – Director (1951–64) and Chairman (1970–74) of Conservative Research Department.

J. William Fulbright – Democrat US Senator for Arkansas 1945–74 and Chairman, Senate Committee on Foreign Relations 1959–74.

Félix Gaillard – French Prime Minister 1957–58.

Hugh Gaitskell – Labour MP for Leeds South 1945–63. Minister of Fuel and Power 1947–50, Chancellor of the Exchequer 1950–51, Leader of the Opposition 1955–63.

Thomas Galbraith – Conservative MP for Glasgow Hillhead 1948–82. Civil Lord of the Admiralty 1957–59, Under-Secretary, Scottish Office 1959–62, PS, Ministry of Transport 1963–64.

Charles de Gaulle – With Macmillan in North Africa, becoming President of the French Committee of National Liberation in 1943. Head of French Provisional Government 1944–46, French Prime Minister 1958–59 and first President of the Fifth Republic 1959–69.

Patrick Gordon Walker – Labour MP for Smethwick 1945–64, for Leyton 1966–74. Commonwealth Relations Secretary 1950–51, Foreign Secretary 1964–65, Education and Science Secretary 1967–68.

Sidney Greene – General Secretary of the NUR 1957–75.

Julian Greenfield – Central African Minister of Education 1954–58, of Law 1956–63, of Home Affairs 1962–63.

James Griffiths – Labour MP for Llanelli 1936–70 and Deputy Leader 1956–59. Minister of National Insurance 1945–50, Colonial Secretary 1950–51, Welsh Secretary 1964–66.

Jo Grimond – Liberal MP for Orkney and Shetland 1950–83 and Party Leader 1956–67.

Georgios Grivas – Leader of the EOKA terrorists in Cyprus 1955–59.

Andrei Gromyko – Soviet Ambassador to the US 1943–46, to UK 1952–53, Foreign Minister 1957–85.

James Hagerty – White House press secretary 1953–61.

Patrick Buchan-Hepburn, 1st Baron Hailes – Conservative MP 1931–57 and Chief Whip 1948–55. Governor-General of the West Indies Federation 1958–62.

Quintin Hogg, 2nd Viscount Hailsham – Succeeded 1950. Conservative MP for Oxford 1938–50 and Party Chairman 1957–59. Renounced peerage in 1963. Conservative MP for St Marylebone 1963–70. First Lord of the Admiralty 1956–57, Minister of Education 1957, Lord President of the Council 1957–59 and 1960–64, Lord Privy Seal 1959–60, Education and Science Secretary 1964, Lord Chancellor 1970–74 and 1979–87.

Sir William Haley – BBC Director-General 1944–52. Editor of *The Times* 1952–66.

Sir Robert Hall – Director, Cabinet Office Economic Section 1947–53, government economic adviser 1953–61.

Walter Hallstein – President, Commission of the European Economic Community 1958–67.

Dag Hammarskjöld – UN Secretary-General 1953–61.

Hans Hansen – Danish Foreign Minister 1953–58, Prime Minister 1955–60.

John Hare, 1st Viscount Blakenham – Conservative MP for Woodbridge 1945–63 and Party Chairman 1963–65. War Secretary 1956–58, Minister of Agriculture, Fisheries and Food 1958–60, of Labour 1960–63, Chancellor of the Duchy of Lancaster 1963–64.

William Harper – Leader of the opposition Dominion Party in the Central African Federation 1959–62. He helped to found the new right-wing Rhodesia Front party which won the December 1962 Southern Rhodesia elections and was a senior minister in the new government until forced to resign by Ian Smith in 1968.

Averell Harriman – US Ambassador to USSR 1943–46, to Britain 1946, at large 1961, 1965–69. Democrat Governor, New York State, 1955–58. Under-Secretary of State for Far Eastern Affairs 1961–63, for Political Affairs 1963–65.

Roy Harrod – Oxford economist, biographer of John Maynard Keynes (1951) and regular correspondent with his erstwhile publisher, Harold Macmillan, on economic issues.

Abdel-Qadir Hatem – Egyptian lieutenant colonel and spokesman, especially on intelligence matters.

Sir William Hayter. Ambassador to the USSR 1953–57, Deputy Secretary, Foreign Office 1957–58. Warden of New College, Oxford 1958–76.

Anthony, 1st Viscount Head – Conservative MP for Carshalton 1945–60. War Secretary 1951–56, Minister of Defence 1956–57. High Commissioner to Nigeria 1960–63, to Malaysia 1963–66.

Denis Healey – Labour MP in Leeds 1952–92 and Deputy Leader 1980–83. Defence Secretary 1964–70, Chancellor of the Exchequer 1974–79.

Edward Heath – Conservative MP in Bexley 1950–2001 and Chief Whip 1955–59. Minister of Labour 1959–60, Lord Privy Seal (with responsibility for European negotiations) 1960–63, President of the Board of Trade 1963–64, Leader of the Opposition 1965–70, 1974–75, Prime Minister 1970–74.

Derick Heathcoat Amory, 1st Viscount Amory – Conservative MP for Tiverton 1945–60. Minister of Agriculture, Fisheries and Food 1954–58, Chancellor of the Exchequer 1958–60. High Commissioner to Canada 1961–63.

Sir Laurence Helsby – First Civil Service Commissioner 1954–59, Permanent Secretary, Ministry of Labour 1959–62, Joint Permanent Secretary of the Treasury and Head of the Home Civil Service 1963–68.

Arthur Henderson – Labour MP 1923–24, 1929–31, 1935–66. Commonwealth Relations Secretary 1947, Air Secretary 1947–51.

Christian Herter – Republican Governor of Massachusetts 1953–57, US Under-Secretary of State 1957–59, Secretary of State 1959–61, US Trade Representative 1962–66.

Charles Hill – Conservative MP for Luton 1950–63. Postmaster-General 1955–57, Chancellor of the Duchy of Lancaster 1957–61, Minister of Housing and Local Government and of Welsh Affairs 1961–62. Chairman, Independent Television Authority 1963–67, of BBC governors 1967–72.

Viscount Hinchingbrooke – Courtesy title of Alexander Montagu, 10th Earl of Sandwich (succeeded 1962, renounced 1964). Conservative MP for South Dorset 1941–62. President, Anti-Common Market League 1962–84.

Sidney Holland – National Party Prime Minister of New Zealand 1949–57.

Sir Roger Hollis – Director-General of MI5 1956–65.

Keith Holyoake – National Party Prime Minister of New Zealand 1957 and 1960–72. Governor-General of New Zealand 1977–80.

Sir Alec Douglas-Home, 14th Earl of Home – Succeeded 1951. Conservative MP for Lanark 1931–45, 1950–51. After renunciation sat for Kinross and Western Perthshire 1963–74. PPS to Neville Chamberlain 1937–39. Commonwealth Relations Secretary 1955–60, Leader of the Lords 1957–60, Lord President of the Council 1957, 1959–60, Foreign Secretary 1960–63, 1970–74, Prime Minister 1963–64, Leader of the Opposition 1964–65.

Sir Evelyn Hone – Governor of Northern Rhodesia 1959–64.

Samuel, 6th Viscount Hood – Minister, British Embassy in Washington 1958–62. Deputy Under-Secretary of State, Foreign Office 1962–69.

Lord John Hope – Conservative MP 1950–64. PS, Foreign Office 1954–56, Commonwealth Relations Office 1956–57, Scottish Office 1957–59. Minister of Works 1959–62.

Sir Frederick [Derick] Hoyer Millar – High Commissioner in Germany 1953–55, Ambassador to West Germany 1955–57, Permanent Secretary, Foreign Office 1957–61.

Sir Richard Hull – Last CIGS 1961–64 (the post then became Chief of the General Staff, which he held 1964–65), CDS 1965–67.

George Humphrey – US Treasury Secretary 1953–57.

Hussein – King of Jordan 1952–99.

Sir Harry Hylton-Foster. Conservative MP 1950–59. Solicitor-General 1954–59. Speaker of the Commons 1959–65.

Hastings (Pug), 1st Baron Ismay – Commonwealth Relations Secretary 1951–52, Secretary-General of NATO 1952–57.

İsmet İnönü – Turkish Prime Minister 1923–24, 1925–37, 1961–65 and President (1938–50).

Cheddi Jagan – Allegedly very left-wing Chief Minister of British Guiana 1953, 1961–64. After independence as Guyana was President 1992–97.

Sir Gladwyn Jebb, 1st Baron Gladwyn – Ambassador to UN 1950–54, to France 1954–60. Subsequently a leading Liberal politician and pro-European.

Robert Jenkins – Conservative MP for Dulwich 1951–64.

Lyndon Johnson – Democrat US Senate majority leader 1955–61, Vice-President 1961–63, President 1963–69.

Aubrey Jones – Conservative MP for Birmingham Hall Green 1950–65. Minister of Fuel and Power 1955–57, of Supply 1957–59. Chairman, National Board for Prices and Incomes 1965–70.

Keith Joseph – Conservative MP for Leeds North East 1956–87. PPS (1957–59), PS (1959–61), Commonwealth Relations Office, President of the Board of Trade 1961–62, Minister of Housing and Local Government and of Welsh Affairs 1962–64, Social Services Secretary 1970–74, Industry Secretary 1979–81, Education and Science Secretary 1981–86.

Louis Joxe – French Minister of Education 1960, 1962, Minister for Algerian Affairs 1960–62, Minister of Administrative Reform 1962–66, Minister of Justice 1966–68.

Konstantinos Karamanlis – Prime Minister of Greece 1955–58, 1958–61, 1961–63, 1974–80, President 1990–95.

Kenneth Kaunda – Leading Northern Rhodesia nationalist from 1953, becoming Prime Minister in 1964 and President 1964–91.

Rashidi Kawawa – Prime Minister of Tanganyika, January–December 1962.

D. H. (Harold) Kay – Joined M&Co in 1943. Sent to Africa after 1945, he signed up many indigenous authors and built up M&Co's African educational publishing before he left the firm in 1968.

Urho Kekkonen – Finnish Prime Minister 1950–53, 1954–56, President 1956–82.

John Fitzgerald Kennedy – Democrat US Senator for Massachusetts 1953–60, President 1960–63.

Robert Kennedy – US Attorney General 1961–64.

Jomo Kenyatta – Sentenced for alleged involvement in Mau Mau in 1953 and released in 1961. Kenyan Prime Minister 1963–64 and President 1964–78.

Nikita Khrushchev – First Secretary of the Communist Party of the Soviet Union 1951–64 and Chairman of the Council of Ministers 1958–64.

David Maxwell-Fyfe, 1st Earl of Kilmuir – Conservative MP 1935–54. Deputy Chief British Prosecutor at Nuremburg. Home Secretary 1951–54, Lord Chancellor 1954–62.

Cecil Harmsworth King – Cousin of 2nd Viscount Rothermere. Chairman, Daily Mirror Newspapers Ltd 1951–63, International Publishing Corporation 1963–68.

Nobusuke Kishi – Japanese Foreign Minister 1956–57, Prime Minister 1957–60.

Ronald Knox – Private tutor to Macmillan 1910, and chaplain at Oxford during his time there. A celebrated theologian and Bible translator who converted to the Roman Catholic Church in 1917.

Samuel Knox-Cunningham – Conservative MP for South Antrim 1955–70. PPS to Macmillan 1959–63.

Jens Krag – Danish Foreign Minister 1958–62, Prime Minister 1962–68.

Antony, Viscount Lambton – Conservative MP for Berwick-upon-Tweed 1951–73.

Halvard Lange – Foreign Minister of Norway 1946–63, 1963–65.

George Petty-Fitzmaurice, 8th Marquess of Lansdowne – Lady Dorothy's second cousin. PS to Foreign Office 1958–62, Minister of State, Colonial Office 1962–64, Commonwealth Relations Office 1963–64.

Sir Frank Lee – Permanent Secretary, Ministry of Food 1949–51, Board of Trade 1951–60, Joint Permanent Secretary of the Treasury 1960–62.

Sir Harry Legge-Bourke – Conservative MP for Ely 1945–73, Chairman of the 1922 Committee 1970–72.

Seán Lemass – Irish Deputy Prime Minister 1957–59, Prime Minister 1959–66.

Alan Lennox-Boyd, 1st Viscount Boyd of Merton – Conservative MP for Mid-Bedfordshire 1931–60. Minister for Transport and Civil Aviation 1952–54, Colonial Secretary 1954–59.

Geoffrey Lloyd – Conservative MP 1931–45, 1950–74. Minister of Information 1945, Minister of Fuel and Power 1951–55, Minister of Education 1957–59.

Selwyn Lloyd – Conservative MP for The Wirral 1945–76. Minister of Supply 1954–55, Minister of Defence 1955, Foreign Secretary 1955–60, Chancellor of the Exchequer 1960–62, Lord Privy Seal and Leader of the Commons 1963–64, Speaker of the Commons 1971–76.

Henry Cabot Lodge Jr – US Ambassador to the UN 1953–60, to South Vietnam 1963–4, 1965–67, to West Germany 1968–69.

Eric Louw – South African Foreign Minister 1957–63.

Patrice Lumumba – Congolese Prime Minister from independence in June until his overthrow in September 1960.

John McCone – Chairman of US Atomic Energy Commission 1958–61, Director of the CIA 1961–65.

Malcolm MacDonald – Labour MP 1929–31 and National Labour MP 1931–35, 1936–45. Colonial Secretary 1935, 1938–40, Dominions Secretary 1935–38, 1938–39. High Commissioner to Canada 1941–46, to India 1955–60, to Kenya 1964–65. Governor/Commissioner for South East Asia 1946–55, of Kenya 1963–64. Co-Chair, International Conference on Laos 1961–62.

Thomas MacDonald – New Zealand Minister of Defence 1949–57 and Foreign Secretary 1954–57. NZ High Commissioner to Britain 1961–68.

John McEwen – Deputy Prime Minister of Australia and Leader of Country Party 1958–71.

John Maclay – National Liberal MP for Montrose 1940–50, for West Renfrewshire 1950–64. Minister of State, Colonial Office 1956–57, Scottish Secretary 1957–62.

Alan Maclean – General list editor and board director at M&Co from 1954. Former diplomat, brother of Soviet defector Donald Maclean.

Iain Macleod – Conservative MP for Enfield West 1950–70 and Party Chairman 1961–63. Minister of Health 1952–55, of Labour and National Service 1955–59, Colonial Secretary 1959–61, Chancellor of the Duchy of Lancaster and Leader of the Commons 1961–63, editor of the *Spectator* 1963–65, Chancellor of the Exchequer 1970.

Daniel Macmillan – Macmillan's eldest brother. Chairman and Managing Director of M&Co 1936–63.

Maurice Macmillan – Macmillan's son. Conservative MP for Halifax 1955–64 and in Surrey 1966–84. UK delegate, Council of Europe and WEU 1960–63. EST 1963–64, Chief Secretary, Treasury 1970–72, Employment Secretary 1972–73, Paymaster-General 1973–4. Chairman, M&Co 1963, 1967–70.

Robert S. McNamara – US Defense Secretary 1961–68. President of the World Bank 1968–81.

Makarios III – Archbishop and Ethnarch of Cyprus 1950–77. Exiled for his support for *enosis* and EOKA 1956–59. President of Cyprus 1960–74, 1974–77.

Sir Roger Makins – With Macmillan in North Africa. Ambassador to the US 1953–56, Joint Permanent Secretary of the Treasury 1956–59, Chairman, UK Atomic Energy Authority 1960–64.

Norman Manley – Chief Minister of Jamaica 1955–62.

Sir Milton Margai – Sierra Leone Chief Minister 1954–61, Prime Minister 1961–64.

Ernest Marples – Conservative MP for Wallasey 1945–74. PS, Ministry of Housing and Local Government 1951–54, of Pensions and National Insurance 1954–55, Postmaster-General 1957–59, Minister of Transport 1959–64.

John Marshall – National Party New Zealand Deputy Prime Minister 1957, 1960–72, Prime Minister 1972.

René Massigli – With Macmillan in North Africa, where he was de Gaulle's Commissioner for Foreign Affairs 1943–44. French Ambassador to Britain 1944–54 and Secretary-General of the French Foreign Ministry 1954–56.

Angus Maude – Conservative MP for Ealing South 1950–58, for Stratford-upon-Avon 1963–83. Editor of *Sydney Morning Herald* 1958–61. Paymaster-General 1979–81.

Reginald Maudling – Conservative MP for Barnet 1950–79. EST 1952–55, Minister of Supply 1955–57, Paymaster-General (with responsibility for European negotiations) 1957–59, President of the Board of Trade 1959–61, Colonial Secretary 1961–62, Chancellor of the Exchequer 1962–64, Home Secretary 1970–72.

Adnan Menderes – Prime Minister of Turkey 1950–60. Overthrown by a military coup and executed in 1961.

Pierre Mendes-France – French Prime Minister 1954–55 and leader of the French Radical Party until 1957.

Krishna Menon – Indian High Commissioner to the UK 1947–52, Minister of Defence 1957–62.

Sir Robert Menzies – Leader of Australian Liberal Party 1945–66 and Prime Minister 1939–41, 1949–66.

Livingston (Libby) Merchant – US Assistant Secretary of State for European Affairs 1953–56, 1958–59, Ambassador to Canada 1956–58, 1961–62, Under-Secretary of State for Political Affairs 1959–61.

Pierre Messmer – French Governor of Cameroun 1956–58, of French Equatorial Africa 1958, High Commissioner for French West Africa 1958–59. French Defence Minister 1959–69, Minister for Overseas Departments and Territories 1971–72, Prime Minister 1972–74.

Anastas Mikoyan – First Deputy Premier of the Soviet Union 1955–64.

Percy, 1st Baron Mills of Studley – Macmillan's adviser at the Ministry of Housing and Local Government 1951–52. Minister of Power 1957–59, Paymaster-General 1959–61, Minister without Portfolio 1961–62.

Dom Mintoff – Prime Minister of Malta 1955–58, 1971–84.

Iskander Mirza – Governor-General (1955–56) then President (1956–58) of Pakistan.

Joseph Mobutu – Commander-in-Chief of the Congolese army. He overthrew Lumumba in 1960 and, after another coup in 1965, became President 1965–97.

Sir John Moffat – Liberal Party Leader, Central African Assembly 1954–62.

Guy Mollet – French Socialist leader, Prime Minister 1956–57, Secretary of State under de Gaulle 1958–59.

Walter, 1st Viscount Monckton of Brenchley – Conservative MP 1951–57. Minister of Labour and National Service 1951–55, of Defence 1955–56, Paymaster-General 1956–57. Chairman of Midland Bank 1957–64, of Advisory Commission on Central Africa 1960.

Jean Monnet – With Macmillan in North Africa. President, Action Committee for a United States of Europe 1956–75.

Bernard, 1st Viscount Montgomery of Alamein – Wartime commander, CIGS 1946–48, Deputy SACEUR 1951–58.

Herbert Morrison – Labour MP 1923–24, 1929–31, 1935–59. Macmillan's chief as Minister of Supply 1940, Home Secretary 1940–45, Lord President and Leader of the Commons 1945–51, Foreign Secretary 1951, Deputy Leader of the Labour Party 1945–56.

John Morrison – Conservative MP for Salisbury 1942–65. Chairman of the 1922 Committee 1955–64.

Louis, 1st Earl Mountbatten of Burma – SAC, South East Asia 1943–46, Viceroy (1947) and Governor-General (1947–48) of India. First Sea Lord 1955–59, CDS 1959–65.

Bob Murphy – Worked with Macmillan and Eisenhower in North Africa 1942–43. US Ambassador to Japan 1952, Assistant Secretary of State for UN affairs 1953, Deputy Under-Secretary of State 1953–59, Under-Secretary of State for Political Affairs 1959.

Gerald Nabarro – Flamboyant Conservative MP for Kidderminster 1950–64, for South Worcestershire 1966–73.

Walter Nash – New Zealand Labour Finance Minister 1935–49, Prime Minister 1957–60.

Gamal Abdel Nasser – Egyptian Prime Minister 1954–56 and President 1956–70.

Sir Wilfred Neden – Chief Industrial Commissioner, Ministry of Labour 1954–58.

Jawaharlal Nehru – Indian Prime Minister and Minister of External Affairs 1947–64.

Richard Nixon – Republican US Vice-President 1953–61, President 1969–74.

Joshua Nkomo – Leading campaigner for black majority rule in Southern Rhodesia and founder of Zimbabwe African Peoples Union in 1962.

Kwame Nkrumah – Prime Minister of Gold Coast/Ghana 1952–60, President 1960–66.

Lauris Norstad – SACEUR 1956–62.

Nuri al-Said – British-backed central figure in Iraqi politics from 1930 until his murder in the 1958 revolution.

Julius Nyerere – Formed Tanganyikan African National Union in 1954. Prime Minister 1960–62, President 1962–64 of Tanganyika and 1964–85 of Tanzania (after merger with Zanzibar).

Milton Obote – Ugandan Prime Minister 1962–66, President 1966–71, 1980–85.

Sir Con O'Neill – Ambassador to Finland 1961–63, to EEC 1963–65. Assistant Under-Secretary (1957–60), Deputy Secretary, Foreign Office 1965–68, 1969–72.

David Ormsby-Gore – Maurice Macmillan's brother-in-law. Conservative MP for Oswestry 1950–61. Minister of State, Foreign Office 1957–61. Ambassador to the US 1961–65.

Sir Thomas Padmore – 2nd Secretary at the Treasury 1952–62, Permanent Secretary, Ministry of Transport 1962–68.

Vijaya Pandit – Indian Ambassador to the USSR 1947–49, to the US 1949–51, High Commissioner to the UK 1954–61.

Lester (Mike) Pearson – Canadian External Affairs Secretary 1948–57, Prime Minister 1963–68.

Giuseppe Pella – Italian Foreign Minister 1953–4, 1957–8, 1959–60, Prime Minister 1953–4.

Sir William Penney – A physicist. After wartime work on the Manhattan atomic weapons project, he led postwar development of Britain's atomic and nuclear weapons. Chairman of the United Kingdom Atomic Energy Authority 1962–67.

John Drummond, 17th Earl of Perth – Minister of State, Colonial Office 1957–62.

Pierre Pflimlin – French Minister of Agriculture 1947–49, 1950–51, Minister of Finance 1955–56, 1957–58 and briefly Prime Minister during the Algerian crisis of May 1958. He resigned with the other MRP ministers from de Gaulle's government in 1962.

Souvanna Phouma – A nephew of King Sisavang Vong of Laos, he served as Prime Minister of Laos 1951–54, 1956–58, 1960 and from 1962, though his efforts to preserve political balance ended when he was ousted by the Communist Pathet Lao in 1975.

Phoumi Nosavan – With CIA backing, Phoumi became the right-wing strongman of Laos, seizing power in December 1960. Forced into a coalition with Phouma in 1962, he was ousted by a coup in April 1964.

Antoine Pinay – French Economic Minister 1948–49, 1950–52, Prime Minister 1952, Foreign Minister 1955–56, Finance and Economic Affairs Minister 1958–60.

Christian Pineau – French Finance Minister 1948, Foreign Minister 1956–57.

Sir Edwin Plowden – Chairman, Atomic Energy Authority 1954–59, Committee on Treasury Control of Public Expenditure 1959–61.

Georges Pompidou – French Prime Minister 1962–68, President 1969–74.

Oliver, 1st Baron Poole – Conservative MP for Oswestry 1945–50, Party Chairman 1955–57, 1963.

Enoch Powell – Conservative MP for Wolverhampton South West 1950–74, Ulster Unionist MP for South Down 1974–87. FST 1957–58, Minister of Health 1960–63.

Sir Richard Powell – Permanent Secretary, Ministry of Defence 1956–59, Board of Trade 1960–68.

John Profumo – Conservative MP for Kettering 1940–45, for Stratford-upon-Avon 1950–63. PS, Colonial Office 1957–58, Foreign Office 1958–59, Minister of State, Foreign Office 1959–60, War Secretary 1960–63.

Abd al-Karim Qasim – Led the 1958 Iraqi revolution. Prime Minister of the Iraqi Republic from 1958 until his execution during the 1963 coup.

Donald Quarles – US Deputy Defense Secretary 1957–59.

Cyril, 1st Viscount Radcliffe – Director-General of Ministry of Information, 1941. Chaired the boundary commissions on Indian independence. Appointed a law lord in 1949, he chaired important inquiries into Cyprus policy (1956), the workings of monetary policy (1957–59) and security procedures (1961–62).

Tunku Abdul Rahman – Prime Minister of Malaya/Malaysia 1957–70.

Sir Victor Raikes – Conservative MP 1931–57. Suez Group member.

Michael Ramsay – Bishop of Durham 1952–56, Archbishop of York 1956–61, Archbishop of Canterbury 1961–74.

Adam Rapacki – Polish Foreign Minister 1956–68.

Martin Redmayne – Conservative MP for Rushcliffe 1950–66 and Chief Whip 1959–64.

William Rees-Mogg – City (1960–61), Politics and Economics (1961–63), Deputy (1964–67) Editor of the *Sunday Times*. Editor of *The Times* 1967–81.

Sir Patrick Reilly – Ambassador to the USSR 1957–60, to France 1965–68. Deputy Under-Secretary, Foreign Office 1960–64.

Juliet Rhys-Williams – A former Liberal, she became acquainted with Macmillan through her chairmanship of the European League for Economic Co-operation 1948–64. Although Secretary (1947–58) and Chairman (1958–64) of the United Europe Movement, she opposed the closer and narrower type of European integration introduced by the 1957 Treaty of Rome.

Sir John Richardson – Macmillan's physician, who according to John Wyndham generally called on him once a month.

David Robarts – Chairman, National Provincial Bank 1954–68, National Westminster Bank 1969–71.

Alf Robens – Labour MP for Wansbeck 1945–50, for Blyth 1950–60. Minister of Labour and National Service 1951. Chairman, National Coal Board 1961–71.

Sir Frank Roberts – Ambassador to Yugoslavia 1954–57, to NATO 1957–60, to USSR 1960–62, to West Germany 1963–68.

Sir Brian Robertson – Commander-in-Chief, Middle East Land Forces and Governor of the Suez Canal Zone, 1950–53. Chairman, British Transport Commission 1953–61.

John Kemp, 1st Viscount Rochdale – Industrialist. President, National Union of Manufacturers 1953–56, Chairman, Cotton Board 1957–62, Chairman, National Ports Council 1963–67.

Walt Rostow – US economist and Director of Policy Planning 1961–66, National Security Advisor 1966–69.

Esmond Harmsworth, 2nd Viscount Rothermere – Conservative MP 1919–29. Chairman, Daily Mail General Trust Ltd 1932–71.

Sir Anthony Rumbold – Assistant Under-Secretary, Foreign Office 1957–60. British Minister, Paris Embassy 1960–63. Ambassador to Thailand 1965–67, to Austria 1967–70.

Dean Rusk – Served in US State Department 1947–51. US Secretary of State 1961–69.

Michael Hicks Beach, 2nd Earl St Aldwyn – PS, Ministry of Agriculture, Fisheries and Food 1954–58, Conservative Chief Whip in the Lords 1958–78.

Robert (Bobbety) Cecil, 5th Marquess of Salisbury – Macmillan's kinsman through marriage. Leader of the Lords 1942–45, 1951–57, Commonwealth Relations Secretary 1952, Lord President of the Council 1952–57. President of the Monday Club 1961–72.

Duncan Sandys – Churchill's son-in-law. Conservative MP for Norwood 1935–45, for Streatham 1950–74. Minister of Works 1944–45, of Supply 1951–54, of Housing and Local Government 1954–57, of Defence 1957–59, of Aviation 1959–60, Commonwealth Relations Secretary 1960–64, Colonial Secretary 1962–64. Founder member of European Movement, 1947.

Saud – King of Saudi Arabia 1953–64.

Lawrence Lumley, 11th Earl of Scarbrough – Conservative MP 1922–29, 1931–37. Lord Chamberlain 1952–63.

Albert-Hilger van Scherpenberg – State Secretary, West German Foreign Ministry 1958–61.

Gerhard Schröder – West German Interior Minister 1953–61, Foreign Minister 1961–66, Defence Minister 1966–69.

Antonio Segni – Italian Prime Minister 1955–57, 1959–60, President 1962–64.

George Douglas-Hamilton, 10th Earl of Selkirk – Paymaster-General 1953–55, Chancellor of the Duchy of Lancaster 1955–57, First Lord of the Admiralty 1957–59, Commissioner-General for South East Asia 1959–63.

Sir Hartley, Lord Shawcross – UK Chief Prosecutor at Nuremburg. Labour MP for St Helens 1945–58. Attorney-General 1945–51, President of the Board of Trade 1951. Chairman, Royal Commission on the Press 1961–62.

Margaret Shepherd – Chairman of the Conservative women's organisation 1960–63.

Emmanuel Shinwell – Labour MP 1922–24, 1928–31, 1935–70 and Parliamentary Party Chairman 1964–67. Minister of Fuel and Power 1945–47, War Secretary 1947–50, Minister of Defence 1950–51.

Sir Evelyn Shuckburgh – Private Secretary to the Foreign Secretary 1951–54. Assistant Under-Secretary (1954–56) Deputy Under-Secretary (1960–62), Foreign Office. Assistant Secretary-General, NATO 1958–60. Ambassador to NATO 1962–66, to Italy 1966–69.

Ian Smith – Chief Whip of Welensky's United Federal Party in the Central African Federation 1958–61. Returning to Southern Rhodesian politics he founded the Rhodesia Front in 1962, becoming Deputy Prime Minister 1962–64 and Prime Minister 1964–79.

Christopher Soames – Churchill's son-in-law. Conservative MP for Bedford 1950–66. PS, Admiralty 1957–58. War Secretary 1958–60, Minister of Agriculture, Fisheries and Food 1960–64. Ambassador to France 1968–72. Vice-President, European Commission 1973–77. Governor of Rhodesia 1979. Lord President and Leader of the Lords 1979–81.

Sir Frank Soskice – Labour MP 1945–55, 1956–66. Solicitor-General 1945–51, Attorney-General 1951, Home Secretary 1964–65, Lord Privy Seal 1965–66.

Paul-Henri Spaak – Belgian Prime Minister 1938–39, 1947–49, Foreign Minister 1939–46, 1947–49, 1954–57, 1961–66. NATO Secretary-General 1957–61.

Adlai Stevenson – Democrat Governor of Illinois 1949–53 and nominee for US presidential elections 1952 and 1956. US Ambassador to UN 1961–65.

Richard Stokes – Labour MP 1938–57. Lord Privy Seal 1951.

John Strachey – Left-wing Labour MP 1929–31, 1945–63. Minister of Food 1946–50, War Secretary 1950–51.

Sir William Strath – Head of the Cabinet Office Central War Plans Secretariat, and author of the 1955 report on the potential effects on Britain of a thermonuclear attack. Permanent Secretary, Ministry of Supply 1959, of Aviation 1959–60.

Franz-Josef Strauss – West German Defence Minister 1956–62, Finance Minister 1966–69. Minister President of Bavaria 1978–88.

Lewis L. Strauss – Chairman of the US Atomic Energy Commission 1953–58. US Secretary for Commerce 1958–59.

James, 1st Viscount Stuart of Findhorn – Married to Dorothy Macmillan's sister Rachel. Conservative MP 1923–59 and Chief Whip 1941–48. Scottish Secretary 1951–57.

Huseyn Shaheed Suhrawardy – Prime Minister of Pakistan 1956–57.

Sukarno – President of Indonesia 1945–67.

Philip Cunliffe-Lister, 1st Earl of Swinton – Conservative MP 1918–35. President of the Board of Trade 1922–23, 1924–29, 1931, Colonial Secretary 1931–35, Air Secretary 1935–38, Minister Resident in West Africa 1942–44, for Civil Aviation 1944–45, Chancellor of the Duchy of Lancaster 1951–52, Commonwealth Relations Secretary 1952–55.

Sir Gerald Templer – High Commissioner of Malaya 1952–54, CIGS 1955–58.

Vincent Tewson – TUC General Secretary 1946–60.

U Thant – UN Secretary-General 1961–71.

Roy Thomson – Canadian media magnate who acquired Scottish Television in 1957, the Kemsley newspapers (including the *Sunday Times*) in 1959 and *The Times* in 1966.

Peter Thorneycroft – Conservative MP for Stafford 1938–45, for Monmouth 1945–66 and Party Chairman 1975–81. President of the Board of Trade 1951–57, Chancellor of the Exchequer 1957–58, Minister of Aviation 1960–62, of Defence 1962–64.

Sir Burke Trend – Deputy Cabinet Secretary 1956–59. Third Secretary (1959–60), Second Secretary (1960–62) at the Treasury. Cabinet Secretary 1963–73.

Moïse Tshombe – President of Congo rebel province of Katanga 1960–63. Prime Minister of Congolese coalition government 1964–65.

Sir James Turner – President of the National Farmers' Union 1945–60.

Robert (Robin) Turton – Conservative MP for Thirsk and Malton 1929–74. Minister of Health 1955–57.

Nathan Twining – Chairman, US Joint Chiefs of Staff 1957–60.

Eamon de Valera – Irish Prime Minister 1937–48, 1951–54, 1957–59, President 1959–73.

Georges Vanier – Governor-General of Canada 1959–67.

Hendrik Verwoerd – Principal architect of apartheid and South African Prime Minister 1958–66.

Donald Wade – Liberal MP for Huddersfield West 1950–64, Chief Whip 1956–62, and Deputy Leader 1962–64.

Sir Derek Walker-Smith – Conservative MP for Hertfordshire 1945–83. PS, Board of Trade 1955–56, EST 1956–57, Minister of Health 1957–60. Chairman of the 1922 Committee 1951–55.

George (Geordie), 1st Viscount Ward of Witley – Conservative MP for Worcester 1945–60. PS, Admiralty 1955–57, Air Secretary 1957–60.

Harold Watkinson – Conservative MP for Woking 1950–64. PS, Ministry of Labour and National Service 1952–55, Minister of Transport and Civil Aviation 1955–59, of Defence 1959–62.

Sir Roy Welensky – Prime Minister of Central African Federation 1956–63.

John Wheeler-Bennett – Historian of Nazi Germany, biographer of George VI (1958) and Macmillan author.

Sir Edgar Whitehead – Prime Minister of Southern Rhodesia 1958–62.

Jock Whitney – US Ambassador to the UK 1957–61.

George Wigg – Labour MP 1945–67, Paymaster-General 1964–67.

Eric Williams – Prime Minister of Trinidad and Tobago 1956–81.

Paul Williams – Conservative MP for Sunderland South 1953–64. Active in the Suez Group, he went on to chair the Monday Club.

Tom Williamson – Labour MP 1945–48. General Secretary, National Union of General and Municipal Workers 1946–61.

Robert Willis – General Secretary, London Typographical Society 1945–64.

Harold Wilson – Labour MP for Ormskirk 1945–50, for Huyton 1950–83. President of the Board of Trade 1947–51. Shadow Chancellor of the Exchequer 1955–61, Shadow Foreign Secretary 1961–63, Leader of the Opposition 1963–64, 1970–74. Prime Minister 1964–70, 1974–76.

Richard Wood – Conservative MP for Bridlington 1950–79. Joint Parliamentary Secretary at Ministry of Pensions and National Insurance 1955–58, at Ministry of Labour 1958–59, at Ministry of Power 1959–63. Minister of Pensions and National Insurance 1963–64, Minister of Overseas Development 1970–74.

George Woodcock – Assistant General Secretary (1947–60) and General Secretary (1960–69) of the TUC.

Frederick Marquis, 1st Earl of Woolton – Conservative Party Chairman 1946–55, Lord President of the Council 1945, 1951–52, Chancellor of the Duchy of Lancaster 1952–55.

John Wyndham, 1st Baron Egremont – With Macmillan in North Africa. Macmillan's Private Secretary 1957–63.

Sir Thomas Yates – General Secretary, National Union of Seamen 1947–60.

Kenneth Younger – Labour MP 1945–59. Minister of State, Foreign Office 1950–51. Shadow Home Secretary 1955–57.

Valerian Zorin – Russian Deputy Minister of Foreign Affairs and delegate to the UN Security Council 1956–65.

Fatin Zorlu – Turkish Ambassador to NATO 1952–54, Minister of State 1955–57, Foreign Minister 1955–60.

Sir Solly Zuckerman – Chief Scientific Adviser to the Ministry of Defence 1960–66, to the British government 1964–71.

Philip de Zulueta – Private Secretary to the Prime Minister 1955–64.

Macmillan's Cabinets

January 1957

Harold Macmillan	*Prime Minister*
Lord Kilmuir	*Lord Chancellor*
Lord Salisbury	*Lord President* (on resignation in March 1957, replaced by Home and, in Sept 1957 by Hailsham)
R. A. Butler	*Lord Privy Seal*
	Home Secretary
Peter Thorneycroft	*Chancellor of the Exchequer* (on resignation in Jan 1958, replaced by Heathcoat Amory)
Selwyn Lloyd	*Foreign Secretary*
Alan Lennox-Boyd	*Colonial Secretary*
Lord Home	*Commonwealth Relations Secretary*
Sir David Eccles	*President of the Board of Trade*
Charles Hill	*Chancellor of the Duchy of Lancaster*
Lord Hailsham	*Minister of Education* (see below)
John Maclay	*Scottish Secretary*
Derick Heathcoat Amory	*Minister of Agriculture, Fisheries and Food* (see below)
Iain Macleod	*Minister of Labour and National Service*
Harold Watkinson	*Minister of Transport and Civil Aviation*
Duncan Sandys	*Minister of Defence*
Lord Mills	*Minister of Power*
Henry Brooke	*Minister of Housing and Local Government*
	Minister of Welsh Affairs

Additions: Sept 1957

Geoffrey Lloyd   *Minister of Education* (replacing
                          Hailsham)
Reginald Maudling   *Paymaster-General* (office enters Cabinet)

Addition: Jan 1958

John Hare   *Minister of Agriculture, Fisheries and
                          Food* (replacing Heathcoat Amory)

October 1959 (following the general election)

Harold Macmillan   *Prime Minister*
Lord Kilmuir   *Lord Chancellor*
Lord Home   *Lord President* (replaced by Hailsham in
                          July 1960 reshuffle)
                          Commonwealth Relations Secretary
                          (replaced by Sandys in July 1960
                          reshuffle)
Lord Hailsham   *Lord Privy Seal* (replaced by Heath in July
                          1960 reshuffle)
                          Minister of Science
Derick Heathcoat Amory   *Chancellor of the Exchequer* (on
                          resignation in July 1960, replaced by
                          Selwyn Lloyd)
R. A. Butler   *Home Secretary*
Selwyn Lloyd   *Foreign Secretary* (replaced by Home in
                          July 1960 reshuffle)
Iain Macleod   *Colonial Secretary* (replaced by Maudling
                          in Oct 1961 reshuffle)
Reginald Maudling   *President of the Board of Trade* (see
                          below)
Charles Hill   *Chancellor of the Duchy of Lancaster*
                          (replaced by Macleod in Oct 1961
                          reshuffle)
Sir David Eccles   *Minister of Education*
Lord Mills   *Paymaster-General* (replaced by Brooke in
                          Oct 1961, whilst Mills remained in
                          Cabinet as *Minister without Portfolio*)

Ernest Marples	*Minister of Transport*
Duncan Sandys	*Minister of Aviation* (replaced by Thorneycroft in July 1960 reshuffle)
Harold Watkinson	*Minister of Defence*
John Maclay	*Scottish Secretary*
Edward Heath	*Minister of Labour and National Service* (replaced by Hare in July 1960 reshuffle)
John Hare	*Minister of Agriculture, Fisheries and Food* (see below)
Henry Brooke	*Minister of Housing and Local Government*
	Minister of Welsh Affairs (replaced in both portfolios by Hill in Oct 1961 reshuffle)

Additions in the July 1960 reshuffle

| Peter Thorneycroft | *Minister of Aviation* (replacing Sandys) |
| Christopher Soames | *Minister of Agriculture, Fisheries and Food* (replacing Hare) |

Addition in the Oct 1961 reshuffle

| Frederick Erroll | *President of the Board of Trade* (replacing Maudling) |

July 1962 Cabinet re-constitution following the 'Night of the Long Knives'

Harold Macmillan	*Prime Minister*
R. A. Butler	*Deputy Prime Minister*
	First Secretary of State
Lord Dilhorne	*Lord Chancellor*
Lord Hailsham	*Lord President*
	Minister of Science
Edward Heath	*Lord Privy Seal*
Reginald Maudling	*Chancellor of the Exchequer*
Henry Brooke	*Home Secretary*
Lord Home	*Foreign Secretary*

Duncan Sandys	*Commonwealth Relations Secretary*
	Colonial Secretary
Frederick Erroll	*President of the Board of Trade*
Iain Macleod	*Chancellor of the Duchy of Lancaster*
Sir Edward Boyle	*Minister of Education*
John Boyd-Carpenter	*Paymaster-General*
Ernest Marples	*Minister of Transport*
Peter Thorneycroft	*Minister of Defence*
Michael Noble	*Scottish Secretary*
John Hare	*Minister of Labour and National Service*
Christopher Soames	*Minister of Agriculture, Fisheries and Food*
Sir Keith Joseph	*Minister of Housing and Local Government*
	Minister of Welsh Affairs
Enoch Powell	*Minister of Health*
Bill Deedes	*Minister without Portfolio*

Acknowledgements

I am very grateful to the present Earl of Stockton and the other Macmillan trustees both for entrusting the task of editing these diaries to me, and for their patience. Particular thanks should go to Philippa Blake-Roberts. I only hope that they will feel that their trust has been repaid.

The editing process has been lengthy and has involved the consultation of large amounts of published and archival material. I should gratefully acknowledge that my earlier ESRC research grant L124251002 to research the history of the Cabinet committee system, despite initially delaying the start of work on the diaries, has provided information invaluable in completing it. And thanks must go to the Fulbright Commission and all my erstwhile colleagues at Westminster College, Fulton for a year in Missouri during which I was able to consult relevant material in the Eisenhower and Kennedy Presidential libraries. A very welcome travel grant from the Westfield Trust facilitated archival checks of various of the more arcane references in the diaries, whilst an equally welcome sabbatical from my teaching duties at Queen Mary University of London enabled me at last to finish the work.

I am grateful to the archivists at the Eisenhower and Kennedy Presidential libraries and at The National Archives in London for their assistance, and for permission to quote material in their possession. A number of other archivists were no less helpful. Particular thanks should go to Colin Harris and his colleagues in the Department of Western Manuscripts at the Bodleian Library, Oxford, to Robin Harcourt-Williams at the archives of the Marquess of Salisbury at Hatfield House, to Alysoun Sanders at Macmillan Publishers Ltd, to David Clover at the Institute of Commonwealth Studies, to Anny Mochel at the OECD and to my former student Emma White at Bromley archives. The kind permission of the present Marquess of Salisbury and of Clarissa, Countess of Avon to quote from material in the Salisbury archives should also be gratefully acknowledged.

I have benefited over the years from the advice of many colleagues and friends too numerous to mention here. In particular, however, I should like to thank Richard Aldrich, Simon Ball, Oliver Bange, Lewis

Baston, Vernon Bogdanor, Roger Broad, Theodore Bromund, the late Lord Chelmer, Martin Cohen, Virginia Davis, James Ellison, David Faber, Gary Haines, Peter Hennessy, Lord Howe of Aberavon, Laura James, Colin Jones, Jens Kreuzfeldt, Charles Loft, Spencer Mawby, Lord Norton of Louth, James Obelkevich, Sue Onslow, Roland Quinault, James Reid, Peter Rose, Anne Rudelt, Julie Stepney, D. R. Thorpe, David Torrance, Nigel West, and Ken Young. I should also record my appreciation of the efforts of Tania Adams in helping to nurse this work through to production, and of Nick de Somogyi and Anthony Hippisley, who proved as meticulous and helpful as copy-editor and copy-reader as I could have wished for.

Finally, I would like to thank Anthony Goff at David Higham Associates and Georgina Morley and Natasha Martin at Macmillan for both their support and patience. Amongst the more bizarre excuses they must have had to put up with over the years for authorial dilatoriness must be mine of breaking a leg by falling down steps at the British Library. Editing Harold Macmillan's diaries has taken me much longer than I ever imagined. I would like to close by thanking my wife Christine for her love, support and encouragement through the various vicissitudes along the way.

PETER CATTERALL
London, June 2010

Index

www.panmacmillan.com